USER'S MAP TO GOING PLACES

PART ONE

1 Meeting the Demands of College Writing
2 The Writing Process
3 Writing Paragraphs in College

Writing in College *presents a strategies-based overview of what you need to know for writing in college, with a variety of exercises. You'll have the chance to address questions of purpose and audience, learn the basics of the writing process, and determine your own writing goals.*

PART TWO

4 Description
5 Example
6 Narration
7 Process
8 Classification
9 Cause and Effect
10 Comparison and Contrast
11 Definition
12 Argument

Paragraph Writing and Patterns of Thinking *walks you through nine commonly used patterns of paragraph development—description, illustration and example, narration, process, classification, cause and effect, comparison/contrast, definition, and argument. You will learn the elements of paragraph structure specific to each pattern, as well as develop thinking and writing skills that will help you succeed in your writing assignments.*

PART THREE

13 Essay Structure and the Writing Process
14 Types of Essays
15 Paraphrase, Summary, and Quotation
16 The Documented Essay
17 Writing in Class: Short-Answer and Essay Tests

Going to the Next Level: Essay Writing and Patterns of Thinking *prepares you to succeed with the college essay. You'll practice using each pattern of organization in an essay, as well as try your hand at a "mixed mode" essay using two or more patterns of organization. Part Three also gives you the chance to practice and develop important reading-thinking-writing processes that include how to paraphrase, summarize, and quote sources, write a research paper (including how to find and use sources to avoid plagiarism), and prepare for a variety of in class tests and essay exams.*

PART FOUR

18 The Simple Sentence
19 Beyond the Simple Sentence: Compounds, Coordination, and Subordination
20 The Sentence Fragment
21 Comma Splices and Run-Ons
22 Editing Verb Errors: Agreement, Irregular Verbs, and Consistency
23 Pronoun Agreement, Case, and Consistency
24 Adjectives and Adverbs
25 Punctuation
26 Mechanics

The Writer's Guidebook *is a valuable resource and workbook for grammar review and practice and covers sentence basics, sentence variety, punctuation, and grammar and mechanics. This part of the book is flexible; it may be part of your in-class work with your instructor or serve as an out-of-class reference or practice book for you to use on your own to improve your skills.*

PART FIVE

27 Vocabulary
28 Critical Reading, Thinking, and Writing

Reading and Thinking Critically *helps you build vocabulary and improve your word choice and tone when writing. Part Five also addresses critical reading skills, featuring a number of reading selections for you to respond to and discuss. Exercises will help you read interactively and craft responses before, during, and after reading a selection to deepen your understanding of the text.*

The McGraw·Hill Companies

Going Places

EDITOR IN CHIEF **Michael Ryan**
EDITORIAL DIRECTOR **Beth Ann Mejia**
PUBLISHER **David S. Patterson**
SENIOR SPONSORING EDITOR **John Kindler**
DIRECTOR OF DEVELOPMENT **Dawn Groundwater**
DEVELOPMENT EDITOR **Gillian Cook**
MARKET DEVELOPMENT MANAGER **Molly Meneely**
EXECUTIVE MARKETING MANAGER **Allison Jones**
EDITORIAL COORDINATOR **Jesse Hassenger**
SENIOR PRODUCTION EDITOR **Catherine Morris**
MANUSCRIPT EDITOR **Jennifer Gordon**
ART DIRECTOR **Preston Thomas**
DESIGN MANAGER **Andrei Pasternak**
TEXT DESIGNER **Maureen McCutcheon, Glenda King**
COVER DESIGNER **Andrei Pasternak**
ILLUSTRATOR **Thompson Type**
PHOTO RESEARCH MANAGER **Brian J. Pecko**
SENIOR PRODUCTION SUPERVISOR **Richard DeVitto**
COMPOSITION **10/12 Sabon by Thompson Type**
PRINTING **45# Influence Gloss, Quebecor World, Dubuque**
COVER **Front cover: © Digital Vision/Getty; Back Cover: © Alexander Hafemann/Photodisc/Getty**

Going Places

Published by McGraw-Hill, an imprint of The McGraw-Hill Companies, Inc., 1221 Avenue of the Americas, New York, NY 10020.

This book is printed on acid-free paper.

1 2 3 4 5 6 7 8 9 0 QPD / QPD 0 9 8

Student Edition ISBN: 978-0-07-340710-4
Student Edition MHID: 0-07-340710-0

Instructor's Edition ISBN: 978-0-07-327814-8
Instructor's Edition MHID: 0-07-327814-9

Credits: The credits section for this book begins on page 617 and is considered an extension of the copyright page.

Library of Congress Cataloging-in-Publication Data

Bailey, Richard E., 1952–
Going places : paragraph to essay / Richard E. Bailey ; Linda Denstaedt.—1st ed.
p. cm.
Includes index.
ISBN-13: 978-0-07-340710-4 (alk. paper)
ISBN-10: 0-07-340710-0 (alk. paper)
ISBN-13: 978-0-07-327814-8 (alk. paper : instructor's ed.) 1. English language—Paragraphs—Problems, exercises, etc. 2. Report writing—Problems, exercises, etc. 3. College readers. I. Denstaedt, Linda. II. Title.
PE1439.B294 2009
808'.042076—dc22
2008045687

www.mhhe.com

FEATURES

Knowing how important writing is to you in school and on the job, the authors of *Going Places* have developed features to help you draw on your experiences outside the classroom and to bring into play all dimensions of verbal communication: reading, thinking, speaking, listening, and writing. The assignments and topics focus on practical application of the writing process—so your efforts in this course, and all the writing you do, will help you get where you want to go in life.

GOING PLACES INCLUDES

Research-based and instructor- and student-tested **M-Series design** that delivers course content in the ways you learn best.

Interactive Visual Chapter Openers with "Think First" writing prompts kick-start each chapter and get you ready to write.

"Going Places" features that open chapters in Parts I–III invite you to connect the chapter's writing activity with your personal, school, and work lives and to develop these connections by brainstorming and sharing your ideas with friends in class.

"At a Glance" annotated student writing samples in each chapter in Parts II and III point out important elements of effective writing, such as thesis statements, topic sentences, supporting details, unity, and coherence.

"A Professional's Take," brief reading selections written by professional writers in each chapter of Part II, show how the experts use the same patterns of organization as you do.

"__________ Thinking" sections in each chapter in Part II, such as "Description Thinking" or "Narration Thinking," help you focus and develop your thoughts in relation to the chapter's main concepts.

"________ in Process" sections in each chapter in Parts II and III, such as "Classification in Process" or "Cause and Effect in Process," walk you through the steps of the writing process. Discover which forms of prewriting work best for you, what challenges you may encounter when drafting and revising, and which errors might need special attention as you edit.

Checkpoints help you stay on point throughout the chapter and connect each chapter's ideas to your own habits, beliefs, and goals:

- **"Ask Yourself"** for critical thinking and quick self-check
- **"Talk about It"** for sharing ideas with peers
- **"A Writer's Response"** for low-pressure writing practice

CourseSmart is a new way to find and buy eTextbooks. At CourseSmart you can save up to 50% off the cost of a print textbook, reduce your impact on the environment, and gain access to powerful web tools for learning. CourseSmart has the largest selection of eTextbooks available anywhere. CourseSmart eTextbooks are available in one standard online reader with full text search, notes and highlighting, and email tools for sharing notes between classmates.

REFLECT
- Identify strengths
- Set goals

Reflection Exercises at the end of each chapter in Part II give you a chance to evaluate your own learning and progress, before moving on to something new.

15 Professional Readings in Part V help you connect critical reading and the writing process, as each reading is followed by comprehension and discussion questions as well as a list of writing assignments.

Integrated Technology icons appear in the margins of the book to let you know where you can go online for extra practice.

CONTENTS

PART 1: Writing in College

Meeting the Demands of College Writing 2

Writing in College 4
Purpose and Form in Writing 5
Focus and Content 9
Critical Reading and Thinking 13
Five Strategies for Reading and Thinking Critically 13
READING
from "On Baking," by Richard Sennett 15
READING
from "Mother Tongue," by Amy Tan 16
Set Goals and Become a Reflective Student 17
Reflective Writing 17

The Writing Process 20

The Writing Process 23
Prewrite: Write Before You Write 23
Talk 24
Cluster 24
Brainstorm 25
Freewrite 27
Review Your Prewriting and Define Your Topic 28
Draft: Focus and Organize 29
Consider Your Audience 29
Focus Your Topic Sentence 30
Organize and Connect Ideas and Details 31
Revise: Read Critically, Then Rewrite 33
Revise Strategically 34
Read Critically 34
READING
from "Growing Up Game," by Brenda Peterson 35
Use Response Groups 35
Revise with a Plan 36
Edit 37
Eliminate Your Usual Errors 37
Reflect 39
Identify Successes 39
Set Goals 40

Writing Paragraphs in College 42

Paragraph Structure 45
Assignments and Topics 46
The Topic Sentence 47
Focus Your Topic Sentence 48
From Prewrite to Topic Sentence 50
Supporting Details 52
Elaborate on Your Major Supporting Details 54
Be Specific 56
Concluding Sentence 57
Paragraph Organization 59
Unity and Coherence 62
Order Your Details 63

PART 2: Paragraph Writing and Patterns of Thinking

4 Description 66

THE DESCRIPTION PARAGRAPH AT A GLANCE *69*

The Description Paragraph at a Glance *69*

DESCRIPTION THINKING *70*

Elements of Description *70*
Get Started *70*
Organize Your Thinking *71*
Comparisons and Description Thinking *73*

DESCRIPTION IN PROCESS *74*

Select an Assignment *74*
Prewrite: Write Before You Write *75*
- Brainstorm *75*
- Freewrite *75*

Draft: Focus and Organize *75*
- Consider Your Audience *76*
- Topic Sentence *76*
- Unity and Coherence *76*
- Concluding Sentence *77*
- Write a First Draft *77*

A PROFESSIONAL'S TAKE

from *Nickel and Dimed*, by Barbara Ehrenreich *78*

Revise: Read Critically, Then Rewrite *79*
- Revision in Action *79*
- Read Critically *80*
- Revise with a Plan *80*

Edit *81*
Reflect *83*

5 Example 84

THE EXAMPLE PARAGRAPH AT A GLANCE *87*

The Example Paragraph at a Glance *87*

EXAMPLE THINKING *88*

Elements of Example *88*
Get Started *88*
- General to Specific *89*

Types of Examples *91*
- Related Examples *91*
- Extended Examples *92*
- Examples as Proof *93*

Elaborate on Examples *93*
Organize Your Thinking *96*

EXAMPLE IN PROCESS *98*

Select an Assignment *98*
Prewrite: Write Before You Write *99*
- Brainstorm *99*
- Freewrite *99*

Draft: Focus and Organize *100*
- Consider Your Audience *100*
- Topic Sentence *100*
- Unity and Coherence *100*
- Concluding Sentence *101*
- Write a First Draft *101*

A PROFESSIONAL'S TAKE

From *Life of Pi*, by Yann Martel *102*

Revise: Read Critically, Then Rewrite *103*
- Revision in Action *103*
- Read Critically *104*
- Revise with a Plan *105*

Edit *105*
Reflect *109*

Narration 110

THE NARRATION PARAGRAPH AT A GLANCE *113*

The Narration Paragraph at a Glance *113*

NARRATION THINKING *114*

Elements of Narration *114*

Get Started *115*

Narration and Specific Detail *117*

Make Connections *119*

NARRATION IN PROCESS *120*

Select an Assignment *121*

Prewrite: Write Before You Write *121*
- Cluster *121*
- Talk *122*

Draft: Focus and Organize *122*
- Consider Your Audience *122*
- Topic Sentence *123*
- Unity and Coherence *123*
- Concluding Sentence *124*
- Write a First Draft *124*

A PROFESSIONAL'S TAKE

From "Ping: The Risk of Innovation: Will Anyone Embrace It?" by G. Pascal Zachary *125*

Revise: Read Critically, Then Rewrite *126*
- Revision in Action *126*
- Read Critically *127*
- Revise with a Plan *128*

Edit *128*

Reflect *131*

Process 132

THE PROCESS PARAGRAPH AT A GLANCE *135*

The Process Paragraph at a Glance *135*

PROCESS THINKING *136*

Elements of Process *136*

Get Started *137*

Organize Your Details *140*

Key Details *141*

PROCESS IN PROCESS *143*

Select an Assignment *143*

Prewrite: Write Before You Write *143*
- Talk *144*
- Brainstorm *144*

Draft: Focus and Organize *144*
- Consider Your Audience *144*
- Topic Sentence *145*
- Unity and Coherence *145*
- Concluding Sentence *146*
- Write a First Draft *146*

A PROFESSIONAL'S TAKE

From "Polly Want a PhD?" by Mark Caldwell *147*

Revise: Read Critically, Then Rewrite *147*
- Revision in Action *148*
- Read Critically *149*
- Revise with a Plan *150*

Edit *150*

Reflect *153*

Classification 154

THE CLASSIFICATION PARAGRAPH AT A GLANCE *157*

The Classification Paragraph at a Glance *157*

CLASSIFICATION THINKING *158*

Elements of Classification *158*

Get Started *158*

Provide Examples of Categories *160*

Avoid Stereotyping *164*

CLASSIFICATION IN PROCESS *165*

Select an Assignment *165*

Prewrite: Write Before You Write *166*
- Brainstorm *166*
- Cluster *166*

Draft: Focus and Organize *166*
- Consider Your Audience *166*
- Topic Sentence *167*
- Unity and Coherence *167*
- Concluding Sentence *168*
- Write a First Draft *168*

A PROFESSIONAL'S TAKE

From *BusinessWeek*, by Karen Kline *169*

Revise: Read Critically, Then Rewrite *170*
- Revision in Action *170*
- Read Critically *171*
- Revise with a Plan *172*

Edit *172*

Reflect *175*

Cause and Effect 176

THE CAUSE AND EFFECT PARAGRAPH AT A GLANCE *179*

The Cause and Effect Paragraph at a Glance *179*
- One Cause, One Effect *179*
- One Cause, Multiple Effects *180*
- Multiple Causes, One Effect *180*

CAUSE AND EFFECT THINKING 181

Elements of Cause and Effect *181*

Get Started *182*

Cause and Effect Details *183*

Organize Your Thinking *184*

CAUSE AND EFFECT IN PROCESS *187*

Select an Assignment *187*

Prewrite: Write Before You Write *188*
- Cluster *188*
- Talk *188*

Draft: Focus and Organize *188*
- Consider Your Audience *188*
- Topic Sentence *189*
- Unity and Coherence *189*
- Concluding Sentence *190*
- Write a First Draft *190*

A PROFESSIONAL'S TAKE

From *Psychology Today*, by Laurence Steinberg *191*

Revise: Read Critically, Then Rewrite *191*
- Revision in Action *192*
- Read Critically *193*
- Revise with a Plan *194*

Edit *194*

Reflect *197*

Comparison and Contrast 198

THE COMPARISON AND CONTRAST PARAGRAPH AT A GLANCE *201*

The Comparison and Contrast Paragraph at a Glance *201*
- Subject-by-Subject Organization *201*
- Point-by-Point Organization *202*

COMPARISON AND CONTRAST THINKING 204
Elements of Comparison and Contrast 204
Get Started 204
Points of Comparison and Contrast 205
Begin with Points of Comparison and Contrast 206
Begin with Details and Discover Points of Comparison and Contrast 206
Select and Elaborate on Details 209
COMPARISON AND CONTRAST IN PROCESS 210
Select an Assignment 210
Prewrite: Write Before You Write 211
Talk 211
Brainstorm 212
Draft: Focus and Organize 212
Consider Your Audience 212
Topic Sentence 212
Unity and Coherence 212
Concluding Sentence 213
Write a First Draft 213
A PROFESSIONAL'S TAKE
From *Time Bind*, by Arlie Hochschild 214
Revise: Read Critically, Then Rewrite 215
Revision in Action 215
Read Critically 217
Revise with a Plan 217
Edit 217
Reflect 221

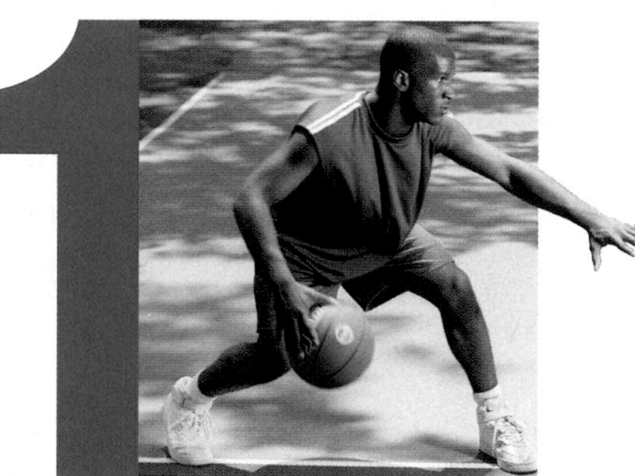

11 Definition 222
THE DEFINITION PARAGRAPH AT A GLANCE 225
The Definition Paragraph at a Glance 225
DEFINITION THINKING 226
Elements of Definition 226
Get Started 227
Examples and Details 228
Negatives 230
DEFINITION IN PROCESS 231
Select an Assignment 231
Prewrite: Write Before You Write 232
Cluster 232
Freewrite 232
Draft: Focus and Organize 233
Consider Your Audience 233
Topic Sentence 233
Unity and Coherence 233
Concluding Sentence 234
Write a First Draft 234
A PROFESSIONAL'S TAKE
From *Care of the Soul*, by Thomas Moore 235
Revise: Read Critically, Then Rewrite 235
Revision in Action 236
Read Critically 237
Revise with a Plan 238
Edit 238
Reflect 241

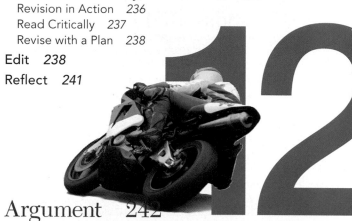

12 Argument 242
THE ARGUMENT PARAGRAPH AT A GLANCE 245
The Argument Paragraph at a Glance 245
ARGUMENT THINKING 246
Elements of Argument 246
Get Started 247
Review Evidence 248
Acknowledge Another Viewpoint 249
ARGUMENT IN PROCESS 252
Select an Assignment 253
Prewrite: Write Before You Write 253
Freewrite 253
Talk 254
Draft: Focus and Organize 254
Consider Your Audience 254
Topic Sentence 254
Unity and Coherence 254
Concluding Sentence 255
Write a First Draft 255
A PROFESSIONAL'S TAKE
From *The Economist* 256
Revise: Read Critically, Then Rewrite 257
Revision in Action 257
Read Critically 258
Revise with a Plan 259
Edit 259
Reflect 263

PART 3: Going to the Next Level: Essay Writing and Patterns of Thinking

13 Essay Structure and the Writing Process 264

THE ESSAY AT A GLANCE *267*

The Essay at a Glance *267*
Elements of Essay Structure *269*
Essay Structure in Outline Form *269*
Get Started *271*
Assignments and Topics *271*
Prewrite *273*
Introductions *274*
  Guidelines for Writing an Effective Introduction *274*
Develop a Thesis *277*
  Guidelines for Writing an Effective Thesis *277*
The Body of the Essay *280*
  Thesis and Topic Sentences *280*
  Supporting Details *284*
  Develop an Essay Plan *286*
  Unity and Coherence *288*
Conclusions *291*
  Guidelines for Writing an Effective Conclusion *291*
Revise and Edit Your Essay *294*
  Guidelines for Revising and Editing Your Essay *295*
Titles *295*
Final Review *296*

14 Types of Essays 298

THE ESSAY STRUCTURE AT A GLANCE *301*

The Essay at a Glance *301*
Elements of the Essay *302*
The Writing Process *303*
Essays with One Pattern of Organization *304*
Description *304*
  Description Refresher *306*
Example *308*
  Example Refresher *310*
Narration *310*
  Narration Refresher *313*
Process *313*
  Process Refresher *315*
Classification *316*
  Classification Refresher *318*
Cause and Effect *319*
  Cause and Effect Refresher *321*
Comparison and Contrast *321*
  Comparison and Contrast Refresher *324*
Definition *325*
  Definition Refresher *328*
Argument *328*
  Argument Refresher *331*
Essays with Multiple Patterns of Organization *331*
The Mixed-Pattern Essay at a Glance *331*
Final Review *335*

Paraphrase, Summary, and Quotation 336

Use Sources Correctly 339

Paraphrase 339

- Acknowledge Sources 341

Plagiarism 343

- Copy and Paste 343
- Close Paraphrase 345

Summary 346

- Capture the Main Idea of a Story 347

READING

from "Lives Changed in a Split Second," by Charles Wheelan 347

- Capture the Key Details of a Story 349

READING

from "A Deadly Toll Is Haunting Football," by Ira Berkow 349

- Provide an Overview of a Textbook, Magazine, or Journal Article 350

READING

from "Homework, a School Reform That Works," by Jonathon Rauch 351

READING

from "The Violent Games People Play," by Hazel Muir 352

Quotation 354

- Choose Quotations 354
- Introduce Quotations 354

Suggestions for Daily Practice 361

The Documented Essay 362

THE DOCUMENTED ESSAY AT A GLANCE 365

The Documented Essay at a Glance 365

Elements of the Documented Essay 367

Get Started 368

Locate Information 368

- Internet Sources 368
- Periodical Literature 370
- Library Catalog and Reference Books 371

PROCESS INFORMATION 372

Types of Information 372

- Facts and Statistics 372
- Authoritative Opinion 372
- Cases and Examples 373

Take Notes 373

Integrate Sources 376

- In-Text Citations 376

Document Sources 378

Cite Different Types of Sources 379

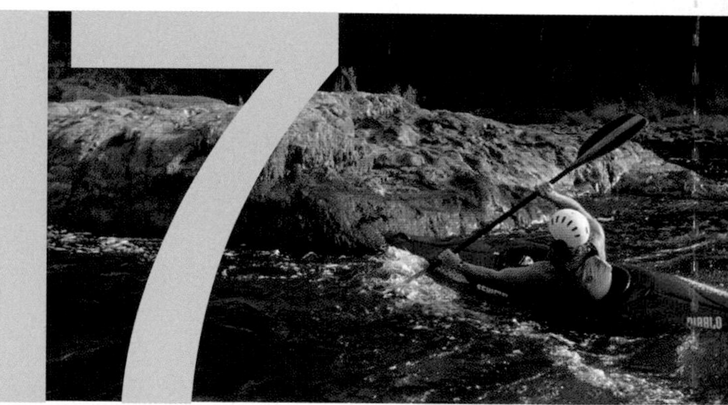

Writing in Class: *Short-Answer and Essay Tests* 384

THE IN-CLASS ESSAY AT A GLANCE 387

The In-Class Essay at a Glance 387

Elements of In-Class Writing 389

Types of In-Class Writing 389

Sentence-Length Short Answers 389

Paragraph-Length, Short Essay Answers 391

Essay-Length Answers 393

How to Prepare for In-Class Writing 395

PART 4: The Writer's Guidebook

The Simple Sentence 397

An Introduction to the Simple Sentence *397*

Find Subjects and Predicates *398*

The Subject *399*
- Nouns *400*
- Pronouns *400*
- Gerunds *400*
- Tips for Finding the Simple Subject *401*
- Subjects and Prepositional Phrases *402*
- Subjects in Questions and Commands *404*

The Predicate *406*
- Action Verbs *406*
- Linking Verbs *408*
- Helping Verbs and Verb Phrases *410*

Beyond the Simple Sentence: *Compounds, Coordination, and Subordination* 413

Build on the Simple Sentence: Compound Subjects and Compound Predicates *414*
- Compound Subjects *414*
- Compound Predicates *416*

The Compound Sentence and Coordination *418*
- Use a Comma and a Conjunction *418*
- Use a Semicolon and a Conjunctive Adverb *421*
- Use a Semicolon *422*

The Complex Sentence and Subordination *424*
- Subordination and the Relative Clause *428*

The Sentence Fragment 435

Types of Fragments *436*
- Noun Phrase Fragments *436*
- Adjective Phrase Fragments *436*
- Prepositional Phrase Fragments *437*
- Verbal Phrase Fragments *437*
- Dependent Clause Fragments *439*

Comma Splices and Run-Ons 445

Comma Splices *445*
- Identify Comma Splices *446*
- Correct Comma Splices *447*

Run-Ons *451*
- Identify Run-Ons *451*
- Correct Run-Ons *453*

Editing Verb Errors:
Agreement, Irregular Verbs, and Consistency 459

Verbs and Verb Agreement 460
- Verbs 460
- Subject and Verb Agreement 461
- Additional Verb Agreement Problems 466

Irregular Verbs 471

Consistent Verb Tense 474

Pronoun Agreement, Case, and Consistency 477

Pronoun Agreement 478
- Detect Errors in Pronoun Agreement 480
- Indefinite Pronouns and Agreement 483

Pronoun Case 485
- Compound Subjects and Objects, Sentences with *Than* and *As* 487

Pronoun Consistency 489

Adjectives and Adverbs 493

Adjectives 494

Adverbs and the -ly Ending 495

Good/Well, Bad/Badly, Real/Really 497

Adjectives: Comparatives and Superlatives 498

Adverbs: Comparatives and Superlatives 500

Hyphenated Adjectives 501

Punctuation 503

Commas 503
- Commas and Conjunctions 504
- Commas and Introductory Modifiers 505
- Commas and Interrupters 507
- Commas in a Series 509

Semicolons and Colons 513
- Semicolons 513
- Colons 513

Quotation Marks 516
- Complete-Sentence Quotations 516
- Partial Quotations 516
- Indirect Quotations 518
- Internal Quotations and Titles 519

Apostrophes 520
- Possessive Forms 520
- Contractions 521
- Plurals 522

Mechanics 525

Spelling 525
- Basic Spelling Rules 526
- Commonly Misspelled Words 530
- Commonly Misused Words 531

Capitalization 542

Numbers 546

Abbreviations 548

PART 5: Reading and Thinking Critically

Building Vocabulary 550

Collect Vocabulary Daily *552*

Use a Dictionary and Thesaurus *554*

- Get Acquainted with a Dictionary *555*
- Use a Dictionary Effectively *555*
- Get Acquainted with a Thesaurus *558*
- Use a Thesaurus Effectively *558*
- Write with a Thesaurus and a Dictionary *561*

Improve Word Choice *563*

- Precise Nouns and Verbs *563*
- Tone *564*
- Denotation and Connotation *565*
- Appropriate Word Choice *566*

Critical Reading, Thinking, and Writing 570

Critical Reading *573*

Five Strategies for Effective Reading *573*

- Preview *573*

"Edision and the Kinetoscope," by John Belton *574*

- Ask Questions *575*
- Connect to Prior Knowledge *576*
- Identify Important Information *576*
- Reread *576*

Read with a Pen *578*

READING

"A Simple Glass of Water," by Ted Fishman *579*

ADDITIONAL READINGS

"Too Much Homework, Too Little Play," by Kathy Seal *580*

"In Defense of Zoos" from *The Life of Pi*, by Yann Martel *583*

"Night Walker," by Brent Staples *585*

"You've Got Hate Mail," by Lydie Raschka *588*

"The Body of the Beholder," by Michele Ingrassia *591*

"Dogs Need a Best Friend, Too," by Michelle Slatalla *594*

"Hitting Bottom: Why America Should Outlaw Spanking," by Emily Bazelon *598*

"How Space Junk Works," by John Fuller *601*

"The Ice Bear Cometh, Wearing Nothing but a Speedo," by Lewis Gordon Pugh *604*

"Anatomy Lessons: A Vanishing Rite for Young Doctors," by Abigail Zuger *606*

"Privacy Lost: These Phones Can Find You," by Laura M. Holson *609*

"The Replacement," by Sanford J. Ungar *612*

"Desperate to Learn English," by Alice Callaghan *615*

GOING PLACES

Getting to Know Yourself

Most of us have ideas and beliefs we do not think about or question. Maybe you love art. Perhaps you are concerned about the environment. When someone asks you to write about these topics, you may be surprised by what you discover. Writing is actually a great way to learn about yourself. It may be challenging at first, but it is worth the effort.

BRAINSTORM

Brainstorm a list of subjects you really care about. Then select the two or three most important ones. When did these subjects become important? Has their importance to you changed over time? What caused that change?

The "Write" Audience

Whenever you write, ask yourself who your reader is. Just as you shift gears when you stop talking to a friend outside of class and address an instructor instead, you need to adjust how you write, what you choose to say, and the words you use when you write for different readers. Depending on your audience and the context, you might be a student, a friend, a granddaughter, and a coworker all in one day. If you write a paper for an instructor and then e-mail a friend, you are writing for two very different readers. Being sensitive to your tone and language, professionally and personally, will help you communicate more effectively.

DISCUSSION

Who is the person you find it easiest to talk to? Why? Who do you find it most difficult to talk to? Why? Turn and talk to a classmate about these two people, and describe what it feels like to talk to them.

Get Ahead: Moving Toward Successful Writing

Knowing what you want to say (subject and focus), why you are saying it (purpose), how you will say it (form), and who you are saying it to (reader/audience) will give you a head start on any writing project. If you take the time to reflect on and explore your ideas, you will make the writing process less frustrating and the end result more successful. By becoming a successful writer in college, you will be prepared for almost any career. Going Places boxes like this one in each of the chapters in Parts I, II, and III will show you how the skills learned in that chapter can help you get ahead in the classroom, the working world, and your personal life.

DISCUSSION

Brainstorm for a minute or two, recalling times in school or at home that you had to write. For each instance, recall the subject, purpose, form, and audience you wrote for. Then turn and talk to a classmate, describing one of these writing experiences.

Meeting the Demands of College Writing

CHAPTER 1

CHAPTER OVERVIEW

- Writing in College
- Purpose and Form
- Focus and Content
- Critical Reading and Thinking
  - *Five Strategies*
- Set Goals

THINK FIRST

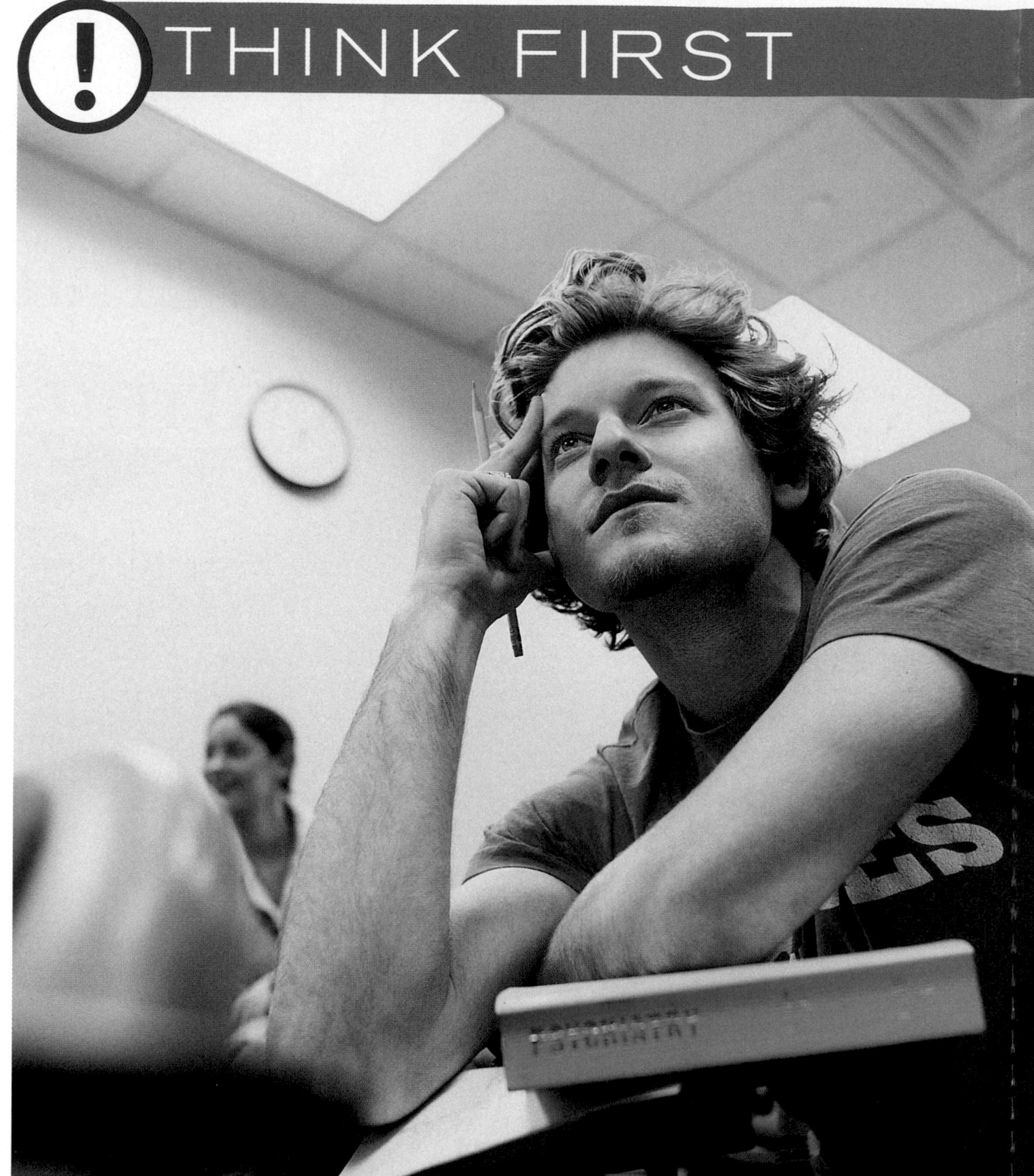

Does learning involve pleasure, hard work, or both? What makes learning fun? Recall a positive and a negative experience you had in school. Write a paragraph about these two experiences. Be specific about the time, place, subject, and people involved.

Writing in College

Take out a piece of paper and a pen. In college your writing will often begin with an assignment. Assignments have a purpose. In some cases, you will write to explore ideas and make connections between one idea and another or between classroom learning and the real world. More often you will write to convey information or to demonstrate what you know about course content. Finally, you will sometimes write to persuade, to change your reader's mind and possibly to motivate someone to act. More often than not, the reader of your writing will be the instructor who provides you with a subject. The form of your writing will vary, from journal entry to summary, from paragraph to essay, from short-answer and essay test to report and term paper.

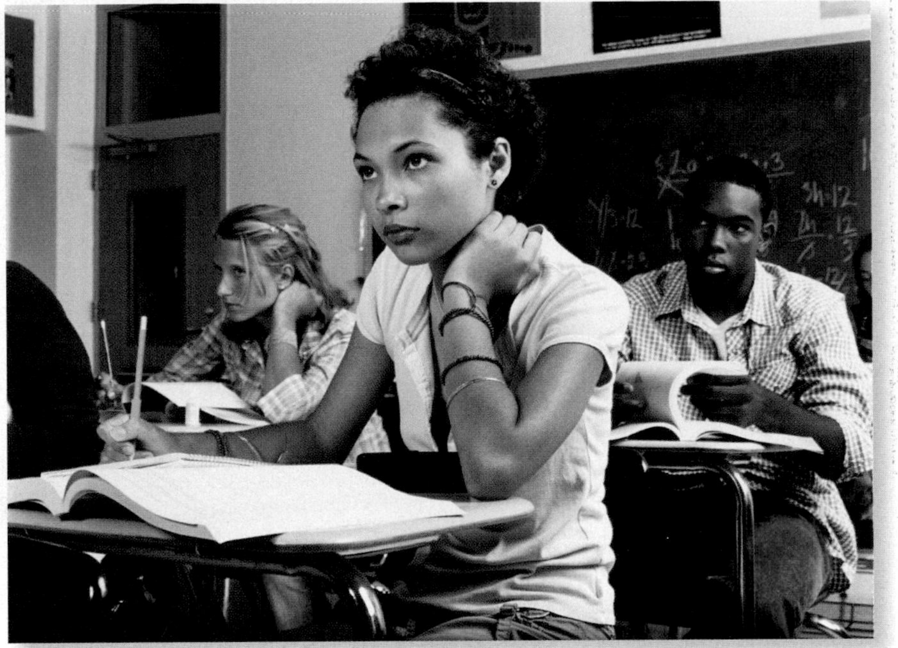

Purpose and Form in Writing

The reason you write is your **purpose.** You write to reflect, to inform, and to persuade. Purpose will often determine the **form** your writing takes, the way it is organized and presented. For example, when you write to figure something out, you do not write a memo to yourself; you keep your thoughts and words flowing in a journal entry. In contrast, when you write to inform or to persuade, you do so with a reader in mind. Readers of academic writing look for organization, supporting detail, and correct use of language. Readers of workplace writing look for the same things.

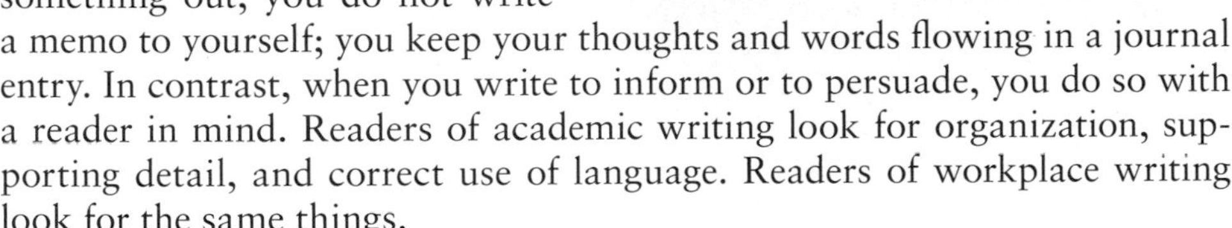

In school, you will often write paragraphs and essays; in the workplace, you will often write memos and reports. When writing to inform or persuade, always pay attention to form. Ask yourself these questions:

Who am I writing for?

What do I want to say?

What is this writing supposed to look like?

Moreover, in most academic writing, keep in mind these guidelines when considering word choice and style:

Minimize your use of first-person pronouns: *I, my, me.*

Minimize your use of contractions: *isn't, don't, won't.*

Avoid slang and the kind of informal language you use in casual conversation.

EXERCISE 1-1 Purpose in Home and Work Writing

Directions: *Circle the purpose that best relates to each of the forms of writing listed. For each form of writing, indicate the subject (what it is about) and who will read it. Some forms of writing may have more than one purpose. The first one has been done for you.*

Purpose

A. **Think on paper:** Explore your thoughts, ideas, feelings, and beliefs.

B. **Convey information:** Share what you know and what you have learned.

C. **Persuade your reader:** Change your reader's mind, motivate your reader to do something.

EXAMPLE

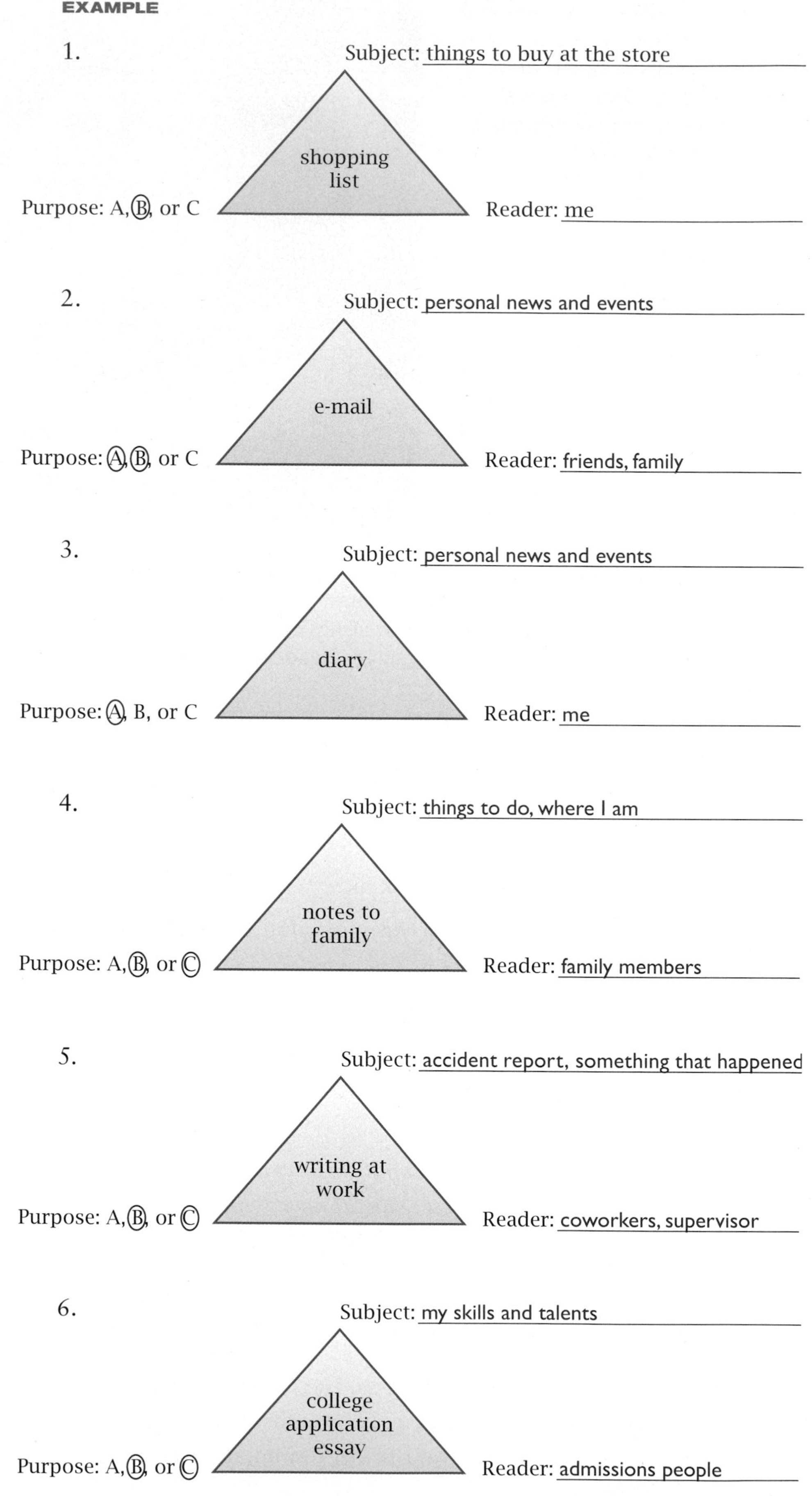
1.
Subject: things to buy at the store
shopping list
Purpose: A, (B), or C
Reader: me
2.
Subject: personal news and events
e-mail
Purpose: (A), (B), or C
Reader: friends, family
3.
Subject: personal news and events
diary
Purpose: (A), B, or C
Reader: me
4.
Subject: things to do, where I am
notes to family
Purpose: A, (B), or (C)
Reader: family members
5.
Subject: accident report, something that happened
writing at work
Purpose: A, (B), or (C)
Reader: coworkers, supervisor
6.
Subject: my skills and talents
college application essay
Purpose: A, (B), or (C)
Reader: admissions people

EXERCISE 1-2 Purpose in College Writing

Directions: *Circle the purpose that best relates to each of the forms of college writing listed below. (Some forms of writing will have more than one purpose.) Indicate possible subjects and readers for each form of writing.*

Purpose

A. **Think on paper:** Explore your thoughts, ideas, feelings, and beliefs.
B. **Convey information:** Share what you know and what you have learned.
C. **Persuade your reader:** Change your reader's mind, motivate your reader to do something.

EXAMPLE

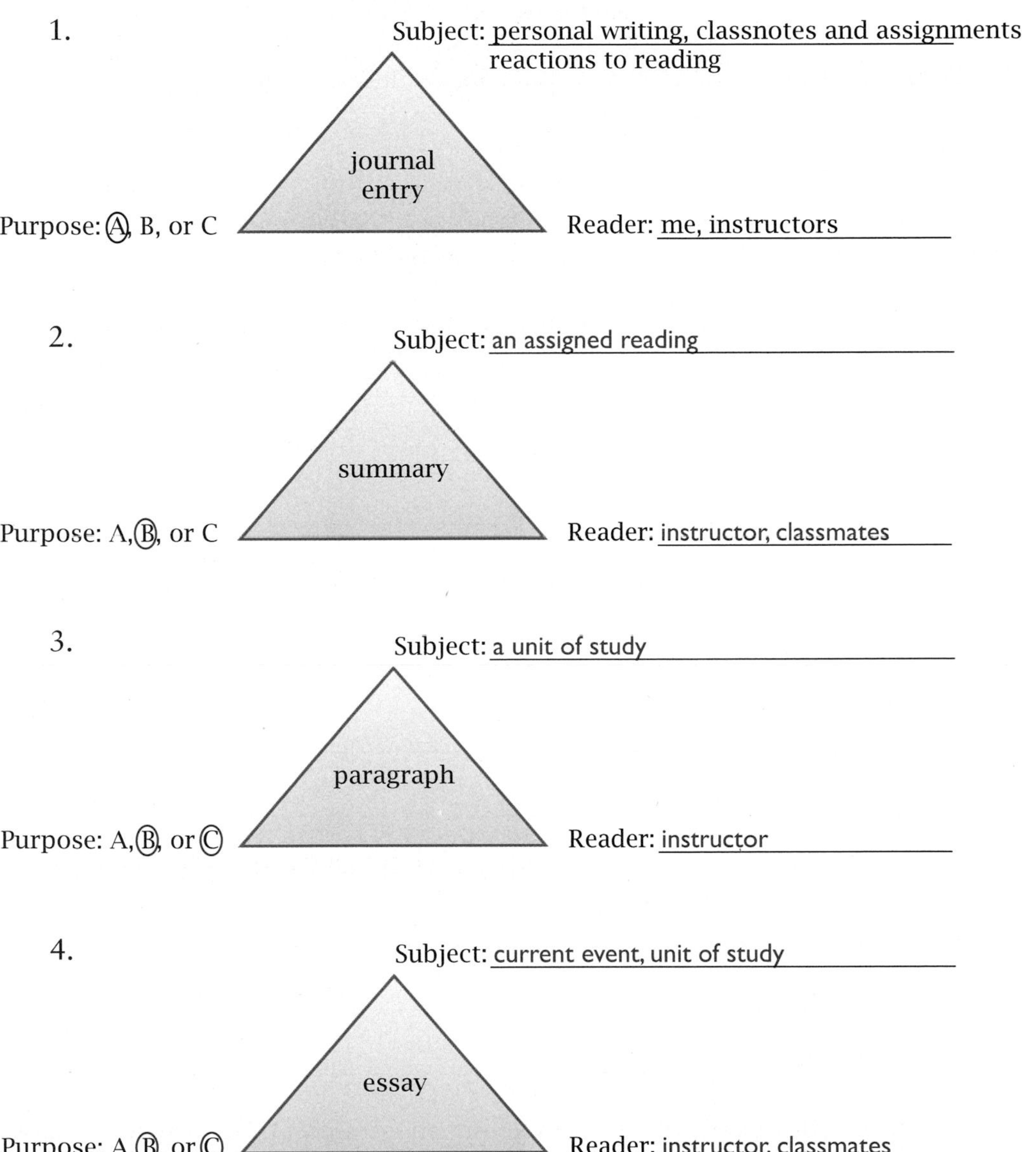

5.

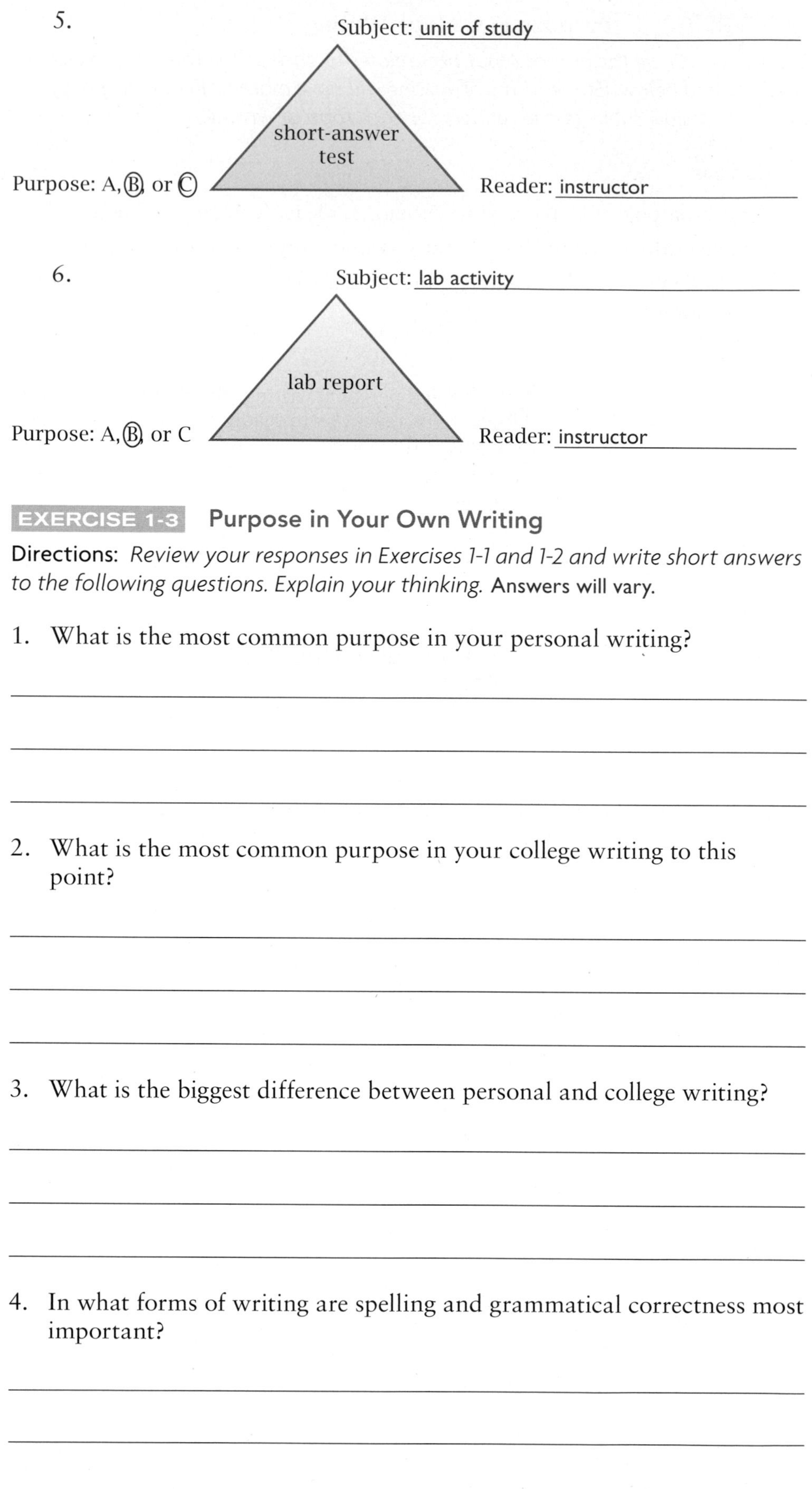

6.

EXERCISE 1-3 Purpose in Your Own Writing

Directions: *Review your responses in Exercises 1-1 and 1-2 and write short answers to the following questions. Explain your thinking.* Answers will vary.

1. What is the most common purpose in your personal writing?

____

____

____

2. What is the most common purpose in your college writing to this point?

____

____

____

3. What is the biggest difference between personal and college writing?

____

____

____

4. In what forms of writing are spelling and grammatical correctness most important?

____

____

____

Focus and Content

The focus of your writing will vary according to your purpose for writing. In assignments asking you to think on paper (journal writing, for example), the content may be personal. As you explore ideas or think on paper, the focus is on you, the writer, and the subject you are writing about. You do not worry about your reader's reaction. You are the primary audience.

In writing assignments in school, you are asked to convey information and show your understanding of course material. Your content is academic in reports, short-answer tests, papers, and exams. You demonstrate your knowledge to a professor. The focus is on the subject and the reader.

In argument and persuasion, you demonstrate your knowledge to a professor by stating and supporting an opinion. The focus is on the writer, the subject, and the reader. There is a subject—for example, Should the legal drinking age be lowered? There is an audience—a reader who is not convinced it is a good idea. Along with the evidence you present, there is your personal knowledge of the subject that you include to influence the reader's thinking.

The following samples of student writing illustrate the relationship between focus and writing content.

A. Unedited Student Journal Entry

FOCUS: The writer

What is so great about drinking? I do not get enjoyment, pleasure, or satisfaction from it. It seems like everyone my age is drinking just to get drunk and stupid. People drink to be more social and or to enhance life. Life would be boring without alcohol right? Not in my opinon. I like to talk to and aproach people, I can act goofy and stupid, and I can enjoy myself. People have found it hard to believe that I do not enjoy drinking. I suppose it is odd, considering most eighteen-year-olds pass the weekends with getting hammered and wasted at parties. Ive been there and done that. Ive had a good time too. People get hurt physically and mentally when drinking. People will say things they do not mean or do things they would not do when they were sober. I imagine this is another reason why so many people do drink: A temporary solution to life's problems.

FORM AND PURPOSE
The journal entry focuses on the writer's experiences, thoughts, and beliefs.

FOCUS
The writer is the audience. He is not worried about who might read his journal. The use of "I" is acceptable in this form of writing. Spelling and grammatical correctness are not big issues because this writing is not for an outside audience.

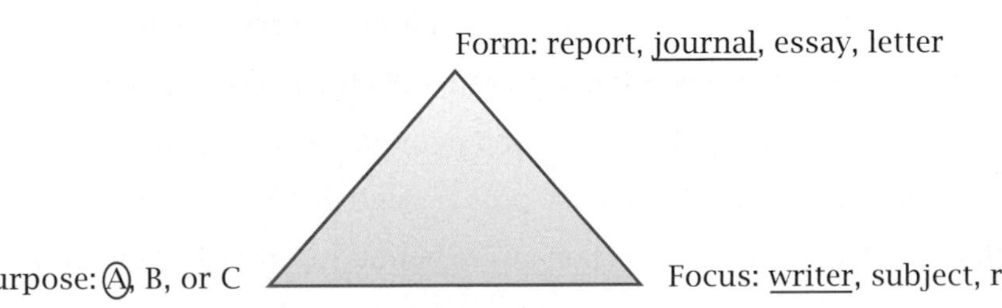

FORM AND PURPOSE
This report focuses on the subject, explaining the test process. The writer provides detailed observations and tries to answer questions the reader might have about the workplace.

FOCUS
The focus here is also on the reader. This report was written for a supervisor or other professional in the field to read, so spelling and grammatical correctness are very important.

B. Report on Workplace Visit for Physics Class

FOCUS: The subject and the reader

This facility was doing tests on truck frames, with the goal of making trucks lighter by reducing the mass of the frame. The manufacturer needs to be sure the truck frame is strong enough to be safe in normal operation. A number of tests were devised to obtain data. Technicians outfitted a vehicle with instrumentation and took it to an appropriate site so data could be collected and recorded. Test situations included travel over rough terrain, ordinary highway mileage, and sudden shocks such as those caused by potholes. After data were recorded, the vehicle was then returned to the test facility, where the recorded data were, in effect, played over and over. In a few weeks' time, the vehicle was subjected to a lifetime of road wear. Engineers analyzed the results.

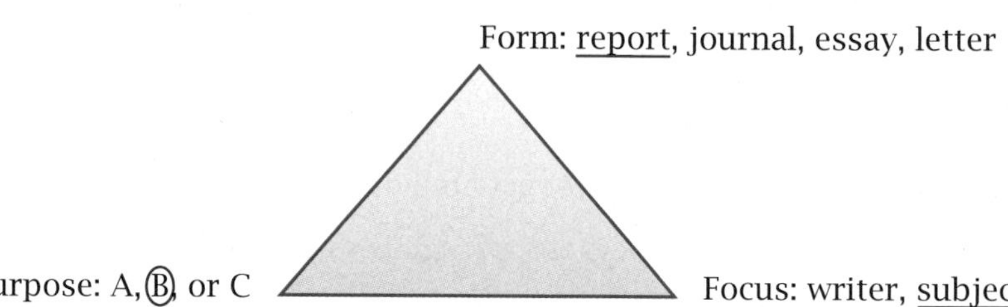

FORM AND PURPOSE
This discussion question response focuses on detailed knowledge of a reading assignment. The writer quotes the essay by Maya Angelou and provides a thorough response.

FOCUS
The focus is also on the reader. The careful writing, use of quotations, and detailed explanations show that this writer knows what the professor wants. The content and careful writing persuades the reader that the writer is disciplined, informed, and capable of critical thinking. The writer avoids first-person pronouns and slang.

C. Response to Discussion Question in Literature Textbook

FOCUS: The writer, the subject, and the reader

Young Maya Angelou was ashamed that Mama could show off her ignorance in the presence of a woman as great as Mrs. Flowers. To Angelou the way Mama used incorrect grammar in front of a gentlewoman was a sign of ignorance. She did not understand why Mama could not remember her verbs. Why did Mama always say "is" when she talked about more than two people? Why did Mama insist on calling her "Sister Flowers"? Why did Mama have to embarrass her so much? To Angelou, Mrs. Flowers was the definition of elegance. Angelou felt that Mrs. Flowers deserved a proper greeting. Mama's improper speech never bothered Mrs. Flowers. She understood the difference between ignorance and poor education. Mama had her own intelligence even if she did not use proper English. They spoke easily with each other. Mrs. Flowers and Mama were bound together by how they were alike in a prejudiced and sexist society. They both understood that money and appearance were not what make a person great. What seemed like a strange relationship at the time was really a relationship of respect. She discovered years later that a formal education was all that separated them.

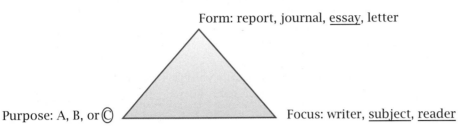

Form: report, journal, <u>essay</u>, letter

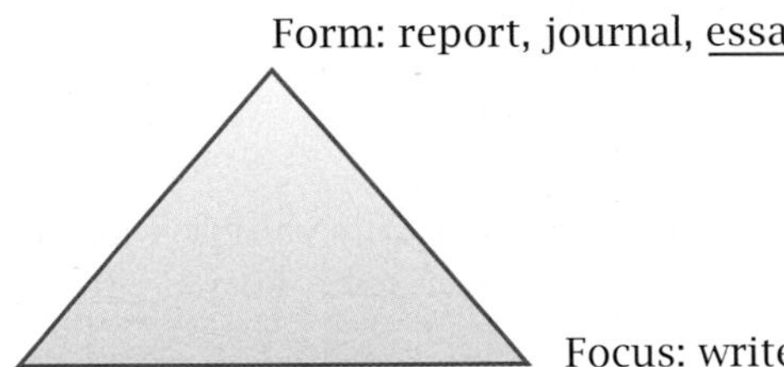

Purpose: A, B, or (C) Focus: writer, <u>subject</u>, <u>reader</u>

EXERCISE 1-4 **Form, Purpose, and Focus**

Directions: *Read the following passages. Underline the form of writing that best describes each passage and underline the focus of each passage. Circle the primary purpose.*

1.

All of a sudden, rock music is getting way too popular. More and more young people are forming their own bands. They are even changing their appearance. Kids who always had short hair are coming out with "college hair." Kids who used to be all but invisible are dying their hair green and sporting chained wallets. Even the ones who used to sell drugs want to become rock stars as their next source of income. The competition is suddenly so steep that the odds of being successful have declined. In addition, the sound is uniform. It is all hardcore bandwagon noise. Where is the originality? They just follow the crowd. The popularity of rock, and the idea that anyone can play, means everything sounds the same—and bad, at that.

Form: report, <u>journal</u>, essay, letter

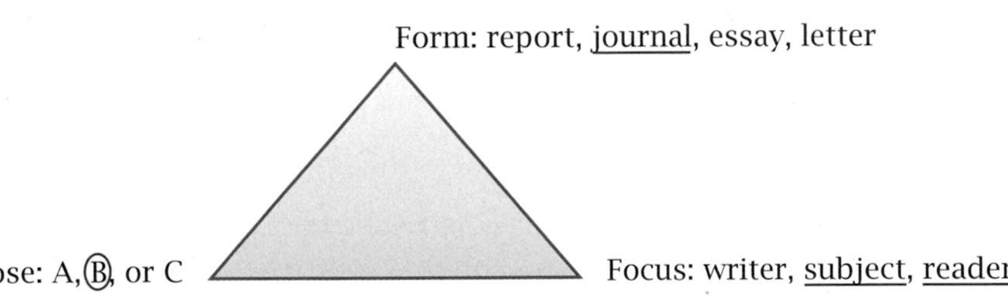

Purpose: A, (B), or C Focus: writer, <u>subject</u>, <u>reader</u>

2.

Vehicle 33 arrived at the scene of the accident at 2:25 p.m. Scene was the southwest corner of Canfield and Beck. Two-car collision. Driver of one car, middle-aged male, was unconscious, breathing 25 bpm, bleeding from the mouth. Trauma to the head and face. Situation called for airway management. C-collar was applied. Patient was boarded, oxygen administered high flow, transported by ALS. Driver of the other car, 18-yr-old female, was sitting on the curb, responsive. Quick survey indicated possible fracture of ulna, right arm; lacerations. Fracture was splinted. Patient was stable when transported to emergency.

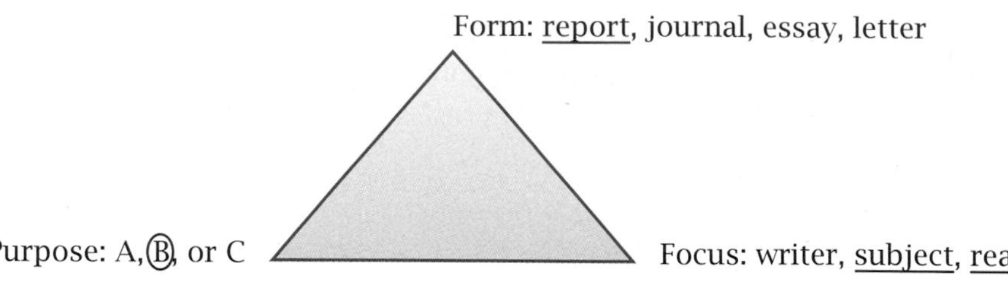

3.

I worked on your campaign last year in the Cleveland area. Your stance on water quality and Ohio's participation in the Great Lake Alliance was very important to me. In fact, that issue sold me on your candidacy.

For that reason, I urge you to alter your stated position on future funding for the EPA. I know you are a member of the committee that will recommend funding, and I know you are a man of conscience and vision. The EPA has been an important factor in the cleanup of Lake Erie. Cutting its funding and its ability to regulate industry along the water's edge will have long-term and, I fear, negative effects on one of Ohio's greatest natural resources.

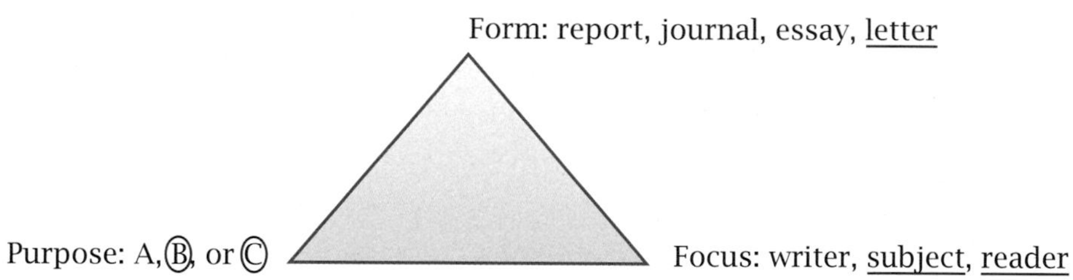

4.

In Walter E. Williams's article "Making a Case for Corporal Punishment," Williams expresses his opinion on this controversial subject. He states that the old-fashioned way of whipping misbehaved children produces more civilized young people. Parents today do not discipline their kids the way they used to. Children in today's society are hostile and disrespectful toward adults. Williams believes that whipping these children, as a form of punishment, would make them as respectful as the children of yesterday. By disciplining children, parents and other figures of authority would have more control over the children of today.

Form: report, journal, <u>essay</u>, letter

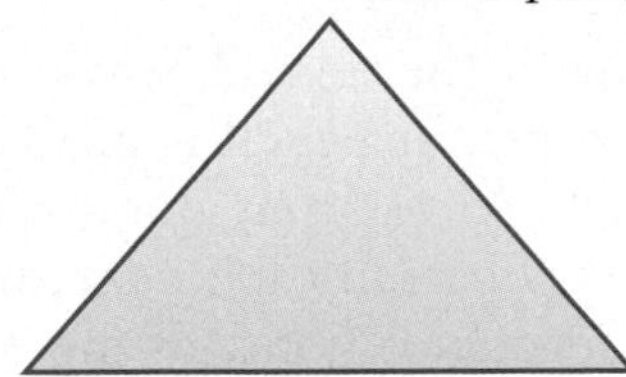

Purpose: A, (B), or (C)

Focus: writer, <u>subject</u>, <u>reader</u>

5.

FROM: sadsoul22@omni.com
DATE: Sun, 13 Oct 2002 19:44:29 EDT
SUBJECT: Your 2B
TO: Professor Safer
Sorry i did not turn in my essay! i'll take care of it, as soon as i can. the past week has been tough, my kids have a serious case of ear infection and the flu for two weeks now, so it has been pretty challenging for me. and on top of that we left to canada friday and i just got back two hours ago. I'm done with my most of the work and i'm working as hard as i can. so sorry for the delay. is tomorrow ok?
your student, Sue

Form: report, journal, essay, <u>letter</u>

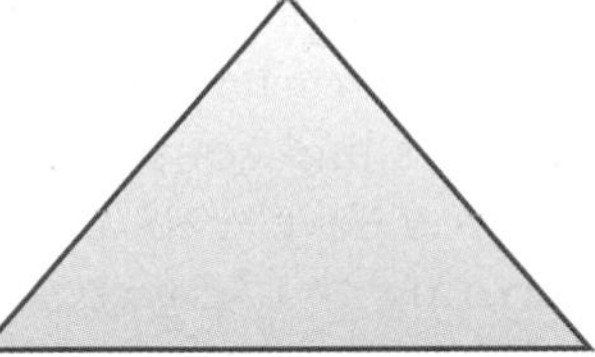

Purpose: A, (B), or C

Focus: writer, <u>subject</u>, <u>reader</u>

Critical Reading and Thinking

See Chapter 28 for a more detailed discussion of critical reading.

Because of the volume of reading required in college, your academic survival will depend on your becoming a critical reader. You need to identify your purpose for reading, apply strategies to help you read effectively, and monitor your comprehension.

Five Strategies for Reading and Thinking Critically

These five strategies will help you develop your critical reading and thinking skills. Apply these strategies before, during, and after reading materials for your classes. Apply them also to essays written by your peers. Learning to be a critical reader will also help you become a better writer.

1. Read with a pen.
2. Ask questions.
3. Make personal connections.
4. Determine important information and ideas.
5. Draw inferences.

Read with a Pen

Be an active reader and interact with the text. Always read with a pen or pencil. A highlighter is good, but a pen or pencil is probably better. With a highlighter, you can cover too much, so you may not always select the most important information. Instead, as you read each page, use a pen or pencil to underline the most important ideas, jot notes in the margins, circle key terms, and trace connections across the page. Reading with a pen helps you interact with and work on what you are reading.

Ask Questions

In this chapter, you have started to ask questions about writing. What is the form being used? What are the purpose and focus of a particular piece of writing? Ask these questions about everything you read. Ask yourself what the writer's main idea is and what supporting details the writer provides. As you work through the chapters in Part II of this text and learn about different patterns of organization, you will ask more questions about the organization of what you read. For example, does it tell a story? Does it compare and contrast two items or points of view? Does it explain the steps in a process?

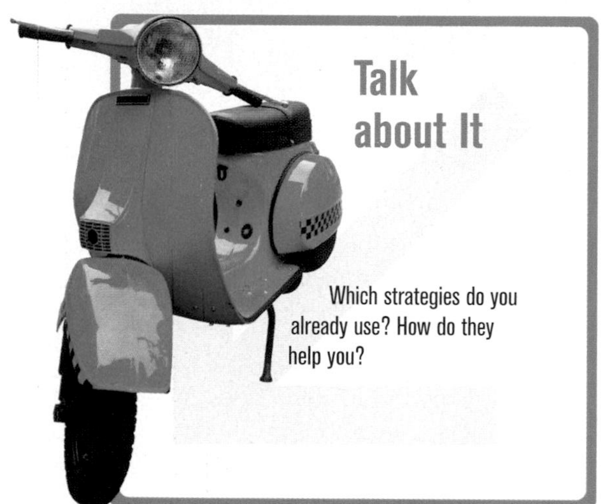

Talk about It

Which strategies do you already use? How do they help you?

Make Personal Connections

The meaning of what you read comes from both the page and from you. You bring knowledge to the page. What you read might remind you of people, events, ideas, and opinions you are familiar with or have thought about. Use a pen to briefly note these personal connections. Briefly note connections with things you have read too. When you read, you create a web of meaning that consists of what you know, what you have read, and what you are currently reading. Sometimes personal connections can lead you astray, so monitor your thinking to stay connected to the subject of the material you are reading.

Determine Important Information and Ideas

Everything you read is not of equal importance. Some ideas are more important than others. You can get an idea of what is important by reading titles and headings and the first and last sentences of paragraphs, by looking for bold type and italicized type, and by checking for marginal notes and boxes. If you are reading a textbook, survey the chapter and look for review sections and anything that specifically announces what is important. In other types of reading, look for the same information or for ideas that appear in more than one place. Anything that is repeated is probably important.

Draw Inferences

Critical reading involves *drawing inferences.* You want to be able to point to the facts. However, you also want to *read between the lines.* When you make an **inference,** you use facts and information in the text to make an informed guess about what the author is saying. For instance, in the response to a question about a reading on page 10, the writer asserts, "Mrs. Flowers and Mama were bound together by how they were alike in a prejudiced and sexist society." Here the writer has put two and two together. She has made a connection between separate statements of fact in the reading and come to a conclusion. The conclusion is not explicitly stated by Angelou, but given the facts, the inference makes sense.

Now notice how the reader of the following excerpt has read with a pen.

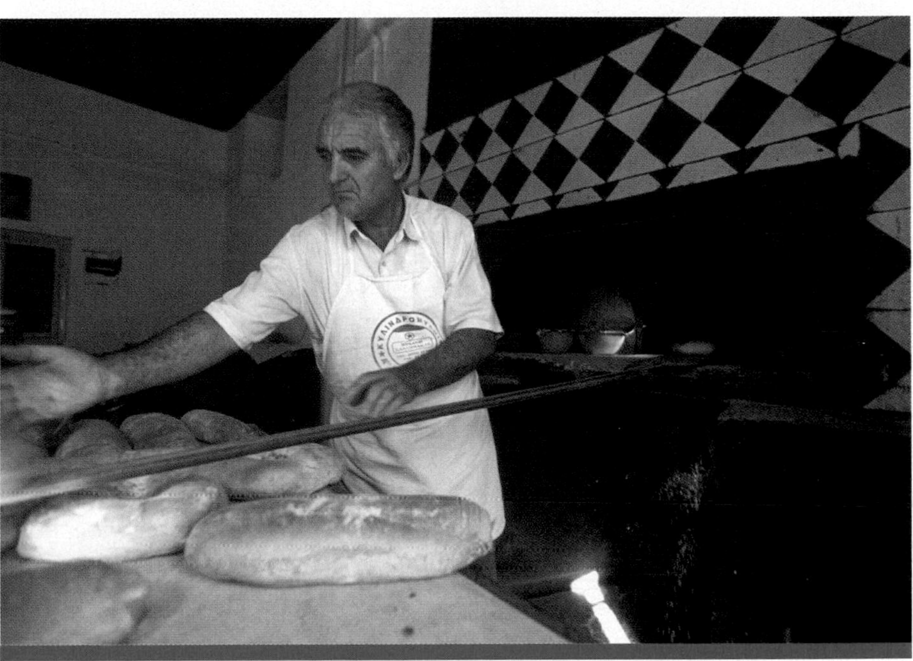

from "On Baking"
by RICHARD SENNETT

A year or so ago, I went back to the Boston bakery where twenty-five years ago, in researching *The Hidden Injuries of Class*, I had interviewed a group of bakers. Back then, the bakers worried about upward social mobility among themselves; they feared their children would lose their Greek roots in becoming more American. And the bakers were certain Boston's white Anglo-Saxon Protestants looked down on immigrant Americans like themselves—perhaps a realistic assessment.

PERSONAL CONNECTION
Talked about this in sociology.

INFERENCE
Immigrants faced prejudice in America.

Work in the bakery bound the workers self-consciously together. The bakery was filled with noise; the smell of yeast mingled with human sweat in the hot rooms; the bakers' hands were constantly plunged into flour and water; the men used their noses as well as their eyes to judge when the bread was done. Craft pride was strong, but the men said they did not enjoy their work, and I believed them. The ovens often burned them; the primitive dough beater pulled human muscles; and it was night work, which meant these men, so family-centered, seldom saw their families during the week.

PERSONAL CONNECTION
I love the smell of a bakery.

But it seemed to me, watching them struggle, that the ethnic solidarity of being Greek made possible their solidarity in this difficult labor—good worker meant good Greek. The equation of good work and good Greek made sense in the concrete, rather than the abstract. The bakers needed to cooperate intimately in order to coordinate the varied tasks of

INFERENCE
Lots of pressure on people to do the right thing in a new country.

QUESTION
What does berate mean?
"to scold angrily"

the bakery. When two of the bakers, brothers who were both alcoholic, showed up plastered on the job, others would berate them by referring to the mess they were making of their families and the loss of prestige of their families in the community where all the Greeks lived. Not being a good Greek was a potent tool of shame, and thus of work discipline. When I returned to the bakery years later, I was amazed at how much had changed.

The reader uses all the strategies we have mentioned as he reads this essay with a pen. He underlines important details. He makes personal connections to himself and to other classes he has taken. Although his comment about loving the smell of bread may not be relevant to understanding Sennett's purpose, it demonstrates he is personally engaged in the reading. Plus, he makes an inference about the pressures these bakers face by connecting his thinking about prejudice to the inference in the third paragraph. Finally, he also asks and answers a question to define a difficult but important word.

EXERCISE 1-5 Reading Critically

Directions: *Read the following excerpt and try out the strategies for critical reading we have detailed above. Read with a pen. Place a P in the margin and write a word or two about the personal connection you make with the reading. Underline one or two sentences that seem important. Place a Q in the margin and ask a question. Place a C in the margin where you make a connection between what is said in different places in the reading.* Answers will vary.

from "Mother Tongue"
by AMY TAN

Writer's Response
Tell about a time you helped a parent solve a problem.

Lately, I have been giving more thought to the kind of English my mother speaks. Like others, I have described it to people as "broken" or "fractured" English. But I wince when I say that. It has always bothered me that I can think of no way to describe it other than "broken," as if it were damaged and needed to be fixed, as if it lacked a certain wholeness and soundness. I have heard other terms used, "limited English," for example. But they seem just as bad, as if everything is limited, including the people's perceptions of the limited English speaker.

I know this for a fact, because when I was growing up, my mother's "limited" English limited my perception of her. I was ashamed of her English. I believed that her English reflected the quality of what she had to say. That is, because she expressed them imperfectly her thoughts were imperfect. And I had plenty of empirical evidence to support me: the fact that people in department stores, at banks, and at restaurants did not take her seriously, did not give her good service, pretended not to understand her, or even acted as if they did not hear her.

My mother has long realized the limitations of her English as well. When I was fifteen, she used to have me call people on the phone to pretend I was she. In this guise, I was forced to ask for information or even to complain and yell at people who had been rude to her. One time it was a call to her stockbroker in New York. She had cashed out her small portfolio and it just so happened we were going to go to New York the next week, our very first trip outside California. I had to get on the phone and say in an adolescent voice that was not very convincing, "This is Mrs. Tan."

And my mother was standing in the back whispering loudly, "Why he did not send me check, already two weeks late. So mad he lie to me, losing me money."

And then I said in perfect English, "Yes, I'm getting rather concerned. You had agreed to send the check two weeks ago, but it has not arrived."

EXERCISE 1-6 **Form, Purpose, and Focus**

Directions: *Underline the form of writing that best describes the passage from Amy Tan's essay, "Mother Tongue," and underline the focus of the passage. Circle the primary purpose.*

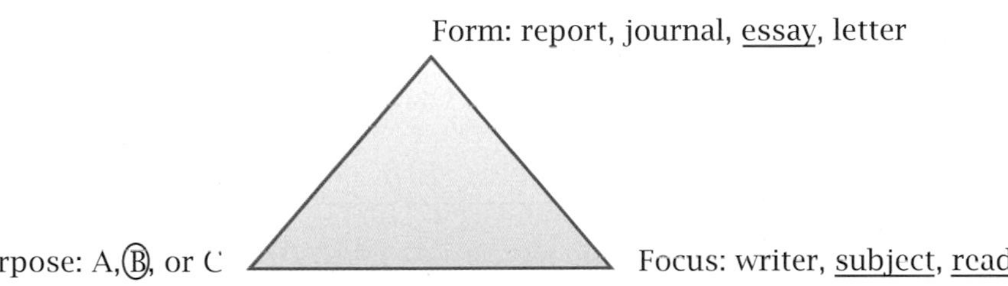

Set Goals and Become a Reflective Student

Improving your writing will depend on your awareness of your own strengths and weaknesses. To monitor your progress, develop the habit of keeping track of the skills you need to improve. Reflect on your work and set goals for improving your writing. Doing so will help you become a better writer and a more effective student.

Reflective Writing

Reflective writing helps you examine your attitudes about issues, explore your feelings about events in your life, and recognize your achievements. Reflective writing is most effective when you write regularly. This enables you to reread your thoughts, identify your strengths, and set goals. Over time you can recognize how your thinking and writing have changed.

1. *Keep a journal to capture your personal experience of learning to write.* Reread your journal regularly. Journaling enables you to see trends that might help you solve a writing problem or identify a successful strategy.

2. *Write every day.* Establish a place and time when you can write every day. Write for at least ten minutes. Use your daily writing to explore topics that are important to you at that time. Aim for quantity in your writing. Try to write a little more every day. Use your daily writing to apply what you are learning about the sentence, the paragraph, and the essay. Try to do new things with your writing.

EXERCISE 1-7 Setting Goals

Directions: *Answer the following questions to help you explore your previous writing experiences and to help you set goals for improvement.* Answers will vary.

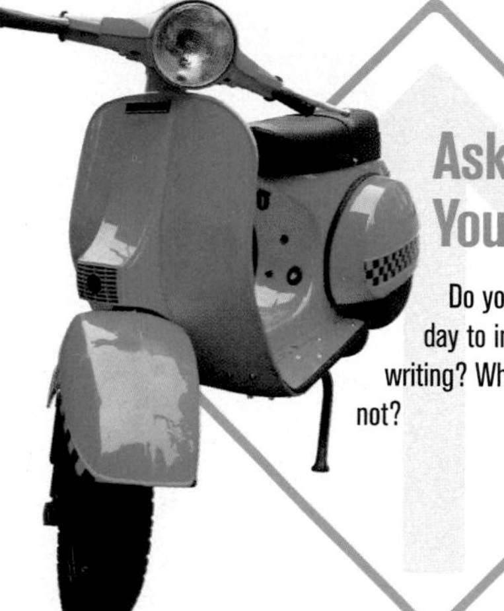

Ask Yourself
Do you write every day to improve your writing? Why or why not?

1. What kinds of papers do you like to write?

____

____

____

2. Who taught you to write your first successful paper? What was the subject? What made the paper good?

____

____

____

3. What kinds of papers do you not like to write?

____

____

____

4. Describe one assignment in particular that was very difficult for you.

____

____

____

EXERCISE 1-8 Applying What You Have Learned

Directions: *Apply what you have learned in this chapter to analyze what you described in Exercise 1-7 as assignments you liked to write and those you did not like to write.* Answers will vary.

1. An assignment you liked to write:

Form: report, journal, essay, letter

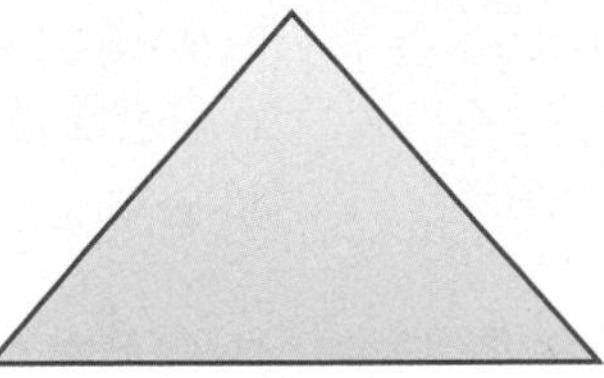

Purpose: A, B, or C

Focus: writer, subject, reader

2. An assignment you did not like to write:

Form: report, journal, essay, letter

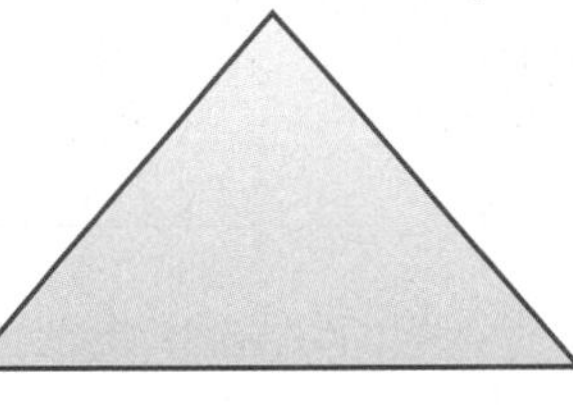

Purpose: A, B, or C

Focus: writer, subject, reader

3. What do you like about writing and what do you believe you do well?

____

____

____

4. According to your analysis in these exercises, what do you need to work on to be more effective as a college writer?

____

____

____

CHARTING YOUR COURSE WITH THE WRITING PROCESS

Prewrite: Think Through Ideas

You may be surprised by how much you know about a wide range of topics. Freewriting in your journal, brainstorming, or talking ideas through with a friend will help you discover what you know now and what your attitudes are on a subject. When you sit down to write, you will not be starting from scratch. That alone will make your first draft more successful.

BRAINSTORM

Think about a complex task you do with confidence, such as preparing for a trip, planning a party, or purchasing something important. How do you prepare? What are the steps you take to get ready? Brainstorm for five minutes, recording as many ideas and details as you can.

Revise and Get Organized

Revising a paper is a lot like reviewing your wardrobe. What works and what does not? Can you get that jacket to look good, or should you just chuck it? Are those ripped jeans OK, or do they give people the wrong impression of you? When revising a paper, you ask similar questions. Can a passage be altered to be more persuasive, or should you just take it out? Is colloquial language appropriate, or should you be formal? Is the structure of the paper sound? Do you have details to support your point? It takes a careful eye to revise a paper. You rethink your ideas and conclusions based on information and insights you gain during the writing process.

DISCUSSION

Turn and talk to a classmate about the writing process. What do you like best about it? What do you like least? What do you think you need to work on the most to become a better writer?

From Good Editing to Getting a Job

When applying for a job, be sure to edit your resume and cover letter. Potential employers view errors in your application as signs of carelessness. Incorrect grammar and spelling will contradict the message you convey about your talents. Your employer has good reason to be picky; in the workplace, the ability to express yourself reflects not only on you but on your employer. Good editing will give you a better shot at getting—and keeping—a job.

BRAINSTORM

Good editing often depends on having another person look at your writing. Who would you trust to read and comment on your writing? Make a list of at least three people.

2

CHAPTER

The Writing Process

CHAPTER OVERVIEW

- The Writing Process
- Prewrite
- Draft
- Revise
- Edit
- Reflect

THINK FIRST

Many students seek college degrees to help them build a future. In that future, they see meaningful work that also earns them a living. Describe the work environment you see in the photograph. What kind of work do you think the man does? What do you think his coworkers are like?

The Writing Process

I use a three-step approach to writing papers: Read the assignment, type the paper, turn it in. If this sentence describes your approach to writing, it will be a big shift to think of writing as a process. There are several reasons why you should change your approach to writing. First, a process approach allows you to relax. Good writers know that what they write at the beginning of the process may not appear in the final draft. Second, writing takes time and energy. Good writers want to be efficient. Third, you need strategies to make writing decisions. Knowledge of the process helps you make good decisions as you write.

The writing process is rarely a neat step-by-step process. Here is a helpful five-step model.

Step 1—Prewrite: This step involves thinking, making preliminary notes, and doing exploratory writing. In the prewriting and drafting stages of the process, you experiment with various responses to an assignment. If these experiments do not work, it does not matter because you can try again. This experimental attitude enables many writers to do their best work.

Step 2—Draft: After prewriting, you put pen to paper. You write sentences and paragraphs to express what was in sketchy form in your prewriting. When you draft, you flesh out your ideas. Once you have a first draft, it is a good idea to have a reader look at it and respond. Doing so gives you ideas for improving your writing.

Step 3—Revise: During revision, you move, cut, and add content to your writing. You organize it logically to make your points more forcefully. Even at this stage, nothing is written in stone. Writing involves revision at every step of the process. You revise your prewriting when you draft. You revise your first draft when you write a second draft. Even when you edit, you may review everything you have written and make meaningful changes in your writing.

Step 4—Edit: After revising, you edit your work. You fix grammar, spelling, punctuation, capitalization, and anything else that will distract a reader. When you edit, you also fine-tune word choice and style so your writing is appropriate for an academic audience.

Step 5—Reflect: The edited revision is your best effort. At this point, it is good to reflect on what you have done, noticing those parts of the writing you like and those that are still challenging and need improvement.

REVISION IN ACTION
Watch for these boxes throughout the chapter. They indicate the importance of revision at various points in the writing process. Writing is recursive. You constantly look back before moving forward. Revision in Action reminds you to look back and improve on good writing you have already done.

Prewrite: Write Before You Write

How do I get started? All writers begin by facing the blank page. It can be intimidating. A positive approach and an experimental attitude are essential. Prewriting generates thinking and ideas on a topic.

Prewriting is thinking and writing *before* you write. You explore what you know before you begin to draft. **Talking** to someone about your ideas can be useful because it is fast and interactive. You find out what your ideas are and get ideas from the person you talk to. **Clustering** is another form of prewriting. You jot down ideas and draw their connections to related ideas

TOPIC 2: Gathering Information
www.mhhe.com/goingplaces

and details. **Brainstorming** is listing everything you can think of related to your topic. You accept everything that comes to mind. Finally, **freewriting** is continuous writing to explore your topic. It is thought written down. Before you draft, take ten or fifteen minutes to prewrite on your subject.

Talk

Talking is relaxed and natural. It does not require you to make a commitment the same way writing does. As you talk to someone about your topic, you explore your thinking and respond to the listener, who helps you by adding ideas or personal experiences that develop your topic further.

PEER CONVERSATION

MULTILINGUAL TIP
If you can't think of a word in English, perhaps your partner can help you.

EXERCISE 2-1 Talking to Find a Topic

Directions: *Have a conversation with another student to prepare for the writing exercise that follows. Briefly describe a childhood leisure activity, something you especially enjoyed. You might talk about playing a sport, picnicking with your family, going to a relative's house, drawing at the kitchen table, or going to the park.*

- *Take turns talking for five minutes.*
- *Begin by discussing the childhood activity of your choice, but allow the conversation to remind you of other activities.*
- *As you recall events, include facts, details, examples, and the exact words you used or heard.*

MULTILINGUAL TIP
If you don't know how to express a thought, leave a blank. You can consult a dictionary later.

EXERCISE 2-2 Writing about Your Conversation

Directions: *Write for 5 to 10 minutes about your conversation with your classmate. Begin by writing a sentence that introduces your topic. Review the following list of sentences that might introduce the topic of drawing at the kitchen table. Then write a similar sentence to introduce your topic.*

- *My love of art began with a box of crayons and a coloring book.*
- *If you want to create artists, burn coloring books.*
- *Crayons, scissors, glue, and paper make hours of fun and memories.*

Cluster

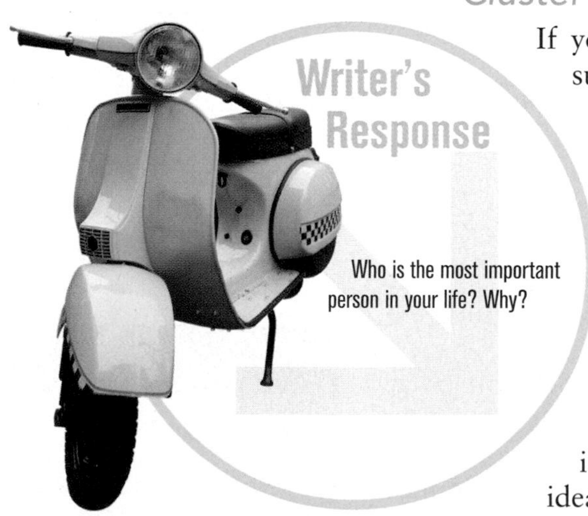

Writer's Response
Who is the most important person in your life? Why?

If you are a visual thinker, clustering will help you picture a subject. You begin with a key term from your writing assignment and branch out to possible topics, related ideas, and supporting details. For each new idea, you add additional lines and ovals as you extend your thinking. When you cluster, push for at least four or five topic chains. This is experimental work, so you want to be flexible and open to new thinking.

In a matter of minutes, clustering can help you see potential relationships between your ideas and supporting details. It also helps you be specific. Each time you add new links to the chain, you are narrowing the subject, making it smaller and more detailed, or you are imagining a new idea that might lead to a whole set of different details.

Here is an example of clustering on the topic of taking a vacation.

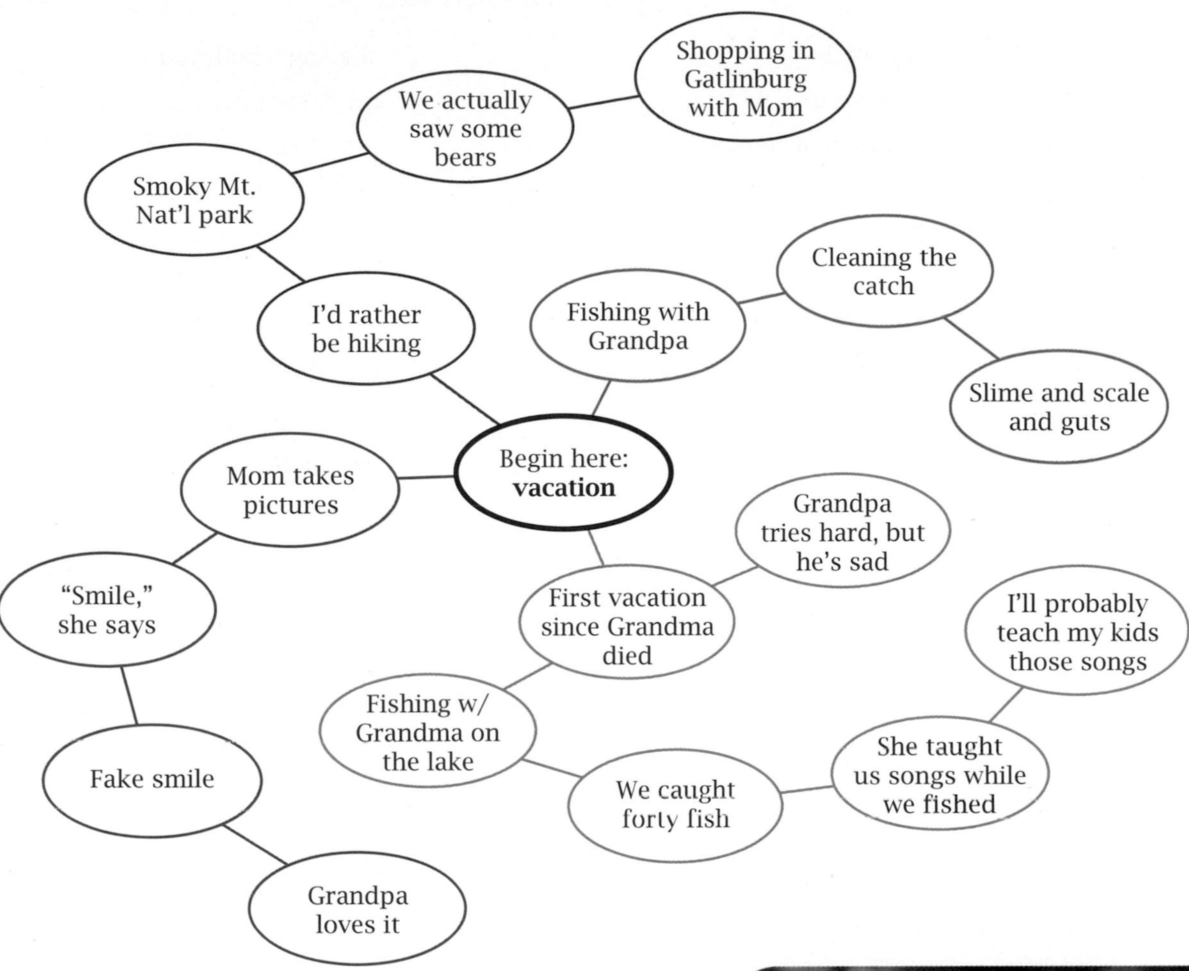

EXERCISE 2-3 **Clustering to Find a Topic**

Directions: *Use the clustering diagram as a model for generating possible topics. Examine the photograph "Boy Fishing" to further prompt your thinking on the topic of childhood. As you look at it, think about how this photograph connects to you. What does it remind you of? What view of childhood does it suggest to you? Then practice clustering on a separate sheet of paper.*

Boy Fishing

Brainstorm

Brainstorming is clustering without the ovals and lines. It can be as simple as randomly listing as many ideas about a topic as you can think of. It can also involve *piggybacking*. In this case, you review your random list and find categories of ideas to explore further. More is better in brainstorming. Here is an example of brainstorming on the topic of childhood:

Random Listing

flashlight tag	sharing a bedroom
reading groups	my first bike
Spiderman comics	food fights
Halloween	raking leaves
Boy Scouts	Willard, my dog
my first fish	making Christmas cookies
soccer games	pick-up baseball
Billy moving away	mowing lawns
my secret ring	lemonade stands
the Santa lie	hating dance lessons

Here is an example of piggybacking. The writer has chosen three categories of ideas to explore further: firsts, holiday traditions, and jobs.

Firsts

fish

fishing pole that broke the first time I used it

girlfriend—Lucy in sixth grade who was a foot taller than me

two-wheel bike

time I broke a window playing ball

Holiday Traditions

time I got caught soaping windows on Halloween

making Christmas cookies—cornflake wreaths and gingerbread people

cutting out pumpkins—I got to dig out the insides and draw the faces

going Christmas caroling at the retirement home

going to Grandma's on Christmas Eve

Jobs

lemonade stand with my friend Billy who drank all the lemonade

raking leaves in the neighborhood

mowing the Petersons' lawn—my first business

taking out the garbage and discovering maggots in the trash can

EXERCISE 2-4 Brainstorming to Find a Topic

Directions: *Brainstorm a list of childhood memories on a separate sheet of paper. Use the lists above as models for brainstorming on your own.*

Freewrite

The key to freewriting is staying loose. Keep your hand moving. When you talk, you do not stop to correct your grammar. Instead, you allow lapses in grammar and thinking. Freewriting is the same. You do not need to worry about spelling and grammar because freewriting is not for an audience; it is just for you.

Be messy. It is fine to jump around when you freewrite. There is no real logic to it. Change subjects and look for new directions to follow. Freewriting enables you to recall forgotten memories, uncover ideas that have personal value, and understand attitudes in a new or deeper way. Here is an example of freewriting by a student named Christina.

Christina's Freewrite

I could talk with my family and friends forever. Me standup in front of people and tell a speech, no way! I become extremely nervous I feel my heart pounding, I cannot take a breath while my face turns red. I took speech it did not help. My eyes are always focused on the paper, I cannot make eye contact, and I do not know what to do. Last semester in my history class, I experienced all the symptoms one can go through. I also gave a speech in Spanish and could not maintain eye contact. If the instructor decides to ask me a question or read what I wrote sitting down I am fine. Stand in front of the class? Forget it. I volunteer to give speeches. I want to improve. They keep getting worse. I do extensive research on all my speeches and almost memorize the whole thing. Still nervous. I write very little on my note cards, which forces me to keep eye contact. Find a focal point and fix my eyesight on it. Which is a little better. They see my face and not just the top of my forehead.

Childhood Entertainment

EXERCISE 2-5 Freewriting to Find a Topic

Directions: *Examine the cartoon of the boy playing video games to prompt memories of childhood. Then freewrite on a separate sheet of paper for five to ten minutes without stopping. Allow your thinking and writing to wander. As you do so, you may discover memories or ideas that surprise you.*

Review Your Prewriting and Define Your Topic

Prewriting is the beginning. It is not a first draft. Take a few minutes and review the ideas and memories generated about childhood in your prewriting. Use the following exercises to help you define a topic.

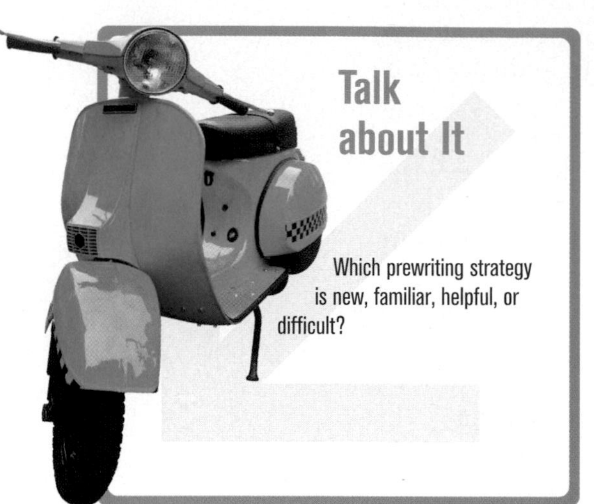

Talk about It
Which prewriting strategy is new, familiar, helpful, or difficult?

EXERCISE 2-6 **Defining Your Topic**

Directions: *List the possible topics you generated from talking, clustering, brainstorming, and freewriting. A couple of topics have been provided as models.*

- *Write a phrase or two to describe each possible topic.*
- *Indicate which prewriting strategy you used to discover each topic.*
- *Then use the questions that follow to select the topic you will use to write a paragraph.*

Possible Topics	*Prewriting Strategy*
my dog Willard	freewriting
we grow up too fast	clustering

1. ______________________________
2. ______________________________
3. ______________________________
4. ______________________________
5. ______________________________

Which topic interests you the most? ______________________________

____

Which topic generated the most interesting ideas? ______________________________

____

Which topic generated the most interesting details or examples? ______________________________

____

Which topic seems most clearly organized on paper? ______________________________

____

The topic I will explore further is ______________________________

____

Select the prewriting strategy that is most effective for you. Some students use two or more strategies to explore a topic. Find out what form of prewriting works best for you and then use it in the future. Remember to maintain an experimental attitude, trying other forms of prewriting from time to time. You may discover that particular forms of prewriting are best suited to specific topics or writing assignments.

EXERCISE 2-7 **Choosing a Prewriting Strategy**

Directions: *Review your prewriting work and answer the following questions to determine which strategy is most effective for you.*

1. Which strategy is easiest for you to use? Why? ____________________

____

2. Which strategy generates the deepest thinking? Why? ____________________

____

3. Which activity provides the most interesting topic? Why? ____________________

____

4. Which strategy would you like to use again? Why? ____________________

____

Draft: Focus and Organize

What do I want to say? Who will read this paragraph? Drafting organizes prewriting into readable text. Your job in the first draft is to identify your main point, organize your prewriting into a logical structure, and shape it to meet a reader's expectations. At this point you define your topic, formulate a topic sentence, select and explain supporting details, and end with a convincing concluding sentence.

Remember, you will probably write multiple drafts of a paper. You will read peers' papers, and they will read yours. Peer review will give you more ideas. Most writers make substantial changes as they write and rewrite. Drafting enables you to improve your writing to the point where it satisfies both you and your audience.

Gateway

TOPIC 4: Outlining, Drafting, and Revising
www.mhhe.com/goingplaces

MULTILINGUAL TIP
Writing multiple drafts is not an indication of poor writing skills.

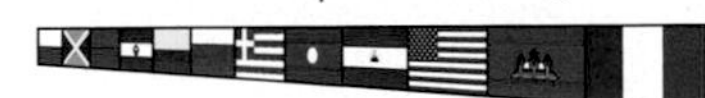

Consider Your Audience

When you draft, you shift from writing for yourself to writing for your audience. In prewriting, you did not have to worry about what is acceptable for an audience; now you do. In drafting, you provide specific details, such as names of people and places that are obvious to you but that your audience may not know. You provide careful descriptions, such as sensory detail and exact dates and times that you know all about but that your audience does not. Finally, you consider any specific knowledge you have of your subject that your audience might not have.

At this stage of the process, you also start to eliminate slang and make your language more formal. For example, you write, "I was going to," not "I was gonna." Remember that by paying careful attention to your language, you convey respect for your audience and yourself.

Ask questions like these when considering your audience:

- Who will read this paragraph and what do they expect?
- How much do they know about my topic?
- How much do they need to know about my topic to understand the point I want to make?
- How might they react to what I have to say?

EXERCISE 2-8 Determining What You Want to Say

Directions: *Read your prewriting for the topic you chose in Exercise 2-6. Gather together all the ideas and details you generated about it. You may want to do additional brainstorming, freewriting, clustering, or talking about it. Then respond to the prompts below. Remember to be specific enough so your audience understands the point you are making.* Answers will vary.

Topic: ______________________________

A. Write a topic sentence that states the point you want your audience to understand.

____

____

B. List five to seven details, examples, or reasons from your prewriting that explain your topic sentence. Circle the two or three most convincing details, examples, or reasons.

____

____

____

____

MULTILINGUAL TIP
Although you may not be accustomed to beginning with a strong or direct point, it is expected in academic writing.

Focus Your Topic Sentence

Focus is essential to good writing, and it begins with your topic sentence. The topic sentence states the main idea of a paragraph. It is often the first sentence. Think about your assignment. You have a topic and something to say about it. So your topic sentence should focus on these two things: topic and point. Develop this 1 (topic) + 1 (point) approach. Getting this sentence focused will also focus the paragraph.

Take a few minutes to step back and analyze your first sentence. Are you specific enough? Ask questions to focus your topic sentence. An easy way to start is by asking who, what, when, where, why, and how.

First Draft of Topic Sentence

(topic) (point)

Vacations in a cramped car and equally small tent created an unbreakable family bond.

1 + 1

Focusing Questions

Who went on vacation? Me, my brother, and the dog

What vacation? The vacation we took the year my brother left for college

When? When I was in sixth grade

Where? Pike's Peak

Why did we go on vacation? To spend time together before he left for college

How did we camp? He and I slept in a small pup tent together. It was crowded.

Second Draft of Topic Sentence

(topic) (point)

Two brothers and a dog in a pup tent created laughter and a bond of love.

1 + 1

EXERCISE 2-9 **Focusing Your Topic Sentence**

Directions: *Rewrite and focus your topic sentence from Exercise 2-8 making sure to clearly state your topic and the point you want to make about it.* Answers will vary.

Organize and Connect Ideas and Details

Paragraph **unity** means every idea and detail supports the topic sentence. In your paragraph, all the supporting details need to relate to the topic sentence in your paragraph. Furthermore, there should be a *reason* why you present details in the order that you do. When the order of your details makes sense, your draft is coherent. Paragraph **coherence** means there is a clear, smooth flow of ideas in the paragraph, brought about by careful organization and the use of appropriate transition words and phrases.

MULTILINGUAL TIP

Stay on the topic; do not digress. Otherwise the reader will be confused.

Drafting your paper involves transforming your prewriting and making significant changes in the content of your paragraph to make it logical. The organization of your draft cannot be random. The order in which ideas and details occur has an impact on your audience, and the content has to make sense.

Depending on your focus and purpose, you can use one of the following methods to organize your paragraph:

- ***Spatial:*** Describing an object or place from top to bottom, back to front, left to right, and so on.
- ***Chronological:*** Describing events or the steps in a process in the order in which they occur.
- ***Order of importance:*** Describing either the most important or the least important details first.
- ***Simple to complex:*** Describing the simple details first and working toward more complex ones.

For example, here are some different ways you could organize details related to the topic of casino gambling:

Topic: The pleasures of casino gambling

Spatial

The pool and gardens—from right to left
The lobby and rooms—from downstairs to upstairs
The casino gambling area—from front to back

Chronological

First visit, 1989, Atlantic City
Second visit, 1995, Atlantic City again
Third visit, 2003, The Venetian, Las Vegas

Ask Yourself
What transitions do you already use?

Order of Importance

Get some rest
Eat some good food
See a couple shows

Simple to Complex

Play the games and come home with some money
People watching
Different places to eat (reasonable prices)
The games

Transitions

Transition words signal the connections you make between ideas and details in your writing. They give your paragraph coherence and help the reader see how everything fits together. This table shows some commonly used transition words.

Additional Detail	Contrast	Sequence	Logical Connectors	Time
consequently furthermore and in addition moreover also in the same way	however but yet nevertheless on the contrary on the other hand	first second third generally furthermore finally in the first place also last	consequently therefore thus hence in conclusion indeed in the final analysis	after as soon as at first then at last finally before later next soon in the first place in the meantime

MULTILINGUAL TIP
Review the transitions. Learn the meaning of all the words. Do not omit any words in a phrase.

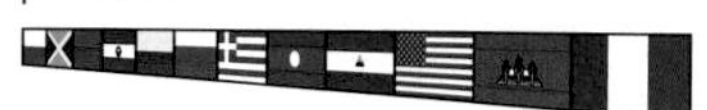

EXERCISE 2-10 **Ordering the Details in Your Paragraph**

Directions: *Using the key details, ideas, and examples you generated to support your topic sentence in Exercise 2-8, create a logical order for the details in your paragraph. Try using spatial order, chronological order, order of importance, or simple to complex order. Indicate the transition words you think will be most useful.* Answers will vary.

____

____

____

____

____

____

Transition Words: ______________________________

Here is an example of a first draft of Christina's writing.

Christina's First Draft

Giving a speech is a nerve-wracking challenge for most people. There are few things folks are more afraid of. The signs and symptoms of nerves are totally obvious to see. The speaker's cheeks turn bright read. Her voice starts to quiver and crack. Even in college courses, some speakers sound like teenagers going through puberty. Another symptom is the struggle to maintain eye contact. Some speakers stare off into space. Most keep their eyes down, focused on their papers or note cards. Then there are those rockers and tappers, the ones who go completely nuts. Some speakers rock back and forth without knowing it, fidgeting and fiddling, making it totally distracting to watch them. Others are all wound up, so full of nervous energy, they tap pencils or pens like crazy, distracting the reader even more. Then there is the Statue of Liberty. This poor guy is petrified. He does not move a muscle through the whole speech.

REVISION IN ACTION
Christina changes her focus, details, and organization in the first draft.

FOCUS
In this draft, Christina leaves behind the first-person focus of her prewriting. This is an important step in adapting her ideas to an academic audience.

SUPPORTING DETAILS
Her supporting details describe how some speakers display their nervousness during a speech.

UNITY AND COHERENCE
She uses transition terms to show she is adding detail and to create a coherent paragraph. Plus, she stays on the subject, making her paragraph unified. However, her paragraph seems inconclusive because she has no concluding sentence.

Revise: Read Critically, Then Rewrite

Will a reader understand what I know about my topic? How can I get an *A*? A draft is your beginning, but there is more to do. Experienced writers often say the end product is not at all what they thought they would write when they began. Revision means rethinking. Give yourself time to do this important step.

As you revise, read critically. Look for evidence that you have achieved your purpose. Identify what you did well and where your paper is weak. Listen to the views of other readers. Ask yourself these questions:

- Did I keep my readers' interest?
- Were my readers confused? What can I do to reduce their confusion?

- Can I try something new? What do other writers in my class do that I could try? What do professional writers do that I could try?

As you revise, be open to adding, cutting, or reorganizing your writing. College students often say too little about their subjects, so be prepared to add details and explanations. Adding details can mean you need to cut information that is not relevant to your topic. Finally, by moving around ideas and details in your draft, you often see new possibilities. Here are three useful strategies for revising your work.

Revise Strategically

Strategy 1: Add

Add new details, examples, and explanations that answer questions raised by your readers. Add sentences that connect or relate one part of your paper to another. To ensure a more coherent paragraph, add appropriate transitions.

Strategy 2: Cut

Cut details, examples, and explanations that your readers did not understand or that did not connect directly to the topic. Do not be afraid to cut deeply. If you need to, you can always put something back in the essay. Cutting from and adding to your draft will help you see your writing in a new light.

Strategy 3: Reorganize

Reorganize your work so that it looks, feels, and reads differently. Sometimes what you write at the end of a paragraph or paper works better at the beginning. Reorganizing may help you discover appropriate transition words and phrases so that you produce a more coherent paragraph.

Read Critically

Critically reading published writers will help you improve your writing. Look closely at their writing and try to apply what they do in your writing. As you read, ask these questions:

- How does the writer present information?
- What does the writer do that I admire?
- How does the writer solve a problem that I have in my writing?
- Is there a technique in the professional model that I can try?

EXERCISE 2-11 Reading Critically

Directions: *Read the paragraph from "Growing Up Game" three times, following the instructions below.* Answers will vary. Example answers shown.

1. *First reading:* Read without a pen or pencil. Simply try to understand the author's subject and purpose. Then, in a sentence or two, write your view of the author's purpose.

The writer explores her early attitude about hunting.

2. *Second reading:* Underline two sentences that express Peterson's subject and purpose. Circle the details that support or explain her purpose as you read the rest of the paragraph.
3. *Third reading:* Place a checkmark in the margin next to a sentence or two that you admire. Label what the writer is doing.
4. *Rethinking after a close reading:* In a sentence or two, write your view of the author's purpose.

The writer recognizes her connection to the animal they have hunted. They are both creatures. She learns something about life and death.

from "Growing Up Game"
by BRENDA PETERSON

This hunting trip was the first time I remember eating game as a conscious act. My father and Buddy Earl shot a big doe and she lay with me in the back of the tarp-draped station wagon all the way home. It was not the smell I minded; it was the glazed great, dark eyes and the way that head flopped around crazily on what I knew was once a graceful neck. I found myself petting this doe, murmuring all those graces we had been taught long ago as children. Thank you for the sacrifice, thank you for letting us be like you so that we can grow up strong as game. But there was an uneasiness in me that night as I bounced along in the back of the car with the deer.

✓ details provide description

✓ actions provide an example

Use Response Groups

A real audience tells you if your writing says what you think it says. In a response group of your peers, you are both a writer and a reader. Response groups work most effectively when readers avoid focusing on problems in the writing or on trying to fix them. Effective groups discuss the strengths as well as weaknesses of the writing.

You can form a response group with three to four members of your class. Here are some guidelines for how to make effective use of a response group:

MULTILINGUAL TIP
Do not feel uncomfortable getting feedback from your peers. They can provide good insights, especially native speakers of English

Guidelines for an Effective Response Group

As a Writer

- Distribute copies of your work to group members.
- After you read your work aloud, listen quietly and take notes as the group members talk.
- When members are done talking, ask for clarification of any comments you did not understand. Also ask for advice on specific problems you are having with your writing (topic sentence, including enough relevant details, etc.) or ask for ideas to expand your paragraph.
- Thank the group for their comments.
- Collect the copies so you can use their notes or comments for your revision.

As a Reader

- Identify the point or purpose of the paragraph or essay.
- Identify the topic sentence and key words that state the purpose. Does the topic sentence grab your interest?
- Discuss key details, examples, or reasons. Notice the details or examples that grab your interest. Are they connected?
- Notice places where the writing is confusing, inconsistent, or underdeveloped.
- Identify the conclusion. What does the writer emphasize in the conclusion?

EXERCISE 2-12 **Forming a Peer Response Group**

PEER CONVERSATION

Directions: *Form a response group with three or four members of your class. Using the guidelines listed above, take turns sharing your writing and listening to the group respond to your work.*

Revise with a Plan

Here is Christina's revision plan and revised first draft. In her revised paragraph, added text is in bold font. Text she deleted from her first draft is crossed out.

REVISION IN ACTION
Christina takes control of her paragraph structure. She cuts and adds to create unity and coherence. She changes her (a) topic sentence, (b) informal language, (c) transition terms, and (d) concluding sentence.

Christina's Revision Plan: Focus my paragraph's purpose

1. Rewrite my topic sentence to clarify my purpose.
2. Add transition terms to connect my points and create coherence.
3. Cut informal language not appropriate for academic writing.

TOPIC SENTENCE
Christina replaces vague words with specific ones to focus her topic sentence and purpose.

TRANSITION TERMS
She adds transition words and phrases. She also repeats "those who" to make the supporting details fit together, enhancing the coherence of the paragraph.

INFORMAL LANGUAGE
She cuts "totally" and "Poor guy," which are informal and not appropriate for academic writing.

Christina's Revised Paragraph

Giving a speech ~~is a~~ **can be** nerve-wracking ~~challenge~~ for **both the speaker and the audience** ~~most people~~. **In fact,** there are few things folks are more afraid of. The signs and symptoms of nerves are ~~totally~~ obvious to see. **For instance,** ~~The~~ a speaker's cheeks often turn bright **red** ~~read~~. **and** Her voice ~~starts to~~ quivers and cracks. ~~Even in college courses~~, Some speakers sound like teenagers going through puberty. Another symptom is the struggle to maintain eye contact. ~~Some speakers~~ **There are those who** stare off into space., **and those who** ~~Most~~ keep their eyes down, focused on their papers or note cards. Then there are **the** ~~those~~ rockers and tappers, ~~the ones who go completely nuts. Some speakers rock back and forth without knowing it,~~ **who** fidget~~ing~~ and fiddl~~ing~~, making it totally distracting to watch them. ~~Others are all wound up, so full of nervous energy, they tap pencils or pens like crazy, distracting the reader even more. Then there is~~ **Finally, we come to** the Statue of Liberty. This ~~poor guy~~ **speaker** is petrified. He does not move a muscle through the whole speech. **It can be agonizing for some speakers to make even a three-minute speech, and it is just as agonizing for the audience, especially in a college speech class. They know their turn might be next.**

EXERCISE 2-13 Revising Your Draft

Directions: *Review the peer feedback and your own assessment of your writing. Add, cut, and reorganize to clarify your paragraph's meaning and purpose.*

Edit

I am terrible with grammar. Is there no quick way to edit? Too often, students simply scan their papers before turning them in for a grade. If an error finds them, they correct it, but they are not searching for errors. Good editing is a focused, systematic search. To edit effectively, you need to anticipate the errors you make, search for those errors, and correct them.

Eliminate Your Usual Errors

It is important to know what mistakes you consistently make. This is easier than it sounds. You may already know, for example, that your spelling is weak. When your instructors return work to you, they will alert you to errors that appear in your papers. Keep a tally of errors and search for them when you edit your work. The following seven editing strategies will help you do a thorough job when you edit your work.

Strategy 1: Use a Checklist

Your instructors may provide you with an editing checklist for papers; in the meantime, use the following universal checklist.

YOUR EDITING CHECKLIST

Words

______ I removed unnecessary contractions.

______ I removed informal language.

______ I checked my capitalization.

______ I corrected all spelling errors by consulting a dictionary, a peer editor, or my computer spell-check, being sure to look for words my computer spell-check missed.

Sentences

______ I checked all end punctuation marks.

______ I used complete sentences with subjects and verbs.

______ I proofread all my sentences so their meaning is clear.

______ I removed sentence fragments.

Paragraphs

______ I indented all new paragraphs.

EXERCISE 2-14 Editing Your Paragraph

Directions: *Use the preceding checklist to review your paragraph.*

Strategy 2: Eliminate One Error at a Time

Read your paper several times using the following guidelines. Concentrate on one error at a time.

- *Read each sentence individually or read your paragraph backward, from the last sentence to the first, so you read each sentence in isolation.*
- *Look for spots that signal a consistent error.* If you know you have trouble with punctuation, look at those sentences that might require commas, semicolons, colons, or apostrophes.

FOCUS ON ONE COMMON ERROR
Use the lessons and activities in the Writer's Guidebook to practice proofreading for a specific error that recurs in your writing. Read your work carefully with this single error in mind.

Strategy 3: Read Your Work Aloud

Use one of the following approaches:

- *Read aloud slowly.* Listen and look closely at each sentence. Watch for missing words, words missed by spell-check, and confusing language.
- *Read aloud to a classmate.* If you have difficulty reading certain parts of your writing, those parts probably need editing. Often you will find problems with sentence structure and grammatical errors.

Strategy 4: Highlight Signal Words

Highlight words that signal punctuation. For example, highlight all the coordinating conjunctions and then use the rules for items in a series or compound sentences to determine the need for commas. (See Chapter 25 for work on the comma.)

Strategy 5: Use Computer Aids—Spell-Check and Grammar-Check

Your computer's grammar-check alerts you to confusing or grammatically incorrect sentences. Use it as an aid. If the computer questions your sentences, you should too. However, like spell-check, grammar-check can be unreliable. To the computer, "I would hope in the back" is just as correct as "I would hop in the back." It takes a human reader to know the difference and to select the correct words and spelling. Computer aids do not replace careful proofreading and knowing how to make good decisions about grammar.

Strategy 6: Use Proofreading Peers

Proofread your paper with someone who has an objective eye. Tell this person about the errors you are inclined to make. Read your paper aloud, or ask your proofreading peer to do so, and search for your errors. Proofreading works best with two sets of eyes.

Strategy 7: Double-Check Your Work

If you are writing for a college assignment, reread the instructions. Check for specific directions that define length, content, typing format, or other requirements. If you are writing for your job, be sure you know what your boss's expectations are before you turn in your work.

Here is Christina's edited paragraph. Added text is in bold font. Text she deleted from her first draft is crossed out.

Christina's Edited Paragraph

Giving a speech can be nerve-wracking for both the speaker and the audience. In fact, there are few things people are more afraid of. The signs and symptoms of nerves are obvious ~~to see~~. For instance, ~~a~~ **the** speaker's cheeks ~~often~~ turn bright red, and her voice quivers and cracks. Some speakers sound like teenagers going through puberty. Another symptom is the struggle to maintain eye contact. There are ~~those~~ **speakers** who stare off into space, ~~those~~ **speakers** who keep their eyes down, focused on their papers or note cards~~. Then there are the rockers and tappers,~~ **and speakers** who fidget and fiddle, making it ~~totally~~ **almost completely** distracting to watch them. Finally, we come to the Statue of Liberty. This speaker is petrified. He does not move a muscle through the whole speech. It can be agonizing for some speakers to make even a three-minute speech, and it is just as agonizing for the audience, especially in a college speech class. **because** They know their turn might be next.

EXERCISE 2-15 Final Editing of Your Paragraph

Directions: *Use at least two of the editing strategies listed above to produce a final edited draft of your paragraph.*

Christina's Final Draft

Giving a speech can be nerve-wracking for both the speaker and the audience. In fact, there are few things people are more afraid of. The signs and symptoms of nerves are obvious. For instance, the speaker's cheeks turn bright red, and her voice quivers and cracks. Some speakers sound like teenagers going through puberty. Another symptom is the struggle to maintain eye contact. There are speakers who stare off into space; speakers who keep their eyes down, focusing on their papers or note cards; and speakers who fidget and fiddle, making it almost completely distracting to watch them. Finally, there is the Statue of Liberty. This speaker is petrified. He does not move a muscle through the whole speech. It can be agonizing for some speakers to make even a three-minute speech, and it is just as agonizing for the audience, especially in a college speech class because they know their turn might be next.

Reflect

Successful students are reflective. They think about what they did, what worked, and what did not work, so they can make good decisions the next time around. For that reason, at the end of the writing process, you will be asked to think about the work you did, the decisions you made, what you learned, and what challenges you still face.

Identify Successes

Remember what you do well and what you enjoy. Becoming a good writer involves recognizing and using your strengths.

EXERCISE 2-16 Reflecting on Your Success

Directions: *Take a few minutes to reflect on your successes. Write one or two sentences that explain two things you have learned from this chapter and how you successfully applied them to your writing. Use a specific example from your work to support what you say.*

____

____

____

____

____

____

MULTILINGUAL TIP
Locate the writing centers on your campus. Find out available days and hours. Some provide online support.

Gateway
TOPIC 3: Focusing on a Central Idea
www.mhhe.com/goingplaces

Set Goals

As you move forward, set realistic goals. Use your successes to identify changes in your writing. Become aware of breakthroughs in your use of skills and strategies and strive to create additional breakthroughs. Remember that small achievements add up to large gains.

EXERCISE 2-17 Identifying Your Challenges

Directions: *Now that you have examined your successes, determine what challenges lie ahead. Rate yourself using the following scale—1 indicates a task that you consider a challenge most of the time, and 5 indicates a task for which you have the required skills and strategies.* Answers will vary.

Prewriting

____ 1. I prewrite to explore my ideas and think more deeply about a topic.

Drafting

____ 2. I focus my paragraphs with a clear purpose.

____ 3. I organize my ideas and make connections.

____ 4. I insert details, examples, and reasons to explain my thinking.

____ 5. I eliminate irrelevant details to enhance the unity of my writing.

____ 6. I use transition words and phrases to provide coherence.

Revising

____ 7. I read critically to identify and use the successful techniques of other writers.

____ 8. I identify the strengths and weaknesses in my papers.

_____ 9. I apply specific revision strategies to my papers.

_____ 10. I am flexible and willing to make changes in my writing.

Editing

_____ 11. I employ all or some of the following editing strategies:

- _____ Use a checklist.
- _____ Eliminate one error at a time.
- _____ Read my work aloud.
- _____ Use spell-check or grammar-check on my computer.
- _____ Use a proofreading peer.
- _____ Double-check the assignment and expectations.

Be Specific: Details Matter

"I will have the stuffed-crust pan pizza with extra cheese, ham, and pineapple." "One venti double nonfat caramel latte, please." When you place an order, you do not just say simply "pizza" or "coffee." You need to be specific to get what you want from the person taking your order. Similarly, when developing a paragraph, you need to be specific to get the response you want from your reader. Vague, unsupported statements—like vague orders—will not make your point.

DISCUSSION

Turn and talk to a classmate about something you are very picky about, such as your food, how you listen to music, the way you want a closet or drawer arranged. Provide as much specific detail as you can.

Your Opener

Whether you are preparing an oral presentation or writing a paragraph, nothing hooks an audience like a great first sentence. Whether structured deductively (stating your point right away) or inductively (beginning with your evidence), what you say first makes an impact; it establishes purpose and direction. You do not have to write your opener first. In fact, the best hooks are often discovered well into the writing process.

DISCUSSION

Television commercials need to have a hook. Watch TV and focus on commercials. Look for two or three examples of a good hook that grabs the viewer's attention. Tell a classmate about what you saw and how the commercial introduced its topic.

Writing on the Job

In the working world, you will often carry a project through from idea to completed project. Say, for example, that an assistant at a nonprofit agency is given his boss's vague notes from a meeting and asked to write a grant letter. He might ask his boss some questions and do additional research to make sure the information in the letter is accurate, the arguments for giving money are persuasive, and the tone is confident. Or suppose a parent writes a brief proposal about how to raise test scores in her school; if the board approves her plan, the school will have to follow the proposal to see that the initiatives and programs she suggested are created and carried through.

DISCUSSION

Turn and talk to a classmate about a project idea that you would like to see through to completion. What is it? Who would be involved? When and where? What is the purpose of the project? What potential difficulties do you see?

CHAPTER 3

Writing Paragraphs in College

CHAPTER OVERVIEW

- Paragraph Structure
- Assignments and Topics
- Supporting Details
- Concluding Sentence
- Paragraph Organization
  - *Unity and Coherence*
  - *Order Your Details*

THINK FIRST

To start thinking about ideas for paragraphs you might write, describe what you see in this photo. After you write a careful description, consider these questions. What does the photo remind you of? What issues or ideas would you like to explore in connection with the photo?

Paragraph Structure

A paragraph explores a clearly focused topic in a number of related sentences. The main idea—the main point an author wants to make about the topic—is stated in the **topic sentence.** Sentences following the topic sentence explore and explain the main idea. They provide **supporting details** that relate directly to the specific focus of the paragraph. Supporting details come in a variety of forms, such as examples, facts, and stories. The type of support you provide in your paragraph depends on your purpose for writing. A **conclusion sentence** restates the main point or comments about the main idea of the paragraph.

MULTILINGUAL TIP

A topic sentence that includes the topic and controlling idea is expected in English. It is not considered rude or impolite.

EXERCISE 3-1 **Paragraph Structure**

Directions: *Read the two paragraphs below and answer the questions that follow.*

Paragraph A

Many people go to stores because they have great deals. Some stores carry items for 30 percent less than the price at other places. I bought dress clothes from Nordstrom until I found out that I could get the same suits, shirts, ties, and shoes from local stores for a third less. What about the stores that do not have bargains? When I am walking by a store and see something I like, I walk in. Stores display products in windows that get customers' attention. The store changes as it gets in new products so customers have to keep looking. Merchandising executives decide how they want everything set up for a reason. They want to maintain the company's image, which could be hip and fashionable or just young and contemporary. It is the visual manager's job to set up the store using those guidelines, and it is the associate's job to organize and color coordinate all the products. This creates a pleasing and welcoming look for the store which will keep you coming back.

Paragraph B

Seeing a movie in the theater has its advantages. One advantage of going to a theater to watch a movie is the extremely large movie screen. Also the sound in a theater is loud and dynamic. The big screen and sound can be a huge advantage when watching battle scenes in an action movie, such as *The Fellowship of the Ring.* The viewer experiences battle scenes on the largest scale possible. Another advantage is refreshments. A bucket of popcorn and a soda go with a movie much like peanut butter goes with jelly. For people who do not like to wait to see a movie, the biggest advantage to going out is seeing a movie as soon as it is released. Then again, there are a few disadvantages. You miss part of the movie if you go to the bathroom. If you sit near talkers or hear cell phones ring, it is hard not to be upset. Then there is everybody's favorite: being kicked in the back of your chair by the antsy kid sitting behind you. Finally, there is cost. A movie experience can easily cost thirty dollars or more. For these reasons, it may be best to go to the theater only on rare occasions, mainly for big spectacle movies.

1. Which of the two paragraphs seems better organized? List and explain two or three things the writer does to organize her content.

Paragraph B seems better organized. The writer stays on the subject. She repeats the terms "advantages" and "disadvantages." The writer also uses the words "one," "another," and "finally."

2. Briefly explain what makes the other paragraph seem confusing and poorly organized.

Paragraph A is confusing because the writer changes from one subject to another. The focus of the paragraph is not clear.

Assignments and Topics

College writing usually begins with an assignment. Your instructor makes the assignment, or you choose one from a book. Your job as a writer is to respond to that assignment. From the assignment you generate a topic and then provide your reader with a focused, detailed discussion of that topic.

Here is everybody's favorite assignment: What did you do last summer? Maybe you worked at an amusement park. If you did, your work at the amusement park becomes your topic. Your reader expects you to say something focused and detailed about this topic.

In many classes, especially those for disciplines other than English, your assignment will be very specific. It will be designed to trigger writing that shows what you have learned. Here are some focused assignments:

- Name and describe the three kinds of rock we have studied in this unit.
- Discuss the domestic and international impact of the Marshall Plan.
- Describe two or three approaches to determining level of consciousness in initial patient assessment.

These assignments include key terms ("three kinds of rock," "domestic and international impact," "approaches, level of consciousness, patient assessment") that define the topic.

If you are faced with a less specific assignment, the job of generating a topic is more challenging. Suppose your assignment is to write about stress. Your first task is to identify a specific topic related to stress that you can write about. For example, you could begin by listing specific causes of stress in a person's life. Then you could select one—the stress of being a single parent, for instance—and narrow it down by asking, What makes being a single parent so stressful?

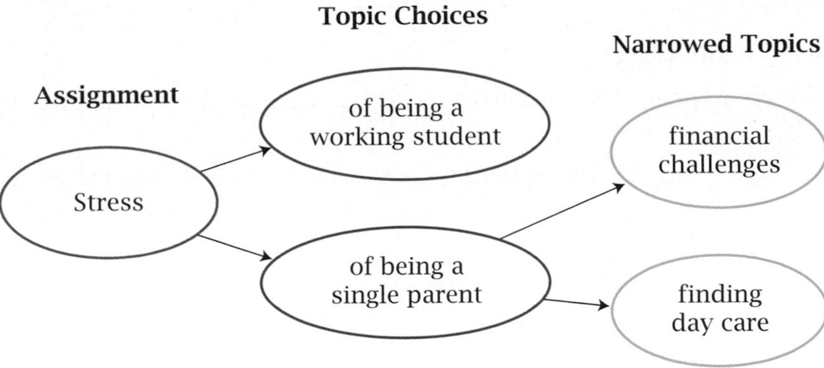

Assignment: Stress

Specific Topic: Single parents stress over finding day care for their children.

The Topic Sentence

A good topic sentence makes a specific point about a topic. It establishes the position you are taking on the topic. It prepares the reader for what you are going to talk about. If you are given a focused assignment, often your topic sentence involves formulating a sentence using key terms from the assignment.

Assignment: What evidence do you see of help for people with disabilities on this campus?

Topic Sentence: There is considerable evidence of help for people with disabilities on this campus.

Writer's Response
Describe something that causes stress for you.

Assignment: What kind of an impact does television have on the lives of young people?

Topic Sentence: Television has a very definite impact on the lives of young people, mostly negative.

With general assignments, however, you have to generate and narrow down a topic yourself. In these cases, when you formulate a topic sentence, try to avoid a vague topic sentence that lacks focus and is too broad to discuss in a paragraph, or a specific topic sentence that is so limited there is nothing to say about it.

Assignment: Stress

Topic Sentences

Vague: Single parents have lots of things to worry about.

Too Specific: My daughter caught a cold at day care last week.

Focused: Finding quality day care for their children is real source of stress for single parents.

Assignment: Travel

Topic Sentences **Vague:** Airport security is simply maddening these days.

Too Specific: Last week I stood in line for an hour and a half while TSA officials searched older women.

Focused: Airport security procedures have slowed down travel, especially at the check-in stage.

EXERCISE 3-2 **Vague Versus Specific Topic Sentences**

Directions: *Read the following topic sentences. Place a V for vague next to those topic sentences that are not adequately focused. Place an S next to topic sentences that are too specific.*

__V__ 1. When I think of marriage, I want someone with that certain something.

__S__ 2. My friend DL started smoking when he was 14.

__V__ 3. Saturday morning television is a wasteland.

__S__ 4. Liquid crystal display monitors are affected by cold temperatures.

__V__ 5. I know a lot about cars.

__V__ 6. Organized sports are what is wrong with high school; end of conversation.

__S__ 7. I like to lie under a shade tree on a warm summer day and take a long nap.

__S__ 8. What we call "flu" is actually a virus.

__S__ 9. Last fall Dorine's father grew the largest pumpkin in Cass County.

__V__ 10. Women: can't live with them, can't live without them.

Focus Your Topic Sentence

To write a focused topic sentence, develop the habit of asking yourself, What exactly am I saying about my topic? What do I want the reader to understand? Ask questions to focus your topic sentence. An easy way to start is to ask who, what, where, when, why, and how?

Vague: Championship wrestling is really cool.

"Really cool" does not direct the reader's attention to anything specific about championship wrestling. Ask yourself a question like, What makes championship wrestling cool?

Focused: Championship wrestling has continuous action, which makes it very entertaining.

"Continuous action" focuses the reader's attention on a specific dimension of wrestling and connects that aspect of wrestling to its entertainment value.

Too Specific: Last week I lost 2 pounds.

This sentence states a fact. It does not really focus the reader's attention on a subject. There are very few additional details you can add to create a meaningful paragraph. Ask yourself a question like, How did I lose the weight?

Focused: Losing weight is possible only when a person makes hard choices many times a day.

"Losing weight" is the subject; "hard choices many times a day" focuses the reader's attention on a specific dimension of the subject.

To visualize the process of narrowing your topic, it might help to use this graphic.

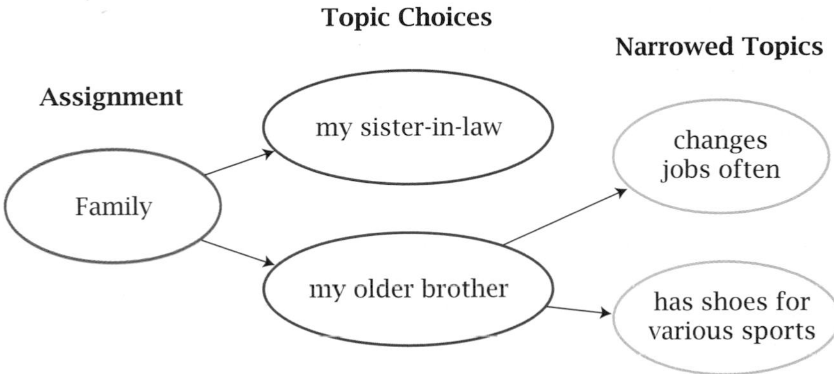

Topic Sentence: My brother has a special pair of shoes for each sport he plays.

EXERCISE 3-3 Writing Focused Topic Sentences

Directions: *For each of the following topics, use the graphic above to narrow your topic. Then write a focused topic sentence that makes a specific point about the topic. Underline the terms that direct the reader's attention to the specific focus of the topic.* Answers will vary. Example answers shown.

1. Swimming

Waking up every morning to go to swimming practice taught me a lot about self-discipline.

2. Textbooks

Textbooks are written with aids to help a student learn content and study effectively.

3. Musical instruments

Renting a musical instrument is perfect for a young child starting a music program.

Ask Yourself
Are you too general or too specific when you write?

4. Household chores

Young family members given household chores contribute to family life and learn responsibility.

5. Old age

Many senior citizens work in stores to keep active and make extra money.

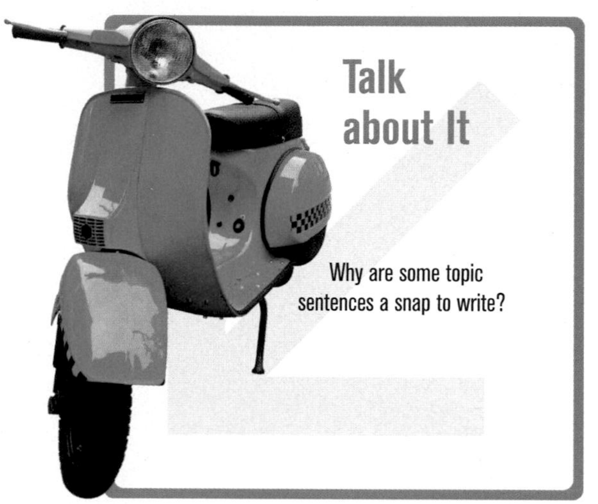

Talk about It
Why are some topic sentences a snap to write?

6. Insects

Summer brings annoying insects and requires outdoor and indoor management of these pests.

7. Bottled water

Many soft drink producers and food conglomerates have gotten into the water business since bottled water became so popular.

8. Mountains

Campgrounds high in the Rockies are primitive but adequate for the prepared camper.

9. Jewelry

Jewelry requiring piercing in unconventional places increases the risk of infection and disease.

10. Math

My junior high math teachers helped me learn the study skills I need to be successful in higher math.

From Prewriting to Topic Sentence

In Chapter 2, you saw that prewriting is a way of exploring what you know about your topic. Prewriting is also a way of narrowing and focusing your topic. The end result of talking, clustering, brainstorming, and freewriting about your topic is therefore likely to be a focused topic sentence about your assignment and the specific details you need to develop the main idea of your paragraph.

Here is an illustration of a student using clustering and freewriting to explore what he knows about his topic. A focused topic sentence is the by-product of his work.

Assignment: Write a cause and effect paragraph that explains how people can get into debt.

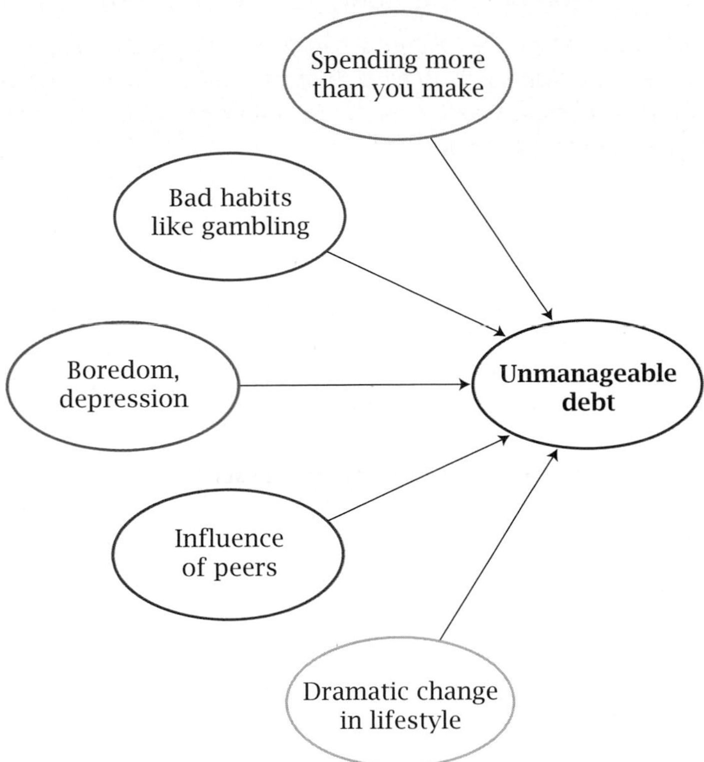

Freewrite

How can you not be in debt when you spend your money foolishly? I have friends who love those casinos. Once or twice a month they go. They drop a lot of cash. One guy says, "I always say I am up a few hundred, even if I am down a grand." Down a grand. Down a grand! I can't imagine those words ever coming out of my mouth. Other friends bet on sports. They have bookies they call. They place bets. Then Saturday comes. They win and lose. Over time maybe it evens out but some get in debt up to their ears. It's kind of a club. They gamble. Their peers gamble. Some get cash against credit cards. One guy I know went to the Indian casino near the college he went away to. By November all his money was gone. Bad decisions. These are bad decisions about how to have fun.

Topic Sentence: Problems with debt are often caused by bad decisions about how to have fun.

Prewriting is an act of discovery. In the process of exploring what he knows about his topic, this student discovers the point he wants to make. He states this point in his topic sentence.

EXERCISE 3-4 **Finding Topic Sentences in Your Prewriting**

Directions: *Choose two of the following topics. Explore each topic using two methods of prewriting (talking, clustering, brainstorming, freewriting) on a separate sheet of paper. Then, for each topic, formulate a focused topic sentence for a paragraph you could write about it.*

1. Difficult classes

Topic Sentence: ______________________________

____

2. Television

Topic Sentence: ______________________________

____

3. Athletics

Topic Sentence: ______________________________

____

4. Fashion

Topic Sentence: ______________________________

____

5. Goals

Topic Sentence: ______________________________

____

Gateway

TOPIC 5: Writing Unified Paragraphs and Essays
www.mhhe.com/goingplaces

Supporting Details

Be specific. This is one of the most common demands made of writers in college. Readers of college writing want to see content. The details you provide support the topic sentence in your paragraph, and the kind of details you offer will vary according to the purpose of your paragraph. You might use description, examples, narrative, facts, or statistics. You might talk about the steps in the process of carrying out a lab experiment or the causes and effects of inflation. The chapters in Part II of this book give you extensive practice at developing and organizing various kinds of supporting details.

A useful way to picture the supporting details in your paragraph is to write an outline of the **major details** you plan to include. Identifying the major details helps focus your paragraph.

Topic Sentence: My brother has a special pair of shoes for each sport he plays.

A. Walking shoes, usually found by the back door
B. Two pairs of running shoes in the garage, always muddy
C. Baseball cleats that he does not use anymore
D. Three pairs of Converse Allstars, his basketball shoes

Topic Sentence: The secret to a good homemade pizza is getting the crust of the pizza just right.

A. Buy raw dough at the local Italian market.

B. Roll it out on a cookie sheet—very thin.

C. Bake it twice.

D. High temperature (the key detail!).

In the first illustration, the writer outlines the major examples she will use to support her topic sentence; in the second, the writer outlines the process of making the crust for a pizza. In both topic sentences, the writers state what they want the reader to understand about their focused topics. In the outlines of major supporting details, the writers make decisions about the specific content of their paragraphs.

EXERCISE 3-5 Outlines and Major Supporting Details

Directions: *Fill in the outlines below with major supporting details that would provide specific content for each topic sentence.* Answers will vary. Example answers shown.

1. A fun and entertaining vacation requires specific planning beforehand.

   A. Examine possible spots.

   B. Research fun things to do in the surrounding area.

   C. Develop a budget.

   D. Pack only the necessities.

2. Saturday morning television can have negative consequences for children.

   A. Constant advertising makes them materialistic.

   B. When they are sitting, they are not exercising.

   C. Sometimes they learn antisocial behaviors.

   D. Small children are exposed to violent cartoons.

3. Even though I know fast food is not good for me, there are a few places I just cannot resist.

   A. Wendy's double burger is my favorite.

   B. I will eat anything at Taco Bell.

   C. Theater popcorn (with lots of butter) is my weakness.

   D. Burger King's fries are the greatest.

4. The cost of operating a car can keep a young person very busy earning money.

   A. A financed car has interest costs.

   B. A financed car means full-coverage insurance.

   C. Forty-five dollars for a tank of gas!

   D. Repairs.

5. Quality leisure time has to satisfy a few specific needs I have in my life.

   A. Time alone: I need quiet.

   B. Time in nature: I need to get away.

   C. Exercise: I need to keep moving.

   D. Music: I need to hear music when I am relaxing.

Elaborate on Your Major Supporting Details

The most common shortcoming in college writing is that students do not say enough. They do not elaborate, and they do not explain. When you write, if you are going to be specific, you have to tell the reader what you know. For each major supporting detail, you can often add one, two, or even three sentences of explanation. These are called **minor details.**

Topic Sentence: My brother has a special pair of shoes for each sport he plays.

A. Walking shoes, usually found by the back door
B. Two pairs of running shoes in the garage, always muddy
C. Baseball cleats that he does not use anymore
D. Three pairs of Converse Allstars, his basketball shoes

In this outline, the writer might add two or three sentences of explanation (minor details) for each major detail:

Topic Sentence: My brother has a special pair of shoes for each sport he plays.

Major Detail

I. He has two pairs of walking shoes, usually found by the back door.

Minor Details

A. He leaves them in the same place my dad takes off his work boots.
B. This means there is always a huge pile of shoes right by the door.
C. It really makes my mother angry.

Major Detail

II. He also has two pairs of running shoes in the garage, always muddy.

Minor Details

A. He runs every morning, rain or shine.

B. When it rains, his shoes pick up mud.

C. He tracks the mud in on his shoes, getting mud all over the garage.

Major Detail

III. Then there are the baseball cleats, which he does not use anymore.

Minor Details

A. He played baseball in high school and in a league for a year or two after high school.

B. That was two or three years ago, but he still has those cleats, in the heap by the back door.

Major Detail

IV. Finally, there are the three pairs of Converse Allstars, his basketball shoes.

Minor Details

A. One pair is worn down to nothing.

B. Another pair is brand new.

C. Then there is the pair he wrote all over when he graduated from high school.

In this illustration, the writer provides additional visual details (pile of muddy shoes by the back door), more information about her brother's running habits and background, and some proper names (Converse Allstars). Note that the writer maintains equal emphasis, providing a similar amount of elaboration for each detail.

EXERCISE 3-6 Elaborating

Directions: *Choose an outline you wrote for Exercise 3-5 and elaborate on the supporting details you provided. For each detail, write two or three sentences of elaboration.* Answers will vary. Example answers shown.

Major Detail: Time alone: I need quiet.

Minor Details

1. I do not want to hear the announcements from work.
2. I do not want to hear complaining customers.
3. I need silence to think.
4. __________

Major Detail: Time in nature: I need to get away.

Minor Details

1. Sometimes I go driving through the park.
2. I also like to sit by the river.
3. Even at home, I can look out the window and enjoy nature.
4. ______

Major Detail: Exercise: I need to keep moving.

Minor Details

1. Sometimes I exercise in the basement.
2. I like to go for a run, too.
3. I prefer forms of exercise I can do by myself.
4. ______

Major Detail: Music: I need to hear music when I relax.

Minor Details

1. I like to listen carefully, preferably on my iPod.
2. If I am in the car, I will probably listen to classical.
3. It has to be music from my collection. I need control.
4. ______

MULTILINGUAL TIP
You may need to work with a dictionary to assist in providing specific details.

Be Specific

Your reader needs specific detail. It is not enough to say your brother has lots of shoes. From the illustration earlier in this chapter (page 49), the reader now knows about at least eight pairs of shoes and the specific brand name (Converse Allstars) of some of them. Effective writers develop the habit of being specific about places and times, dimensions and sizes, and proper names.

Vague Details	*Specific Details*
a big house	a two-story, four-bedroom house with a three-car garage
last year	the end of November, just before Thanksgiving
my high school biology teacher	Mr. Perry, my high school biology teacher
a bad smell	the stench of burning rubber
a short vacation somewhere nice	three nights in the Standish Hunting Lodge
expensive clothes	a black leather YSL belt that cost fifty-nine dollars

EXERCISE 3-7 **Specifying Details**

Directions: *Transform each of the vague details below into a specific detail. Keep place and time, dimensions and sizes, and proper names in mind when you work.* Answers will vary. Example answers shown.

1. A snack

Ants on a log: celery, peanut butter, and raisins; a Coke

2. Older people

The older people I see at church: Gladys, who has a warm hug for everyone; her husband Irv, who smiles a big smile and likes to tell you what he did in the war

3. The newspaper

Stacks of papers left on my porch every day after school, tied together with twine; on Sundays, special color inserts that fall out and have to be retrieved

4. Electronic device

The answering machine we bought recently; it is digital and records lots of messages; I am the only one in the family who knows how to use it

5. Clutter

Open the kitchen drawer by the phone: paper clips; keys that do not unlock anything; dried-up sticks of gum; twenty-one ink pens, most of which do not even write

Concluding Sentence

Your paragraph's point is stated in the topic sentence, then backed up with the supporting details. Finish your paragraph with a sentence that restates or comments on the main idea. The concluding sentence emphasizes the point; sometimes it also makes a transition to the main idea of the next paragraph. Like the topic sentence, it helps the reader know what your paragraph is about and your purpose for writing it.

EXERCISE 3-8 **Analyzing Paragraphs**

Directions: *Read each paragraph, underline the topic sentence, and number the major details. Then answer the questions that follow.*

People go to tanning booths for a variety reasons. Some people start going to tanning booths at a young age, in high school, for example.[1]They say they like the way they look when they have a nice tan. They spend a lot of time and money keeping themselves tan. They cannot just go once in a while. They have to go all the time, or their tan will fade. Looks are not the only reason they do this.[2]Some individuals go right before vacation to get some color. That way when they get to the beach, their tan is already started, and nature can then take over.[3]Finally, there are those people who are simply addicted to tanning. Some women go so often that their skin gets discolored and blotchy. They know they should take a break, but they do not listen. Their skin is already wrinkled, and sometimes these women are still quite young. It is important to them that they look tan year-round. Going to a tanning booth once in a while, maybe before a vacation, might be acceptable, but compulsive tanning is just plain dangerous.

1. What is the topic of the paragraph?

People go to tanning booths for a variety of reasons.

2. What is the focus of the topic sentence?

The topic sentence is not very focused. "A variety of reasons" is vague.

3. What kind of supporting detail is used?

The writer cites and explains reasons for tanning.

4. What is the purpose of the paragraph?

The purpose of the paragraph is to express disapproval of frequent tanning.

Increasing the amount of fish in a person's daily diet has health benefits.[1]First, fish is easier to digest than red meat. Eating more fish improves digestion and reduces colon problems.[2]In addition, seafood contains little or no fat. Consequently, people in cultures where fish is a significant part of the diet have a lower incidence of obesity.[3]Plus, the fats found in fish actually have a positive effect on consumer's health. For example, fish oil can lower an individual's cholesterol. Research shows that the omega-3 fatty acids found in fish benefit the heart and vascular system. There may even be favorable effects for those suffering from autism, Alzheimer's disease, and attention deficit disorder. Researchers claim that people who eat fish live longer.

1. What is the topic of the paragraph?

The topic is eating fish.

2. What is the focus of the topic sentence?

The focus of the topic sentence is the health benefits of eating fish.

3. What kind of supporting details are used?

The writer cites examples of health benefits.

4. What is the purpose of the paragraph?

The purpose of the paragraph is to inform the reader.

Video games can be educational in a positive way.[1]The first time I saw a video game, I knew I had to play. I was around four years old. Some of my relatives were playing "Super Mario Brothers" for the Nintendo Entertainment System (NES) at my grandparents' house. I did not play that day, but I knew I would.[2]Soon after, when I got that NES at Christmas, I was a happy boy. I sat and played games all day, every day. As often as I could, I would go to Hollywood Video and rent a new game.[3]Once, when I was five, I rented a role-playing game. It required a whole lot of reading. That was not something I could do too well, but I had fun anyway. In fact, that game inspired me to start learning to read.[4]The first words I can remember figuring out were "continue" and "game over." Knowing the difference between those words helped a lot. I also learned a little math from remembering my high scores. I have been playing video games ever since I got that NES. I would like to think that I learn a little something from every new game that I play. It may not be that important, but I learn something.

1. What is the topic of the paragraph?

The topic of the paragraph is video games.

2. What is the focus of the topic sentence?

The focus is the educational value video games can have.

3. What kind of supporting details are used?

The writer tells a story about his video game play to support his point.

4. What is the purpose of the paragraph?

The purpose of the paragraph is to inform readers that video games are not all bad.

Paragraph Organization

It is common to place the topic sentence at the beginning of a paragraph. Doing so sends a clear message to the reader: This is what I am talking about in this paragraph. When you begin a paragraph with a topic sentence, you are using **deductive order.**

MULTILINGUAL TIP
Learn a variety of ways to organize a paragraph in English. Compare this process to formal writing in your native language.

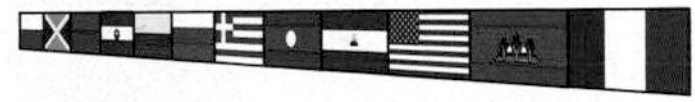

Topic: Math in daily life

People use math all the time in daily life. When a woman goes shopping, she adds up the prices of her items before she gets to the checkout line to avoid overspending. At least once a month, people have to balance their checking accounts. Sometimes a consumer will have to figure out

TOPIC SENTENCE
Supporting details come after the topic sentence: examples of everyday uses of math.

loan terms (when buying a new car, for example) and which approaches to financing the purchase will be most economical. In my own case, when I work at the family store all summer, I balance a cash box every day. Monthly I write out a budget and mail checks to pay bills. I rarely use a calculator for these routine chores, and I believe my mind is sharper for it.

However, there are times when it makes sense to place the topic sentence at the end of a paragraph. When you begin with your supporting details, you "hook" your reader and create interest in your topic. When it comes at the end of a paragraph, your topic sentence states the main idea as a conclusion. Beginning with details and ending a paragraph with your topic sentence is called **inductive order.**

Details come first in this paragraph.

Topic: Knitting

When I was thirteen years old, I came down with the flu. I was stuck in the house for a week. My grandmother came to visit me to see how I was feeling. She had a crazy idea that she would teach me how to knit. She thought that it might help pass time. Well, bless her heart, she tried. She brought me yards of pretty blue yarn and two knitting needles. My mom and grandma sat on the couch with me, trying to explain the concept of "knit one, pearl two." It just did not work. I practiced and practiced. The most that I could come up with was an odd-shaped potholder. My grandmother and my mother gave me the impression any woman could knit. They had me convinced that I would have an afghan in no time. They were right, if you want to call an odd-shaped potholder an afghan. Every once in a while, I pick up my mom's needles and give it a try. Those horrible memories come back. I remember: I cannot do this, and furthermore, I do not like it. Knitting is one of those "woman things" I just do not get.

TOPIC SENTENCE

EXERCISE 3-9 Deductive and Inductive Order

Directions: *Underline the sentence that works best as a topic sentence for each of the following lists. To make a unified paragraph, cross out those detail sentences that do not support the topic sentence. On a separate piece of paper, rewrite the sentences to form a paragraph, organizing the detail sentences so they logically support the topic sentence. Use either a deductive or inductive order for each list.*

EXAMPLE

1. He puts a lot of thought into the art he gets.
2. The first time I looked in the mirror and saw a thirty-something mom looking back at me, I thought of getting a tattoo.
3. His tattoos are a collection of significant and meaningful things in his life.
4. He is able to display his devotion on his skin for all to see.

5. Skeptics who do not understand another's love for living art have to look at the fan of body art.
6. Therefore, anyone can understand the fan by studying his tattoos.
7. The fan of body art has sentimental feelings about tattoos.

Deductive order: 5, 7, 1, 3, 4, 6. Delete 2.

Skeptics who do not understand another's love for living art have to look at the fan of body art. The fan of body art has sentimental feelings about tattoos. He puts a lot of thought into the art he gets. His tattoos are a collection of significant and meaningful things in his life. He is able to display his devotion on his skin for all to see. By understanding his tattoos, you begin to understand him.

Paragraph A

1. Late fees are ridiculous.
2. If you pay with a credit card, you have to pay later, which can be a hassle.
3. Credit cards are not for everyone.
4. If you are not careful, it can take forever to pay off a bill.
5. Credit cards can be a big hassle.
6. Not all businesses take credit cards, like fast-food places.
7. Some people end up using them for petty things like gas and food, and before they know it they owe more money than they ever imagined.
8. The interest rates can go through the roof.
9. Sometimes the card gets bent or scratched, and it will not work.
10. There can be problems if you get behind on your bill.
11. There is nothing more to pay.
12. When you buy things with cash, on the other hand, it is a done deal.
13. That can be a hassle, but it is when it works that the real trouble starts.

Ask Yourself
Do you generally use deductive or inductive order for your paragraphs?

Deductive order: 5, 9, 13, 7, 2, 10, 1, 8, 4, 12, 11, 3. Delete 6.

Paragraph B

1. Teams get together often for pizza parties after games or practices.
2. A good soccer player controls the ball with his head up high and his eyes on the field, not on the ball.
3. In high school, soccer games are two forty-minute periods.
4. It is a great place to meet nice guys and make friends.
5. There is a lot of practice involved in learning to dribble down the field.
6. Soccer teaches the value of control and endurance.
7. Soccer players need endurance to stay ahead in the game.

8. It is definitely a game of coordination, body position, and skill.
9. The main skill is running back and forth down the field, trying to maneuver around opponents, and still having the soccer ball under control.
10. Spending lots of time together both on and off the field improves performance as a team.
11. Sometimes a defenseman will not get a break until halftime comes, and then it is back on the field for the second half.
12. Faced with physical and mental challenges in every game, team members learn to trust and depend on one another.

Deductive order: 6, 8, 5, 2, 9, 7, 11, 12. Delete 1, 3, 4, 10.

Paragraph C

1. She was new to the area.
2. For example, all of the kids who learned their times tables 1 through 12 got to go to Showbiz Pizza.
3. Cleaning her cage had its down side.
4. Her name was Scarlett.
5. I learned a great deal and had a blast doing it.
6. I learned all of my times tables that year.
7. What I remember best is that we had a guinea pig in our class.
8. I was one of the winners.
9. I was selected to take care of her at home over the Christmas holiday.
10. Mrs. Kress was creative and full of life.
11. I will never forget my fourth-grade teacher, Mrs. Kress.
12. She was orange and brown in color, with long hair.
13. The smell was terrible.
14. They were actually edible.
15. She always held contests.
16. We had a great time in class that year.
17. We made donuts in class once.

Inductive order: 11, 1, 10, 15, 2, 8, 6, 17, 14, 7, 4, 12, 9, 3, 13, 16, 5.

MULTILINGUAL TIP
Learn the elements of unity and coherence in academic writing. They may differ from those in your native language.

Unity and Coherence

In a well-written paragraph, the main idea is stated in the topic sentence, and all the supporting details relate to that main idea, forming a **unified** paragraph. Further, in a well-written paragraph, the details of the paragraph have a clear logical relationship. They fit together and *work together,* forming a **coherent** paragraph. When you go off the subject in a paragraph, introducing new ideas unrelated to the topic, your writing lacks unity. When you do not indicate connections between the details in your paragraph, your writing lacks coherence. Here is a paragraph that lacks unity and coherence.

TOPIC 6: Coherence In and Between Paragraphs
www.mhhe.com/goingplaces

Some of my most enjoyable memories are of my grandparents. I am sure most children are spoiled by their grandparents as I was by mine. When I would feel sick and had to stay home, I would go over to my grandma's and be pampered like a prince. She would give me a bell to ring to be answered on every waking call. As a society we have many prejudices, which lead to the separation of young and elderly people and the prevention of communities coming closer together. We should take various steps to control these prejudices and create a better environment for older people. Many are locked up in nursing homes and are never seen by the rest of society. Some of us have prejudices because we never take the time to get to know older people. We tend to only see their flaws and do not appreciate the contributions they have made.

TOPIC SENTENCE
The sentence focuses on grandparents and memories.

This memory relates directly to the main idea of the paragraph.

Here the writer goes off the subject. He introduces a new idea—society having prejudices against elderly people—and leaves behind the discussion of memories and grandparents.

This writer has two important topics in his paragraph: memories of his grandparents and the poor treatment of elderly people in our society. One topic is personal and specific; the other is impersonal and general. Given proper focus, either would be a suitable topic for a paragraph or an essay. In this paragraph, however, the writer fails to do either topic justice.

Here is a revision of the above paragraph. The writer focuses on the more general topic. Not only is this paragraph unified around the main idea, "elderly people can make a contribution," it is also a coherent paragraph because of the writer's use of transition words and phrases.

Given half a chance, elderly people can make an important **contribution** to our society. **For example,** these days it is common to find a senior citizen working as a greeter in a department store. They are friendly and helpful, pointing a shopper in the direction of linens or plumbing supplies. **Seniors are also** visible in schools these days. In the local school in my community, **they stand** at crosswalks and help young children across the street. **They work** in the cafeterias and on playgrounds. Some are in the classroom in lower grades, reading to students and, at times, helping little children learn to read. Some seniors get involved in health care **as well. They drive** patients to appointments, work in blood drives, and make a real difference in people's lives. **A final contribution is they remember** what life was like in the past. They can recall what it was like to live through a world war or what it was like coming to this country. **They remember** fashions and fads and the funny and tragic parts of life. If we do not listen, we lose what they know forever. No one wants to be locked away. Seniors are too important to push aside: in so many ways, they can make our lives richer and better.

TOPIC SENTENCE
Unity means all the details of the paragraph relate to the main idea. *Coherence* refers to the order and flow of ideas and details.

The *coherence* of a paragraph is enhanced by the use of transition words and phrases. In this paragraph the writer uses "for example," "also," "as well," "a final."

Coherence is also enhanced when a writer repeats key terms. In this paragraph the writer repeats the key term "contribution."

The writer also uses a recurring sentence structure: "they stand," "they work," "they drive," "they remember," "they remember."

Order Your Details

How you present your supporting details matters a great deal. It is not enough to simply list them in the order you thought of them. There has to be a reason they occur in the order they do.

Details may be presented in **chronological order.** This means they are organized by time, the order in which they happened. In a narrative paragraph, you begin at the beginning of the story and tell what happens next. This is true in process paragraphs as well.

In description writing, spatial order makes sense. When you use **spatial order** you might describe an object or place by beginning outside, then moving inside, working from left to right, or moving from top to bottom.

In writing about causes and effects, or in comparison and contrast writing, it is useful to organize details from **simple to complex.** You begin by explaining relatively simple details, then transition to more complicated details and ideas.

In persuasive writing, **order of importance** gives maximum impact to your details. You often save the most important, most persuasive detail for last.

Use transition words and phrases to signal the order of your details and enhance the coherence of your paragraph. Here is a list of commonly used transition words and phrases.

MULTILINGUAL TIP

Study transition words and phrases. Be sure to include all the words in the phrases.

Additional Detail	Contrast	Sequence	Logical Connectors	Time
consequently	however	first	consequently	after
furthermore	but	second	therefore	as soon as
and	yet	third	thus	at first
in addition	nevertheless		hence	then
moreover	on the contrary	generally	in conclusion	at last
also	on the other hand	furthermore	indeed	finally
in the same way		finally	in the final analysis	before
		in the first place		later
		also		next
		last		soon
				in the first place
				in the meantime

TOPIC 7: Developing and Organizing Paragraphs www.mhhe.com/goingplaces

EXERCISE 3-10 Writing with Unity and Coherence

Directions: *Write a short paragraph in response to the following assignments. Survey the list of transition words and phrases and select the transitions you need to enhance the coherence of your writing.*

1. Write a short paragraph about your first job. Describe the process of learning to do the job well. Begin with a topic sentence that states the main idea of your paragraph. Use transition words relating to sequence to organize the details of your paragraph.

2. Write a short paragraph about a disappointing trip you took. Begin with a topic sentence that states the main idea of your paragraph. Be specific about where and when you took the trip. Tell what happened. Use transition words relating to time to organize the details of your paragraph.
3. Write a short paragraph about a goal you have set for yourself, why it is important, and what benefits achieving it will have. Begin with a topic sentence that states the main idea of your paragraph. Use transition words relating to additional detail to organize the details of your paragraph.

TAKING THE READER THERE THROUGH DESCRIPTION

Seeing Is Believing

"That man outside looks odd." *Odd* seems like a description word, when in fact it is not. What is odd to one person might not be odd to another. To explain odd, you need concrete, specific details. Look again: "He is tugging a lock of brown hair on the side of his head. He is dressed in a black three-piece suit with a pink tie. He is in his late fifties. If you get close enough to him, you can smell pipe tobacco and hear him talking about mathematical equations." Description takes the reader to the scene. We might need to call the local university and ask if they are missing a genius; we probably do not need to call the police. There is odd, and then there is odd. Careful description matters.

DISCUSSION

Turn and talk with a classmate to answer the following questions: Do you know someone who seems odd? Remember where you saw that person. Describe the person. Think about appearance, actions, and conversations. Use several senses to describe this "odd" person.

What I Mean Is . . .

In the paragraphs and essays you write in college, good description will always make a significant difference. Whether you are looking through a microscope or conducting a physics experiment, careful observation and description will help your reader understand exactly what you observed. If you report on a music performance, it will not be enough to say, "It was a big band in a big room." What is big? Are eight instruments a big band? Are forty-three instruments a big band? Is a big room one that seats two hundred or two thousand? In art appreciation, describing a painting as "a colorful country scene" will be just the beginning. You will need to mention the three yellow haystacks and the barn with its door half open. Description is a writer's basic tool for any class.

BRAINSTORM

Think about your favorite place. Why do you like it? For example, you might make a statement about a restaurant. You might write, "The Purple Pickle Restaurant is a place with a really good atmosphere." You would then illustrate what you mean by "atmosphere" with specific descriptions of the restaurant, the food, or the customers. As you brainstorm, list examples and details that explain why you like it.

Details Matter

On the job, careful observation is essential. A health care employee needs to assess symptoms and convey them clearly to other practitioners. A police officer on the scene of an accident notes traffic conditions, weather, damage, and the individuals involved in the accident. In food service, recipes depend on exact descriptions of ingredients. For example, if a recipe calls for cheese, the cook needs to know if the cheese is sliced, shredded, or grated and if the recipe requires parmesan or gorgonzola. Precise detail can make a critical difference. Description is dependent on precise word choice.

RESUME BUILDER

Any job requires you to learn precise vocabulary. Words are one tool necessary to do a good job. Think about your job. What specific language do you use just at work? Make a list of ten precise words that are necessary for you to do a good job. Then write a sentence or two to explain why these words are essential to doing your job well.

4

Description

CHAPTER OVERVIEW

- THE DESCRIPTION PARAGRAPH AT A GLANCE
- DESCRIPTION THINKING
  - Elements of Description
  - Organize Your Thinking
  - Comparisons and Description Thinking
- DESCRIPTION IN PROCESS
  - Prewrite
  - Draft
  - A Professional's Take
  - Revise
  - Edit
  - Reflect

THINK FIRST

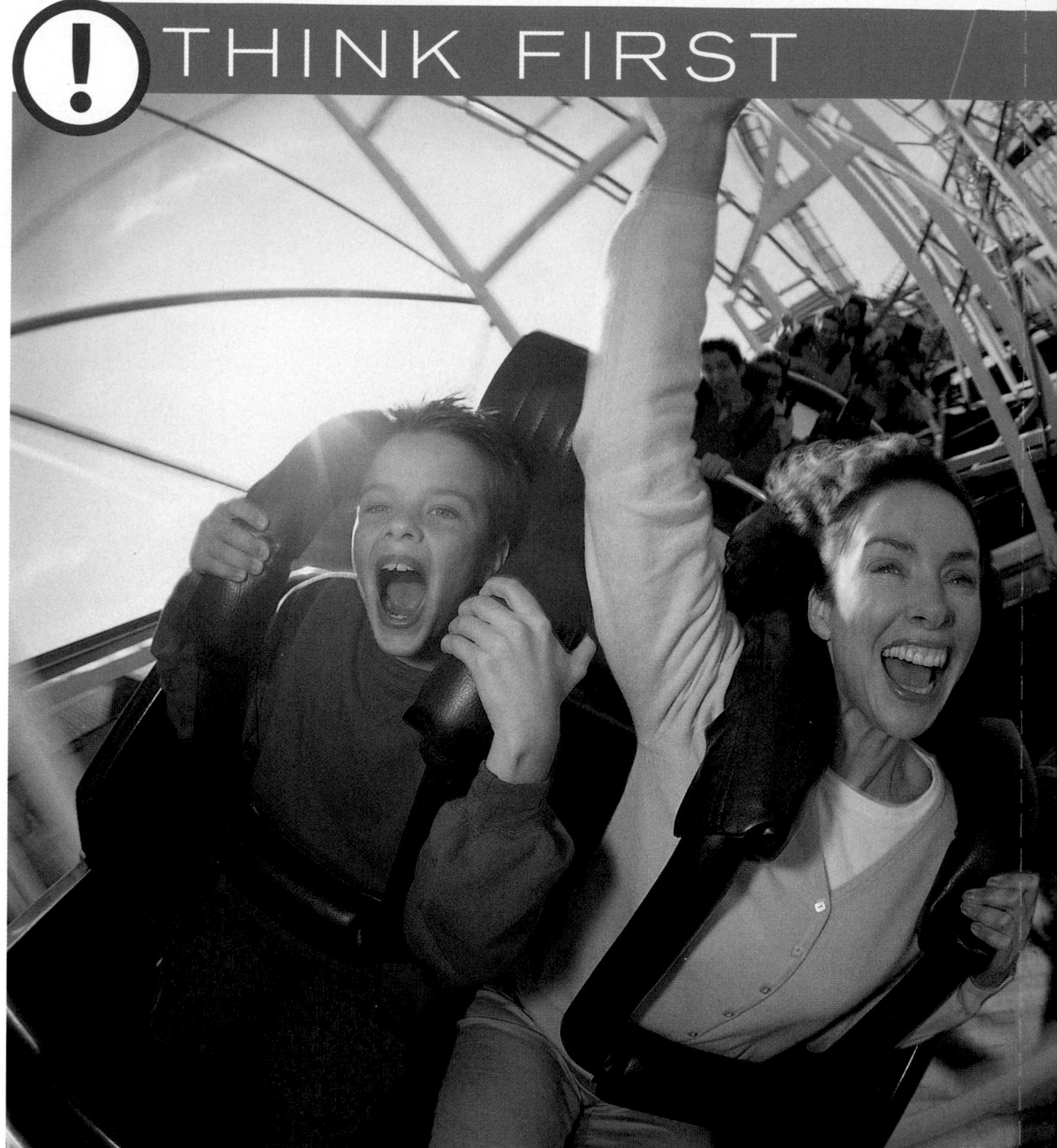

Write a description of what you see in this photograph. Begin with a sentence that states the general impression you get. Then use your senses to describe what you see in the scene. Get the details down. Make your description a word painting so that if you read it to someone over the phone, the other person would see exactly what you see.

At a Glance

THE DESCRIPTION PARAGRAPH AT A GLANCE

A description paragraph has three basic parts: a topic sentence, supporting details, and a concluding sentence. The topic sentence states the dominant impression. The paragraph support provides concrete details to make a vivid impression on the reader. The details combine to convey the writer's purpose. The concluding sentence restates or emphasizes the dominant impression.

The Description Paragraph at a Glance

ASSIGNMENT Write about a region, city, neighborhood, or building and describe the living conditions of the people who live in it. Describe this place using details that convey a dominant impression.

Mumbai, a famous city in India, has slum areas where poor people live in the worst conditions possible. (1) **In these places,** known as chawls, people barely make it through the day. In a chawl, homes are built out of scrap materials found in the garbage. People use pieces of metal or cardboard for roofs. Walls are built like a camper tent since bricks are impossible to afford. These homes keep them sheltered but not warm or safe from the weather. Often these homes do not survive severe weather conditions and have to be rebuilt. (2) **In addition,** the biggest problem people face is getting water. Each morning, they wake up before the sun rises to line up near a government-provided water pump. Everyone has to carry enough water to last them the rest of the day. The water is always cold since it is expensive to heat, so daily bathing is unpleasant. (3) **Finally,** chawls are usually built near sewage areas, garbage dumps, railroad tracks, or even runways for airplanes. Chawl residents have to live with the stench of human excrement, spoiled food, and the roaring noise of trains and planes. Sewers get backed up causing water to overflow, increasing the risk of disease. Moreover, rats live in these slums, and they carry diseases. These slum conditions make life extremely difficult every day.

TOPIC SENTENCE
The writer uses key words from the assignment and states the dominant impression.

SUPPORTING DETAILS
The writer uses multiple senses to describe the chawl: (a) sight—description of the homes; (b) touch—description of the water; (c) sound and smell—description of the area where chawls are built.

ORDER AND TRANSITIONS
The writer uses a list to describe the slum in three ways. He begins with "in these places" and adds a second description and a final description of the place.

CONCLUDING SENTENCE
The writer emphasizes the dominant impression and impact of this impression on the people who live there.

DISCUSSION QUESTIONS

1. Can you identify the supporting detail that best illustrates the dominant impression stated in the topic sentence?
2. Why is it effective?

PEER CONVERSATION

DESCRIPTION THINKING

Effective descriptions make a point by creating a dominant impression using sensory details and comparisons. The dominant impression, sensory details, and comparisons are the basic elements of description.

Elements of Description

How does description thinking work? Below is a brief summary of the elements you should keep in mind when writing a description paragraph.

- ***Dominant impression:*** The topic sentence states your impression of the person, place, or object being described. It states your attitude or feeling about it. A chawl, for example, is a depressing place.
- ***Sensory description:*** Effective sensory description consists of specific details gathered through the five senses: sight, sound, smell, taste, and touch. In the sample paragraph, the writer provides vivid detail to capture what a chawl is like.
- ***Comparisons:*** Many supporting details are hard to describe. For this reason, writers use comparisons to indicate what something is similar to or like.

Get Started

The details in good description need to work together to create a dominant impression. Good description consists of both general observations and very specific concrete details.

In the following example, a student has brainstormed a list of general observations and the specific details that illustrate them in preparation for writing a description paragraph about a coffee shop she visits.

The Coffee Shop

General Detail	*Concrete Detail*
nice atmosphere	classical music piped in (esp. piano and classical guitar)
	just enough noise to drown out surrounding conversation
	like a bookstore but better: more sociable, yet private

good smells	fresh bagels grilled sandwiches prepared for lunch
spacious	eighteen to twenty tables—plenty of room to be alone to read and sip coffee
courteous help	May, fiftyish, brown hair. "Want a mug today, hon?" "Take all the time you want"
good light	track lighting, ochre walls, lots of windows

Good description depends on the use of precise language. In this student's work, when she mentions track lighting and ochre walls, you get a much more vivid impression of the coffee shop's interior than from the term "good light." Notice the writer includes a comparison detail too: "like a bookstore but better: more sociable, yet private." In this exploration, all the details add up to a vivid description of the coffee shop. The general observations have value as well. In addition to helping the student get to the concrete details, the general observations help her formulate a topic sentence.

Topic Sentence: The coffee shop, because of its inviting atmosphere and friendly employees, is a great place to pass time.

EXERCISE 4-1 **Finding the Details**

Directions: *Go to a public place where you can sit undisturbed. Decide on a focal point—a person, a place, or an object. Make as many observations as you can and record them as notes. Try to cover as many of the senses as you can in these observations. If it is useful, make comparisons as well. When you have finished, review your notes and write a couple of sentences that sum up your impression.*

Writer's Response
Are you a people watcher? Why?

Organize Your Thinking

Good description comes more easily if you think systematically about your subject. If you describe an object or place, organize your thinking by moving from top to bottom, front to back, or left to right.

A graphic organizer can help you think in an organized way. Draw a diagram of the place you are describing or make a sketch of the object. This gives you a visual sense of what you are describing; you can use this diagram to organize your description and suggest additional description details.

Figure 4-1 is the diagram the student made of the coffee shop she described as "a great place to pass time"; it includes the notes the student made.

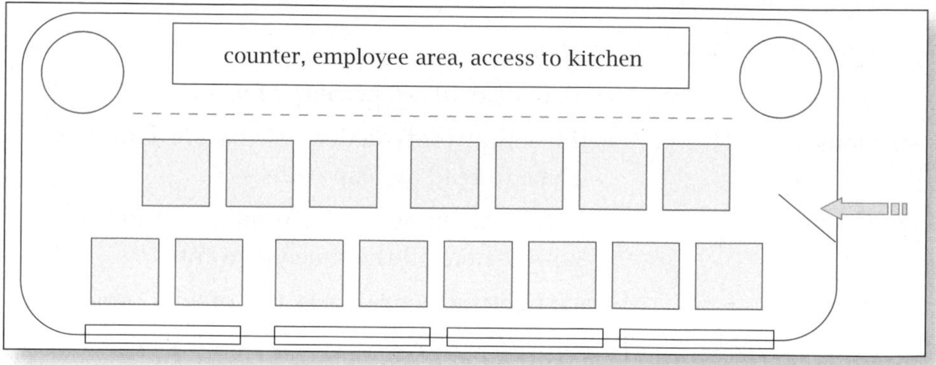

FIGURE 4-1 Student Diagram of Coffee Shop

I forgot about the comfy chairs (the circles)! You can really relax in this place. The coffee shop is long. It is deep. Seating along the windows on the left of the entrance is the best. Booths on the right, tables on the left, along the windows. Artwork on the walls I forgot that too. A photo of a man with a giant piece of bread!

If you describe a person, organize your thinking by listing his or her physical characteristics or personality traits. A t-chart can be helpful to organize your description of a person. Figure 4-2 is a t-chart a student used to list the physical and personality traits of a close friend.

Physical Characteristics	Personality Traits
Clothes—always khakis or shorts. A brown braided belt that is too big, hangs down like a dog's tongue. T-shirt with "dogshirt" written on the front. (Get close and he smells like a dog!)	Sloppy, but good sloppy. Really easy to be with. A dog lover.
Dark hair, almost black. Parted on the left. Long hair, over the ears, full in the back. Usually looks like he is just out of bed. Sticky-up hair, esp. in the back. Matted hair.	The most laidback person in the world. Capable of sleeping long hours.
Terrible shoes. Tennies with the toes ripped open. Muddy shoes, shoes practically falling off his feet. Do not get too close, they smell bad!	Known him for years. When we were kids, if there was a puddle, he walked through it. Seemed like he was always wet.
Powerful legs. You can tell this guy is a jock. Angry red scar on his forearm from a recent surgery.	He may be laidback, he may seem lazy, but on the football field, he is an animal. Naturally, he loves the mud on the football field.

FIGURE 4-2 T-Chart Showing Physical and Personality Traits

On a t-chart, try to include both concrete details, which you see on the left in this illustration, and general observations, which you see on the right. The right column will be especially useful for finding the words to describe your dominant impression.

EXERCISE 4-2 **Organizing Your Thinking**

Directions: *Use one of the graphic organizers shown to organize the work you generated for Exercise 4-1. If you prefer, picture a new person, place, or thing and use one of the graphics to help you think of sensory details that describe it. Be sure to work toward a dominant impression that you can sum up in a sentence or two.* Answers will vary.

Comparisons and Description Thinking

In ordinary conversation, we naturally compare one thing to another. Your father's overcooked hamburger looks like a hockey puck on a bun. When your grandfather pulls into the driveway at your house, his big old car reminds you of a parade float. The tiny hat your grandmother wears to church looks like two scoops of vanilla ice cream. Comparisons help us see things clearly. They convey a sense of what we are describing.

EXERCISE 4-3 **Comparing in Description**

Directions: *Read the description paragraph below. Underline the comparisons you see. Then answer the questions that follow.*

New York City is bustling and alive. The streets are filled with yellow cabs zipping up the streets and honking. They buzz around corners like bees in search of honey stopping to pick up a fare, then buzzing away. A delivery truck blocks traffic as the driver unloads slim envelopes and stacks of brown boxes before he disappears into a building. Every corner has a vendor. The smell of onions and peppers draw a lunch-hour crowd to stainless steel carts selling hot dogs, coffee, and drinks. The sidewalks are filled with people weaving in and out of traffic like professional dancers on a dance floor. Small children tug on their mothers' hands and shout over honking horns. Tourists wander and point as they open a map and fight the wind to keep it steady as they check their location. New York City is a whirlwind of energy twenty-four hours a day.

Senses: sight and sound

Comparison

Senses: sight

Senses: smell

Comparison

Senses: sight, touch, and hearing

Senses: sight, touch

PEER CONVERSATION

DISCUSSION QUESTIONS

1. How many comparisons did you find in this description?
2. How do the comparisons contribute to the overall description?
3. Reread the paragraph looking for sensory detail. Which sensory details do you like best? Why?

Process

DESCRIPTION IN PROCESS

Good description writing benefits from using the writing process: prewriting, drafting, revising, and editing.

Select an Assignment

In college you will be asked to write descriptions in a variety of contexts and assignments. In these cases, it is important to respond directly to the assignment. Also, your description will be most effective if you provide your reader with plenty of specific detail.

EXERCISE 4-4 Selecting an Assignment for a Description Paragraph

Directions: *Review the assignments listed below. Choose the one you know the most about and think is best suited to an effective description paragraph.*

1. Describe a person, place, or thing that has value to you or to society.
2. Recall a place you visited that made you feel uneasy or even frightened. Describe the place in detail.
3. Think about the advantages of being a young, middle-aged, or older person. Describe a person you know who really lives those advantages.
4. Working conditions contribute positively or negatively to the work you do. Describe the working conditions of a workplace you know well. Create a positive or negative dominant impression that reveals your attitude toward this workplace.
5. Technology is everywhere in modern American education. Describe a technology that really makes a difference in your learning in a particular subject or discipline.
6. Select a photograph from a magazine or newspaper that creates a powerful impact on the viewer. State the impression and describe the photograph to convey this impression to a reader. Attach the photograph to your paragraph.

7. Describe a fashion fad that you like or dislike.
8. Describe a classroom with an atmosphere that contributes positively or negatively to learning.
9. Describe an animal you find to be odd, funny, or threatening.
10. Choose your own topic.

Prewrite: Write Before You Write

When you describe, you are building a word picture for your reader. To ensure you include all the relevant details, it helps to be systematic about your work. Take nothing for granted. Imagine that your reader has never seen what you are describing. Use plenty of sensory detail—including specifics of size, color, and shape—and comparisons with familiar objects, places, or people. Even the smallest details are important in description.

For description, combine two prewriting strategies: brainstorming and freewriting.

PREWRITE
- Talk
- Cluster
- Brainstorm
- Freewrite

Brainstorm

Brainstorming allows you to systematically explore what you know about your subject. You can create a list of as many ideas as you can think of about a topic. You can also organize the list as a way to generate more ideas that are connected to your main point.

EXERCISE 4-5 **Brainstorming**

Directions: *On a separate sheet of paper, brainstorm for ten minutes on the assignment that you chose in Exercise 4-4. Write the assignment at the top of the page. Then list as many description details as you can (use all your senses), as well as details of items you could compare to your subject. Include ideas about your topic as well as description details.*

Freewrite

Freewriting helps you explore the dominant impression you want to create. If you brainstorm first, your freewriting can focus on your dominant impression and your attitude toward the topic. Focused freewriting should expand your current thinking.

EXERCISE 4-6 **Focused Freewriting**

Directions: *On a separate sheet of paper, freewrite for ten minutes on the assignment that you chose in Exercise 4-4. You might start with a detail from your brainstorming but focus on your attitude toward your subject and the dominant impression you aim to create. Ask yourself, What is my attitude toward this topic? What does it mean to me?*

DRAFT
- Consider your audience
- Formulate your topic sentence
- Outline for unity and coherence
- Write a conclusion sentence
- Compose your first draft

Draft: Focus and Organize

After prewriting, you usually have a hunch about what you want to include in your paragraph. You can point to three or four concrete details you really like. You know the dominant impression you wish to explore.

Consider Your Audience

Before you draft, consider your reader. Begin by rereading the assignment. Identify the key words in the assignment. What kind of description is the reader expecting? Think about how to organize your paragraph so your reader can make sense of the description and understand why you are describing the topic in this way. Use the following questions to consider how to convey your dominant impression to an audience:

- Why is my topic important?
- What do I want my readers to understand?
- What details will help them understand and connect to my perspective?

PEER CONVERSATION

EXERCISE 4-7 **Considering Your Audience**

Directions: *Use the questions above to think critically about which specific details to include in your paragraph and how you will use them to convey your dominant impression to an audience. Talk with a classmate to clarify your purpose and decide on the description details you will use. Take notes on this conversation and add it to your prewriting.*

Topic Sentence

To begin, write a clear topic sentence that echoes the key words from the assignment. If you are not sure of your dominant impression, relax. Often the dominant impression becomes clear after you have written a first draft. Remember, revision can happen as you write, so you can always state the dominant impression in the conclusion or rewrite the topic sentence as you are drafting or when you have finished your first draft.

Ask Yourself

Do you relax or get tense when you write a paper?

Unity and Coherence

Your paragraph should be unified around a main idea. That means all the description details relate to that idea. Be careful not to go off the subject. Remember too that that your details need to fit together to form a coherent paragraph.

Description is often organized using spatial order. For example, a room can be described by moving from front to back, left to right, or by the placement of furniture to the left or right of an important focal point. You may want to try some commonly used transition terms based on spatial order.

TRANSITIONS BASED ON SPATIAL ORDER	
to the right	below
to the left	in front
close by	in back
above	in the center

Many writers mix spatial order transitions with other types of transition terms. Transitions based on priority and importance can be used to emphasize key details. The following is a list of commonly used transition terms based on priority and importance.

TRANSITIONS BASED ON PRIORITY OR IMPORTANCE

To Show Priority

always

certainly

definitely

never

obviously

To Show Importance

most

equally

absolutely

Concluding Sentence

A concluding sentence restates the topic sentence or emphasizes the dominant impression. Before writing your conclusion, carefully reread your paragraph to be clear about what you want to emphasize. Do your details create a dominant impression? What point would you like to make in the paragraph?

EXERCISE 4-8 Planning Your First Draft

Directions: *On a separate sheet of paper, write a topic sentence that echoes the key words from the assignment topic you selected and states the dominant impression you want to convey. Make a short outline to organize your description details.*

See "Supporting Details" in Chapter 3 for detailed explanation of outlining.

Write a First Draft

You have chosen your topic, decided on the dominant impression you want to convey, and organized the description details you will use. Now it is time to write a first draft of your paragraph. As you write, you may think of details that are not in your brainstorming and freewriting. Make use of any new ideas and details that are important and relevant.

EXERCISE 4-9 Writing Your First Draft

Directions: *Write a draft of your paragraph. Use the following checklist as a guide.*

FIRST DRAFT CHECKLIST

- _____ My topic sentence states the dominant impression of my paragraph and echoes key terms in the assignment.
- _____ I included sensory details to help a reader picture my description and understand the dominant impression.
- _____ I inserted transitions to organize the description by spatial order or by priority or importance.
- _____ My concluding sentence restates my dominant impression and emphasizes some aspect of my dominant impression.

A PROFESSIONAL'S TAKE

Here is a description by Barbara Ehrenreich, from her book *Nickel and Dimed:*

To say that some place is the worst motel in the country is, of course, to set oneself up for considerable challenge. I have encountered plenty of contenders in my own travels—the one in Cleveland that turned into a brothel at night, the one in Butte where the window looked out into another room. Still, the Clearview Inn leaves the competition in the dust. Room 133 contains a bed, a chair, a chest of drawers, and a TV fastened to the wall. I plead for and get a lamp to supplement the single overhead bulb. Instead of the mold smell, I now breathe a mixture of fresh paint and what I eventually identify as mouse droppings. But the real problems are all window- and door-related: the single small window has no screen, and the room has no AC or fan. The curtain is transparently thin; the door has no bolt. Without a screen, the window should be sensibly closed at night, meaning no air, unless I'm willing to take my chances with the bugs and the neighbors. Who are the neighbors? The motel forms a toilet-seat shape around the parking lot, and I can see an inexplicable collection. A woman with a baby in her arms leans in the doorway of one room. Two bunches of teenagers, one group black and the other white, seem to share adjoining rooms. There are several unencumbered men of various ages, including an older white man in work clothes whose bumper sticker says, "Don't steal, the government hates competition"—as if the income tax were the only thing keeping him from living at the Embassy Suites right now. When it gets dark I go outside and look through my curtain, and yes, you can see pretty much everything, at least in silhouette. I eat the deli food I've brought with me from a Minneapolis supermarket and go to bed with my clothes on, but not to sleep.

EXERCISE 4-10 A PROFESSIONAL'S TAKE

Directions: *Using the first draft checklist as your guide, identify the elements of an effective description paragraph in the professional model.*

Revise: Read Critically, Then Rewrite

What if your reader does not "get it"? In description, writers often assume the reader can see the person, place, or object they are describing. As a result, they leave out critical description detail. It helps if you have someone read and talk with you about your writing.

REVISE
- Read critically
- Develop a revision plan

Revision in Action

Revision is rethinking a draft and making decisions to improve the quality of your writing. You read critically, plan your revision, and revise the writing. Here is an example of revision by a student named Martin.

The full version of Martin's sample is available online.

Assignment: Describe a person, place, or thing you value highly.

Martin's First Draft

All the world is digital, but I have an analog Timex wrist watch. (1) **First and most important,** the analog wrist watch is simple and beautiful. The face of the watch is round. There are black Arabic numerals. There are thin black stems for hands. There is no month, no date or day of the week. It just gives me the time of day. (2) **In addition to being beautiful,** this watch is environmentally friendly. There are no batteries to replace because it has to be wound. The tiny machine inside works based on a mainspring that has tension. I pinch the stem between my thumb and forefinger and turn it back and forth. I often find myself winding it. This does make it noisy. When I hold it to my ear: it ticks. When it is lying by my bed at night, I can hear it. (3) **Last,** the watch is cheap. If I lose it, I buy another one. No matter what other people think, I still like my simple analog watch.

TOPIC SENTENCE
Martin states the thing he will describe.

SUPPORTING DETAILS
He describes the physical appearance of the watch, how it works, and the cost.

ORDER AND TRANSITIONS
He begins with order of importance, but continues with a list.

CONCLUDING SENTENCE
Martin makes a comment that states his attitude toward the watch.

Revision Plan: Revise the topic sentence to connect to the assignment and clarify the dominant impression. Reorder, cut, and add details to support the dominant impression. Change the paragraph to objective description by removing first-person pronouns.

Martin focuses his revision on improving the dominant impression. He also decides to make the writing more appropriate for an academic audience by removing the first-person pronouns.

Martin's Revised Draft

All the world is digital, but a simple Timex wrist watch still has value. **The insides** of an analog Timex watch might be the most valuable because it is a tiny machine. It works by creating tension on a mainspring, so it

TOPIC SENTENCE
Martin revises his topic sentence by inserting the dominant impression.

SUPPORTING DETAILS
He cuts irrelevant description and adds details to describe why a simple watch has value.

ORDER AND TRANSITIONS
He uses spatial order to clarify the description.

CONCLUDING SENTENCE
The conclusion now emphasizes the key words from the assignment.

does not use a battery. Therefore, it has to be wound to keep tension on the mainspring and the watch ticking. This reminds its wearer that time matters. **The outside** of a Timex wrist watch is simplified beauty. This watch has a round white face and black Arabic numerals. The hands are thin, black stems. There is no month, no date or day of the week to clutter the simple face. No matter what other people think, a Timex is a simple reminder to value time.

PEER CONVERSATION

DISCUSSION QUESTIONS Which changes in the revision most improve Martin's paragraph? Why?

Read Critically

MULTILINGUAL TIP
Bring your draft to the writing center on your campus.

Pay attention to how other writers do what you are trying to do. It helps if you read your peers' papers so you can compare your work to theirs. Do their paragraphs have a dominant impression that makes sense to a reader? Do they provide enough description details so a reader can understand the dominant impression? Revision gives you a chance to get things right.

PEER CONVERSATION

EXERCISE 4-11 **Reading Peer Papers**

Directions: *Exchange papers with another student. Be a critical reader and make suggestions you think will improve your classmate's first draft. Also identify what your classmate did well. Make notes in the margin as you read to remember your suggestions. After you read, discuss your suggestions. Use the guidelines in the revision checklist.*

REVISION CHECKLIST

_____ Does the topic sentence connect to the assignment and state the point of the paragraph?

_____ Does the writer stay on the subject through the paragraph?

_____ Does the writer provide a variety of description detail?

_____ Does the paragraph have effective transitions?

_____ Does the concluding sentence summarize the point or emphasize the dominant impression of the paragraph?

Revise with a Plan

Reread your assignment before revising. Some description paragraphs can be written in first person, but most require an objective description, which requires a shift to third-person pronouns.

EXERCISE 4-12 **Revising Your Draft**

Directions: *Develop a revision plan and revise the draft of the paragraph you wrote for Exercise 4-9.*

Edit

To make your description count, edit for careless errors. Careless punctuation and grammar can lose your reader. Work to make your writing as perfect as possible. In any class, not just for an English course, your instructors want to see that you care about your work. Focus your editing with this personalized checklist.

EDIT
- Search and correct
- Self-edit

YOUR EDITING CHECKLIST

_____ Spelling: List any words you misspelled in your last paper:

____

_____ Punctuation: List two punctuation errors from your last paper:

____

_____ Capitalization: List any capitalization errors from your last paper:

____

_____ Other errors: List any errors your instructor has pointed out in graded work:

____

____

To Prepare Your Draft for an Academic Audience

_____ Remove first-person pronouns: *I, me, my.*

_____ Remove second-person pronouns: *you, your.*

_____ Use third-person pronouns: *he, she, it, they.*

MULTILINGUAL TIP
Proofread for missing articles.

EXERCISE 4-13 Revising and Editing Practice

Directions: *Read the following paragraph that was written in response to the assignment below. The paragraph contains errors that require revising and editing. Then answer the questions that follow.*

Assignment: Write about a region, city, neighborhood, or building and describe the living conditions of the people who live in it. Describe this place using details that convey a dominant impression.

(1) ____________________________________. (2) People and noise are everywhere. (3) Driving in the city is more than unpleasant! (4) Rush hour is unbearable. (5) Cars are backed up bumper to bumper. (6) Everyone constantly honks their horn. (7) Once traffic starts moving, drivers cut in and out of traffic, racing to the next red light. (8) They cannot seem to go fast enough. (9) Few people remember how to be courteous behind the wheel. (10) ______________, neighbors can be a nuisance. (11) The houses

are so close that everything a family does in their home can be heard by their neighbors. (12) If you looked in a neighbor's window you would see they are watching the same show, and you are just one big family. (13) Even the backyards are not very peaceful, because of the barking dogs plus summer brings the personal problems outside. (14) Children argue over games, and teen's shout and fight, but the domestic arguments are the most unpleasant. (15) A couple shouting insults across the front lawn as if they are in the privacy of their kitchen is embarrassing. (16) Cities are crowded and unpleasant places where living is rarely peaceful, and privacy does not exist.

apostrophe error

Revising

__b__ 1. Which sentence should be inserted in blank 1? The sentence would state the dominant impression and serve as the topic sentence.

a. Privacy is not possible in a city.

b. City living is unpleasant.

c. City living has its downside, but I love it anyway.

d. You cannot get away from noise and people in the city.

__d__ 2. Select the order of sentences 5, 6, 7, 8, and 9 that provides the most logical sequence of ideas and supporting details. If appropriate, choose "no change is necessary."

a. 5, 9, 6, 7, 8

b. 9, 5, 6, 7, 8

c. 5, 7, 8, 6, 9

d. no change is necessary

__d__ 3. Which word or phrase should be inserted in blank 10? The word or phrase would serve as a clear transition between the writer's two ideas in this paragraph.

a. Next

b. Also

c. In addition

d. Even more unpleasant

__a__ 4. Which sentence should be cut to improve the focus of the paragraph? If appropriate, choose "no change is necessary."

a. sentence 12

b. sentence 13

c. sentence 16

d. no change is necessary

Editing

__c__ 1. Choose the option that corrects the error in sentence 6. If appropriate, choose "no change is necessary."

a. Everyone is honking their horn.

b. Everyone honks at the driver in front of them.

c. Up and down the road, horns make a terrible racket.

d. no change is necessary

__d__ 2. Choose the option that corrects the error in sentence 11. If no error exists, choose "no change is necessary."

a. are so close and everything

b. are so close; everything

c. are so close: everything

d. no change is necessary

__c__ 3. Choose the option that corrects the error in sentence 13. If no error exists, choose "no change is necessary."

a. dogs, plus summer

b. dogs, moreover, summer

c. dogs. Plus summer

d. no change is necessary

4. Proofread for an apostrophe error in the paragraph and correct the error.

Talk about It

Which do you use more, comparisons or sensory details?

EXERCISE 4-14 Searching and Correcting

PEER CONVERSATION

Directions: *Exchange papers with a proofreading peer and proofread each other's work. In addition to spelling, punctuation, and capitalization, find out what other errors your classmate has on his or her checklist; tell your classmate what errors you have on your checklist.*

EXERCISE 4-15 Self-Editing

Directions: *Carefully rewrite your paper, correcting the errors you and your classmate found. Give yourself time to set aside the finished paper. Then come back to it and read your final draft one last time, using your checklist as a guide.*

Reflect

Take a moment and reflect on what you have learned.

REFLECT
- Identify strengths
- Set goals

EXERCISE 4-16 Identifying Strengths and Setting Goals

Directions: *Review your writing and your writing process. On a separate sheet of paper, write answers to these questions:*

- *What did you do well in the paragraph you wrote?*
- *What did you enjoy working on in this chapter?*
- *What have you learned that you will apply in future writing assignments?*

GOING PLACES

TAKING SHORTCUTS AND SCENIC ROUTES WITH EXAMPLES

For Example . . .

One of the first rules of good communication is to be specific. General statements like "My brother is annoying" or "My boss is the greatest" might convey the speaker's main idea, but they do not have much impact on the listener. Real communicative power comes in the form of specific examples: "My brother refuses to take phone messages for me, he teases me relentlessly about my taste in clothes, and he sold my CD collection." "My boss mentors me, pays me well, and she gave me her tickets to the baseball game tonight." Specific examples provide weight and strength to any point you may make. Use them often.

DISCUSSION

Turn and talk with a classmate to answer the following questions: Who is annoying to you? Or who is a great influence in your life? Give several specific examples to illustrate just how annoying or great this person is.

Drawing Your Reader In

While logic is the foundation of all academic writing, the strongest piece of writing is more than that. Your work also needs to be *engaging.* The surest way to draw your reader in is through the use of examples that, in addition to providing the basic evidence for your writing, also evoke laughter, sympathy, anger, or fear. Whether you choose to focus on a battle in the Vietnam War, the migratory patterns of birds, or an interpretation of a Rita Dove poem, your writing will receive greater attention if readers can find something to latch on to.

BRAINSTORM

College instructors want specifics in your work. Brainstorm a list of college assignments that asked you to provide specific examples.

The Lessons of the Past

In the business world, practicality comes first. Theories about efficiency and philosophies of customer relations have their place, but the usual questions of the business world are more mundane: How many boxes can we get to Cleveland by Thursday? What are Anna's job responsibilities? How much will it cost to develop a new product, and how much revenue will it bring in? Hence, in a business setting, your ability to draw effectively on real-world events and facts by employing examples is essential. For instance, if you want to convince your boss to take a risk on a new product, you will probably need to demonstrate how similar products have fared in the past or how many paying customers would be interested. The more specifically you can support your claims, the more credibility your ideas will have.

RESUME BUILDER

Think about your current job. What is your job title? What are your job responsibilities? List two or three specific examples to illustrate how you are an effective and efficient employee.

Example

CHAPTER 5

CHAPTER OVERVIEW

- THE EXAMPLE PARAGRAPH AT A GLANCE
- EXAMPLE THINKING
  - Elements of Example
  - Types of Examples
  - Elaborate on Examples
  - Organize Your Thinking
- EXAMPLE IN PROCESS
  - Prewrite
  - Draft
  - A Professional's Take
  - Revise
  - Edit
  - Reflect

THINK FIRST

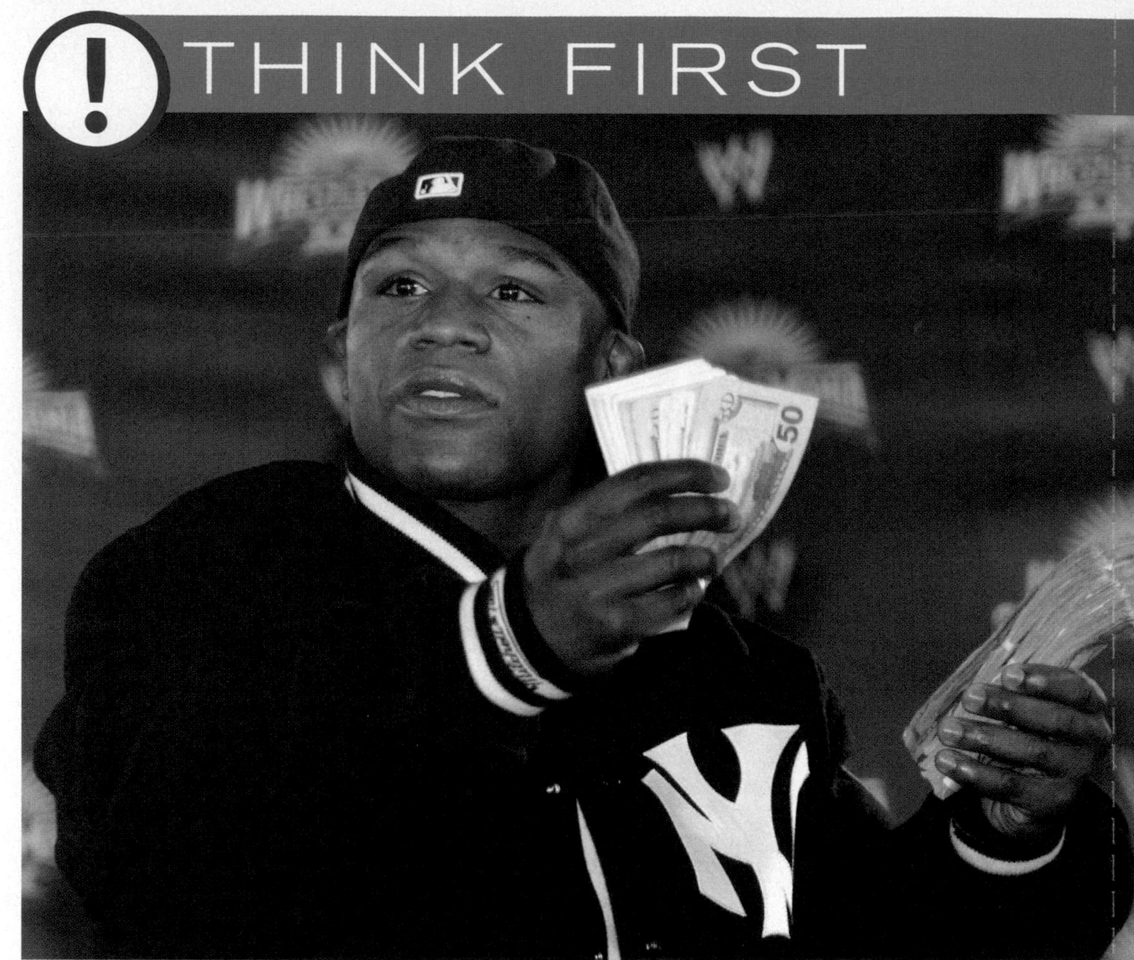

PEER CONVERSATION

Turn and talk to a classmate about this photo. Why do you like it or dislike about it? What is money for? What problems does it cause? How do you spend money? After your conversation, write a short paragraph that states your attitude toward money. Include several examples that illustrate how you feel about it.

At a Glance

THE EXAMPLE PARAGRAPH AT A GLANCE

An example paragraph has three basic parts: a topic sentence, supporting details, and a concluding sentence or sentences. The topic sentence is usually the first sentence in an example paragraph. The major supporting details consist of one or more examples. These examples are supported and explained through the use of facts and specific details that make the examples clear and interesting. The concluding sentence emphasizes the point of the paragraph.

The Example Paragraph at a Glance

ASSIGNMENT Some of the individuals we have studied this semester snatched success from the jaws of defeat. Write a paragraph discussing two or three examples.

Some of the individuals we studied this semester had the uncanny ability to turn adversity into success. (1) **For example,** Abraham Lincoln might have been considered a failure. He failed at business twice. He suffered a nervous breakdown. He was defeated in elections multiple times before he was elected president in 1860. (2) **Another example** is Thomas Edison. As a child, Edison was considered retarded, but he learned to imagine things. He tried over ten thousand experiments before he successfully invented the incandescent bulb. (3) **A final example** is Langston Hughes. His father sent him to Columbia University to become an engineer. However, Hughes loved poetry and dropped out of college and worked at menial jobs to pursue his dream. Eventually Hughes became a major American poet. Faced with failure, these famous men discovered that they could make something happen.

TOPIC SENTENCE
The writer repeats the key words from the assignment and then adds her opinion about successful people.

EXAMPLES AND DETAILS
The writer provides three examples of men who overcame failure to succeed. Each example gives facts and details to show how the men overcame failure as well as how they succeeded.

ORDER AND TRANSITIONS
The examples are organized in a list. Each transition introduces the "next" example.

CONCLUDING SENTENCE
The writer restates the topic sentence by rephrasing it.

DISCUSSION QUESTIONS

1. Identify the specific, minor details in each example that help make the point of the example.
2. Which of these facts and details do you find most effective?

PEER CONVERSATION

EXAMPLE THINKING

You use examples in every aspect of your life. When you tell friends about your busy weekend, you use specific examples to convince them you are exhausted. You might say you worked eight hours at the laundry folding shirts and unbuttoning buttons, wrote a three-page essay on poverty in the 1920s, and studied angles and formulas for a geometry test. Writing for college, you will use examples to explore a topic, explain a concept, or support an argument.

Elements of Example

Typically, an example paragraph includes a point, examples, and facts or details. Below is a brief description of the elements you should keep in mind when writing an example paragraph.

- ***Point:*** A topic sentence makes a point. It states your main idea and what you want a reader to understand. In the sample above, the writer makes a point about adversity and success. The point is stated at the beginning of the paragraph. The examples and details that follow help the reader understand the point.
- ***Examples:*** Examples illustrate and explain the point made in the topic sentence. They should be fresh, interesting, and relevant. Readers will immediately connect good examples to their own experience and to the topic. In the illustration, the reader can connect with the examples because the writer provides the proper names of actual people and makes specific remarks about these historical examples.
- ***Facts and details:*** Specific facts and details help you elaborate and develop your examples. You want the reader to understand how the examples illustrate the point. It is not enough simply to cite the example; you need to help the reader see the example the way you see it. Langston Hughes changed careers. He worked menial jobs before becoming a successful poet. He faced adversity and persevered.

Get Started

Examples explain what you mean. They help you think more clearly about the point you would like to make; they also help your reader begin to grasp your meaning. The sooner you get specific, the sooner you begin to make progress in your writing.

Suppose you are taking a course in health, and on the first day of class, you are asked to write a paragraph on your formula for maintaining good health. Experienced students learn to "think in three's." An experienced student asks herself, "What are the three most important things a person does to maintain good health?" She divides her subject into three manageable subtopics, three examples of what she knows about healthy living. Then she gets specific. This process of thinking in three's, moving from a topic or assignment to manageable subtopics, can be pictured like this:

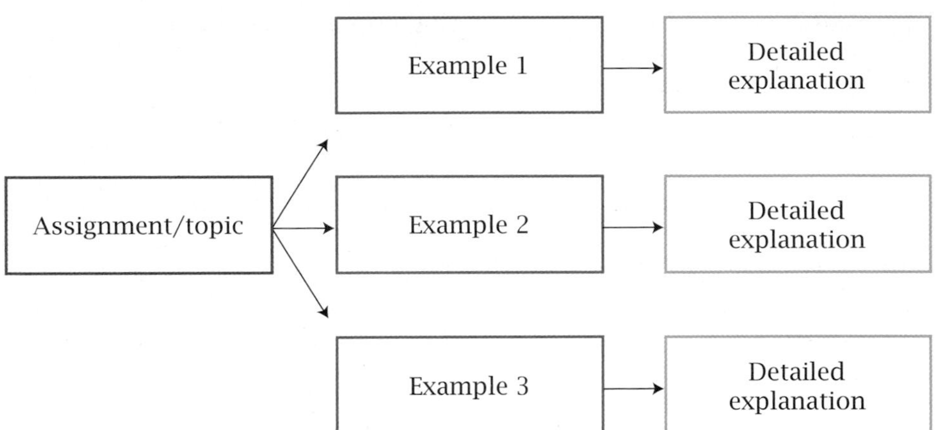

Learning to divide your topic like this is the beginning of effective example thinking. Is three the magic number? Of course not. You might think of two important approaches to maintaining good health, or four, or even five. The important thing is the narrowing of your thinking, your movement from general to specific. Effective students actually make two moves: first from topic to examples, and then from examples to details.

General to Specific

An effective example paragraph moves from a general topic to the specific and detailed examples that support it. Notice in this example how the writer gets specific to explain a healthy lifestyle:

Topic Sentence: Good health is built each day by making healthy lifestyle choices.

Example 1: Choose a healthy diet by using USDA Dietary Guidelines for the five basic food groups.

Details: Eat a variety of fruits, vegetables, bread or grains, dairy products or cheese, and meat, fish, or fats every day.

Example 2: Forget the gym. Start a daily exercise program that can fit easily into a busy schedule.

Details: Grab 15 to 30 minutes at lunch. Walking or climbing the stairs is an aerobic exercise that improves heart and lung health. Yoga, tai chi, or stretching at your desk will reduce stress and tone muscles.

Example 3: Go to bed on time. Good health is more likely if you get plenty of rest.

Details: Studies have shown there is a connection between good rest and a person's resistance to illness. Less rest means lower resistance. Those who do not make sure they sleep well and enough are more likely to get sick.

EXERCISE 5-1 General to Specific

Directions: *For each of the general topics and topic sentences below write three specific examples that could support them.* Answers will vary. Example answers shown.

1. **General:** Children

Topic Sentence: Divorce can have a lasting impact on children.

Specific:

Example 1: Some children withdraw.

Example 2: Other children respond with aggression.

Example 3: Some children have trust issues in relationships.

2. **General:** Education

Topic Sentence: Reading is an essential life skill.

Specific:

Example 1: People need to read on the job.

Example 2: They also need reading to conduct daily business.

Example 3: People need to read to maximize leisure time as well.

3. **General:** Employment

Topic Sentence: A global economy impacts jobs and employment.

Specific:

Example 1: When jobs are shipped overseas, there is a negative impact.

Example 2: It helps to be bilingual in a global economy.

Example 3: Immigration issues become important in a global economy.

Types of Examples

You can use different types of examples to support your topic sentence. Often you will cite multiple examples to support your main idea. Sometimes these will be several related examples and sometimes contrasting examples. At other times you will find an extended example serves your purpose best.

Related Examples

Examples build support and convince readers to adopt your point of view. While writers vary the number of examples they use, they are careful to connect them. Sometimes writers connect similar examples; sometimes they connect contrasting examples.

Topic Sentence: Success comes from being creative.

Similar Examples

- Joe Cossman made millions in mail-order selling ant farms, potato spud guns, and shrunken heads.
- Similarly, Bill Gates is expanding his billion-dollar business in computers to online banking and interactive TV.

Contrasting Examples

- Madonna makes millions as a huge rock sensation because she creatively changes her music to keep up with trends and shocks audiences.
- In contrast, Oprah Winfrey invents creative ways she and others can give away millions of dollars to help underprivileged people.

Ask Yourself

Do you examine your examples to connect them for a reader?

EXERCISE 5-2 Similar and Contrasting Examples

Directions: *Use your own experience, television advertisements, magazines, or newspapers to find examples to support the topic sentences below. Provide two similar examples and one contrasting example for each topic sentence.* Answers will vary. Example answers shown.

1. **Topic Sentence:** Credit cards can be the road to financial ruin.

Example: The lure of low monthly payments encourages people to buy now and pay later.

Similar Example: Making minimum payments will make it almost impossible to pay off a credit card debt.

Contrasting Example: Paying off a credit card each month offers the ease of purchasing with credit but avoids the high interest that causes some people problems.

2. **Topic Sentence:** Athletes serve as role models to the world.

Example: Michael Jordan serves as a role model on the court and off for his involvement with Boys and Girls Club of America and Special Olympics.

Similar Example: Deion Sanders donates his time and money to help sick children and people who are homeless.

Contrasting Example: The drug addiction of Jamal Lewis and drug-related death of Ken Caminiti serve only as models of trouble.

3. **Topic Sentence:** Good study habits are the key to success in college.

Example: My friend Omar studies all the time. He is on his way to becoming a dentist.

Similar Example: Over the past few weeks, I have learned to do a little homework every day, and the results have been positive.

Contrasting Example: My friend Sheila, on the other hand, always waits until the night before a test to open her books. She is now on academic probation.

Extended Examples

A single extended example can support a point or claim. Students use this approach when they have a single convincing example and can elaborate with facts and details, or when they have a narrative that illustrates their point. For example, you might tell the story of a disastrous haircut to illustrate that communication is important.

To extend a single example, a writer will provide additional information by answering the six basic questions: who, what, when, where, why, and how. Here is a paragraph in which an extended example is used to illustrate the writer's point.

Sometimes people wish for things before they are ready for them. I will always remember turning twelve. I wanted to be a grown-up, so I wished for a pair of nylons. I was not disappointed. I got a pair of Hanes that looked like a second pair of legs when I took them out of the box to put them on. For that birthday, I also got a blue and silver three-speed bike. It had a black seat, and thin black tires. After breakfast the day after my birthday, wearing my nylons, of course, I raced out of the house to meet my best friend Connie. She met me on the sidewalk, got her bike, and we rode around the neighborhood showing our friends. Just before I left for home, I remembered the nylons, but they were ruined. They hung in shreds on my legs. I realized that even though I wanted to be a grown-up, I was not ready to be a lady at twelve.

TOPIC SENTENCE

Who: A twelve-year-old girl.
What: She wished for nylons to feel grown-up.
When: It was her twelfth birthday.
Where: She rode her bike around the neighborhood wearing her nylons.
Why: She did not realize nylons were for ladylike activities and not for riding bikes.
How: She ruined her nylons riding her bike.

CONCLUDING SENTENCE

EXERCISE 5-3 Writing an Extended Example

Directions: *Choose one of the topic sentences below and write a paragraph using an extended example to develop the main idea. Do your work on a separate sheet of paper.*

1. A good teacher can make all the difference in the world.
2. A bad teacher can make all the difference in the world.
3. Coworkers can make a bad job tolerable.
4. Coworkers can make a good job intolerable.

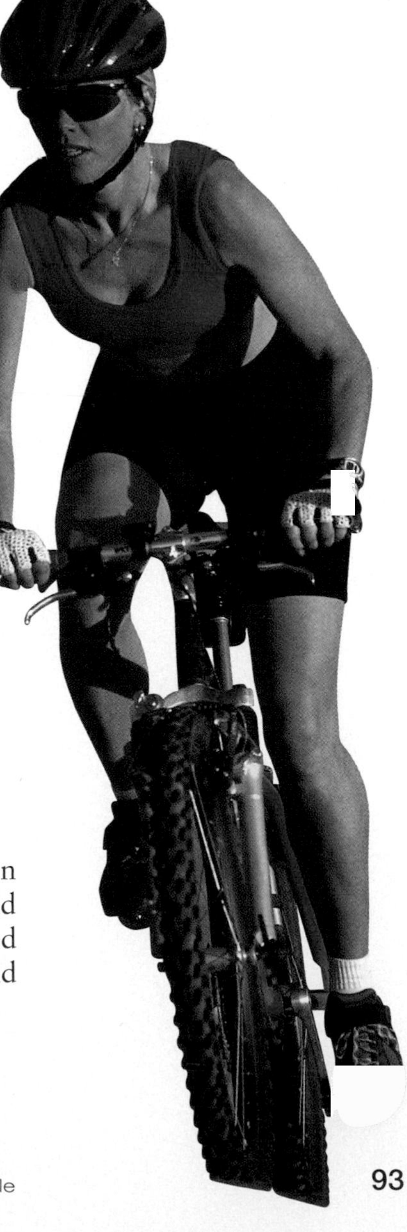

Examples as Proof

An example paragraph can provide proof of a point or claim. When used in this way, it is best to state the point in the topic sentence. Then you can decide if you will use multiple examples or a single extended example to prove your point.

EXERCISE 5-4 Examples as Proof

Directions: *"People have to find an approach to fitness that works best for them." Write a paragraph in which you use either a number of related examples or an extended example to prove this claim.*

Elaborate on Examples

Citing an example is just the beginning. For your example to really function in your writing, you need to explain it. You need to say what it means and explain what you want your reader to understand. This explanation is called *elaboration*. Note the contrast between the following simple examples and the elaborated versions of them that follow:

Here the writer cites two examples to develop the main idea in the topic sentence. Neither example is elaborated. on.

Simple Examples

The small town often felt the force of nature. For example, there was a river that flowed through the town. Also, because the town was located in the snow belt, it was not unusual for five to ten inches of snow to fall in a few hours' time.

Here the writer elaborates on the two examples. He shows how the river was a force of nature and the impact that snow had on the community. The impact of flooding and heavy snow helps the reader appreciate what the writer means by "felt the force of nature."

Elaborated Examples

The small town often felt the force of nature. For example, there was a river that flowed through the town. Every spring, if there was heavy rain, the river would rise, overflow its banks, and tear through people's backyards, carrying away swingsets, overturning doghouses, and leaving a sea of mud on lawns. Also, because the town was located in the snow belt, it was not unusual to have five to ten inches of snow fall in a few hours' time. One year it snowed for three days, accumulating five feet of snow. Schools and businesses closed. People stayed home from work and climbed up on their roofs to shovel snow off. Some roofs collapsed under the weight of the snow.

Elaboration ensures that your reader connects your example to the main idea. It drives your point home.

EXERCISE 5-5 Elaborating on Your Examples

Directions: *Provide an example that supports the main idea of each of the following topic sentences. Then provide additional details that explain and support the example.* Answers will vary. Example answers shown.

EXAMPLE

Topic Sentence: Divorce can have a lasting impact on children.

Example 1: Losing one parent and the security of the family unit can cause loneliness and insecurity in elementary-age children.

Details: Young children understand the sadness of having one parent leave the house. However, they cannot explain their feelings or express them. As a result, young children may have feelings of resentment or embarrassment that never get resolved and affect other relationships.

Example 2: In addition, living in a single-parent home puts pressure on teens who often take on the responsibilities of the missing parent.

Details: Teens may take on child care of younger siblings or increase duties to maintain the house. These added responsibilities reduce their relationships with friends and push them into adulthood too early.

1. **Topic Sentence:** Reading is an essential life skill.

Example 1: Adults who cannot read cannot perform basic life skills.

Details: These adults cannot balance a checkbook, fill out job applications, read drug labels, or understand directions for preparing food.

Example 2: Moreover, students who cannot read are at risk of dropping out of school.

Details: Government statistics state that in the last twenty-five years, over six million Americans have dropped out of high school.

2. **Topic Sentence:** A global economy impacts jobs and employment.

Example 1: The clothing industry may be the hardest hit by the impact of a global economy and employment.

Details: Jobs have shifted to companies outside the United States where wages are cheaper.

Example 2: Furthermore, technology telephone support centers also have been outsourced to countries like Canada, Mexico, and India.

Details: This trend suggests that one in nine white-collar jobs are at risk of being outsourced to other countries.

Organize Your Thinking

If you use two or three examples to make a point, be sure to think about the order in which you present those examples. How you organize your ideas and details can affect, negatively or positively, the impact you have on a reader. Two common ways of organizing your use of examples are chronological order and order of importance.

In chronological order, you begin in the past and move to the present, or begin in the present and move to the past.

Topic Sentence: I have always had a hard time learning French.

Example 1: In Madame Bidwell's class last semester, I struggled with verb tense.

Example 2: In middle school French, the only French word I could really pronounce was the name that Madame Vey gave me, Benois.

Example 3: I learned to count in French by watching television when I was very young, but counting and speaking are two different things.

Writer's Response
Which form of organization do you use most, chronological order or order of importance?

The order used in this sentence outline begins in the present and moves to the past. In fact, the impact on the reader might be stronger if the student reversed the order, beginning with the example of counting and finishing with his recent experience of trying to learn French verbs.

When using order of importance, writers often save the best for last. The idea is that the last example makes the greatest impact on the reader. The opposite approach, however, can also be effective. You can begin with your most persuasive example to convince the reader of the importance of your main idea, using the example to pull the reader in.

Topic Sentence: Studies show that young drivers are at considerable risk on the road.

Example 1: They tend to drive fast and overestimate their reaction time and ability to control their vehicle.

Example 2: They often have the radio turned on, probably at high volume, which distracts them from the road.

Example 3: They frequently have friends in the car with them, which significantly enhances the risk of accident and injury.

These three examples all explain the risk young drivers face. Which is the most important? The answer may be determined by interpretation, by personal experience, or by the data from the studies. Whatever the order, writers should use transitions to indicate their thinking about importance. In this case, transitions related to impact would be appropriate.

Topic Sentence: Studies show that young drivers are at considerable risk on the road.

For example, they often have the radio turned on, probably at high volume, which distracts them from the road.

More importantly, they tend to drive fast and overestimate their reaction time and ability to control their vehicle.

Finally, the most important reason young drivers are at risk is that they frequently have friends in the car with them, which significantly enhances risk of accident and injury.

EXERCISE 5-6 Organizing Your Thinking

Directions: *For each topic sentence, indicate the order in which you would present the following examples. In the space provided, indicate whether you recommend chronological order or order of importance. Briefly explain the reasons for your choices.* Answers will vary. Example answers shown.

EXAMPLE

Topic Sentence: Although high school sports may distract students' attention from their studies, there are definite benefits from these programs.

__2__ The students learn about teamwork.

__1__ The students have to manage their time effectively.

__3__ The students' spare time is organized around physical activity.

Order of importance. Because so many young people are now overweight, I think the physical fitness aspect of sports is the most important.

1. **Topic Sentence:** A good school is vital to an inner-city community.

__3__ A school that sets high standards will encourage positive behaviors that help children in the long run.

__2__ A good school provides kids with role models.

__1__ A good school is vital to a community if it offers kids a safe place to be and a chance to do things after school.

Order of importance. Safety and role models seem most important in an inner-city school.

2. **Topic Sentence:** The options available on cars these days are amazing.

__3__ New models have GPS systems, sensors to indicate the distance of the car from curbs and other cars, and, of course, amazing sound systems.

__1__ My first car had an AM radio, and that was it.

__2__ Then came FM radios, cassette players, and ultimately CD players.

__4__ The sound systems in some cars can even be synchronized with the driver's iPod and telephone.

Chronological order. The improvements in car options are listed from the writer's first car to cars today.

3. **Topic Sentence:** Many academic subjects have immediate practical applications in everyday life.

__3__ A course in health will identify issues and lifestyle decisions that have far-reaching consequences.

__2__ Mathematics is useful in the grocery store, at the car dealership, and at the bank.

__1__ Psychology gives a person the skills to size up other people, read their motives, and understand their behavior.

Order of importance. The psychology example can be used every day in many encounters with people. The other examples are more specific and might be used less often.

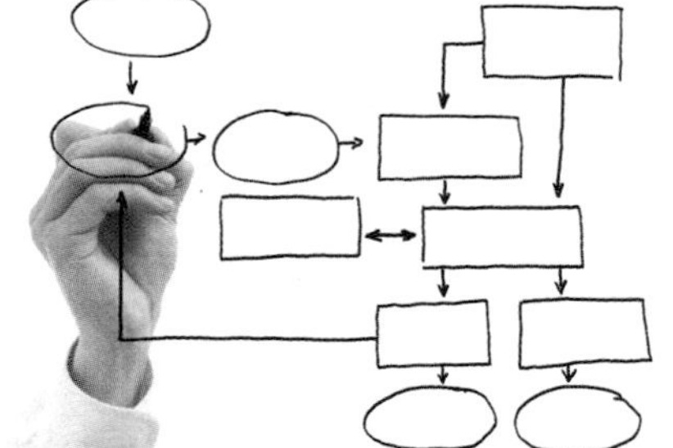

Process

EXAMPLE IN PROCESS

Good example writing benefits from using the writing process: prewriting, drafting, revising, and editing.

Select an Assignment

In college you will be asked to write a variety of assignments. Most of them will require you to find an example to illustrate your point. Sometimes the examples will come from your experience. Other times the examples will come from the reading and research you are doing for the course.

EXERCISE 5-7 Selecting an Assignment for an Example Paragraph

Directions: *Review the assignments listed below. Choose the one you know the most about and believe is best suited to an effective example paragraph.*

1. Explain the advantages of organized sports in school.
2. Explain the disadvantages of organized sports in school.
3. Provide examples of the difficulties of being a kid today.

4. Explain the advantages of being married (or being single).
5. Provide strategies for saving money.
6. Give your tips for getting good grades.
7. List some strategies for getting fired.
8. Name an important person in your life.
9. Describe some approaches for staying thin or gaining weight.
10. Respond to the following quote by Eleanor Roosevelt: "You gain strength, courage, and confidence by every experience in which you really stop to look fear in the face. . . . You must do the thing you cannot do."

Prewrite: Write Before You Write

PREWRITE
- Talk
- Cluster
- Brainstorm
- Freewrite

Perhaps the two most important words in college writing are "for example." But your examples are only as good as your details because examples do not explain themselves. That is the writer's job.

Before you start writing, do some prewriting to discover the specific details that will really make your examples work. Remember that you have a variety of prewriting techniques to choose from: talking, clustering, brainstorming, and freewriting. For this mode, focus on brainstorming and freewriting.

Brainstorm

Use brainstorming to list the examples you could use in your paragraph. Try "thinking in three's" if it helps. List three examples and specific details that go with each example. Then try again: three different examples with specific details. After you find the breakdown of your topic you like best, analyze your examples and details, assessing their connection to your assignment. What is your point? Will the examples help you make your point?

EXERCISE 5-8 **Brainstorming**

Directions: *Brainstorm on your topic for about ten minutes. Use a separate sheet of paper. List a variety of examples to explore the assignment you have chosen. Try listing your examples in chronological order.*

Freewrite

Use freewriting to elaborate on and explore your examples. You can follow leads, discover new details that may lead to important ideas. To get to additional detail for each example, use the six basic questions: who, what, when, where, why, and how.

EXERCISE 5-9 **Freewriting**

Directions: *Freewrite on your topic for ten minutes. Explore as many examples as you can think of. Try to provide several sentences of explanation for each example.*

Draft: Focus and Organize

DRAFT

- Consider your audience
- Formulate your topic sentence
- Outline for unity and coherence
- Write a conclusion sentence
- Compose your first draft

Prewriting helps you see your subject more clearly. Then you can select what interests you and build on it. In the next phase of the writing process you add content. However, you also think more about what the writing means and the point you want to make. You analyze the content to decide what examples and details will be most effective.

Consider Your Audience

Read the assignment again. Think about who will read your paragraph. If you had a conversation with your audience about this topic, they could ask you questions. They could pull information out of you and ask for clarification. What questions would your audience ask? What do you know that they do not know?

Your paragraph will have to stand on its own. It will have to speak for itself. As you think about your topic and your audience, consider these questions:

- Why is my topic important?
- What do I want my reader to understand?
- Which examples will most effectively illustrate my point?
- Which examples will need some explanation?

EXERCISE 5-10 **Considering Your Audience**

PEER CONVERSATION

Directions: *Use the questions above to think critically about the point, examples, and details you want to include in your paragraph. Talk with a classmate to explore what you know and want to say. Test your examples and details on this classmate. Take notes on this conversation and add them to your prewriting.*

Topic Sentence

Writers often write and rewrite topic sentences as they work on their writing. At this point in the writing process, think of your topic sentence as a work in progress. A clear topic sentence will state your point, echo the assignment, and help organize the details from your prewriting.

Unity and Coherence

Paragraphs with examples have a cumulative effect. The evidence adds up. When you draft your paragraph, think about the case you are building for your viewpoint. Examine your examples and details, and be alert to those details that might lead readers astray, taking them off the subject.

You want your paragraph to be unified—clearly focused on one idea. Remember, too, that your readers want to feel that you are in control of the discussion, that you are leading the way. The best way to create this impression is by using appropriate transition terms. These terms make connections, which create coherent text. In example writing, transitions related to examples and priority or importance are useful in helping your reader follow your thinking.

TRANSITIONS BASED ON EXAMPLE	
for example	in this case
a second (and third) example	to illustrate
for instance	

TRANSITIONS BASED ON PRIORITY OR IMPORTANCE	
however	in particular
more important	specifically
equally important	of course
better	certainly
worse	in fact

Concluding Sentence

Plan your concluding sentence. A concluding sentence summarizes the point of the paragraph. Sometimes it does this by referring back to the most important example and at other times by restating the main idea expressed in the topic sentence.

EXERCISE 5-11 **Planning Your First Draft**

Directions: *On a separate sheet of paper, write a topic sentence that echoes the key words from the assignment topic you selected. Then organize and outline your details.*

See "Supporting Details" in Chapter 3 for detailed explanation of outlining.

Write a First Draft

Think of your outline as a roadmap. If you follow it, you will reach your destination, which is a rough draft of your paragraph. As you work toward this goal, however, pay attention to what your writing is telling you. If you have difficulty developing and explaining an example, that might be a reason to cut it from your draft. If you find that you have a great detail to add about another example, that might be an indication that your paragraph could be developed with an extended example, rather than multiple examples.

As they draft, writers often go back and revise their outlines. If you decide to do that, it is probably the right thing to do. There is more than one way to get to your destination.

MULTILINGUAL TIP

Bring your draft to the writing center on your campus.

EXERCISE 5-12 **Writing Your First Draft**

Directions: *Write a draft of your paragraph. Use the following checklist as a guide.*

FIRST DARFT CHECKLIST

______ My topic sentence states the point of my paragraph.
______ My topic sentence echoes key terms in the assignment.
______ I inserted transitions to make connections between my examples visible.
______ I included relevant supporting details to explain the examples.
______ My concluding sentence summarizes the point and emphasizes the significance of my topic.

A PROFESSIONAL'S TAKE

Here is Yann Martel's use of examples, from his book *Life of Pi:*

In the literature can be found legions of examples of animals that could escape but did not, or did and returned. There is the case of the chimpanzee whose cage door was left unlocked and had swung open. Increasingly anxious, the chimp began to shriek and to slam the door shut repeatedly—with a deafening clang each time—until the keeper, notified by a visitor, hurried over to remedy the situation. A herd of roe-deer in a European zoo stepped out of their corral when the gate was left open. Frightened by visitors, the deer bolted for the nearby forest, which had its own herd of wild roe-deer and could support more. Nonetheless, the zoo roe-deer quickly returned to their corral. In another zoo a worker was walking to his work site at an early hour, carrying planks of wood, when, to his horror, a bear emerged from the morning mist, heading straight for him at a confident pace. The man dropped the planks and ran for his life. The zoo staff immediately started searching for the escaped bear. They found it back in its enclosure, having climbed down into its pit the way it had climbed out, by way of a tree that had fallen over. It was thought that the noise of the planks of wood falling to the ground had frightened it.

EXERCISE 5-13 A PROFESSIONAL'S TAKE

Directions: *Using the first draft checklist as your guide, identify the elements of an effective example paragraph in the professional model.*

Revise: Read Critically, Then Rewrite

Sometimes an example is not as effective as you hoped it would be. Sometimes you forget to explain a critical detail. It helps if you have someone read and talk with you about your writing. It helps if you read your peers' papers so you can compare your work to theirs. Do their paragraphs make a point? Is their point expressed in a topic sentence? Do their examples connect to support their point? Can you identify transition terms that help the reader make connections? Revision gives you a chance to get things right.

REVISE
- Read critically
- Develop a revision plan

Revision in Action

Revision is rethinking a draft and making decisions to improve the quality of your writing. You read critically, plan your revision, and revise the writing. Here is an example of revision by a student named Theresa.

The full version of Theresa's sample is available online.

Assignment: Write about a person who was important in your life. Provide examples that illustrate why that person was important.

Theresa's First Draft

My mother taught me the importance of family fun. Family is the focus of my mother's life. She is always happy and works hard to keep the whole family together. And not just on holidays and birthdays. We make time for family fun during the week. (1) **For example,** one of her favorite family events is movie night. She likes to do family movie nights. Instead of going out, we rent a movie and pop popcorn. **Even though** we are a lot older and a lot bigger, we all climb onto the sofa and eat out of the same huge bowl filled with buttered popcorn. She likes to rent a comedy so we all laugh together. **These days,** movie night is a double-feature. We rotate who gets to pick the second movie. Another family fun event is game night. She likes to play games. (2) **After dinner,** we do the dishes and pull out the games. She especially likes to play cards. Rummy is our favorite game. **We laugh** a lot more than we win because everyone cheats. **We love** the competition, and **we argue** over who is cheating because we all cheat. It is like a war between us. I think cheating and getting away with cheating are more important than winning the game. So I have gotten really good at looking innocent. Sometimes we play until two o'clock in the morning. Family fun nights taught me how important a family is and how special my mother is as well.

TOPIC SENTENCE
Theresa chooses key words from the assignment: "person" and "important" to write a 1 + 1 topic sentence.

SUPPORTING DETAILS
She explains why family fun is important and provides two examples. Each example has minor details that describe the activity and why it is fun.

ORDER AND TRANSITIONS
Theresa uses a variety of transitions. She uses example ("for example"), comparison ("even though"), and time ("these days," "after dinner") word or phrase transitions. She also uses repetition ("we laugh," "we love," "we argue").

CONCLUDING SENTENCE
Theresa adds a comment that restates the topic sentence.

Revision Plan: Revise the topic sentence to clearly state the purpose of the paragraph. Create transitions to connect the major details—two types of family fun. Cut minor details to focus the paragraph on the two examples and the new point in the topic sentence.

TOPIC SENTENCE
Theresa emphasizes family values, then adds how she learned that.

SUPPORTING DETAILS
Theresa cuts details that are less important to focus each example. She relates each example to the main idea of the paragraph: the two events emphasize the importance of family to her mother.

ORDER AND TRANSITIONS
Theresa names the two examples of family events—movie night and game night. She uses transitions to list details.

CONCLUDING SENTENCE
Theresa restates the topic sentence and adds the comment that her mother is special.

Theresa's Revised Draft

Family values are important, and my mother has taught me this with weekly family events. **Movie night is one of her favorite family events.** Instead of going out, we rent a movie and pop popcorn. Even though we are a lot older and a lot bigger, we all climb onto the sofa and eat out of the same huge bowl filled with buttered popcorn. She always rents a comedy so we all laugh together. Crowding together to laugh and relax has made our family close. **Game night is another family fun event.** After dinner, we do the dishes together and pull out the games. She especially likes to play cards. Rummy is our favorite game. We laugh a lot more than we win because everyone cheats. She loves the competition, so we argue over who is cheating. Sometimes we play until after midnight, but it is not hard to get up the next day because family fun helps us all relax. Family fun nights have taught me the importance of family, and how special my mother is as well.

PEER CONVERSATION

DISCUSSION QUESTIONS Which changes in the revision most improve Theresa's paragraph? Why?

Read Critically

Half the task of revising well is reading well. Critical reading is a search for the characteristics of effective writing: topic sentence, supporting examples and details, transitions, and concluding sentence. Critical reading involves making careful comparisons between your writing and that of your peers. Pay attention to how other writers do what you are trying to do.

PEER CONVERSATION

EXERCISE 5-14 Reading Peer Papers

Directions: *Exchange papers with another student. Be a critical reader and make suggestions to improve and clarify your classmate's first draft. Also identify what your classmate does well. Make notes in the margin as you read to remember your suggestions. After you read, you will discuss your suggestions. Use the following guidelines.*

REVISION CHECKLIST

_____ Does the topic sentence connect to the assignment and state the point of the paragraph?

_____ Does the writer stay on the subject through the paragraph?

_____ Does the writer cite examples and then elaborate sufficiently on the examples?

_____ Does the paragraph have effective transitions that establish connections between examples and details?

_____ Does the concluding sentence emphasize the point of the paragraph?

Revise with a Plan

Effective example paragraphs are focused and specific. As you review the comments from your classmate, consider whether your paragraph is adequately focused. Look for the point you are making in your topic sentence. Is it clear? Look at your examples. Do they prove your point? Do you include enough details to adequately explain your examples?

EXERCISE 5-15 **Revising Your Draft**

Directions: *Write a revision plan and use it to revise the first draft of the paragraph you wrote for Exercise 5-12.*

Edit

The ideas in your work matter, but if your content is expressed in language that contains careless errors, readers may focus on the errors and miss your point. Invest time in getting your work as close to perfect as possible. In any class, not just for an English course, your instructors want to see that you care about your work. Focus your editing using this personalized checklist.

EDIT
- Search and correct
- Self-edit

YOUR EDITING CHECKLIST

_____ Spelling: List any words you misspelled in your last paper:

____

_____ Punctuation: List two punctuation errors from your last paper:

____

_____ Capitalization: List any capitalization errors from your last paper:

____

_____ Other errors: List any errors your instructor has pointed out in graded work:

____

____

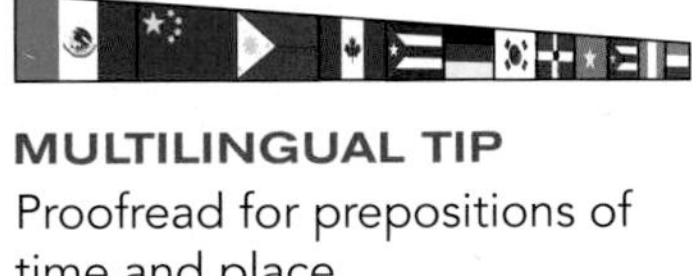

MULTILINGUAL TIP

Proofread for prepositions of time and place.

To Prepare Your Draft for an Academic Audience

_____ Minimize first-person pronouns: *I, me, my.*

_____ Minimize second-person pronouns: *you, your.*

_____ Use third-person pronouns: *he, she, it, they.*

EXERCISE 5-16 **Revising and Editing Practice**

Directions: *Read the following paragraph that was written in response to the assignment below; it contains errors that require revising and editing. Then answer the questions that follow.*

Assignment: Television shows compete for viewers. What makes a hit show? Write an example paragraph to discuss a single show or several shows you love or hate.

(1) Reality television provides totally unimaginative, brain-numbing entertainment. (2) *Survivor* was the first big hit with a simple concept. (3) Sixteen strangers flew to a remote island, formed tribes, ate bugs, faced challenges like making fire and voted each other off the island. (4) It seemed like a totally ridiculous show. (5) Unfortunately, it clicked with viewers and remained popular. (6) ____________________, television producers imagined new scenarios in which people win, lose, cry, and look foolish. (7) Love became the next hot competition in *the Bachelor.* (8) Women flocked to their televisions to watch competitors engage in a fairy tale romance. (9) ____________________, they created twists to the love story. (10) In *Joe Millionaire,* young women competed to marry a dashing young millionaire who was really a blue-collar worker. (11) Eventually, producers invent more terrible reality television to make millions of viewers sit on the edge of their couches. *The Amazing Race, American Idol,* and *Top Chef* all drew big ratings. (12) It seems that we are getting more and more terrible reality programming. (13) Critics recently predicted the end of reality television. (14) ____________________.

capitalization error

Revising

_b_ 1. Which transition word or phrase should be inserted in blank 6?

a. To my surprise

b. As a result

c. In addition

d. Furthermore

_a_ 2. Which word or phrase should be inserted in blank 9? The word or phrase would serve as the best transition between the writer's ideas in this paragraph. If no transition is needed, choose "no transition is necessary."

a. Next

b. Soon

c. Eventually

d. no transition is necessary

_b_ 3. Which sentence should be cut to improve the focus and reduce repetition in the paragraph? If no sentence needs to be cut, choose "no change is necessary."

a. sentence 11

b. sentence 12

c. sentence 13

d. no change is necessary

Talk about It

Is repetition a good or bad thing? Why?

_c_ 4. Which sentence should be inserted in blank 14? The sentence would serve as the concluding sentence. If no conclusion sentence is necessary, choose "no conclusion is necessary."

a. However, I counted five new reality shows this fall.

b. In conclusion, *Dancing with the Stars* is one more horrible example to prove my point.

c. Obviously, reality television is not dead because brain-numbing shows draw viewers and make money.

d. no conclusion is necessary

Editing

_b_ 1. Choose the option that corrects the error in sentence 3. If no error exists, choose "no change is necessary."

a. faced challenges, like making fire, and voted

b. faced challenges like making fire, and voted

c. faced challenges, like making fire; and voted

d. no change is necessary

_c_ 2. Choose the option that corrects the pronoun reference error in sentence 9. If no error exists, choose "no change is necessary."

a. women

b. viewers

c. producers

d. no change is necessary

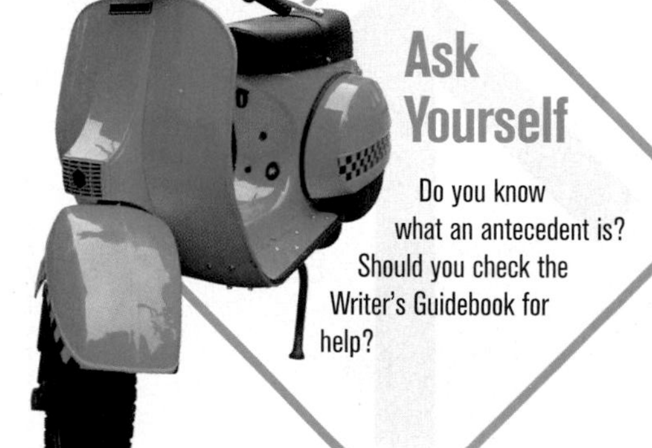
Ask
Yourself
Do you know
what an antecedent is?
Should you check the
Writer's Guidebook for
help?

_b_ 3. Choose the option that corrects the error in sentence 11. If no error exists, choose "no change is necessary."

a. producers are inventing more terrible reality television

b. producers invented more terrible reality television

c. producers had invented more terrible reality television

d. no change is necessary

4. Proofread the paragraph for a capitalization error and correct the error.

EXERCISE 5-17 Searching and Correcting

PEER CONVERSATION

Directions: *Exchange papers with a classmate and proofread each other's work. In addition to spelling, punctuation, and capitalization, find out what other errors your classmate has on his or her class checklist; tell your classmate what errors you have on your checklist.*

EXERCISE 5-18 Self-Editing

Directions: *Carefully rewrite your paper, correcting errors you and your classmate found. Give yourself time to set aside the finished paper. Then come back to it and read your final draft one last time, using your checklist as a guide.*

Reflect

Take a moment and reflect on what you have learned.

REFLECT
- Identify strengths
- Set goals

EXERCISE 5-19 Identifying Strengths and Setting Goals

Directions: *Review your writing and your writing process. On a separate sheet of paper, write answers to these questions:*

- *What did you do well in the paragraph you wrote?*
- *What did you enjoy working on in this chapter?*
- *What have you learned that you will apply in future writing assignments?*

GOING PLACES

REVEALING THE WORLD THROUGH NARRATION

Once Upon a Time . . .

Is there any phrase in the English language more arresting than "once upon a time"? We have all heard it a thousand times, but it still evokes a simple-hearted enthusiasm, an anticipation of what is to come. It seems that in almost any context and at any age, we enjoy hearing stories. Mastering the skills of narration will benefit you in many different contexts. Wherever you are and whatever you are doing, it is always nice (and useful!) to be able to tell a good story.

DISCUSSION

Turn and talk with a classmate to answer the following questions: What recent movie have you seen that is particularly memorable? Can you describe a specific scene or event in the movie and explain why it is memorable?

The Story of the Essay

There are many ways to structure an essay, but perhaps the most interesting, at least from a reader's point of view, is narration. Try to think of your essay as a story: Who (or what) are the main "characters"? What kinds of things does your reader need to know about them in order for them to seem convincing? What happens to them? What kind of conclusion is the essay building toward? The next time you sit down to write about a physics lab, think about the ways in which you can transform your writing into more than just a recitation of facts; try to make those facts into a coherent narration.

BRAINSTORM

For which college courses or college assignments might you be expected to write a narration? Brainstorm a list of courses or assignments for which you would write a narration to make a point or to engage a reader.

The Story of Your Life

Like everyone else, people in the business world are interested in stories. Keep this in mind as you put together your resume—try to think of it as a story of your working life. Following proper formatting guidelines, shape your resume so that it presents a snapshot of your career and of you as a person. Similarly, in a job interview, do not restrict yourself to short yes and no answers; rather, treat the interview as an opportunity to reveal something about yourself. Remember, your interviewer is looking for someone that he or she wants to see five days a week. Do not be afraid to present yourself as interesting and captivating as you really are.

RESUME BUILDER

Prior experience is a powerful tool for convincing a future boss to hire you. Think of a job you would like. What experience have you had that might convince an interviewer that you are perfect for the job? Write the story of this experience on a separate sheet of paper.

Narration

CHAPTER 6

CHAPTER OVERVIEW

- THE NARRATION PARAGRAPH AT A GLANCE
- NARRATION THINKING
  - Elements of Narration
  - Narration and Specific Detail
  - Make Connections
- NARRATION IN PROCESS
  - Prewrite
  - Draft
  - A Professional's Take
  - Revise
  - Edit
  - Reflect

THINK FIRST

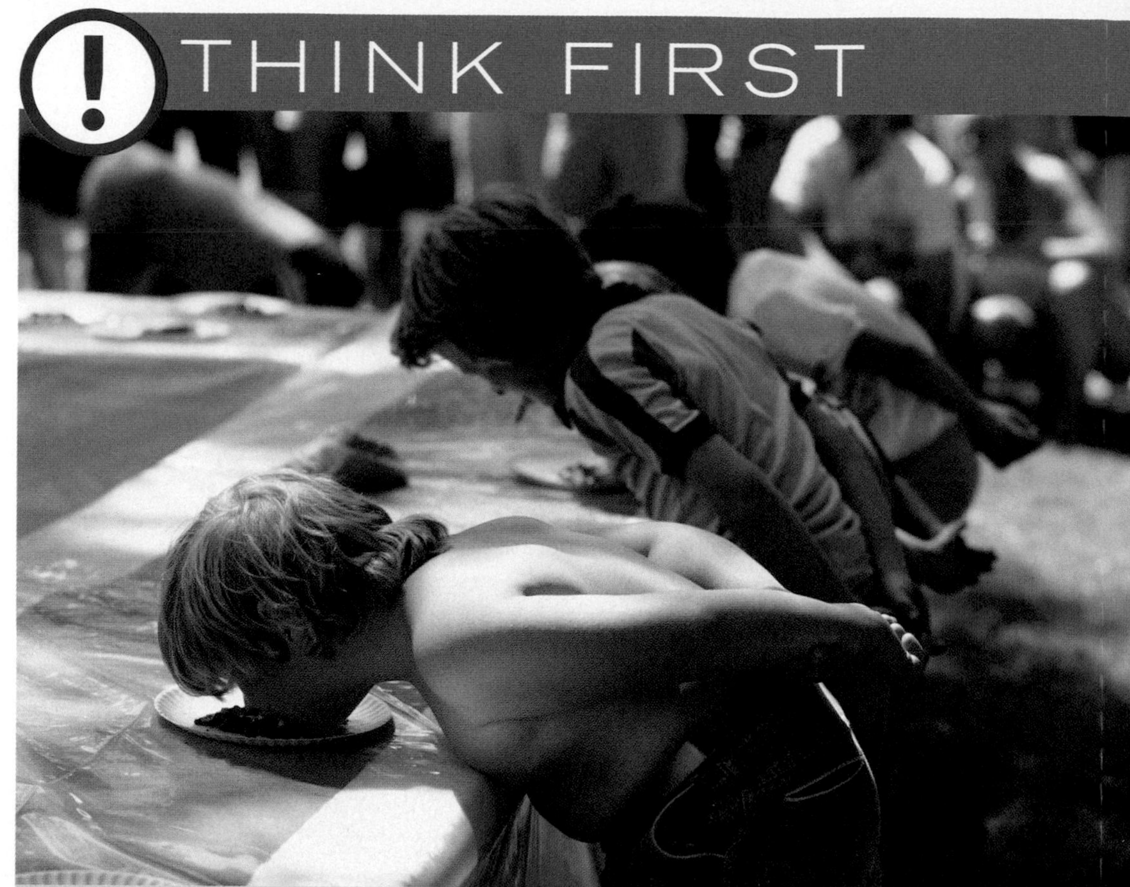

Think of an event that involved winning or losing. Write a paragraph describing the event so a reader can picture the scene and understand who was involved, the crucial actions that took place, the outcome of the event, and your point.

At a Glance

THE NARRATION PARAGRAPH AT A GLANCE

A narration paragraph has three basic parts: a topic sentence, supporting details, and a concluding sentence or sentences. The topic sentence in a narration paragraph can be the first or last sentence of the paragraph. The supporting details provide specific information about the scene, the actors, the action, and the outcome. These details are most often organized in chronological order. The conclusion may be several sentences long. Its purpose is to convey the impact of the event as well as to illustrate the claim the writer is making.

The Narration Paragraph at a Glance

ASSIGNMENT Life experiences teach us lessons. Tell a story that relates to something you believe to be true. Consider experiences that taught you a lesson or changed your view of something in some way.

Fear is often the best teacher, and it taught me a lesson about foolishness. (1) **One hot day** in July, Mike and I were bored. So we started the challenge-wars. Soon it was obvious that he could spit farther and run faster than I could. Then he challenged me to climb the corkscrew tree in my backyard. The tree was huge. It seemed to shade the entire block. It had all the right branches in all the right spots, so it was great for climbing. (2) **Immediately,** I leaped into the tree. I knew this tree and was sure I could climb to the top and finally beat Mike at something. (3) **Before long,** I was halfway up the tree, and I was winning. The branches were getting smaller. That is when I stopped and thought, "This is stupid." But I did not listen to my fears. I climbed higher. (4) **When I got to the top,** the wind was strong, and the branches swayed back and forth. I froze and was afraid to climb down. (5) **Soon,** Mike got frightened and climbed down. He knew I was in trouble and tried to talk me down, but I was too afraid. **So** he called the fire department. I clung to the branches as I swayed in the wind. I thought about how stupid I was to climb so high. (6) **Finally,** the fire truck arrived, and they raised the ladder and helped me down. The whole neighborhood gathered to watch the rescue. (7) **Worse,** one neighbor called my

TOPIC SENTENCE
The writer uses key words from the assignment.

SUPPORTING DETAILS
1. The writer describes the scene and the actors. The relationship between Mike and the writer helps a reader make sense of the actions that follow.
2–5. The writer describes actions and thoughts related to the competition.
6–7. The writer describes the outcome of the competition.

ORDER AND TRANSITIONS
The writer uses time order to tell the story of an important lesson. The last transitions emphasize the final event.

CONCLUDING SENTENCES
The writer states two lessons and makes two points: one about foolishness and the other about fear.

mother, who blew her top when she arrived home and found me sitting on the porch with a firefighter. That day I learned that I will do foolish things to win. More importantly, I also learned that fear is a good thing, and I should listen to it.

PEER CONVERSATION

DISCUSSION QUESTIONS

1. Identify the supporting detail that best illustrates the point of the topic sentence.
2. How many sentences does the writer use to describe this detail?
3. Why is it effective?

Thinking

NARRATION THINKING

In conversation, it is natural for all of us to tell stories. In writing, however, effective narrations are carefully constructed, using these basic elements: scene, actors, actions, and outcome. A writer combines these elements to make a point. You tell a story for a reason.

Elements of Narration

Effective narration takes the reader to the scene of an event, introduces the actors or important people, shows these people in action, and reveals the outcome.

- ***Scene:*** Details about scene tell where and when an event took place—for example, in the corkscrew tree in the writer's backyard.
- ***Actors:*** Details about the actors in a narration tell who is important and who had an impact on the event's outcome. The writer climbed the tree because of Mike.
- ***Actions:*** Details about action are the heart of effective narration. A writer decides which actions are crucial to the point of the narration. Once the writer reached the top of the tree, he could not climb down.
- ***Outcome:*** Details about outcome provide an ending, but they also emphasize the point. The reader wants to know what happened. In college writing, the reader wants to know why the story is important. The writer learned a valuable lesson the day he was stuck at the top of a tree.

Get Started

An effective narration paragraph contains a clear point stated in the topic sentence, narration elements to illustrate the story, and a clear conclusion to state the impact of the event. In the clustering diagram, you can see how a student pieced together a narration response to a specific assignment in a science class.

Assignment: Describe a breakthrough in your learning about physics this semester.

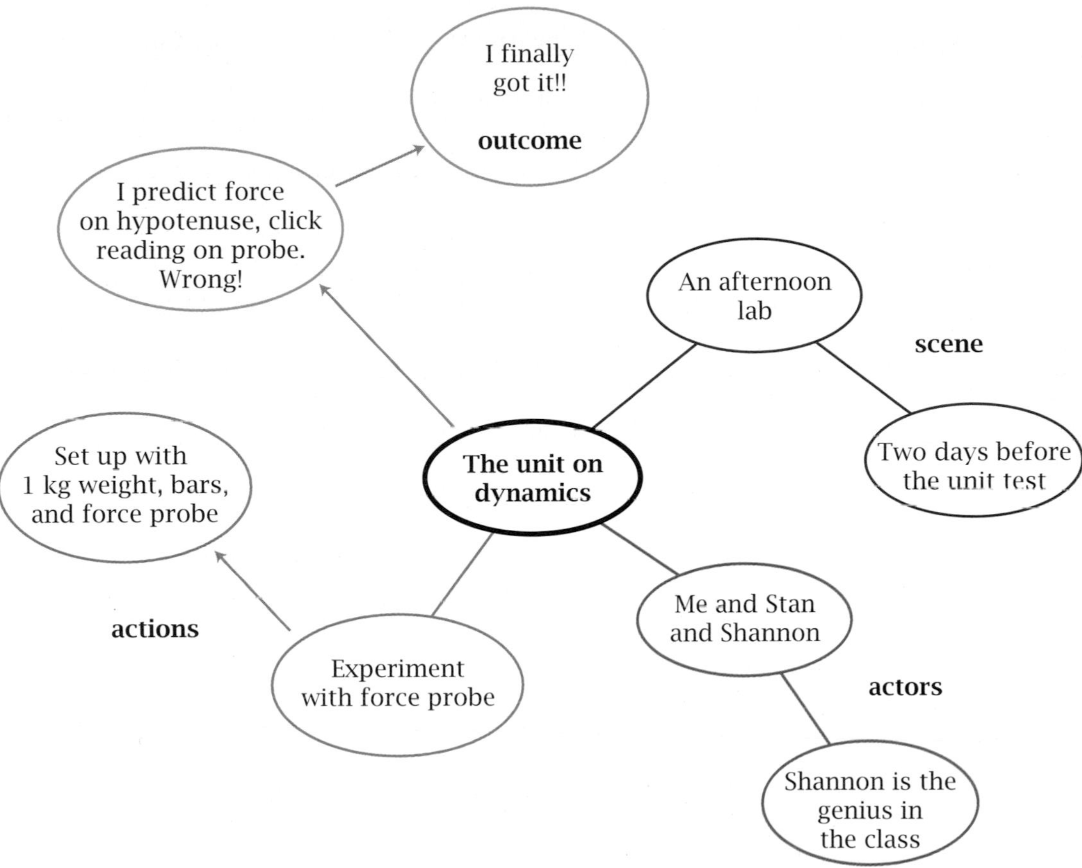

When you pay attention to all the elements of narration, the story will make its point more effectively. In this clustering exercise, the student covers all the details, scene, actors, actions, and outcome. He notes that Shannon is the genius in the class. He indicates the specific experiment the students ran and when it happened in relation to the unit exam. These narration details provide the skeleton for the story the student will tell in the final version of the paragraph. At this point, it is possible for him to formulate a topic sentence that incorporates key terms from the assignment and points at the important content of the paragraph.

Topic Sentence: My breakthrough in physics learning came during a study session a few days before the unit test on dynamics.

EXERCISE 6-1 Elements of Narration

Directions: *Pick two of the topics listed below and use the four elements of effective narration to plan a story you could tell that would support each one. To find details for each element, cluster on a separate sheet of paper. Then fill in your answers in the space provided.* Answers will vary.

EXAMPLE

Topic: Sometimes just a little extra effort can make all the difference in the world.

Scene: Breckenridge, Colorado. The construction site, "The Gold Camp," where I worked as a laborer for Fisher Plumbing

Actors: Kenny, the owner; Bill, the foreman; the other laborers on the job.

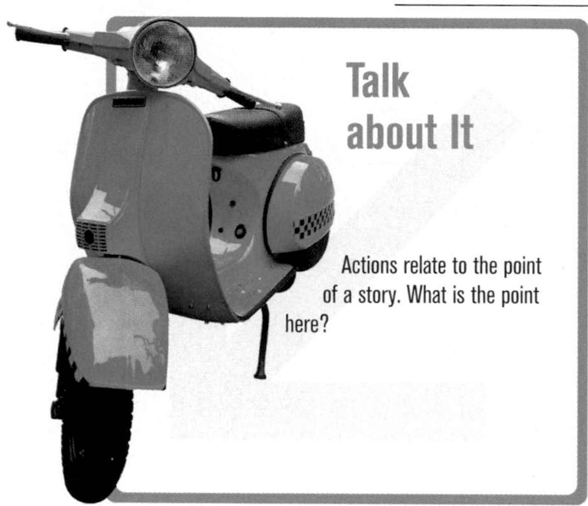

Talk about It

Actions relate to the point of a story. What is the point here?

Actions: (1) I am ordered to do a difficult job. (2) I spend a long afternoon digging underneath a footing full of rocks. (3) Kenny tells Bill to get the backhoe.

Outcome: I impressed the owner by not giving up on a really hard job. As a result, he liked my attitude and gave me a chance to do some better jobs.

1. **Topic:** Making mistakes is an essential part of learning.

Scene: ______________________________

____

Actors: ______________________________

____

Actions: ______________________________

____

____

Outcome: ______________________________

____

2. **Topic:** Money spent quickly is not always spent wisely.

Scene: ____

____

Actors: ____

____

Actions: ____

____

____

Outcome: ____

____

3. **Topic:** In times of crisis, people show their true colors.

Scene: ____

____

Actors: ____

____

Actions: ____

____

____

Outcome: ____

____

Narration and Specific Detail

The elements of narration are scene, actors, actions, and outcome. The real content, however, is in the details you provide. For each of these elements, you want to think about what your reader needs to know for your narration to make sense. It might not be necessary to elaborate on all the elements of your narration. Your critical thinking task here is to focus on only those elements that are important and provide essential support for your point.

Scene Actors Actions Outcome	In your narration, which of these elements is most important? Which requires elaboration and explanation?

When the student responding to his assignment in physics examined the elements of his narration, he decided to provide additional details about the actors and actions involved.

Elements	Details	Elaboration
Scene	afternoon lab two days before the test	
Actors	Shannon and Stan	Shannon is the brain. Taking the course for refresher. A future teacher. Makes me do all the work. Asks me to explain my thinking as I do it.
Actions	We set up the exp. 1 kg weight, bars, force probe	I don't understand why the force on the long bar (hypotenuse) is not the same as the short one. We set it up. I predict. Click the force probe. Wrong! We draw a couple triangles and do the addition. I finally get it.
Outcome	I get it.	What I now understand is the experiment is a practical instance of the vector addition problems we have been doing in the book.

Part of your thinking task here is to elaborate only on those details relevant to the point you wish to make and essential to your reader's understanding. Doing so will ultimately improve the unity of the paragraph you write.

EXERCISE 6-2 Narration Detail

Directions: *Choose one of the topics from Exercise 6-1 and elaborate on the key details you provided for the elements of narration. Choose only those details most relevant to the point you want your narration to make.* Answers will vary.

Scene: ____

Key Detail: ____

Elaboration: ____

____

____

Actors: ____

Key Detail: ____

Elaboration: ____

____

____

Actions: ____

Key Detail: ____

Elaboration: ____

____

____

Outcome: ____

Key Detail: ____

Elaboration: ____

____

____

Ask Yourself

Elaboration helps a reader see action more clearly. Do you elaborate?

Make Connections

Good narration helps the reader see the connections between details. Transition words and phrases make these connections explicit. In the narration paragraph at the beginning of this chapter, on page 113, for example, the writer uses these transition words and phrases: *one hot day, immediately, before long, when I got to the top, soon, so, finally, worse,* and *that day.* These transitions help the writer use chronological order to organize his details. They make the story coherent.

EXERCISE 6-3 Making Connections

Directions: *Read the paragraph below and underline the transition words and phrases the writer uses. In the margin, note the elements of narration as they appear in the paragraph: scene, actors, actions, and outcome.*

> The Fourth of July is family day. My family gathers at Uncle Mark's cottage on the lake. My father cooks four or five slabs of ribs. Aunt Jill brings her famous potato salad and dump cake, and everyone contributes food or entertainment. This year Uncle Mark added an unusual contribution

scene: time and place
actors
actors

action

action

actor

action

action

action

to the picnic, his new fiancée whom he met on the Internet. Uncle Mark has trouble finding girlfriends, so we were all eager to meet her. We were disappointed when he showed up by himself. He said she would be along a little later. About an hour later, Mark, my dad, my brother-in-law Stan, and I were playing horseshoes and teasing Uncle Mark about his computer fiancée. Just then a blue Ford Focus drove up and parked. It was the girlfriend. My dad said, "What is that on the side of her car?" We all stared, then blinked to be sure we were seeing correctly. Hanging from the side of her car was the handle and hose of a gas pump. She had driven off with the whole thing and did not even know. It was the funniest thing I ever saw. We just could not stop laughing. Later, even Uncle Mark continually broke into laughter as he introduced Kim to the family. She was very embarrassed, but we made her feel like part of the family and shared our own ridiculous stories. Eventually, she did not feel like a total fool. However, we did take pictures of her car. From now on, every Fourth of July we will tell that story. That is what happens in a big family. If you do something funny, everyone hears about it, and no one forgets. After all, laughter is the glue that holds a big family together.

DISCUSSION QUESTIONS

PEER CONVERSATION

1. Where is the topic sentence in this paragraph?
2. What details in the story best demonstrate the point of the paragraph?
   Answers will vary.

Process

NARRATION IN PROCESS

Whatever the assignment in college, in order to write effective narration, it helps to remember the steps in the writing process. In this section you will use a process approach to write a single paragraph that tells a story and supports a claim.

Select an Assignment

In college you will be asked to write assignments on a variety of topics. For some of them, narration will be a useful way to explore the topic. Before you tell a story, however, be sure the point of the story relates to the assignment.

EXERCISE 6-4 Selecting an Assignment for a Narration Paragraph

Directions: *Review the assignments listed below. Choose the one you know the most about and think is best suited to an effective narration paragraph.*

1. Getting help in school at just the right time can be critical. Recall a time when you or someone you know sought help and it made an important difference.
2. Consider the value of punishment or the damage it can do. Tell a story about a time you were punished properly or improperly.
3. Good employees make an important difference in the workplace. Tell a story about a good (or bad) employee, explaining what this person did (or did not do) at work.
4. Being surprised can be both pleasant and unpleasant, depending on the people and circumstances involved. Recall a pleasant or unpleasant surprise and explain its positive or negative impact.
5. Being disappointed or frightened can teach you a valuable lesson. Write about a lesson you or someone you know learned from such an experience.
6. Write a story about playing a sport.
7. Tell a story about how you learned to manage money.
8. Recall a time when you changed your mind about something or someone and write about that experience.
9. Relate a story about a trip you took.
10. Choose your own topic.

Writer's Response
Good writing can come from trouble. Write about trouble you have seen.

Prewrite: Write Before You Write

When you tell a story, it is easy to overlook important details. Your reader will want to know about everything: where and when the story took place, who was involved, what happened, and what the outcome was. Before you start writing, do some prewriting to make sure you touch on all the important elements of narration. Prewriting will help you discover what you have to say about your topic. Remember that you have a variety of prewriting techniques to choose from: talking, clustering, brainstorming, and freewriting. Try clustering and talking for this mode.

PREWRITE
- Talk
- Cluster
- Brainstorm
- Freewrite

Cluster

Clustering enables you to think systematically about the story you want to tell. It helps you keep track of various parts of your narration, such as details about place and time, people, actions, and outcome. It also lets you see the connections between details and get ideas about how to focus your topic.

EXERCISE 6-5 **Clustering**

Directions: *Cluster on your assignment for ten minutes. Be sure to include details relating to the elements of the narration: actors, scene (place and time), actions, and outcome. List as many narration details as you can.*

Talk

Talking enables you to discover additional details for the story you tell. When you combine talking with clustering, you take your thinking deeper. As you tell your story to a classmate, you may remember more details. Capture your new thinking on paper after you finish talking.

EXERCISE 6-6 **Talking about the Assignment**

PEER CONVERSATION

Directions: *Turn to your neighbor in class or find another interested listener. Tell this person the story you focused on in your clustering. Be specific about important information. Include details about scene, actors, actions, and outcome. Then be a critical listener to your neighbor's story. Listen without interrupting. When the speaker finishes, ask questions or offer suggestions. Identify what was clear and what was not clear.*

Draft: Focus and Organize

Prewriting helps you get ideas and details down on paper. You may have more to say now than you did before. You may also have a better idea about the point your narration paragraph will make.

DRAFT
- Consider your audience
- Formulate your topic sentence
- Outline for unity and coherence
- Write a conclusion sentence
- Compose your first draft

Consider Your Audience

Now that you have selected your topic, consider who will read your paragraph. Chances are your reader was not at work with you when your coworker came in late or at your house when you got punished for doing something wrong. Your reader does not know any of the specifics about the story you are going to tell. When you tell your story, you might have to provide some information that is obvious to you but essential for your reader to know in order to understand the point of the story. Use the following questions to consider how to convey your point to an audience:

- What special meaning does this topic have for me?
- What do I want my audience to understand about this story?
- What details relating to time, place, people, and actions are important to help my audience understand my meaning?

EXERCISE 6-7 **Considering Your Audience**

PEER CONVERSATION

Directions: *Use the questions above to think critically about the specific details to include in your paragraph and how you will use them to convey your point to an audience. Talk with a classmate to clarify your purpose and the details that will convey your point. Take notes on this conversation and add it to your prewriting.*

Topic Sentence

In a first draft, writers often write and rewrite topic sentences. At this point in the writing process, think of your topic sentence as a work in progress. A clear topic sentence will state your point, echo the assignment, and help organize the details from your prewriting. In a narration paragraph, the topic sentence might not be the first sentence of the paragraph. As you write, decide on the best place for your topic sentence.

Unity and Coherence

Your narration will be focused on a specific point you wish to make. As you work, watch for details that go off the subject. For your paragraph to be unified, all the details should relate to the main idea of the paragraph.

Narration is typically organized by chronological order. The story is told in sequence from the first action to the last action or outcome. A writer who uses transition terms indicating chronological order helps the reader follow the story.

TRANSITIONS BASED ON CHRONOLOGICAL ORDER	
first	then
second	soon
third	moreover
to begin with	to conclude
next	eventually
in addition	finally

Narration paragraphs can also be organized by priority or importance. To do this, the writer would emphasize key actions using transition terms that show impact and create emphasis.

TRANSITIONS BASED ON PRIORITY OR IMPORTANCE	
also	likewise
another	plus
as a result	worse than that
at the same time	better yet
consequently	thus
equally important	most importantly

EXERCISE 6-8 Transitions and Chronological Order

Directions: *This narration is written in chronological order. Write in an appropriate transition term to introduce each action. Use both types of transition terms, choosing from the boxes on page 123.* Answers will vary.

Sometimes nosy neighbors can be a good thing. One rainy night in October, my mom and I could not sleep. We watched a movie and folded laundry until after midnight. (1) After Mom shoved a last load in the dryer, we tried to wait for it to finish, but we were too exhausted. I went to bed, and Mom fell asleep on the couch. (2) Then I heard someone beating on the front door. It sounded like they were trying to break in. (3) At first, I thought I was dreaming, but when I opened my eyes, the pounding was still there. I sat straight up in bed and looked at the clock. It was 1:13 a.m., and I had only been asleep a little while. (4) At the same time, I heard Mom open the door. Our neighbors were shouting that the house was on fire. I raced down the stairs and out onto the lawn. (5) For ten minutes we watched the house, but there were no flames. (6) Finally, we realized the smoke was from the dryer vent. Our neighbors were frightened over nothing. At first, my mother and I were irritated, but later we were grateful for our nosy neighbors who want to keep us safe.

DISCUSSION QUESTIONS

PEER CONVERSATION

1. Which actions did you emphasize by using transitions based on impact?
2. Why did you choose these actions? Answers will vary.

Concluding Sentence

Plan your concluding sentence. Try to avoid ending your narration paragraph with the last thing that happened. Go one step farther and state the meaning or point of the narration.

See "Supporting Details" in Chapter 3 for detailed explanation of outlining.

EXERCISE 6-9 Planning Your First Draft

Directions: *On a separate sheet of paper, write a topic sentence that echoes the key words from the assignment topic you selected. Then organize and outline your details.*

Write a First Draft

Now that you have chosen your topic, decided on the point you want to make, and selected the details you will use to support your claim, you are ready to write a first draft of your paragraph. As you write, you may think of details that were not in your clustering. Remember that most writers say too little in their first draft. It is better to write too much than too little: you can always cut back later. Make sure your paragraph has a lot of sensory detail.

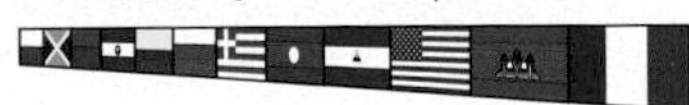

MULTILINGUAL TIP
Bring your draft to the writing center on your campus.

EXERCISE 6-10 **Writing Your First Draft**

Directions: *Write a draft of your paragraph. Use the following checklist as a guide.*

FIRST DRAFT CHECKLIST

______ My topic sentence states the point of my paragraph.
______ My topic sentence echoes key terms in the assignment.
______ I include relevant supporting details.
______ I inserted transitions to make obvious connections between narration details.
______ My concluding sentence summarizes the point of my narration and emphasizes the significance of my topic.

A PROFESSIONAL'S TAKE

Here is G. Pascal Zachary's use of narration from a *New York Times* article, "Ping: The Risk of Innovation: Will Anyone Embrace It?"

The Prius has become one of the hottest cars in America—an amazing development, because this hybrid-electric car requires some rather large changes in how people behave. I learned the need for Prius-style adaptation early this month, when I rented a Prius from Budget Rent A Car in Seattle. Much to my embarrassment, I could not get it to go forward. Once I got going and arrived at my destination, I could not figure out how to put it in reverse. Fortunately, another Prius owner on the premises—they seem to be everywhere these days—gave me a quick lesson. You start the Prius by pressing a button on the dashboard, not once but twice. To put it in drive or reverse, you manipulate a very small stick protruding from the dashboard. The next morning, I awoke before dawn and started the Prius, but no matter how many times I pressed the button, I could not get it to move. I finally called Budget roadside assistance, and a polite man talked me back from my private technology disaster. It turns out that I had failed to tap the brake while moving the gear shifter in a certain inexplicable way. I do not think I

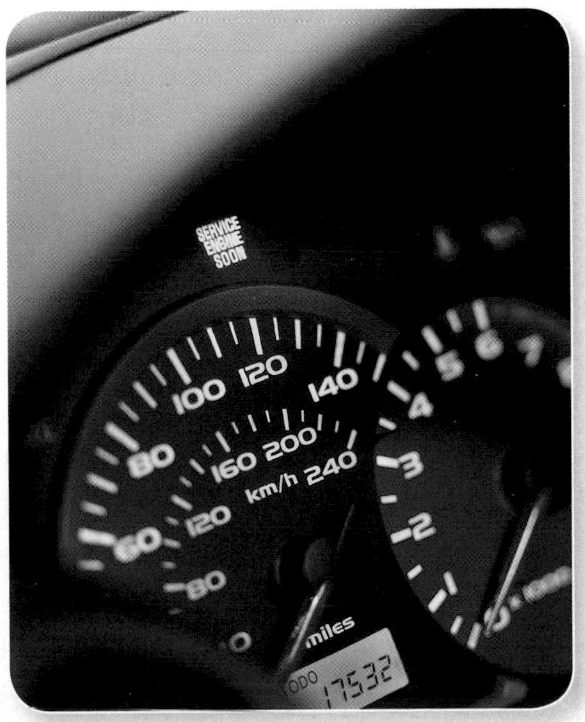

can adapt to the behaviors required by the Prius. But thousands of people are, and Toyota, its maker, is reaping the benefits.

EXERCISE 6-11 A PROFESSIONAL'S TAKE

Directions: *Using the first draft checklist as your guide, identify the elements of an effective narration paragraph in the professional model.*

Revise: Read Critically, Then Rewrite

REVISE
- Read critically
- Develop a revision plan

What if your reader does not "get it"? Narration paragraphs generally have two common problems. One problem is assuming readers understand something they do not so that you leave out a critical detail. Adding the missing detail will help readers understand the narration and your point. A second problem is that the paragraph is not sufficiently focused. Maybe you include too many people or places or try to tell too much of the story. If you identify the most important or exciting part of the narration and expand on just that brief time period, you will help readers better understand your point.

Revision in Action

The full version of Sara's sample is available online.

Revision is rethinking a draft and making decisions to improve the quality of your writing. You read critically, plan your revision, and revise the writing. Here is an example of revision by a student named Sara.

Assignment: Not everyone relaxes in exactly the same way. Tell about a time when you found that you did not agree with your friends on how to relax.

TOPIC SENTENCE
Sara connects to the assignment by stating she disagrees with friends and identifies a specific way to relax—*a good night out.*

SUPPORTING DETAILS
She tells the story of a good night for her friends and a bad night for her to illustrate the topic sentence. She uses many minor details to make her point clear.

ORDER AND TRANSITIONS
The story is told in chronological order. Her transitions indicate time and impact.

Sara's First Draft

My friends and I disagree about what makes a good night out. Just the other night, I went to Rocco's Club with some friends. It was a **Saturday night,** and the place was packed with people. There were no empty tables. I love hip-hop music, but the noise totally killed it. My friends did not seem to mind. I found an empty chair. They immediately started to dance. **To make matters worse,** all the cute guys had their girlfriends with them. The few single guys there all seemed to have attitude problems. Most of them looked like they had had too much to drink already. I joined my friends on the dance floor. I was having fun after a few songs, and the band did not seem so loud. **Even** that was short-lived. Some strange guy came over, and he started dancing with me. I enjoyed myself **at first.** It was actually fun until he put his hands on my waist and pulled me close. I love to dance, but I hate even the smallest physical contact with a stranger. I quickly walked off the floor. **Luckily** he got the point and did not follow me. **Before long** the place got more crowded and very smoky. The air was so bad it was hardly possible to breathe. My friends were having a great time, but I was not. That is when I realized that maybe nightclubs are not fun to me anymore.

CONCLUDING SENTENCE
She states the different views of the evening to emphasize the point of her topic sentence.

Revision Plan: Revise my topic sentence and purpose. Focus on the major details and actions. Cut irrelevant personal details. Cut informal language to sound sophisticated and thoughtful. Although my assignment is a personal narrative, I will start fewer sentences with "I."

Sara's Revised Draft

Fun is a personal thing: what is fun for one person is not always fun for someone else. Like my girlfriends, I love hip-hop music, so we planned a night of fun at Rocco's Club. However, **after fifteen minutes** of crowds, smoke, and head-splitting noise, they were having fun, but I was not. "Check out the men," Lisa said. **In fact,** the men were a big part of the problem. All the cute men had girlfriends hanging all over them. The few dateless men seemed to have attitude problems. **After fifteen more minutes,** a tall, athletic guy asked me to dance. It was actually fun until he put his hands on my waist and pulled me close. **After all,** he was just a sweaty stranger. **As soon as the song was over,** I quickly walked off the floor, found my girlfriends, and said, "Let's leave." They looked shocked; they were enjoying the smoke, loud music, and sweaty strangers. **Two hours of torture** went by as I watched my friends dance with one guy after another. **Finally,** they reluctantly agreed to leave. On a Saturday night, at a smoky club packed with sweaty men, I learned what fun is not.

TOPIC SENTENCE
Sara revises her topic sentence to clearly state an idea about fun—*it is a personal thing.*

SUPPORTING DETAILS
Sara focuses on thirty minutes. She focuses on the action and stops starting sentences with "I." She cuts irrelevant details about her experience and adds details to focus on the differences between her view and the view of her friends.

ORDER AND TRANSITIONS
Sara uses time and impact to focus the narrative and the point.

CONCLUDING SENTENCE
Sara restates and makes a comment on her experience.

DISCUSSION QUESTIONS Which changes in the revision most improve Sara's paragraph? Why?

PEER CONVERSATION

Read Critically

Critical reading is a search for the characteristics of effective writing: topic sentence, supporting details, transitions, and concluding sentence. Critical reading also involves careful analysis of the content. Are there sufficient details? Are some details irrelevant? Is the narration focused? These are basic questions, but they are essential to remember as you read peer papers.

PEER CONVERSATION

EXERCISE 6-12 **Reading Peer Papers**

Directions: *Exchange papers with another student. Be a critical reader as you make suggestions to improve your peer's first draft. Also identify what your classmate did well. Make notes in the margin as you read to remember your suggestions. After you read, you will discuss your suggestions. Use the following guidelines.*

REVISION CHECKLIST

_____ Does the topic sentence connect to the assignment and state the point of the paragraph?

_____ Does the writer stay on the subject throughout the paragraph?

_____ Does the writer provide enough detail in the paragraph?

_____ Does the paragraph have effective transitions?

_____ Does the concluding sentence emphasize the point of the paragraph?

Revise with a Plan

Before you revise your paragraph, reread your assignment. Some narrations can be written in first person. If your assignment indicates that third person is preferable, you need to prepare your writing for an academic audience.

EXERCISE 6-13 **Revising Your Draft**

Directions: *Develop a revision plan and revise the first draft of the paragraph you wrote for Exercise 6-10.*

Edit

EDIT
- Search and correct
- Self-edit

The ideas in your work matter, but if your content is expressed in language that contains careless errors, readers may focus on the errors and miss your point. Invest time in getting your work as close to perfect as possible. In any class, not just for an English course, your instructors want to see that you care about your work. Focus your editing using this personalized checklist.

MULTILINGUAL TIP
Proofread for chronological order.

YOUR EDITING CHECKLIST

_____ Spelling: List any words you misspelled in your last paper:

____

_____ Punctuation: List two punctuation errors from your last paper:

____

_____ Capitalization: List any capitalization errors from your last paper:

____

_____ Other errors: List any errors your instructor has pointed out in graded work:

____

____

To Prepare Your Draft for an Academic Audience

_____ Minimize first-person pronouns: *I, me, my.*

_____ Minimize second-person pronouns: *you, your.*

_____ Use third-person pronouns: *he, she, it, they.*

EXERCISE 6-14 **Revising and Editing Practice**

Directions: *Read the following paragraph that was written in response to the assignment below; it contains errors that require revising and editing. Then answer the questions that follow.*

Assignment: Life experiences teach us lessons. Tell a story that states something you believe to be true. Consider experiences that taught you a lesson or changed your view of something in some way.

(1) The only true "punishment" I can remember was when I was in Junior High School. (2) After working all summer, I had saved enough money to buy a stereo with incredible speakers for my bedroom. (3) It had a CD player. (4) Before that I had a cassette player, but I wanted to get rid of it. (5) In January, semester report cards were handed out and I did not do so well, my grades were terrible. (6) I have always disliked science, and I have never done very well in it. (7) At first, I tried to hide my report card, but my parents caught on after 2 weeks and demanded to see it. (8) Before giving it to them, I edited the grades that I earned. (9) ________________, my mother was not fooled, and she grounds me until my dad comes home from work that evening. (10) He chose to take away my brand-new prized possession, but there was a catch. (11) He did not want the entire component. (12) he took only the speakers. (13) He thought that looking at the component would be a constant reminder of my wrongdoing. (14) I was forced to look at my brand-new stereo without being able to hear it for a week. (15) I never did anything like that again.

error in how numbers are written

Revising

__a__ 1. Which sentence below would work best as a topic sentence for the paragraph?

a. An effective punishment can change a person's behavior.

b. Never lie about your report card.

c. My father really knew how to punish me.

d. Who wears the pants in your family?

__d__ 2. The first sentence is not always the topic sentence of a narration. In this paragraph, where would you place the topic sentence you selected in question 1?

a. replace sentence 1

b. after sentence 1

c. replace sentence 14

d. after sentence 15

__b__ 3. Which sentences should be cut to improve the focus of the paragraph and reduce irrelevant details? If no sentences need to be cut, choose "no change is necessary."

a. sentences 3, 4, 6, and 7

b. sentences 3, 4, and 6

c. sentences 3, 4, 6, and 14

d. no change is necessary

__a__ 4. Which word or phrase should be inserted in blank 9? The word or phrase would serve as a clear transition between the writer's ideas in this paragraph.

a. However

b. Without hesitation

c. Next

d. Since

Editing

__c__ 1. Choose the option that corrects the capitalization error in sentence 1. If no error exists, choose "no change is necessary."

a. Junior High school

b. Junior high school

c. junior high school

d. no change is necessary

__a__ 2. Choose the option that best edits sentence 5.

a. In January, semester report cards were handed out. I did not do well.

b. In January, semester report cards were handed out, in which I did not do so well. My grades were terrible.

c. In January, semester report cards were handed out, I did not do so well. My grades were terrible.

d. In January, when semester report cards were handed out, and I did not do so well, my grades were terrible.

__b__ 3. Choose the option that corrects the error in sentence 9. If no error exists, choose "no change is necessary."

a. she grounded me until my dad comes home from work that evening.

b. she grounded me until my dad came home from work that evening.

c. she grounds me until my dad came home from work that evening.

d. no change is necessary

4. Proofread the paragraph for an error in how numbers are written and correct the error.

EXERCISE 6-15 **Searching and Correcting**

Directions: *Exchange papers with a classmate and proofread each other's work. In addition to spelling, punctuation, and capitalization, find out what other errors your classmate has on his or her checklist; tell your classmate what errors you have on your checklist.*

EXERCISE 6-16 **Self-Editing**

Directions: *Rewrite your paper, correcting errors you and your classmate found. Give yourself time to set aside the finished paper. Then come back to it and read your final draft one last time, using your checklist as a guide.*

Reflect

Take a moment and reflect on what you have learned.

REFLECT
- Identify strengths
- Set goals

EXERCISE 6-17 **Identifying Strengths and Setting Goals**

Directions: *Review your writing and your writing process. On a separate sheet of paper, write answers to these questions:*

- *What did you do well in the paragraph you wrote?*
- *What did you enjoy working on in this chapter?*
- *What have you learned that you will apply in future writing assignments?*

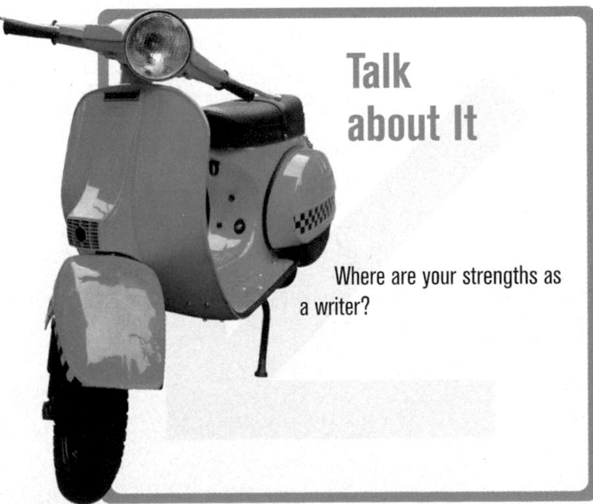

Talk about It

Where are your strengths as a writer?

GOING PLACES

Thinking in Terms of a Process

Some tasks can be done in a moment, without much thought. It does not take a lot of preparation and concentration to make a sandwich or fill the car with gas. Then again, other tasks are more complicated, and the important ones can require a great deal of thought and effort. How, for example, does one graduate from college? or maintain a successful relationship? or find the right job? Tasks like these require you to think in terms of a process. Graduating from college cannot be accomplished in a single night's studying. It requires a series of small accomplishments achieved over four years—quizzes taken, readings done, classes attended. By turning your attention to the immediate task at hand, you can more easily and effectively fulfill your master goal.

DISCUSSION

Turn and talk with a classmate to describe a process you have used to achieve a goal. For example, how did you find your current job? How do you achieve good grades? How do you balance work, school, and home responsibilities? List the steps you use to achieve one of these tasks.

The Essay as a Process

Writing an essay is a process. If you feel dizzy trying to imagine how you are going to get from an empty white sheet of paper to a great grade on a finished product, try breaking the whole thing down into manageable steps: brainstorming, freewriting, talking with friends to figure out what you want to write about; homing in on your topic and roughing out a thesis; writing a first, very rough, draft; redrafting and rewriting; editing for typos and spelling; and then handing in your finished essay. If you think of writing as a series of steps you know how to do, instead of allowing yourself to be daunted by the entire process of writing, you should be able to face any assignment.

BRAINSTORM

Reflect on your writing process by reviewing the list of steps in the Chapter Overview at the beginning of this chapter. Select two steps in the process you use to write for courses other than English. Explain why these steps are helpful to you.

Big Goals, Small Steps

Your first day on the job is never easy. In addition to adjusting to a new work environment, new coworkers, and possibly a new city, you need to learn, on a very basic level, *how to do your job.* The change from rookie to reliable veteran does not happen overnight. You gradually learn what your colleagues know, such as terminology, computer programs, the basics of how your new company operates. Then you begin to acquire more complex skills and, eventually, become knowledgeable about your position and field. By concentrating on learning one new task at a time and discovering how multitasking itself is a process, you can become a dependable and effective employee.

RESUME BUILDER

A major difference between novices and experts is the ability to identify and solve problems. Experts identify problems and connect them to past experience in order to determine solutions. What problems do you face at work? How does your ability to solve them show you are to some degree an expert? On a separate sheet of paper, write about a time you solved a problem at work.

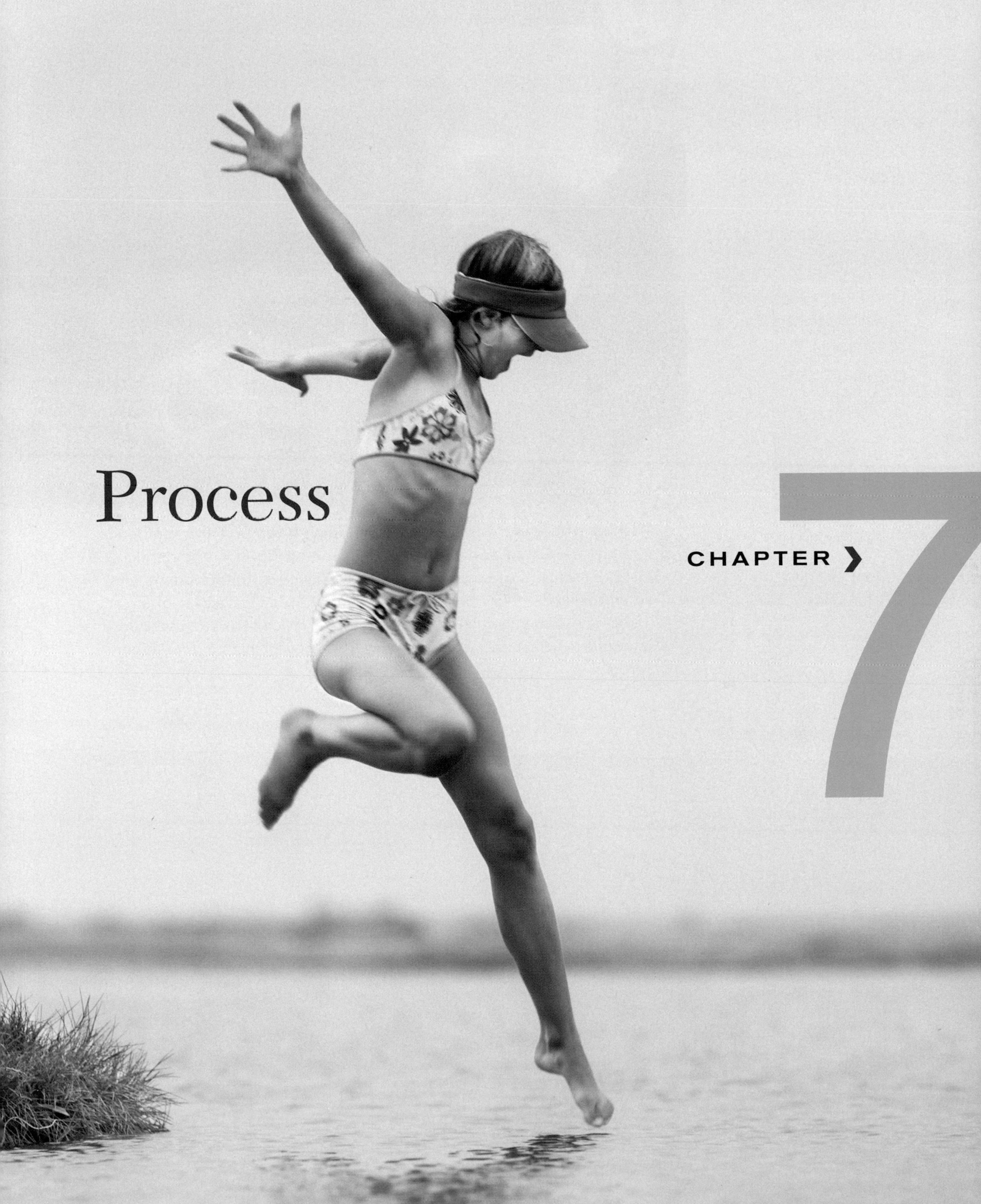

Process

CHAPTER ❯ 7

CHAPTER OVERVIEW

- THE PROCESS PARAGRAPH AT A GLANCE
- PROCESS THINKING
  - Elements of Process
  - Organize Your Details
  - Key Details
- PROCESS IN PROCESS
  - Prewrite
  - Draft
  - A Professional's Take
  - Revise
  - Edit
  - Reflect

THINK FIRST

Process writing explains how to do something. Having a dinner for friends is a process that takes planning and organization. Consider the steps you take to arrange a successful dinner. What will you do before, during, and after the dinner? Now, on a separate sheet of paper, make a list of three other activities you do every day that involve following a process to be successful. Select one and write a paragraph describing the steps in the process.

At a Glance

THE PROCESS PARAGRAPH AT A GLANCE

To explain a process, a writer identifies the key details that make it work well or poorly and suggests ways it could be improved. The topic sentence of a process paragraph states the purpose of the paragraph. Some paragraphs explain how something works or how to perform a process. Others explain how a process can be improved. The supporting details usually explain the steps of the process in chronological order. Transition terms establish and highlight the coherence of the details. The conclusion states the effects or impact of the process on the work, the product, or the people involved.

The Process Paragraph at a Glance

ASSIGNMENT Describe or explain a government process, such as voting a candidate into office, passing a bill into law, or appointing a Supreme Court justice.

The legislative process of making a bill into a law is very complicated from beginning to end. (1) **First,** the person or group that sees the need for a bill must find a member of Congress to sponsor and introduce the bill. A member of either the House or the Senate can introduce a bill. Typically a member of Congress is contacted, meetings take place, needs are assessed, and work begins on the bill in the congressperson's office. (2) **Next,** the bill is named, numbered, and sent to a committee that considers the bill's impact on people, the law, and the federal budget. More information is sought. Hearings may be called. Staff members for a number of congresspersons now start to work on the bill. (3) **Typically** the bill goes through a series of reviews and changes as a result of the work of committees and subcommittees. (4) **Then,** if a bill makes it through this review and change process, it is published in a committee report, gets a place on the legislative calendar, and is debated in the House or Senate. However, it is not law yet. (5) **Next,** the bill must go through a voting process that can change it. Often both Houses of the Congress debate, offer changes, and

TOPIC SENTENCE
The writer uses key words from the assignment and clearly states the point of the paragraph.

SUPPORTING DETAILS
The steps in the process are sequenced in chronological order. Some steps have additional explanation (steps 1, 2, and 5).

ORDER AND TRANSITIONS
The steps are organized by chronological order and introduced by transitions. The concluding sentence uses a transition to emphasize the final comment.

CONCLUDING SENTENCE
The writer comments on the difficult and complicated process of making a bill into a law.

work toward a compromise version that satisfies both Houses. (6) **Finally,** even if it passes, the new legislation can be vetoed by the president. Obviously, bills go through a significant change process and do not become laws easily.

DISCUSSION QUESTIONS

PEER CONVERSATION

1. This paragraph is organized chronologically. Has the writer indicated the most important step or key detail in the process?
2. If you think the most important step is indicated, what is it? If not, what do you think it is? Why?

Thinking

PROCESS THINKING

Like narration, process description is very common in conversation. You tell someone how to download a game from the Internet. You ask someone how to change the setting on the digital clock in your car. Sometimes you evaluate a process, explaining the best way to prepare for running a marathon or how to avoid difficulty when enrolling for classes online.

In college writing, you build on this skill you have in conversation. However, as is the case with all college writing, you have to think about an academic audience that looks for precise detail and careful use of language.

Elements of Process

The elements of process are purpose or end result, the participants and materials involved in arriving at the result, the order in which steps occur, and the key details involved in the process.

- *Purpose:* The purpose of the process is often stated in the topic sentence.
- *Participants and materials:* In processes involving people, discussion of the participants is useful. For example, in the illustration, consider how many people are involved in the legislative process. In those processes involving materials, such as equipment, tools, ingredients, components, facts, and information, detailed explanation of each can be helpful.

- *Steps and order:* Process thinking takes a complex activity and reduces it to steps that are manageable to discuss. Introducing legislation probably involves hundreds of distinct actions. In a paragraph discussion of the process, however, those actions are covered in three or four steps. Organization is important in this area of process thinking, too. The supporting details (which are the steps in the process) and the transition words and phrases are key to communicating how a process works.
- *Key details:* When you evaluate a process, critical thinking comes into play. Not everyone has exactly the same approach to a process. Experience teaches us special ways of doing things that ensure a better outcome. Often there is a key detail you need to emphasize in your paragraph. Without this detail, the process might fail or fall short of achieving maximum success.

Writer's Response

What gets you started in the morning?

Get Started

Effective process writing explains a process in a detailed, organized manner. In the topic sentence, you identify the process in question, then proceed to discuss it in clear language, paying attention to detail and order and providing any specialized information a reader might need to fully understand the process. In the brainstorming exercise shown here, you can see a student's initial exploration of an important process: making a good cup of coffee.

Purpose	Participants and Materials
What is the purpose of coffee?	What participants? Do it by yourself.
Wakes you up.	Type of pots: stove top, perk, drip, espresso, <u>pots with timers.</u>
Goes great after a meal.	Instant coffee too (yuck).
Needed for conversation, like with friends in a coffee shop.	Grind your own, buy it ground.
Keeps you awake studying.	Flavored coffees (yuck).
	You need a good cup.
	Styrofoam cup, the worst.
	Stiff paper cup, less worse.
	China cup, too delicate.
	Gimme a mug heavy enough to knock someone out.
	Cream and sugar.
	Whiskey (Irish coffee).

Steps and Order	Key Detail(s)
Fill the pot with water (has to be cold water).	Easy pot, like one with a timer.
Put in the coffee.	Convenient!
Turn it on.	Good coffee.
Wait. Wait. I hate to wait.	Good mug.
If the coffee sits in the pot and gets old, it smells.	A timer pot means you have coffee when you wake up in the morning.
Drink it.	
Clean up.	
Before—decide on kind of coffee.	
During—how to fix it up (two sugars).	
Continuous stirring (put spoon in materials list), love the clang.	
Maybe choose something to eat with it.	

Your goal in your early thinking about your subject is to be as thorough as possible. Include everything you can think of that is related to your topic. Later in the thinking process, you will use some of these ideas and details and reject others. In the exploration shown here, the student moves systematically through the process of making coffee. He knows a lot. He specifies what he does not like: instant coffee, flavored coffee, Styrofoam cups. He specifies what he does like: a mug. He mentions the pot with the timer twice and underlines "I hate to wait," suggesting a possible point of interest to him.

As you think about your topic and get ideas down on paper, you will probably develop a feel for a possible focus for your paragraph. However, as you get started, be inclusive. Here is this student's tentative topic sentence:

Topic Sentence: Good coffee is necessary to get going in the morning, and the key is the right pot.

EXERCISE 7-1 Elements of Process

Directions: *Choose one of the processes listed below and brainstorm to get started thinking about the topic. Look at all four elements of process thinking. When you finish, formulate a tentative topic sentence on the process.*

- *Learning to ride a bike*
- *Losing five pounds in one week*
- *Breaking a bad habit*

Purpose: ______________________________

____

Participants and Materials: ______________________________

____

____

Steps and Order: ______________________________

____

____

Key Detail(s): ______________________________

____

____

Topic Sentence: ______________________________

____

Organize Your Details

A common challenge in process writing is reducing a number of actions to a few steps. Remember, a reader of academic writing does not want to read about the eighteen steps involved in the process you have chosen to examine. Not only do you risk losing your reader (and getting a low grade), but you also lose an opportunity to provide the kind of detail your academic reader values. Your job is to reduce the eighteen steps to a manageable number. For this reason, you may need to group steps into categories or stages in the process, making transitions from one stage of the process to another.

Consider the coffee example from earlier in this section. Here are all the steps based on the student's brainstorming:

1. Decide on the type of coffee.
2. Fill the pot with water.
3. Put the coffee in the basket.
4. Pack it.
5. Plug in the coffeemaker or put it on the stove.
6. Take the basket out of the pot.
7. Fix the coffee (cream, sugar, etc.).
8. Choose something to eat with the coffee.
9. Drink it.
10. Stir continuously.

Returning to this list, this student organizes his details, cutting and adding as he works.

Step 1: Get the right materials.

- a. coffee pot
- b. coffee

} Make it easy on yourself. Get one of those pots you can program to go on by itself. No waiting in the morning.

- c. cup or take-it-with-you mug

Step 2: Program the machine the night before.

- a. fill the reservoir with water
- b. put one of those cartridges in the basket
- c. go to bed

Step 3: Wake up and smell the coffee (I hate waiting!).

- a. pour the coffee, add two sugars
- b. turn on the TV, listen to traffic updates, drink the coffee, and wake up
- c. fill your road mug and head for school
- d. cleanup is a snap with those cartridge thingies

This student has reduced the process of making coffee to three main steps. In the process of organizing his details, his thinking has become more focused, which has caused him to select specific details from his initial exploration. He shifts his focus to convenience. This shift in focus means that some of his initial thoughts—about types of pots and different grinds of coffee, for example—are no longer relevant to his purpose. His new purpose is explaining how to get good coffee in the morning in the most convenient way.

EXERCISE 7-2 **Organizing Your Details**

Directions: *Return to the brainstorming you did in Exercise 7-1. Organize your process details into three or four major steps. Below outline the process and draft a topic sentence stating your purpose in explaining the process.*

See "Supporting Details" in Chapter 3 for detailed explanation of outlining.

Step 1

a. ______________________________

b. ______________________________

c. ______________________________

Step 2

a. ______________________________

b. ______________________________

c. ______________________________

Step 3

a. ______________________________

b. ______________________________

c. ______________________________

Step 4

a. ______________________________

b. ______________________________

c. ______________________________

Purpose: ______________________________

____

Talk about It

Are you a big idea or a detail person? Is it challenging to limit yourself to four steps?

Key Details

Processes run smoothly (or poorly) because of where they occur, who helps (or does not help), environmental factors, quality of the materials used, and the level of experience of those involved. Whether you are writing about how to do a process or how to improve a process, process thinking becomes critical thinking when you notice the key details involved and explain why they are essential.

PEER CONVERSATION

EXERCISE 7-3 Identifying Key Details

Directions: *Read the following paragraph. With a classmate, answer the discussion questions that follow.*

PURPOSE
The topic sentence states the purpose of the paragraph: what steps to take to wake up to a good cup of coffee.

MATERIALS
Materials include the following: (1) programmable coffeemaker, (2) automatic shut-off, (3) coffee filter packs, (4) coffee mug and travel mug.

STEPS AND ORDER
The supporting details explain the steps of the process. The writer uses four transitions to indicate the steps and emphasis of the paragraph.

IMPACT
The concluding sentence comments on the effects of the process.

Waking up to a good cup of coffee requires having the right machine and planning ahead. (1) The most important step in the process is buying the right equipment. Look for a programmable coffeemaker. This enables you to set your coffeemaker the way you set your alarm and wake up to the smell of coffee already brewed. Mr. Coffee offers an inexpensive model that is easy to use. Slightly more expensive is the Krups Programmable Coffee Maker, "the coffee is ready when you are." The Krups comes with an automatic shut-off so you do not have to remember to turn it off as you rush out the door. Once you have all the right equipment, a daily three-step routine delivers great morning coffee. (2) To start, set up the pot before you go to bed. Make this simpler by purchasing coffee in filter packs. This decision will make coffee-making effortless and reduce cleanup as well. (3) Next, set out a cup for your first cup of the day and your travel mug. (4) Last, wake up to fresh coffee. The smell will urge you out of bed. Waking up to fresh brewed coffee improves a coffee-lover's attitude toward the day to come.

DISCUSSION QUESTIONS

PEER CONVERSATION

1. What is the key detail in this paragraph? choosing the right equipment
2. What transition words or phrases does the student use? once, to start, next, last.

EXERCISE 7-4 Your Key Details

Directions: *Review your brainstorming and outline from Exercises 7-1 and 7-2. In the space below, briefly describe the key details in the process.* Answers will vary.

PROCESS IN PROCESS

Writing about a process can help you understand it and communicate that understanding to others. Process writing can also focus on improving a process. In college writing, you will use process description and analysis in a variety of courses: in science labs, in writing accompanying calculations in mathematics, in criminal justice, and in hospitality programs.

In this section, you will use a process approach to write a single paragraph that describes or explains a process.

Select an Assignment

When you write about a process in a college course, your primary concerns are how the process works, why it is important, and what can be done to improve it.

EXERCISE 7-5 Selecting an Assignment for a Process Paragraph

Directions: *Review the assignments listed below. Choose the one you know the most about and think is best suited to an effective process paragraph.*

1. Explain how to search for information on the Internet.
2. Describe the process of getting registered for college classes.
3. Outline the steps involved in taking out a loan.
4. Describe how to handle a customer complaint at work.
5. Review the process of getting a tan at a tanning booth.
6. Explain how to buy a used car.
7. Explain the causes of a war or another historical event.
8. Describe a process that you use every day at home, school, or work.
9. Explain the process of a disease or a process used to manage a disease.
10. Choose your own topic.

Prewrite: Write Before You Write

When you write a process paragraph, you have a specific purpose in mind. You want a reader to understand the process; in addition, you may want to explain how the steps impact the people and work involved. To get started, you might try these two prewriting strategies: talking and brainstorming.

PREWRITE
- Talk
- Cluster
- Brainstorm
- Freewrite

Talk

Talking enables you to analyze the process and get input from a classmate. Use this conversation to extend your thinking and identify the elements that need more explanation.

PEER CONVERSATION

EXERCISE 7-6 **Talking about It**

Directions: *Turn to a classmate or find an interested listener. Describe your process: its purpose, participants and materials, steps, and key detail(s). Be specific and include details so your listener understands your process. Then be a critical listener to your partner's process thinking. Listen without interrupting. When your partner finishes, ask questions or offer suggestions. Identify what was clear and what was not clear.*

Brainstorm

Brainstorming enables you to examine all areas of your topic quickly and efficiently. Remember the elements of process writing: purpose, participants and materials, steps and order, and key detail(s). Ask yourself, What do I know about this process? What does the reader need to know to understand it? Jot down as many idea and details as you can.

EXERCISE 7-7 **Brainstorming**

Directions: *On a separate sheet of paper, brainstorm for ten minutes on the assignment you chose in Exercise 7-5. List the elements of the process and include as many details as possible. Then identify the key detail(s) and consider the impact of the detail(s) on the people or work.*

Draft: Focus and Organize

DRAFT

- Consider your audience
- Formulate your topic sentence
- Outline for unity and coherence
- Write a conclusion sentence
- Compose your first draft

After prewriting, you probably have a feel for what you want to include in your paragraph. You can identify your purpose for explaining the process and list the participants and materials, the steps in the process, and the key detail(s).

Consider Your Audience

Before you draft, consider the background of your readers. What do they know about this process? What terms will be new to them? If you identify and define new information and key terms, it will help readers follow your train of thought. Also, remember that no two people complete a process in exactly the same way. What is the most important step in the process from your perspective? Use the following questions to consider how best to convey the process you are explaining to an audience:

- What terms do I need to define to explain the process?
- What essential steps and methods do I need to include?
- What do I want my audience to understand about this process?

EXERCISE 7-8 **Considering Your Audience**

PEER CONVERSATION

Directions: *Talk with a classmate about your topic. Use the questions above to think critically about the key terms, essential steps, and specific details to include as you explain the process to an audience. Take notes on this conversation and add new ideas and details to your prewriting. Talk to a different classmate to gain another perspective and clarify your thinking.*

Topic Sentence

To begin, write a clear topic sentence that echoes the key words from the assignment and states the purpose of your paragraph. Be aware that you may change your topic sentence or move it to a different location in the paragraph during revision.

Ask Yourself
Which transitions do you always use?

Unity and Coherence

Your goal is a unified paragraph. That means all the details you include should be relevant to the main point of your paragraph. Be sure you do not go off the subject, including details that are interesting to you but not directly related to the discussion at hand.

Steps in a process are typically organized by sequence or chronological order. Your careful use of transition words and phrases will enhance the coherence of your paragraph.

TRANSITIONS BASED ON CHRONOLOGICAL ORDER	
first	then
second	soon
third	afterward
finally	simultaneously
next	

Some students use transitions based on priority or importance to indicate the key steps in a process.

TRANSITIONS BASED ON PRIORITY OR IMPORTANCE	
most	certainly
equally	definitely
absolutely	never
always	obviously

Concluding Sentence

A concluding sentence states the importance of the process or underscores the point your paragraph makes about improving the process.

EXERCISE 7-9 **Planning Your First Draft**

See "Supporting Details" in Chapter 3 for detailed explanation of outlining.

Directions: *On a separate sheet of paper, state the purpose of your process paragraph. Then write a topic sentence that echoes the key words from the assignment you selected and states the purpose of your process paragraph. Make a short outline to organize the paragraph. Write a concluding sentence that comments on the process.*

Write a First Draft

Write a first draft of your paragraph. As you write, select only the relevant ideas and details from your brainstorming or outlining. It may be helpful at this point to reconsider the order of what you have written and the transition terms you plan to use. Look for the details that seem most important for readers to notice so they can understand your purpose. Be sure to provide adequate explanation of these details.

EXERCISE 7-10 **Writing Your First Draft**

Directions: *Write a draft of your paragraph. Use the following checklist as a guide.*

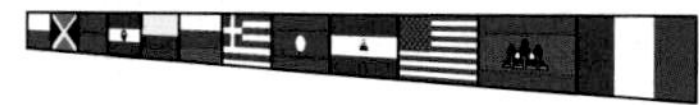

MULTILINGUAL TIP
Bring your draft to the writing center on your campus.

FIRST DRAFT CHECKLIST

______ My topic sentence states the point of my paragraph.

______ My topic sentence echoes key terms in the assignment.

______ I have included process details related to time, place, material, and people involved in the process.

______ I have organized the process into three to four steps and used transitions to show the relationship between the steps and details.

______ My concluding sentence summarizes the point of my process analysis.

A PROFESSIONAL'S TAKE

Here is Mark Caldwell's use of process in a short *Discover Magazine* article entitled "Polly Want a PhD?"

It's not just what the parrots say that makes them seem eerily human; it's the level of intelligence they easily demonstrate. Consider Griffin's [a parrot] performance on a test Pepperberg [a researcher] devised to see whether the birds could use a mirror image of an object to manipulate it. Children don't typically master that skill until they're 3 years old. In the experiment, a nut is concealed underneath the lid of a box. The nut is attached to a wire that runs up through a slit in the lid and connects to a paper clip for the parrot to yank. The slit branches out into three tracks, each of which ends in a hole through which the nut can be pulled. The trick is that two of the three slits are blocked by obstructions that can only be seen by looking in a mirror that reflects a backward view of what's inside the box. Most humans who try to solve the puzzle are baffled, but Griffin, watching intently from his perch on the lab counter, will demand to be brought over, peer into the mirror for perhaps half a second, triumphantly zip the nut down the right track, jerk it up through the opening, and grab it.

EXERCISE 7-11 A PROFESSIONAL'S TAKE

Directions: *Using the first draft checklist as your guide, identify the elements of an effective process paragraph in the professional model.*

Revise: Read Critically, Then Rewrite

REVISE
- Read critically
- Develop a revision plan

Process analysis is complex. Revision in process writing means rethinking and evaluating your explanation of the process. Ask yourself a few questions as you reread your first draft. What is your purpose? Are you explaining how something works, how to perform a process, or how a process can be improved? Do you provide all the essential steps and necessary explanation? Is there any unnecessary detail you could cut? Revision gives you a chance to read critically and to reorganize, clarify, or cut.

Revision in Action

The full version of Deidre's sample is available online.

Revision is rethinking a draft and making decisions to improve the quality of your writing. You read critically, plan your revision, and revise the writing. Here is an example of revision by a student named Deidre.

Assignment: Describe, explain, or analyze a process that you know well.

TOPIC SENTENCE
Deidre states the process and the focus of the process paragraph in her topic sentence.

SUPPORTING DETAILS
She explains the process step by step. She lists the steps using technical language.

ORDER AND TRANSITIONS
Deidre inserts transitions for some steps in the process that emphasize the point in her topic sentence—*getting the process right.*

Deidre's First Draft

Providing CPR can save a person's life; the important thing is starting CPR early and getting the process right. The **first important step** is to assess the patient. Not every unconscious person needs CPR. I look, listen, and feel for breathing, heartbeat, and pulse. If all three are negative, I proceed with CPR. I use universal precautions, such as gloves and a mask. **It is best** to move the patient to a hard, flat surface so compressions have maximum effect. I learned that CPR consists of breathing and compressions. To help a patient breathe I tilt her head back to open her airway. **Then** I apply the mask and give one long breath, until the diaphragm rises. **At this point,** I start CPR. Give another breath and start chest compressions, fifteen compressions for each breath, two breaths a minute. If I have a buddy responder, it is a good idea to change positions, one doing breathing and maintaining airway, the other doing compressions. **Every so often,** I stop and check for respiration and heartbeat. Doing CPR is hard work, but when I save a life, it is definitely worth it.

Revision Plan: Revise my topic sentence to focus on my purpose: to explain how a process can be effective. Adjust organization to emphasize effectiveness, especially placing emphasis on the key detail in the process. Add another important detail: CALL 911! Revise my concluding sentence to comment on my topic sentence. Shift to third person.

Deidre's Revised Draft

Cardiopulmonary Resuscitation (CPR) is hard work, but knowledgeable responders save lives. Responders must know the correct procedures so their responses are automatic. The **first important step** is to assess the patient. Not every unconscious person needs CPR. Responders should look, listen, and feel for breathing, heartbeat, and pulse. If all three are negative, they should have someone call 911 and prepare for CPR. **It is best** to move a patient to a hard, flat surface so compressions have maximum effect. **However,** responders should check for serious back or neck injuries before moving the patient. **Next,** responders should use universal precautions, such as gloves and a mask, to protect themselves and the patient from infection. **Now** they can begin CPR. CPR consists of alternating breathing and compressions to provide a patient with oxygen. **First,** responders should tip a patient's head back to open his or her airway. They should apply a mask and give one long breath, until the patient's diaphragm rises. Responders should then give another breath and start chest compressions, fifteen compressions for each breath, two breaths a minute. Chest compressions involve placing both hands, the heel of one hand, the other on top of that, between the patient's nipples. A compression should be no more than 1½ inches deep. Giving compressions is hard work. If there is another person available, it is a good idea to change positions at five-minute intervals, with one person doing breathing and maintaining the airway and the other doing compressions. **Every so often,** it is important to stop and check for respiration and heartbeat. Providing CPR can save a person's life; the important thing is starting CPR early and getting the process right.

TOPIC SENTENCE
In her revised draft, Deidre uses formal language and emphasizes that saving a life requires specific skills. She adds a second sentence to explain why knowledge can make a difference.

SUPPORTING DETAILS
She adds significant detail to her explanation, particularly about how to give chest compressions.

ORDER AND TRANSITIONS
Deidre divides the paragraph into two major parts: (1) steps before CPR, and (2) steps during CPR. She rearranges the order of her minor details to connect all the steps that are done before and during CPR. She also uses two kinds of transitions: importance and time. This emphasizes her point in the topic sentence that knowledge can save a life

CONCLUDING SENTENCE
Deidre revises her conclusion sentence to emphasize the key detail—*starting early and doing it correctly.*

DISCUSSION QUESTIONS Which changes in the revision most improved Deidre's paragraph? Why?

PEER CONVERSATION

Read Critically

Critical reading is a search for the characteristics of effective writing: topic sentence, supporting details, transitions, concluding sentence. It is also a search for clarity of purpose.

EXERCISE 7-12 Reading Peer Papers

PEER CONVERSATION

Directions: *Exchange papers with another student. Be a critical reader and make suggestions to improve your peer's first draft. Also identify what your classmate did well. Make notes in the margin as you read to remember your suggestions. After you read, discuss your suggestions. Use the following guidelines.*

REVISION CHECKLIST

_____ Does the topic sentence connect to the assignment and state the point of the paragraph?

_____ Does the writer divide the process into three to four steps?

_____ Does the writer provide enough detail to explain the steps in the process?

_____ Does the paragraph have effective transitions?

_____ Does the concluding sentence emphasize the point of the paragraph?

Revise with a Plan

Time controls the order and transitions in a process paragraph. As you review the comments from your classmate, consider how focusing on time might make your paragraph more effective. In addition, look at the details you have included. Do they explain the process? Are they relevant?

EXERCISE 7-13 **Revising Your Draft**

Directions: *Develop a revision plan and revise the first draft of the paragraph you wrote for Exercise 7-10.*

Edit

EDIT
- Search and correct
- Self-edit

In any class, not just for an English course, your instructors want to see that you care about your work. Focus your editing with this personalized checklist.

MULTILINGUAL TIP
Proofread "command" forms; make sure you omitted the subject pronoun "you."

YOUR EDITING CHECKLIST

_____ Spelling: List any words you misspelled in your last paper:

_____ Punctuation: List two punctuation errors from your last paper:

_____ Capitalization: List any capitalization errors from your last paper:

_____ Other errors: List any errors your instructor has pointed out in graded work:

To Prepare Your Draft for an Academic Audience

_____ Minimize first-person pronouns: *I, me, my.*

_____ Minimize second-person pronouns: *you, your.*

_____ Use third-person pronouns: *he, she, it, they.*

EXERCISE 7-14 **Revising and Editing Practice**

Directions: *Read the following paragraph that was written in response to the assignment below; it contains errors that require revising and editing. Then answer the questions that follow.*

Assignment: Explain a process you use at home, school, or work. State the impact of the process and support your point with specific details.

(1) Making enemies out of your neighbors, should never be a difficult task. (2) Following three easy steps will send Mr. Johnson through the roof. (3) The first rule of thumb is to always show disrespect. (4) Begin responding to hello with a menacing glare. (5) Follow this up by responding with the term "Yo!" (6) This will send Mr. Johnsons mind meandering through corridors of shock. (7) With some neighbors this will be enough. (8) ____. (9) You may need to create more animosity in the air using sound waves. (10) Arrange a playlist of grind core metal to disrupt the still of the night. (11) Begin your social gathering at midnight. (12) Plan a large gathering on a business day. (13) If it begins earlier you may risk Mr. Johnson still being awake. (14) The most important piece of the puzzle is to be sure that everyone stays all night. (15) ______________, the climactic moment is upon you. (16) The day after the party, in the mid-afternoon, Mr. Johnson will knock on your door, keep your wits about you because he is certain to be upset. (17) When he blames you for not being able to rest the night before. (18) Smile and slam the door. (19) If you have the nerve to follow these instructions you can easily make enemies with your neighbors.

sentence fragment

Revising

__a__ 1. Is sentence 2 relevant?

a. yes

b. no

__a__ 2. Which sentence should be inserted into blank 8 to provide a transition? If no sentence is needed, choose "no transition is necessary."

a. For others, however, more effort will be required.

b. Mr. Johnson's mind is easy to disturb.

c. Making enemies is not advised for good neighborhood relations.

d. no transition is necessary

__b__ 3. Select the order of sentences 10, 11, 12, and 13 to provide the most logical sequence of ideas and supporting details. If the order is correct, choose "no change is necessary."

a. 10, 13, 11, 12

b. 12, 10, 11, 13

c. 10, 12, 11, 13

d. no change is necessary

__c__ 4. Which word or phrase should be inserted in blank 15?

a. Therefore

b. Once in a while

c. Finally

d. Indeed

Editing

__a__ 1. Choose the option that corrects the error in sentence 1. If no error exists, choose "no change is necessary."

a. Making enemies out of your neighbors should never be a difficult task.

b. Making enemies, out of your neighbors, should never be a difficult task.

c. Making an enemy out of your neighbor, should never be a difficult task.

d. no change is necessary

Ask Yourself
Do you insert commas where you would take a breath? What does the Writer's Guidebook say about commas?

__c__ 2. Choose the option that corrects the error in sentence 6. If no error exists, choose "no change is necessary."

a. This will send Mr. Johnsons' mind meandering through corridors of shock.

b. This will send Mr. Johnson mind meandering through corridors of shock.

c. This will send Mr. Johnson's mind meandering through corridors of shock.

d. no change is necessary

__b__ 3. Choose the option that corrects the error in sentence 16. If no error exists, choose "no change is necessary."

a. The day after the party, in the mid-afternoon, Mr. Johnson will knock on your door, keep your wits about you, because he is certain to be upset.

b. The day after the party, in the mid-afternoon, Mr. Johnson will knock on your door. Keep your wits about you because he is certain to be upset.

c. The day after the party, in the mid-afternoon; Mr. Johnson will knock on your door, keep your wits about you because he is certain to be upset.

d. no change is necessary

4. Proofread the paragraph for a sentence fragment and correct the error.

EXERCISE 7-15 Searching and Correcting

PEER CONVERSATION

Directions: *Exchange papers with a peer and proofread each other's work. In addition to spelling, punctuation, and capitalization, find out what other errors your classmate has on his or her checklist; tell your classmate what errors you have on your checklist.*

EXERCISE 7-16 Self-Editing

Directions: *Rewrite your paper, correcting errors you and your classmate have found. Give yourself time to set aside the finished paper. Then come back to it and read your final draft one last time, using your checklist as a guide.*

Reflect

Take a moment and reflect on what you have learned.

REFLECT
- Identify strengths
- Set goals

EXERCISE 7-17 Identifying Strengths and Setting Goals

Directions: *Review your writing and your writing process. On a separate sheet of paper, write answers to these questions:*

- *What did you do well in the paragraph you wrote?*
- *What did you enjoy working on in this chapter?*
- *What have you learned that you will apply in future writing assignments?*

GOING PLACES

Organizing Your World

That is not where that goes! We make sense of the world by organizing it—by sorting things, people, events, and ideas. Think of a kitchen cupboard. Open the doors and most likely you will see objects stored according to their size, use, and materials: glasses on the first shelf; next to them, coffee cups and saucers; on the shelf above, dinner plates, salad plates, and dessert dishes. Think about movies. There are comedies, action movies, date movies, and horror movies.

This is classification. It serves a purpose. It answers a need. The philosopher William James said the world is a "humming-buzzing confusion" until we organize it through experience. James says this work of organizing goes on continuously; it is never complete. So, we create categories, and they work—for a while. For example, at one time, our category for CEO meant a white male. Then we re-created our categories, making them more inclusive. A CEO could be male or female, white or black or Hispanic. How we organize the world and understand our place in it is a work in progress. Classification is at the heart of this work.

DISCUSSION

Talk with a classmate to answer the following questions: How do you find your way around a grocery store, electronics store, or home repair store? How does a place like that use classification to make shopping quick and easy?

Your Program of Study

Are you studying heath care? That field of study is divided into different categories: nursing, x-ray technology, dental assistance, or emergency response. How about business? The college curriculum divides the business field into a number of categories: accounting and finance, marketing and advertising, and administration and human resources. These distinct fields focus on money, on sales, and on the management of personnel and operations. A student going into business might also consider whether her future is in corporate work, small business, a family business, or a limited partnership. These broader categories are determined by the size of the operation. For each of these categories, the college curriculum helps you build a knowledge base and develop skills in math, science, social science, and humanities that are relevant to optimum job performance. The college curriculum provides countless examples of classification at work.

BRAINSTORM

Think about the career you are interested in pursuing. Create several lists to help you explore what this career possibility might mean. Consider the type of education required, the different types of work environments, the various types of responsibilities, and the kinds of people with whom you might interact.

Job Description

In the workplace, classification defines an employee's responsibilities and pay scale. For years we have distinguished between white-collar and blue-collar employees, those who make a salary and those who make an hourly wage, those who work with their minds and those who work with their hands. This division of the workforce allows us to see the big picture and describe work in broad strokes. However, a closer look changes the picture. Blue-collar employees can be classified as skilled or unskilled, and on the job, skilled workers use sophisticated technology, exhibit high levels of expertise, and demonstrate important critical-thinking skills. The classification "those who work with their hands" just does not fit the facts. New classifications are necessary, such as "knowledge workers," for example. What color is their collar?

RESUME BUILDER

Use classification to examine what makes you an effective and efficient worker. Identify two or three job categories at your place of work. Then list the characteristics or requirements of each job. Where are you currently in the organization? What would you have to do to move to a more responsible position?

CHAPTER 8

Classification

CHAPTER OVERVIEW

- THE CLASSIFICATION PARAGRAPH AT A GLANCE
- CLASSIFICATION THINKING
  - Elements of Classification
  - Provide Examples of Categories
  - Avoid Stereotyping
- CLASSIFICATION IN PROCESS
  - Prewrite
  - Draft
  - A Professional's Take
  - Revise
  - Edit
  - Reflect

! THINK FIRST

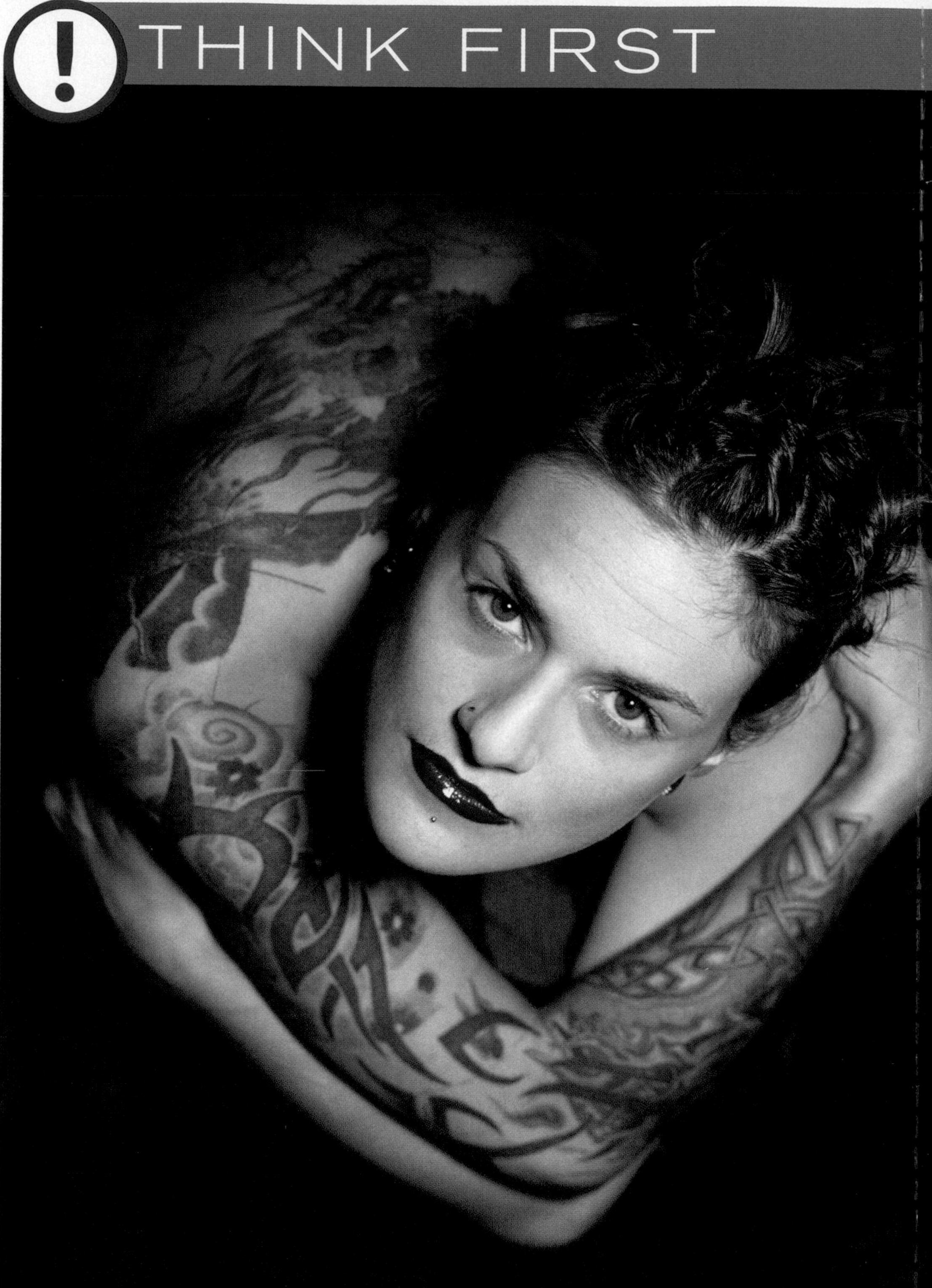

Everyone is getting a tattoo these days. Why? Brainstorm to develop a list of all the people you can think of with tattoos. Sort the individuals on your list into categories based on their reasons for getting a tattoo. Then write a paragraph in which you describe the various types of people who are getting tattoos.

At a Glance

THE CLASSIFICATION PARAGRAPH AT A GLANCE

A classification paragraph has three basic parts: a topic sentence, supporting details, and a concluding sentence. The topic sentence of a classification paragraph serves multiple purposes. It states the key words from the assignment, names the topic to be discussed, and lists the categories to be described in the paragraph. The supporting details in the body of the paragraph consist of examples that describe and illustrate each category. The concluding sentence may restate the topic sentence or make a comment about the categories included in the paragraph.

The Classification Paragraph at a Glance

ASSIGNMENT As election day draws near, discuss the types of voters you see out there.

There are several different types of voters: the wealthy, working-class, and one-issue voter. **The first type,** the wealthy, are mostly rich entrepreneurs that vote based on their economic self-interest. They vote for tax cuts. They vote for small government. They do not mind jobs being moved offshore because they are the bosses. They make money anyway. More often than not, wealthy voters vote Republican because that is the party of the entrepreneur. **The next type** is the working-class voter. These voters want effective solutions to their troubles; they see government as the source of such solutions. They want government to protect jobs. If they are laid off, they want retraining. They want affordable health care. They want the minimum wage to be raised. Working-class voters usually vote Democratic, for the candidate who understands bread-and-butter issues. **Then there are the one-issue voters.** Sometimes they are wealthy; sometimes they are from the working class. They want one thing: an end to abortion, a ban on same-sex marriages, freedom to own a gun, or limits on immigration. Often one issue is so important to these voters that they pay little attention to anything else. If the Republicans own their issue, that is how they vote. If the Democrats have the right idea on an issue, he is in their camp. Whether a wealthy, working-class, or one-issue voter, the fact remains that voting is the civic duty of every American.

TOPIC SENTENCE
The student's topic sentence states the different types of voters.

SUPPORTING DETAILS
For each type of voter she discusses, the student provides detailed explanation.

ORDER AND TRANSITIONS
Transitions from descriptions of one type of voter to the next are clearly stated.

CONCLUDING SENTENCE
In her concluding sentence, the student reiterates the three categories and connects them to an important idea: "civic duty."

PEER CONVERSATION

DISCUSSION QUESTIONS

1. What reasons can you suggest for presenting the types of voters in the order the student has chosen?
2. Suppose the assignment was to write about why people do not vote. How would you classify nonvoters? Why?

Thinking

CLASSIFICATION THINKING

Classification begins with the recognition of difference. It involves careful observation, which in turn leads to careful thinking. When you classify, you make a complex topic more focused and easier to understand. You help the reader see your subject in a new way, perhaps in a way he or she has never considered before.

Elements of Classification

The important elements of classification thinking are purpose, basis for classification, categories, and examples.

- *Purpose:* Classification serves a purpose. It imposes order on information to meet your needs or the needs of a reader. For example, you notice different types of people voting on election day and begin to think critically about what brings people to the polls.
- *Basis for classification:* To impose order on information, you need a basis for classification. In the case of types of voters, you consider what could be the basis of classification to distinguish among voters.
- *Categories:* From purpose and a basis for classification come the categories you will use. In the case of types of voters, you might identify older voters, soccer moms, and teenagers voting for the first time.
- *Examples:* Within categories, examples provide the specific detail in classification thinking. You discuss specific examples of types of voters, or you provide descriptive detail to elaborate on each category.

Get Started

Classification thinking moves from general to specific. You begin with a topic, divide the topic into general categories, and then move toward specific examples that illustrate each category. How you divide your topic depends on your purpose, which then leads to the basis for classification.

Take a very general subject like popular music. There are many possibilities for classification. One student might be interested in guitar music, another in instrumental music. Their different purposes result in different bases for classification.

Topic	*Interest/Purpose*	*Basis for Classification*
Popular Music	To explore the influence of the electric guitar	Types of music in which electric guitar is used
	To discuss the pleasures of nonvocal, instrumental music	Types of popular nonvocal instrumental music

The importance of the electric guitar and the pleasures of instrumental music are two different purposes for classifying popular music. Approaching classification with these purposes in mind, one student would focus on different types of music in which the electric guitar is prominent, using categories such as blues, rock, and jazz. Another student would focus on different types of instrumental music—categories such as jazz, orchestral, techno—that people find enjoyable. These different approaches to classification would lead to topic sentences that reflect the specific focus and purpose for classification:

> The influence of the electric guitar can be heard in many categories of popular music.
>
> A rich variety of instrumental music is available in popular music today for the enjoyment of the interested listener.

EXERCISE 8-1 Purpose and Classification

Directions: *For each topic, state two different interests you have related to the subject. Then explain how each interest provides you with a basis for classification.* Answers will vary.

EXAMPLE

Topic: Reading materials

A. I'm interested in reducing the amount of clutter in my house. I will classify reading materials based on whether I plan to keep them or get rid of them.

B. I'm interested in planning what I will read over the next few months. I'll classify reading materials based on whether they are something I really enjoy or something I read for personal improvement.

1. **Topic:** Hobbies/pastimes

A. I'm interested in finding a hobby that does not cost me a lot of money. I'll classify hobbies based on expense.

B. I'm also interested in aviation. I'll classify hobbies based on what I can learn about aviation in the process of doing them.

2. **Topic:** Students

A. I'm annoyed by the fact that not all students are as serious as I am about my studies. I'll classify students based on their reasons for being in college.

B. I'm interested in those students who already know exactly what they want to do. I'll classify students based on how they determined their academic and career goals.

3. **Topic:** Shoppers

A. I'm interested in those shoppers who come to the cash register with boxes of coupons they have clipped from the newspaper. I'll classify shoppers based on the effort they put into being a "smart shopper."

B. I'm interested in shoppers who have quality as their number one goal for shopping. I'll classify shoppers based on their desire or indifference to the importance of quality when they shop.

Provide Examples of Categories

Classification serves a purpose. You decide on categories because doing so helps you explore what interests you about your topic. Your next task is to be specific—to cite and discuss specific examples in your categories.

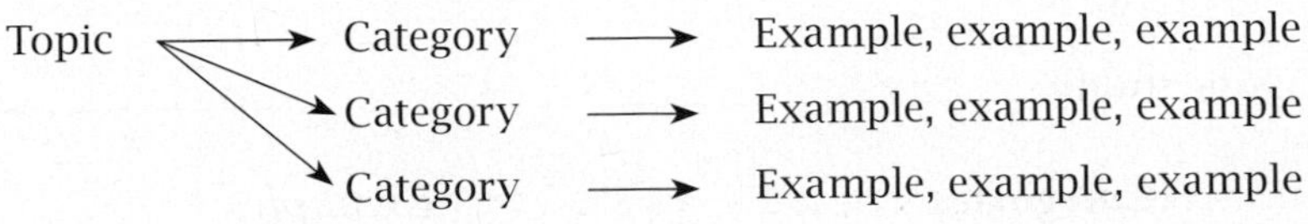

For instance, the student who explores the influence of the electric guitar in popular music would cite specific examples, as shown here:

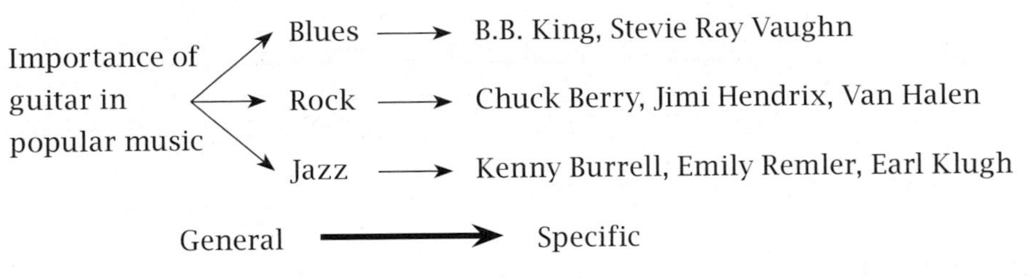

Examples, of course, are always more complex than their categories. Jimi Hendrix was not only a rock musician. His style of play also drew upon the blues category. A student examining popular music with a different purpose would have different categories and arrive at many different specific examples. The important thing in this work is to be clear about your purpose and focus.

EXERCISE 8-2 **Topics, Categories, and Examples**

Directions: *Using the model below as a guide, divide each topic into categories. Be sure your categories reflect a clear purpose and basis for classification. Once your categories are in place, provide specific examples for each category. Then write a topic sentence that states the topic and purpose for classification for each one.* Answers will vary.

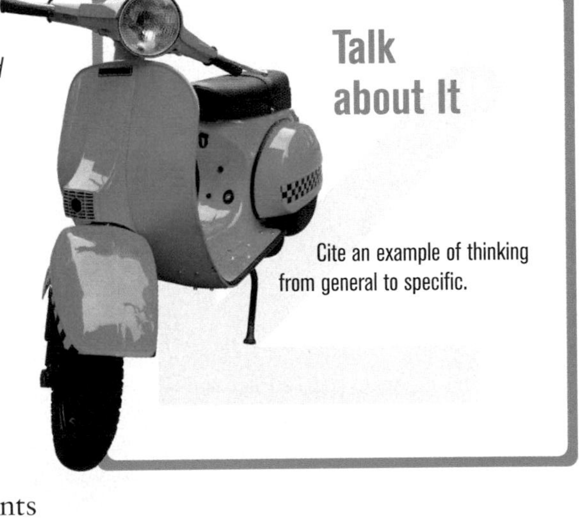

Talk about It
Cite an example of thinking from general to specific.

EXAMPLE

Topic: Parents

Basis for Classification: Approaches to discipline

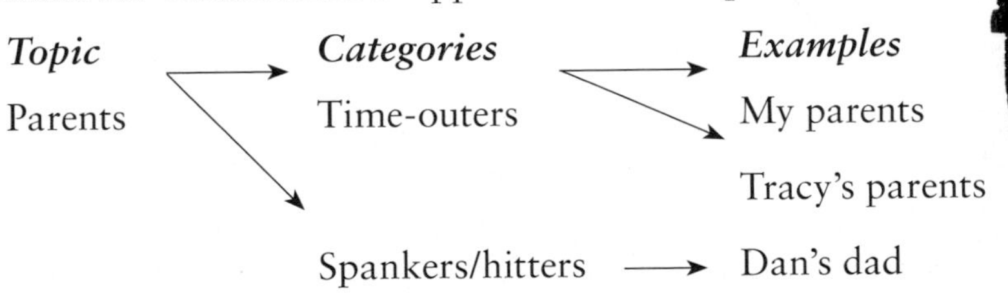

Topic Sentence: Not all parents have exactly the same approach to disciplining their children.

1. **Topic:** Friends

Basis for Classification: ______________________

Topic	*Categories*	*Examples*
Friends	______________	______________
		______________
		______________
	______________	______________
		______________
		______________

Topic Sentence: ______________________

____

2. **Topic:** Expenses

Basis for Classification: ______________________

Topic	*Categories*	*Examples*
Expenses	______________	______________
		______________
		______________
	______________	______________
		______________
		______________

Topic Sentence: ______________________

____

EXERCISE 8-3 Categories and Examples Working Together

Directions: *Good examples persuade the reader that a category is accurate. Also, examples help a reader understand why classification is a helpful way of thinking about a subject. To explore further the relationship of categories and examples, provide one example to explain how each category below relates to the general topic and supports the topic sentence.* Answers will vary.

EXAMPLE

Topic: Fashion fad

Topic Sentence: Fads often emphasize an antisocial or subversive effect of fashion.

Category A: Tattoos and piercings Tattoos and piercings have shock value. For example, pierced eyebrows and nostrils are visible and shocking. It is impossible to look at a person and not see a pierced eyebrow or nostril. When the piercings are recent, they look red, angry, and painful.

Category B: Low-cut tanks and shirts Low-cut tanks and shirts also have shock value. For example, it is common to see young women showing both belly and cleavage. It is brash. It says, I'll uncover myself if I want to. When these articles of clothing are combined with jeans worn low on the hips, maximum exposure is the result.

1. **Topic:** Part-time jobs

Topic Sentence: A part-time job can be categorized in two ways: mindless and for-the-money-only or an opportunity to learn something directly connected to your career goal.

Category A: A mindless part-time job for money only ______________

____

____

Category B: A part-time job that provides a chance to learn something

____

____

2. **Topic:** Extracurricular activities

Topic Sentence: Some extracurricular activities are strictly related to socializing and having fun, whereas others are related to classroom learning and skill development.

Category A: Activities that are strictly related to socializing and having fun

____

____

Category B: Activities related to classroom learning and skill development

___

___

3. **Topic:** Stress

Topic Sentence: Stress comes in various forms—for instance, family-related stress and work-related stress.

Category A: Family-related stress ___

___

___

Category B: Work-related stress ___

___

___

Avoid Stereotyping

Stereotyping occurs when you categorize someone or something using oversimplified and possibly biased criteria. Often, good classification thinking occurs in response to a stereotype. You realize, "Not all female bosses are pushy." "Not all men are chauvinist pigs."

Because individuals vary, stereotypes always distort the truth. Consequently, when you are considering a group, you need to develop broad categories that will include the range of different types of individuals in that group. Once you have established categories, you can think more critically, classifying the individuals that fall within your categories. For example, you might analyze female bosses as follows:

Female bosses bring a variety of personal characteristics to the workplace.

1. Some are hard-driving like male bosses.
2. Others quietly delegate work.
3. Others are good at bringing people together and building consensus.

Classifying like this enables you to avoid stereotyping. The spacious categories provide room for individual differences, and you avoid the appearance of saying all individuals are alike. In your analysis, you do not oversimplify and distort the truth.

CLASSIFICATION IN PROCESS

Good classification writing is an invitation to think critically about your subject. When you think carefully, you typically revise and refine your ideas. For that reason, like all writing, classification writing benefits from using the writing process: prewriting, drafting, revising, and editing.

Select an Assignment

In this section, you will write a single paragraph that uses classification to define categories. You will also provide specific examples to explain those categories.

EXERCISE 8-4 Selecting an Assignment for a Classification Paragraph

Directions: *Select a topic from the list below. Choose the one you know the most about and think is best suited to an effective classification paragraph.*

1. For most people, free time is a valuable commodity. Briefly discuss different ways to make valuable use of free time.
2. Not all parents are the same. Describe different approaches to parenting.
3. Educators talk about different kinds of learning styles. What are some different kinds of teaching styles you have observed this semester or in past classes?
4. A good budget is essential to effective money management. What types of expenses should a person keep track of to be an effective money manager?
5. Careless eating habits contribute to a rapidly expanding waistline. What types of eating should a weight-conscious person be on the lookout for?
6. Talents
7. Entertainment
8. Historical events
9. Illnesses
10. A topic from your other courses

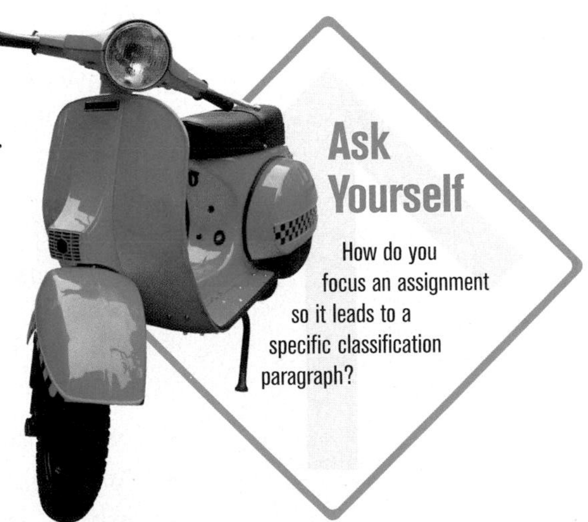

Ask Yourself
How do you focus an assignment so it leads to a specific classification paragraph?

Prewrite: Write Before You Write

PREWRITING
- Talk
- Cluster
- Brainstorm
- Freewrite

When writing a classification paragraph, you begin by thinking about your purpose and the basis for classifying your topic. Once you know how you will classify your topic, you can generate useful categories and examples through focused exploration. For classification, try brainstorming and clustering as methods of exploring your subject.

Brainstorm

Brainstorming helps you get a quick look at what you know. This means getting some words and ideas on paper. When you put your thoughts in writing, you can see more clearly how the pieces fit together and what to do next.

EXERCISE 8-5 **Brainstorming**

Directions: *Brainstorm on your topic to come up with several different ways you could break it into categories. Choose the most useful way to classify information about your topic and use it to brainstorm a list of at least three categories you could use in your paragraph.*

Cluster

Classification depends on purpose, a basis for classification, categories, and examples. Use clustering to explore various elements of classification.

EXERCISE 8-6 **Clustering**

Directions: *Cluster for ten minutes on the categories you identified in Exercise 8-5 to come up with examples that illustrate or explain them.*

Draft: Focus and Organize

DRAFT
- Consider your audience
- Formulate your topic sentence
- Outline for unity and coherence
- Write a conclusion sentence
- Compose your first draft

In classification writing, focus is essential. You want to be sure your categories are useful and serve your purpose for classifying the topic in the way you have. You also must ensure that your examples fit the categories and are not stereotypes. So as you draft, you focus and organize your prewriting to double-check your thinking.

Consider Your Audience

Read the assignment again. Think about your audience. Your classification system should provide your reader with a useful way of looking at your topic. Here are some questions to keep in mind as you consider your audience:

- Why is this topic important?
- What do I want my reader to understand about my topic?
- Why is classification helpful in a discussion of this topic?

EXERCISE 8-7 **Considering Your Audience**

Directions: *Talk with a classmate about your topic. Use the questions on page 166 to think critically about the key terms and specific details to include as you explain your classification to an audience. Take notes on this conversation and add new* *ideas and details to your prewriting. Talk to a different classmate to gain another perspective and clarify your thinking.*

PEER CONVERSATION

Topic Sentence

The topic sentence of a classification paragraph links the topic and the categories you will explore.

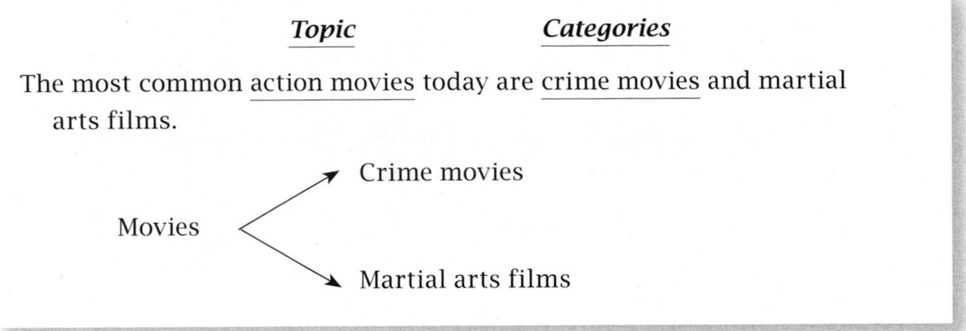

Topic
Categories
The most common action movies today are crime movies and martial arts films.
Crime movies
Movies
Martial arts films

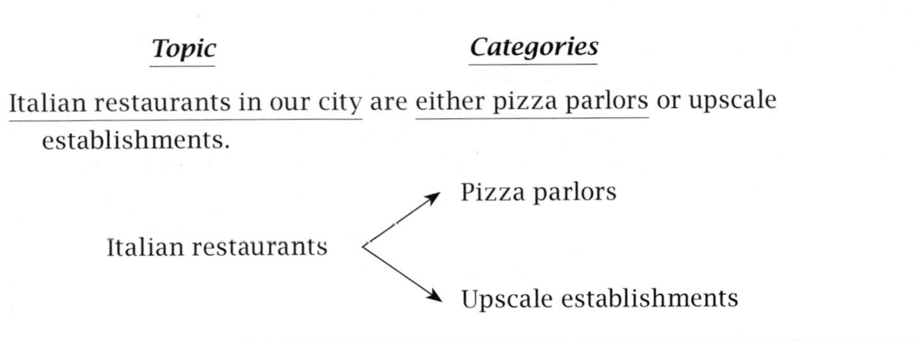

Effective topic sentences in classification paragraphs use parallelism. **Parallelism** means the terms describing the categories are related in meaning and are the same parts of speech, usually nouns, verbs, or adjectives. In the examples above, the categories are expressed with parallel nouns, *movies* and *films, parlors* and *establishments*. In addition, each noun is preceded by an adjective, *crime* flicks and *martial arts* films, *pizza* parlors and *upscale* establishments.

Unity and Coherence

Before you draft, outline your paragraph and check your details. To plan a unified paragraph, make sure everything in your paragraph relates to your topic sentence. Choose transitions that make the relationship between your examples visible to a reader. Transitions also emphasize examples.

TRANSITIONS TO EXPRESS CONTRAST

yet	on the contrary
in contrast	however
nevertheless	notwithstanding
though	nonetheless
on the other hand	otherwise
after all	at the same time

TRANSITIONS FOR EXAMPLES	
for example	furthermore
moreover	too
also	in the second place
again	in addition
even	more
next	further
last	lastly
finally	besides
first	secondly

Concluding Sentence

A concluding sentence states the importance of your categories or underscores the point your paragraph makes about your subject.

EXERCISE 8-8 Planning Your First Draft

See "Supporting Details" in Chapter 3 for detailed explanation of outlining.

Directions: *On a separate sheet of paper, write a clear topic sentence that states the main idea and the purpose of your classification paragraph. Following your topic sentence, list the categories and examples you will use to develop your paragraph. Make a short outline to organize the paragraph. Write a concluding sentence that restates your main idea.*

Write a First Draft

Review all of your prewriting and check your outline. Then write a first draft of your paragraph. It is a good idea to refine sentences and rethink organization and details. As you write, keep emphasis in mind. As you develop your ideas and explain categories and examples, try to use a similar amount of detail

MULTILINGUAL TIP

Bring your draft to the writing center on your campus.

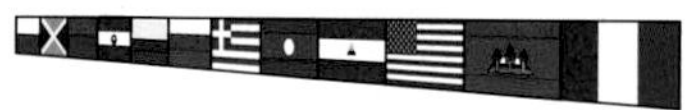

EXERCISE 8-9 Writing Your First Draft

Directions: *Write a first draft of your paragraph. It is better to write too much than too little. You can always cut back later. Make sure your paragraph has sufficient detail, explanation, and appropriate transitions so that a reader will understand how the examples fit with the categories you establish. Use the following checklist as a guide.*

FIRST DRAFT CHECKLIST

_____ My topic sentence states the topic and categories to be described in my paragraph.

_____ My topic sentence echoes key terms in the assignment.

_____ I inserted transitions to make the categories easily recognizable.

_____ I included relevant examples and supporting details to explain the categories.

_____ My concluding sentence makes a comment on my topic.

A PROFESSIONAL'S TAKE

Here is Karen Kline's use of classification, from a short article in *BusinessWeek:*

There is a link between birth order and personality type, as examples of successful business people show. For instance, first-born entrepreneurs tend to be more extroverted and confident than their younger siblings. In a business where somebody needs to maintain a high PR profile, you could imagine that it might be easier if you're naturally extroverted and confident, especially if you'll be called on to talk to the media as the public face of your company. First-borns also tend to be more assertive and authoritarian, dominant and inflexible. They're good at executing a plan, following it, and driving others to follow it in a disciplined way. Conformist, task-oriented, disciplined, and concerned with getting things done right—all these traits are naturally found in first-borns. All those sound like leadership qualities that would be helpful for business owners. What about the downside of first-borns? They tend to be concerned about and fearful of losing their position or rank. So, they might find it threatening to bring on partners, or get defensive about admitting their own errors. Then again, second-borns have a lot of the classic entrepreneur personality traits: They're creative, risk-taking, flexible, and more likely to embrace new paradigms than first-borns are. They're also more relationship-focused, more concerned about fairness and justice, less academic and more interested in the international scene than their older siblings. They may drop out of college, like Bill Gates did, who is a second-born. Does that mean second-borns are more likely to start their own businesses, given the risks involved? Perhaps. But sometimes they're the ones who start a company, and then hire some disciplined, authoritarian first-borns to come in and turn their creative ideas into a reality. Second-borns, who often have a highly empathic nature, are often found in the service businesses, where relationships are crucial.

EXERCISE 8-10 A PROFESSIONAL'S TAKE

Directions: *Using the first draft checklist as your guide, identify the elements of an effective classification paragraph.*

Revise: Read Critically, Then Rewrite

REVISE
- Read critically
- Develop a revision plan

Few writers get things perfect in one draft. Now that you have a first draft, you need to do the additional work of reading it critically and revising. Go back to your draft and ask yourself, Is my purpose clear? Do my categories make sense? Do the examples I have included adequately explain my categories? Revision gives you a chance to rethink, to add and cut content, and to get closer to your intended meaning.

Revision in Action

The full version of Denny's sample is available online.

Revision is rethinking a draft. You read critically, plan your revision, and revise the writing. Quality revision will also improve your future writing. Here is an example of revision by a student named Denny.

Assignment: Every summer, thousands of Americans flock to amusement parks. Write a paragraph about the different types of people who go to amusement parks.

TOPIC SENTENCE
Denny lists three types of people who go to amusement parks.

SUPPORTING DETAILS
He describes the categories of park-goers and provides specific details to illustrate the ways they have a good time.

ORDER AND TRANSITIONS
His transitions list the types: "to begin," "second category," "final category." He adds the word "category" to connect the examples to the assignment.

Denny's First Draft

Every summer the usual maniacs, family fun seekers, and shade seekers crowd into America's amusement parks, hoping to find a good time. **To begin with,** we have the maniacs. These are usually young people in t-shirts, shorts, and flipflops, screaming at their friends at the top of their lungs. The maniacs go on the highest roller coaster as many times as possible. **Along with** the roller-coaster maniacs, we have the game idiots who throw hoops at Coke bottles and darts at balloons, hoping to win a stuffed animal the size of a phone booth. These maniacs and idiots are joined by the junk food fools who stuff their faces with hot dogs, corn dogs, and Ding Dongs, eating until they puke all over their feet. Now that is what I call fun. **A second category** of fun seeker is the average American family. We're talking little kids on rides that move at walking speed. Kids love animals. They love amusement parks. They tire their parents out, but hey, weren't the parents little kids once too? Oh, and do not forget those cameras. The family fun seekers take pictures all day long. **A final category** is the shade seekers. These are usually grandparents who have escaped from the rest of the family. They want shade, they want quiet. Good luck! Sometimes these grandparents have little kids sleeping on blankets in the shade. It is kinda cute. Also in the shade, you just might find one of the junk food fools cleaning you know what off his feet. It takes all kinds. Amusement parks are for the slightly crazy and those, like those grandparents, with little or no choice in the matter.

Revision Plan: Create an academic tone by eliminating informal language and minimize use of "I" and "you." Make the transitions similar. Cut extra details that are interesting but not essential to the description of the three categories of park-goers.

Denny edits word choice in this draft and uses third person. This makes the paragraph more appropriate for an academic audience.

Denny's Revised Draft

Every summer the usual maniacs, family fun seekers, and shade seekers crowd into America's amusement parks. The maniacs, **the largest category of park-goers,** are usually young people in t-shirts, shorts, and flip-flops. They race from one roller coaster to another and scream wildly as they ride the highest roller coaster as many times as possible. They never get tired. **In addition to** the roller-coaster maniacs, there are the game maniacs, who play games all day. They throw hoops at Coke bottles and darts at balloons, hoping to win that special stuffed animal. Then there are the **families, the second category:** moms and dads with little children on rides that move at walking speed. **Occasionally** the dads (or moms) slip away to go on a real ride. **Generally,** the family fun seekers take pictures, eat corn dogs and cotton candy, and buy identical t-shirts as souvenirs. **The quietest category** is made up of shade seekers. These are usually grandparents who have escaped from the rest of the family. They want peace and quiet. **Sometimes** the shade seekers sleep next to little children on blankets in the shade. Amusement parks try to offer something for everyone; as long as they do not run out of roller coasters, games, corn dogs, kiddy rides, and shade, people will probably be happy.

TOPIC SENTENCE
Denny shortens his topic sentence to focus on the categories of park-goers.

SUPPORTING DETAILS
He cuts one example from the maniacs category and adds details to the average American family and shade seeker categories.

ORDER AND TRANSITIONS
Denny's decision to cut and focus impacts his transitions. He uses three parallel transitions that name each category. He also uses transitions to connect the details in each category.

CONCLUDING SENTENCE
Denny comments and lists the things that draw people to amusement parks.

DISCUSSION QUESTIONS Which changes in the revision most improved Denny's paragraph? Why?

PEER CONVERSATION

Read Critically

When you read a peer's paper, you can get insights into your own writing. Beginning with the topic sentence, read with classification in mind. Notice if the writer uses sufficient examples and details to explain the categories. Pay attention to how other writers do what you are trying to do.

PEER CONVERSATION

EXERCISE 8-11 **Reading Peer Papers**

Directions: *Exchange papers with another student. Consider the significant changes that Denny made between his first draft and his revision. Be a critical reader and make suggestions to improve and clarify your peer's first draft. Make notes in the margin as you read to remember your suggestions. After you read, you will discuss your suggestions. Use the following guidelines.*

Revise with a Plan

Before you revise your paragraph, reread your assignment. Be sure that you provide a detailed response to the assignment. Remember that most college writing should be written in the third person. As you revise, remember to prepare your writing for an academic audience.

EXERCISE 8-12 **Revising Your Draft**

Directions: *Develop a revision plan and revise the first draft for the paragraph you wrote for Exercise 8-9.*

Edit

EDIT
- Search and correct
- Self-edit

The ideas in your work count. The content matters. Classification paragraphs often use specific types of punctuation: colons and semicolons. Check out how to use them correctly in Chapter 25, page 513. Also, focus your editing using this personalized checklist.

MULTILINGUAL TIP
Proofread for verb tense.

YOUR EDITING CHECKLIST

_____ Spelling: List any words you misspelled in your last paper:

____

_____ Punctuation: List two punctuation errors from your last paper:

____

_____ Capitalization: List any capitalization errors from your last paper:

____

_____ Other errors: List any errors your instructor has pointed out in graded work:

____

To Prepare Your Draft for an Academic Audience

_____ Minimize first-person pronouns: *I, me, my.*

_____ Minimize second-person pronouns: *you, your.*

_____ Use third-person pronouns: *he, she, it, they.*

EXERCISE 8-13 **Revising and Editing Practice**

Directions: *Read the following paragraph that was written in response to the assignment; it contains errors that require revising and editing. Then answer the questions that follow.*

Assignment: Examine a current trend. Identify the types of people that engage in this trend. Use specific examples to explain the categories.

(1) Cosmetic procedures can be classified as beauty maintenance, age reduction, or obsessive reconstruction. (2) Cosmetic surgery is not just for the rich and famous. (3) Every day across the nation, cosmetic surgeons performed procedures that range from simple injections to major reconstruction. (4) Beauty maintenance is accomplished in the office on a lunch-hour. (5) Botox is the most popular procedure. (6) ____________________. (7) Injection's of Botox are quick, fairly inexpensive, and instantly improve appearance. (8) Age reduction generally requires reconstructive surgery and a hospital stay which include tummy tucks, liposuction, eyelid surgery, and partial or full face-lifts are the most common and they can remove ten, twenty, or thirty years. (9) Unfortunately, cosmetic surgery becomes a crazed obsession for a few individuals. (10) They completely reconstruct their faces. (11) And mold their bodies with repeated surgeries. (12) At the appearance of the smallest wrinkle, they panic and schedule another surgery. (13) Michael Jackson is a perfect example of the obsessive use of cosmetic surgery. (14) ____________________.

apostrophe error

Revising

__a__ 1. The topic sentence does not have to be the first sentence in a paragraph. Identify the topic sentence. Then select the best order for sentences 1, 2, and 3 to establish the topic and clarify the purpose of the paragraph. If the order is correct, choose "no change is necessary."

a. 2, 3, 1

b. 3, 1, 2

c. 3, 2, 1

d. no change is necessary

__c__ 2. Which sentence should be inserted into blank 6? The sentence would provide the best specific details to support the topic sentence.

a. Botox reduces or removes frown lines for people eighteen to sixty-five.

b. Surgeons treat medical procedures like spa services.

c. However, laser hair removal, chemical peels, and microdermabrasion top the list as well.

d. Compared to a facelift, Botox is a walk in the park!

__c__ 3. Which sentence should be cut to improve the focus of the paragraph? If nothing should be cut, choose "no change is necessary."

a. sentence 2

b. sentence 12

c. sentence 13

d. no change is necessary

__b__ 4. Which sentence should be inserted into blank 14? The sentence would provide a concluding sentence that restates the topic and makes a comment.

a. These days, anyone can be young and beautiful for a price.

b. Beauty is big business, and there is a cosmetic surgeon willing to serve any category of patient.

c. In my opinion, any cosmetic surgery is a waste of money.

d. In conclusion, cosmetic surgeons perform procedures on men and women every day.

Editing

__a__ 1. Choose the option that corrects the error in sentence 3. If no error exists, choose "no change is necessary."

a. Every day across the nation, cosmetic surgeons perform procedures that range from simple injections to major reconstruction.

b. Every day across the nation, cosmetic surgeons performed a procedure that range from simple injections to major reconstruction.

c. Every day across the nation, cosmetic surgeons have performed procedures that range from simple injections to major reconstruction.

d. no change is necessary

__c__ 2. Choose the option that corrects the error in sentence 8. If no error exists, choose "no change is necessary."

a. Age reduction generally requiring reconstructive surgery and a hospital stay. Tummy tucks, liposuction, eyelid surgery, and partial or full face-lifts are the most common and they can remove ten, twenty or thirty years.

b. Age reduction generally requiring reconstructive surgery and a hospital stay, which include tummy tucks, liposuction, eyelid surgery, and partial or full face-lifts, are the most common. They can remove ten, twenty or thirty years.

c. Age reduction, which includes tummy tucks, liposuction, eyelid surgery, and partial or full face-lifts, generally requires reconstructive surgery and a hospital stay. These surgeries can remove ten, twenty, or thirty years.

d. no change is necessary

Writer's
Response
Find two short sentences in your paragraph and combine them in two different ways.

__b__ 3. Choose the option that corrects the error in sentence 11. If no error exists, choose "no change is necessary."

a. delete sentence 11

b. combine sentence 10 with sentence 11

c. combine sentence 11 with sentence 12

d. no change is necessary

4. Proofread the paragraph for an apostrophe error and correct the error.

EXERCISE 8-14 Searching and Correcting

PEER CONVERSATION

Directions: *Exchange papers with a peer and proofread each other's work. In addition to spelling, punctuation, and capitalization, find out what other errors your classmate has on his or her checklist; tell your classmate what errors you have on your checklist.*

EXERCISE 8-15 Self-Editing

Directions: *Carefully rewrite your paper, correcting the errors you and your classmate found. Give yourself time to set aside the finished paper. Then come back to it and read your final draft one last time, using your checklist as a guide.*

Reflect

Take a moment and reflect on what you have learned.

EDIT
- Identify strengths
- Set goals

EXERCISE 8-16 Identifying Strengths

Directions: *Review your writing and your writing process. On a separate sheet of paper, write answers to these questions:*

- *What did you do well in the paragraph you wrote?*
- *What did you enjoy working on in this chapter?*
- *What have you learned that you will apply in future writing assignments?*

GOING PLACES

GETTING SOMEWHERE (AND KNOWING HOW YOU DID) WITH CAUSE AND EFFECT

Targeting Cause, Gauging Effect

1. The king died, and then the queen died.

2. The king died, and then the queen died of grief.

The difference between these two sentences involves only two words but a whole world of meaning. Every day, we exercise a basic component of critical thinking: asking ourselves why something happened. If you like what happened—let's say, you managed to talk a police officer out of giving you a speeding ticket—you might ask yourself how you can get it to happen again, by examining the chain of cause and effect that led up to the event. Where were you driving? Exactly how fast were you going? Why were you speeding? What did you say to the officer when you were stopped? On the other hand, if you do not like what happened—let's say you got the ticket and a hefty fine—you will need to follow the chain of events back far enough so that you can keep it from happening again.

BRAINSTORM

Identify an important event in your life. Brainstorm the causes and the effects of it. List as many as you can.

Making Your Case in Class

You will often find yourself arguing about cause and effect in papers and in classroom discussion. Remember that every statement you make about "what caused what" is, in fact, a claim, and implies an argument. What were the causes of the Civil War? Why do so few Americans vote? Why didn't the engine start? Why did the mixture of two chemicals form a noxious gas? Being able to argue convincingly for the cause (or combination of causes) you think most relevant will make the difference between persuading your audience and leaving them doubting your conclusions.

DISCUSSION

Turn and talk with a classmate about a college course in which you explained the causes or effects of an event. Did you deal primarily with causes or effects? How do you know?

Working It Out

Cause and effect analysis is a skill you need in virtually any job. You may assemble data on consumer buying patterns or changes in the way you market a product. In the medical field, you may note physical symptoms carefully, consider the patient's history, and perform the necessary tests before making a proper judgment as to causes of a condition. Going the extra mile in analyzing a situation can make the difference between success and failure in your chosen career.

RESUME BUILDER

Interviewers love to ask job applicants to talk about something they did that they are proud of. They also want to know what caused them to do it. What would your answer be in this situation?

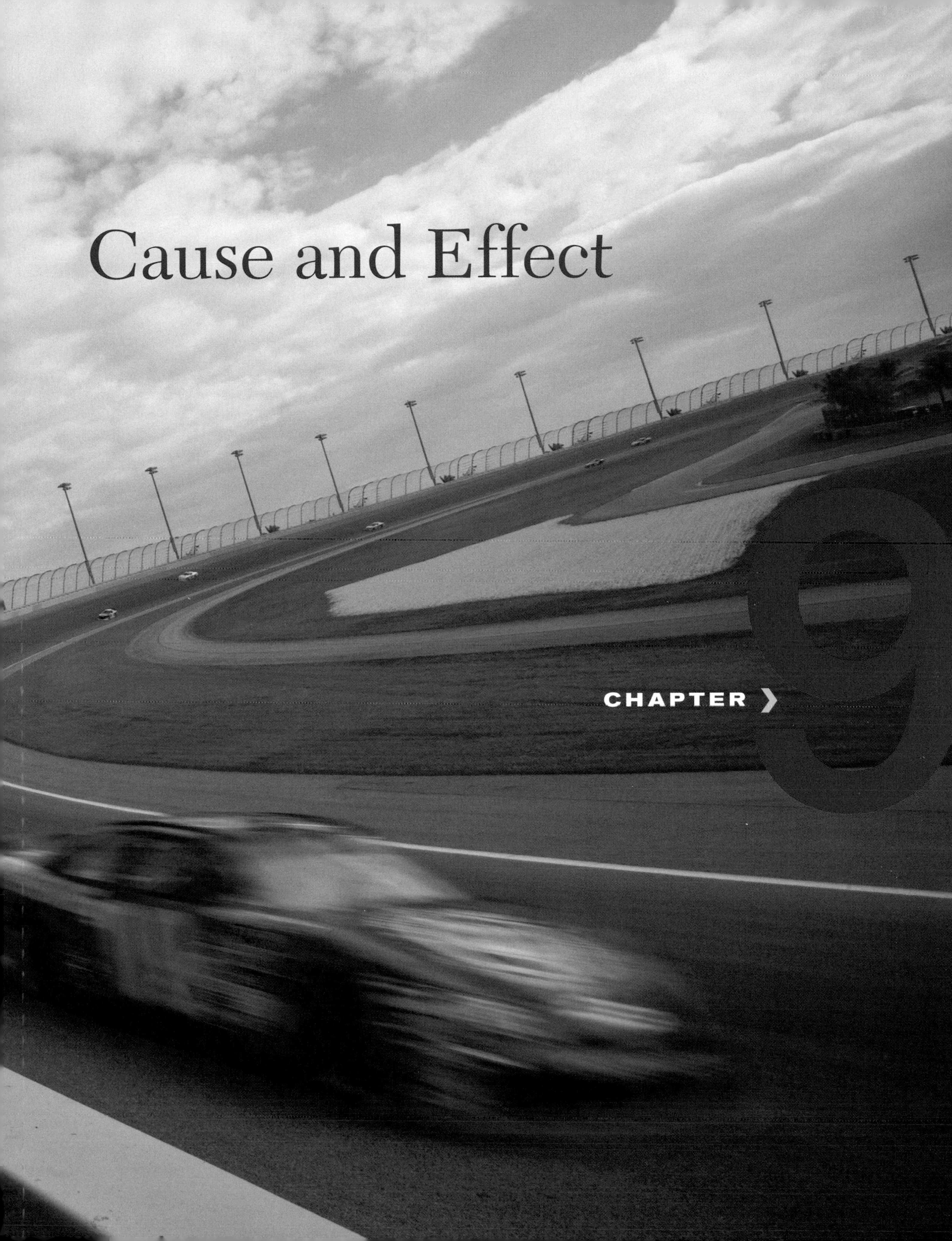

Cause and Effect

CHAPTER 9

CHAPTER OVERVIEW

- THE CAUSE AND EFFECT PARAGRAPH AT A GLANCE
- CAUSE AND EFFECT THINKING
  - Elements of Cause and Effect
  - Cause and Effect Details
  - Organize Your Thinking
- CAUSE AND EFFECT IN PROCESS
  - Prewrite
  - Draft
  - A Professional's Take
  - Revise
  - Edit
  - Reflect

THINK FIRST

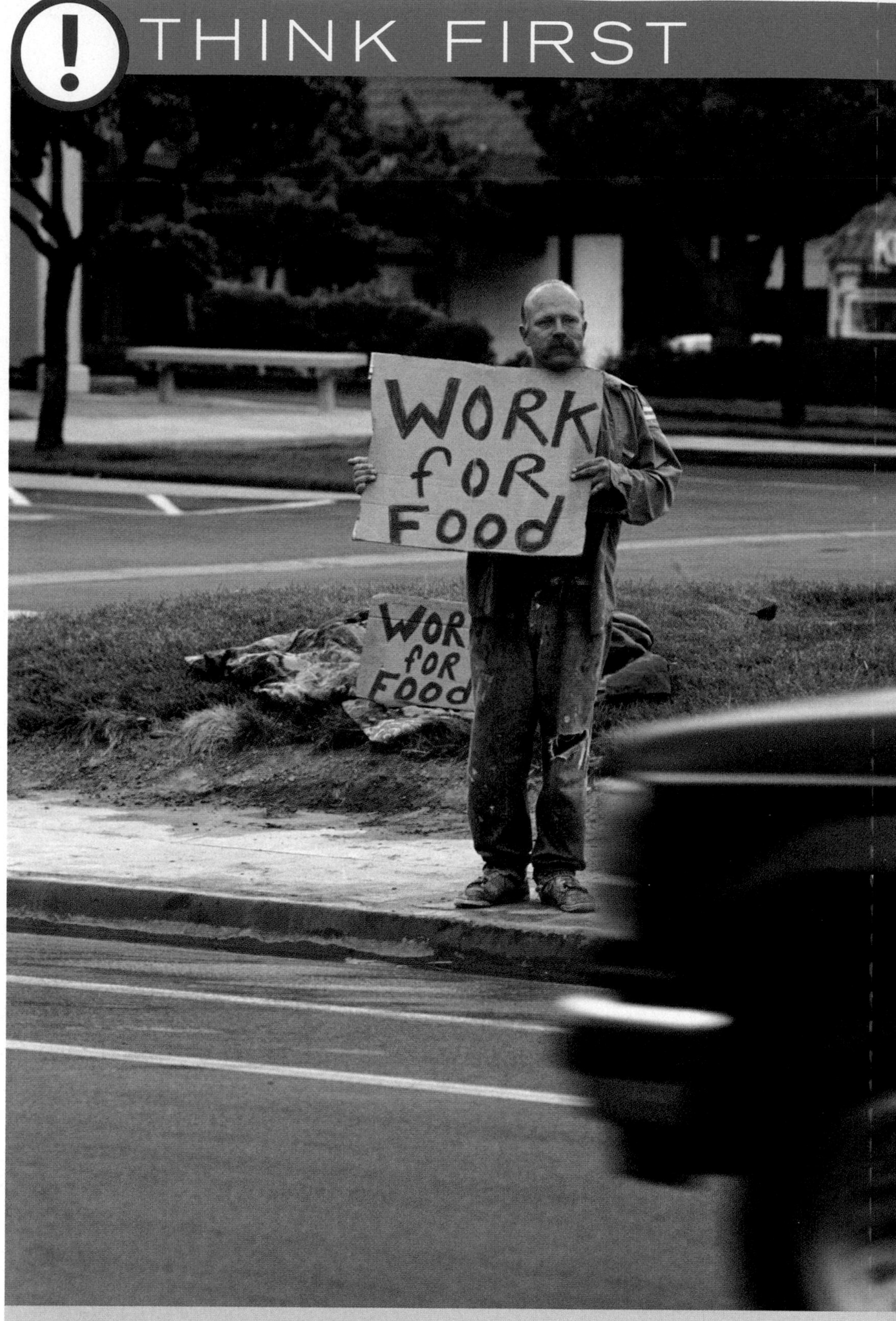

Poverty and homelessness are not simple problems. What are the causes and the effects? Write a paragraph in which you examine a cause or an effect of poverty or homelessness.

At a Glance

THE CAUSE AND EFFECT PARAGRAPH AT A GLANCE

In cause and effect analysis, students use evidence to explain how or why something happened (causes) or the consequences (effects) of certain actions or events. For example, when asked to analyze the causes of a traffic accident, your knowledge about other accidents will help you identify the probable causes. You also might want to examine the facts, make diagrams of the accident scene, interview witnesses, and review the effects of the accident in order to determine the actual cause or causes.

In a cause and effect paragraph, the topic sentence frequently states the problem or situation and the focus of the paragraph. The supporting details provide examples, facts, or reasons to illustrate and explain the point made by the topic sentence. The concluding sentence makes a comment on the issue or emphasizes a key cause or effect related to it.

There are three typical paragraph structures: one cause and one effect, multiple causes and one effect, and one cause followed by multiple effects.

The Cause and Effect Paragraph at a Glance

One Cause, One Effect

ASSIGNMENT Examine the cause and effect of an environmental factor on learning.

Studies show that lead paint can reduce a young child's ability to learn. (1) **Even though** laws were passed in 1999 to ban lead use, lead poisoning is a major threat to young children. Lead paint is the primary cause of lead poisoning in young children. For example, the paint used in low-income housing and older school buildings contains potentially dangerous levels of lead. (2) **Studies show** children living in housing that is old and deteriorating are most susceptible to lead poisoning. Children from birth to age five are the most at risk for learning difficulties. (3) **Studies link** lead poisoning to reading difficulties and problems with attention. These problems have a singular effect: young children exposed to lead paint may sustain serious damage that affects their ability to learn.

TOPIC SENTENCE
The writer uses a key word from the assignment—"learn"—and states a specific environmental factor—"lead paint."

SUPPORTING DETAILS
The writer uses details about laws and studies to support his point.

ORDER AND TRANSITIONS
The writer's first transition ("Even though") suggests changes in laws have not corrected this problem. Then he uses two parallel transitions ("Studies show" and "Studies link") to repeat key words from the topic sentence.

CONCLUDING SENTENCE
The writer restates the topic sentence.

One Cause, Multiple Effects

ASSIGNMENT Write a cause and effect paragraph to illustrate the following quote: "If you think you can do a thing or think you can't do a thing, you're right"—Henry Ford.

TOPIC SENTENCE
The student cites the quotation from the assignment.

SUPPORTING DETAILS
The details all relate to a single individual: multiple effects of can-do thinking in the life of a father.

ORDER AND TRANSITIONS
The student's repeated use of "think" makes connections between details in the paragraph. The term "also" contributes to the coherence of the paragraph as well.

CONCLUDING SENTENCE
The student makes a connection with the assignment and reiterates that his father confirms the truth of Henry Ford's belief.

Henry Ford said, "If you think you can do a thing or think you can't do a thing, you're right." This statement, in my experience, is very true. My father is a good example. He **thinks** he can do something, and he is right. He proposed greatly expanding operations in his work. When he met with the district manager of the company he worked for, the manager asked: "Can you do this?" My father answered, "I **think** I can." The manager pressed him. "I don't want to know if you **think** you can. I want to know if you can do it." "I can do it," my father said, and he did it. He **also** thought he could tear the kitchen out of our house and install a brand-new one. He planned, he studied, and he drew diagrams. Then he ordered a custom-designed kitchen. When it was delivered to the house, he and I had already done the demolition of the old one. In a weekend, he installed the new kitchen, floor to ceiling. I thought he was crazy to attempt it, but he thought he could do it, and he was right. His can-do attitude causes him to attempt all sorts of things he might not do if he did not **think** he could. In my father's case, Henry Ford was definitely right.

Multiple Causes, One Effect

ASSIGNMENT Examine the causes or effects of sibling rivalry.

TOPIC SENTENCE
The writer focuses the topic sentence on one effect (sibling rivalry) and three causes.

SUPPORTING DETAILS
The writer explains three causes of sibling rivalry: position in the family, gender, and favoritism.

ORDER AND TRANSITIONS
The writer lists the three causes. The transitions identify each cause.

CONCLUDING SENTENCE
The writer comments on sibling rivalry.

Birth order, gender, and family dynamics can cause sibling rivalry. (1) **An unavoidable cause** of sibling fights is position in the family. For example, the oldest child is inevitably given more responsibility or freedom. Younger sisters or brothers may feel jealous, and a fight will break out, but no one is the winner in this fight. (2) **Another predictable cause** of sibling rivalry is gender. Parents may not notice that they expect boys to do outdoor chores and girls to do house cleaning. They may not see that their attitudes create stereotypical roles and problems between the siblings. (3) **Yet another common cause** of sibling rivalry is parents playing favorites. Parents may not even realize they treat the child that does his homework without whining in a special way. Consequently, parent favoritism causes tension and fights between the siblings. To a certain extent, sibling rivalry is probably an inevitable and normal condition in families with more than one child.

DISCUSSION QUESTIONS

PEER CONVERSATION

1. These three paragraphs illustrate cause and effect thinking. What situations, problems, or issues in your life came to mind when you were reading them?
2. Discuss an issue you recall with a classmate. Is it an example of one cause and one effect, one cause and multiple effects, or multiple causes and one effect?

Thinking

CAUSE AND EFFECT THINKING

Cause and effect analysis begins with a situation or problem. Your car will not start. Your coworker gets a raise that you expected to get. You are not working up to your potential in school. The doctor tells your mother that her cholesterol is too high. These situations have causes. They also have effects that are the result of the causes. In addition these effects can have consequences.

The complex relationship of causes and effects can be pictured in this diagram. The pollution in a nearby lake has specific causes; further, there are consequences of the effects of the pollution.

Causes	Effect	Consequences
1. Septic tanks are overflowing into the ground water. 2. Fertilizer run-off from farm fields is also getting into area streams. 3. Untreated waste water from a chemical plant is spilling into the lake.	A polluted lake	1. Fish are dying. 2. Swimming is hazardous.

Elements of Cause and Effect

To get started, consider these elements of cause and effect thinking.

- ***Problem or situation:*** The topic sentence states the problem, situation, or event and establishes the focus of the paragraph. The paragraph usually focuses on either cause or effect.

- *Causes:* Causes are the reasons, circumstances, or conditions that bring about a problem or situation. Supporting details for a paragraph focusing on causes examine and explain these reasons, circumstances, or conditions. For example, lead paint causes learning problems in children. How does this happen? Supporting details elaborate on the cause.
- *Effects:* Effects are the outcomes or consequences of a problem or situation. Supporting details for a paragraph focusing on effects examine and explain these outcomes or consequences. Sibling rivalry, for example, is the effect or result of various family dynamics.

Get Started

Time is an important aspect of cause and effect thinking. Causes occur prior to a situation or problem; effects occur afterward. In the illustration shown here, a student uses a graphic organizer to analyze her situation in a math class.

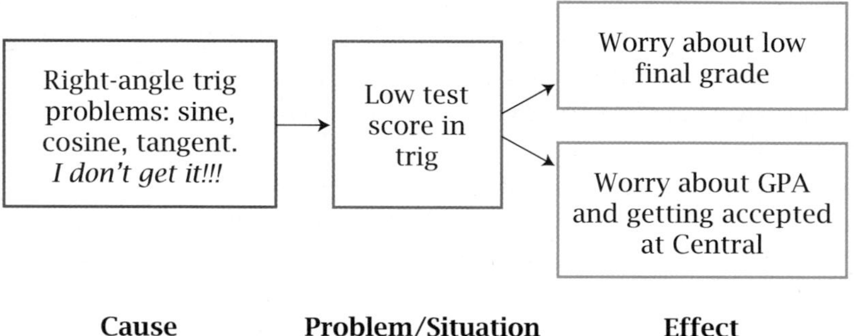

The diagram provides a snapshot of a problem she faces. The immediate situation is a low test score. She has diagnosed the cause of the problem: She is having trouble with right-angle trig problems in the class. She has also identified two effects of the problem: that her final grade in the class may suffer because of the low test score and, as a result of a lower GPA, she might not get accepted into the college of her choice.

Cause and effect analysis like this invites critical thinking. In her next move, the student can make a decision to examine either the cause or the effects of the problem in more detail. The decision she makes focuses her thinking further and determines the content of her paragraph.

> **Topic Sentence:** Because of my low grade on the most recent math test, my final grade in the course could be a *C*, and that may affect my application to Central.

EXERCISE 9-1 **Getting Started**

Directions: *On a separate sheet of paper, use a graphic organizer to analyze two of the following situations. (Use the student sample above as a model.) Indicate* *multiple causes and multiple effects as needed. Beneath the graphic organizer, write a topic sentence indicating your decision to focus on the cause(s) or effect(s).*

- *Satisfaction (or dissatisfaction) with your current job*
- *Progress (or lack of progress) toward your career goal*
- *Success (or difficulty) you are currently having in a course*

Cause and Effect Details

For the sake of unity and focus, it is usually best to focus on either causes or effects. Being clear about your focus helps you think systematically about the situation or problem you have chosen as your topic. In order to identify relevant details, you need to carefully analyze the problem.

In this diagram, the student having trouble in her math class focuses on the reasons, circumstances, and conditions that brought about her low test score.

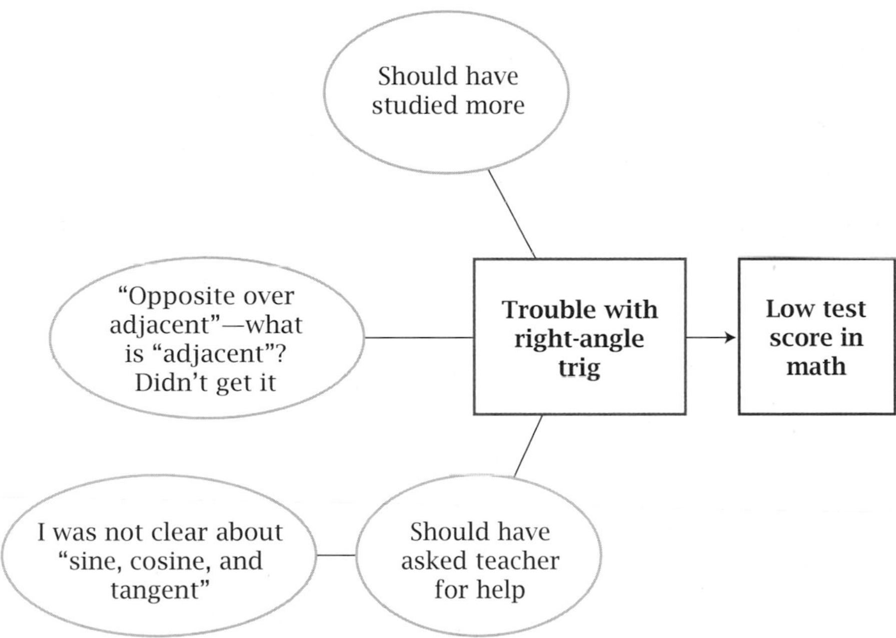

Details elaborating on the cause ⟶ the problem

These details are in the past tense. They focus on circumstances and conditions that preceded the student's poor performance on her math test. The analysis is valuable to the student because she can now address the causes and possibly rectify the problem.

Suppose this student decided to focus on effects. In that case, she would elaborate on the consequences of the problem.

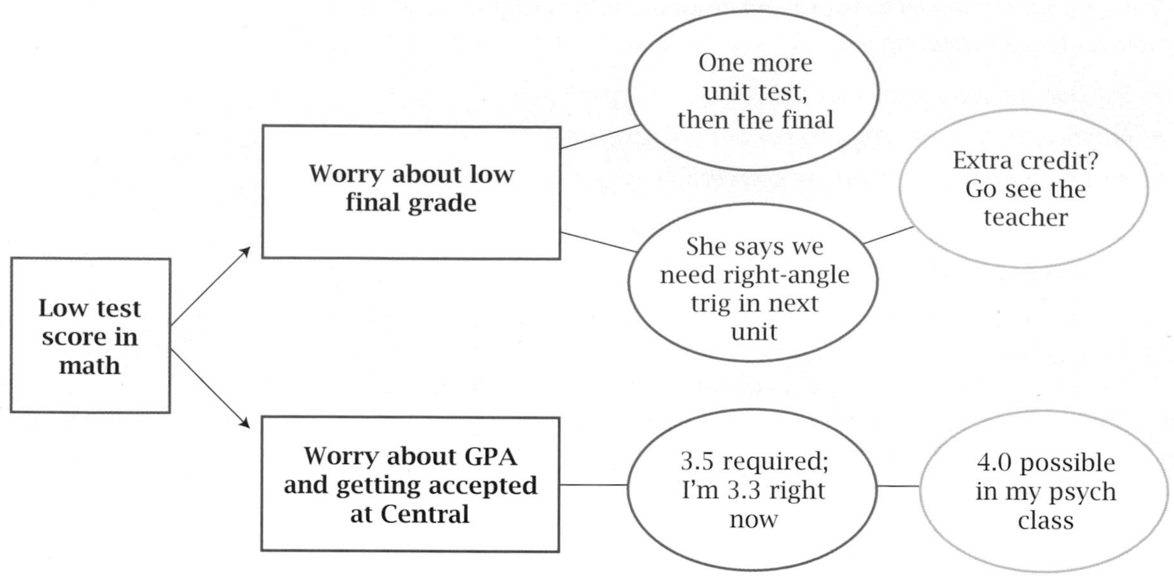

Talk about It
When faced with a challenge, do you focus more on the past and the causes or the future and the effects?

When the student elaborates on effects, the emphasis is more on the future and what happens next.

After your initial reflection on your topic in cause and effect analysis, make a conscious decision to focus on either causes or effects.

EXERCISE 9-2 **Getting Focused on Causes or Effects**

Directions: *On a separate sheet of paper, use a graphic organizer to examine either causes or effects related to one of the following topics. Look for supporting details that explain the reasons, circumstances, or conditions that led up to the problem (causes) or that illustrate the outcomes and consequences (effects) resulting from it.*

- *Young people watching too much TV*
- *A recurring family argument*
- *A bad habit*

Organize Your Thinking

How you organize your cause and effect thinking may be influenced by either the importance of events or when they happened (time). All cause and effect details are not necessarily equal. Consequently, you may organize your thinking by proceeding from the least important to the most important detail. On the other hand, multiple causes or effects might not occur simultaneously, in which case it makes sense to organize them according to when they happened. In this illustration, the student uses order of importance to organize her details.

Low Test Score in Math

Cause

__3__ "Opposite over adjacent"—what does that mean?

__4__ Not clear about what sine, cosine, and tangent are

__2__ Should have asked instructor for help

__1__ Should have studied more

Notes: It makes sense to organize my details by order of importance. First of all, I should have studied more. I knew I was not "getting" the problems in right-angle trig, but I did not apply myself. Second, and even more important, in addition to studying, I should have gone to see the instructor right away. I knew what the problem areas were—I did not get "opposite over adjacent" or exactly what sine, cosine, and tangent are. How can I figure out answers to questions when I do not even know what the terms mean?

The student's notes reflect her thinking as she fits the pieces together in her analysis of the causes of her low grade. Here is the same student's analysis of the effects of receiving a low test grade. In this instance, she relies on chronological order.

Effects

__1__ Worry about low final grade

  __C__ One more unit test, then the final

  __B__ She says we need right-angle trig for next unit

  __A__ Go see instructor about extra credit

__2__ Worry about GPA and getting accepted at Central

  __A__ 3.5 required; I am 3.3 right now

Notes: It makes sense to order these details chronologically. The short-term consequence of doing poorly on the test is that I might get a low grade in the class. The long-term effect is that I might not get into Central. I need to go see the instructor. I do not understand right-angle trig. She said everything we do after this involves right-angle trig so I need to know that. If I ace the next unit test and do really well on the final, maybe I can 4 point the class and keep my GPA where I want it.

EXERCISE 9-3 Organizing Your Details

Directions: *The following topic has multiple possible causes and effects. In the spaces provided, indicate how you would organize these details. Write a short paragraph explaining whether you used order of importance or chronological order and the reasons for your choice.* **Answers will vary.**

Topic: Premarital sex

Causes

_____ Drug and/or alcohol use

_____ Peer pressure

_____ Influence of the media

_____ Lyrics in songs

_____ Content of TV shows and movies

_____ Emotional needs that are not being met in other relationships

_____ Relationships in the home

_____ Relationships with other members of the opposite sex

_____ Self-esteem issues

Form of Organization: ______________________________

____

____

Effects

_____ Pregnancy

_____ Mental health problems

_____ Depression

_____ Loss of concentration in school

_____ Lack of effort in friendships

_____ Promiscuity

_____ Lower grades

_____ Physical health problems

Form of Organization: ______________________________

____

____

Writer's Response

What are some causes and effects of premarital sex?

CAUSE AND EFFECT IN PROCESS

You analyze an idea, event, or problem with cause and effect writing. A focused, organized paragraph helps your reader understand the complexities of your topic. To make your points clear and simple, you need to provide detailed explanations of causes and effects.

Select an Assignment

When asked to write about causes and effects in college, you will often analyze ideas, events, or problems to determine a focus for your paragraph. This work may require research or outside reading.

EXERCISE 9-4 Selecting an Assignment for Cause and Effect Paragraph

Directions: *Choose the assignment you know the most about and think is best suited to an effective cause and effect paragraph.*

1. Explain the impact of science or technology on education, health, or daily life.
2. Describe a computer application you struggle to understand.
3. Provide a description of the performance of your sound system.
4. Explain the negative causes or effects of a historical event.
5. Relate the circumstances concerning a friend who does not pay you money he owes you.
6. Explain a tricky communication problem you have had with a teacher or a boss.
7. Give the details of conflicts with your parents.
8. Explain why a parent, spouse, or significant other does not trust you.
9. Provide the recipe for a dish that everyone raves about, or for one that does not taste right to you.
10. Relate the circumstances that are the basis of your problem with reading, math, or speaking in front of groups.

Prewrite: Write Before You Write

PREWRITE
- Talk
- Cluster
- Brainstorm
- Freewrite

To reduce your topic to manageable terms, allow yourself to explore your subject before you write. Careful analysis involves thinking and rethinking. You may find it most productive to cluster and talk to organize and focus your topic. You may also wish to freewrite to put examples, reasons, and facts down on paper so you know what you have to say about a subject.

Cluster

Clustering enables you to see how ideas and details connect and relate to one another. You can use clustering to think about the sequence of causes and effects in a particular situation.

EXERCISE 9-5 Clustering

Directions: *Cluster on your assignment for ten minutes. Use a separate sheet of paper. List as many causes and effects as you can. Remember to include examples, facts, and reasons that explain and illustrate the causes and effects.*

Talk

Talking enables you to explore your topic and clarify your thinking. Talk about your analysis of the problem or situation. Are you focused on causes or effects? Do you have specific ideas and details to support your thinking? When you combine talking with clustering, you take your thinking deeper. Capture your new thinking on paper after you finish talking.

EXERCISE 9-6 Talking about It

PEER CONVERSATION

Directions: *Turn to your neighbor in class or find another interested listener. Show this person your clustering work and talk about the causes or effects related to your topic. Be specific about important information. Include examples, facts, and reasons. Then be a critical listener to your neighbor's topic. Listen without interrupting. When the speaker finishes, ask questions or offer suggestions. Identify what was clear and what was not clear.*

Draft: Focus and Organize

DRAFT
- Consider your audience
- Formulate your topic sentence
- Outline for unity and coherence
- Write a conclusion sentence
- Compose your first draft

In cause and effect thinking, it is essential to be clear about your focus. Are you talking mainly about causes or effects? For example, a storm came through town and downed power lines. The cause is obvious and simple. What if you focused on the effects of the storm? As you prepare to write, be clear in your mind about your focus.

Consider Your Audience

Read the assignment again and think about who will read your paper. Your instructor is interested in analytical thinking. Use the following questions to consider how to focus your paragraph on causes or effects and how you will support your thinking for your audience.

- What does my reader expect of my paragraph?
- Is my paragraph about causes or effects?
- What do I want a reader to understand about my topic?

Then ask these questions:

- What supporting details do I have to develop my ideas?
- Why are these supporting details important? Do I need to explain any of them to my reader?

EXERCISE 9-7 **Considering Your Audience**

PEER CONVERSATION

Directions: *Use the questions above to think critically about your focus and the supporting details you will use to explain your analysis in your paragraph. Talk with a classmate to clarify your focus, examples, facts, and reasons. Take notes on this conversation and add them to your prewriting.*

Topic Sentence

Students often revise and refine their topic sentences as they work through the writing process. In cause and effect writing, your topic sentence controls the rest of the paragraph. Be sure you clearly state whether the paragraph will deal with causes or effects. Some paragraphs may require a second sentence that explains the topic or hooks a reader with an interesting fact.

Unity and Coherence

Is your paragraph primarily about causes or effects? To write a unified paragraph, it is important that you focus on one or the other and include relevant details. Transitions between details will make your paragraph coherent.

Cause and effect paragraphs are typically organized using transitions based on causes or effects. Writers use these transition terms so readers can easily shift their attention to the next cause or effect being discussed.

In some cases, however, you may want to use transitions based on importance or chronological order.

TRANSITIONS RELATED TO CAUSES AND EFFECTS

Causes

the first (second, third) cause	the first (second, third) reason
yet another factor	because
is caused by	results from

Effects

one important effect	a first (second, third) outcome
then	next
therefore	thus
so	however
consequently	as a result
hence	therefore

TRANSITIONS BASED ON IMPORTANCE OR CHRONOLOGICAL ORDER

To Show Importance

more important	equally important	better
worse	in particular	specifically
of course	certainly	in fact

To Show Chronological Order

to begin with	first of all	next
second	in addition	moreover
then	third	finally

Concluding Sentence

A concluding sentence comments on the idea, event, or problem after you have analyzed it. It states the causes or effects related to it. You may find this easier to do after you reread your first draft.

EXERCISE 9-8 Planning Your First Draft

Directions: *On a separate sheet of paper, write a topic sentence that echoes the key words from the assignment topic you selected and focuses your paragraph on causes or effects. Then organize and outline your paragraph and supporting details. Write a concluding sentence that comments on your cause and effect paragraph.*

See "Supporting Details" in Chapter 3 for detailed explanation of outlining.

Write a First Draft

Review your prewriting and check your outline. Then write a first draft of your paragraph. Writers often reconsider the order of what they have written and the transition terms they use; they add additional examples, facts, or reasons. Look for the details that seem most important for readers to notice so they can understand your purpose.

EXERCISE 9-9 Writing Your First Draft

Directions: *Write a draft of your paragraph. Use the following checklist as a guide.*

MULTILINGUAL TIP
Bring your draft to the writing center on your campus.

FIRST DRAFT CHECKLIST

_____ My topic sentence states the point of my paragraph.

_____ My topic sentence echoes key terms in the assignment.

_____ I have included details related to cause or effect in the paragraph.

_____ I have organized my discussion and used transitions to show the relationship between ideas and details.

_____ My concluding sentence summarizes the point of my cause and effect analysis.

A PROFESSIONAL'S TAKE

Here is Laurence Steinberg's use of cause and effect, from a short article in *Psychology Today:*

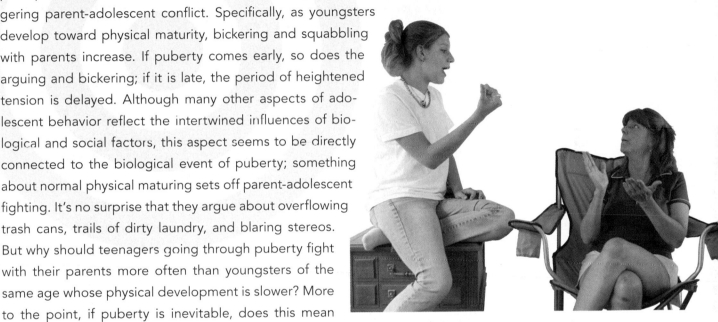

My own studies point to early adolescence—the years from ten to thirteen—as a period of special strain between parents and children. But more intriguing, perhaps, is that these studies reveal that puberty plays a central role in triggering parent-adolescent conflict. Specifically, as youngsters develop toward physical maturity, bickering and squabbling with parents increase. If puberty comes early, so does the arguing and bickering; if it is late, the period of heightened tension is delayed. Although many other aspects of adolescent behavior reflect the intertwined influences of biological and social factors, this aspect seems to be directly connected to the biological event of puberty; something about normal physical maturing sets off parent-adolescent fighting. It's no surprise that they argue about overflowing trash cans, trails of dirty laundry, and blaring stereos. But why should teenagers going through puberty fight with their parents more often than youngsters of the same age whose physical development is slower? More to the point, if puberty is inevitable, does this mean that parent-child conflict is, too?

EXERCISE 9-10 **A PROFESSIONAL'S TAKE**

Directions: *Using the first draft checklist as your guide, identify the elements of an effective cause and effect paragraph in the professional sample.*

Revise: Read Critically, Then Rewrite

Revision means rethinking. Ask yourself a few questions as you reread your first draft. Is your problem, situation, or event clearly stated? Is your focus on causes or effects? Are you explaining a combination of causes or the effects and impact on people or situations? Revision gives you a chance to read critically and then cut, reorder, or clarify.

REVISE
- Read critically
- Develop a revision plan

Revision in Action

Revision is rethinking a draft through a series of actions and decisions to improve the quality of your writing: Read critically, plan revision, and revise the writing. Here is an example of revision by a student named Roberto.

The full version of Roberto's sample is available online.

Assignment: Write a cause and effect paragraph that explains how people can get into debt.

Roberto's First Draft

TOPIC SENTENCE
Roberto focuses his paragraph on three problems.

SUPPORTING DETAILS
He provides details on each problem. His details explain how each problem causes unmanageable debt.

CONCLUDING SENTENCE
Roberto restates the topic sentence, including the key term "causes."

Three problems can cause unmanageable debt. Possibly, **the most difficult problem** to face is losing a job. This situation changes people's lifestyle. With a steady job and paycheck, people are sure they can make the mortgage, car, and living expenses. They might have a budget, but they always have extra money to spend. Life is easier when people have a steady job. Without a job they struggle to pay the bills, and they start paying for rent, groceries, and utilities with credit cards. This leads to growing debt. Sometimes this debt might even keep people from getting another job because an employer will see they have bad credit. **However, the most common problem** is spending habits. It is simple: People spend more money than they make. People spend money because they are bored or they are trying to keep up with friends who have more money. Credit cards make money easy to spend until people hit their limit and cannot pay their monthly bills. This problem leads to increasing debt. Debt like this can cause depression and then more spending until the debt is unmanageable. **Finally, another problem** is gambling. Gambling is a bad habit that leaves many people in extreme debt. Gamblers believe they will win the next time. So they spend their paychecks and then get cash advances in the hopes of winning back the lost paycheck. In the end, they lose everything. Although, they can pay off credit cards with minimum payments, they still owe money for years to come. Plus, gamblers must always fight the hope that they might win it all back. These are a few causes of unmanageable debt that should be avoided.

Revision Plan: Narrow my topic to credit card debt. Focus my paragraph so a reader can understand the causes of unmanageable credit card debt. Cut irrelevant details and insert specific, relevant details. Focus on causes and state the effect in the topic sentence.

Roberto's Revised Draft

Unmanageable credit card debt has three causes: overspending, misusing credit, and carrying debt on the card. Probably, the **most significant cause** is overspending. People can use plastic to buy anything they want, even if they do not have the money to pay for it. Credit card companies suggest that easy credit causes people to spend 12–18 percent more on purchases than they would if they paid cash. **However,** misusing credit causes as much debt as overspending. Many people use credit to pay for emergencies or special purchases. This debt can be paid off quickly. The trouble starts when people use credit to pay for basic needs like groceries, medical expenses, rent, or utilities. **The most damaging cause** is carrying credit card debt. With 14–18 percent interest on the unpaid balance, it can take years to pay off the balance. Plus, the interest will cost more than the original charge. These days credit cards make life easy, but they require self-control and money management skill; otherwise, major debt is a likely outcome.

TOPIC SENTENCE
Roberto uses key words from the assignment and clearly states the effect (unmanageable credit card debt) as well as the three causes he will explain in his paragraph.

SUPPORTING DETAILS
Roberto does not discuss effects in his revision. Roberto includes facts about credit card debt to explain the causes.

ORDER AND TRANSITIONS
Roberto uses transitions based on importance or priority. He begins with the most significant cause and ends with the most damaging cause.

CONCLUDING SENTENCE
He comments on the effects of credit cards.

DISCUSSION QUESTIONS Which changes did Roberto make in his revision that most radically improved his paragraph? Why?

PEER CONVERSATION

Read Critically

Critical reading is a search for the characteristics of effective writing: topic sentence, supporting details, transitions, concluding sentence. It is also a search for clarity of purpose.

EXERCISE 9-11 Reading Peer Papers

PEER CONVERSATION

Directions: *Exchange papers with another student. Consider the significant changes that Roberto made between his first draft and his revision. Be a critical reader and make suggestions to improve your peer's first draft. Also identify what your classmate did well. Make notes in the margin as you read to remember your suggestions. After you read, you will discuss your suggestions. Use the following guidelines.*

REVISION CHECKLIST

______ Does the topic sentence connect to the assignment and state the point of the paragraph?

______ Does the writer focus on causes or effects?

______ Does the writer provide enough detail to explain causes or effects?

______ Does the paragraph have effective transitions?

______ Does the concluding sentence emphasize the point of the paragraph?

Revise with a Plan

Reread your assignment before revising. Some assignments may require you to focus on causes, while others may require a focus on effects. Be sure your focus matches the assignment. In addition, simplify your paragraph. It is not too late to narrow your topic and cut irrelevant details.

Cause and effect paragraphs are complex. This can cause a writer to include more information than is necessary. Reread your paragraph and the notes from your peer conference. Where can you focus or cut? After you cut, where do you need to add relevant details?

EXERCISE 9-12 **Revising Your Draft**

Directions: *Develop a revision plan and revise the paragraph you wrote for Exercise 9-9.*

Edit

EDIT
- Search and correct
- Self-edit

The ideas in your work count. The content matters. Focus your editing using this personalized checklist.

MULTILINGUAL TIP
Proofread for transition phrases related to cause and effect.

YOUR EDITING CHECKLIST

_____ Spelling: List any words you misspelled in your last paper:

____

_____ Punctuation: List two punctuation errors from your last paper:

____

_____ Capitalization: List any capitalization errors from your last paper:

____

_____ Other errors: List any errors your instructor has pointed out in graded work:

____

____

To Prepare Your Draft for an Academic Audience

_____ Minimize first-person pronouns: *I, me, my.*

_____ Minimize second-person pronouns: *you, your.*

_____ Use third-person pronouns: *he, she, it, they.*

EXERCISE 9-13 **Revising and Editing Practice**

Directions: *Read the following paragraph that was written in response to the assignment below; it contains errors that require revising and editing. Then answer the questions that follow.*

Assignment: Write a paragraph to examine the causes and effects of technology on the ways people meet, date, or communicate.

(1) Since 1993 Internet communication has created opportunities and problems. (2) Today, MySpace is the hottest site online to meet young people; however, it is also a supermarket for predators. (3) Young people flock to the site, posting photos and real personal information and search for new friends. (4) However, a predator can also simply search, click, and connect to a young victim. (5) Why is it so easy? (6) First, MySpace does not require verification of a persons identity. (7) This makes the online Community open to a wide range of users. (8) Unfortunately, users can create a fake identity, age, address, e-mail, and photograph. (9) ________________, predators can exchange messages with complete anonymity. (10) ________________, these websites cannot legally kick registered sex offenders off the sites. (11) Moreover, if social networking websites tried to remove registered sex offenders, they could only remove the ones that provide a real name. (12) Last, even if MySpace removed sex offenders, they can go to a dozen other sites like Friendster or My Yearbook, so the problem is not really solved. (13) Ebay had similar problems with fraud when it first started. (14) Obviously, the problem will not be resolved by sites, therefore, Internet users must use caution when communicating online.

comma splice

Revising

__a__ 1. Which sentence(s) should be deleted to focus the topic sentence and the opening of this paragraph? If no sentences need to be cut, choose "no change is necessary."

a. 1

b. 1 and 4

c. 1 and 5

d. no change is necessary

__b__ 2. Which word or phrase should be inserted in blank 9? The word or phrase would serve as the best transition between the specific details the writer is using to support his point.

a. Next

b. As a result

c. In addition

d. In fact

___a___ 3. Which word or phrase should be inserted in blank 10? The word or phrase would serve as the best transition between the writer's major points in the paragraph.

a. Second

b. As a result

c. In addition

d. Unfortunately

___c___ 4. Which sentence should be cut to improve the focus of the paragraph? If no sentence needs to be cut, choose "no change is necessary."

a. sentence 9

b. sentence 11

c. sentence 13

d. no change is necessary

Editing

___a___ 1. Choose the option that corrects the error in sentence 3. If no error exists, choose "no change is necessary."

a. Young people flock to the site, posting photos and very personal information and searching for new friends.

b. Young people flock to the site, posting photos and real personal information and search for new friends.

c. Young people flock to the site and post photos and real personal information and search for new friends.

d. no change is necessary

___b___ 2. Choose the option that corrects the error in sentence 6. If no error exists, choose "no change is necessary."

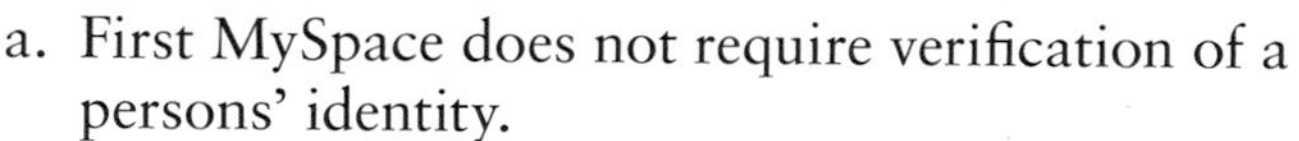

a. First MySpace does not require verification of a persons' identity.

b. First, MySpace does not require verification of a person's identity.

c. First, MySpace doesn't require verification of a persons identity.

d. no change is necessary

Ask Yourself
What punctuation rules do you apply to your writing automatically? How did you learn them?

___b___ 3. Choose the option that corrects the capitalization error in sentence 7. If no error exists, choose "no change is necessary."

a. Online Community

b. online community

c. Online community

d. no change is necessary

4. Proofread the paragraph for a comma splice error and correct the error.

EXERCISE 9-14 **Searching and Correcting**

PEER CONVERSATION

Directions: *Exchange papers with a proofreading peer and proofread each other's work. In addition to spelling, punctuation, and capitalization, find out what other errors your classmate has on his or her checklist; tell your classmate what errors you have on your checklist.*

EXERCISE 9-15 **Self-Editing**

Directions: *Carefully rewrite your paper, correcting errors you and your classmate found. Give yourself time to set aside the finished paper. Then come back to it and read your final draft one last time, using your checklist as a guide.*

Reflect

REFLECT

- Identify strengths
- Set goals

Take a moment and reflect on what you have learned.

EXERCISE 9-16 **Identifying Strengths and Setting Goals**

Directions: *Review your writing and your writing process. On a separate sheet of paper, write answers to these questions:*

- *What did you do well in the paragraph you wrote?*
- *What did you enjoy working on in this chapter?*
- *What have you learned that you will apply in future writing assignments?*

CHOOSING ROUTES WITH COMPARISON AND CONTRAST

GOING PLACES

Making Daily Decisions

Think about the last time you made a purchase—say you were looking for running shoes. In order to decide what to buy, you almost certainly compared different brands according to the qualities that were important to you—for example, sole construction, support and cushioning, ventilation, and looks. And you did this more or less automatically, without thinking explicitly about choosing the criteria. So why do you have to learn about "comparison and contrast" in textbooks? It is important to become fully conscious of what you are doing when you compare and contrast things in order to apply these same skills to more complicated situations. Imagine that you are trying to persuade someone to see one movie over another. To do this effectively, you have to be aware of the criteria that matters to that other person and present the two movies accordingly.

BRAINSTORM

Choose a movie that you have seen and really liked. Then brainstorm a list of other movies that are similar. What elements or qualities do they have that make them similar?

On the Other Hand . . .

Comparing and contrasting for a particular purpose is an important aspect of critical thinking and of writing. You might draft a proposal for a solution to a social problem like homelessness and present two alternatives (one of which you favor), or you might present two methods of performing an experiment, explaining why you chose one over the other. In order to make the best case for your position, you will need to have relevant information to make a fair comparison and contrast.

DISCUSSION

Talk with a classmate to answer the following questions: What is your favorite course? What is your least favorite course? Compare and contrast these two courses. What makes your response to these courses different?

Which One Would You Choose?

If you are involved in purchasing anything for your business—from office supplies to next season's clothing—you are required to choose from among a number of options, and you have to base your decision on specific criteria, such as cost, quality, availability, and variety. Comparison and contrast is not just useful for buying things, of course. A mechanic compares different repair jobs in order to prioritize them, while a dental assistant compares a patient's x-rays between visits to determine whether treatment by the dentist is required. The more practice you have in comparing and contrasting effectively, the better you will be at your job.

RESUME BUILDER

Think about a job you want. To prepare for an interview, you might think about the similarities and differences between your current job and the job you want. What skills do you need to change jobs? List two or three skills you will need. What skills do you currently use that you might also apply in your new job? List specific skills that are similar in both jobs.

Comparison and Contrast

CHAPTER 10

CHAPTER OVERVIEW

- THE COMPARISON AND CONTRAST PARAGRAPH AT A GLANCE
- COMPARISON AND CONTRAST THINKING
  - Elements of Comparison and Contrast
  - Points of Comparison and Contrast
  - Select and Elaborate on Details
- COMPARISON AND CONTRAST IN PROCESS
  - Prewrite
  - Draft
  - A Professional's Take
  - Revise
  - Edit
  - Reflect

THINK FIRST

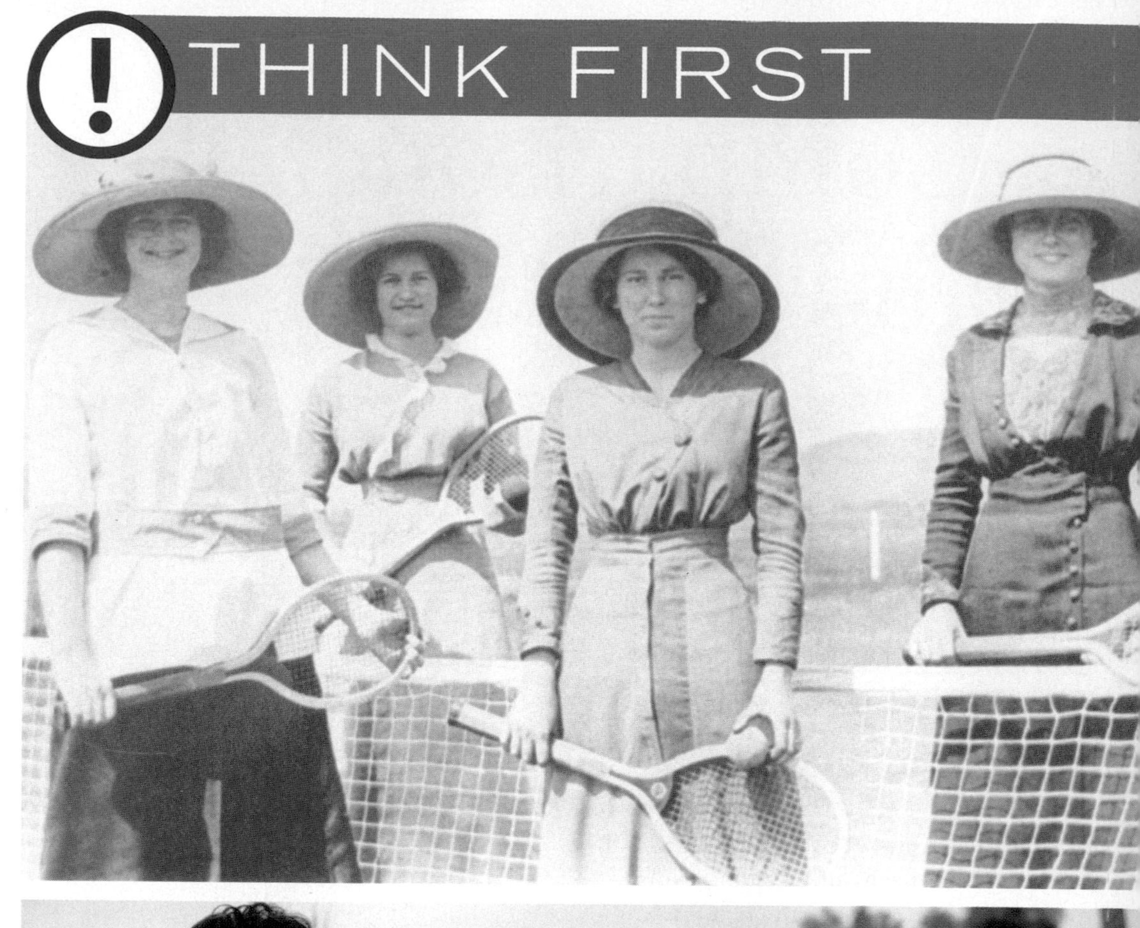

Write a paragraph describing these two photographs of tennis players. Focus on how the players are alike or different.

At a Glance

THE COMPARISON AND CONTRAST PARAGRAPH AT A GLANCE

Comparison and contrast analysis begins when you have to make a decision about two situations, ideas, or objects. An effective paragraph compares or contrasts two things that have something in common. For example, you want a job, but you cannot decide which one will provide the best opportunities. Your instructor wants you to evaluate two paintings, but you are not sure what criteria to use. To think critically, you make lists of points to consider, examine the common and contrasting characteristics, give equal consideration to each alternative, and reach a decision.

Comparison and contrast paragraphs are generally focused on either comparisons or contrasts. The topic sentence states the two things to be compared or contrasted and the writer's position on the similarities or differences. The supporting details provide specific examples, reasons, or details to explain the points of similarity or difference. These details are examined in both things being compared or being contrasted. A concluding sentence restates the main idea or makes a comment on the things being compared or contrasted.

Comparison and contrast paragraphs are structured in two ways: subject by subject and point by point. In **subject-by-subject organization,** you take turns focusing on each subject, including all the points about one subject and then all the points about the other subject. In **point-by-point organization,** you focus the discussion on each point. First you state a point and then include details about each subject. You proceed through the other points in the same way.

Ask Yourself

What factors do you consider when you compare two courses? Two coworkers?

The Comparison and Contrast Paragraph at a Glance

Subject-by-Subject Organization

ASSIGNMENT Compare or contrast two approaches to a recreational activity and show why one approach is superior.

TOPIC SENTENCE
The writer states his purpose: to show that pools have advantages. He will contrast pools and lakes to do this.

CONTRAST POINTS
The writer contrasts a pool and a beach by focusing on three points of contrast: accommodations, recreational options, and water quality.

ORDER AND TRANSITIONS
The writer discusses the three points in connection to pools, using transition terms to list and state importance. When he shifts to the discussion of lakes, he uses a transition showing contrast ("on the other hand"). He uses transition terms to list the same three points.

CONCLUDING SENTENCE
The writer restates her preference for pools.

Subject by Subject

Topic Sentence: Pools have advantages that lakes cannot provide.

First—Subject A: Pools

Point 1: Accommodations

Point 2: Recreational options

Point 3: Water quality

Next—Subject B: Lakes

Point 1: Accommodations

Point 2: Recreational options

Point 3: Water quality

(Subject A) Pools have advantages that lakes cannot provide. (Point 1) **For one thing,** the *accommodations* are almost always more comfortable at a pool. Pool-goers walk on a cement deck. **Moreover** the pool supplies comfortable chairs, tables, and umbrellas. Nearby, a snack bar offers convenient access to drinks and accessories such as tanning lotion or batteries. (Point 2) **An added** benefit is the *recreational options.* Pools almost always have diving boards, slides, and fountains. There is often a hot tub as well. (Point 3) **Most important,** the water quality is predictable. At a well-run facility, the water is usually very clean. There are no leaves floating on the surface and no bacteria waiting to infect the swimmer. (Subject B) **On the other hand, consider a lake.** (Point 1) **First,** the *accommodations* are natural. There are sand, waves, and sun. Beach-goers lie on a towel in the sand. The wind blows sand in their faces. Snack bars are not within walking distance or even on the beach itself. (Point 2) **In addition,** waves are the only *recreational option.* (Point 3) **Last,** because a beach is natural, the *water quality* is unpredictable. A swimmer might find dead fish floating next to him or her. A hot summer day can increase growth of bacteria in the water, so swimming is actually a health hazard. Unless you are a nature-purist or a risk-taker, a pool offers a relaxing day in the sun without health hazards.

Point-by-Point Organization

ASSIGNMENT Compare or contrast two consumer products and indicate your preference.

Point by Point

Topic Sentence: These days, cell phones have so much in common; it may be difficult to choose between two competing brands.

Point 1: Features

Subject A: voice mail, text and video messages, e-mail, camera

Subject B: voice mail, text and video messages, e-mail, camera

Point 2: Specifications

Subject A: Motorola 3.5 ounces, three colors (black, silver, red)

Subject B: Samsung 3.3 ounces, three colors (pink, blue, black)

Point 3: Phone Price

Subject A: Free with activation and media package

Subject B: Free with activation and media package

Point 4: Media Package Plan

Subject A: Media package plan of your choice offering voice, text and video messaging, game viewing, and Internet

Subject B: Media package plan of your choice offering voice, text and video messaging, game viewing, and Internet

These days cell phones have so much in common, it may be difficult to choose between two competing brands. (Point 1) **One selling point** is the *features* of the phone. (Subject A) A Motorola RAZR offers multimedia messaging, e-mail, video playback, and Bluetooth® capabilities. (Subject B) **Likewise,** a Samsung SYNC phone offers the same features. (Point 2) **Other considerations** are the *specifications*: weight and color. (Subject A) **Again,** Motorola offers a light and compact phone weighing only 3.83 ounces. **In addition,** the phone comes in traditional and new colors: black, silver, and red. (Subject B) **Similarly,** Samsung offers a 3.95 ounce phone in similar color choices: black, pink, and charcoal. These phones capture the attention of both young and more mature users. (Point 3) **Plus,** the phones both have an appealing *price*—$49.99 with activation. (Point 4) **Finally,** the plan may be the only difference, but package deals make even this point irrelevant. (Subject A) The Motorola phone is free with the purchase of any media package. The user can purchase a package to fit her needs. (Subject B) The Samsung phone is included in the same package. With so much in common, a phone purchase might come down to color. Red anyone?

TOPIC SENTENCE
The writer chooses two related things to purchase: a Motorola and Samsung cell phone. She also states her purpose to illustrate that because cell phones are so much alike, it is difficult to choose one. She will illustrate her view by comparing them.

COMPARISON POINTS
The writer compares two cell phones using four categories: features, specifications, price, and plan.

ORDER AND TRANSITIONS
The writer connects the four points using transition terms to list the common traits.

CONCLUDING SENTENCE
The writer comments on the one choice a buyer has that separates the two phones—color.

DISCUSSION QUESTIONS

1. Which paragraph is easier to follow? Why?
2. Which paragraph makes greater use of transition words and phrases?
3. When you compare and contrast, which form of organization are you more likely to use?

PEER CONVERSATION

COMPARISON AND CONTRAST THINKING

When you compare and contrast, you look for similarities and differences in two people, places, ideas, or things. You compare and contrast to make a point to a reader. A compare or contrast paragraph includes three elements: a focus on similarities or differences; points of comparison or contrast; and details, reasons, or examples to support those points.

Elements of Comparison and Contrast

These are the basic elements of effective comparison and contrast paragraphs.

- ***Purpose of your comparison or contrast:*** The topic sentence identifies the two subjects being discussed and indicates the purpose of the discussion, such as choosing between two different cell phones.
- ***Points of comparison or contrast:*** The middle section of the paragraph states the points by which the items will be compared or contrasted and examines each one using these points. In the case of cell phones, points of comparison or contrast might be weight and color, price, and the billing packages that come with the phones.
- ***Details, reasons, and examples:*** Details, reasons, and examples elaborate on each point and provide support for the main idea of the paragraph. It is not enough simply to say "weight and color." You need to provide some explanation of what this means.

Get Started

Why are you writing a comparison and contrast paragraph? Comparison and contrast thinking proceeds from having a clearly defined purpose. You use this mode to identify similarities or differences, to evaluate items, or to indicate a preference for an idea, person, place, or thing. How has your work environment changed since the new manager took charge? Which of the two teams in the NBA finals is most likely to win? Why do you prefer one instructor over another?

A clear statement of purpose focuses your inquiry. Here are three topic sentences that state the purpose of comparison and contrast paragraphs written on the topics above:

- ***Work environment:*** Several important changes have occurred since the new manager started.
- ***NBA finals:*** Because of their inside game and 3-point shooting, the Pistons are likely to beat the Spurs in the NBA finals.

- ***Instructor preference:*** Mr. Gruber's use of visual aids and his sense of humor make his class much more interesting than Dr. Koll's economics class.

EXERCISE 10-1 Thinking about Purpose

Directions: *For each of the following topics, write a topic sentence stating the purpose of comparing and contrasting them.* Answers will vary.

EXAMPLE

Buying clothes online and buying them in a store: For the consumer who is difficult to fit, buying clothes in a store is much better than buying them online.

1. Old cars and new cars: ______________________________

____

____

2. Female and male shopping habits: ______________________________

____

____

3. Two singers or popular performers: ______________________________

____

____

4. Television when you were a kid and television today: ______________________________

____

____

5. News from TV and news from print media: ______________________________

____

____

Points of Comparison and Contrast

The focus of comparison and contrast thinking is points of comparison and contrast between two ideas, places, objects, or people and the details that help you explain these points. Once you have an idea of your purpose, you might take two different approaches to get started.

Begin with Points of Comparison and Contrast

Sometimes you begin comparison and contrast thinking with a clear idea of your points of comparison and contrast. For example, you want to compare the attraction of two destination cities for spring break. Your points of comparison are (1) how easy they are to reach, (2) climate, and (3) what there is to do when you get there. In this case, you can proceed to listing and exploring details.

The side-by-side diagram in Figure 10-1 displays this thinking process. The student begins with her points of comparison and works back and forth across columns, filling in details that relate to each point. The purpose of her thinking process is to explore why one destination city is better than another.

Begin with Details and Discover Points of Comparison and Contrast

What if you do not know what your points of comparison are? In this case, you begin by listing details. It is probably best to examine the subject you know the most about first, listing all the details you can think of, then turn to the second subject.

The side-by-side diagram in Figure 10-2 illustrates the thinking process of a student who compares and contrasts exercising at home to exercising in a gym. He fills in details in the exercise-at-home category first, then moves to his second subject, exercising at a gym, using the details in the left column to generate details in the right column. When he finishes, he examines his list and notes possible points of comparison and contrast. The purpose of his thinking process is to determine which place will produce the best exercise results. The points of comparison for this student seem to be ease of access, variety of exercises, and the impact of other people on the process.

City #1	City #2
Point 1: How easy is it to get to Twelve hours by car	**Point 1: How easy is it to get to** Eighteen hours by car
Point 2: Climate 75–80 degrees, little chance of rain	**Point 2: Climate** 80–90 degrees, never rains, higher humidity
Point 3: What to do there Beach, sunbathing and body surfing, parasailing, great clubs at night	**Point 3: What to do there** Beach, sunbathing and body surfing, parasailing, great clubs at night, visit family friends (they know all the latest places to eat and cool places to go at night)

FIGURE 10-1 Listing and Exploring Details

Working Out at Home	Working Out at a Gym
Less emphasis on machinery	State of the art machines
Weights	Elliptical, weight machines
NordicTrack machine	Stairmaster, rowing machines
Working out in the laundry room	Working out in public
Walking and jogging outside	Always inside
Weather can be a factor	Any kind of weather
Can't be as noisy (listen to TV loud)	No choice over music or TV station
No need to have fancy clothes	Want to look good

FIGURE 10-2 Listing Details for the Subject You Know Best

EXERCISE 10-2 Points of Comparison and Contrast

Directions: *Choose two of the following subjects and fill in the charts with details related to them.*

- *If you know what your points of comparison and contrast will be, number them, write them in the columns provided, and list your supporting details under each point (see Figure 10-1).*
- *If you do not know what your points of comparison and contrast will be, list details in the column for the subject you know best. Use this list to generate details for the other column, and then note possible points of comparison and contrast in the space provided.*

When you are finished, write a sentence or two stating what your points of comparison and contrast are (see Figure 10-2). Answers will vary.

1. Tests

Essay Tests	*Multiple-Choice Tests*
________________	________________
________________	________________
________________	________________
________________	________________
________________	________________
________________	________________
________________	________________
________________	________________

Points of Comparison: ______________________________

____

____

2. Where to do homework

Doing Homework at School	*Doing Homework at Home*
______________	______________
______________	______________
______________	______________
______________	______________
______________	______________
______________	______________
______________	______________
______________	______________

Points of Comparison: ______________________________

____

____

3. Types of class

Face-to-Face Classes	*Online Classes*
______________	______________
______________	______________
______________	______________
______________	______________
______________	______________
______________	______________
______________	______________
______________	______________

Points of Comparison: ______________________________

____

____

Select and Elaborate on Details

As you explore your subject in comparison and contrast thinking, you are likely to generate a lot of details; far more, in fact, than you can use in a paragraph. Consequently, it is important to be selective. Choose only those details that are most significant and helpful in explaining similarity or difference. It is probably better to have two or three good details to elaborate on than six or seven details you simply list. It is easier on your reader and more persuasive.

Here are details selected by the student comparing home and gym workouts.

Topic Sentence: Although working out at home is more convenient, the advantages of exercising in a gym outweigh mere convenience.

Working Out at Home	Working Out at the Gym
Point 1: Ease of access Always open. Go downstairs or step outside.	**Point 1: Ease of access** Have to leave the house. Collect clothes, shoes, get in the car, drive.
Point 2: Variety of exercises Home loses here. Cannot compete with the gym.	**Point 2: Variety of exercises** Gym has greater variety: elliptical, weight machines, StairMaster, rowing machines, pool, track, sauna, massage.
Point 3: Influence of other people Have to be quiet, so do not disturb the family. Home loses here, too.	**Point 3: Influence of other people** Everyone is in the same boat.

EXERCISE 10-3 Selecting and Elaborating on Your Details

Directions: *Choose the topic you care most about from Exercise 10-2 and, in the space below, write a topic sentence for it. Then use the side-by-side chart to fill in points of comparison and contrast, along with the most important details related to each point.*

Topic Sentence: ____

____

____

Talk about It

Which comparison and contrast approach do you prefer? Subject-by-subject or point-by-point? Why?

Subject 1	*Subject 2*
Point 1: ____________ ____________ ____________ ____________	Point 1: ____________ ____________ ____________ ____________
Point 2: ____________ ____________ ____________ ____________	Point 2: ____________ ____________ ____________ ____________
Point 3: ____________ ____________ ____________ ____________	Point 3: ____________ ____________ ____________ ____________

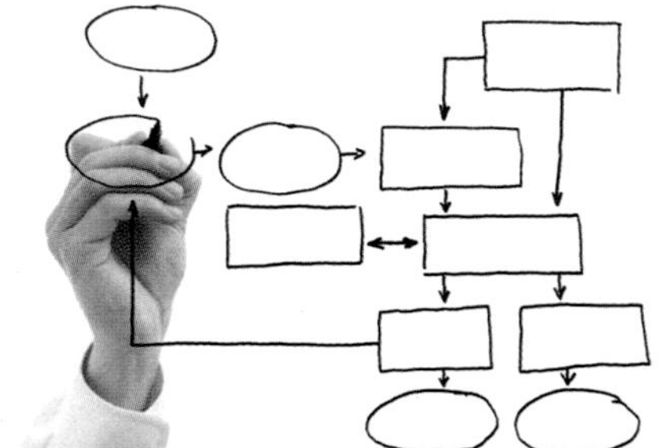

Process

COMPARISON AND CONTRAST IN PROCESS

Effective comparison or contrast writing systematically examines a topic. You determine the purpose of your writing, establish points of comparison and contrast, then identify and elaborate on supporting details.

Select an Assignment

In your college courses, comparison and contrast writing calls for attention to detail and meticulous organization. This challenging thinking and writing activity cuts across all disciplines.

EXERCISE 10-4 **Selecting an Assignment for a Comparison and Contrast Paragraph**

Directions: *Review the assignments listed below. Choose the one you know the most about and think is best suited to a comparison and contrast paragraph.*

1. Compare or contrast an expensive hobby and an inexpensive hobby.
2. Compare or contrast living at home or getting an apartment.
3. Compare or contrast driving an older car or driving a new car.
4. Compare or contrast two vacations, parties, or dates.
5. Compare or contrast a past job and a current job.
6. Compare or contrast why it is better or worse to be the boss rather than the worker.
7. Compare or contrast which job is better—a desk job or a manual labor job.
8. Compare or contrast two ideas, events, people, or objects you recently studied.
9. Compare or contrast two people you know who have made a difference in the community.
10. Compare or contrast two different approaches to solving the same problem in your community.

Prewrite: Write Before You Write

You have a lot to keep track of in comparison and contrast writing, which is all the more reason to take full advantage of the writing process. Talk to classmates and interested others about your ideas. Use brainstorming to get your ideas and details down on paper so you are clear about your thinking.

PREWRITE
- Talk
- Cluster
- Brainstorm
- Freewrite

Talk

Talking enables you to explore what you know in an unthreatening format. You can also get input from a classmate to help you determine your purpose for writing and your points of comparison or contrast. Use conversation to get started thinking.

EXERCISE 10-5 **Talking about It**

PEER CONVERSATION

Directions: *Turn to your neighbor in class or find an interested listener. Explore the two subjects you wish to compare and contrast. As you talk, be sure to consider the purpose for your paragraph and the points of comparison and contrast you have in mind. Be specific and include details. Then be a critical listener to your neighbor's comparison and contrast thinking. Listen without interrupting. When the speaker finishes, ask questions or offer suggestions. Identify what was clear and what was not clear.*

Brainstorm

Using the side-by-side approach illustrated in the thinking section of this chapter, brainstorm on your subject. List your points of comparison and contrast and the details for each subject. If you are unsure of your points of comparison and contrast, list as many details as you can, review your brainstorming, and look for two to three points that organize your thinking.

EXERCISE 10-6 **Brainstorming**

Directions: *On a separate sheet of paper, brainstorm for ten minutes on the assignment that you chose in Exercise 10-4. At the top of the paper, write a sentence expressing your tentative purpose. Then use the side-by-side approach to list the points of comparison or contrast about your topic. When you finish, identify your points of comparison and contrast.*

Draft: Focus and Organize

DRAFT

- Consider your audience
- Formulate your topic sentence
- Outline for unity and coherence
- Write a conclusion sentence
- Compose your first draft

After prewriting, you should have a sense of your purpose for the paragraph. In addition, you can list your points of comparison and contrast, and you have generated a number of details to provide the substance of your paragraph. Your next step is to focus, organize, and draft your paragraph.

Consider Your Audience

Reread your assignment. Look for key words in the assignment, and make sure you incorporate the words and ideas into your plan for your paragraph. As you take audience into consideration, it may help to keep these questions in mind:

- Why is this topic important?
- What do I want my reader to understand about it?
- What special knowledge about this subject do I have that might require explanation for a reader to understand?

EXERCISE 10-7 **Considering Your Audience**

PEER CONVERSATION

Directions: *Use the questions above to think critically about the purpose of your paragraph and the points and details to include in it. Talk with a classmate to try out your thinking on an audience. Take notes on this conversation and add any new ideas and details to your prewriting.*

Topic Sentence

The topic sentence in a comparison or contrast paragraph identifies the two things being compared or contrasted and states the main idea of the paragraph. Review your prewriting, especially anything you wrote relating to purpose and points of comparison and contrast. Do not be afraid to reconsider and revise your thinking.

Unity and Coherence

Planning well will help you write a unified paragraph. Be sure you know what your points of comparison and contrast are and which details are needed to explain those points. Eliminate those details that do not relate to these points. Then, think about the order in which you present your points of comparison and contrast. It might be effective to lead off with an important point, or perhaps you want to save the best for last. Changing the order of your ideas can help you understand something about your topic that eluded you before.

In your comparison and contrast paragraph, you will make extensive use of transition words and phrases because you are discussing two subjects at the same time. In addition, you will have two or three points of comparison and contrast, along with supporting details relating to these points. Transition words and phrases will make it easier for you to handle multiple ideas and details.

TRANSITIONS BASED ON COMPARISON		
again	as well as	likewise
both	in the same way	similarly
in addition	also	

TRANSITIONS BASED ON CONTRAST		
although	but	however
in contrast	moreover	on the contrary
on the other hand	opposite of	

Concluding Sentence

Plan your concluding sentence. A concluding sentence makes a comment on the position stated in the topic sentence. It can also restate the purpose of the paragraph.

EXERCISE 10-8 Planning Your First Draft

Directions: *On a separate sheet of paper, write a topic sentence that echoes the key words from the assignment topic you selected. Then organize and outline your details. Look back at pages 201–203 in this chapter for help with planning point-by-point or subject-by-subject structure.*

See "Supporting Details" in Chapter 3 for detailed explanation of outlining.

Write a First Draft

Now that you have chosen your topic, decided on your position, and selected the examples and details, you can write a first draft of your paragraph. At this point, it is better to write too much than too little: You can always cut back later. Make sure your paragraph has sufficient detail and explanation so a reader understands your position.

EXERCISE 10-9 **Writing Your First Draft**

Directions: *Write a draft of your paragraph. Use the following checklist as a guide.*

FIRST DRAFT CHECKLIST

______ My topic sentence states the purpose of my paragraph.

______ My topic sentence echoes key terms in the assignment.

______ I have clearly defined points of comparison and contrast.

______ I have included details to explain these points.

______ I have organized my discussion and used transitions to show the relationship between ideas and details.

______ My concluding sentence emphasizes the point of my paragraph.

A PROFESSIONAL'S TAKE

Here is Arlie Hochschild's use of comparison and contrast, from her book *Time Bind:*

Psychologist Reed Larson and his colleagues studied the daily emotional experiences of mothers and fathers in fifty-five two-parent Chicago families with children in the fifth to eighth grades. Some of the mothers cared for children at home, some worked part time, others full time, while all the fathers in the study worked full time. Each participant wore a pager for a week, and whenever they were beeped by the research team, each wrote down how he or she felt: "happy-unhappy, cheerful-irritable, friendly-angry." The researchers found that men and women reported a similar range of emotional states across the week. But fathers reported more "positive emotional states" at home; mothers, more positive emotional states at work. This held true for every social class. Fathers like Bill Avery relaxed more at home; while mothers like Linda Avery did more housework there. Larson suggests that "because women are constantly on call to the needs of other family members, they are less able to relax at home in the way men do." Wives were typically in better moods than their husbands at home only when they were eating or engaging in "family transport." They were in worse moods when they were doing "child-related activities" or "socializing" there. Men and women each felt most at ease when involved in tasks they felt less obliged to do, Larson reports. For women, this meant first shift work; for men, second.

EXERCISE 10-10 A PROFESSIONAL'S TAKE

Directions: *Using the first draft checklist as your guide, identify elements of an effective comparison and contrast paragraph in the professional model.*

Revise: Read Critically, Then Rewrite

Revision gives you a chance to get things right. Even if you have carefully analyzed, focused, and planned your first draft, you have done this work alone. You will always benefit from having an outside reader.

REVISE
- Read critically
- Develop a revision plan

Revision in Action

Revision is rethinking a draft to improve the quality of your writing: You read critically, plan your revision, and revise your writing. Quality revision will also improve your future writing. Here is an example of revision by a student named Barbara.

The full version of Barbara's sample is available online.

Assignment: Examine an important dietary issue in our country today, such as increasing levels of obesity, the use of food supplements, or the growth of organic foods in the marketplace.

Barbara's First Draft

Organic foods are widely available in our country today, to the benefit of both the animals providing the food and the humans consuming it. **The first benefit** of organic foods is a more ethical approach to food production. **In the traditional food industry,** animals spend more of their lives in cages, usually standing in their own feces. Some never see the outdoors at all. **In contrast,** animals raised in the organic food industry are sometimes called "free-range animals." They get to go outside and play. They live the lives that God intended them to live. If I were a cow or a chicken, I would want to be outside. **A second benefit** of organic foods is fewer growth hormones and antibiotics. **In traditional meats,** cows are fed grains to make them fatten up nicely. Unfortunately, grains make them sick, which means they are pumped full of antibiotics. Growth hormones also are used to fatten beef faster. It is all about efficiency. The problem is, if cows get antibiotics and hormones, we get them too when we eat the cows. **Unlike these producers,** organic producers do not depend on these drugs. Their animals take their time. Holistic medicine expert Dr. Richard King suggests that organic and natural meat products are even more important than organic and natural fruits and vegetables. Fruits and vegetables,

TOPIC SENTENCE
Barbara repeats key words from the assignment and states her position on the benefits of organic foods for both animals and humans.

SUPPORTING DETAILS
She uses examples, facts, and reasons to support each point stating how organic food production benefits both animals and people.

ORDER AND TRANSITIONS
She uses a point-by-point order contrasting the methods of organic food producers and traditional food producers. She uses a combination of enumeration and contrast transitions.

CONCLUDING SENTENCE
Barbara comments on the value of organic food.

he says, can be washed. You cannot wash chemicals out of the tissues of meats. Organic meats seem to offer a significant dietary gain for people. They may cost more, and that is a problem, but organic products are better for the creatures on both sides of the food chain.

Revision Plan: Keep the good details and transitions but reorganize the content. Begin with people to make them sound more important than animals. Cut first-person pronouns.

TOPIC SENTENCE
Barbara revises her topic sentence to focus on health.

SUPPORTING DETAILS
She adds fruits and vegetables to include all organic foods.

ORDER AND TRANSITIONS
Barbara uses point-by-point order to contrast organic food production and traditional food production. Her transitions indicate the major points and the contrasting details for each type of production.

CONCLUDING SENTENCE
She comments on the cost and benefits of organic products.

Barbara's Revised Draft

Organic foods are widely available in our country today, which benefits both the humans consuming them and, in the case of meats, the animals providing the food. **For example,** more organic fruits and vegetables are now available. **While** most broccoli and cauliflower on the shelves have residues of fertilizer, pesticides, and herbicides on them, organic products do not. This means they are safer to eat and better for you. **In addition,** organic meats are now on the market, which are much better to eat. **In traditional meat production,** cows are fed grains and growth hormones so they reach slaughter weight faster. Grains make them sick, which means they need antibiotics. If cows get antibiotics and hormones, the consumer gets them in his hamburger and steak. **Unlike these producers, organic producers** do not depend on drugs. They allow their animals the time to grow naturally. They are what the organic food industry calls "free-range" animals: better for the animals, better for the consumer. **A final benefit** of organic foods is a more ethical approach to food production. **In the traditional food industry,** animals spend most of their lives in cages. Many stand and sleep in their own feces. Chickens live their whole lives indoors. It is hard to see how human well-being can come from such inhumane treatment of animals. In organic food production, animals live in a natural environment. They may cost more, but organic products are better all around for the creatures on both ends of the food chain.

PEER CONVERSATION

DISCUSSION QUESTIONS What changes did Barbara make in her revision to improve her paragraph? Why?

Read Critically

Half the task of revising well is reading well. Critical reading is a search for the characteristics of effective writing: topic sentence, supporting examples and details, transitions, and concluding sentence. In comparison and contrast writing, pay attention to a writer's approach to organization. Is it point by point or subject by subject? Also, note how effective the supporting details are. Watch for repetition and lists. Does the writer elaborate and explain his or her details?

MULTILINGUAL TIP

Bring your draft to the writing center on your campus.

EXERCISE 10-11 **Reading Peer Papers**

Directions: *Exchange papers with another student. Consider the significant changes that Barbara made between writing her first draft and her revision. Be a critical reader and make suggestions to improve your peer's first draft. Also identify what your classmate did well. Make notes in the margin as you read to remember your suggestions. Use the following guidelines.*

PEER CONVERSATION

REVISION CHECKLIST

_____ Does the topic sentence connect to the assignment and state the point of the paragraph?

_____ Does the writer clearly define points of comparison or contrast?

_____ Does the writer provide enough details to elaborate on these points?

_____ Does the paragraph have effective transitions?

_____ Does the concluding sentence emphasize the point of the paragraph?

Revise with a Plan

Reread your assignment before revising. Be sure the paragraph you have drafted is an appropriate response to the assignment. Also, review everything you have written, including prewriting. If you need to add to your paragraph, you might have ideas and details in your prewriting that you can revise and improve on. If you need to cut from your paragraph, think about how those cuts will enhance the unity of your paragraph.

EXERCISE 10-12 **Revising Your Draft**

Directions: *Develop a revision plan and revise the paragraph you wrote for Exercise 10-9.*

Edit

The ideas in your work count. The content matters. Focus your editing with this personalized checklist.

EDIT
- Search and correct
- Self-edit

MULTILINGUAL TIP
Proofread for correct comparative and superlative forms; correct distinction between a few/few/a little/little.

YOUR EDITING CHECKLIST

_____ Spelling: List any words you misspelled in your last paper:

____

_____ Punctuation: List two punctuation errors from your last paper:

____

_____ Capitalization: List any capitalization errors from your last paper:

____

_____ Other errors: List any errors your instructor has pointed out in graded work:

____

____

To Prepare Your Draft for an Academic Audience

_____ Minimize first-person pronouns: *I, me, my.*

_____ Minimize second-person pronouns: *you, your.*

_____ Use third-person pronouns: *he, she, it, they.*

EXERCISE 10-13 **Revising and Editing Practice**

Directions: *Read the following paragraph that was written in response to the assignment below; it contains errors that require revising and editing. Then answer the questions that follow.*

Assignment: Write a comparison and contrast paragraph to examine two approaches to organizing your home, work, or school life.

(1) ________________________________. (2) First, many people think a handheld personal digital assistant (PDA) is better because it is a mini-computer. (3) They can connect a PDA to their computer at work and at home to synchronize items on their calendars. (4) A PDA makes it easy for a person to keep track of appointments and contact information. (5) In addition, they have access to the Internet, and some even have word processors and spreadsheets. (6) What anyone does with a spreadsheet is beyond me. (7) ____________, there are some disadvantages. (8) For one thing, the keyboards and displays are small and hard to read in addition, it can be irritating to constantly charge the batteries. (9) Some users do not like the fact that they rely on it and when they need it, the battery is dead. (10) On the other hand, a paper day planner may be more convenient for

work and personal appointments. (11) There is no computer to boot up at work or at home, no synchronization process to go through, and no batteries to charge. (12) ________________. (13) The handheld device is fine for some people but definitely not without it's problems.

commonly confused word: its

Revising

__b__ 1. Which sentence should be inserted in blank 1? The sentence would include key words from the assignment and state the purpose of the paragraph.

a. Handheld devices are not all they are cracked up to be; nevertheless, people love these personal digital assistants (PDAs).

b. Handheld devices are replacing day planners, but are they all they are cracked up to be?

c. There are many differences between a day planner and a PDA.

d. If you compare a day planner and a PDA, you will choose the one right for you.

__b__ 2. Which word or phrase should be inserted in blank 7? The word or phrase would serve as a best transition between points that describe a PDA.

a. Also

b. Nevertheless

c. In addition

d. Surprisingly

__b__ 3. Which sentence should be cut to improve the focus of the paragraph? If no sentence needs to be cut, choose "no change is necessary."

a. sentence 4

b. sentence 6

c. sentence 9

d. no change is necessary

__a__ 4. Which sentence, if any, should be inserted in blank 12? The sentence would provide the best specific details to support sentence 10. If no sentence needs to be added, choose "no sentence should be inserted."

a. Making changes simply requires erasing.

b. Plus, who needs a keyboard and a word processing program to write down an appointment?

c. In addition, planners have space for contact information in the back.

d. no sentence should be inserted

Editing

c 1. Choose the option that corrects the error in sentence 5. If no error exists, choose "no change is necessary."

a. In addition, they have access to the Internet, and some PDAs even have word processors and spreadsheets

b. In addition, a PDA have access to the Internet, and some even have word processors and spreadsheets.

c. In addition, a PDA has access to the Internet, and some even have word processors and spreadsheets.

d. no change is necessary

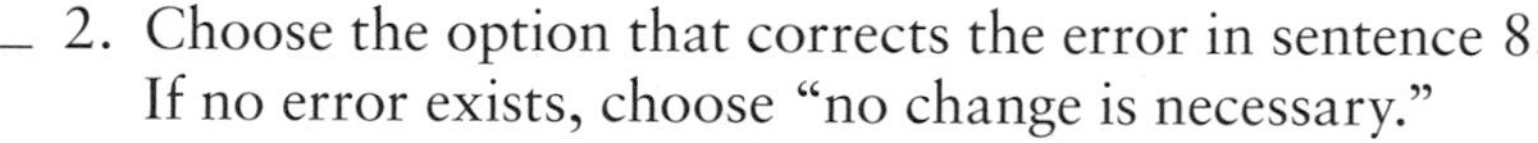

Writer's Response
What kinds of technology have improved your life? How has it been improved?

c 2. Choose the option that corrects the error in sentence 8. If no error exists, choose "no change is necessary."

a. For one thing, the keyboards and displays are small and hard to read, in addition, it can be irritating to constantly charge the batteries.

b. For one thing, the keyboards and displays are small and hard to read, additionally, it can be irritating to constantly charge the batteries.

c. For one thing, the keyboards and displays are small and hard to read; in addition, it can be irritating to constantly charge the batteries.

d. no change is necessary

a 3. Choose the option that corrects the punctuation error in sentence 9. If no error exists, choose "no change is necessary."

a. Some users do not like the fact that they rely on it, and when they need it, the battery is dead.

b. Some users do not like the fact that they rely on it and, when they need it, the battery is dead.

c. Some users do not like the fact that they rely on it. And when they need it the battery is dead.

d. no change is necessary

4. Proofread the paragraph for an error with a commonly confused word and correct the error.

PEER CONVERSATION

EXERCISE 10-14 Searching and Correcting

Directions: *Exchange papers with a peer and proofread each other's work. In addition to spelling, punctuation, and capitalization, find out what other errors your classmate has on his or her checklist; tell your classmate what errors you have on your checklist.*

EXERCISE 10-15 Self-Editing

Directions: *Rewrite your paper, correcting errors you and your classmate found. Give yourself time to set aside the finished paper. Then come back to it and read your final draft one last time, using your checklist as a guide.*

REFLECT
- Identify strengths
- Set goals

Reflect

Take a moment and reflect on what you have learned.

EXERCISE 10-16 Identifying Strengths and Setting Goals

Directions: *Review your writing and your writing process. On a separate sheet of paper, write answers to these questions:*

- *What did you do well in the paragraph you wrote?*
- *What did you enjoy working on in this chapter?*
- *What have you learned that will apply in future writing assignments?*

GIVING THE JOURNEY MEANING WITH DEFINITION

What Did You Say Again?

Imagine you are describing a movie you just saw to one of your friends. If you were to say, "It's a screwball comedy, but a little on the dark side," you might hear this response: "What's a 'screwball comedy'? And what do you mean by the 'dark side'?" Your friend is asking you to define your terms, and, in order for the conversation to move forward, you will have to do so. Definition, then, is one way of establishing a basis for an intelligent discussion. You may also find that your notion of a word's meaning will change after talking about it with others.

BRAINSTORM

Brainstorm a list of words you use with your close friends or at work that your family members might not understand.

Definition: A Basis for Argument

In class discussion, you will need to carefully define your terms. Suppose you are discussing assisted suicide. At the outset, you should be sure that you and your listeners understand how you define the term. For example, you might say, "In referring to 'assisted suicide,' I am limiting this discussion to cases in which terminally ill patients—as opposed to physically healthy persons—are aided by others in ending their life." Limiting the argument by defining your terms clarifies an unmanageably large topic.

DISCUSSION

Talk with a classmate to define the following terms: hack, spam, phishing, floss, earjacking, *and* subwoofing. *See if you both define them in the same way.*

Definition on the Job

Definition is obviously key to classroom teaching: "an isosceles triangle is . . . ," "democracy is most commonly defined as . . . ," "Freud defined the ego as. . . ." But it plays a role in many other jobs as well. A librarian would need to define an "online database" for someone new to the world of electronic research; a physician's assistant might need to explain the phrase "complete workup" to an anxious patient; an employee training a new hire would have to define the jargon of the particular business. Similarly, the kind of definition that clarifies a decision, position, or policy is a part of most jobs: for example, a government official might state the technical definition of an "assembly" in discussing the need for a license for a planned public meeting, while a server in a restaurant might have to clearly define the "early bird special" in order to avoid an argument with eager customers.

RESUME BUILDER

Before you go for an interview, research the language that you will need to use to converse with your future employer. To practice, make a list of the essential words you need to understand in your current job. Why are these words important?

CHAPTER 11

Definition

CHAPTER OVERVIEW

- THE DEFINITION PARAGRAPH AT A GLANCE
- DEFINITION THINKING
  - Elements of Definition
  - Examples and Details
  - Negatives
- DEFINITION IN PROCESS
  - Prewrite
  - Draft
  - A Professional's Take
  - Revise
  - Edit
  - Reflect

THINK FIRST

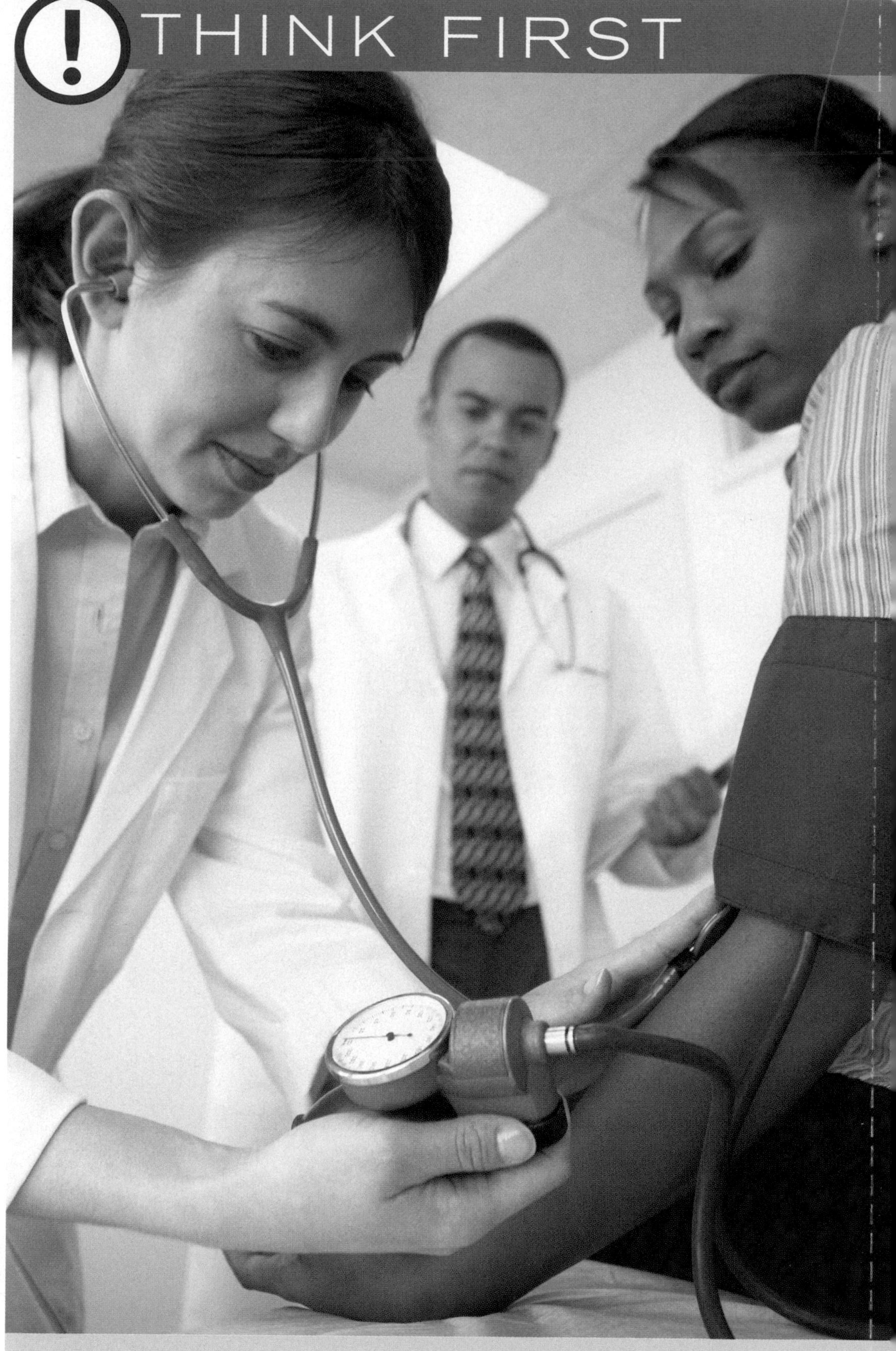

Write a paragraph in which you define what health means to you. Elaborate on your ideas, explaining your definition in detail.

At a Glance

THE DEFINITION PARAGRAPH AT A GLANCE

A good definition paragraph should not only define a term, phrase, or concept but also illustrate or demonstrate its meaning. For example, a construction trades instructor might ask you to write a paragraph defining the term *flush*. A simple answer is that flush is achieved by creating a continuous plane with two adjacent objects. However, in order to help someone understand that simple definition, you might describe how important creating flush walls is to the construction of a house, or you might explain the process of building a flush wall. Either of these approaches will more specifically define *flush*.

A definition paragraph has three parts: a topic sentence, supporting details, and a concluding sentence. Generally, definition paragraphs are short and specific. The topic sentence states the term to be defined and possibly gives a general definition. The sentence that follows may state a reason for defining the term. The supporting details describe, explain, or illustrate the definition using specific examples or facts. The concluding sentence restates the definition in simple terms.

The Definition Paragraph at a Glance

ASSIGNMENT Write a paragraph that defines the term *work ethic.*

A work ethic is a person's attitude about work. **For example,** some people believe work is valuable and necessary for a good life. They work for pay, but they also work for the satisfaction work brings. Because of this positive work ethic, they feel that when they work, they are using their time productively. They are making something of their lives. A negative attitude about work is **also** a work ethic. **In contrast** to those who embrace work are those who avoid work at all costs. They feel work takes something from them. They work for money because they want the money, not because they like or love the work. There is little or no satisfaction from a job well done. **Those with a positive work ethic** are probably more inclined to work for the fun of it. In their homes, they are cleaners and fixers and organizers. They have hobbies. They are perpetual activity machines. **Those people with a negative work ethic** might be less inclined to do work like this. They can walk around a mess and sit on the couch. They can see

TOPIC SENTENCE
The writer repeats the definition term from the assignment and defines work ethic as an attitude.

SUPPORTING DETAILS
The writer cites examples of two different attitudes to work, positive and negative, to provide a definition of the term *work ethic.*

ORDER AND TRANSITIONS
The writer uses transition words as he alternates between his two examples. He also uses repeating terms, "those with a positive," to structure his discussion.

a sink full of dishes and look the other way. In other areas of life, they may be happy people, but work is not one of their sources of happiness. Positive or negative, a work ethic is about attitude and the effect of that attitude on what people do with their lives.

DISCUSSION QUESTIONS

PEER CONVERSATION

1. Does this definition seem accurate? Discuss people you know who have either a positive or a negative attitude about work.
2. Do you agree or disagree with this definition of work ethic? What does it overlook? What would you add to it?

Thinking

DEFINITION THINKING

Sometimes a one-sentence definition is sufficient. You pull down your *Webster's* dictionary, copy a phrase or two, and away you go. In academic writing, however, you may need to provide more detailed definitions of terms and concepts, so that you and your reader have a shared understanding of their meanings. Providing clear definitions forces you to clarify your own thinking about a topic and allows you to discuss complex issues.

Elements of Definition

There are some basic elements of an effective definition paragraph. These elements enable you to focus and elaborate on a useful definition.

- ***Group or category:*** In a topic sentence, it helps to associate the term, concept, or idea you want to define with a group or category. A work ethic is an *attitude*. Placing work ethic in this category enables you to talk about positive and negative feelings and how they translate into actual behaviors.
- ***Examples:*** A good definition often makes use of examples. Once a work ethic is defined as an attitude, you can cite examples of attitude, positive and negative, and in so doing add useful detail to your definition.
- ***Negatives:*** When you define a term using negatives, you focus on misconceptions—what people erroneously think about your subject. You say what your subject is not. Often this form of definition is a two-

statement maneuver. You state what your subject is not; then you state what it is. *A work ethic is not simply a desire to make a lot of money; it is an attitude about work.*

Get Started

Good definitions begin with general statements. To make a general statement about the term you are defining, it helps to connect it to a group or category. The group or category then provides you with new ways of thinking in detail about examples and specific details that will illustrate your definition.

There may be several categories into which you can fit your term. Clustering can be a useful way to start your definition thinking. In this example, the student identifies ways of thinking about a hobby.

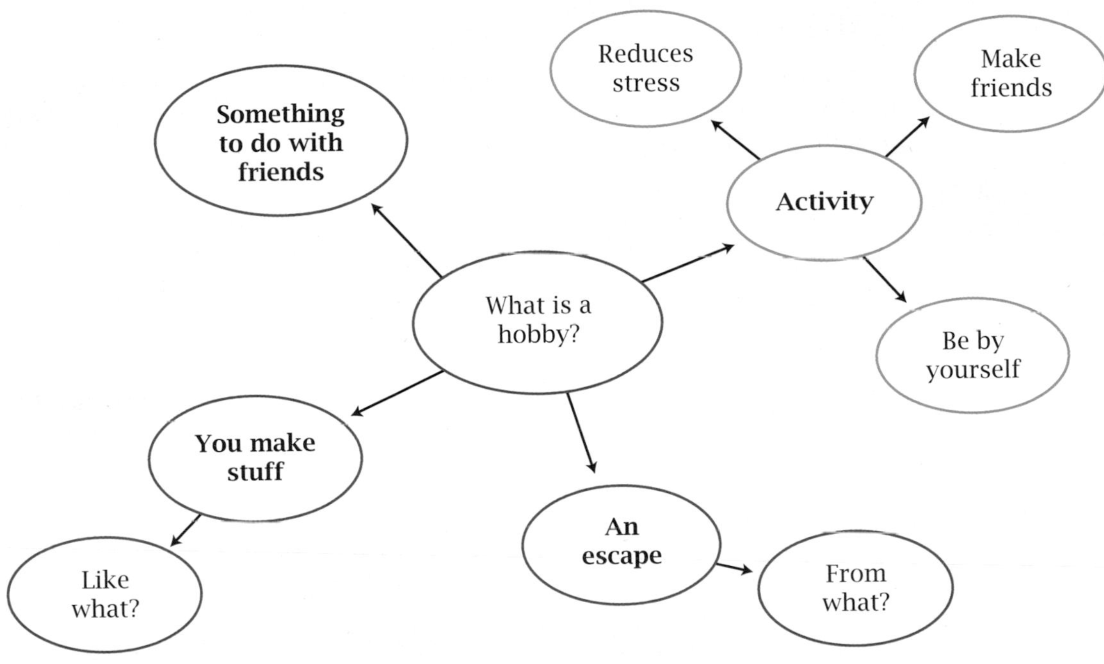

This student's clustering can be summarized as follows:

Term	*Category*
A hobby is	an escape.
A hobby is	something you do.
A hobby is	something you do to make stuff.
A hobby is	something to do with friends.
A hobby is	**an activity that reduces stress.**

The sentence in bold type indicates the sentence this student liked best from his clustering.

EXERCISE 11-1 Definitions and Categories

Directions: *Pick three terms from the list below. Write a sentence that associates the term to be defined with a group or category. To look for possible categories, do some clustering on a separate sheet of paper. Write your best definition sentence in the space provided.* Answers will vary.

Terms: *comfort food, a budget, music, courage, religion*

	Term		*Category*
1.	____________	is	____________.
2.	____________	is	____________.
3.	____________	is	____________.

Examples and Details

As you think further about the term you are defining, it helps to consider examples. Examples lead you to details; details force you to consider whether your definition actually fits the facts.

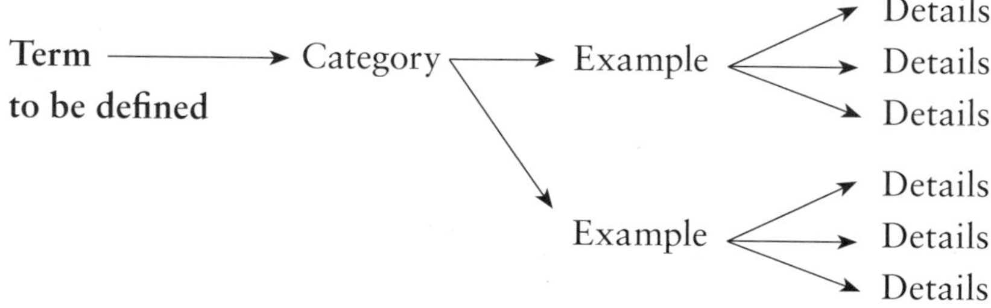

In the case of the student defining hobbies, he decides on a category, a stress-reduction activity, and then lists examples, as shown here.

Term		Category
A hobby	is a	stress-reduction activity.
Examples		**Details**
1. woodworking		done in a relaxing setting
		physical work
		complex—varieties of woods, tools
		no deadlines
		beautiful products of the work
2. working out		done alone or with friends
		visible outcomes (weight loss, improved muscle tone)
		strenuous physical work

These examples and details elaborate on the student's definition sentence. Both woodworking and working out are examples of hobbies, and the details he uses to describe the examples relate to the category of stress reduction, especially *relaxing setting*, *no deadlines*, and *visible outcomes*. Based on this preliminary exploration of his definition, it appears to fit the facts. Now, the student freewrites about the thinking behind his definition of the term *hobby:*

> In both these examples, I note stress is reduced by physical activity. Stress is a mental thing. Physical activity is like stress medicine. A hobby is stress medicine! Also, in both examples, the individual has control over the activity. He can decide if he wants to do it or not. He is in control. He is the boss. A hobby is not something you do because you have to do it. It is something you do because you want to do it.

EXERCISE 11-2 Definitions, Examples, and Details

Directions: *Select two topics from Exercise 11-1 and write your definition sentences for them in the spaces provided below. Then cite two or three examples for each definition and two or three details for each example. When you finish working on the examples, write a few notes to comment on the accuracy of your definition.* Answers will vary.

Term *Category*

1. ______________ is ______________________.

Examples *Details*

____

____

____

Notes on My Definition: ______________________

Term *Category*

2. ______________ is ______________________.

Examples *Details*

Notes on My Definition: ______________________

Negatives

Often there can be disagreement on a key definition. In fact, disagreement on a definition is likely to be the starting point of a protracted discussion. For this reason, it can be useful to think of negative definitions. Doing so says to an academic reader, "I am not talking about *that*. I am talking about *this*."

> Higher education *is not* training that enables a person to make a living. Higher education is enrichment that enables a person to make a life.
>
> Rock music *is not* just three chords played at high volume. Rock music is three chords and in-your-face lyrics.

These definition statements are argumentative. They prepare a writer to write *against* another person's point of view. What is the difference between making a living and making a life? The definition promises to explore that distinction. What does it mean to say the listener is an outlaw? The sentence defining rock music promises to say both what the music is and what it says.

In the student sample on hobbies, he formulated both a positive and a negative definition:

> A hobby *is not* something you do because you have to do it. It is something you do because you want to do it.

A sentence like this establishes your territory. It sets your view apart from competing views.

EXERCISE 11-3 **Establishing Your Territory**

Directions: *Choose the topic from Exercises 11-1 and 11-2 that you care about the most. Write a negative and a positive definition statement about your subject.*
Answers will vary.

Topic: ______________________________

______________ is not ______________________________ .

It is ______________________________ .

Process

DEFINITION IN PROCESS

Definition writing begins with the exploration of a single word or phrase. As you move through the writing process, you develop your ideas, testing and refining your definition.

Select an Assignment

In college writing, definition is a basic writing task that demonstrates your understanding of course content. It is also the starting point for more ambitious thinking and writing.

EXERCISE 11-4 **Selecting an Assignment for a Definition Paragraph**

Directions: *Review the assignments listed below. Choose the one you know the most about and think is best suited to an effective definition paragraph.*

1. Provide a definition of a good job.
2. Define an operation or product that is important in the work you do.
3. Define a term you use at work that is essential to success.

4. Describe a personal value you know best, such as loyalty, consideration, responsibility, compassion, dedication, respect, or acceptance.
5. Define a social problem you have witnessed, such as discrimination, homelessness, physical or mental abuse, apathy, or poverty.
6. Define a word or phrase from your favorite subject that means more to you as you study the subject, such as writing life, patient-community, open dialogue, naturalization, or the lens of popular media.
7. Define a key phrase or slang term that describes an activity you love that others may not understand.
8. Give a definition of a food you love that might be unusual or unique.
9. Define relaxation, fun, or happiness.
10. Provide a definition of a topic of your own choosing.

Prewrite: Write Before You Write

PREWRITE
- Talk
- Cluster
- Brainstorm
- Freewrite

Use prewriting to explore your topic. It is useful to start with a clear destination in mind. However, many writers feel they have really succeeded when they end up writing something they did not expect to write when they began.

Be open to new ways of understanding your subject. Trust the writing process to help you find something important to say. For definition, try clustering and freewriting as ways of exploring what you know about your word and subject.

Cluster

Clustering enables you to see your ideas and details. It also helps you focus on elements of definition and think about how to organize your writing. It is not too early in the writing process to think about the order in which you present your ideas.

Talk about It

Which combination of prewriting strategies is most effective? Why does this combination work so well?

EXERCISE 11-5 Clustering

Directions: *Cluster on your assignment for ten minutes. Use a separate sheet of paper. Remember to try to include details to explain important ideas in your definition.*

Freewrite

Freewriting helps you explore your ideas further. At this point in the process, what you write does not have to be perfect. You want to get everything down on paper that you know about your subject. If ideas and details lead to new material you have not yet thought of, that is even better. In freewriting, you put everything on the table for consideration.

EXERCISE 11-6 Freewriting

Directions: *Write for ten minutes on your subject. Because this is definition, think about the class or category your subject fits into, as well as examples and details that will help you write a good definition.*

Draft: Focus and Organize

In definition thinking, it helps to keep in mind who your definiton is for and why it matters. In a college class, for example, a student's definition of attendance might be coming to class regularly. To the instructor, in contrast, attendance might involve coming to class, participating in discussions, and coming for conferences during office hours. If part of the student's grade is based on attendance, the precise definition of that term would matter a great deal.

DRAFT
- Consider your audience
- Formulate your topic sentence
- Outline for unity and coherence
- Write a conclusion sentence
- Compose your first draft

Consider Your Audience

More often than not, the main reader of your writing in college is your instructor. Your instructor is interested in clarity and detail. You need to convince the reader that your definition is important. In addition, you need to persuade your reader that your definition fits the facts. That means your main idea and supporting details have to work together. Use the following questions to consider how to explain your approach to your reader:

- Why is this subject important?
- What point do I want the reader to understand about my term?
- What details will make my definition more persuasive?

EXERCISE 11-7 **Considering Your Audience**

PEER CONVERSATION

Directions: *Use the questions above to think critically about the subject you are defining and the details you will use to develop your ideas. Talk with a classmate to clarify your thinking. Take notes on this conversation and add them to your prewriting.*

Topic Sentence

At this point in the writing process, think of your topic sentence as a work in progress. As you write, your understanding of your assignment and what you have to say about it may change. For now, a clear topic sentence should echo the assignment, state the term you are defining, and possibly connect the term to a category or group.

Unity and Coherence

Your task is to produce a coherent paragraph that is unified around a single controlling idea. As you draft, watch for details and ideas that go off the subject. A unified paragraph contains only those details relevant to the point your paragraph makes. The coherence of your paragraph will be enhanced by the use of appropriate transition words and phrases. Because you rely on examples and details to elaborate your definition, it is appropriate to use transitions related to example.

TRANSITIONS BASED ON EXAMPLE		
for example	for instance	in this case
to illustrate	in addition	moreover
on the other hand		

If the order of your examples is based on importance, it may also be useful to think about transitions related to priority and impact in this paragraph.

TRANSITIONS BASED ON PRIORITY OR IMPORTANCE

however	more important	equally important
better	worse	in particular
specifically	of course	certainly
in fact		

Concluding Sentence

Plan your concluding sentence. A concluding sentence restates or rephrases the definition and the point of the paragraph.

See "Supporting Details" in Chapter 3 for detailed explanation of outlining.

EXERCISE 11-8 Planning Your First Draft

Directions: *On a separate sheet of paper, write a topic sentence that echoes the key words from the assignment topic you selected. Then organize and outline your details.*

MULTILINGUAL TIP

Bring your draft to the writing center on your campus.

Write a First Draft

So far you have chosen your term and selected the ideas and details you will use to define it. Now that you have decided on the approach you want to use to organize your material, you can write a first draft of your paragraph. As you write, be sure to explain your details. Make sure your paragraph has sufficient detail and explanation so a reader understands why your definition of this word or phrase is important.

EXERCISE 11-9 Writing Your First Draft

Directions: *Write a draft of your paragraph. Use the following checklist as a guide.*

FIRST DRAFT CHECKLIST

_____ My topic sentence states the point of my paragraph.

_____ My topic sentence echoes key terms in the assignment.

_____ I have included examples and details to fully explain the definition in the paragraph.

_____ I have organized my discussion and used transitions to show the relationship between examples and details.

_____ My concluding sentence summarizes the definition in my paragraph.

A PROFESSIONAL'S TAKE

Here is Thomas Moore's use of definition, from his book *Care of the Soul:*

Care of the soul is a fundamentally different way of regarding daily life and the quest for happiness. The emphasis may not be on problems at all. One person might care for the soul by buying or renting a good piece of land, another by selecting an appropriate school or program of study, another by painting his house or his bedroom. Care of the soul is a continuous process that concerns itself not so much with "fixing" a central flaw as with attending to the small details of everyday life, as well as to major decisions and changes. Care of the soul may not focus on the personality or on relationships at all, and therefore it is not psychological in the usual sense. Tending to things around us and becoming sensitive to the importance of home, daily schedule, and maybe even the clothes we wear, are ways of caring for the soul. When Marsilio Ficino wrote his self-help book, *The Book of Life,* five hundred years ago, he placed emphasis on choosing colors, spices, oils, places to walk, countries to visit—all very concrete decisions of everyday life that day by day either support or disturb the soul. We think of the psyche, if we think of it at all, as a cousin to the brain and therefore something essentially internal. But ancient psychologists taught that our own souls are inseparable from the world's soul, and that both are found in all the many things that make up nature and culture.

EXERCISE 11-10 A PROFESSIONAL'S TAKE

Directions: *Using the first draft checklist as your guide, identify elements of an effective definition paragraph in the professional model.*

Revise: Read Critically, Then Rewrite

REVISE
- Read critically
- Develop a revision plan

Revision gives you a chance to rethink. In definition writing, rethinking is key. A first draft gets just one angle on your term and subject. You might find that another angle is more effective. Be open to new thinking as your proceed with this step in the process.

Revision in Action

Revision involves rethinking a draft to improve the quality of your writing: You read critically, plan your revision, and revise your writing. Quality revision will also improve your future writing. Here is an example of revision by a student named Taryn.

The full version of Taryn's sample is available online.

Assignment: To finish our unit on vocabulary and slang, pick a slang term used commonly by a subgroup and explain what it means.

Taryn's First Draft

Kicking is a slang term for a form of relaxation that young people enjoy in our world today. **My first example** of kicking is summer vacation. Some kids between high school graduation and college kick all summer long. They sleep until one in the afternoon, then get up and lie around. Just lying around is almost kicking, but not quite. Without some friends around and without movies, it does not really qualify as kicking. Friends and movies are essential. During the summer, if you can get close to water, like the pool or a beach somewhere, that is kicking in style. **Kicking can also** occur on a daily basis during the school year. I am kicking every day after school. However, it is only reruns that are on TV and I am all by myself, so sometimes I just catch up on my sleep. Technically, when you are sleeping, you are not kicking. You are just asleep. **The most important example of an all-around kicking experience** is the Friday night, Waiting to Exhale party. The girls all get together and fill the room with pillows. They get the right movies and, of course, junk food. No one feels bad about what they eat when they kick. This is be good to yourself time. To be kicking, you have to get relief from something. And waiting to exhale, you cannot have any boys. Kicking is not about anything serious. It is about being with your girls and getting as deeply relaxed as possible. Be careful. You might not want to come back.

TOPIC SENTENCE
Taryn defines kicking as a slang term and identifies a subgroup in her topic sentence.

SUPPORTING DETAILS
She uses three examples to define kicking. All of her details focus on young women. Taryn explains when this activity is and is not kicking.

ORDER AND TRANSITIONS
Taryn uses "first" and "also" as transitions. Her final transition indicates she is also considering order of importance.

CONCLUDING SENTENCE
Taryn concludes with several sentences to define kicking.

Revision Plan: Connect my examples so they define kicking by focusing on the essential details and cutting irrelevant details. Rethink my transitions. Cut first-person pronouns. Keep the casual tone that also helps define kicking.

Taryn's Revised Draft

Kicking is a slang term for a form a relaxation that many young women enjoy in our world today. For some young women, **the most common form** of kicking is accomplished on summer vacation. They sleep until one in the afternoon, then get up and just lie around. This is kicking, **but it is not the best form** of kicking. Without girlfriends around, and more importantly, without movies, it is good kicking, but it is not really great. A **second form of kicking** takes place after school. However, if it is only reruns on TV and there is no one there to share with, it is kicking, but **not great kicking.** To be great, it has to be **planned.** It has to be premeditated. The most important all-around kicking experience is the Friday night, *Waiting to Exhale* form of kicking. This is a **planned** event. The girls all get together and fill the room with pillows. They rent a number of romance movies and settle in for a long evening with Denzel Washington. And, of course, they eat a lot of junk food. No one feels bad about what they eat when they kick. This is be-good-to-yourself time. Kicking is not about anything serious. It is about being with girlfriends and getting as deeply relaxed as possible. Some girls get so relaxed, they do not want to come back.

TOPIC SENTENCE
Taryn keeps her original topic sentence but focuses the subgroup.

ORDER AND TRANSITIONS
Transition terms and repeated words connect the examples and define kicking. Taryn also uses "the most common" and "the most important" to introduce her two major points.

SUPPORTING DETAILS
She defines *kicking* by describing the key factors that create a common understanding of it. She then adds details that show a more sophisticated definition of it. Each point adds to the reader's understanding of *great kicking*.

CONCLUDING SENTENCE
Shifting to third person improves Taryn's concluding sentences.

DISCUSSION QUESTIONS Identify two or three details that make Taryn's revised paragraph a more effective definition of kicking.

PEER CONVERSATION

Read Critically

As you serve as a critical reader for a classmate, you are also getting ideas about how you might improve your own paragraph. Critical reading is a search for the characteristics of effective writing: topic sentence, supporting examples and details, transitions, and concluding sentence. It is also a study of how classmates organize their thinking and the types of supporting details they use to define a subject. Pay attention to how other writers do what you are trying to do.

EXERCISE 11-11 Reading Peer Papers

PEER CONVERSATION

Directions: *Exchange papers with another student. Consider the significant changes that Taryn made between writing her first draft and her revision. Be a critical reader and make suggestions to improve your peer's first draft. Also identify what your classmate did well. Make notes in the margin as you read to remember your thoughts and suggestions. After you read, you will discuss your suggestions. Use the following guidelines.*

REVISION CHECKLIST

______ Does the topic sentence connect to the assignment and state the point of the paragraph?
______ Does the writer focus on definition?
______ Does the writer provide enough detail to clearly define the term?
______ Does the paragraph have effective transitions?
______ Does the concluding sentence emphasize the point of the paragraph?

Revise with a Plan

Reread your assignment. Make sure the paragraph you have written relates directly to your assignment. Look back at all your prewriting for ideas and details you may have missed when you wrote your first draft. It may also be helpful to think about cutting ideas and details to make room for more relevant material. Finally, this is a good time to consider rearranging the ideas and details in your paragraph.

EXERCISE 11-12 **Revising Your Draft**

Directions: *Develop a revision plan and revise the paragraph you wrote for Exercise 11-9.*

Edit

EDIT
- Search and correct
- Self-edit

The small things make all the difference. A misspelled word or an incorrect capitalization can instantly change your reader's view of your work—for the worse. You cannot afford to take that chance. In all your classes, not just English, you should get your writing as close to perfect as you can. If possible, read your work out loud. Listen to it. Look for the errors you know you make. Focus your editing using this personalized checklist.

MULTILINGUAL TIP
Proofread for prepositions and articles.

YOUR EDITING CHECKLIST

______ Spelling: List any words you misspelled in your last paper:

____

______ Punctuation: List two punctuation errors from your last paper:

____

______ Capitalization: List any capitalization errors from your last paper:

____

______ Other errors: List any errors your instructor has pointed out in graded work:

____

____

To Prepare Your Draft for an Academic Audience

Minimize first-person pronouns: *I, me, my.*

Minimize second-person pronouns: *you, your.*

Use third-person pronouns: *he, she, it, they.*

EXERCISE 11-13 Revising and Editing Practice

Directions: *Read the following paragraph that was written in response to the assignment below; it contains errors that require revising and editing. Then answer the questions that follow.*

Assignment: Define an activity, a job, an attitude, or a perspective that might be misunderstood.

(1) Cheerleading may be the most misunderstood team sport. (2) A team sport is defined as something played by a group of teammates who practice, execute strategys, and compete to accomplish a goal. (3) ______________, cheerleading squads practice daily to learn complicated routines. (4) It might even be said that they practice every bit as hard as the players in any team sport. (5) Their cheer routines are performed at games, but they are also prepared for local, state and national compititions. (6) Teams from schools compete, are judged, and are eliminated. (7) Some of them advancing in the competition and ultimately taking trophies back to their schools. (8) These tournaments are very similar to those in which players in team sports compete. (9) Furthermore, cheerleaders are gymnasts who execute flips and dangerous pyramids in their routines. (10) These gymnastic performances require sophisticated strategies to ensure accurate timeing and safe execution. (11) Moreover, cheerleading is a physically demanding sport, cheerleaders must be in top physical condition, like other athletes, they compete for scholarships to major universities. (12) ______________. (13) ______________.

strategies

competition

sentence fragment

tournaments

timing

Revising

b 1. Which word or phrase should be inserted in blank 3? The word or phrase would focus the first point the writer is making to define cheerleading.

a. First

b. Like any team sport

c. In brief

d. Similarly

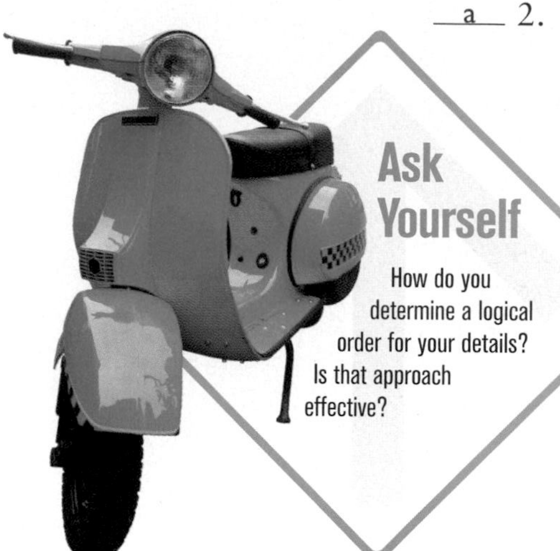
Ask Yourself
How do you determine a logical order for your details? Is that approach effective?

a 2. To arrange the details of this paragraph in a logical order, select the change that is most logical. If the order is correct, choose "no change is necessary."

a. Move sentences 9, 10, and 11 so they follow sentence 4.

b. Reverse the order of sentences 1 and 2.

c. Begin the paragraph with sentence 3.

d. no change is necessary

d 3. Which sentence should be inserted in blank 12? The sentence would provide specific support details for sentence 7. If no sentence is necessary, choose "no change is necessary."

a. I had a friend who won a scholarship to college.

b. Competitions are usually held on weekends and rarely attended by fans.

c. Cheerleaders compete with other high schools.

d. no change is necessary

b 4. Which sentence should be inserted into blank 13? The sentence would provide a conclusion that restates the definition.

a. Spectators at sporting events see cheerleaders as noisy or cute, but they do not see the work it takes to be a cheerleader.

b. Cheerleading is more than shouting cheers at a football game; it is a competitive and demanding sport.

c. Obviously, shouting "Go Team Go" is not the only thing cheerleaders do.

d. Like football and basketball, cheerleading is a sport.

Editing

d 1. Choose the option that corrects the error in sentence 9. If no error exists, choose "no change is necessary."

a. Furthermore, cheerleaders are gymnasts, who execute flips and dangerous pyramids in their routines.

b. Furthermore, cheerleaders are gymnasts who execute flips, and dangerous pyramids in their routines.

c. Furthermore cheerleaders are gymnasts and they execute flips and dangerous pyramids in their routines.

d. no change is necessary

__a__ 2. Choose the option that corrects the error(s) in sentence 11. If no error exists, choose "no change is necessary."

   a. Moreover, because cheerleading is a physically demanding sport, cheerleaders must be in top physical condition. Like other athletes, they compete for scholarships to major universities.

   b. Moreover, cheerleading is a physically demanding sport and cheerleaders must be in top physical condition, like other athletes; they compete for scholarships to major universities.

   c. Moreover, cheerleading is a physically demanding sport. And cheerleaders must be in top physical condition, like other athletes. They compete for scholarships to major universities.

   d. no change is necessary

3. Proofread the paragraph for spelling errors.

4. Proofread the paragraph for a sentence fragment and correct the error.

EXERCISE 11-14 Searching and Correcting

Directions: *Exchange papers with a peer and proofread each other's work. In addition to spelling, punctuation, and capitalization, find out what other errors your classmate has on his or her checklist; tell your classmate what errors you have on your checklist.*

PEER CONVERSATION

EXERCISE 11-15 Self-Editing

Directions: *Carefully rewrite your paper, correcting errors you and your classmate found. Give yourself time to set aside the finished paper. Then come back to it and read your final draft one last time, using your checklist as a guide.*

Reflect

Definition writing puts you to the test. You made sophisticated decisions to apply your previous learning to this paragraph. Take a moment and reflect on what you have learned.

REFLECT
- Identify strengths
- Set goals

EXERCISE 11-16 Identifying Strengths and Setting Goals

Directions: *Review your writing and your writing process. On a separate sheet of paper answer these questions:*

- *What did you do well in the paragraph you wrote?*
- *What did you enjoy working on in this chapter?*
- *What have you learned that you will apply in future writing assignments?*

That Is Your Opinion

Much language activity is neutral. Casual conversation at home, classroom discussion, talk about a new person at work—in these contexts we are showing interest in each other, sharing information, or just passing the time of day. Then again, even casual conversation can have an edge. The give-and-take of talk can also become a contest. One person says the best pizza in town is at Paisano's; the other makes a strong case for Milano Pizzeria. There is a difference of opinion, and suddenly there is an argument. The focus of the argument is crust, sauce, toppings, restaurant atmosphere, the help, and price. The argument about where to find the best pizza involves a careful (and passionate) analysis of what pizza is, how and where pizza is eaten, and why we like what we like. Such things are a matter of opinion, but from this argument comes a more detailed understanding of our subject—in this case, pizza.

BRAINSTORM

Do you have opinions? Sure you do. Make a list of your opinions, big and small. Then select three and write a sentence or two about each one.

Make Your Case

The writing you do in college will frequently be persuasive because it will ask you to evaluate. "Most," "best," "least," "worst"—when you write in college, you need to make a case for your reader. Why do kids drop out of school? *The most common reason is . . .* This approach to the subject suggests that there are many reasons, that they are not all equal, and that the writer is going to make a case for what she feels is the most common. What if there is a difference of opinion? Then the writer has to dig down and present evidence. She has to use information to convince her reader that her view is on target. Persuasion often involves finding facts that fit your gut feeling and then presenting those facts to win over your reader.

DISCUSSION

Talk with a classmate to answer the following questions: What is the most pressing problem facing your neighborhood, your city, or your state? How can this problem be solved? What gut feelings do you have to support your solution? What facts do you have to support your solution? Do you agree on how to solve this problem?

Sounds Like a Plan

On the job, you may have ideas about how to fine-tune processes and procedures. You assess the situation, think critically, and propose a plan of action. Often, however, it is not that easy. You have to persuade your coworkers and your boss that your plan makes sense. This requires careful observation and evidence. It also involves knowing how to appeal to others for their support. Convince coworkers that your plan reduces stress and reduces work, and you will have them on board. Convince your boss that your plan makes for greater efficiency and higher profits, and you will have a chance of seeing your plan taken seriously.

RESUME BUILDER

There are processes and procedures you know well at work. Maybe you have a faster or better way to do something. Maybe you have a suggestion for handling customers. In what ways could your job be made more efficient or effective? What facts or details can you use to support your idea for change?

CHAPTER 12

Argument

CHAPTER OVERVIEW

- THE ARGUMENT PARAGRAPH AT A GLANCE
- ARGUMENT THINKING
  - Elements of Argument
  - Review Evidence
  - Acknowledge Another Viewpoint
- ARGUMENT IN PROCESS
  - Prewrite
  - Draft
  - A Professional's Take
  - Revise
  - Edit
  - Reflect

THINK FIRST

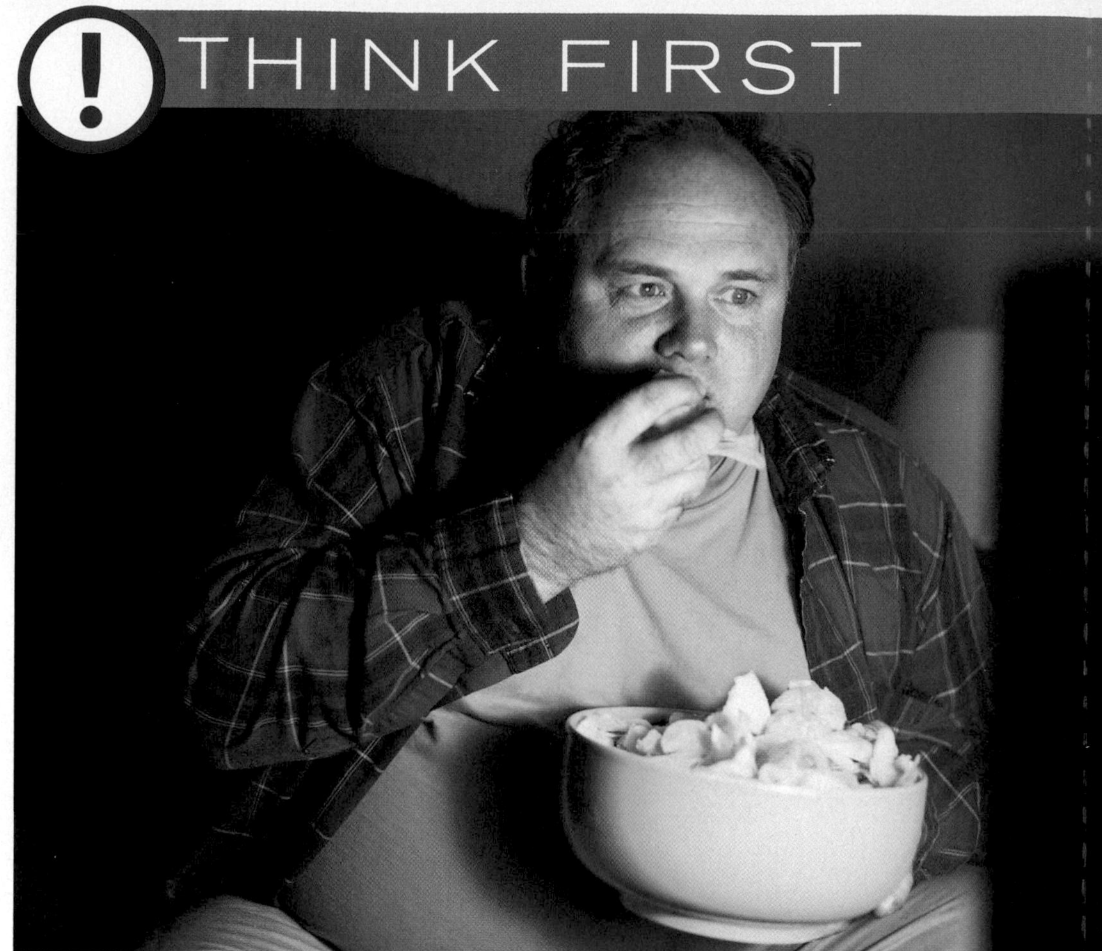

This man is relaxing. This man is engaging in a self-destructive behavior. Which is it? Write a paragraph in which you persuade the reader that one or the other viewpoint is accurate. Explain your reasons.

At a Glance

THE ARGUMENT PARAGRAPH AT A GLANCE

Argument begins with a difference of opinion. There are two or more competing viewpoints on an issue, problem, or situation; and as a writer, you need to take a stand. An effective argument paragraph crisply defines the issue, problem, or situation, and then provides reasons and evidence for the stand you have taken.

Argument works best when the writer provides convincing information and compelling reasons. Your topic sentence states your position or the claim of your argument. This opener is followed by details that explain the reasons for the argument. These details are usually ordered by importance, starting or ending with the most important details. Your final sentence clinches the argument, sums it up, and makes a powerful appeal to your reader.

The Argument Paragraph at a Glance

ASSIGNMENT What is the best lifestyle choice a person can make to increase mental and physical health?

The best lifestyle choice a person can make to increase his or her mental and physical health is to decrease stress. Stress has been shown to have a negative impact on both mental and physical health. **For example,** people often deal with stress in one of two ways: They act out, which involves arguing, yelling, physical violence directed at others, and self-destructive behavior; or they withdraw inward, becoming depressed and isolated. **Those who deal with stress by** arguing or hurting others merely add to the stress in their lives. How can they possibly be happy when they hurt those they love? **Those who turn to** self-destructive behaviors, such as alcohol or drug use, are likely to do physical harm to themselves. **In contrast, those who turn inward** shut themselves away from people and experiences that might actually help them deal with the source of their stress. They concentrate on their troubles, which only compounds their stress. People who decrease their stress can take pleasure in family and friends. **In addition,** an individual's health is enhanced when he or she is less stressed. **To the**

TOPIC SENTENCE
The student echoes the key words in the assignment and focuses on a specific health issue.

SUPPORTING DETAILS
The student discusses the consequences of stress, presenting them as reasons why stress has a negative effect on mental and physical health.

ORDER AND TRANSITIONS
The student begins with the most important reason stress is negative: It hurts both the individual and other people. Then she shifts to the effects of stress on the individual alone.

CONCLUDING SENTENCES
At the end of the paragraph, the student restates the assignment language and, in her last two sentences, emphasizes the point of her argument.

extent that stress causes a person to direct negative energy both outward and inward, mental and physical health are going to be compromised. Live well. Minimize stress.

DISCUSSION QUESTIONS

PEER CONVERSATION

1. What would be the effect of reversing the order of evidence in this paragraph?
2. What other lifestyle choices affect mental and physical health?
3. In your opinion, which of these other choices is the most important? Why?

Thinking

ARGUMENT THINKING

Argument is a special form of problem solving. You begin with a problem or issue. Should we lower the legal drinking age? What is your view? You have to settle matters in your own mind first. Then you have to anticipate the views of an audience. What do others think? Then you turn to reasons—why you think you are right and what you believe to be the basis for opposing views. Finally, you present the evidence to support your position and explain your reasoning. If you want your argument to prevail, you need to be focused and logical.

Elements of Argument

These are the basic elements of argument thinking.

- *A claim:* Your topic sentence states a position or claim you are promoting.
- *Reasons, evidence, or details:* The body of your paragraph proves your claim with supporting details or evidence. Argument paragraphs use both personal and expert evidence. This evidence can be facts, examples, narrative, or compelling testimony.
- *Conceding other viewpoints:* Argument involves topics about which there is a difference of opinion. It is common and useful to acknowledge other viewpoints in your argument paragraph. In the sample above, for instance, the writer concedes that diet and sleep can both contribute to physical and mental health.

Get Started

In academic writing, you have to take a stand. Readers of college writing do not want to see, "In the end every person has to make up his or her own mind." No, your reader wants *you* to *make up your mind* and present detailed reasoning to make a case for your point of view. Doing so shows the reader you can think critically. It shows the reader you know your subject.

Suppose you are presented with a question like this: Should students be able to use calculators in their math classes? Maybe you take the stand expressed in the following topic sentence. Then you list reasons to support your claim.

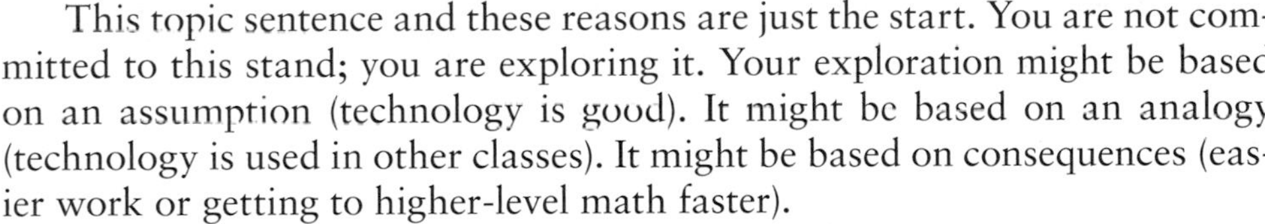

Writer's Response

When you argue, how do you support a claim you make? What kind of evidence is most effective?

Topic Sentence: Students should definitely be able to use calculators in their math classes.

Reasons

A. Technology makes the job easier. Why not use it?

B. Technology is widely used in other classes: word processors, with spell-check, for example.

C. Technology helps math students get to higher-level math ideas faster.

This topic sentence and these reasons are just the start. You are not committed to this stand; you are exploring it. Your exploration might be based on an assumption (technology is good). It might be based on an analogy (technology is used in other classes). It might be based on consequences (easier work or getting to higher-level math faster).

EXERCISE 12-1 Taking a Stand

Directions: *Write a sentence that states your position on each of the following issues in the spaces provided. Then briefly list two or three reasons or details to support your view. Indicate whether your reasons are based on assumption, on analogy, or on consequences.* Answers will vary.

1. Is it a good idea to give money to a homeless person standing on a street corner?

Topic Sentence: ______________________________

____

____

Reasons

A. ______________________________

B. ______________________________

C. ______________________________

Reasons based on assumption/analogy/consequences: ____________

2. Should a parent's signature be required for young people to have access to birth control?

Topic Sentence: ______________________________

____

____

Reasons

A. ______________________________

B. ______________________________

C. ______________________________

Reasons based on assumption/analogy/consequences: ______________

3. Should juvenile offenders who commit violent crimes be tried as adults?

Topic Sentence: ______________________________

____

____

Reasons

A. ______________________________

B. ______________________________

C. ______________________________

Reasons based on assumption/analogy/consequences: ______________

Review Evidence

Once you identify reasons for your position on a topic, you need to provide evidence. Your argument is only as good as your evidence. Evidence might consist of personal narrative, observation and example, or expert opinion and data that show the validity of your reasons.

In the example that follows, the student argues for the use of calculators in the classroom using all three forms of evidence to support his argument.

This evidence supports the student's first reason: "Technology makes the job easier."

Personal Narrative

Technology makes the job easier. In fifth-grade math, we did long division problems for weeks at a time with Mrs. Mann. The work was tedious and took forever. Everyone hated it. The only thing it taught some kids was to hate math. Long division with a calculator takes seconds. By hand, it takes a very long time.

Observation and Example

My math class this semester, science class last semester; friends' classes where they go to college. Calculators okay.

Expert Opinion

Patricia Campbell, a math professor at the University of Maryland, states in the *Washington Post,* "I would want a child to know how to add and subtract two and three digit numbers. However, I do not want to spend class time adding and subtracting five and six digit numbers. I would rather spend class time doing other math" (www.education-world.com/a_curr/curr072.shtml).

Expert opinion and data can be particularly useful in argument paragraphs. For a detailed explanation of how to go about finding expert opinion and data, see Chapter 16, "The Documented Essay."

EXERCISE 12-2 Reviewing Evidence

Directions: *Select a topic that interests you from Exercise 12-1. Write your topic sentence in the space provided and list evidence, such as personal narrative, examples, or expert opinion that supports your argument.* Answers will vary.

Topic Sentence: ______________________________

____

____

Evidence: ______________________________

____

____

____

____

____

____

____

____

Acknowledge Another Viewpoint

Argument involves the explanation of reasons that support a viewpoint. It is important that your viewpoint fits the facts. As you formulate opinions and review evidence, you will become aware of opposing views. What makes your viewpoint preferable? Is it more reasonable? Does it fit the facts better?

Your initial tendency may be to avoid thinking about views that are contrary to your own. Taking them into consideration, however, may actually help you better understand the basis of your viewpoint and strengthen your position.

In the case of using calculators in math classes, the student examines the opposing view and a few reasons to support it.

Opposing View: Calculators should not be used in math classes.

A. Students might not learn fundamentals of math.

B. Students become dependent on machines and cannot think without their help.

These reasons seem valid. Learning the fundamentals is important. Being able to think without the help of machines is important. Simply to dismiss these reasons would actually hurt this student's argument for the use of calculators in the classroom. His task then is to acknowledge these opposing reasons, to concede them, and in so doing, qualify his position. Another way of thinking of this is that the writer gives a little ground. He admits the value of another way of looking at the issues.

Topic Sentence: Students should definitely be able to use calculators in their math classes.

concede opposing reasons

A. It is true that students might not learn fundamentals.

B. It is true that students might become dependent on machines and be unable to think without their help.

qualifier

C. For this reason, students should not use calculators until they have mastered the fundamentals.

D. After that, if technology makes the job easier, why not use it?

supporting reasons

E. Technology is widely used in other classes: word processors, with spell-check, for example.

F. Technology helps math students get to higher-level math ideas faster.

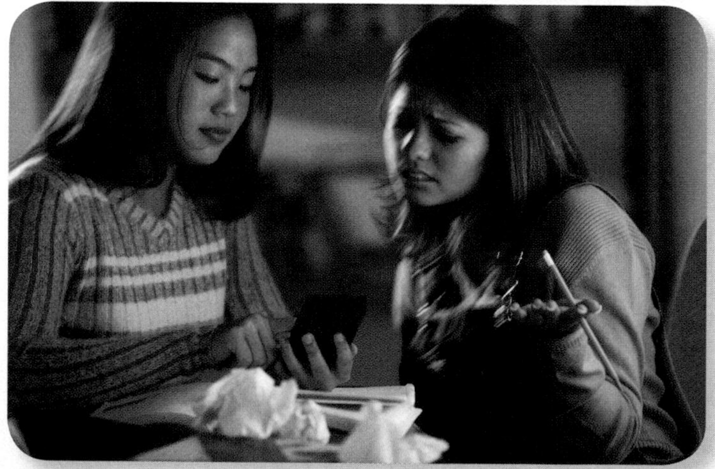

Because he has acknowledged opposing reasons, the student's argument is now stronger. A reader cannot object, saying, "Wait, what about kids who do not know how to multiply?" In his qualifier, he has answered this objection. When you qualify your position on an issue, you soften it slightly. You move from saying something is *always* true to saying something is *frequently* true or true *under certain conditions.*

The moves a student makes when framing an argument can be pictured as follows.

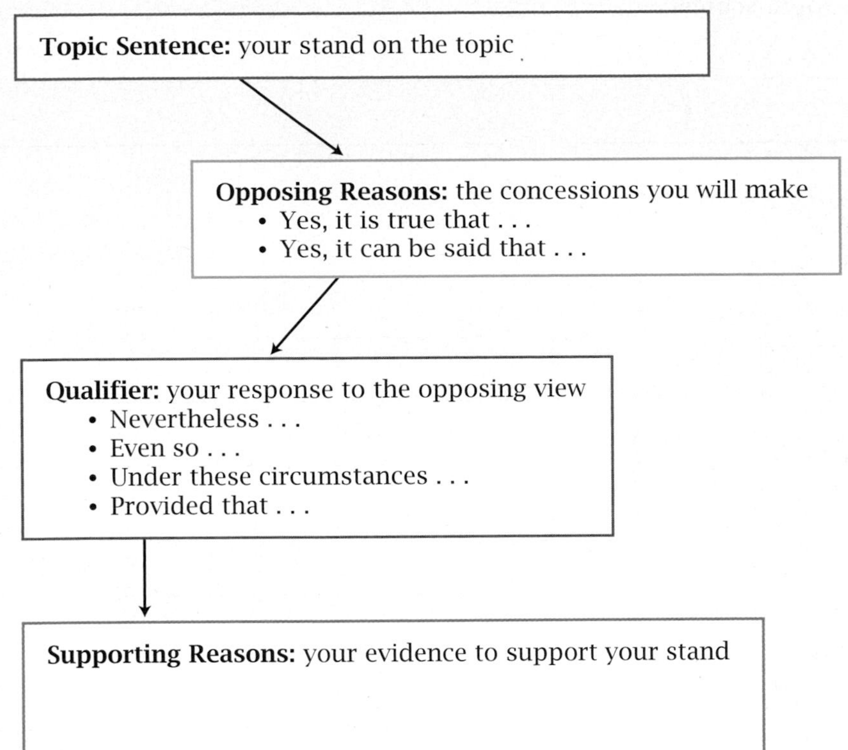

Topic Sentence: your stand on the topic
Opposing Reasons: the concessions you will make
• Yes, it is true that . . .
• Yes, it can be said that . . .
Qualifier: your response to the opposing view
• Nevertheless . . .
• Even so . . .
• Under these circumstances . . .
• Provided that . . .
Supporting Reasons: your evidence to support your stand

EXERCISE 12-3 Acknowledging an Opposing Viewpoint

Directions: *Review the topic you worked on in Exercises 12-1 and 12-2. You have taken a stand on an issue and reviewed evidence that supports your position. Now consider the opposing viewpoint. Using the diagram below, list two or three reasons that support the opposing viewpoint and then qualify your position on the issue to reflect those reasons.* Answers will vary.

EXAMPLE

Assignment: State your opinion on mothers working outside the home and the possible impact on their children.

Topic Sentence: Mothers working outside the home is often necessary for the well-being of the family and is ultimately good for children.

Opposing Reasons

It is true that A. Small children may be looked after in day care rather than in the home, which is not optimum.

It is true that B. Older children can be unsupervised after school, which has risks.

Qualifier

C. Nevertheless, in cases where these supervision issues are addressed properly, women in the workplace can be a good thing.

Supporting Reasons

D. Working mothers contribute significantly to family income.

E. Working mothers provide positive role models for both their female and male children.

Your Topic Sentence: ______________________________

____

____

Opposing Reasons

It is true that A. ______________________________

____

____

It is true that B. ______________________________

____

____

Qualifier

C. ______________________________

____

Supporting Reasons

D. ______________________________

____

E. ______________________________

____

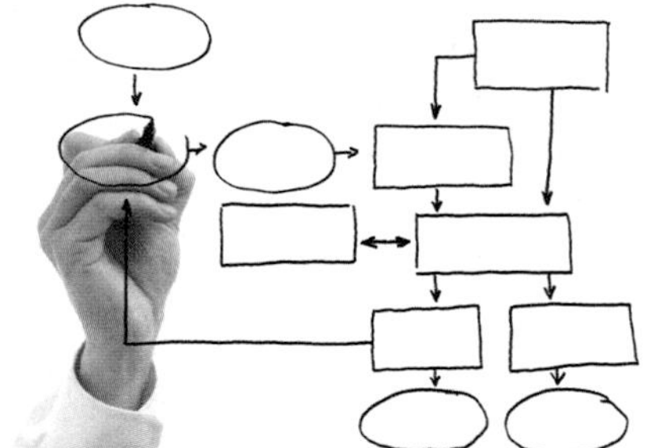

Process

ARGUMENT IN PROCESS

Argument often begins with something you read or hear. You think, *Wait a minute. That is not right.* This reaction triggers an investigation of your position on the subject, on opposing viewpoints, and on evidence. Argument is about examining your beliefs and opinions, determining their foundations, and squaring them with the facts.

Select an Assignment

In college courses, students need to persuade the reader that they are informed, that they have mastered the content. They also need to demonstrate fairness and openness to other viewpoints. When you take a position on a subject, you must include the evidence to the contrary in your discussion.

EXERCISE 12-4 **Selecting an Assignment for Argument Paragraph**

Directions: *Review the assignments listed below. Choose the one you know the most about and think is best suited to an effective argument paragraph.*

1. Should there be a total ban on smoking in all public places?
2. Should age limits be reconsidered for things like credit cards?
3. Should the limit on the legal age for drinking be raised or lowered?
4. Should schools have rigid control over dress code?
5. Should affirmative action be part of college admission?
6. Should admission standards be compromised for individuals with exceptional athletic ability?
7. Should the government create a health insurance plan for everyone?
8. Should the government restrict marriage, adoption, or parental rights?
9. Discuss a current rule or law that needs to be changed.
10. Select a subject from a current course or a subject of your choice.

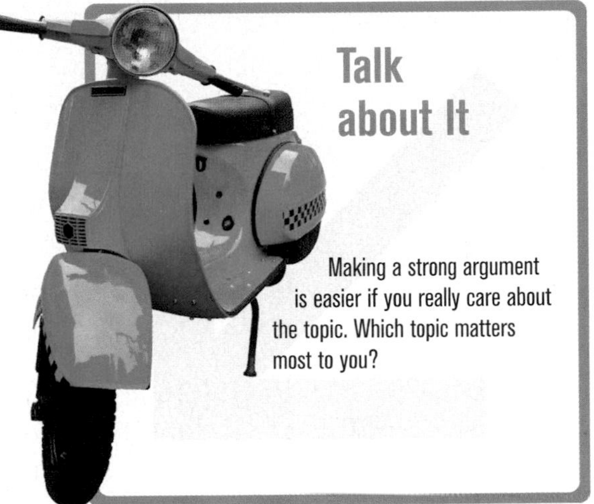

Talk about It

Making a strong argument is easier if you really care about the topic. Which topic matters most to you?

Prewrite: Write Before You Write

Argument pushes you to examine your beliefs and opinions. It requires you to explore a subject from multiple viewpoints. We often have arguments in casual conversation. For that reason, after your initial exploration of your topic, it may help to square off with classmates and test your ideas.

PREWRITE
- Talk
- Cluster
- Brainstorm
- Freewrite

Freewrite

Explore your topic with freewriting. Work fast. Get your ideas down on paper. Find out what you know about your subject and why you believe what you believe. As you work, try to look at more than one point of view on your subject. Be open to new thinking as you write.

EXERCISE 12-5 **Freewriting**

Directions: *Freewrite on your subject for ten minutes. Take a stand on your topic and examine any facts, examples, and reasons related to your viewpoint. In addition, explore opposing points of view. Be open to new thinking. You may discover that a new or different claim will emerge.*

Talk

Talking enables you to test your idea and benefit from the give-and-take that comes in conversation. Capture your new thinking on paper after you finish talking.

PEER CONVERSATION

EXERCISE 12-6 **Talking about It**

Directions: *Turn to your neighbor in class or find another interested listener. Tell this person about your subject and state the opinion you explored in your freewriting. Explain both sides of the argument as you see it. Then listen to your classmate's viewpoint. Take notes to capture his or her views. Then be a critical listener and speaker to your partner's argument.*

Draft: Focus and Organize

When writing an argument, it is essential to be clear about your viewpoint. What is your position on your topic? What examples and reasons can you cite to support your position? What facts support your position? What facts go against your position?

Consider Your Audience

In argument writing, considering your audience will strengthen your argument and your paragraph. Identifying counterarguments can be helpful. Review your prewriting to find the important ideas you want to use in your paragraph. Use the following questions to consider your audience.

- Why is this topic important?
- What do I want my reader to understand about my topic?
- What objections would a reader have to my position on this subject?
- What is my response to those objections?

PEER CONVERSATION

EXERCISE 12-7 **Considering Your Audience**

Directions: *Use the questions above to think critically about your topic, opinion, and reasons. Talk with a classmate to clarify your thinking. Take notes on this conversation and add them to your prewriting.*

Topic Sentence

In an argument paragraph, your topic sentence establishes your topic and states your viewpoint. Write a topic sentence that clearly states your position.

Unity and Coherence

Staying on point is important in argument. If you go off the subject, you lose your reader. A unified argument paragraph focuses on ideas and details related to the main idea of the paragraph.

In addition to unity, coherence will add strength to your argument. Think ahead about your transitions. Transitions make the relationships among ideas, details, and reasons visible for the reader. Consider using these transitions related to evidence and conclusions in your argument paragraph.

Concluding Sentence

When writers place the topic sentence at the beginning of a paragraph, the concluding sentence generally restates the claim and emphasizes the writer's viewpoint.

EXERCISE 12-8 Planning Your First Draft

Directions: *On a separate sheet of paper, write a topic sentence that states your claim and connects to your assignment. Then use the topic sentence to outline your supporting details. Although your transitions may change in your first draft, include transitions in your outline to plan how the forms of proof will support your argument.*

See "Supporting Details" in Chapter 3 for detailed explanation of outlining.

Write a First Draft

As you write a first draft, remember that it is better to write too much than too little; you can always cut back later. Put all the evidence you have into your first draft. In a second draft you can cut what a reader does not find convincing. Also, be sure to explain your ideas and reasons.

MULTILINGUAL TIP

Bring your draft to the writing center on your campus.

EXERCISE 12-9 Writing Your First Draft

Directions: *Write a draft of your paragraph. Use the following checklist as a guide.*

FIRST DRAFT CHECKLIST

_____ My topic sentence states the claim of my argument paragraph.

_____ My topic sentence echoes key terms in the assignment.

_____ I inserted transitions to make connections between supporting details visible.

_____ I included multiple forms of proof (facts, examples, or testimony) to convince my reader.

_____ I included reasons that explain the evidence.

A PROFESSIONAL'S TAKE

The use of argument from *The Economist*

The two main arguments against being helped into death are both of the "slippery slope" sort. The first is that it is hard to know where the boundary lies. Should a patient be three days, three months or three years away from death when the help is given? If the criterion is that a patient should be terminally ill, how should "terminally" be defined? Is it logical to distinguish between terminally ill and chronically ill, if a chronically ill person wants to die but may have years to live? Should people in good physical health but emotional distress be allowed help in dying? This is a matter of where to draw the line. The even tougher counter-argument is that the whole process is dangerously open to abuse. To many, legal doctor-assisted suicide is a harbinger of evil, the start of a slide into a time of state-condoned euthanasia when the frail and the handicapped will be bullied into dying prematurely, doctors will become executioners, and the terminally ill will be offered the "treatment" of death instead of relief from pain. Death, after all, is cheaper than treatment. It is not hard to imagine health-insurance companies and managed-care organizations agreeing to pay for barbiturates that kill rather than pills that merely reduce pain. The strongest practical argument the defenders of a ban on doctor-assisted suicide can make is that, though some people would benefit from help in dying, a greater number are vulnerable to potential abuse from such a system; therefore, society has an interest in asking the state to protect their lives. The trouble is that this argument leaves dying people preserved in a state of suffering without any chance to choose oblivion instead. Even more important, it assumes that a law for doctor-assisted suicide cannot be drafted in a way that would prevent its abuse.

EXERCISE 12-10 A PROFESSIONAL'S TAKE

Directions: *Using the first draft checklist as your guide, identify elements of an effective argument paragraph in the professional model.*

Revise: Read Critically, Then Rewrite

Before you revise your paragraph, examine the strengths in a classmate's argument paragraph. Then look at your argument paragraph with fresh eyes. Revision gives you a chance to rethink.

REVISE
- Read critically
- Develop a revision plan

Revision in Action

Revision is rethinking a draft to improve the quality of your writing: Read critically, plan revision, and revise the writing. Quality revision will also improve your future writing. Here is an example of revision by a student named Diana.

The full version of Diana's sample is available online.

Assignment: What can the informed individual do to make a difference on an environmental issue today? Be specific.

Diana's First Draft

A small thing consumers can do that would have a big environmental impact is to stop using plastic bags at the grocery story. **On one hand,** plastic bags are convenient. They are lighter and nicer to carry than paper. They take up less room at home and in the landfill. They cost the grocery store only a penny each. **However,** according to the *New York Times,* plastic bags take more than a thousand years to break down in a landfill. That is bad for the environment. **Furthermore,** there are a lot of plastic bags blowing around out there. According to the Progressive Bag Alliance, the world uses between 100 billion and a trillion plastic bags a year (Conway). Hard to imagine. **How about paper?** Is that a good option? Not really. **While** paper bags are biodegradable and some are even made from recycled paper, they are not environmentally friendly to make. The process uses lots of water, and water is polluted in the process. **The best solution,** it turns out, is to take reusable bags with you to the store. They will save you money because pretty soon stores will start charging you for paper or plastic bags. Using them will also help save the environment. It will give you something to do with all those bags your mother has been saving all these years. Heck, you will probably never run out.

TOPIC SENTENCE
Diana uses key words from the assignment and states a specific action an individual can take.

SUPPORTING DETAILS
Diana provides details about using plastic bags. Then she explores two ways a person can stop using them. She provides facts, details, and reasons to support her argument.

ORDER AND TRANSITIONS
She uses a variety of transitions to connect major and minor points in her paragraph. She clearly indicates the key point in her argument ("best solution").

CONCLUDING SENTENCE
Diana use two sentences to conclude and makes two comments about reusable bags.

Revision Plan: Remove the informal language. Work on the conclusion of my paragraph. Check order and transitions.

TOPIC SENTENCE
Diana revises her topic sentence.

SUPPORTING DETAILS
Diana concedes that plastic bags are convenient and inexpensive. She adds detail to explain convenience. Diana also adds detail on the paper bag option in this draft.

ORDER AND TRANSITIONS
She uses parallel sentences to move the argument from plastic to paper to reusable bags. Her transitions connect facts, details, and reasons in each major point.

CONCLUDING SENTENCE
Diana revises her concluding sentences, focusing responsibility on each person.

Diana's Revised Draft

A small thing every consumer can do to have a big environmental impact is stop using plastic or paper bags at the grocery store. **Plastic bags are truly convenient.** Plastic bags are lighter and easier to carry than paper bags. They take up less room at home, and they cost the grocery store only a penny each, which means they are cheap for the consumer. **Howver,** according to the *New York Times,* plastic bags take more than a thousand years to break down in a landfill. That is bad for the environment. **Furthermore,** the number of plastic bags used is staggering. According to the Progressive Bag Alliance, the world uses between 100 billion and a trillion plastic bags a year (Conway). **Paper bags are not a much better option.** While paper bags are biodegradable and some are even made from recycled paper, they are not environmentally friendly to make. They take up a lot of landfill space and are slow to degrade. **Moreover,** the Environmental Protection Agency reports that they take more energy to make than plastic bags (Conway). The process uses lots of water and causes water pollution. **Reusable bags are the best solution.** To encourage consumers to reuse bags, some European countries have started to tax consumers. **For every** bag a consumer takes, a fee is added to his or her grocery bill. **As soon as** that happens in this country, reusable bags will become common practice. It will be more economical for consumers, and reusable bags will be environmentally friendly. Choosing not to use plastic or paper bags makes a difference on an important environmental issue. The sooner each person gets started, the better.

Works Cited

Conway, Chris. "Taking Aim at All Those Plastic Bags." *New York Times.* April 1, 2007: B2. Print.

PEER CONVERSATION

DISCUSSION QUESTIONS What changes affect the tone of Diana's paragraph? Cite and discuss two or three specific examples.

Read Critically

When you read a peer's paper, you will gain skill at reading your own writing more critically. Read systematically. Think about difficulties you had when you wrote your paragraph. Look for ways your classmate handled similar difficulties in his or her writing.

EXERCISE 12-11 Reading Peer Papers

PEER CONVERSATION

Directions: *Exchange papers with another student. Consider the strengths and weaknesses of Diana's argument paragraph. Be a systematic reader and identify the claim, points, evidence, and explanation. Also identify what your classmate did well. Make notes in the margin as you read to remember your suggestions. After you read, you will discuss your suggestions. Use the following guidelines.*

REVISION CHECKLIST

_____ Does the topic sentence connect to the assignment and state the point of the paragraph?
_____ Does the writer take a position and provide evidence for the argument?
_____ Does the writer provide enough detail to explain the evidence?
_____ Does the writer take other viewpoints into consideration?
_____ Does the paragraph have effective transitions?
_____ Does the concluding sentence emphasize the point of the paragraph?

Revise with a Plan

Reread your assignment before revising. Be sure your focus matches the assignment. In addition, review the elements of argument and look for them in your paragraph. Do you take a clear position? Do you provide reasons and explain them? Do you take an opposing viewpoint into account? Do you qualify your argument based on them? Reread your paragraph and the notes from your peer conference. Make changes accordingly.

EXERCISE 12-12 Revising Your Draft

Directions: *Develop a revision plan and revise the paragraph you wrote for Exercise 12-9.*

Edit

EDIT
- Search and correct
- Self-edit

In argument writing, facts matter. However, nothing is more persuasive than carefully edited writing. If your reader is distracted by careless errors, your argument is in trouble. This is true in English class and in all classes you take in college. Focus your editing using this personalized checklist.

YOUR EDITING CHECKLIST

_____ Spelling: List any words you misspelled in your last paper:

____

_____ Punctuation: List two punctuation errors from your last paper:

____

MULTILINGUAL TIP

Proofread for correct pronoun use.

______ Capitalization: List any capitalization errors from your last paper:

____

______ Other errors: List any errors your instructor has pointed out in graded work:

____

____

To Prepare Your Draft for an Academic Audience

______ Minimize first-person pronouns: *I, me, my.*

______ Minimize second-person pronouns: *you, your.*

______ Use third-person pronouns: *he, she, it, they.*

EXERCISE 12-13 Revising and Editing Practice

Directions: *Read the following paragraph that was written in response to the assignment below; it contains errors that require revising and editing. Then answer the questions that follow.*

Assignment: Select a topic about which you have a strong opinion. Write an argument paragraph stating your position on the topic. Use specific facts, details, and examples to argue and support your position, taking into account how others may disagree with your point of view.

(1) Animal rights groups argue that there is no reason to hunt animals, that it is inhumane, and that the animals are little more than target practice for the hunters. (2) Hunters argue otherwise they insist that hunting is much more than simply pointing a gun or a bow in the direction of game animals and taking close aim. (3) Ask bird hunters how often they miss or never even have a chance to take a shot at there prey. (4) They will describe the years of target practice, tracking or dog training required to be a successful bird hunter. (5) No, hunting is not about killing. (6) ________________. (7) A family-oriented tradition passed from father to son, hunting provides an excellent opportunity for bonding between parents and children and can offer lots of time for personal reflection. (8) Some fathers and sons have quality time together fishing. (9) While they are hunting, they enjoy watching the sun come up, walking in silence and listening to the birds, and breathing the fresh air. (10) ________________, hunters eat what they kill, and they respect the regulations and limits set

run-on

by game management policies so game is not overhunted. (11) Actually hunters play an important role in holding the ecosystem in balance. (12) Thinning the population of wildlife that is moving into urban areas. (13) Hunters also protect the food supply and the health of the remaining wildlife. (14) The positive effects of hunting far outweigh the negatives both for the hunter personally and for the ecosystem as a whole.

Revising

__b__ 1. Which sentence should be inserted in blank 6? The sentence would state the argument and serve as the topic sentence.

a. Hunting should be valued by nonhunters.

b. Hunting is an American tradition that requires skill and adherence to a code of ethics.

c. Animal rights groups are wrong about hunting.

d. Everyone has their own point of view about hunting: some like it; some do not.

__d__ 2. Select the order of sentences 2, 3, 4, and 5 to provide the most logical sequence of details to present the position of the paragraph and support the topic sentence. If the order is correct, choose "no change is necessary."

a. 5, 2, 3, 4

b. 2, 5, 3, 4

c. 2, 3, 5, 4

d. no change is necessary

__c__ 3. Which word or phrase should be inserted in blank 10?

a. Second

b. As a result

c. In addition

d. In any case

Ask Yourself
Which revision strategy do you prefer? Adding, cutting, or rearranging details?

__b__ 4. Which sentence should be cut to improve the unity of the paragraph? If no sentence needs to be cut, choose "no change is necessary."

a. sentence 1

b. sentence 8

c. sentence 13

d. no change is necessary

Editing

_d_ 1. Choose the option that corrects the error in sentence 1. If no error exists, choose "no change is necessary."

a. Animal rights groups argue, that there is no reason to hunt animals, that it is inhumane, and that the animals are little more than target practice for the hunters.

b. Animal rights groups argue that there is no reason to hunt animals; that it is inhumane; and that the animals are little more than target practice for the hunters.

c. Animal rights groups argue that there is no reason to hunt animals. That it is inhumane, and that the animals are little more than target practice for the hunters.

d. no change is necessary

_b_ 2. Choose the option that corrects the spelling error in sentence 3. If no error exists, choose "no change is necessary."

a. Ask bird hunters how often they miss or never even have a chance to take a shot at there pray.

b. Ask bird hunters how often they miss or never even have a chance to take a shot at their prey.

c. Ask bird hunters how often they miss or never even have a chance to take a shoot at there prey.

d. no change is necessary

_a_ 3. Sentence 12 is a fragment. Choose the option to correct this sentence error.

a. combine sentence 11 and 12

b. combine sentence 12 and 13

c. cut sentence 11

d. cut sentence 12

4. Proofread the paragraph for a run-on sentence and correct the error.

EXERCISE 12-14 Searching and Correcting

PEER CONVERSATION

Directions: *Exchange papers with a peer and proofread each other's work. In addition to spelling, punctuation, and capitalization, find out what other errors your classmate has on his or her checklist; tell your classmate what errors you have on your checklist.*

EXERCISE 12-15 Self-Editing

Directions: *Rewrite your paper, correcting errors you and your classmate found. Give yourself time to set aside the finished paper. Then come back to it and read your final draft one last time, using your checklist as a guide.*

Reflect

Take a moment and reflect on what you have learned.

REFLECT

- Identify strengths
- Set goals

EXERCISE 12-16 Identifying Strengths and Setting Goals

Directions: *Review your writing and your writing process. On a separate sheet of paper, answer these questions:*

- *What did you do well in the paragraph you wrote?*
- *What did you enjoy working on in this chapter?*
- *What have you learned that you will apply in future writing assignments?*

TOPIC 9: Arguing a Point
www.mhhe.com/goingplaces

Exchanging Ideas: Thinking in Expository Mode

If you find yourself in disagreement with a friend or family member about a political or personal issue, think about how and why you disagree. Supporting your beliefs with details and examples and conveying them in a civil, respectful tone will contribute to the strength and coherence of your message. Through a full exchange of ideas, you will come to a better understanding of others' opinions and your own.

BRAINSTORM

Make a list of two or three hot topics you argue about in your family. Divide a sheet of paper in half. Choose one topic, and on one side write "My view"; on the other side, write "Their view." Make a list of opinions, reasons, and beliefs on both sides. Which opinions, reasons, and beliefs are based on facts? What are the facts?

Studying Techniques

An important part of studying is knowing what to study. When studying for an exam, be sure to consider the format—essay, multiple choice, short answer, or a combination of the three. If the exam includes an essay component, ask yourself about the key points in the material the exam covers, list these points, and make a note of examples and details that support them. If the exam is multiple choice, you may want to concentrate more on memorizing facts, such as dates or formulas. It is usually wise to focus on material that was emphasized in class, so check your notes.

DISCUSSION

Turn and talk to a classmate about the kinds of tests you like and dislike. What are the reasons for your respective positions? Do you agree or disagree?

Multitasking: Staying Organized

At work, it is not unusual to be faced with several tasks simultaneously. This is where your organizational and outlining skills come into play. Many people find it helpful to write out a to-do list that outlines what needs to be done and in what order. Planning and structuring will make the tasks less daunting. Organizing will help you get the job done quickly and effectively.

RESUME BUILDER

Recall a time when your organization skills paid off. What were the circumstances? Who else was involved? What did you do? Why did it matter? Write a paragraph that captures the important dimensions of this incident. Think of your audience as a prospective employer.

Essay Structure and the Writing Process

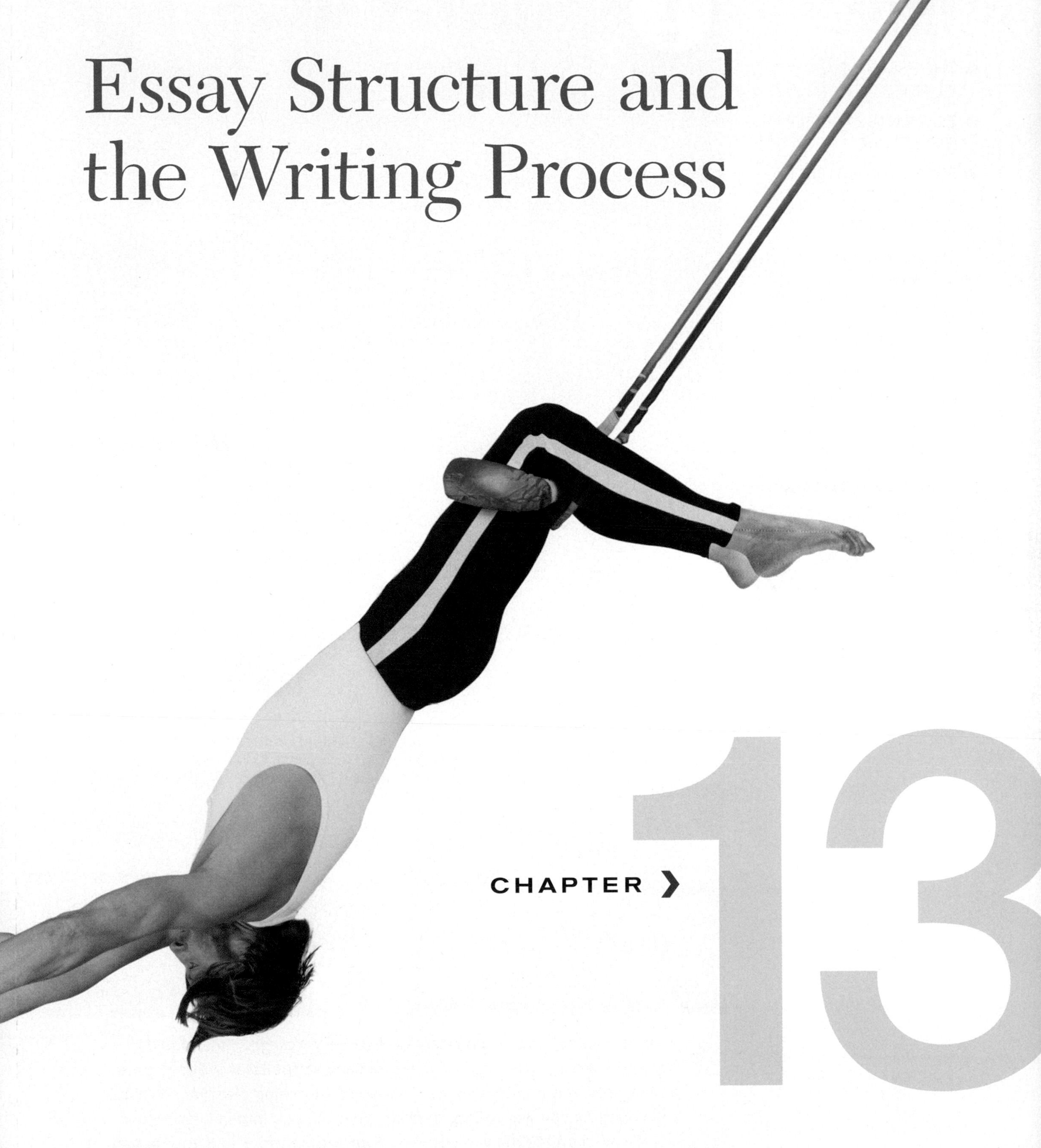

CHAPTER ❯ 13

CHAPTER OVERVIEW

- THE ESSAY AT A GLANCE
- ELEMENTS OF ESSAY STRUCTURE
- ESSAY STRUCTURE IN OUTLINE FORM
- GET STARTED
    - Assignments and Topics
    - Prewrite
    - Introductions
    - Develop a Thesis
    - The Body of the Essay
    - Conclusions
    - Revise and Edit Your Essay
    - Titles
    - Final Review

THINK FIRST

Writing an essay can be a process of discovery. You go places you did not know were on the map. To start thinking about essay writing, write a paragraph about a time when you made a surprising discovery. What did you think you were going to find? What did you find instead? How do you account for the gap between your expectations and your actual experience?

At a Glance

THE ESSAY AT A GLANCE

An essay is a multiple-paragraph paper. At the very least, your readers will expect to see three or four or possibly five or six paragraphs in the essays you write. They will read for both structure and content. An essay has an introduction, a body, and a conclusion. Using the forms of thinking and writing you learned in Part II, an essay conveys information in an organized fashion. The content may be personal observation or information you get from assigned reading.

The Essay at a Glance

ASSIGNMENT Use classification to explore one of the following topics: types of dates, jobs, learning experiences, parents, or homes.

Just Another Excuse

Her hands were sweating, and her heart was racing. Her divorce was final, and this was her first date in fifteen years. She felt like a teenager again. She had bought the perfect dress and shoes and had her nails done. They were going to his favorite Italian restaurant. However, her stomach was in knots. Then the phone rang. Sorry, he said, but he had to catch a jet for Paris. The business deal just could not wait. Well, she thought, I'm not waiting either. The more a woman dates, the more she is likely to realize that there are three types of men, each with his own distinctive style. For her own peace of mind, a woman who starts dating again has to recognize these types.

The first type is Richie Rich. He wears expensive suits and travels everywhere. He knows all the fine restaurants and all the witty words to say. He thinks the woman in his life should be honored by his presence and laugh at all his jokes. Because of his wealth, he thinks he can get away with any smooth excuse. **For example,** there is a good chance Richie will cancel a date because he has a business meeting with his boss, which could very well be a meeting with a topless dancer at a local establishment. **Then again,** Richie might have to fly to Hawaii to clinch a business deal, when in

The writer begins with a dramatic situation to engage the reader.

THESIS STATEMENT
She ends her introduction with a sentence that establishes the focus of the essay.

TOPIC SENTENCE
She identifies the first type.

SUPPORTING DETAILS
The writer's details, in this paragraph and those that follow, explain the various types of men.

EXAMPLES
The writer cites instances of deception, using transition phrases to connect them.

fact he is making a deal with a flight attendant. **Then** there is the canceled lunch date because his client is in town, when in fact it is his ex-wife. Richie's money, smooth talk, and fine dining can be impressive, but who needs the Richies of the world or their lame excuses?

CONCLUDING SENTENCE

TOPIC SENTENCE
The writer's use of "another type" is an effective transition.

SUPPORTING DETAILS
The writer uses examples in this paragraph, too.

Another type is Mama's Boy. He is well mannered and understanding. He is a wonderful cook. What Boy does not reveal is that he still lives at home with Mama. **One Boy** will cancel a date because his mama is upset, and he is treating her to dinner. He is telling a half-truth. He has to walk five steps to the kitchen table to treat Mama to dinner. **Another Mama's Boy,** if a lady actually accepts a date with him, will force his lady to share him with his mama, who calls his cell phone to give him her grocery list, remind him of his dental appointment, and who knows what else. No sane woman needs this.

CONCLUDING SENTENCE

TOPIC SENTENCE
The writer introduces a third type of man.

Set apart from Richie Rich and Mama's Boy is Average Joe. He is in a class by himself. Joe is the honest type. He is hard-working and respectable. He makes a decent living at a decent job and enjoys life immensely. Joe respects a woman because he, in turn, wants to be respected. Deeply embedded within his personality is his honesty. If Joe calls and says he has to work a double shift, there is no reason to question him. If he changes plans because he is going hunting, he really is going hunting. If he says he loves you, he is telling the truth.

CONCLUSION
The shift in focus here tells the reader the essay is moving toward closing. The body paragraphs tell the reader what the writer has learned; the conclusion explains how she uses what she has learned.

A smart woman will ask a few questions before a date. Where do you work? Do you have your own place? Have you been married before? How big is your family? What is your favorite restaurant? If his replies are "Microsoft, I have my own apartment, married three times, I'm an only child, Italian," then it might be a good idea to look elsewhere. It is not that difficult to distinguish between the Richies, Boys, and Joes. It is definitely worth saying no and waiting for the right guy.

DISCUSSION QUESTIONS

PEER CONVERSATION

1. What is your opinion of the title of the essay? Is it a good title? Why or why not?
2. What is the purpose of this essay?
3. Do you agree with the order in which the writer presents different types of men? Why or why not?

ELEMENTS OF ESSAY STRUCTURE

Here are the basic elements of an effective essay.

- *Introduction:* When you write an essay, you present information, but you also present yourself to the reader. For this reason, the introduction is like an invitation. It draws the reader in, states and focuses the topic, and conveys the topic's importance. "Her hands were sweating" is a dramatic opening. The reader wants to know why and what happens next.
- *Body:* The body of the essay provides the content, the support for the main idea of the essay. You examine and develop related ideas, making connections and explaining how the pieces fit together. Your job in the body of the paper is to control the communication.
- *Conclusion:* Finally, the conclusion signals a release. It says to the reader, "I'm finishing up. Here is something to think about."

The relationship of the essay to the paragraph is shown in the box. Note that the paragraph—with its topic sentence, supporting details, and concluding sentence—is the basis for the body paragraphs in the essay.

RELATIONSHIP OF PARAGRAPH TO ESSAY

Paragraph	Essay
Topic sentence states the main idea of a focused paragraph.	Introduction and **thesis statement** establish the focus of the essay.
Supporting details explore the main idea of the paragraph. The writer elaborates and explains, maintaining the unity and coherence of paragraph content.	**Body paragraphs** explore the main idea of the thesis. The writer provides supporting details in each paragraph, maintaining the unity and coherence of the essay content.
Conclusion sentence restates the main idea of the paragraph.	**Conclusion paragraph** sums up the content of the essay, restating the thesis.

ESSAY STRUCTURE IN OUTLINE FORM

A convenient way to visualize the structure of your essay is to use a formal outline. The outline consists of your thesis statement and the topic sentences and supporting details for each paragraph you write. Many students outline repeatedly during the writing process. They use an outline after they pre-write to provide structure to their ideas. While they draft, they may go back

See "Supporting Details" in Chapter 3 for detailed explanation of outlining.

to their outline to alter the structure. They revisit their outline when they prepare to revise. Here is a formal outline, also known as the *alphanumeric outline*.

Thesis statement: ______________________________

I. Topic sentence: ______________________________

   A. Major detail

      1.

      2.

      3.

   B. Major detail

      1.

      2.

      3.

   C. Major detail

      1.

      2.

      3.

II. Topic sentence: ______________________________

   A. Major detail

      1.

      2.

      3.

   B. Major detail

      1.

      2.

      3.

   C. Major detail

      1.

      2.

      3.

Conclusion

Here is a formal outline of the at-a-glance essay at the beginning of this chapter:

Thesis: For her own peace of mind, a woman who starts dating again has to recognize these types.

I. The first type is Richie Rich.
   A. Expensive suits
   B. Travels everywhere
   C. Honors a woman with his presence
   D. Likely to cancel a date
      1. Business meeting with boss (topless dancer)
      2. Business trip to Hawaii (date with flight attendant)
      3. Canceling date with client to see ex-wife.

II. Another type is Mama's Boy.
   A. Good manners
   B. Good cook
   C. Also likely to ruin a date
      1. Mama is upset and he cancels
      2. He talks to Mama on the phone during the date
      3. Clients in town

III. Set apart from Richie Rich and Mama's Boy is Average Joe.
   A. Honest and hard-working
   B. Respects a woman, wants respect in return
   C. Tells the truth

Conclusion

GET STARTED

An essay assignment is an invitation for you to show what you know about a subject. Because it is a form of writing with multiple paragraphs, the essay challenges you to assert relationships among many ideas and details. You give your audience a big picture. That picture has to be in focus.

Assignments and Topics

Essay assignments in courses other than English will frequently focus on specific content. For example, in an American history class, you will be asked to explain multiple causes of the War of 1812, or in a psychology class, you will be asked to define and illustrate common defense mechanisms. In these cases, your task is to read your assignments carefully, identify key terms, and organize your writing accordingly.

In other instances when you are given a more general assignment, your job will be to identify a topic and break it down into subtopics you can treat in the body paragraphs of your essay. Look at the following diagrams that show how one student broke down both a specific assignment and a general assignment into topics and subtopics.

Specific Assignment: Discuss the causes of the War of 1812 covered in our reading and course lectures.

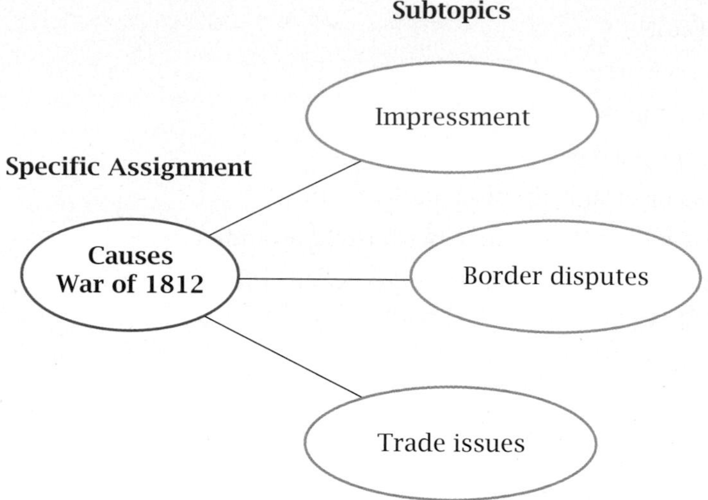

General Assignment: Sports

Possible Topics

General Assignment

Subtopics

Sports

Hockey

Football

Baseball

Rules of the game

Strategy and drama

Fifth game of World Series

The illustrations show the writer's process with two assignments: one specific and one general. The writer begins by narrowing the assignments to identify possible topics, then narrowing the topics further to find subtopics. Effective writers often think in three's. They break down a topic into three manageable subtopics that can be explored in individual paragraphs.

EXERCISE 13-1 Selecting an Assignment

Directions: *Review the following assignments. Choose the one you know the most about and think could be the basis for an effective essay.*

1. Describe an attitude or value of people your age that you object to. How is the attitude or value expressed? Be specific about how we see it, hear it, and know it. Then explain your main reasons for objecting to it.
2. In our culture of celebrity, we see and hear from famous people all the time. Some celebrities use fame for good causes. Cite and discuss a few examples.
3. Nature can be a source of both calm and terror. Recall an experience you had in nature that was very positive or frightening. Be specific about when and where the experience took place, as well as its outcome.
4. Technology has made new forms of communication possible. Discuss the safety issues involved in online communication and what precautionary steps people can take to ensure their safety.
5. The best way to save money is to have a budget that helps you keep track of cash flow. How would you classify your expenses? Which type of expense could most easily be controlled and help you spend money wisely?
6. Discuss a popular form of entertainment—for example, slasher movies or a particular singing group. What makes it so entertaining? Be specific about your reasons.
7. Learning requires maturity, preparation, and readiness. Not everyone is ready to learn at the same time. Compare and contrast two learning experiences involving a particular subject in school that yielded very different results. In your discussion, consider reasons for the different results.

Writer's Response
Write about a personal experience related to the topic that interests you.

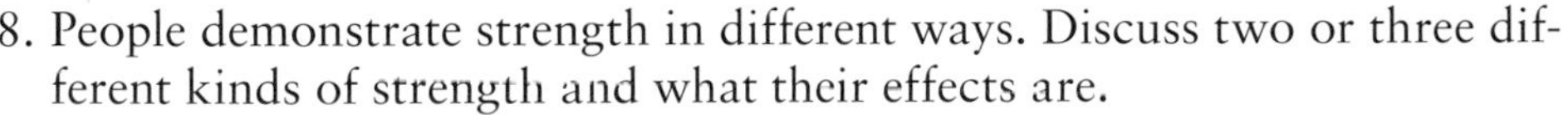

8. People demonstrate strength in different ways. Discuss two or three different kinds of strength and what their effects are.
9. It is common now for young people to live together before getting married. What is your view on this issue? Discuss reasons for and against the practice.
10. Choose your own topic.

Prewrite

When you write an essay, you follow the steps of the writing process. Those steps are prewriting, drafting, revising, and editing. Prewriting gives you a chance to explore what you know about your subject. You probably already have a preferred type of prewriting—talking, clustering, brainstorming, or freewriting—that you automatically turn to when you start the writing process.

EXERCISE 13-2 **Prewriting**

Directions: *Carefully read the assignment you selected. Do some prewriting to explore what you know about it and identify subtopics you could discuss in individual paragraphs. Begin with the type of prewriting you like best. Then use one of the other types of prewriting, too. Do your work on a separate sheet of paper.*

Introductions

Introductions should grab the reader's attention and set the tone of the essay. They should also establish the importance of the topic and focus the essay with a thesis statement.

The approach you choose for your introduction will vary according to the form of writing you do. A personal essay might have an informal tone, whereas a report you write for a science class will be all business. Here are two introductions for an essay on keeping a house clean.

Unfocused Introduction for Personal Essay

In our world today, everyone has to do things they do not want to do. These things are called jobs or maybe even chores. There are jobs you do at home, jobs you do at work, and jobs you do at school. One of the chores a person has to do around the house is vacuum the rug.

Focused Introduction for Personal Essay

Every morning I wake up and find dog hair all over the house. It is on the area rug in the living room, the carpet in my room, and the stairs that lead to the basement and upstairs. My dog is a Norwegian elkhound. Her very thick hair sheds a lot in the summer. I hate seeing dog hair in the house, but I do not like leaving her outside on hot summer days. That is why I depend on my vacuum cleaner. If I did not have a vacuum cleaner, the carpet and the rugs in the house would always be covered with dog hair. The vacuum is just one convenience device I use on a regular basis. It is useful for special jobs, regular cleaning, and even for some jobs outside the house.

The unfocused introduction states the obvious, then states the obvious again. It reads as if anyone could have written it. In the focused introduction, on the other hand, the writer does not sound like anyone; she sounds like herself. What she has to say about keeping her house clean is interesting because of the detail she provides. You sense attitude and personality in the writing. Here are some guidelines for writing a focused and interesting introduction.

Guidelines for Writing an Effective Introduction

Start with a Snappy First Sentence

My hard drive crashed.

She washed my mouth out with soap, then smacked my face.

Macbeth was a fool.

Spare change?

Tell a Captivating Story

She washed my mouth out with soap, then smacked my face. Then she made me run out to the apple tree in our yard to pick a switch. Grandma explained to me that she was going to whip my bottom with the switch that I brought back. She also told me that if the switch was not just right, I would be punished even more. To hear her say this to me was unbelievable. That was how she punished. In the process, she taught obedience, respect, and responsibility.

Cite and Explain Two or Three Specific Details

Macbeth was a fool. To begin with, he was a superstitious fool who listened to witches and allowed himself to be seduced by prophesy. He was also an ambitious fool. He was one of Duncan's favorites. If he had not been so ambitious, Macbeth would have lived a happy life and enjoyed power and wealth. To make matters worse, he allowed himself to be shamed into action by his wife. Shakespeare's play shows us a fool brought to ruin by superstition, ambition, and a foolish desire to "be a man."

Refer to Something You Have Read

Spare change? In the essay "On Compassion," Barbara Ascher asks why people feel compelled to give gifts to homeless people. She comes to the conclusion that they do it out of compassion. Compassion, she says, "is a feeling of pity or empathy." Those who give are not homeless, nor do they know how it feels to be homeless, but somehow they can relate. They probably have been in a situation that required someone else's help. Helping a homeless person makes them feel better about themselves. Nevertheless, many people will not give anything to the homeless, for what they claim to be very good reasons.

Offer a Concession

Compulsory military service? Who could possibly be in favor of such a thing? Two young people finish high school. He has made plans to work and go to school, and she has been accepted to an excellent university out of state. Neither of them wants to set aside those plans for a year or two and go into the service. Waiting a year or two, it seems clear, would be a setback, a long and needless delay to their plans for starting their lives. That argument may have merit. However, there are some very good reasons to consider exactly just such a delay.

Begin with a Compelling Fact or Statistic

Remember, anytime you borrow a quotation, fact, or statistic from another writer, you need to identify your source.

See Chapter 16 for help on documenting your sources.

"Well I thought that was what you meant!" Does this statement sound familiar? Miscommunication happens all the time. According to Deborah Tannen, 93 percent of communication is expressed nonverbally (129). Maybe that explains why communication breaks down so often. To communicate effectively, it is necessary to both listen and look.

Begin with an Analogy or Comparison

Living together is like pulling through the drive-through at McDonald's. It does not cost much. You get what everyone else has. You expect little from it. In contrast, marriage is like cooking a gourmet meal at home. It takes time. There is a lot of preparation and cleanup. However, in the end, you have something filling and wonderful. You have something that lasts. Marriage is hard work, but in the end, its benefits outweigh those of just living together.

Include a Focused Thesis Statement

The thesis states the point you want to make in your essay. It sums up the paper. It can appear at the beginning, middle, or end of your introduction paragraph.

EXERCISE 13-3 **Your Introduction**

Directions: *Review your prewriting to identify ideas for writing your introduction. Write the first two or three sentences of your introduction in the space provided.*

____

____

____

____

Now underline the guidelines listed below that helped you focus your thinking for writing an effective introduction.

Guidelines

Snappy first sentence
Captivating story
Two or three specific details
A reference to something you have read
A concession
Begin with a compelling fact or statistic
Begin with an analogy

Develop a Thesis

Your thesis puts your particular fingerprint on your topic. It sums up the content of your essay, and it states the main point or idea you will explore. It answers your reader's question: *What is this essay really about?* Typically readers look for your thesis statement at the end of your introduction paragraph. An effective thesis is specific, has edge, and states the divisions of your topic.

MULTILINGUAL TIP
In the United States, readers appreciate a direct approach. State your point early in the essay.

Guidelines for Writing an Effective Thesis

Include a Specific Controlling Idea

Like the topic sentence in a paragraph, the thesis statement lets the audience know there is a plan behind the writing. However, the thesis statement promises more than the topic sentence. Because of its complexity, a thesis leads to multiple paragraphs of discussion. The differences between a topic sentence and a thesis statement are illustrated in these examples.

Assignment: Discuss the causes of the War of 1812 covered in our reading and course lectures.

Topic Sentence: The most important cause of the War of 1812 was the British navy's practice of impressment.

This topic sentence limits the discussion to one cause of the War of 1812.

Thesis Statement: The most important causes of the War of 1812 were the British navy's practice of impressments, border disputes, and Britain's interference with trade between the US and countries in Europe.

This thesis statement states the main idea of the essay and the topics of each body paragraph (impressments, border disputes, and trade interference).

In the case of a general assignment, the writer narrows her topic and thinks in three's, breaking her topic into subtopics that can be explored in separate body paragraphs.

Assignment: Sports

Topic Sentence: One thing that makes baseball challenging is the rules of the game.

Thesis Statement: Because of the complex rules of the game, baseball often involves strategy and drama.

Notice the key words in the topic sentence, *challenging* and *rules,* as opposed to those in the thesis statement, *complex rules, strategy,* and *drama.* In a single paragraph, the writer might explore two or three examples of rules that make baseball challenging. In an essay, on the other hand, the writer can do much more. She can explore two or three examples of rules and then explain how those rules enable managers and players to make strategy and add to the dramatic tension of a good game.

Like a topic sentence, a thesis statement is most effective when it is specific and focused, as opposed to vague and unfocused. It should be possible to read a thesis statement and predict what the body of the essay will explore.

Vague Thesis Statement: Some people are terrified of flying.

Focused Thesis Statement: Because of their terrible fear of flying, some travelers have special rituals they follow both before and while they fly to minimize anxiety.

The focused thesis statement enables the reader to predict the writer will discuss these questions: Why is the writer so afraid of flying? What is her before-flying ritual? What is her in-air ritual that minimizes anxiety?

State How the Topic Will Be Divided into Subtopics

A good thesis ensures that the content will be organized and specific. It indicates what subtopics you will address in the body of your paper.

Vague Thesis Statement: The art fair is enjoyable for a variety of reasons.

Specific Thesis Statement: To me, the art fair is enjoyable because of the ambiance in the park, tasty local food, and the good deals on ceramics and paintings.

The first thesis does not provide the reader with a preview of the essay's content because it is not specific about why the art fair is enjoyable. The second thesis divides the topic into three subtopics: ambiance, local food, and good deals. The reader can look forward to a discussion of these subtopics in the body of the essay, probably in the same order they are presented in the thesis.

Avoid Making a Big Announcement, Such as "In This Paper, I Will Tell You about . . ."

A common problem students have is making a ponderous statement, such as "In this essay, I will talk about . . ." Usually a heavy-handed thesis like this can be revised by cutting the "I will talk about" and working with what comes next.

Heavy-Handed Thesis: ~~In this essay I will write about~~ the problems students face in the financial aid office at this college.

Revised Thesis: Students face major problems at this college in the financial aid office: long waits, delays before funds are released, and rare referrals to scholarship opportunities at the institution.

A focused thesis shows that you have done your thinking before writing. The heavy-handed thesis is general. The revised thesis focuses the essay on three specific problems. Writing a specific thesis makes your work as a writer much easier.

EXERCISE 13-4 Vague Versus Focused Thesis Statements

Directions: *Read the following thesis statements. Place a* V *next to those that are vague,* F *next to those that are focused, and* A *next to those that make an announcement. For those that are focused, jot down two or three questions you think the writer promises to explore in the body of the essay. Rewrite those that are not focused. The first thesis is done for you.* Answers will vary. Example answers shown.

_F_ 1. Since Saturday morning television is designed to sell small children a lot of worthless junk, parents need to monitor what their kids watch.

1. What kind of worthless junk?

2. What is a good process for monitoring TV watching?

____

_V_ 2. The cougar is an endangered species in Florida.

____

____

____

F 3. Older siblings either make life easier or a living hell for their brothers and sisters.

1. How do older siblings make life a living hell?

2. How do they make life easier?

____

A 4. I am going to tell you why hockey is the greatest sport on earth.

____

____

____

F 5. Advances in technology are visible in a number of new films coming out of Hollywood.

1. What specific technologies?

2. What new films, in particular, make use of this technology?

3. Does technology really improve a film that much? In what way?

EXERCISE 13-5 **Formulating Your Thesis**

Directions: *Review your prewriting and thoughts about your introduction. Then write a tentative thesis for your essay in the space provided.*

____

____

____

The Body of the Essay

Explain. College writing requires detailed explanation. Your audience wants information: evidence that you have mastered course content as well as details from your personal observation and experience that indicate careful thinking. In response to an assignment, you formulate a focused thesis statement that says something substantive about the topic. That thesis statement is then explained by focused topic sentences.

Thesis and Topic Sentences

A focused thesis statement narrows your topic and identifies those ideas you plan to discuss in the body of the paper. From your thesis come your topic sentences. In a good essay, that connection is both necessary and obvious. Some assignments are formulated so you can easily extract key terms and write a focused thesis statement. In your thesis, in turn, are the key terms that become part of your topic sentences.

Assignment: Discuss a technological device in your home that has changed your family dynamics or caused significant differences of opinion between family members.

In this assignment, the key terms are *technological device, family dynamics,* and *significant differences of opinion.* A thesis statement, along with topic sentences related to it, might look like this:

Thesis Statement: A telephone answering machine on our phone has changed the family dynamics in our house, eliminating one source of conflict while creating new ones.

Topic Sentence 1: The answering machine has eliminated a continuous source of conflict: lost or undelivered phone messages.

Topic Sentence 2: A new source of conflict, however, is how long messages are left (or are not left) on the recorder.

Topic Sentence 3: While message management is still a problem, an even more bothersome problem is that an answering machine means less privacy in phone communication.

In this illustration, the student's thesis statement leads to precise topic sentences. From each topic sentence, the student would write a detailed paragraph developing the idea with specific details.

In the case of general assignments, you need to limit and narrow the topic as shown below. The illustration, beginning with "Cathedral" on the left, shows a student narrowing an assignment to write on the short story "Cathedral," by Raymond Carver. He moves from assignment to topic and from topic to subtopics.

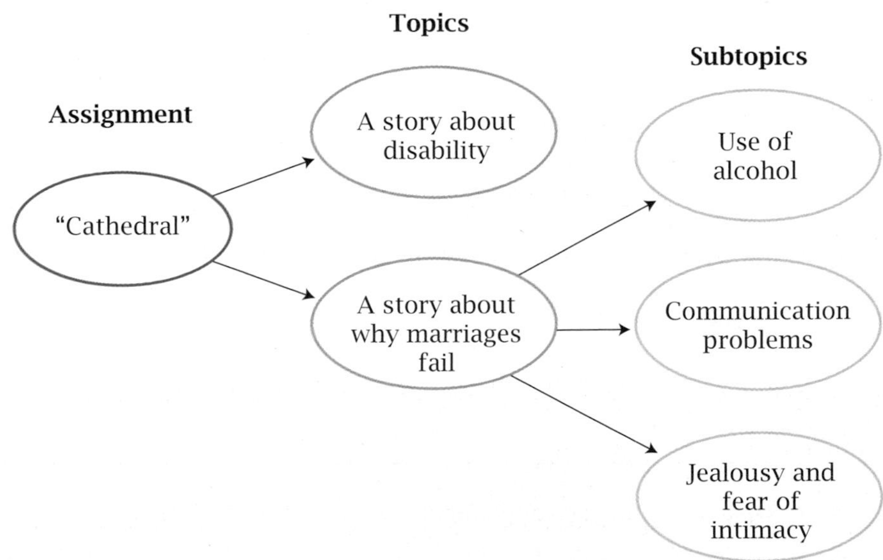

Assignment: Write an essay on the short story "Cathedral" by Raymond Carver.

Thesis Statement: Raymond Carver's short story "Cathedral" explores a troubled marriage, in particular, the impact of alcohol, poor communication, and jealousy on the narrator's marriage.

Topic Sentence 1: The narrator's marriage is in trouble because of alcohol abuse.

Topic Sentence 2: Communication problems plague the failing marriage and complicate the conflicts.

Topic Sentence 3: Jealousy causes the narrator to fear intimacy, creating more conflicts.

Thesis statements and topic sentences tell readers where they are, what is being discussed, and what connections are being made between ideas. These guide sentences also establish the logic of your writing. There should be a reason for visiting the ideas and details of each subtopic in the order you have chosen.

EXERCISE 13-6 Writing Focused Thesis and Topic Sentences

Directions: *For each of the following general assignments, use the graphic on page 281 to narrow the assignment and write a focused thesis statement. Then write two or three topic sentences that echo key terms from the thesis. The first one has been done for you.* Answers will vary.

EXAMPLE

Topic: Health care

Controlling Idea: alternative medicines

Thesis: Using the Internet as a source of information, many young people take control of their health care, using alternative medications and dietary supplements to treat themselves.

Topic Sentence 1: The Internet has expanded people's access to information about health.

Topic Sentence 2: Alternative medications are effective for some ailments.

Topic Sentence 3: Dietary supplements are a useful treatment in some cases.

1. **Topic:** Transportation

Controlling Idea: ______________________________

Thesis: ______________________________

____

____

Topic Sentence 1: ______________________________

____

Topic Sentence 2: ______________________________

____

Topic Sentence 3: ______________________________

____

2. **Topic:** Math

Controlling Idea: ______________________________

Thesis: ______________________________

____

____

Topic Sentence 1: ______________________________

____

Topic Sentence 2: ______________________________

____

Topic Sentence 3: ______________________________

____

3. **Topic:** Childhood

Controlling Idea: ______________________________

Thesis: ______________________________

____

____

Talk about It

No two people have the same view of a topic. Tell about someone who might disagree with you, and why.

Topic Sentence 1: ______________________________

____

Topic Sentence 2: ______________________________

____

Topic Sentence 3: ______________________________

____

EXERCISE 13-7 Your Thesis and Topic Sentences

Directions: *Review your prewriting, ideas about an introduction, and tentative thesis. Thinking ahead about the essay you will write, compose your thesis and two to four topic sentences in the space below. Revise your thesis as needed.*

Thesis: ______________________________

____

____

Topic Sentence 1: ______________________________

____

Topic Sentence 2: ______________________________

____

____

Topic Sentence 3: ______________________________

____

____

Topic Sentence 4: ______________________________

____

____

Supporting Details

The ultimate goal of an essay is to deliver the content. Readers of academic writing look for specific detail. Your movement toward greater specificity can be pictured as a stairway, with the most general content at the top, becoming increasingly more specific as you move downward.

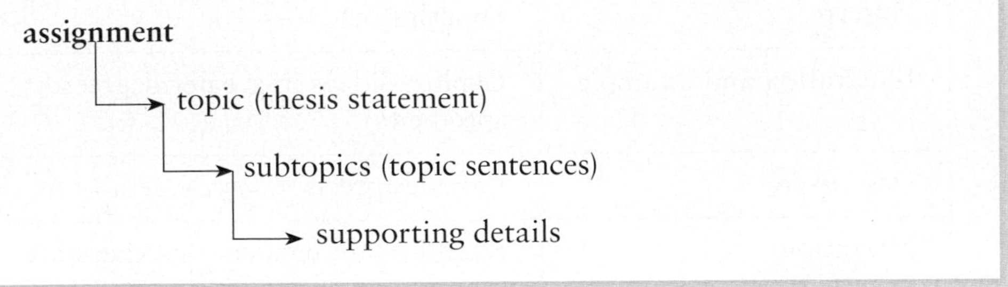

This pattern of relationships can be pictured in outline form.

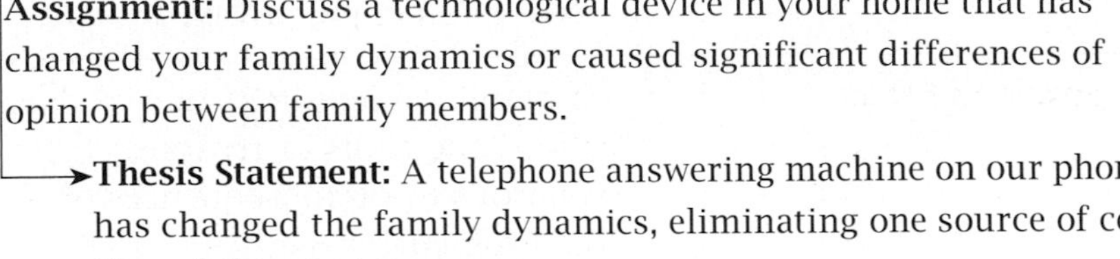

Assignment: Discuss a technological device in your home that has changed your family dynamics or caused significant differences of opinion between family members.

→**Thesis Statement:** A telephone answering machine on our phone has changed the family dynamics, eliminating one source of conflict while creating new ones.

THESIS STATEMENT
The student's **thesis statement** echoes key terms from the assignment.

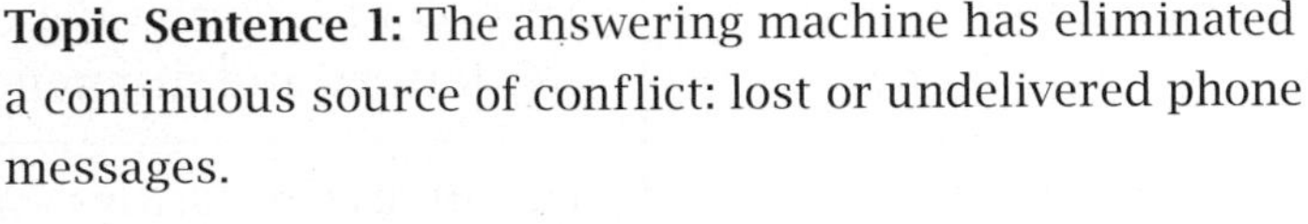

Topic Sentence 1: The answering machine has eliminated a continuous source of conflict: lost or undelivered phone messages.

TOPIC SENTENCE
This topic sentence echoes "source of conflict" from the thesis. The student will use examples to develop the main idea of this paragraph.

→**Detail A:** Lost messages from friends

→**Detail B:** Lost messages from family members

→**Detail C:** Lost work-related messages

Topic Sentence 2: A new source of conflict, however, is how long messages are left (or are not left) on the recorder.

The student's topic sentence makes a direct reference to the thesis of the essay.

→**Detail A:** Some people never even listen to their messages

The student will use examples to develop the main idea of the paragraph.

→**Detail B:** Some people never delete their messages

→**Detail C:** Some people delete theirs and others' messages

Topic Sentence 3: While message management is still a problem, an even more bothersome problem is that an answering machine means less privacy in phone communication.

The topic sentence refers back to the thesis.

→**Detail A:** The call that came in from my girlfriend

The student will use narration to develop the main idea of this paragraph.

This outline shows a pattern of support at each level: thesis, topic sentence, supporting details. Your ultimate destination is specific detail: facts, statistics, description, and examples that support, explain, and illustrate your thesis. Typically, the content of body paragraphs is organized in one or more of the organizational patterns shown in the following chart:

See Chapter 14 for detailed examples of essays written using these different patterns.

Pattern	Description
Illustration and Example	Explores ideas in greater degrees of specificity
Description	Provides precise sensory detail
Narration	Examines an incident or experience, focusing on specific place, time, people, events, and outcomes
Process	Explains a procedure by describing steps involved, props and equipment used, and people involved
Cause and Effect	Explores "symptoms" of a problem, prior conditions or reasons, solutions to or consequences of the problem
Classification	Sorts content into types, detailing similarities and differences
Comparison and Contrast	Examines similarities and differences in point-by-point or subject-by-subject organization
Definition	Specifies meaning of terms or important ideas: component parts, function or purpose, origins, illustrations
Argument	Explains opinions, examining their reasons and foundations

Develop an Essay Plan

To plan your essay, make a tentative outline, beginning with your thesis, followed by each topic sentence and the details that support the main ideas stated in those topic sentences. Then stand back and look at your outline. Think about what kind of plan works best—whether spatial or chronological, order of importance, or simple to complex are the best ways of presenting your ideas.

EXERCISE 13-8 The Essay Plan and Logical Order

Directions: *Review the thesis and topic sentences that follow. Indicate the order of topic sentences that seems most logical to you. Write a sentence justifying your thinking. The first one is done for you.*

EXAMPLE

Thesis: Travel is valuable to young people because it helps them learn about different ways of life, shows them different geographic regions, and makes them appreciate home.

__3__ **Topic Sentence:** Travel is valuable because it makes young people appreciate home.

__2__ **Topic Sentence:** Travel helps young people learn about other people.

__1__ **Topic Sentence:** Travel shows young people different geographic regions.

Explanation: Begin with the body paragraph on different regions because young people have to get someplace before they encounter different ways of life. The paragraph about appreciating home makes sense last because young people feel this appreciation after the trip is over.

The samples in the pages that follow illustrate five-paragraph structure. In any assignment, however, students may elect to organize their ideas using fewer or more paragraphs, depending on the complexity of the assignment.

1. **Thesis:** Students face major problems at this college in the financial aid office: long waits, delays before funds are released, and only rare referrals to scholarship opportunities at the institution.

   __3__ **Topic Sentence:** The financial aid office would do students a service by posting current information about scholarship opportunities.

   __1__ **Topic Sentence:** Perhaps the biggest headache about the office is the long wait and lack of organization when you arrive.

   __2__ **Topic Sentence:** Many students complain about delays in fund release once financial aid is approved.

Explanation: Put the body paragraphs in the same order as they appear in the thesis statement.

2. **Thesis:** The local art fair is enjoyable because of the ambiance in the park, the tasty local food, and the good deals on ceramics and paintings.

   __3__ **Topic Sentence:** New painters and ceramic artists emerge every year selling their work at reasonable prices.

   __1__ **Topic Sentence:** Local restaurants set up booths offering taste treats and local specialties.

   __2__ **Topic Sentence:** Parks offer the perfect atmosphere for an art fair.

Explanation: Put the body paragraphs in the same order as they appear in the thesis statement.

3. **Thesis:** Members of my family have served in the military in a number of wars fought by the United States.

   __3__ **Topic Sentence:** My grandfather went ashore at Anzio Beach in Italy.

   __2__ **Topic Sentence:** My great-grandfather served in the military in World War I, but he never actually left the United States.

   __1__ **Topic Sentence:** My father was in Vietnam during the Tet Offensive.

Explanation: Put the paragraphs in chronological order. Start with the oldest person (the great-grandfather) and move to grandfather and then father.

EXERCISE 13-9 Developing Your Essay Plan

Directions: *Write a detailed plan for your essay. Include your thesis, topic sentences, and supporting details. Depending on the complexity of your topic, you might plan on 2, 3, 4, or more body paragraphs to develop your ideas. Organize your ideas and details in a logical order. Do this work on a separate sheet of paper.*

Unity and Coherence

A reader should be able to look up from an essay, then look back without losing track of what the writer is saying. To create coherent text like this, you need to make explicit the connections within and across paragraphs.

In the paragraphs you wrote in Part II of this book, you used transition words to make your writing coherent and connected. In the essay, your job is essentially the same. A web of connections is created when you repeat key terms and write transitional sentences between paragraphs.

Repeat Key Terms in Some or Most of Your Paragraphs

Key terms remind the reader of the essay's focus and give the writer a chance to explain how the discussion in a given paragraph relates to the main idea of the essay.

Write Transition Sentences Between Paragraphs

Paragraphs frequently end with transition sentences. A transition sentence points both backward and forward. It restates the idea of the current paragraph and it points to the main idea of the next paragraph.

The web of connections created by key terms and transition sentences is visible in this illustration:

> **Thesis:** In order to be a responsible pet owner, you should determine what size pet will work with your living environment, figure out how much time and care you can give your pet, and understand that pets become part of the family.

Topic Sentence: To be a responsible pet owner, you must determine what size animal works in your environment. ***[transition sentence]*** In the past year or so, my boys have been learning how to take care of a pet.

Topic Sentence: In order to have a happy, healthy pet, you must provide it with care. ***[transition sentence]*** In short, we tried to bring him up right.

Topic Sentence: Raising an animal is just like raising a child. It becomes part of your family unit.

Conclusion: I think we have been responsible pet owners.

Here is the complete essay with the thesis, topic, and transition sentences shown above.

Sweet Little Pup

Oh my goodness! Someone hit that poor dog. You see it every day on the city streets and freeways, and you wonder, How could this happen? Where are the owners of the pet? The truth is that a lot of people who own pets should not. In order to be a **responsible dog owner,** you should determine what size pet will work with your living **environment,** figure out how much time and care you can give your pet, and understand that pets become **part of the family.**

THESIS STATEMENT

A **responsible dog owner** looks for an animal that fits his or her environment. One cannot keep a Great Dane in a studio apartment. When a single mother and her two boys decided they wanted a pet, they looked for just the right fit. They had two turtles already, but they wanted something more affectionate. They had a long talk about their living arrangements, a three-bedroom townhouse with a small yard. Even though they lacked a lot of **outdoor space,** they decided to purchase a dog. They searched www.petfinder.com and found a cute little male brindle boxer puppy that they named Bruno. He was a frisky little devil and fit their **space** just about right. In the next year or so, the boys learned about how to take **care** of a pet.

TOPIC SENTENCE

TRANSITION SENTENCE

In order to have a happy, healthy pet, you must provide it with care. Dogs cannot explain that they are sick. They have to be watched closely during the first few years. They need to be given two sets of shots. Some dogs are given additional medication to treat them for worms. If its physical needs are met, it does not take long for a dog to adjust to its new home, but that is when the **socializing and training** begins. An obedient dog

TOPIC SENTENCE
"Care" is the main idea of this paragraph.

SUPPORTING DETAILS
The student elaborates on two types of needs: physical and social.

learns to heel and to sit. The dog owner has to teach him to stay out of traffic, which can be very time-consuming. A good dog learns not to jump on people, not to chew things like shoes and furniture, and not to beg for food. In short, much like a child, a dog needs to be **brought up right.**

TRANSITION SENTENCE

TOPIC SENTENCE
In this paragraph the student compares raising a dog to raising a child.

Raising an animal is just like raising a child. It becomes part of the family unit. It feels lonely when the owners are gone, and it loves the owners unconditionally. In addition to love, a dog needs plenty of exercise. It needs to be walked. It loves fresh air. Like a child, it loves to run, and it needs to eat right. Part of caring for a dog is also taking on a long-term commitment. Once again, like children, a dog joins a family for a long time, usually its whole life. That means the dog owner has to organize her life accordingly. She has to find someone to look after the animal when she goes out of town. She has to take care of it if it gets hurt or sick. A pet is not a machine. It goes through stages of life, just like a person does.

CONCLUSION
The writer repeats the first sentence of her introduction

Someone hit that poor dog. There is really no excuse for it. Being a responsible pet owner means looking after the animal's physical, social, and emotional needs. In fact, that is what being a responsible pet owner is all about.

PEER CONVERSATION

DISCUSSION QUESTIONS

1. What is your opinion of the title of this essay?
2. What part or parts of the essay do you find particularly effective? Why?
3. Did the writer overlook anything? If so, would you put this additional detail in an existing paragraph or add a new paragraph? Explain

Conclusions

While introductions prepare the reader for what is to come, conclusions help the reader see how the individual parts of the essay add up. How you finish depends on the form of writing. In a research paper, you might focus on solutions to an important problem. In an essay, you might tell an engaging story so the reader grasps the significance of your thesis. Whenever possible, try to match your conclusion with your introduction.

Guidelines for Writing an Effective Conclusion

Retrieve a Specific Detail

Reread your introduction or the body of your essay and identify an interesting, important, or engaging fact or detail. This detail will emphasize the main point of your paper.

Introduction

Every morning I wake up and find dog hair all over the house. It is on the area rug in the living room, the carpet in my room, and the stairs that lead to the basement and upstairs. My dog Cheyenne is a Norwegian elkhound. . . .

Repeated Detail Conclusion

Cheyenne sheds. There is just no way around it. Nevertheless, I have found ways of keeping up with dog hair and most of the other problems associated with keeping my house clean.

Ask and Answer a Question to Repeat and Reinforce Your Thesis

Introduction

Macbeth was a fool. To begin with, he was a superstitious fool who listened to witches and allowed himself to be seduced by prophesy. He was also an ambitious fool. He was one of Duncan's favorites. If he had not been so ambitious, Macbeth would have lived a happy life and enjoyed power and wealth.

Conclusion Question

Could Macbeth's fate have been different? If he had been a different kind of man, yes, his fate would have been different. As it is, his flaws eventually led to his destruction.

Select a Related Quotation from a Source Mentioned Earlier in the Essay

Use that quotation to explore the important message your essay imparts.

Introduction

Spare change? In the essay "On Compassion," Barbara Ascher talks about feeding the homeless. The writer asks why people feel compelled to give gifts to the homeless. She comes to the conclusion that people do it out of compassion. What does she mean by compassion? Compassion, she says, "is not a character trait like a sunny disposition." These people are not homeless. . . .

Quotation Conclusion

Ascher says that compassion "is learned by having adversity at our windows." Unfortunately, we do not all look out our windows. We are busy. We walk with our heads down. We are in our own world. . . .

Avoid Conclusion Missteps

Writers sometimes make specific mistakes in their conclusions. Avoid these missteps:

- Do not introduce new ideas in your conclusion that you have not discussed in the body of your paper.
- Do not use overly obvious language like "in conclusion," "in summary," or "to sum up."
- Do not simply summarize what you wrote in the body of the paper.

EXERCISE 13-10 Matching Introductions and Conclusions

Directions: *Read the following introductions and conclusions. In the space provided, indicate what the writers have done to match their introduction and conclusion paragraphs.*

1.

Introduction

James Gleick notes in his essay that stress is an "ill defined term." Maybe that is the case because there are many types of stress in our lives. We stress about work, about education, and about political issues that concern us. Perhaps even more than these, we stress about family. What is family stress and where does it come from?

Conclusion

Stress can affect us physiologically, according to Gleick, sometimes in the form of heart ailments. Ironically, family can be both a source and a solution to stress. By being open, honest, and loving with those in our families we find troublesome, we can resolve stressful differences or misunderstandings.

Strategy: quotation from Gleick

2.

Introduction

A gentleman came to the drive-through on my shift and ordered seventeen cheeseburgers. After he paid I told him we would bring his order out to him, then politely asked him to pull into a parking space. "Why do I have to wait," he said. I responded, "Sir, this is fast food, not instant food." When people think of fast-food jobs, they think "easy work." In fact, it is quite the opposite. Managers constantly harass employees, customers complain about service being slow. This is just part of the joy of Burger King. Fast food may be mindless and repetitive, but easy it is not.

Conclusion

Not all customers think we have it made. Some show a little appreciation, which makes the job tolerable. There is an elderly man who comes in singing every morning. He says, "G'morning beautiful!" every time. I look forward to his visit. The next time you visit your local fast-food joint, a smile and hello would make us grill jockeys feel appreciated.

Strategy: retrieve a specific detail about customers

3.

Introduction

It was Christmastime. I was shopping and checking things off my list. At my last stop, when I reached for my wallet, it was gone. The panic was overwhelming. I rushed out and backtracked to the last store. Luck was on my side because there was my wallet, safely in the hands of the saleswoman. Many people are not as lucky. Identity theft has become a costly problem in our society today. It occurs when someone obtains and uses your personal information such as your Social Security numbers, bank and credit accounts, and birth dates. There are simple, preventative steps a person can take that will keep their personal information safe.

Conclusion

It is the bad guys who steal your identity, right? In fact, ID theft was brought to my attention in a personal way. My father suffered from Alzheimer's, and while in my sister's care, his good credit was misused. When he passed away last February, over $40,000 of debt had been charged in his name—by my sister. Statistics show that 47 percent of all ID theft is committed by friends, neighbors, or family members. On a positive note, the situation led me to learn how to protect my information. Knowing what I now know, especially how to take necessary precautions, I feel much safer.

Strategy: ask a question

EXERCISE 13-11 Your Conclusion

Directions: *Review your prewriting, your essay plan, and the plans for the introduction of your essay you wrote in response to Exercise 13-3. In the space below, write the first two or three sentences of your introduction paragraph. Then write the first two or three sentences of your conclusion in the space below it. Check off which of the guidelines for writing an effective conclusion helped you focus your thinking.* Answers will vary.

Introduction: ______________________________

____

____

____

Conclusion: ______________________________

Guidelines

_____ Retrieve a specific detail.

_____ Ask and answer a question that reinforces your thesis.

_____ Select another quotation from a source mentioned earlier in the essay.

EXERCISE 13-12 **Drafting Your Essay**

Directions: *Write a first draft of an essay that responds to the assignment you selected. Be sure the essay has an introduction, body, and conclusion; thesis and topic sentences; and supporting details that are logical and connected.*

Revise and Edit Your Essay

The difference between a pretty good essay and an excellent essay is in the revisions a writer makes. After drafting, many writers simply stop thinking. There is more you can do with your rough draft—much more.

MULTILINGUAL TIP
Bring your essay to the writing center.

Guidelines for Revising and Editing Your Essay

General Guidelines

- Allow yourself enough time to set aside your work so you can come back to it and see it with fresh eyes.
- Always read your essays out loud. Listen to what you wrote. Let your ears be your editor.
- Have a peer read your paper. Ask someone in your class who knows the assignment.
- Remember that revising involves cutting, adding, and moving sentences and whole paragraphs.

Specific Guidelines

- ***The parts of the essay—introduction, body, and conclusion:*** Your essay should have a clear beginning, middle, and end. Be sure your essay consists of multiple paragraphs, at least four or five, possibly more. In addition, be sure that the paragraphs are all similar in length.

If you have one paragraph that makes up 75 percent of the paper, break it up so your essay has similar emphasis on the different ideas and details you discuss. Finally, your conclusion should clearly signal the end is coming, reinforce the main idea of the essay, and give the reader something to think about.

Ask Yourself
What three key terms can you use in your thesis and topic sentences?

- *Focus—thesis and topic sentences:* Your thesis and topic sentences should include key words that indicate the main ideas of your essay. Moreover, the key words may be repeated in transition sentences to help the reader make connections between paragraphs.
- *Supporting details:* Readers of college writing look for specific details. In every paragraph, your essay will be more effective if you have fresh, vivid detail to go with your ideas. It might help to review Chapter 2, page 52, and patterns of organization and paragraph writing in Part II.
- *Connections:* Transition words in your body paragraphs help the reader see connections. A web of connections is created by thesis, topic, and transition sentences.
- *Proofreading:* Check for spelling and capitalization errors. Proofread for those errors you know you are inclined to make. Readers lose patience with writers who make the same mistakes repeatedly. Proofread for sentence variety.

Titles

The title of your paper is the first thing your audience will see. For many students, it is the last thing they think of. Although it does not matter when you put a title on your essay, be sure that your title reflects the content of the essay.

A little thought goes a long way with a title. Suppose you were asked to write an essay about a role model who has had an impact on your life. What would be the most predictable title for such an essay?

My Role Model

When you decide on a title, try to do the opposite of what your audience expects. Here are less predictable titles for essays on an important role model:

Always Ask Questions

We Will Always Have Pickles

Pass the Scissors

The title of your essay should arouse the reader's curiosity. It is an invitation. Make your title an invitation that your audience wants to accept. Be sure to observe rules for capitalization of titles: first word, last word, all other words except articles, conjunctions, and prepositions. Do not underline your title. If you write your essay on a word processor, use the same font size.

Final Review

Once you have revised and edited your essay, and put an appropriate title on it, use this checklist to determine if it is ready for an academic reader.

Gateway

TOPIC 8: Introduction and Conclusions
www.mhhe.com/goingplaces

ESSAY CHECKLIST

_____ My essay has an introduction, body, and conclusion.

_____ My essay has an appropriate and interesting title.

_____ My introduction invites the reader into the essay.

_____ My thesis is focused.

_____ My body paragraphs have focused topic sentences.

_____ My paragraphs have specific supporting details.

_____ I repeat key words and use transition words and sentences.

_____ My conclusion brings the essay to a close.

_____ I have proofread my paper for spelling, capitalization, common errors, and sentence variety.

THE SITUATION IS COMPLICATED

Got a Minute?

In many cases, a short answer just will not do. Life is too complicated. For this reason, you need time to think through complex issues, analyze them, and discover relationships and connections in order to explain what they mean. For instance, it is sometimes said that people spend their entire adult life figuring out their childhood: relationships with parents, siblings, and friends; decisions made, accidents and opportunities that happened. What does it all mean? How did everything happen so fast? How much control did they actually have over what went on around them?

BRAINSTORM

Brainstorm a list of important events, good or bad, that happened in your family life. Then focus on one. List all the people and places connected to the event. What circumstances or conditions led up to it? What were the consequences? How were you personally affected? How were others affected?

Not That Again . . .

Life is defined by repetition, especially life in school. How often do you have the feeling, sitting in class or working on an assignment: *Have I seen this before?* Yet there are benefits in repeated exercise. You build skills. You develop habits of mind. Sometimes you have breakthroughs that make all the difference in the world. Time, place, and people matter in this respect. What you did not understand about math at one place and time, from one particular instructor, suddenly becomes clear to you at another place and time, from a different instructor. Maybe the difference is the person sitting next to you in class. Then again, maybe you are different—more ready to learn, more capable of understanding connections and applications.

DISCUSSION

Turn and talk to a classmate about a class you like or dislike. Why do you feel the way you do? What prior experiences did you have with the class? Were they similar or different?

We Can Work It Out

Mature people learn how to adjust to circumstances. They listen, learn, and adapt. It may not be easy. In the workplace, this kind of agility is highly valued. You work in teams of diverse individuals with a shared goal—to get the job done. Jobs reach completion. Teams dissolve and form again: different people, new adjustments. Then there is the boss. Some make work wonderful; some do not. Either way, as an employee your ability to adjust and to fit in are tested. In the process, you acquire both marketable and social skills.

RESUME BUILDER

Turn and talk to a classmate about a job you really enjoyed. What made it satisfying? What were your coworkers like? Were there any challenges that required you to learn on the job?

CHAPTER 14

Types of Essays

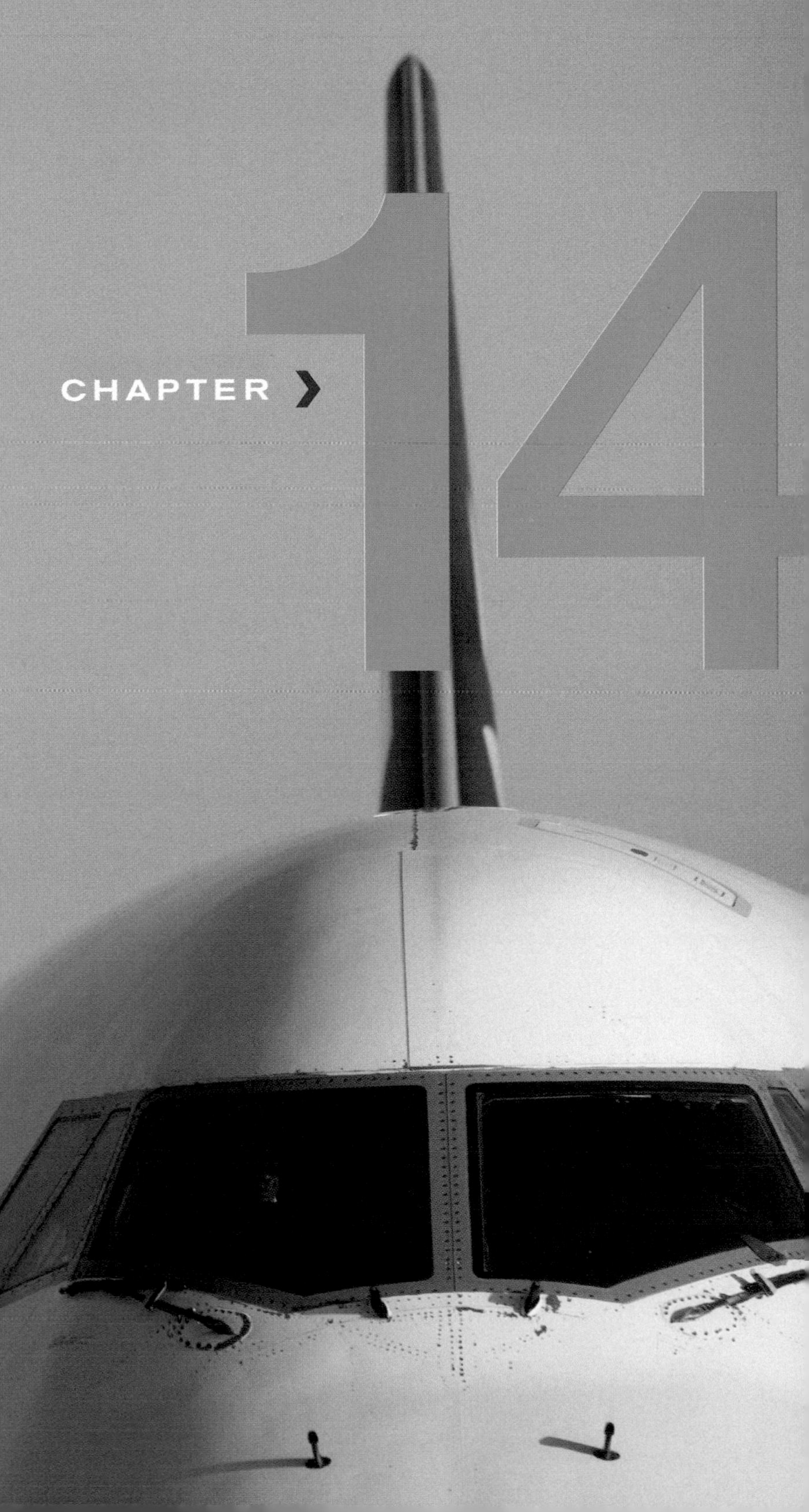

CHAPTER OVERVIEW

- THE ESSAY STRUCTURE AT A GLANCE
  - The Essay at a Glance
- ELEMENTS OF THE ESSAY
- THE WRITING PROCESS
- ESSAYS WITH ONE PATTERN OF ORGANIZATION
- ESSAYS WITH MULTIPLE PATTERNS OF ORGANIZATION
  - The Mixed-Pattern Essay at a Glance
  - Final Review

THINK FIRST

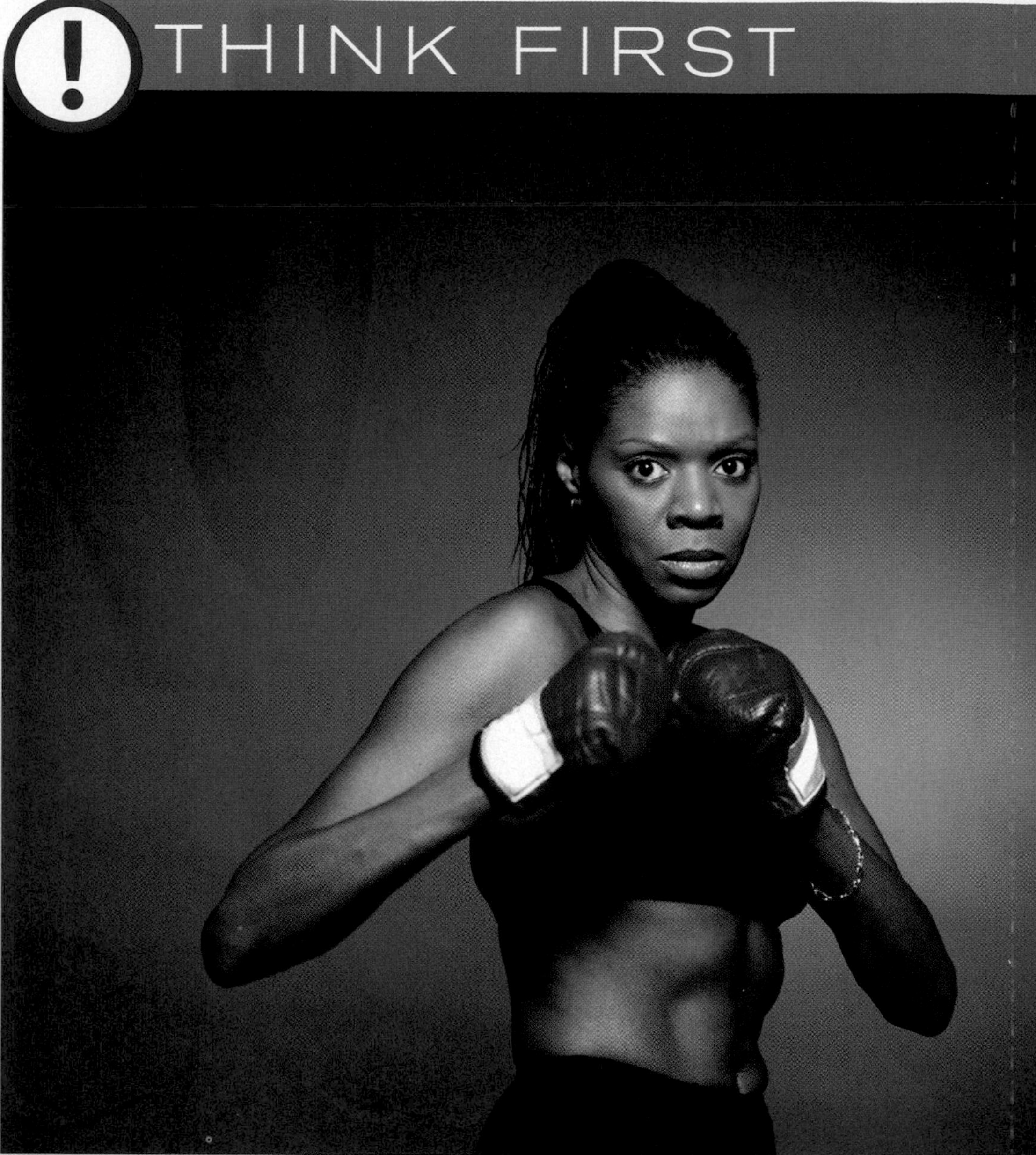

Think about the habits of mind that are essential to being successful in school and the workplace. Pick the area—work or school—that is most important to you right now. Who is your role model? Write a paragraph discussing the characteristics of this person you admire and what he or she has done that you find inspiring and worthy of imitation.

At a Glance

THE ESSAY STRUCTURE AT A GLANCE

Readers of college writing have definite expectations when they see an essay. They expect multiple paragraphs. They expect a beginning, a middle, and an end. They expect the writer to explain how the ideas and details all fit together and make sense. The best students know that good ideas alone are not enough. They have to know their readers' expectations and give them something that looks and sounds like an essay.

The Essay at a Glance

ASSIGNMENT Write an essay about a common problem in contemporary life.

Threat on the Road

The essay's title is a preview of the content.

As she reached the intersection, a car was coming toward her at high speed. It looked like it would run the light. She swerved to avoid hitting the car. Then she rolled down her window and was ready to give him a piece of her mind. However, he slammed on his brakes, got out of his car, and began shouting obscenities at her. He was at fault, yet he was shouting at the blameless driver! She hit the gas pedal and got out of there, fast. There is so much anger on the road these days. Anger is understandable, but sane people do not give in to road rage.

The student begins with a captivating story.

THESIS STATEMENT

Anger on the road, or "road rage," can lead drivers to carry out violent acts against other drivers. People become so angry that they overreact and resort to physical violence, attacking cars or assaulting their drivers with weapons. Race, gender, and age do not play a role in road rage. People who give in to road rage have one thing on their mind: getting even. They think they own the road. They run stoplights intentionally, they make inappropriate lane changes, they tailgate, they speed in and out of traffic, shouting, cursing, and making offensive hand gestures. Probably everyone has done some of these things. **The problem is that some people go too far to prove their point.**

TOPIC SENTENCE

The student provides a number of vivid examples of what drivers do when they act on road rage.

TRANSITION SENTENCE

TOPIC SENTENCE

The student provides examples of road rage going too far. These examples are more detailed than those in the previous paragraph.

Is it necessary to resort to violence to prove a point? Recently a mother of two was killed due to a road rage episode. She was on her way to work when an SUV began tailgating her. In an attempt to get away from the SUV, the woman began speeding. The SUV changed lanes, passed her, and then crossed over in front of her. The SUV slammed on its brakes, causing the woman to turn sharply and crash into a guardrail. She died at the scene. **In another case,** a twenty-year-old man was furious after a fender bender with a thirty-three-year-old woman. He was so infuriated that he dragged her out of her vehicle and forced her to jump from a bridge into the river, where she drowned. **Finally,** a young man almost died recently from a beating he received after a minor car accident. The twenty-six-year-old had gotten out of his SUV to see the damage to his car. The other driver became so enraged that he beat him with a baseball bat.

TRANSITION PHRASE

TRANSITION PHRASE

TOPIC SENTENCES
The student asks an important question in her conclusion.

She uses emphatic final words in the essay.

Where does all this rage come from? What can be done about it? Stress makes people a little crazy, especially when they are in a hurry. Others say there is something about the car, the power it has, and the impersonal space between the driver and other people. People standing in line do not assault each other. In a traffic jam, they sometimes do. Cars cause people to lose control. There has to be a limit. Slow down. Stay calm. Stay alive.

DISCUSSION QUESTIONS

PEER CONVERSATION

1. It can be difficult to think of good titles. Suggest two or three more titles for this essay.
2. The student makes use of examples to develop the ideas in this essay. Is the essay also about definition? cause and effect? Explain.
3. Suppose the student were going to revise this essay. What would you like to know more about? Make two suggestions.

ELEMENTS OF THE ESSAY

As you write essays in response to the assignments in this chapter, keep in mind these important elements.

- ***Introduction:*** Capture your reader's attention with a concise and dramatic story, a surprising statistic, or a vivid description. Your topic matters. Make that clear from the start.
- ***Thesis statement:*** Formulate a thesis statement that states the main idea of the essay and provides the reader with a clear sense of where you will go in the essay. (See Chapter 13 for more on writing a clear thesis statement that avoids heavy-handed announcements or vague statements.)
- ***Body:*** Explore the ideas in your essay in at least three or four consecutive paragraphs. Each paragraph should have a topic sentence that states the main idea and supporting details, such as facts, examples, and reasons, that are presented in a logical order.
- ***Order and transitions:*** The body paragraphs in your essay should be organized using one of the patterns of organization (description, example, narration, process, and so on) discussed in Part II of this text. Use transition words and phrases so your paragraphs are coherent; use transition sentences to indicate the connections between one paragraph and the next.
- ***Conclusion:*** Close the essay with one of the following approaches: (a) Focus on a specific detail in the essay and connect it to the main idea; (b) ask questions to give your reader something to think about; (c) if it is appropriate, offer solutions to a problem.

THE WRITING PROCESS

When you wrote paragraphs, you learned about the writing process: prewriting, drafting, revising, and editing. When you write essays, you take on more complex topics. You have more ideas and details to monitor. Make the writing process work for you. As you write, refer back to this checklist to make sure you spend enough time on each step of the process.

WRITING PROCESS CHECKLIST

Prewriting Approaches

_____ Clustering

_____ Freewriting

_____ Brainstorming

_____ Talking with classmates and people knowledgeable about my subject

Drafting Considerations

_____ Consider my audience

_____ Write a thesis statement

_____ Write topic sentences for each paragraph

_____ Use an outline

_____ Use transitions within paragraphs and transitional sentences between paragraphs

_____ Revise and improve on early ideas

_____ Write a conclusion

Revision Strategies	Editing Activities
______ Read critically	______ Search for and correct errors I know I make
______ Get input from peers	______ Find a peer to proofread
______ Develop a revision plan	______ Use editing checklist
______ Add, cut, and reorganize	

ESSAYS WITH ONE PATTERN OF ORGANIZATION

In the assignments below, you revisit what you learned about writing paragraphs using a pattern of organization, such as description, example, and narration. In these assignments, however, you take your treatment of your topic to the next level.

In the essay, you delve deeper into your subject, offering a more detailed picture. You write multiple paragraphs with a thesis and a topic sentence for each body paragraph. Finally, you bring your discussion to a close with a conclusion that emphasizes the point you have made and leaves your reader with something to think about.

Description

As you saw in the section on paragraph writing, description provides the reader with a concrete, up-close look at your subject. In an essay, you can cover more territory. Often in an essay, you will use description along with other patterns of organization. Here is a description essay. It is not uncommon for students to write description essays in the first person.

ASSIGNMENT Write a descriptive essay about a place that was important in your childhood.

The student begins with an inviting sentence.

THESIS STATEMENT "Three paths" suggests the structure of the paper to come.

TOPIC SENTENCE In her description of this place, the student tells a story.

The Oldest of Five

This is where I got my first kiss, smoked my first cigarette, and buried my first pet. This is where I grew up, the oldest of five, the only girl. All adventure took place in our big backyard. It was heavily wooded with tall birch trees. Three paths led to our favorite places on earth.

The first path led to the "mud hole." It was shaped like a saucer, shallow on the edges, deeper in the center. If we got a good rain, it filled with the blackest, slipperiest, softest mud. **One day we were playing** in the woods when it began to rain. I started to run toward home. We never wore shoes in the summer, and **as I rounded the corner,** I slipped and fell on my side, sliding right through the mud. My brothers rounded the corner just behind me, and down they went, one after the other. **Soon** we had a contest to see who could slide the farthest. Seeing my brothers covered with mud was so funny I started laughing. **When I did,** my brother John threw a pile of mud at me, which hit me in the back of the head. Naturally, I picked up some mud and threw it at him. **Soon** we were all throwing mud until my little brother Nick got mud in his mouth. He ran home crying, and we all followed. I will never forget the look on my mother's face when she saw us, covered in mud, only the whites of our eyes showing. It was the greatest day.

ORDER AND TRANSITIONS
The writer uses transition words and phrases common to the narration pattern of organization, such as "One day," "Soon," and "When I did," which relate to time order.

The second path led to the tree fort. It was in an old pine tree, about seven feet up. It leaned on other trees for support. The fort was not properly constructed, to say the least. **One humid summer day** we had friends visiting. We were all in the tree fort when my little brothers, Gabe and Nick, started jumping. **When** my friend Lynn and I screamed, they jumped harder. **The next thing** we knew, the entire fort came crashing to the ground with us in it. John was the only one hurt; he was leaning against the pine tree with no shirt on. He had the biggest scratches down his back, but that did not stop any of us from rebuilding the fort the next day.

TOPIC SENTENCE

The student tells a story as she describes the place.

ORDER AND TRANSITIONS
Transition words and phrases are commonly used for narration.

The third path led to the railroad tracks at the back of our property. We loved to walk the tracks. Sometimes my brothers would attempt to stop the train by stacking rocks on the track. **One day** when a train came by, we jumped across the water-filled ditch, only to find a fence at the top of the hill. Trapped, we decided to lie on the hillside and wait it out. **As the train sped by,** the wind pushed me onto the ground and I could not lift my head. I worried one of us would fall down toward the tracks. The train went on **forever,** blowing dirt into my eyes and onto my skin. When it **finally passed,** I hugged my brothers in relief. They laughed and said, "That was fun!"

TOPIC SENTENCE

NARRATION

ORDER AND TRANSITIONS
Transition words and phrases are commonly used for narration.

E. B. White wrote, "It is strange how much you can remember about a place like that once you allow your mind to return into the grooves that lead back" (121). This truly was a special place in my life, and there were many good times my brothers and I shared. I actually discovered my childhood again, simply by remembering instead of trying to forget.

Works Cited

White, E. B. "Once More to the Lake." *The Bedford Reader.* Ed. X. J. Kennedy, et al. 6th ed. New York: St. Martin's Press, 1994: 120-26. Print.

DISCUSSION QUESTIONS

PEER CONVERSATION

1. Is the introduction effective? Why or why not?
2. What description detail do you like best in the essay? Why?
3. In addition to description, what does the writer do to get her point across?

EXERCISE 14-1 **Writing a Description Essay**

Directions: *Choose one of the following assignments for a description essay. On a separate sheet of paper, use two forms of prewriting you like best to explore two possible topics related to the assignment. Next, narrow down one of the topics and develop a thesis and subtopics. Use the space provided below (in Exercise 14-2) to formulate your thesis and topic sentences and to plan your essay. Then write your essay.*

Imitation Assignment

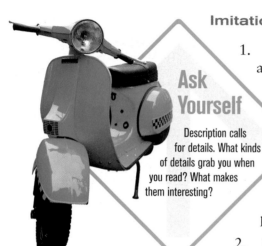

1. Write a description essay using the model as your guide. Describe a place that is important to you. Be sure to give the reader a sense of the spatial organization of the place. Provide details describing some important events that happened there or experiences you had.

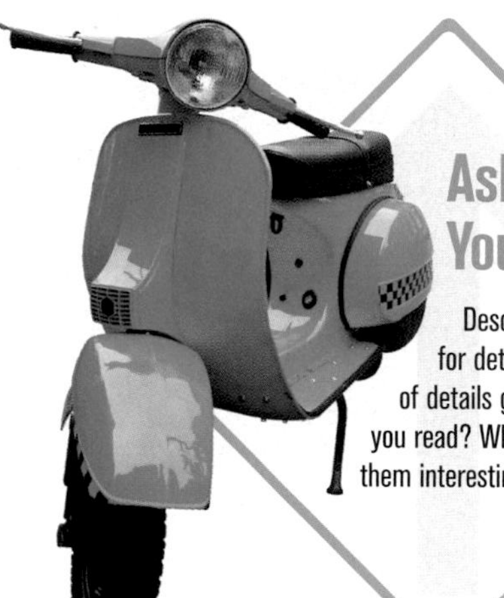

Ask Yourself

Description calls for details. What kinds of details grab you when you read? What makes them interesting?

Focused Assignments

1. Describe a prized possession. What is it? Where did it come from? Why is it important to you? Is the meaning of this possession personal, or is there a public dimension to its value?
2. Pick a stereotype that is common in our society. Describe the stereotype as people commonly think of it, focusing on appearance, actions, and attitudes.
3. Describe an attitude or value of a particular age group with which you take issue. How is the attitude or value expressed? Be specific about how you see it, hear it, and know it. Then explain your main reasons for objecting to it.

General Assignments

1. Describe a difficult class.
2. Use description to detail the ideal job for a college student.
3. Describe the qualities that make a good (or a bad) parent.
4. Describe your worst fear.

Description Refresher

Remember that conveying a dominant impression is essential in effective description writing. Good description depends on sensory detail and frequently uses comparison. For a reminder of these elements of description writing, see these sections of Chapter 4: "Elements of Description" (page 70), "Get

Started" (page 70), "Organize Your Thinking" (page 71), and "Comparisons and Description Thinking" (page 73).

EXERCISE 14-2 Outlining Your Essay

Directions: *When you complete your prewriting, use this outline to plan your description essay.*

This outline calls for three body paragraphs. However, students should know that the five-paragraph essay is an accidental artifact with no basis in actual writing practice.

Placing only two topic sentence slots in this outline might invite students to aim low; placing four or five might cause them to dilute otherwise very good ideas.

Three is a convenient number. Remind students that writers write as many paragraphs as they need to get a job done. Students should feel free to do more or less than is shown in this outline and the outlines that come after it.

Your Topic: ______________________________

Thesis: ______________________________

____

____

Topic Sentence: ______________________________

____

____

A. ______________________________

B. ______________________________

C. ______________________________

Topic Sentence: ______________________________

____

____

A. ______________________________

B. ______________________________

C. ______________________________

Topic Sentence: ______________________________

____

____

A. ______________________________

B. ______________________________

C. ______________________________

Example

On the paragraph level, you briefly elaborate on examples. In an essay, you can go into much more detail, using similar, contrasting, and extended examples to make your point. Here is an example essay.

ASSIGNMENT Discuss the benefits and challenges facing a young person who works.

Overtime

The essay begins with an extended example.

She still gets a call from an elderly man she made friends with when she worked at the retirement home. He says in his deep voice, "Hello, Leah. When are my two girlfriends coming over?" He means Leah and her two-year-old daughter, Natalie. Five years after working at the rest home, Leah still gets calls from Hershel, whom she refers to as "the gentle giant." When they are together, he and Leah talk about their families, school, and about his life "back in the day." He also gives Leah advice when she is having a tough time. There are many benefits and challenges to being a working high school student.

THESIS STATEMENT The writer identifies advantages and disadvantages to working as the focus on the paper.

TOPIC SENTENCE

To begin with, it is fun to meet people from different walks of life. Like Leah, Keianna was a sophomore in high school when she got a job at The Village, a rest home near campus. "I had never seen so many old people in my life," she says. They zipped past her on their motorized wheelchairs, called "hover rounds." Some almost ran over her. She worked in the dining room serving food. "Most of the dining room employees were high school students," Keianna notes, "so I met young and old alike." She grew to love the old people, who liked to see young faces. They liked to see energetic young people as they ran around the room, serving their food quickly and brightening the room.

TOPIC SENTENCE "Other important benefits" provides a transition. The previous paragraph was about a benefit; the current paragraph will also be about benefits.

There are other important benefits to being a working student. In addition to the pay, some employers offer tuition assistance and scholarship funds. If a student works five hundred hours her junior and senior year, she can earn $4,000 for college. A second benefit is learning responsibility. Being on time is a big priority at any job. When kids have a job, they are responsible for their own actions. They also make their own money and have to manage it. Presentation is also important at work. Knowing how to dress properly and speak confidently is a key factor in any work environment. These benefits can make a big difference to a young person.

Then again, there are challenges to working and taking classes. **First and foremost** is fatigue. Working students only have so much energy. Some students work long hours after school, get home late, and have to study tired. They also go to school tired. **A second challenge** is holding down their hours. It is tempting to add on, to take more work, and make more money. Even though it is against the law for high school students to work too many hours, employers will break the law if they have a good employee. Young people like to feel needed. They want to be important. It is difficult to turn down a boss who says, "You are my best worker." Finally, working students are not studying. **In many cases,** the good work they do for an employer is traded for good work they could be doing for a teacher.

TOPIC SENTENCE
"Then again" indicates a reversal of focus. Now the writer talks about the challenges of being a working student. These challenges contrast with the benefits.

ORDER AND TRANSITIONS
The writer uses enumeration to connect details.

Every job has its satisfactions. In every situation, there are trade-offs. Leah does not regret working as a high school student. In fact, she says it was an excellent experience that prepared her for the adult world. However, Leah is only one person. There are other kids who go overboard, working too many hours. They need to be pulled back. They need to be kids.

The essay ends on a balanced note, reminding the reader there are benefits and challenges to being a working student.

DISCUSSION QUESTIONS

PEER CONVERSATION

1. Is the introduction effective? Why or why not?
2. Does the writer reveal her point of view in this essay?
3. In addition to examples, what other patterns of organization do you see in the essay?

EXERCISE 14-3 Writing an Example Essay

Directions: *Choose one of the following assignments for an example essay. On a separate sheet of paper, use the form of prewriting you like best to explore two possible topics related to the assignment. Next, narrow down one of the topics and develop a thesis and subtopics. Use Exercise 14-4 to formulate your thesis and topic sentences and plan your essay. Then write your essay.*

Imitation Assignment

1. Write an example essay using the model as your guide. Cite examples of a social behavior you approve of or object to. Be sure to cite a number of examples, varying the length of the examples you use.

Focused Assignments

1. It is said that adversity builds character. Write an essay in which you agree or disagree with this claim. Discuss how responding to challenges has made you or someone you know a better person. Consider using contrasting examples in your discussion.

2. Modern American life is all about technological devices. Do they improve or complicate our lives? Write an essay in which you examine this question. Cite and discuss a number of examples of technological devices.
3. In a culture of celebrity, such as our own, we see and hear from famous people all the time. Some celebrities use fame for good causes. Cite and discuss a few examples.

General Assignments

1. Give examples of a positive and/or negative role model.
2. Provide examples of abilities you bring to the workplace.
3. Cite the qualities of a good job.
4. Give examples of fads you find amusing.

Example Refresher

Remember that effective example writing depends on including specific details. You present details to make your point. For a reminder of the elements of example writing, see these sections of Chapter 5: "Elements of Example" (page 88), "Get Started" (pages 88–89), and "Types of Examples" (page 91). For a reminder of how to organize example writing, see "Elaborate on Examples" (page 93).

EXERCISE 14-4 **Outlining Your Essay**

Directions: *When you complete your prewriting, copy the outline on page 307 and use it to plan your example essay.*

Narration

You saw in your work on the narration paragraph that a well-told story provides the reader with specific details. In an essay, you can tell one long story, zeroing in on the details that are most significant, or you can tell multiple stories to make a point. Here is a narration essay.

ASSIGNMENT Write a narration essay about a phobia you have. Be sure to draw upon our textbook discussion of phobia in your essay.

No Bones about It

The student begins with a captivating story.

"A dinner party? Great! What time? What should I bring?" I was invited to a dinner party at a new friend's house. It never occurred to me to ask what kind of meat would be served. They were serving chicken and ribs. Most people would be happy with this menu, but not me. Since the age of ten I have been unable to eat meat with bones in it or any meat that looks the way it did when it was alive: I have bonephobia.

THESIS STATEMENT

One of the funniest memories of my bonephobia is when I was in Orlando, Florida. My friends and I went to Medieval Times. We were supposed to have dinner during a horse riding and jousting show. The show started, and they began serving dinner, that is if you consider people wearing rags and throwing food on your plate "serving dinner." There was no silverware. Everything was to be eaten with your hands. We drank our soup out of dented metal bowls. It was all in fun, so I did not mind, until a man came by and threw an entire Cornish hen on my plate. I still remember how it jiggled as it hit the plate. I screamed with surprise and started yelling, "Get it off! Get it off!" I was so upset. I did not know what to do. My friend reached over, picked up the hen, and put it on his plate. I could not calm down at first. When I did, I was very embarrassed. I could not believe the way I reacted. The man sitting next to me, a complete stranger, laughed and said, "Can I have yours?"

TOPIC SENTENCE

In the body of the paper, the student starts right in with a narration to explain what bonephobia is.

She provides specific detail about place, actors, and actions.

Here she gives the outcome of the narration.

TRANSITION SENTENCE

There are many people who actually enjoy eating meat off the bone. I go to the Renaissance Festival in Holly, Michigan, every year, and I see many people buying huge turkey legs. They walk around eating them and seem to enjoy it. It is difficult for me to watch. I am also taken aback by some places that serve seafood. The fish come out cooked with heads still on them. **One year** my friends took me to a seafood restaurant for my birthday. Someone ordered lobster tail. To my surprise they brought the entire lobster. It sat across the table staring at me. I tried to ignore it at first. Then I asked them to put a napkin over it. Everyone thought it was funny that it bothered me. They had lots of fun tormenting me with it for the rest of the evening.

TOPIC SENTENCE
The writer suggests she will look at contrasting examples.

A second narration begins here.

Here is the outcome of the narration.

Some doctors claim they can cure any phobia. In the book *Psychology, an Introduction,* by Benjamin B. Lahey, the author discusses a widely known study published in 1920 by Dr. John B. Watson on classical conditioning. Watson believed that many of our fears are acquired and taught to us. He did a study on counterconditioning. This is a way to "undo" what we were taught to fear. For a situation like mine, a therapist would probably introduce the feared element (chicken bones) gradually. First, a plate of clean chicken bones would be placed in front of me. As I became more comfortable, the therapist might leave small pieces of meat on the bone and have me pick it off and so on. I have heard of experts that try an approach different from Watson's. They claim to help a person overcome a

TOPIC SENTENCE

Here the student uses an extended example.

The student finishes her essay with a small comparison and contrast example.

phobia in twenty-four hours without having that person repeatedly exposed to the feared item(s).

I know a few other people who cannot eat meat off the bone. We all agree that it reminds us that we are eating an animal, which was killed simply for us to eat. If we think about it while eating, the meal is over. On the other hand, I was just talking to my nephew who stated, "Boned chicken is my favorite meat." He thinks that all of the vegetables I eat are gross. When he starts picking on my fear of bones, I just offer him some broccoli.

DISCUSSION QUESTIONS

1. How many stories does the writer tell in the essay?
2. What is the effect of referring to her college textbook in the essay?
3. Compose what you think would be a good thesis for this paper. Then look for a similar statement in the essay itself.
4. Describe what the writer does in her conclusion.

PEER CONVERSATION

EXERCISE 14-5 Writing a Narration Essay

Directions: *Choose one of the following assignments for a narration essay. On a separate sheet of paper, use the form of prewriting you like best to explore two possible topics related to the assignment. Next, narrow down one of the topics and develop a thesis and subtopics. Use Exercise 14-6 to formulate your thesis and topic sentences and to plan your essay. Then write your essay.*

Imitation Assignment

1. Write a narration essay using the model as your guide. Describe a phobia you have and, in the process, recall two or three incidents in which you were keenly aware of this phobia.

Focused Assignments

1. Discuss a person, place, or thing you changed your mind about. Talk about how your attitude about this person, place, or thing was formed. Then tell a story or stories exploring your change of attitude. Be sure to be specific about time, place, people, and events in the stories you tell.
2. We often celebrate our triumphs and our skills, dwelling on the positive. Write an essay about something you are not very good at and wish you were. Tell a story about a specific time you realized your lack of this skill, and consider what difference it makes in your life that you are not good at it.
3. Discuss the relative importance of health in your life. To explore this topic, recall a time when you or someone you know was injured or got sick. Be specific about what happened, including details of time and place. What was the outcome of this experience?

General Assignments

1. Cite a disappointing experience.
2. Give specific details about a technological device.
3. Recall a time when you had amazingly good luck.
4. Tell a story about a challenge you faced in school or on the job.

Narration Refresher

Remember that effective narration depends on using specific details. Your reader needs to know about what happened, when and where, who was involved, and what the outcome was. For a reminder of the elements of narration, see these sections of Chapter 6: "Elements of Narration" (page 114), "Get Started" (page 115), "Narration and Specific Details" (page 117), and "Make Connections" (page 119).

EXERCISE 14-6 Outlining Your Essay

Directions: *When you complete your prewriting, copy the outline on page 307 and use it to plan your narration essay.*

Process

Process analysis is very common in academic writing and writing in the workplace. You will frequently be asked to explain how something works, such as a piece of machinery or cell division.

In the process paragraph you wrote, you saw that a process usually has a key detail that requires explanation. In an essay, you have much more room to focus on one or more of the important components of a process. Here is a process essay.

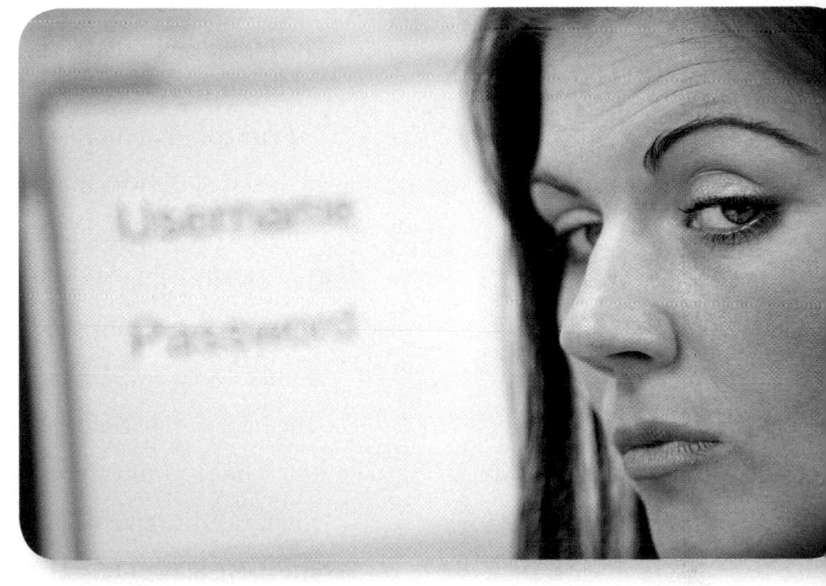

ASSIGNMENT Using process analysis, describe a security issue people should be aware of and how to protect themselves.

Identity Theft: Everyone's Problem

It was Christmastime. He was shopping and checking things off his list. At his last stop, when he reached for his wallet, it was gone. He rushed out and backtracked to the last store. Luck was on his side because there was his wallet, safely in the hands of the saleswoman. Many people are not as lucky as this gentleman. Identity theft has become a costly problem in our society today. It occurs when someone obtains and uses an individual's

The student begins his essay with a captivating story.

THESIS STATEMENT
The writer clearly indicates this is a process essay.

TOPIC SENTENCE
The student identifies important materials needed for this process.

TRANSITION SENTENCE
This sentence in bold takes the reader from one important component of the process to the next.

TOPIC SENTENCE

TOPIC SENTENCE

This conclusion paragraph covers the last step of the process.

personal information such as Social Security numbers, bank and credit accounts, and birth dates. A few simple, preventative steps can keep an individual's personal information safe.

The first step in securing records begins at home. Instead of throwing receipts or pay stubs on the counter, it is wise to purchase a small filing cabinet. This cabinet keeps records neatly organized. At the end of the year, it is possible to sort and keep important papers for future use, discard all unnecessary papers, and start the New Year right. This cabinet keeps personal information in one location, safely under lock and key. **However, all this organizational effort will not work without a paper shredder.** Shred all discarded documents. Catalogs with preprinted order forms inside can contain a person's name and credit card information. Shred the form first before throwing it away. If it is in the garbage, it is public property for anyone to use.

A second step is to take precautions with computer, telephone, and mail communication. Passwords are better than using your mother's maiden name; ensure websites have secure firewalls. **Once the password is established, be on the lookout for irregular requests.** These days it is not uncommon to receive an e-mail from a financial institution requesting a Social Security number and password. A call to that institution invariably proves the request is a hoax. **The same goes for the telephone.** Do not assume that the person on the other end is legitimate. Postal mail is **equally important.** Preapproved credit card applications are sent to households every day. They should be shredded and thrown away. Shredding is the best defense against identity theft.

Finally, individuals should consider asking for a credit report every year. Credit reports identify all open and closed credit accounts, balances on these accounts, and a person's credit rating. This rating can be the difference between purchasing that first home or having doors slammed in one's face. If there is suspicious activity on the report, the following credit reporting agencies can help: Equifax, Experian, or TransUnion. They flag accounts and monitor any subsequent activity. By utilizing these steps, you can effectively prevent identity theft.

DISCUSSION QUESTIONS

PEER CONVERSATION

1. What does the writer do to capture the reader's attention in his introduction?
2. What tool or device is important for identity theft protection?
3. Does the order of the paragraphs make sense? What do you think the writer's reasons were for placing the paragraphs in this order?

EXERCISE 14-7 Writing a Process Essay

Directions: *Choose one of the following assignments for a process essay. On a separate sheet of paper, use the form of prewriting you like best to explore two possible topics related to the assignment. Next, narrow down one of the topics and develop a thesis and subtopics. Use Exercise 14-8 to formulate your thesis and topic sentences and to plan your essay. Then write your essay.*

Imitation Assignment

1. Write a process essay using the model as your guide. Explain the steps involved in becoming a good student. Consider materials, times, places, and people involved in the process. Be sure to identify a key detail.

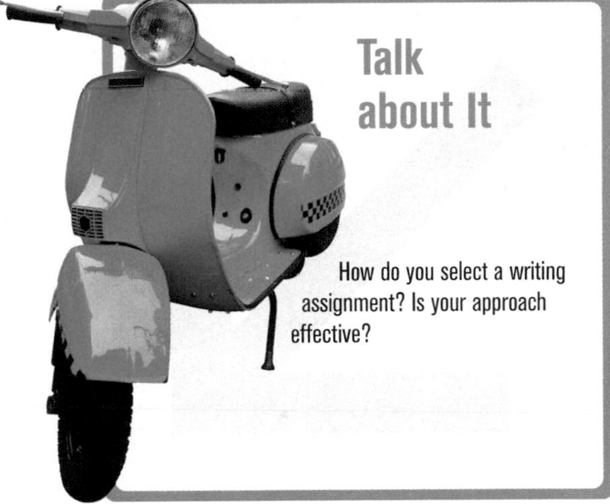

Talk about It

How do you select a writing assignment? Is your approach effective?

Focused Assignments

1. Every so often, people in a household are caught unprepared when they lose power in a storm. What is the best way to prepare for such an inconvenience? And once the power goes out, what steps can be taken to maintain a relatively normal way of life?
2. Complex skills call for smart learning processes. Discuss a complex skill you have, such as playing a musical instrument or speaking a foreign language. Describe the most effective process for acquiring such a skill.
3. Technology has made new forms of communication possible. Discuss the safety issues involved in online communication, such as chat rooms, and what precautionary steps a person can take to ensure safety.

General Assignments

1. Explain the process of gaining too much weight.
2. Describe how to spend almost nothing on a date and still have a very good time.
3. Explain how to overcome a prejudice.
4. What are the steps involved in getting a promotion at work?

Process Refresher

Remember that effective process writing depends on including specific details about the process. These details include when and where the process takes place, what materials are necessary, the people involved in the process, and its key detail. For a reminder on the elements of process writing, see these sections of Chapter 7: "Elements of Process" (page 138), "Get Started" (page 137), "Organize Your Details" (page 140), and "Key Details" (page 141).

EXERCISE 14-8 Outlining Your Essay

Directions: *When you complete your prewriting, copy the outline on page 307 and use it to plan your process essay.*

Classification

You saw in your classification paragraph that sorting detail into categories or types enables you to explain ideas more precisely. In an essay, you have the opportunity to say more about the categories you set forth and why they are important. Classification can make more exact thinking possible. Here is a classification essay.

ASSIGNMENT Write a classification essay in which you discuss different types of people who use the Internet.

Internet Users

The student begins with a general observation—appealing to a common fear.

He cites three examples of video addiction, leading to the focus of the essay—types of Internet users.

THESIS STATEMENT

At one time parents worried about how much television their children watched. Every day a new report came out with alarming statistics: kids were watching four, five, even six hours of television a day. Then came video games. Kids sat in front of television screens, joysticks in hand, completely absorbed by their games. Add the Internet to TV and video games, and the population of the addicted increases significantly. But many Internet users are not kids. They are adult users, and they come in three recognizable types.

TOPIC SENTENCE The writer identifies the first type of user.

ORDER AND TRANSITIONS Repeating the terms "average type user" adds to the coherence of the details in this paragraph.

Less and less you see the average type user. He comes home from work about 5:00 p.m. He strolls up to his computer and checks his e-mail. He finds an e-mail for a bill he was expecting. He pays with his credit card and closes his e-mail. He smiles, knowing he does not have to write a check and that this particular bill is taken care of until next month. That is the last time he is on the computer that day. **The average type user** uses the Internet to save time. **The average type user** takes advantage of the Internet when he can, but he has never depended on the Internet and probably never will.

TOPIC SENTENCE The writer identifies the second type of user.

Another type is the web junk user. These users enjoy being on the Internet and exploring different areas of the web. They are the window shoppers of the Internet world. They forward messages to bring themselves good fortune. My grandfather **used to be** an average type user. He lives in Texas. He would e-mail just to say hello or see how we were doing. **That all changed.** He started e-mailing us ridiculous e-mails about having good luck. **At first** we were his only recipients. **After** a couple of months, the list was enormous. His mail carrier, bingo buddies, and all the people at the VFW are now on his mailing list. He has met thousands of people on the Internet. **They** spend much of their spare time browsing. **They** are infatuated with the power and size of the web. **They** enjoy knowing an article they found will travel around the world. These are the users who congest all of our mailboxes.

After identifying the category, the student cites his grandfather as an example.

ORDER AND TRANSITIONS
Transition words and repetition enhance the coherence of this paragraph.

The third type is the chat room user. These users love being on the Internet. **They** would rather be on the Internet than pick up the phone and call. **They** have more fun in a chat room than at an amusement park. **They** love meeting people on the Internet. **They** love designing their profile, which changes on a daily basis. My sister is this type. She is twenty-three years old. She buys, sells, e-mails, downloads, checks the weather, and even talks to her friends via the Internet. When I visited her last week she was talking to a friend on the computer. She was literally talking through her computer, not typing. I do not understand. Why talk through your computer when you have your cell phone? Chat room users spend all of their spare time on the Internet. Many stay up all night on line. They need it. It is an addiction.

TOPIC SENTENCE

He identifies the type, then illustrates it with a specific example.

I use all the time I save on the Internet deleting junk e-mail. The junk user and chat room addicts are killing me. I am the average user, and I try to enjoy the benefits of the Internet without relying on it too much. Even with the Internet, I still have a life.

In this conclusion the student emphasizes the importance of the topic by discussing an effect: too much unwanted e-mail.

DISCUSSION QUESTIONS

1. State the point of this essay in your own words.
2. For each type of user, the writer provides an example. What is the effect of doing so?
3. Which type of user is the writer?

PEER CONVERSATION

EXERCISE 14-9 Writing a Classification Essay

Directions: *Choose one of the following assignments for a classification essay. On a separate sheet of paper, use the form of prewriting you like best to explore two possible topics related to the assignment. Next, narrow down one of the topics and develop a thesis and subtopics. Use Exercise 14-10 to formulate your thesis and topic sentences and to plan your essay. Then write your essay.*

Imitation Assignment

1. Write a classification essay using the model as your guide. Classify different kinds of animal lovers. For each type, cite an example or two to elaborate and explain.

Focused Assignments

1. Not everyone agrees on the proper approach to disciplining children. Talk about two different approaches and what they teach children.
2. Discuss different types of jobs available to young people today. Consider what these types of jobs offer and what kind of young person they would benefit.
3. The best way to save money is to have a budget that helps you keep track of cash flow. How would you classify your expenses? Which type of expense could most easily be controlled and enable you to spend money more wisely?

Writer's Response

When have you used classification effectively? For what? Why?

General Assignments

1. Classify your friends into different types.
2. Use classification to provide excuses for not getting homework done.
3. There are probably specific kinds of movies you prefer to watch. Use classification to categorize these movies.
4. Classify different types of sports fans.

Classification Refresher

Classification writing involves sorting, dividing an undifferentiated topic into subtopics and categories. Your categories depend on the inclusion of good details if they are to make sense to the reader. You also want to guard against thinking in stereotypes when you classify. For a reminder on the elements of classification writing, see these sections of Chapter 8: "Elements of Classification" (page 158), "Get Started" (page 158), "Provide Examples of Categories" (page 160), and "Avoid Stereotyping" (page 164).

EXERCISE 14-10 Outlining Your Essay

Directions: *When you complete your prewriting, copy the outline on page 307 and use it to plan your classification essay.*

Cause and Effect

In the cause and effect paragraph you wrote, you saw the importance of focusing on causes or effects. The cause and effect essay provides you with greater latitude, inviting you to think critically about both causes and effects. Here is a cause and effect essay.

ASSIGNMENT Select a common problem people face and consider causes or effects.

Sweet Dreams

Have a good sleep. That is the wish of just about every individual. Good sleep is tied to emotional, mental, and physical health. Good sleep, for many, is elusive. What should happen easily and naturally happens only with the help of medications, or it happens not at all. Sleep deprivation affects millions of people a year, possibly every night. Medical literature devotes increasingly more space and discussion to a range of new problems, such as sleep apnea, as well as to old problems, such as insomnia. Why do we have difficulty sleeping, and what are the effects of sleeplessness?

This first sentence goes with the title. It invites the reader in.

THESIS QUESTION
The student uses a question to indicate this is a cause and effect analysis.

One reason people cannot sleep is conditions in the sleep environment. Their sleep is disturbed by **sound.** A barking dog will keep some people awake. The **sound** of blasting music from an upstairs apartment or in a car that drives by is enough to prevent sleep. **Such people** often go into "listening mode." They lie awake waiting for another car to go by. They listen for voices upstairs. **Still** others are kept awake by someone close by. Snoring is a big joke, but not to those whom it keeps awake. Now physicians talk about "restless leg syndrome," a neurological disorder that seems to activate when a person lies down. **Consequently** the afflicted individual is unable to sleep, nor is the person sharing his or her bed.

TOPIC SENTENCE

ORDER AND TRANSITIONS

For each cause, the student provides details and explanation.

Another reason people cannot sleep is worry. They lie awake at night worrying about work, children, or the future. Work is often a culprit. Work is tied in with livelihood. Someone whose work changes or whose income is threatened is likely to lie awake at night, preoccupied with what is happening or about to happen, unable to sleep as a result. **Similarly,** parents may have trouble sleeping if they have a child who is in distress. Parents stay up at night waiting for their teenagers to come home. This wakefulness in fact begins early in their lives as parents. New parents listen for a baby's cry, for the slightest sound. They learn to sleep lightly. **Finally,** people

TOPIC SENTENCE

may suffer sleep deprivation because they worry about the future. Asked why he did not sleep well at night, one patient in a sleep clinic said he lies awake at night thinking about death.

In the conclusion, the student briefly examines the effects of poor sleep.

We need sleep to rest our minds. We also need it to be healthy. People who sleep poorly are more likely to get sick than those who sleep well because lack of sleep affects the immune system. People who are tired also are less able to perform at optimum levels and cannot concentrate as well. Their reflexes and mental agility are affected. Poor performance causes stress. That in turn may affect sleep. It is a vicious cycle.

PEER CONVERSATION

DISCUSSION QUESTIONS

1. This is cause and effect analysis. What pattern of organization does the writer use in the third paragraph?
2. The essay is written mostly in the third person. Where does the writer shift out of third person? Why does she make these shifts?
3. How would you describe the tone of this essay?

EXERCISE 14-11 Writing a Cause and Effect Essay

Directions: *Choose one of the following assignments for a cause and effect essay. On a separate sheet of paper, use the form of prewriting you like best to explore two possible topics related to the assignment. Next, narrow down one of the topics and develop a thesis and subtopics. Use Exercise 14-12 to formulate your thesis and topic sentences and plan your essay. Then write your essay.*

Imitation Assignment

1. Write a cause and effect essay using the model as your guide. Discuss something you changed your mind about. Be specific about what you liked or disliked about it initially as well as your reasons for changing your mind.

Focused Assignments

1. Discuss a physical characteristic about yourself and the effect it has had on your view of yourself. Examine that effect in two or three specific situations.
2. We say sometimes that experience is the best teacher. Write about an experience that taught you a valuable lesson. Be specific about the reasons why the lesson was valuable.
3. Discuss a popular entertainer in the music industry. What makes this person so entertaining? Be specific about your reasons.

General Assignments

1. Discuss going on blind dates.
2. Give the causes and the effects of being good at math.
3. Discuss a bad habit and the consequences of it.
4. Write about having a special skill at work.

Cause and Effect Refresher

Focus is essential in cause and effect writing. It is important that you distinguish between causes and effects and that your reader understands whether you are explaining causes or effects. For a reminder on the elements of cause and effect writing, see these sections of Chapter 9: "Elements of Cause and Effect" (page 181), "Get Started" (page 182), "Cause and Effect Details" (page 183), and "Organizing Your Thinking" (page 184).

EXERCISE 14-12 **Outlining Your Essay**

Directions: *When you complete your prewriting, copy the outline on page 307 and use it to plan your cause and effect essay. Indicate whether your focus is primarily on causes or effects.*

Comparison and Contrast

Like classification, comparison and contrast focuses on similarities and differences. We know something for what it is and for what it is not. Examining similarities and differences is a basic form of inquiry, useful in school, in the workplace, and at home. Here is a comparison and contrast essay.

ASSIGNMENT Using Charles Dickens's *Hard Times* as your starting point, discuss differing views of education.

Possible Minds

The use of education, according to Thomas Gradgrind, a teacher in Charles Dickens's *Hard Times,* is to fill our heads with facts. There is no room for nonsense, play, or wonder. Gradgrind is a "cannon loaded to the muzzle with facts," and he opens fire on the children before him, murdering their imaginations in the process. What is a horse? Bitzer, a Gradgrind success story, answers: "Quadruped. Graminivorous. Forty teeth. . . . Sheds coat in the spring. . . . Hoofs hard. . . . Age known by marks in mouth." In a technical sense, Bitzer's right. That is a horse. Nevertheless, he has missed something. He has missed the majestic animal that excites awe. Education ought to be about awesome possibilities.

The student begins with a specific reference to something he has read.

In my school, Mr. Henke prowled the hallways and cafeteria on stubby legs. He had a hogshead chest and a flat face with a look of total certainty

SUPPORTING DETAILS
This paragraph begins with a statement of fact. Much of the detail in the paragraph is description detail.

on it. Before becoming a principal, he had been a builder. He had measured and sawed lumber to fit, then bashed it into place with his roughing hammer. If it did not fit, he bashed harder. This was also his approach to education. His construction tongue often got the best of him. When riled, he called kids jerks and fools and was not above using tame four-letter words. In the cafeteria, where we inevitably saw him, he pulled lovers apart. "Hey, you should not be doing that here!" He stopped at tables of ninth graders, shooting the breeze. He joked, laughing quickly and without reserve. We liked him. Like us, he was rough around the edges. I do not think he understood kids or that he was even very interested in them. To Mr. Henke, school was a place to keep order. What we learned from him was: Do not neck in the cafeteria. Do not question authority.

TOPIC SENTENCE
The student states his main idea at the end of this paragraph.

TOPIC SENTENCE

This view of school was consistent with the one I learned at home. My father was a businessman. In every interaction, he was selling himself. When I rode with him on his calls, he constantly waved to people he did not know. "You can wave," he said. "It does not cost anything." He had to sell himself before he could sell anything else. As parents will, he made me in his image. I learned to wave. I learned what he called "presentation skills": **how to** talk on the phone, **how to** deal with strangers, **how to** use language to get what I wanted. In school, I had to acquire **useful** learning. **Useful** meant math. My father was **a man of projects.** He drew pictures. He measured and cut. I needed math to size up the world and do **my own projects.** He kept accounts. I needed math to look after my money. Useful also meant reading. I had to learn to read well so I could become an independent learner, like my father.

TRANSITIONS
The writer uses repetition to make his paragraph coherent.

The student uses inductive order in this paragraph, too. It is "details first."

Then I got my hands on literature. **One fall,** I read poetry from an anthology. I also read *Death of a Salesman* and *Othello.* It was not my first encounter with literature. **Up to that time,** reading had not affected me much. It was an information transfer system, a form of work. **That fall,** the terrible longings of Willie Loman, his massive dreams of success and his tragic inability to enjoy simple pleasures, affected me profoundly. At the end of the play, Linda stood over his grave, saying, "We're free, Willie. We're free." It was more than I could stand. Then there was the majestic language of Othello. It was beautiful and dramatic. Reading was fun. In those weeks, education suddenly took on a new meaning.

TRANSITIONS
Words related to time connect the details of this paragraph.

TOPIC SENTENCE
The topic sentence comes at the end of the paragraph.

In his conclusion, the student refers to something read in class.

After that, to me, school became a place where a few thoughtful young people congregated, seeking contact with even more thoughtful older people. It became a place of awesome possibilities. I was still an obedient student, bent upon being useful somehow or other. However, **a little of the Bitzer** in me had died.

He also retrieves a detail from the beginning of the essay.

DISCUSSION QUESTIONS

PEER CONVERSATION

1. Describe the different types of education the writer compares and contrasts in this essay.
2. Titles of essays are supposed to reflect content of the essay. What does the title of this essay mean?
3. What does the writer mean when he says "a little of the Bitzer in me had died"?

EXERCISE 14-13 Writing a Comparison and Contrast Essay

Directions: *Choose one of the following assignments for a comparison and contrast essay. On a separate sheet of paper, use the form of prewriting you like best to explore two possible topics related to the assignment. Next, narrow down one of the topics and develop a thesis and subtopics. Use Exercise 14-14 to formulate your thesis and topic sentences and plan your essay. Then write your essay.*

Imitation Assignment

1. Write a comparison and contrast essay using the model as your guide. Why do we work? What is it for? What does it do for us? Explain two different views of work and its purpose. In your essay, connect those views with specific people you know. Be sure to indicate the view you find most compelling.

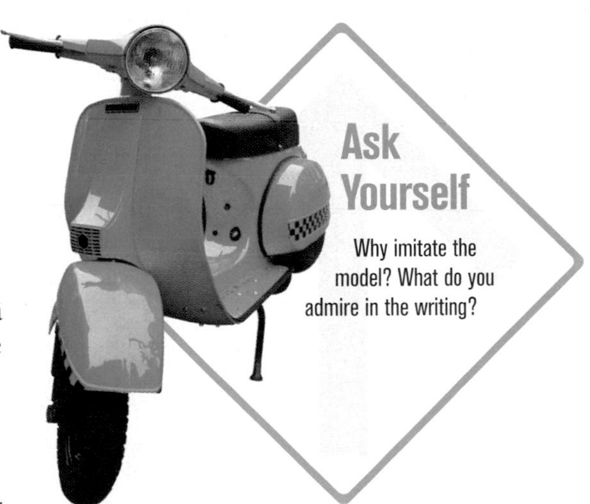

Ask Yourself
Why imitate the model? What do you admire in the writing?

Focused Assignments

1. Change is the law of the universe. Write an essay about a change you have seen occur in a person or place. Provide specific descriptions of the person or place both before and after the change.
2. Discuss two different job positions in your workplace. How are they similar or different in terms of responsibility, relationship to coworkers, and stress levels?
3. Learning requires maturity, preparation, and readiness. Not everyone is ready to learn at the same time. Compare and contrast two learning experiences involving a particular subject in school that yielded very different results. In your discussion, consider reasons for the different results.

General Assignments

1. Compare and contrast a book and a movie made from the book.
2. Compare and contrast two friends you enjoy being with.

3. Compare and contrast views of marriage from the perspective of two different generations.
4. Compare and contrast practical knowledge versus school knowledge.

Comparison and Contrast Refresher

In comparison and contrast writing, you explore similarities and differences, presenting supporting details to illustrate and explain your point. This form of writing poses unique organizational challenges. It may be useful to organize your essay in subject-by-subject format; on the other hand, it may be more effective to use point-by-point organization. For a reminder on the elements of comparison and contrast writing, see these sections of Chapter 10: "Elements of Comparison and Contrast" (page 204), "Get Started" (page 204), "Points of Comparison and Contrast" (page 205), and "Select and Elaborate on Details" (page 209).

EXERCISE 14-14 Outline Your Essay

Directions: *When you complete your prewriting, use this outline to plan your comparison and contrast essay. Choose the approach that works best for your topic.*

Subject-by-Subject Comparison

Topic: ____________________

Thesis: ____________________

____

____

Topic Sentence (Subject 1): ____________________

____

____

A. ____________________

B. ____________________

C. ____________________

Topic Sentence (Subject 2): ____________________

____

____

Point-by-Point Comparison

Topic: ______________________________

Thesis: ______________________________

____

____

Topic Sentence (Point 1): ______________________________

____

____

Subject 1: ______________________________

Subject 2: ______________________________

Topic Sentence (Point 2): ______________________________

____

____

Subject 1: ______________________________

Subject 2: ______________________________

____

Topic Sentence (Point 3): ______________________________

____

____

Subject 1: ______________________________

Subject 2: ______________________________

PEER CONVERSATION

Definition

Definition can be especially important in academic writing, where differences of opinion often rest on different understandings of what something is, where it came from, and how it has changed over time.

The definition essay provides the writer with room to be specific and examine important consequences of a particular definition. Here is a definition essay.

ASSIGNMENT Write an essay in which you explore James Gleick's assertion that stress is an "ill-defined term."

The student leads off with a short quote from a reading in class.

THESIS STATEMENT

TOPIC SENTENCE

SUPPORTING DETAILS
The student tells a story to develop the main idea of this paragraph. He uses transitions related to time.

Family Stress

James Gleick notes in his essay that stress is an "ill defined term." Maybe that is the case because there are many types of stress in our lives. We stress about work, about education, and about political issues that concern us. Perhaps even more than these, we stress about family. What is family stress and where does it come from?

In the immediate family—husband, wife, and children—stress begins with the energy and time required to provide for and support a family. **As soon as** your first child is born and you hold it in your arms, you begin a stressful journey. You are the life support system for this helpless child. **Our first day** home with our first child, we kept her fed, dry, and content. **As the evening progressed,** so did our baby's unhappiness. This escalated into an unceasing crying spell. My wife racked her brain while I pored over our Dr. Spock book looking for causes and solutions to this situation, which was making us both feel helpless and stressed. We had been told at the hospital that our child did not receive a nightly feeding. Through trial and error, we finally realized our daughter was hungry.

TOPIC SENTENCE
To define stress, this student focuses on its sources.

SUPPORTING DETAILS
The student uses both description and illustrations to develop the ideas in this paragraph.

Family stress comes also from worry about the physical and emotional health of your family. As children grow and the number of children increases, you worry about their health, safety, and emotional state. They grow older, they spread their wings, they begin to push, bend, and break all the rules you have put in place to keep them safe and on the right track. Our oldest two children, twenty and seventeen, have both taken up smoking cigarettes. The oldest drinks as if she's twenty-one and the seventeen-year-old has imbibed more times than he should have. The youngest, at thirteen, is constantly on the computer chatting with her friends. She's interested in boys already. A fear of ours is the potential online "admirer" she may encounter. Family stress grows with the family.

TOPIC SENTENCE
The student introduces yet another source of stress.

SUPPORTING DETAILS
The student provides an illustration of stress related to extended family.

Extended family can also be a source of stress: while you love, stick up for, and grow on each other, you also get on each other's nerves. It is just a matter of time before you get caught up in a stressful situation. Holidays provide added stress on the family front. Perhaps it is the coming together of family members who have conflicting personalities or the chaotic activity of hosting the whole family for a meal while surrounded by overactive children. If these holiday gatherings are not equally hosted by all the family members, you have yet another stressful point of contention. In my family the celebration of major holidays has fallen upon three out of six siblings since the passing of our parents. This has caused resentment, primarily between the wives of the siblings who have the gatherings and the spouses of those who will not. Arguing about who hosts the gathering adds to the stress of the holiday season.

To further illustrate, he again refers to his own family as an example.

Stress can affect us physiologically, according to Gleick, sometimes in the form of heart ailments. Ironically, family can be both a source and a solution to stress. By being open, honest, and loving with those in our families we find troublesome, we can resolve stressful differences or misunderstandings. Knowing our limitations in providing for the needs of those dependent upon us, we can minimize daily stress. We can also help alleviate family stress by realizing our contribution to it. Love is the best antidote for family stress. By loving our family members, we can try to understand and overlook differences that cause family stress throughout the years.

In his conclusion, the student refers again to the reading from class.

He ends with an ironic solution to the problem of stress.

DISCUSSION QUESTIONS

PEER CONVERSATION

1. What organization pattern does the writer use in paragraph two for defining family stress?
2. What impact does the writer's use of personal details have in the essay?
3. Where and why does the writer refer to James Gleick?

EXERCISE 14-15 Writing a Definition Essay

Directions: *Choose one of the following assignments for a definition essay. On a separate sheet of paper, use the form of prewriting you like best to explore two possible topics related to the assignment. Next, narrow down one of the topics and develop a thesis and subtopics. Use Exercise 14-16 to formulate your thesis and topic sentences and plan your essay. Then write your essay.*

Imitation Assignment

1. Write a definition essay using the model as your guide. Define a form of stress you deal with in your life. When and where does it occur? What are its causes?

Focused Assignments

1. Young parents with children often disagree on how to discipline their children. What is good discipline? What does it consist of? When does discipline become abuse?
2. Some people have charisma. We see them both in the media and in our daily lives. What is charisma? Where does it come from? What are its consequences? Is everyone charismatic in the same way?
3. People demonstrate strength in different ways. Discuss two or three different kinds of strength and what their effects are.

General Assignments

1. Write a definition essay on planning a budget.
2. Define friendship, using specific details.
3. Write an essay defining imagination.
4. Define motivation and give examples and details explaining it.

Definition Refresher

Definition writing enables you to clarify your terms. Often a definition begins with the writer placing the subject in a category, followed by examples to explain the definition further. For a reminder on the elements of definition writing, see these sections of Chapter 11: "Elements of Definition" (page 226), "Get Started" (page 227), "Examples and Details" (page 228), and "Negatives" (page 230).

EXERCISE 14-16 **Outlining Your Essay**

Directions: *When you complete your prewriting, copy the outline on page 307 and use it to plan your definition essay.*

Argument

In the argument paragraph you wrote, you supported your viewpoint with reasons. In argument essays, you explore multiple viewpoints, examining their reasons and how they fit the facts. Here is an argument essay.

ASSIGNMENT Discuss a viewpoint that you find inaccurate. Identify where the view is in error and argue for a more accurate way of seeing your subject.

Would You Like Fries with That?

The student begins with a captivating story.

A gentleman came to the drive-through on my shift and ordered seventeen cheeseburgers. After he paid I told him we would bring his order out to him, then politely asked him to pull into a parking space. "Why do I have to wait?" he said. I responded, "Sir, this is fast food, not instant food." When people think of fast-food jobs, they think "easy work." In fact, it is quite the opposite. Managers constantly harassing employees, customers complaining about service being slow—this is just part of the joy of Burger King. Fast food may be mindless and repetitive, but easy it is not.

THESIS STATEMENT

TOPIC SENTENCE
The student begins by stating a common view of fast-food work.

I hear it said that the hours in fast-food work are great. This is not true. Burger King opens its doors at 6 a.m. Eight people on **weekdays** and four people on **weekends,** including me, come in at **5 a.m.** to stock the store and prep food. **From 7 a.m. till 2 in the afternoon** there is a constant stream of hungry people. **Between noon and 2 p.m.** the mid-shifters come in and usually work till 7 or 8 p.m. **The closing shift** graces us with their presence at about the same time the mid-shifters are leaving. Things get cleaned and stocked when the store closes between 1 and 3 a.m. On any of these shifts, if someone shows up late, or not at all, the entire system is thrown off, and there is utter chaos. Whatever job position the missing person was supposed to have must be covered by another. Doing the work of two or three people is obscenely difficult!

ORDER AND TRANSITIONS
She uses time to organize the details of this paragraph, going through the daily schedule and explaining what work gets done on each shift.

Some say it is an easy job. That depends on your definition of easy. The endless repetition of easy jobs is awful. My duties consist of drive-through cash, expediting (the handing out of food), counter cash, kitchen worker, or "whipping boy," which is doing all the nasty jobs no one else will. Whipping boy duties include cleaning under the grease vats where congealed grease collects, scrubbing the freezer and "walk-in" fridge, putting away truck shipments, and doing other odd jobs. I started out on cash, and I trained myself on other jobs, so I would not be stuck doing the same thing every day. I love working in the kitchen the best. There is nothing like jumping around a kitchen, making at least five different sandwiches at once, and still getting the food out on time. The adrenaline starts rushing, and I feel like I can do anything. It really is a wonderful feeling.

TOPIC SENTENCE

SUPPORTING DETAILS
She cites and briefly discusses a number of jobs to be done in fast food.

Her descriptive detail here, even though positive in tone, reinforces the impression that fast-food work is demanding.

People think fast-food work is relatively clean. Think again. The big problem at Burger King is grease. There is a pan in the top part of the broiler that holds the grease that evaporates off the burgers and turns back into liquid. This pan must be emptied every other day. I have yet to see anyone get it out without spilling it all over themselves. I find it quite entertaining to watch, but only because I have never had to do it. The grease vats are a real treat. They each hold a fifty-pound block of solid shortening that reaches temperatures of 160 degrees when heated. With every basket of fries, chicken, fish, or "o-rings," the vat gets dirtier. The vats are drained through a tube every few days, and new shortening is put in. Grease spills, leaks, and takes a solid form after a few hours. It looks like a mixture of mashed potatoes and butterscotch pudding. To clean the vats, I use paper towels, degreaser, and a Brillo pad. It takes about one to two hours to do, and I look like I have not showered in weeks when I am done.

TOPIC SENTENCE
She identifies yet another misperception about fast-food work.

SUPPORTING DETAILS
These description details show the other point of view: that fast-food work is not clean, that in fact it can be very dirty work.

Not all customers think we have it made. Some show a little appreciation, which makes the job tolerable. There is an elderly man who comes in singing every morning. He says, "G'morning, beautiful!" every time. I look forward to his visit. The next time you visit your local fast-food joint, a smile and hello would make us grill jockeys feel appreciated.

In her conclusion, the student restates the thesis of the essay: that fast-food workers do not have it made. She also provides an example that contrasts with the one in the introduction.

DISCUSSION QUESTIONS

1. In arguments, writers take issue with viewpoints that are different from theirs. What views does the writer take issue with in this essay?
2. What pattern of organization does the writer use in the body of the paper?
3. Does the writer concede any points in her essay?
4. The essay provides a vivid picture of work in fast food. What detail did you find surprising or effective?

EXERCISE 14-17 Writing an Argument Essay

Directions: *Choose one of the following assignments for an argument essay. On a separate sheet of paper, use the form of prewriting you like best to explore two possible topics related to the assignment. Next, narrow down one of the topics and develop a thesis and subtopics. Use Exercise 14-18 to formulate your thesis and topic sentences and plan your essay. Then write your essay.*

Imitation Assignment

1. Write an argument essay using the model as your guide. Focus on common misperceptions of a group of people, presenting evidence to show why these views are inaccurate.

Focused Assignments

1. Parents often counsel their children not to take time off between high school and college. State your position on this issue. Then discuss the pros and cons of waiting a year or more before starting college after high school.
2. More and more these days, young people live together before getting married. What is your view on this issue? Discuss reasons for and against the practice.
3. In many places in the United States, gay marriage has been a hotly contested issue. What are some reasons to favor gay marriage? What are some reasons to oppose it? In your opinion, what is the best course of action?

General Assignments

1. Present an argument for (or against) restricting immigration into the United States.
2. Argue for (or against) social promotion—passing students when they have not been successful in a course.
3. Present an argument for (or against) requiring national service for all young people after high school.
4. Argue for (or against) providing sex education classes in school.

Argument Refresher

In argument writing, you make a claim that you believe is true, then offer reasons and evidence to support your claim. Argument may also involve a concession: You take another viewpoint into account. For a reminder on the elements of argument writing, see these sections of Chapter 12: "Elements of Argument" (page 246), "Get Started" (page 247), "Review Evidence" (page 248), and "Acknowledge Another Viewpoint" (page 249).

EXERCISE 14-18 Outlining Your Essay

Directions: *When you complete your prewriting, copy the outline on page 307 and use it to plan your argument essay.*

ESSAYS WITH MULTIPLE PATTERNS OF ORGANIZATION

Like paragraphs, essays often have a singular purpose: to explain a process, to classify information, or to compare and contrast ideas. Unlike paragraphs, however, which generally use one pattern of organization, such as description or argument, essays may require more than one pattern of organization. In an essay you write for a psychology class, for example, you might both define and illustrate the defense mechanisms you learned about. In a lab report, you might explain the process involved in an experiment, then consider a cause and effect analysis of the results.

In the workplace, a writer might need to use multiple patterns of organization. Writing up a report on a domestic abuse call, a police officer uses narration to tell exactly what happened at the scene, but the narration will also include important description details such as the bruises on the victim's face and neck.

THE MIXED-PATTERN ESSAY AT A GLANCE

ASSIGNMENT Write an essay about the experience of growing older in U.S. culture.

Youth Rules the World

Our society is obsessed with youth, and I am no exception. I recently started wearing makeup for the first time in my thirty-two years. I never thought I needed it until I saw the old lady in my mirror. "Who is that?"

The essay's title tells the reader what the essay is about.

The writer uses a short personal narration to draw the reader in and make the essay interesting.

THESIS STATEMENT
The sentence clearly identifies the thesis.

TOPIC SENTENCE
The writer defines advertising as the focus in the first paragraph.

TRANSISTIONS
The writer transitions between one example and the next.

TOPIC SENTENCE
The writer's topic sentence indicates this will be a paragraph of classification

TRANSITION
The writer moves from one type to the next.

The writer cites and discusses two different approaches to looking young.

EXAMPLES
The writer cites different examples to support the main idea of the paragraph.

TOPIC SENTENCE

The writer uses an extended example to illustrate the importance of looking youthful in the workplace.

I thought. I am far too young to have permanent lines between my eyebrows. Although I am not self-conscious enough for surgical correction, I did immediately go makeup shopping. Age matters in advertising and in the workplace, leading people to sometimes desperate measures to look young. This is something Natalie Angier addresses in her essay "The Cute Factor." According to Angier, humans are drawn to anything representing youth. Simply put, youth rules our world.

Advertising is saturated with images of youth. Look at the billboards on your way home from work or school. You will not see many older people up there trying to get you to go to a certain casino. Television commercials are **also** full of young people. **For example,** there is the new Band-Aid commercial. It features two children who are the very definition of the word *cute.* Even the little girl's voice is cute. They sing the Band-Aid jingle, and I want to go buy some, even though I already have bandages in my medicine cabinet. Advertisers understand our obsession with youth, and they use it to draw us in.

Measures to keep us young come in two types. Women use creams and makeup to keep themselves looking young. Men and women color their hair when it starts to show signs of age. Women even wear push-up bras as a way to deny what time and gravity have taken. **These are superficial and harmless measures enabling people to hold onto their youth. There are more extreme measures.** Men get hair implants when their hairline starts to recede. Plastic surgery prevents the aging process. A facelift smoothes the skin of a woman's face and neck to recapture youth. Eyelid procedures counteract the sagging that comes with age. Doctors can get rid of age spots and spider veins, as well as lift breasts and buttocks when gravity starts to take its toll. This type of age-defying plastic surgery is a multimillion-dollar industry.

When competing in the workplace, age is a definite factor. For customer service jobs, the employer's preference is young beautiful people. Sales are better and business is increased when there are young, attractive people at the counter. I used to work at a chain pet store. The managers there made it clear that they only wanted pretty young girls at the checkout. They thought it made a bad impression to have older or average-looking people working at the registers. It is not that they refused to hire older people. They simply would not put them on the registers. It is not an uncommon practice.

Youth sells. Since we all crave youth, we all respond better to young people or at least to the appearance of youth. We see it in advertising, in customer service, and in all the products and services sold to keep us young. Angier touches on the causes in her essay. She believes that we are biologically programmed to respond to youth, babies, mainly, but this response has expanded to include youth in general. We cannot help ourselves. We love youth. We want to stay young.

The writer restates the important points of the essay and touches on the reading mentioned in the introduction.

Works Cited

Angier, Natalie. "The Cute Factor." *New York Times* 3 Jan., 2006: F1. Print.

DISCUSSION QUESTIONS

PEER CONVERSATION

1. Does it matter that the thesis of this essay is not the last sentence of the introduction?
2. What patterns of organization does this writer use?
3. The writer mentions two types of measures people use to stay young. Can you think of a third?
4. Which supporting detail in the essay do you find the most effective? Why?
5. What specific details in the conclusion tell you the writer is finishing her essay?

EXERCISE 14-19 **Writing a Mixed-Pattern Essay**

Directions: *Choose one of the following assignments for a mixed pattern essay. Use Exercise 14-20 to help you determine your approach.*

Imitation Assignment

1. Write an argument essay using the model as your guide. Focus on views of older people and the aging process. Provide evidence to show why these views are accurate and/or inaccurate.

Focused Assignments

1. Pick a stereotype that is common in our society. Describe the stereotype as people commonly think of it, focusing on appearance, actions, and attitudes.
2. In a culture of celebrity, such as our own, we see and hear from famous people all the time. Some celebrities use fame for good causes. Cite and discuss a few examples.
3. We often celebrate our triumphs and our skills, dwelling on the positive. Write an essay about something you are not very good at and wish you were. Tell a story about a specific time you realized your lack of this skill, and consider what difference it makes in your life that you are not good at it.

4. Complex skills call for smart learning processes. Discuss a complex skill you have, such as playing a musical instrument or speaking a foreign language. Describe the most effective process for acquiring such a skill.
5. Not everyone agrees on the proper approach to studying. Talk about two different approaches and what their merits are.

General Assignments

1. Discuss the pros and cons of school uniforms.
2. Describe the importance of self-discipline.
3. Describe a prejudice that is overlooked in U.S. society.

EXERCISE 14-20 Determining Your Approach

Directions: *Before you prewrite on your topic, respond to the questions below that will help you discover various approaches to thinking and writing about your topic.*

1. What people, places, things, or ideas can you describe that are important to your topic? Why? What is your dominant impression?

____

____

2. What important idea can you illustrate and explain with examples? Why is this idea important?

____

____

3. Can you tell a story that relates to your topic in an important way?

____

____

4. Is there a process that is relevant to this topic? What is it? Why is it important?

____

____

5. Does classification thinking help you make a point about your topic? How so? What categories or types come to mind? Why are they important?

____

____

6. Is it useful to think about causes in connection to your topic? What about effects? What will this kind of thinking enable you to explain?

____

____

7. Can you use comparison and contrast to explore your topic? Are similarities and differences important in your topic? with respect to what points in particular?

____

____

8. What issue or idea is important in this topic? Can you define the idea or issue for your reader?

____

____

9. Suppose you decide to change your reader's mind about your topic. What reasons would you need to explain to prove your point or points?

____

____

EXERCISE 14-21 **Outlining Your Essay**

Directions: *When you complete your prewriting, copy the outline on page 307 and use it to plan your mixed-pattern essay.*

Final Review

Once you have drafted, revised, and edited your essay, and put an appropriate title on it, use this checklist to determine if it is ready for an academic reader.

ESSAY CHECKLIST

_____ My essay has an introduction, body, and conclusion.

_____ My essay has an appropriate and interesting title.

_____ My introduction invites the reader into the essay.

_____ My thesis is focused.

_____ My body paragraphs have focused topic sentences.

_____ My paragraphs have specific supporting details.

_____ I repeat key words and use transition words and sentences.

_____ My conclusion brings the essay to a close.

_____ I have proofread my paper for spelling, capitalization, common errors, and sentence variety.

STAYING ON COURSE WITH QUOTATION, SUMMARY, AND PARAPHRASE

Summary: A Key to Understanding

Summarizing is a valuable skill, in and out of the classroom. The plot summary of a movie, say, or the summary of an interesting magazine article you read—these could come in handy in a casual conversation. If you encounter something you know you will want to explain later, in writing or in person, you can enhance your memory by consciously identifying and reviewing main ideas, key details, and impressions. This works for anything from a news item to a long, involved novel.

DISCUSSION

Turn and talk to a classmate about a movie you saw recently and liked or disliked very much. Who were the main characters? What happened? Where did the action take place? Why did you respond positively or negatively to the movie?

Avoid Plagiarism: Quote, Quote, Quote!

The process of finding and correctly documenting quotations and other information is necessary to avoid plagiarism. Plagiarism, which has serious ethical and legal repercussions, means taking credit for someone else's work. Using someone else's exact language without giving that person credit is considered plagiarism, but so is paraphrasing—putting their thoughts in your own words—if it is not properly attributed. When you document your sources with internal citations and put together a "Works Cited" page, you give credit where credit is due and inform your reader that specific material in your paper belongs to specific sources.

BRAINSTORM

Make a list of instances when you did not get proper credit for something you said or did. Then focus on one. List all the people and places connected to the event. What circumstances or conditions were involved? What other people were involved? What happened? What were the consequences?

In Other Words: The Art of Paraphrasing

At some jobs, you will be given instructions that, at first, you may not entirely understand. In these situations, it is sometimes helpful to ask a question by paraphrasing or summarizing what your supervisor has just said. For example, instead of asking for a re-explanation, you might say, "So I need to make two photocopies of the file: one to keep in the office, and one to send out to the client. Is that right?" By paraphrasing instructions, you will be able to quickly pinpoint whether you have correctly understood your assignment.

BRAINSTORM

The ability to paraphrase—or say back using your own words—what others tell you depends on your ability to listen well. Brainstorm a few situations in which you need to listen carefully. What are they? With whom do you interact? What are the consequences of listening well or poorly?

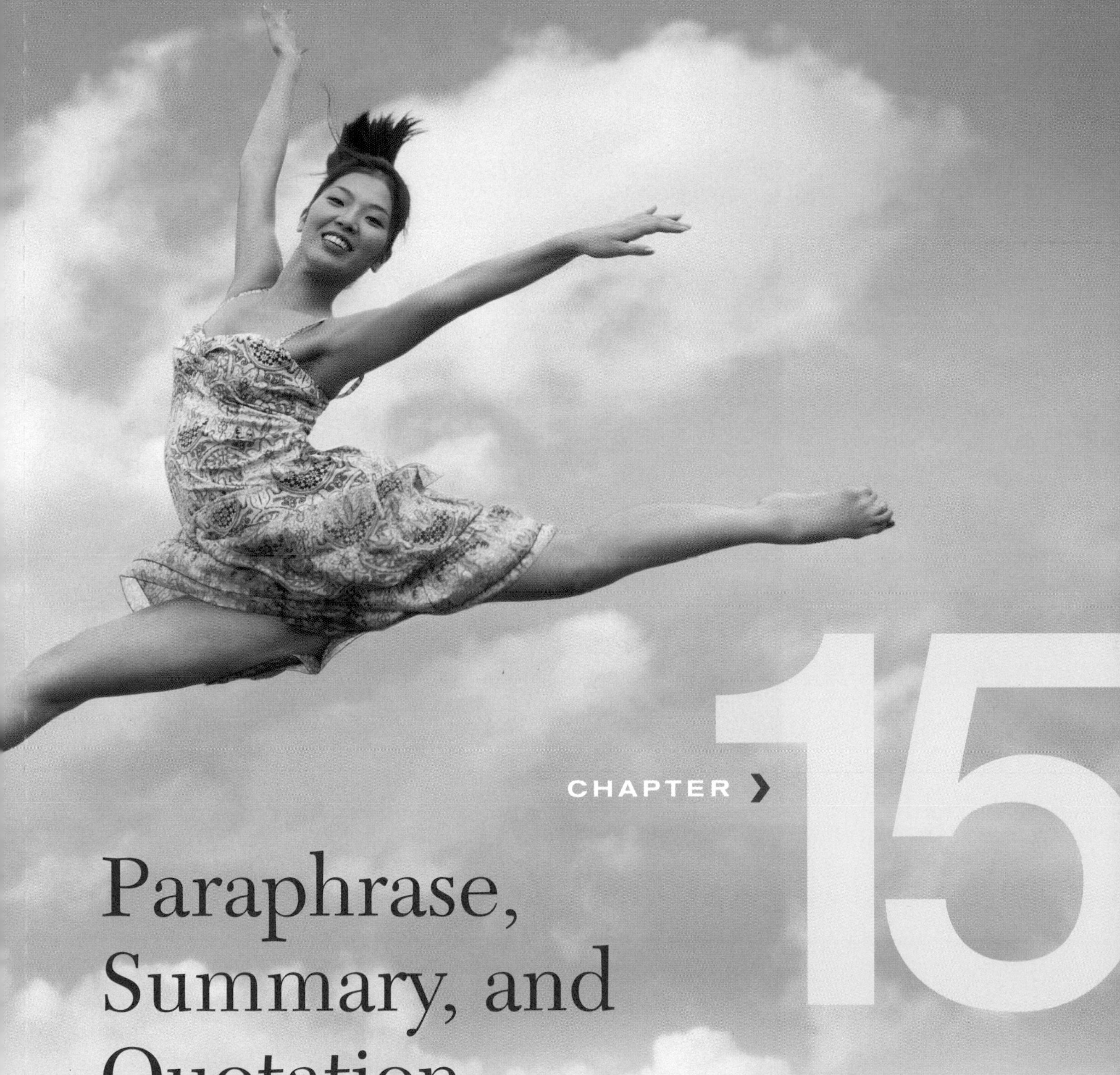

CHAPTER ❯ 15

Paraphrase, Summary, and Quotation

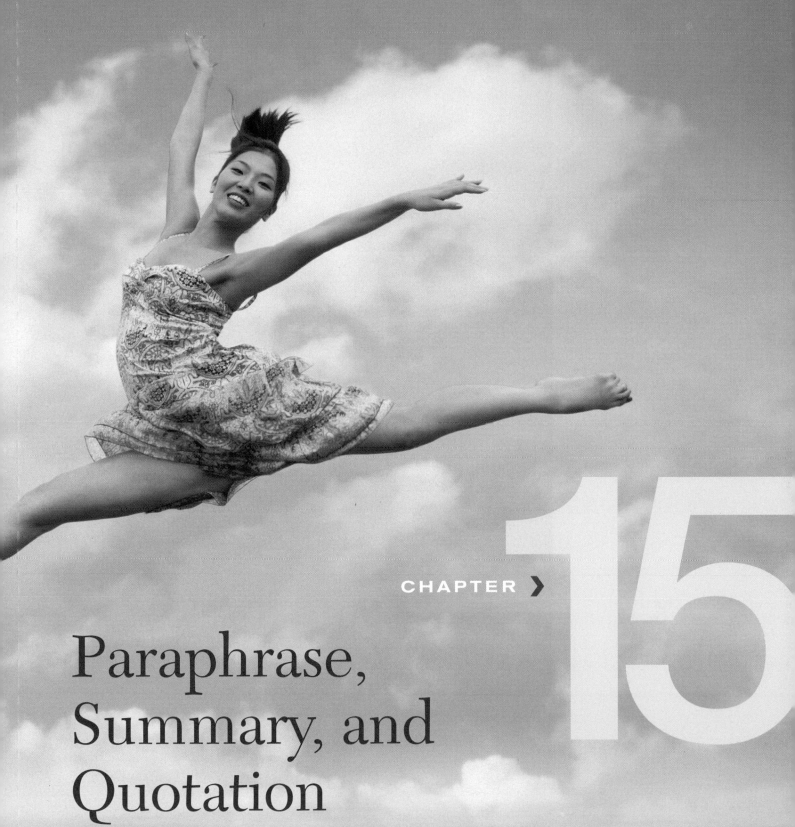

CHAPTER OVERVIEW

- Use Sources Correctly
- Paraphrase
- Plagiarism
- Summary
- Quotation
- Suggestions for Daily Practice

THINK FIRST

Think about the last documentary or newscast you saw. Write a paragraph summarizing what it was about. Who was in it? Where did it take place? What was happening? Why was it important?

Use Sources Correctly

How do I write about what I've read without just repeating what the author says? As a college student, you will often be asked to write about what you read. In doing so, you demonstrate comprehension, recall, and critical thinking. You form connections between what you already know and new information; in the process, you acquire new knowledge.

Two basic forms of writing about what you have read are paraphrase and summary. In paraphrase and summary, you state what you have read using your own words, capturing the most important points and providing the reader with an overview of the passage, article, or textbook chapter. Occasionally you will include a quotation that captures a writer's idea or point of view. Whenever you use paraphrase or summary or quote an author, you must also cite your source in order to avoid plagiarism (see the section on plagiarism on pages 343–346).

Paraphrase

College work involves reading a variety of materials—such as textbooks, articles in coursepacks, and news stories—when you do research. Highlighting identifies important ideas and details. Taking notes and outlining help capture content and the relationship of ideas and details.

Paraphrase goes a step further. When you **paraphrase,** you condense and restate an author's ideas using your own words. Paraphrasing is the most basic skill used in summary. For this reason it deserves continuous practice. Follow these guidelines to write an accurate paraphrase.

Guidelines for Paraphrasing Accurately

1. Read the original passage. Look for the main ideas and key supporting details.
2. Write a sentence that sums up the main idea of the passage.
3. Set aside the text and restate what the author said using your own words. Use synonyms (words that are similar in meaning) to replace words used by the author, break long sentences into shorter ones, and reword sentences so that you are expressing the author's ideas in your own words.
4. Include the author's name and/or the title of the source at the beginning of your paraphrase.
5. Read your paraphrase and compare it to the original.
6. Underline any of the author's words that you have used.
7. Revise your paraphrase to eliminate the author's exact words. Replace them with your own or put quotation marks around the author's words.

When you paraphrase, a short sentence is almost always better than a long one. Also, a good paraphrase reports what an author says; it does not express your opinions on those ideas. Finally, remember that if you use the author's words without quotation marks, you are committing plagiarism, a serious act of academic dishonesty (see section on plagiarism).

The following original sentences come from Richard Sennett's *The Corrosion of Character.*

Original

The bakery was filled with noise; the smell of yeast mingled with human sweat in the hot rooms; the bakers' hands were constantly plunged into flour and water.

Paraphrase

This paraphrase is short and to the point. The writer captures the main idea of Sennett's description.

Sennett reports that it was noisy, hot, and smelly in the bakery, and the work was constant.

Original

The bakers needed to cooperate intimately in order to coordinate the varied tasks of the bakery.

Paraphrase

In her phrase "working together," the writer captures Sennett's idea.

Working together was important.

Original

The bakery no longer smells of sweat and is startlingly cool, whereas workers used to throw up from the heat. Under the soothing fluorescent lights, all is now strangely silent.

Paraphrase

The writer's sentence both sums up Sennett's description and eliminates detail.

The bakery is now a cool, quiet place to work.

In these paraphrases, the student captures the essence of Sennett's ideas. She restates the ideas in her own words and eliminates the very specific details. Notice, too, that the student merely reports on what Sennett wrote. She does not express an opinion or make a judgment about it.

EXERCISE 15-1 Recognizing Effective Paraphrase

Directions: *Following are some sentences from Mary Sherry's essay "In Praise of the F Word." For each sentence, select the paraphrase that most effectively states the main idea of the original sentence.*

__a__ 1. Tens of thousands of eighteen-year-olds will graduate this year and be handed meaningless diplomas.

a. Lots of high school students graduate without full degrees.

b. Many high school graduates will receive meaningless diplomas this year.

c. Tens of thousands of high school graduates will be handed meaningless diplomas this year.

_a_ 2. These diplomas won't look any different from those awarded their luckier classmates.

a. Their diplomas will look like everyone else's diplomas.

b. These kids ought to be really angry.

c. These diplomas aren't worth the paper they are printed on.

_b_ 3. Their validity will be questioned only when their employers discover that these graduates are semiliterate.

a. These kids won't know how to do anything on the job.

b. The meaning of their diplomas won't be questioned until they go to work.

c. These students won't know their diplomas are worthless until they get a job.

_b_ 4. Eventually a fortunate few will find their way into educational-repair shops—adult-literacy programs, such as the one where I teach basic grammar and writing.

a. Educational-repair shops, such as adult-literacy programs, will eventually save a fortunate few.

b. Some of these graduates will eventually go back to school.

c. Naturally these unfortunate individuals will lose their jobs and go back for more education.

Talk about It

Name two things a writer can do to improve the accuracy and quality of a paraphrase.

_b_ 5. There, high school graduates and high school dropouts pursuing graduate equivalency certificates will learn the skills they should have learned in school.

a. They will have to hit the books again, in hopes of eventually making some big bucks.

b. They will pick up basic skills in these programs.

c. Here, high school graduates and high school dropouts pursuing graduate equivalency certificates will make up for lost time.

Acknowledge Sources

Because paraphrase involves writing about what you have read, it is important to acknowledge your sources. In a phrase or sentence before the paraphrase, you should mention the name of the author, the organization he or she is associated with, or the name of the publication from which the information is taken.

> In his description of bakery work in his book *Corrosion of Character,* Richard Sennett points out that at one time it was noisy, hot, and smelly in the bakery, and the work was constant. Working together was important. Twenty-five years later, the bakery is a cool, quiet place to work.

Mary Sherry's essay "In Praise of the F Word" makes a case for failing students instead of passing them along.

It is a good idea to acknowledge your source as soon as you begin to paraphrase. Remember to use the author's full name in your first reference. After the first reference, use the author's last name only. If you do not know the author's name, it is acceptable to mention the name of the publication in which the information appeared.

EXERCISE 15-2 Paraphrasing Practice

Directions: *Paraphrase the ideas in each of the following original sentences. The name of the source is provided in each case. Begin your paraphrase by acknowledging the source. Make sure your paraphrase sentences are short, simple, and to the point. Avoid using more than three consecutive words from the original sentence.*

EXAMPLE

We may have come a long way baby, but the latest Voices of Women opinion poll suggests we still have a long way to go. (United Press International)

Paraphrase: A story published in United Press International suggests women have made a lot of progress, but more work lies ahead.

1. The survey found men are beginning to share the same attitudes toward work as women—with like percentages seeking flexible work hours and the ability to work from home. (United Press International)

Paraphrase: According to United Press International, more men want what women want from work.

2. Leaders of the nation's largest drug prevention program, Drug Abuse Resistance Education, announced on Thursday that they were changing DARE's approach, admitting that the vastly expensive program appears to be ineffective. (Dawn MacKeen, writing for *Salon*)

Paraphrase: Writing for *Salon,* Dawn MacKeen reports that DARE does not work.

3. Joan McCord, cochair of the National Academy of Sciences panel that issued a stinging report on DARE this week, is one of the people who is concerned about the program hurting the children who participate.

Paraphrase: DARE leaders fear the program may do more harm than good.

4. Checking players' weight after practice and the following day to monitor excessive weight loss, and taking mandatory rest breaks in the shade and water breaks during practice and at needed intervals, are essential to help prevent heatstroke. (Ira Berkow, sportswriter for the *New York Times*)

Paraphrase: *New York Times* sportswriter Ira Berkow reports that a number of measures can be taken to prevent heatstroke.

5. Few, if any, countries have adapted notions like automation and virtual reality so widely or embraced them so fully as Japan, where animated films, for example, are consistently the biggest hits. (Howard W. French)

Paraphrase: Howard W. French notes that the Japanese have been at the forefront of technological innovations such as virtual reality.

Plagiarism

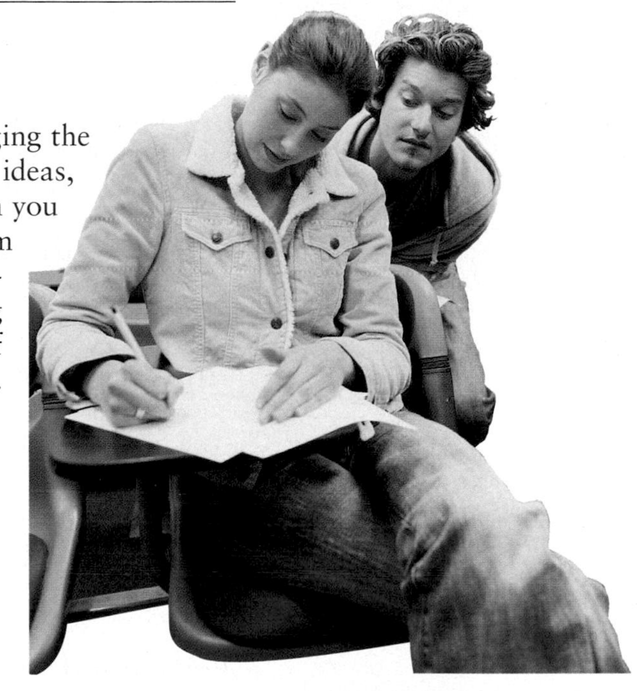

Borrowing another person's writing without acknowledging the source is called **plagiarism.** In some classes, you will use ideas, facts, and details from your reading—for example, when you write a research paper. You will acquire information from books, journals, magazines, newspapers, and the Internet. Some students succumb to the temptation of copying and pasting other people's writing into their papers as if it were their own. To do so is dishonest. It is plagiarism. Plagiarism occurs whenever you

- Use another writer's ideas without giving him or her credit.
- Cite facts or statistics without stating your source.
- Use a quotation by an authority without saying who it is.
- Paraphrase another person's words without acknowledging your source.

Copying another person's words in your writing may result in you receiving a failing grade for the assignment or possibly even the course. Plagiarism can be avoided by careful use of paraphrase, by use of quotation marks if you do borrow someone's writing word-for-word, and by acknowledging your source.

MULTILINGUAL TIP
In the US, written texts are considered the "intellectual property" of the author.

Copy and Paste

The most flagrant instance of plagiarism is simply copying and pasting another person's writing into your paper. Here is an example of this type of plagiarism. The original text is from a website published by the National Stepfamily Resource Center, which published an article called "Democratic Discipline for Stepteens," by Sharon Hanna.

Original

Authoritarian style, the preference of yesteryear, puts the parent/stepparent in total power as the "boss." As such, he or she is dictatorial, strict, and inflexible. The parent or stepparent/child relationship is characterized by fear, distance, coldness, and rigidity.

Plagiarism

This student copies word for word from what he read. Doing so says to the reader, "I wrote this." For stealing another person's words like this, the student could be failed for the assignment.

The dominant parent's word is the law and puts the parent/stepparent in total power as the "boss." As such, he or she is dictatorial, strict, and inflexible. The parent/child relationship is characterized by fear, distance, coldness, and rigidity. In my experience, this type of relationship began early and lasted a long time. It resulted in depressed and rebellious children with low self-esteem.

This student has copied several sentences from the original text into his paragraph without using quotation marks and without acknowledging his source. To avoid plagiarism in this case, the student should acknowledge his source. Then he should either paraphrase the passage or present it as a quotation. It is a good idea to practice all four techniques, shown below, in order to use information effectively and avoid plagiarism.

1. Include the Source in the Paraphrase, with an In-Text Citation

In addition to protecting yourself from the charge of plagiarism, citing an author's name (and the publication in which the piece appeared) indicates that you have done some research, enhancing your credibility.

The dominant stepparent's word is the law. According to Sharon Hanna, writing for the *National Stepfamily Resource Center,* this stepparent wants total control. There is little warmth or closeness in the relationship. It is about giving orders and obedience. In my experience, this type of relationship began early and lasted a long time. It resulted in depressed and rebellious children with low self-esteem.

2. Include the Source in the Paraphrase as a Parenthetical Citation

In the case of a print source, such as a book or journal article, the writer would also include the page number after Hanna in the parenthetical citation.

The dominant stepparent's word is the law. This stepparent wants total control. There is little warmth or closeness in the relationship. It is about giving orders and obedience (Hanna). In my experience, this type of relationship began early and lasted a long time. It resulted in depressed and rebellious children with low self-esteem.

3. Include the Source as a Quotation, with an In-Text Citation

The dominant parent's word is the law. This "authoritarian style," according to *Sharon Hanna,* writing for the *National Stepfamily Resource Center,* "puts the parent/stepparent in total power as the 'boss.' As such, he or she is dictatorial, strict, and inflexible. The parent or stepparent/child relationship is characterized by fear, distance, coldness, and rigidity." In my experience, this type of relationship began early and lasted a long time. It resulted in depressed and rebellious children with low self-esteem.

4. Include the Source as a Quotation, with a Parenthetical Citation

The dominant parent's word is the law. "This authoritarian style, the preference of yesteryear, puts the parent/stepparent in total power as the 'boss.' As such, he or she is dictatorial, strict, and inflexible. The parent or stepparent/child relationship is characterized by fear, distance, coldness, and rigidity" (Hanna). In my experience, this type of relationship began early and lasted a long time. It resulted in depressed and rebellious children with low self-esteem.

Close Paraphrase

In **close paraphrase** the writer changes a few words here and there, possibly rearranging the order of the original, without acknowledging his or her source. Here is an example of close paraphrase. The original text is from an article written by Abraham Thiombiano for the *Dixie Sun Online Edition*, a publication of Dixie State College of Utah.

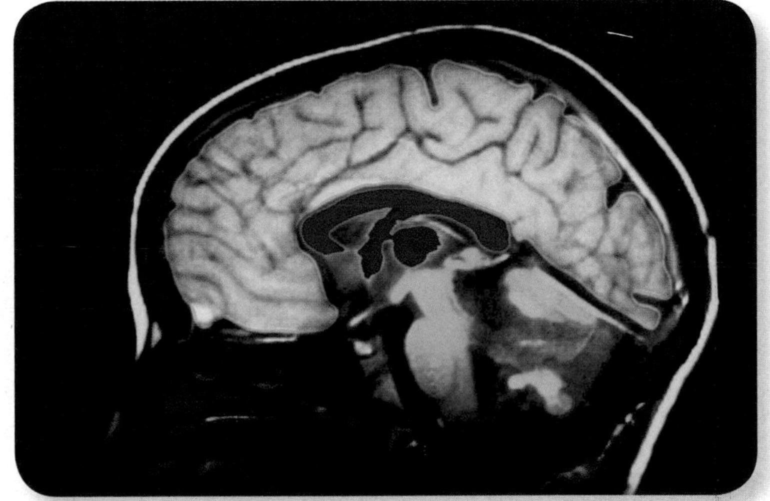

Original

Scientists have come to accept that a few fundamental differences between men and women are biological. It turns out that men's and women's brains, for example, are not only different, but the way we use them differs too. Women have larger connections and more frequent interaction between their brain's left and right hemispheres. This accounts for women's ability to have better verbal skills and intuition. Men, on the other hand, have greater brain hemisphere separation, which explains their skills for abstract reasoning and visual-spatial intelligence.

Plagiarism

In this student's close paraphrase, he makes small changes in phrasing and vocabulary, while retaining the exact order of the sentences in the passage.

Men and women do communicate in different ways. I can tell this from what I have experienced in life so far, and also from the research I have done. Scientists now believe that the basic differences between men

This use of source material would also be considered plagiarism and might result in failure of the assignment or the course.

> and women are a result of biology. They have concluded that men's and women's brains are not only different, but we use them differently too. In women's brains, the left and right hemispheres interact more due to larger connections. This fact explains why women have better verbal skills and intuition. In men's brains, the hemispheres are separated more, a fact that accounts for better ability to reason abstractly and use their visual-spatial intelligence.

This student's close paraphrase is considered to be plagiarism. He does not acknowledge his source. Moreover, he makes only minimal changes to the original text. To avoid plagiarism, this student should paraphrase more carefully or paraphrase and quote some of the original text. He should also acknowledge the source either with an in-text or parenthetical citation as shown below.

Paraphrase with In-Text Citation

"According to" is the most common and useful way to set up an in-text citation of a source.

> Men and women do communicate in different ways. I can tell this from what I have experienced in life so far. Recent brain research also explains why. According to Abraham Thiombiano, writing for the *Dixie Sun,* the brains of women and men are slightly different, particularly with respect to connections between hemispheres. These differences explain difference in form of intelligence: Women are more given to intuitive thought, men to abstract reasoning.

Paraphrase, Quotation, and Parenthetical Citation

Use a parenthetical citation if you do not cite the writer's name in your text.

> Men and women do communicate in different ways. I can tell this from what I have experienced in life so far. Recent brain research also explains: "Women have larger connections and more frequent interaction between their brain's left and right hemispheres. This accounts for women's ability to have better verbal skills and intuition. Men, on the other hand, have greater brain hemisphere separation, which explains their skills for abstract reasoning and visual-spatial intelligence" (Thiombiano).

Summary

A **summary** is a snapshot of what you have read. You summarize to capture the key details of a story, the main ideas of an article, or the important ideas from a textbook reading assignment.

The same basic rules apply in both paraphrase and summary: Acknowledge your source, use your own words, and keep it short. Generally a summary is significantly shorter than the material it summarizes. Here are some guidelines for writing an accurate summary.

Guidelines for Summarizing Accurately

1. Read the original text. Look for the main ideas and key supporting details.
2. Write a sentence that sums up the main point, or thesis, of the author's writing.
3. Use your own words to state the main points the author makes and include them in the same order in which the author presents them.
4. Include, using you own words, information about any important concepts, definitions, procedures, or rules the author discusses.
5. Include the author's name or the title of the source.
6. Read your summary and compare it to the original.
7. Underline any of the author's words you have used and revise your summary to eliminate them, or use quotation marks to indicate you are using the author's exact words.
8. Include the author's opinion, if it is clearly stated. Avoid stating your own opinion or making a judgment of the author in your summary.

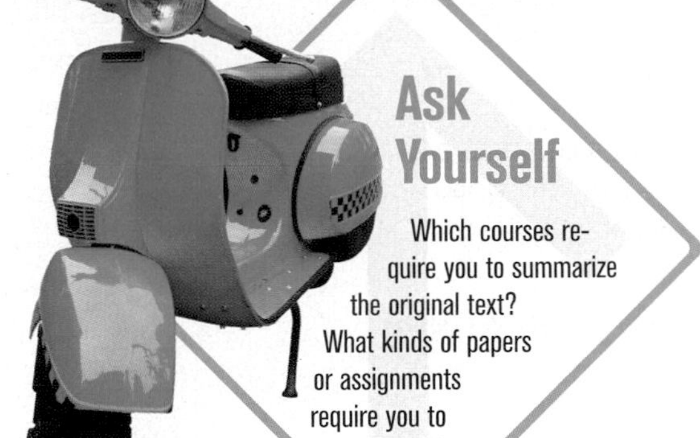

Ask Yourself

Which courses require you to summarize the original text? What kinds of papers or assignments require you to summarize?

Summary is an important skill if you are doing research on a subject. For example, if you are writing about the impact of molds on people with allergies, you might (1) read about people with allergies in a newspaper or magazine; (2) read about competing medical treatments in magazines or journals written for doctors and nurses; and (3) read about the science of mold and its relationship to the environment in your science textbook. In all three instances, summary would be an essential skill for capturing what you read and preparing it for use in your writing. Whether you are reading a newspaper, magazine journal, or a textbook, the same reading and writing skills apply.

Capture the Main Idea of a Story

Stories are central to many areas of academic education. In an investigation of technological innovation, a student might encounter the story of Thomas Edison inventing the light bulb. In an investigation of the American Civil War, a student might encounter stories that explain the course of events in Gettysburg. To summarize these stories, you identify the main idea and important details: what happened, where and when, who was involved, and why it happened. You avoid providing minute detail. Instead, you give an overview.

Summary of an Op-Ed Article

Here is an op-ed article about automobile safety. As suggested above, the main points and proper names have been underlined, and annotations that will serve as the basis of the summary have been made in the margin. A model summary follows.

from "Lives Changed in a Split Second" by CHARLES WHEELAN

WHO
Charles Wheelan and his wife drove an SUV. It was convenient.

WHAT
They drove an SUV. It was a status symbol.

WHAT HAPPENED
They got into a bad accident. The car flipped over.

WHEN AND WHERE

Until the early morning hours of January 3, my wife and I had many reasons to drive a sport utility vehicle. As our only car, it offered space for our two children, the dog, and the things we hauled around, like the Christmas tree. We like being in a big vehicle with a high vantage point in a city full of crazy drivers. Since we take public transportation to work and don't drive much, we could rationalize away the bad gas mileage and the high emissions. And to be honest, an S.U.V. projected a different image than a minivan or station wagon.

But our Ford Explorer felt a lot less practical as we lay smashed upside down in it on Interstate 80 at 4:00 a.m. last Wednesday. My wife was trapped in the passenger seat. Our two daughters hung from their car seats, screaming. The dog was silent. After skidding on a patch of ice, the truck flipped and slid across the median to within a foot of traffic going 65 m.p.h. in the other direction.

I learned a lot of things very quickly. Each of our girls screams in a slightly different way, and I now know that it is a good thing to hear both screams coming from inside a crushed vehicle—because it means that everyone is alive. I learned that I can unhook a child from a car seat upside down in the dark with hands so cold that they have lost nearly all sensation. I know that when there is no other way to get a six-month-old out of a crushed vehicle sitting dangerously close to traffic, you will drag her through broken glass. I learned that strangers will stop in the middle of the night and practice remarkable acts of kindness, including searching through the wreckage for a missing finger.

In the grand scheme of things, we're in great shape. My three-year-old daughter's hand was smashed, and she has lost her right thumb. I don't want to minimize the challenges she faces, but I often visualize the range of possible outcomes, and this one was very, very good.

WHAT
Rollovers are frequently fatal. This article is about what happened to Wheelan's family. It is also about SUVs and safety problems.

WHY
SUVs roll over because they are high and have a narrow wheel base.

He knew SUVs were dangerous and drove one anyway.

Seat belts saved Wheelan's family, not the big vehicle.

Rollovers make up a small fraction of all accidents but are responsible for a disproportionate number of deaths, particularly in S.U.V.'s. And this week the National Highway Traffic Safety Administration gave the Ford Explorer two stars out of a possible five—meaning a 30 to 40 percent chance of flipping in an accident, compared to a less than 10 percent chance for a vehicle with a five-star rating.

Even without the new data, I should have known better. I have followed the Ford Explorer story and have even written about it. True, our truck did not have Firestone tires. Our family was riding on the "good tires"; Ford even sent us a letter to tell us that. But I should have recognized that the tire issue masked the more fundamental problem: S.U.V.'s as a class are more likely to roll over than other vehicles. Indeed, the problem is inherent in vehicles that ride high on a relatively narrow wheel base, which is the most attractive feature of S.U.V.'s.

I do not believe that my family is alive because we were in a big truck. We are alive because of seat belts and car seats. (I will never fully understand how the dog made it, but he did.) I believe that a car with a lower center of gravity would not have been so likely to skid on an icy road, nor would it have flipped so easily when we hit deep snow on the median. Can that be proved in this case? Maybe.

Ford has redesigned the 2002 Explorer to make it less likely to flip and has been eager to settle rollover suits with people involved in far worse accidents than ours in earlier models, including one settled this week involving a Texas woman who was left a quadriplegic. I now know how quickly a rollover can happen. I never should have put my family in that truck or any other like it.

Summary

The article "Lives Changed in a Split Second" describes the dangers of driving an SUV. Charles Wheelan and his wife drove a Ford Explorer because it was practical. Then came a terrible accident. On a Wednesday morning, around 4:00 a.m., the car skidded on ice and rolled over, trapping Wheelan, his wife, and children in the car. In the end, no one was killed or horribly injured, although his daughter lost a finger. The incident reminded Wheelan that SUVs are not safe, something he already knew but chose to ignore. He believes seat belts and car seats saved his family from harm and regrets ever putting his family at risk by driving an SUV.

Capture the Key Details of a Story

Summary is effective both for what it includes and what it leaves out. The summary of "Lives Changed in a Split Second" does not include details about the injury to Wheelan's daughter or the kindness of strangers. These details are interesting but not basic factual information on the story and situation. When you summarize a story, stick to the basic facts: what happened, where, when, why, and who was involved, and the outcome.

EXERCISE 15-3 Capturing the Main Idea and Key Details of a News Story

Directions: *Read the following news story. Underline the main ideas of the story and the key details that support them. Make notes in the margin to provide a basis for your summary. In the space provided, write a short summary of the story.*

from "A Deadly Toll Is Haunting Football" by IRA BERKOW

More than 1000 mourners were expected to file into the Cathedral of St. John the Evangelist on St. John Street in Lafayette, La., this morning to pay final tribute to Eraste Thomas Autin, 18, a local high school football hero who died Wednesday.

It was six days after he had collapsed in 102 degree heat following a voluntary freshman workout at the University of Florida—voluntary, that is, under the NCAA rules, for official workouts are not supposed to begin for another two weeks. He had been in a coma since July 19.

Autin, heavily recruited out of St. Thomas More High School, had accepted a football scholarship to Florida. He planned to major in pre-med and follow in the footsteps of his father, Dr. David Autin. Eraste Autin had been a good student in high school, but he was also a talented athlete. At 6-foot-2, 250 pounds, he played fullback and, it was said, had a shot at starting at that position for the Gators.

Autin's was the second college football related death in the state in the last five months. In February, DeVaughn Darling, a Florida State linebacker, also collapsed and died after a so-called voluntary workout during the off-season. He was, like Autin, 18 years old and a freshman.

The coroner's report on Autin stated that he died from complications of heatstroke. An autopsy on Darling, who died after arduous indoor agility drills, found no definitive cause, although the autopsy also reported that a rare sickle-cell trait may have played a role.

Nonetheless, Autin is the 18th high school or college player since 1995 to die from heatstroke, Dr. Fred

Mueller of the University of North Carolina sports medicine department tracks these statistics.

"It shouldn't be," he said, regarding the number of football deaths by heatstroke. "There has to be more done to prevent these tragedies, and there can be. I think most are preventable."

Mueller said that such deaths reached a high of eight in one year, in 1970, and then began to decrease.

"For a number of years, there were no deaths at all," he said, "but in the last seven years they've begun to creep back up again."

Checking players' weight after practice and the following day to monitor excessive weight loss, and taking mandatory rest breaks in the shade and water breaks during practice and at needed intervals, he said, are essential to help prevent heatstroke. "Many kids don't want to do this," he said, "so someone has got to be watching."

Mueller also wondered what voluntary really meant.

"I teach a class with football players," he said, "and there's a concern about voluntary practice: if you don't show up, it hardly helps your chances of making the football team, or playing more."

Jeremy Foley, the Florida athletic director, seemed to agree.

"It's a two-edged sword," he said. "You want to get players in shape for the official workouts. On the other hand, you don't want to overwork them, but no matter what you do, many of them are so highly motivated—and concerned for their spot in the team—that they'll work out on their own if they have to."

Foley said, yes, there were rest breaks, that water was plentiful and available, and that six coaches were on the field at all times. "Eraste was a hard-working, dedicated kid who was in excellent physical shape," Foley said. "He didn't stumble around on the field, he showed no signs of distress."

Autin's death may or may not be one of the mysteries of life. His mother, Joanie, said there was no reason to believe there was danger, since Eraste had practiced in the heat of Louisiana summers throughout his junior high school and high school years. "He was never sick," she said.

In Mueller's view, however, the overall reasons for the rise in deaths of high school and college football players due to heatstroke can be guessed.

"Proper precautions," he said, "have apparently been relaxed."

The pressures of football, the macho element in football, surely seem to contribute to relaxing such precautions.

An added suggestion here is that twice a year, the team doctor on every high school and college team read to his players and coaches and school administrators the names of the football dead in recent years, and describe the circumstances. Maybe also run a film of Eraste Autin's funeral.

Morbid? Possibly. But lifesaving, possibly, too.

Summary

____

____

____

____

____

____

Provide an Overview of a Textbook, Magazine, or Journal Article

A summary of a magazine or journal article provides an overview. It states the writer's purpose, lists the main ideas, and mentions key details. To write a summary of a textbook, magazine, or journal article, follow the guidelines on page 347.

Here is a short magazine article on the value of homework. The student's notes are shown in the left margin. Notice how, in these notes, the student is already beginning to paraphrase the content of the article. His paraphrased notes serve as the basis for the summary he writes after reading.

from "Homework, a School Reform That Works,"
Atlantic Monthly by JONATHON RAUCH

Suppose I told you that I knew of an education reform guaranteed to raise the achievement levels of American students; that this reform would cost next to nothing and would require no political body's approval; and that it could be implemented overnight by anybody of a mind to undertake it. You would jump at it, right? But Americans haven't jumped at it. They rarely even talk about it.

Talk about school reform has been going on forever.

In 1983 I began my reporting career covering education for a North Carolina newspaper. Then—as now—everyone talked about reforming schools, but I became convinced that one of the key ingredients of successful schooling was being mostly overlooked. Learning depends on what educators call "time on task," which is what the rest of us call attending class and studying.

American schools are remarkably parsimonious with time. The school year is fixed at or below 180 days in all but a handful of states—down from more than 190 in the late nineteenth century, when Saturday-morning sessions were common. The instructional day is only about six hours, of which much is taken up with nonacademic matters. In 1994 a national commission calculated that in four years of high school a typical American student puts in less than half as much time on academic subjects as do students in Japan, France, and Germany.

American kids don't spend much "time on task." The school day is getting shorter. Students in other countries spend twice as much time on academic subjects.

Extending the school day or the school year can get expensive and complicated, and reducing nonacademic electives and gym brings hollers from parents and kids. But there is one quite cheap and uncomplicated way to increase study time: add more homework.

Homework is a low-cost solution to problems with poor performance in American schools.

You may not be shocked to learn that homework raises student achievement, at least in the higher grades. For young children homework appears not to be particularly helpful. Even among older students it is hard to be sure of the extent to which more homework causes higher achievement, because higher achievement also leads to more homework (brighter or harder-working kids will take more-demanding courses). Still, no one doubts that, as all kinds of studies have found, older kids learn more if they study more. Surveying the evidence in 2001, Harris Cooper, an educational psychologist, wrote, "For high school students the effect of homework can be impressive. Indeed, relative to other instructional techniques and the costs involved in doing it, homework can produce a substantial, positive effect on adolescents' performance in school."

Kids in upper grades who do their homework learn more.

You may also not be shocked to learn that, for the most part, American students don't do much homework. Nowadays homework loads among the Ivy-bound

Most American high school students do less than an hour of homework; slightly less than half do no homework at all.

According to this survey, the U.S. ranks last.

superelite can be downright inhumane, but they are the exception. In 1999, according to the National Assessment of Educational Progress, two thirds of seventeen-year-olds did less than an hour of homework on a typical night (in other words, only about ten minutes per subject). Forty percent did no homework at all—up from 34 percent in 1984. In 1995 the Third International Mathematics and Science Survey asked high school seniors (or their equivalents) in twenty countries about study time. "Of twenty nations," says a recent report by the Brookings Institution's Brown Center on Education Policy, "the U.S. ranked near the bottom, tied for the next-to-last position."

Summary

Compared to students in other countries, American students do poorly in school. Discussion of school reform, Jonathon Rauch reports, has been going on forever. Most reform is expensive and controversial. In his *Atlantic Monthly* article Rauch argues that homework is a low-cost solution to the problem of poor performance of students in American schools. Rauch points out that American kids don't spend much "time on task," and the school day is actually getting shorter. The majority of American high school students do less than an hour of homework each day. Slightly less than half do no homework at all. According to the Third International Mathematics and Science Survey of twenty nations, the US ranks next to last in study time.

This summary provides an overview of the *Atlantic Monthly* article. Using careful paraphrase, it captures the main ideas and key details of the article. The student reports what the article says without expressing opinions or making judgments on the content of the story.

Effective summary gets at the main ideas of a source. The more specific detail you provide, the more you risk plagiarizing. Reporting general information and only key details makes your job easier. Remember to report on what someone else says and thinks, not your opinions on the subject.

EXERCISE 15-4 **Summary and Overview**

Directions: *Read the following article. Underline the main ideas and key details such as proper names, make notes in the margin to provide a basis for your summary, and then write a summary in the space provided.*

from "The Violent Games People Play," *New Scientist* by HAZEL MUIR

April 2002, Erfurt, Germany: a 19-year-old runs amok with a pistol at a school. His 20-minute shooting frenzy leaves 17 dead, including himself. April 1999, Littleton, Colorado: two teenagers rampage through Columbine High School with bombs, guns and knives, slaughtering 13 people before committing suicide.

These, and at least 12 other murders since 1997, have been linked to an obsession with violent video games. Is there any scientific evidence that mere games can make children and young adults more aggressive, or possibly even homicidal?

The US Federal Trade Commission says 78 percent of children aged between 13 and 16 can easily buy games aimed at the over-17s. Why is this a problem? Well, to anyone who left gaming behind in the early 1980s, many of today's games are overwhelmingly, sickeningly violent. In *Manhunt,* a first-person 3D game, for instance, the gamer plays a convict reprieved from death row who shoots, beats to death, or suffocates all acquaintances. The more grisly the execution, the greater the accolades earned. And in *Grand Theft Auto: Vice City,* the gamer plays the part of an ex-con trying to recover cash lost in a botched drugs deal. The player mugs people, intimidates jurors, and kills a prostitute.

Psychologists think there may be many reasons why violent games are more harmful to children than vicious movies. Firstly, says Barbara Krahe at the University of Potsdam in Germany, players are actively involved in perpetrating violence, and may begin to perceive using weapons as second nature. Secondly, violent games provide repetitive aggressive experiences that are rewarded by more killing.

The issue is controversial, however. Jeffrey Goldstein, a psychologist at the University of Utrecht in the Netherlands and a consultant to some video games publishers, agrees that there is good evidence that children who are exposed to violent media, including video games, are more aggressive. But he warns it might not be a simple case of cause and effect: Aggressive kids might be most attracted to violent games.

What's more, he says, the experiments that purport to recreate gaming in the lab and measure aggression fail on both counts. Playing a game because a researcher tells you to does not mimic patterns of voluntary gaming. And blasting with noise is not the same thing as a real intent to injure someone.

Like Krahe, most experts agree the way to resolve the question is by monitoring game-playing habits and aggression levels over many years. Goldstein, however, believes the truth may never be known, because aggression is so hard to measure. But he thinks the controversy may recede as game-playing children become parents, teachers, and politicians who don't regard games with fear and suspicion. "In the future, they will be regarded like films or books," he says. "There are good and bad ones—choose carefully."

Summary

A recent article in the *New Scientist* explores the link between video games and violence. Twelve deaths in events such as Columbine have been connected to the perpetrators' obsession with video games. Even though games have ratings and age restrictions, under-age viewers can readily purchase games like *Manhunt* and *Grand Theft Auto,* which include extreme violence. Some psychologists, such as Barbara Krahe from the University of Potsdam, believe video games may have a greater influence on kids than movies because, unlike movies, video games invite kids to participate in repetitive acts of violence. Other psychologists, such as Jeffrey Goldstein, a psychologist at the University of Utrecht in the Netherlands, suggest that violent kids are attracted to violent games, that the games themselves do not cause the violence.

Quotation

A well-chosen quotation can add both authority and color to your writing, but it must be both skillfully introduced and properly integrated in order to be a real asset.

Choose Quotations

Choose your quotations carefully. A poorly chosen quotation indicates a lack of critical thought. Any quotation will not do. Choose a quotation that has one or more of the following qualities:

- It sums up a point of view.
- It illustrates or supports an important point in your summary.
- It has colorful language and is therefore memorable.
- It adds authority to your writing.

Choose a quotation after you have read carefully, absorbed the meaning of what you have read, and summarized the reading. For example, here are quotations from "Lives Changed in a Split Second" and "Homework, a School Reform That Works." These quotations sum up the main idea of each article:

> "I never should have put my family in that truck or any other like it."
>
> "But there is one quite cheap and uncomplicated way to increase study time: add more homework."

EXERCISE 15-5 Choosing Quotations

Directions: *Reread the two articles you summarized, "A Deadly Toll Is Haunting Football" and "The Violent Games People Play." Select a one-sentence quotation from each article that sums up a point of view, has colorful language, or illustrates an important point from each article. Write the sentences below with quotation marks around them and explain why you chose them.* Answers will vary.

1. From "A Deadly Toll Is Haunting Football":

____

____

____

2. From "The Violent Games People Play":

____

____

____

Introduce Quotations

For the sake of variety, learn to use both partial and complete quotations. A partial quotation is a phrase you build a sentence around; a complete quotation is a grammatical sentence that begins with a capital letter and ends with a period. If you are writing a paragraph, you want to use a partial quotation or a very short complete quotation. If you are writing an essay, you might use both partial and complete quotations.

Introducing your quotation has two functions. One, you acknowledge your source and protect yourself from charges of plagiarism. Two, having good sources enhances your credibility. It persuades the reader you know what you are talking about. Here are illustrations of language taken from a reputable source—the first a partial quotation and the second a complete quotation.

Original

from Rick Weiss, "For First Time, Chimps Seen Making Weapons for Hunting," washingtonpost.com

Chimpanzees living in the West African savannah have been observed fashioning deadly spears from sticks and using the tools to hunt small mammals—the first routine production of deadly weapons ever observed in animals other than humans. The multistep spearmaking practice, documented by researchers in Senegal who spent years gaining the chimpanzees' trust, adds credence to the idea that human forebears fashioned similar tools millions of years ago. The landmark observation also supports the long-debated proposition that females—the main makers and users of spears among the Senegalese chimps—tend to be the innovators and creative problem solvers in primate culture.

Partial Quotation

The *Washington Post* reports chimpanzees have been observed making and using weapons, which suggests that "human forebears fashioned similar tools millions of years ago" (Weiss).

Complete Quotation

Chimpanzees have been observed making weapons. According to the *Washington Post,* "The multistep spearmaking practice, documented by researchers in Senegal who spent years gaining the chimpanzees' trust, adds credence to the idea that human forebears fashioned similar tools millions of years ago" (Weiss).

All quotations should be associated with their source. It is the best way to protect yourself from the charge of plagiarism. In addition, when you associate your ideas with a source that has name recognition, such as the *Washington Post,* you enhance the credibility of your writing.

Guidelines for Acknowledging Sources

1. If you are quoting from a magazine or newspaper article, identify the name of the publication. Place your acknowledgment at the beginning of your paraphrase or quotation.

Here is a reference to an article published online by the *Washington Post.*

> The *Washington Post* reports that a large number of high school students work at fast-food restaurants and that McDonald's serves as "the pioneer, trend-setter and symbol" (Etzioni).

2. When you cite a source by the author's name, use the full name and, if possible, include a phrase describing the author's credentials.

Here is a reference to an article by Bernard P. Horn published online by *Frontline.*

> Bernard P. Horn, political director for the National Coalition Against Legalized Gambling, observes, "The American Psychiatric Association and the American Medical Association recognize pathological gambling as a diagnosable mental disorder."

If you include a second quotation by the same author or speaker, use that person's last name only.

> Horn adds that gambling problems in the United States are reaching "epidemic proportions."

3. When you quote from a textbook, article, essay, or book, identify the author, or authors, by name and refer to the article, essay, or book you are quoting from.

> Frances Mayes says of her home in *Under the Tuscan Sun,* "Much of the restoration we did ourselves, an accomplishment, as my grandfather would say, out of the fullness of our ignorance."
>
> In *Dakota: A Spiritual Biography,* Kathleen Norris appreciates "the harsh beauty of a land that rolls like the ocean floor it once was, where dry winds scour out buttes, and the temperature can reach 110 degrees or plunge to 30 degrees below zero for a week or more" (26).

It is best to avoid providing too much information, such as web addresses or dates of publication. It is usually sufficient to introduce and acknowledge your source by stating the name of the author(s) and the title of the source.

EXERCISE 15-6 **Introducing Partial and Complete Quotations**

Directions: *Read the following short excerpts. Write a short paraphrase of each passage. In the first paraphrase select and include a partial quotation. In the second paraphrase, select and include a complete quotation. Write paraphrases with quotations in the spaces provided. Be sure to acknowledge your source in each paraphrase.* Answers will vary.

EXAMPLE

from MSNBC, "The French May Soon Be Sleeping on the Job"

The French already enjoy a 35-hour work week and generous vacation. Now the health minister wants to look into whether workers should be allowed to sleep on the job. France launched plans this week to spend $9 million this year to improve public awareness about sleeping troubles. About one in three French people suffer from them, the ministry says. Fifty-six percent of French complain that a poor night's sleep has affected their job performance, according to the ministry.

Partial Quotation

To combat poor performance in the workplace, MSNBC reports that the French will spend millions this year "to improve public awareness about sleeping trouble" ("The French").

Complete Quotation

According to MSNBC, "France launched plans this week to spend $9 million this year to improve public awareness about sleeping troubles" ("The French").

1. from *Days of Atonement* by Richard Rodriguez (xvii)

Something hopeful was created in California through the century of its Protestant development. People believed that in California they could begin new lives. New generations of immigrants continue to arrive in California, not a few of them from Mexico, hoping to cash in on comedy. It is still possible in California to change your name, change your sex, get a divorce, become a movie star. My Mexican parents live in a house with four telephones, three televisions, and several empty bedrooms.

Partial Quotation

____

____

____

Complete Quotation

____

____

____

2. from Alessandra Stanley, "Sexy Woman Out, Cantankerous Guy In," *New York Times* online

There is still no sexual equality in comedy. For women, historically too easily despised and made the butt of the jokes, the victory is in pulling off a comic character that is both laughable and laudable: Lucy Ricardo in the 50's, Mary Richards in the 70's, and Carrie Bradshaw in the 90's. For men, humor lies in blurring the line between lovable and loathsome: Ralph Kramden, Archie Bunker, and now Larry David.

Partial Quotation

____

____

____

Complete Quotation

____

____

____

3. from Dava Sobel, *Galileo's Daughter*, (73)

December 1615 thus brought Galileo to Rome brandishing new support for Copernicus—derived from observations of the Earth, not the heavens. The tidal motions of the great oceans, Galileo believed, bore constant witness that the planet really did spin through space. If the Earth stood still, then what could make its water rush to and fro, rising and falling at regular intervals along the coasts?

Partial Quotation

____

____

____

Complete Quotation

____

____

____

EXERCISE 15-7 Finding Quotations in Your Reading

Directions: *Read several articles from a newspaper or a news magazine. Find at least five examples each of partial quotations and complete quotations. Copy them exactly as they appear in the article you select, and cite the source.*

EXAMPLE

Source: Deborah Baldwin. "Helping an Old French Art Rise." *New York Times* 27 Nov. 2003: A15.

Scholars say Mr. Kaplan was the first person to put a shift in consumer tastes into the context of a changing workplace and society. Mr. Kaplan is "a superb craftsman, someone working on an important subject and doing justice to it," said Robert Darnton, a Princeton historian who specializes in 17th and 18th century France. "The subject of bread is far more crucial than most modern people appreciate: bread really was the staff of life in early modern Europe, and it deserves such a good historian." Roger Chartier, a French cultural historian and visiting professor at the University of Pennsylvania, said, "He has a very profound, deep knowledge of the archives."

Partial Quotation: Mr. Kaplan is "a superb craftsman, someone working on an important subject and doing justice to it," said Robert Darnton, a Princeton historian who specializes in seventeenth- and eighteenth-century France.

Complete Quotation: Roger Chartier, a French cultural historian and visiting professor at the University of Pennsylvania, said, "He has a very profound, deep knowledge of the archives."

1. **Source:** ____________________

Partial Quotation: ____________________

____

____

Complete Quotation: ____________________

____

____

2. **Source:** ____________________

Partial Quotation: ____________________

____

____

Complete Quotation: ____________________

____

____

3. **Source:** ____________________

Partial Quotation: ____________________

____

____

Complete Quotation: ____________________

____

____

4. **Source:** ____________________

Partial Quotation: ____________________

____

____

Complete Quotation: ____________________

____

____

5. Source: ______________________________

Partial Quotation: ______________________________

____

____

Complete Quotation: ______________________________

____

____

Suggestions for Daily Practice

1. At the end of class, write a short summary of the main points discussed or activities covered.
2. Select a sentence from your textbook. Count the number of words. Write a paraphrase that restates the idea in half the number of words.
3. Select an article from a newspaper that interests you and write a short summary of it.
4. Keep a journal. Make journal entries that summarize your daily activities.
5. Write summaries of movies or television programs you find entertaining.
6. Find a newspaper or magazine article on a subject that interests you. Copy the article's quotations. Count the number of partial and complete quotations.

TOPIC 12: Taking Notes and Incorporating Research
www.mhhe.com/goingplaces

Writer's Response

Daily practice is one way to take charge of your learning. Describe other ways you take charge. Why are they effective?

GOING PLACES

FINDING AND USING SOURCES, ONLINE AND OFF

Hungry for More?

Have you ever seen a movie and found yourself hungry for more information on who was in it, who made it, or what it was based on? To find out, it helps to know how to do research quickly and efficiently. Whether you want to know who played Frodo in Peter Jackson's *The Lord of the Rings* movies or what critics and writers—including W. H. Auden—were saying about *The Fellowship of the Ring* when it was first published in the fall of 1954, online and print sources offer much more than facts; they are a great resource for reviews and other kinds of conversation about the books, films, or music you love.

DISCUSSION

Turn and talk to a classmate about a subject you would like to know more about. How did you become interested in the subject? What do you currently know about it? Why is the subject important to you?

The Internet Versus the Printed Page

The Internet offers a wealth of information that is literally at your fingertips; type a few key words into a search engine, and your computer will return hundreds of sites related to your chosen topic. Be warned, however: Many of these sites will contain irrelevant, highly personal, or downright false information. Anyone with access to a computer and some basic tools can post a site, so be sure to check a site's credibility before citing it. Who wrote it, and who sponsors the site? Why, and for what kinds of readers? Is it well written and carefully edited? Are sources cited? Do the facts presented on the site check out when you compare them to other sources? Evaluating all sources for credibility will ensure that you choose the right ones to cite.

BRAINSTORM

Make a list of websites you visit. How did you find out about these sites? What kind of information do they provide? Is the information reliable and true? How do you know?

Doing Research on the Job

The research skills you hone during college will not simply gather dust after graduation. Finding and managing outside information is an important aspect of many jobs. You could be asked, for example, to locate reliable sales figures (internally) or news stories (externally) that relate to a project you are doing; you might be asked to design a field survey that will help your company determine whether or not to embark on a new venture. Whether you find yourself plowing through years of sales receipts or surfing the Internet for new techniques for building a mousetrap, research skills will aid you in almost any job.

DISCUSSION

Turn and talk to a classmate about the work you expect to do. Take turns talking about the kind of research you might be expected to do on the job.

CHAPTER › 16

The Documented Essay

CHAPTER OVERVIEW

- THE DOCUMENTED ESSAY AT A GLANCE
- ELEMENTS OF THE DOCUMENTED ESSAY
- GET STARTED
  - Locate Information
- PROCESS INFORMATION
  - Type of Information
  - Take Notes
  - Integrate Sources
- DOCUMENT SOURCES
  - Cite Different Types of Sources

THINK FIRST

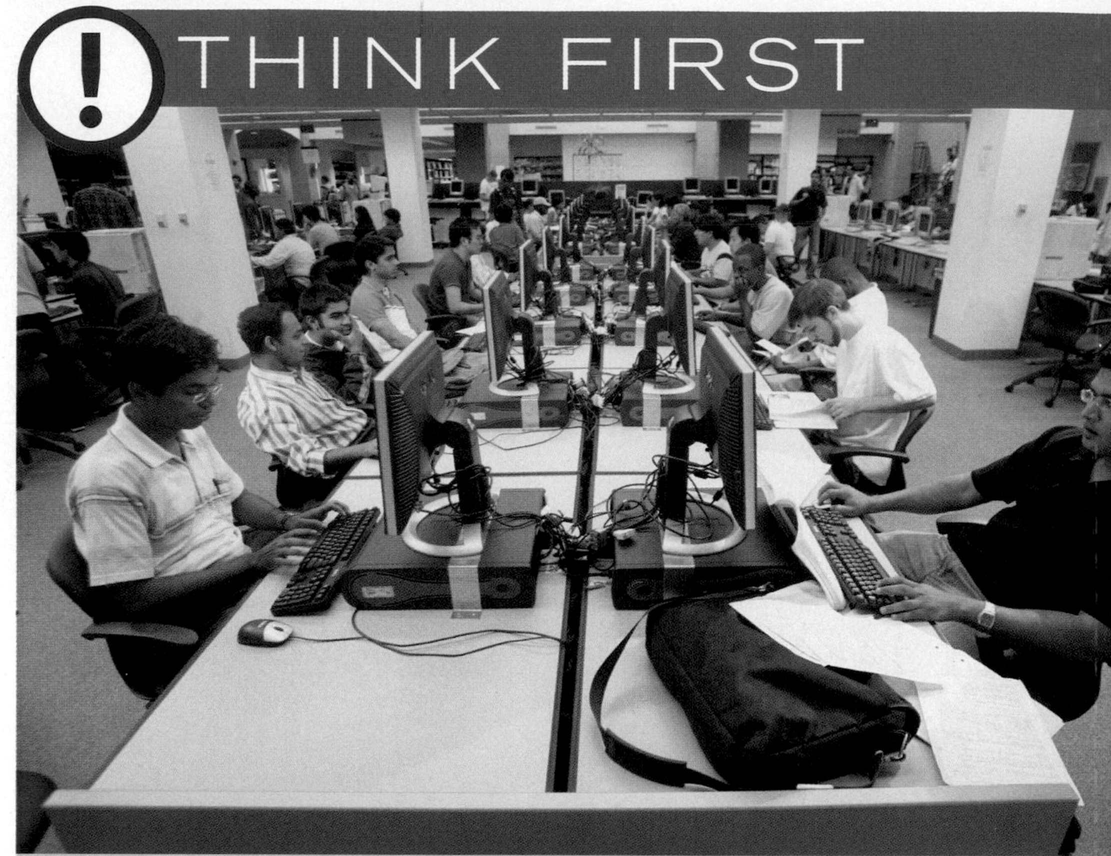

Recall a project you did at school that involved finding and using sources of information. Write a paragraph describing the project. What was it about? What kind of research did you do? What were your strengths and weaknesses?

At a Glance

THE DOCUMENTED ESSAY AT A GLANCE

A documented essay demonstrates your ability to focus on a problem, gather information while distinguishing between different viewpoints, and present what you have learned in a specific format. You are showing your reader that you have digested the information and made judgments about its value by arriving at a reasonable conclusion about an important issue.

The documented essay demonstrates your ability to manage information and use your knowledge of the conventions of college writing. These conventions include the presentation of facts and statistics, quotations, and cases, with specific references to sources in your paper.

The Documented Essay at a Glance

ASSIGNMENT Discuss an environmental issue, preferably a controversial one. Describe the problem and state your opinion on what is to be done about it.

Fritz 1

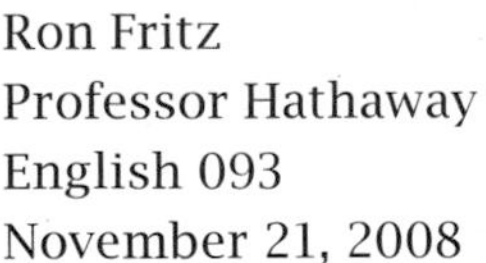

Ron Fritz
Professor Hathaway
English 093
November 21, 2008

Drink Up

Plastic bottles are everywhere these days. They are in the refrigerator, in the office, and on the sidewalk. They are also on the side of the road and floating in rivers and lakes. They pose a significant environmental problem. According to the journal *Environment*, recent data show 23.4 billion plastic bottles of soda were sold in the U.S. in 2000 (Nicholson 6). Indeed, the dramatic increase in plastic bottles is attributed to exactly that use—beverages people drink, only to toss the bottles when they are done. To be perfectly realistic, there appears to be little chance of reversing the trend to use plastic, which is why dramatic efforts to recycle are the only answer.

The student begins with details that dramatize the problem.

To support the observations, she uses statistics.

THESIS STATEMENT
The writer states the main idea of the essay and her opinion about it.

Why don't we go back to glass and aluminum? That is not a solution to the problem. In fact, the trend in plastic use these days is definitely upward. Darryl Young, from the California Department of Conservation, notes that a plastic beverage bottle has become "as common as a cell phone" (qtd in Johnson 1). Californians throw away a billion bottles a year (Johnson 1). In Japan, the use of plastic is expanding at 10 percent a year, and of that production, 413,000 tons of plastic are used for beverages (Yoshihiro 24). In Mexico, polyethylene terephthalate (PET) plastic bottles are fast replacing glass and metal. Producers hope the technology will soon be available for packaging beer in plastic ("Resins" 40). As the technology improves, plastic becomes more attractive for packaging just about everything.

The concluding sentence of this paragraph restates the main idea.

TOPIC SENTENCE
The student presents a second possible solution.

The natural solution is recycling. Unfortunately, PET bottles are not recycled at the rate they should be. Because they are small, fit in a consumer's hand, and are easy to take along on walks and drives, they are more likely to end up in trashcans or worse, on the ground. *Environment* reports that from 1996 to 2000, recycling rates fell from 48 percent to 35 percent. In addition, recycling plastic is more difficult than recycling glass or aluminum. Nicholson points out, "Plastic bottles have to be sorted by color and type of resin, and all extraneous materials have to be removed; in many cases, these processes have to be done by hand" (6). Bottles that end up in landfills are, of course, not biodegradable and take up a tremendous amount of space. Those bottles that are incinerated produce greenhouse gases.

The information in this paragraph, both statistics and quotations, enables the student to discuss obstacles to recycling as a solution to the problem.

TOPIC SENTENCE
The student presents a feasible solution and presents arguments in favor of it.

She presents statistics showing a real financial incentive is possible.

The answer seems to be to appeal to the consumer's pocketbook: make recycling more lucrative. Currently the deposit on plastic bottles is 2.5 to 5 cents. It simply is not enough to motivate people to act responsibly. *Waste News* suggests that Californians lose $26 million a year on unredeemed plastic bottles. That is, the consumer pays the deposit and the bottle is never returned (Johnson 1). The deposit should be doubled, tripled, or even quadrupled. If someone is foolish enough to throw away 25 cents, there will be enterprising people there to pick it up. Moreover, according to *Look Japan,* we are now at a point where PET bottles can now be made from recycled plastic, which "will decrease waste volume and reduce consumption of the petroleum resources used to make PET plastic" (Yoshihiro 24).

This fact makes a connection between recycling and new technology.

Fritz 3

As an environmental issue, plastic bottles are bad, but they are unlikely to go away soon. All the more reason for a policy that makes it very profitable for people to pick up PET bottles and return them.

Works Cited

Johnson, Jim. "A Billion Bottles Litter California; State Report Contends Discarding Portable Containers Is Costly Error." *Waste News* 9.3 (2003): 1. Print.

Nicholson, Robert. "A Lose-Lose Situation." *Environment* 42.10 (2000): 6. Print.

"Resins: Opportunities Downstream." *Chemical Week* 168.11 (2006): 40. Print.

Yoshihiro, Echizenya. "And If One PET Bottle Should Accidentally Fall . . ." *Look Japan* 49.575 (2004): 24. Print.

In her conclusion, the writer refers to a key term from the assignment and restates her argument.

The student's list of works cited tells the reader exactly where her information came from.

The list is written in MLA format, alphabetical by authors' last names or, for those articles without authors listed, by the first word of the title.

DISCUSSION QUESTIONS

1. What is the function of the statistics and quotations used in this paper?
2. How are these statistics and quotations introduced?
3. What do you think "qtd in Johnson" means?

PEER CONVERSATION

ELEMENTS OF THE DOCUMENTED ESSAY

Readers of academic writing have very definite expectations when they see a documented essay. These expectations relate to both form and content. Below is a brief description of the elements you should have in mind when you write a documented essay.

- ***The problem:*** Your work usually begins with a problem or issue. Something is wrong, and there is a public discussion on websites, in newspapers, magazines, and journals about a reasonable approach to addressing this problem. The streets are littered with plastic bottles, for example. What is to be done?
- ***Locating information:*** Readers of the documented essay look for quality information. You need to find good sources and read them with understanding. The evidence you borrow from your sources comes in three forms: facts and statistics, cases and studies, and authoritative opinion. In the at-a-glance essay, for example, the student cites her reading from journals specifically published to address environmental issues.
- ***Processing information:*** Once you locate information, you need to process it. You read, take notes, select what is useful, and integrate it into the essay you write.
- ***Integrating information:*** How you present information matters. If you present information effectively, your essay is more persuasive. You

are expected to use signal phrases ("according to . . .") in the paper, cite authors and publications by name, use in-text citations where necessary, and provide a list of works cited.

GET STARTED

Like most writing in college, documented essays often begin with an assignment. You near the end of a unit of study, and your instructor would now like you to dig deeper into a specific problem, learn what authorities are saying about this problem, and state your opinion about it. Often students begin with an opinion, and in the process of doing their research, their opinion becomes informed. It becomes an opinion based on careful thought about reliable information.

EXERCISE 16-1 Problem and Opinion

Directions: *Select one of the topics below. In a short paragraph, briefly state what you know about the problem and your opinion about it. Do your work on a separate sheet of paper.*

EXAMPLE

Problem: Plastic bottles and the environment
There are plastic bottles everywhere. That's for sure. Especially since bottled water has become so popular. Half the people you see walking down the street are holding onto bottles. What happens to those bottles? Don't they just get thrown away? In my opinion, the use of plastic bottles is very bad. It is probably an environmental disaster. I think they should be outlawed.

1. The use of calculators in lower grades
2. Trying juveniles as adults
3. Boot camp for juvenile offenders
4. Making the morning-after pill available over the counter
5. Same-sex marriage
6. Home schooling
7. Free digital downloads of music
8. Prayer in school

Locate Information

Gateway

TOPIC 11: Researching: Print and Electronic Tools
www.mhhe.com/goingplaces

Your goal in the investigation process is to improve your information literacy. "Just Google it" is not the best formula for success. You need to be informed on a variety of sources of information, many of which are probably available through your college or local library.

Internet Sources

Sitting at your computer, you have access to an abundance of information to get you started. Internet searches are done with search engines.

INTERNET SEARCH ENGINES

- www.google.com
- www.lycos.com
- www.metacrawler.com
- www.altavista.com

These powerful applications search literally hundreds of thousands of sites for key words that you supply. Because it is not uncommon to find thousands of websites that relate to your topic, you need to be as specific as possible in your searches. Then you need to quickly survey a site and make a judgment about whether the information you find there will be valuable to you.

Search Hints

After accessing the search engine of your choice, enter key words that relate to your topic. To avoid an unreasonably large number of "hits," be as specific as possible and use as many terms in a single search as you think apply to your topic.

SEARCH TIP

If you precede each of your terms with a "+" sign, a search engine like Google will return only sites that contain all of the specified terms (as opposed to one of the terms or a combination of them). Adding quotation marks to a phrase (say, "effects of television") will return only sites with that exact phrase:

+ "effects of television" + children + research

For further information on how to search sites for information, look for the "advanced search" link on the home page of the search engine you want to use. There you will find either help or tips on how to search most effectively.

Evaluating Sites

Scan the list of sites your search engine returns. Look at the Internet addresses (URLs, or universal resource locators) of the websites to determine whether they are sponsored by a commercial group (.com), an educational institution (.edu), a government organization (.gov), or a nonprofit organization (.org). Since .com sites are selling something, you should be wary of them.

TYPES OF WEBSITES

- Commercial group (.com)
- Educational institution (.edu)
- Government organization (.gov)
- Nonprofit organization (.org)

Go to specific sites and continue your evaluation. Scroll from the top to the bottom of the site. Check for dates to see if the information is current. Look for "About Us" or "Who We Are" links to learn more about the source of the information. These links will provide information on the organization's background, authors' credentials, and their affiliation with institutions, such as government agencies and universities, or with mainstream publications

If the site passes these initial tests, bookmark it using the "Favorites" or "Bookmarks" function of your Internet browser. Then, either on a note card or in a computer file, record the source and title information, a description of the information you found, and the date you accessed it. Repeat this process for other sites that are likely to have useful information.

Periodical Literature

College and public libraries offer a variety of online periodical databases to help writers search print sources of information more efficiently. Using key words, you can search for articles much as you do on the Internet. Among the databases you might use are the following.

- ***InfoTrac:*** Includes citations from thousands of magazines, journals, and newspapers, many in full text; includes the current year of *The New York Times;* provides excellent coverage of current events, health, business, and much more.

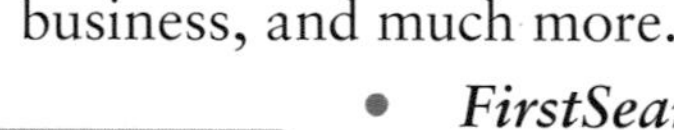

Talk about It
Discuss two or three tips in this chapter that make research both efficient and effective.

- ***FirstSearch:*** Includes specialized databases, many with full-text periodical articles, in fields from accounting to zoology; includes WorldCat (access to the book catalogs of the world's libraries), and WilsonSelect (full-text articles from magazines and journals).
- ***General Reference Center Gold:*** Available twenty-four hours a day via the Internet, provides one-stop access to general interest magazines, business periodicals, reference books, maps, historical images, and newspaper articles; records available with a combination of indexing, abstracts, image, or full-text formats.
- ***Electric Library:*** Content from more than one hundred full-text magazine, newspaper, book, and transcript sources, plus thousands of maps and pictures.

Searching Databases

Key word searches may lead to subtopics, enabling you to narrow your search and be more specific. Follow this four-step process when you do a database search.

1. **Enter terms into the search window of the database.** Narrow your search as much as possible at this stage. Most periodicals databases allow for "Subject," "Author," "Title," and "Key Word" searches, among other options. Check the "Help" section of the database you are using to see how to narrow your searches most efficiently—for example, whether it accepts signs, quotation marks, and/or Boolean operators like AND, OR, NOT, and so on.
2. **Make a quick evaluation of the results of your search.** Along with content descriptions (if any), titles, length, and authorship, consider the

types of periodicals in which articles appear. Depending on your topic, consider popular sources, such as *USA Today, Time,* and *Newsweek,* or more academic or professional publications, such as *Environment, Chemical Week,* and *Waste News.*

3. **If an article is available online, skim it.** Scan the article top to bottom, reading headings and the first sentence of each paragraph. Check for dates to see if the information is current. If the article seems useful, print it out or e-mail a copy of it to yourself (if possible). If you cannot print or e-mail it, record the author's name, the name of the publication, the title of the article, a description of the information you found, the date, and page number(s) on a note card or in a computer file.
4. **If an article is not available, print or copy down the publication information.** Sometimes only the name and publication information, rather than the full text, are available in a search. When that happens, you print or copy down the publication information for articles that look useful and consult the library for a print (or microfilm) copy.

Library Catalog and Reference Books

Library catalogs can be searched by "Subject," "Author," "Title," and "Key Word." Be as specific as possible and include as many search terms as are relevant. Evaluate catalog sources (that is, the actual books or periodicals) for relevance and trustworthiness, authorship, publication information, and dates. Once you have found a book or periodical that passes these initial tests, consult the table of contents and index to find sections and pages that address your topic.

Libraries provide access to reference books and online materials, such as encyclopedias, dictionaries, biography resources, handbooks, and maps and atlases. They also have many sources on geography, politics, and populations, as well as information on countries, states, cities, and business.

EXERCISE 16-2 Locating Information

Directions: *For each of the sources of information described above, write down some key words you would use to search for information on the topic you chose in Exercise 16-1.*

EXAMPLE

Topic: Plastic bottles and the environment

Internet Search: "plastic water bottles" + environment

Periodical Search: plastic bottles, plastic bottles AND environment,

plastic beverage containers AND pollution

Topic: ______________________________

Internet Search: ______________________________

Periodical Search: ______________________________

____

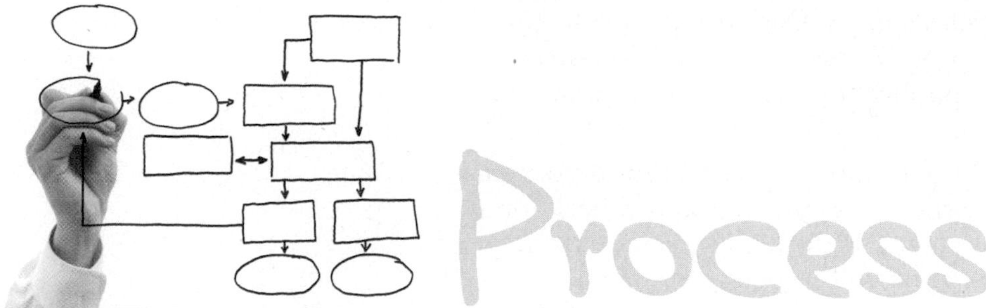

PROCESS INFORMATION

When you write a documented essay, it is important to work efficiently and effectively. You need to locate useful information, process it, and integrate it into your writing.

Types of Information

You will work more efficiently if you have clearly defined types of information in mind when you start your search. Here are three of the most common types of information writers use.

Facts and Statistics

Facts and statistics are numerical data you can use to dramatize a problem and convey the size and dimensions of an issue to a reader.

- According to the journal *Environment,* recent data show 23.4 billion plastic bottles of soda were sold in the U.S. in 2000 (Nicholson 6).
- In Japan, the use of plastic is expanding at 10 percent a year. Of that production, 413,000 tons of plastic are used for beverages (Yoshihiro 24).
- *Environment* reports that from 1996 to 2000 recycling rates have fallen from 48 percent to 35 percent (Nicholson 6).

Facts and statistics also provide support for a viewpoint.

- *Waste News* suggests that Californians lose $26 million a year on unredeemed plastic bottles. That is, the consumer pays the deposit and the bottle is never returned (Johnson 1).

Authoritative Opinion

Authoritative opinion comes from experts whose credentials invite us to believe what they say.

- Darryl Young, from the California Department of Conservation, notes that plastic beverage bottles have become "as common as a cell phone" (qtd in Johnson 1).

In addition to experts with credentials, authoritative opinion can come from journals and respected publications. In the at-a-glance essay, the student writing on plastic bottles refers to *Environment, Waste News,* and *Chemical Week.*

Cases and Examples

Cases and examples are likely to provide you with both factual information and a basis for informed opinion. If you are writing on the topic of same-sex marriages, for example, you can find detailed discussions about gay couples living in states such as New Hampshire, Massachusetts, and California, where specific legislative and judicial actions have addressed this issue. Reading about these cases will give you factual information on the specific disadvantages same-sex couples have experienced because they lack legal marital status. Learning about specific cases will also give you access to informed opinion on the issue.

Take Notes

Once you identify sources you would like to use, you need to process them. Plagiarism is a critical issue at this point. Some students copy large passages from sources into their notes, then copy from their notes to their paper. This is plagiarism. Other students email themselves a full copy of the source, then copy and paste from the source straight into their papers. This also is plagiarism. It is sloppy and dishonest work and will likely result in a failing grade on the assignment and possibly the course.

See page 343 for a more detailed discussion of plagiarism.

Begin with a tentative outline for your paper. What is the problem or issue? What questions will you explore in your reading? What is your viewpoint? Your outline will help you focus your reading and provide you with a system for organizing your notes. This student's very simple outline creates a structure for organized reading and thinking.

Plastic bottles and the environment

I. How big of a problem is this?

II. Doesn't recycling work?

III. What can be done?

As you read, take careful notes on note cards or your computer or on note cards. Here are some tips for recording information.

Take Notes Using Your Computer

1. **Create a folder dedicated to your project.** In this folder keep notes, publication information for your sources, and drafts of the paper you are writing.
2. **Use a new word processing file for each source.** When you take notes on your reading, put these notes in a dedicated Word file. Save the file either by the author's last name or by the first two or three words of the title (for example, Nicholson or "A Billion Bottles").
3. **Follow steps 2–5 in "Take Notes Using Note Cards."**

Source: Author, title

Outline Ref

Notes:

Date of publication, date accessed, page numbers:

FIGURE 16-1 Example Note Card

Take Notes Using Note Cards

1. **Use a separate note card for each source.** If you find an informative source, use a note card for each separate item on your outline.
2. **Record publication information.** For an Internet source, write down the author(s) names, the title of the article, the title of the Web site, the version or edition used, the publisher or sponsor of the site, the date of publication (day, month, year), and the date you accessed the site. If you have accessed an article via the Internet or an online database that also appears in print, you should try to obtain the information listed for print sources as well. For books, newspapers, magazines, and periodicals, write down the author's name(s), the title of the article, periodical, book, newspaper, or magazine; date and place of publication; the publisher; and the page numbers where the information you are using can be found. (See Figure 16-1 for an example note card.)
3. **Use a number or roman numeral on the card to refer to your outline** (see Figure 16-2) and indicate the connection between the notes you take and the structure of your paper.
4. **Take brief notes that paraphrase or summarize information.** Most students take too many notes. Write down only important facts and statistics; names of people, places, and things that you can use in your writing; and quotations from authorities on your subject. Be sure to use your own words. Never copy material word-for-word unless you use quotation marks to indicate you are using the author's exact words. (See Chapter 15 for a detailed treatment of paraphrase and quotation.)
5. **Select appropriate quotations.** Select quotations that sum up an author's point of view, emphasize or illustrate an important point you want to make, or use memorable and colorful language that throws light on the personality or motives of an author. Do not select a quotation that you could easily paraphrase.

EXERCISE 16-3 Processing Information

Directions: *Make an outline with three or four points for the topic you are investigating in the space provided. Then, using the guidelines for taking notes, process the information from one of your sources using the note cards provided.*

Source: Nicholson, Robert, "A Lose-Lose Situation" I.
Environment

Notes: Use of plastic bottles has increased. Recent report of 23.4 billion bottles sold annually in U.S.

42.10 (December 2000) accessed 13 Apr. 2007 <http://find.galegroup.com>

Source: Nicholson, Robert, "A Lose-Lose Situation" II.
Environment

Notes: Actual recycling of plastic bottles is down from 48 percent to 35 percent

42.10 (December 2000) accessed 13 Apr. 2007 <http://find.galegroup.com>

FIGURE 16-2 Numbered Note Cards for Different Outline Points

The student uses separate cards for these notes because they provide facts and statistics related to different points on his outline.

I. ______________________________

II. ______________________________

III. ______________________________

IV. ______________________________

Source:

Notes:

Integrate Sources

To integrate your reading into your work, you should cite your sources by name in your paper and, when appropriate, include in-text citations.

In-Text Citations

An **in-text citation** provides information about your source. You should provide an in-text citation for information in these situations:

- When you use a complete or partial quotation from a source.
- When you refer to facts, statistics, or paraphrased information that can only be found in one specific source.

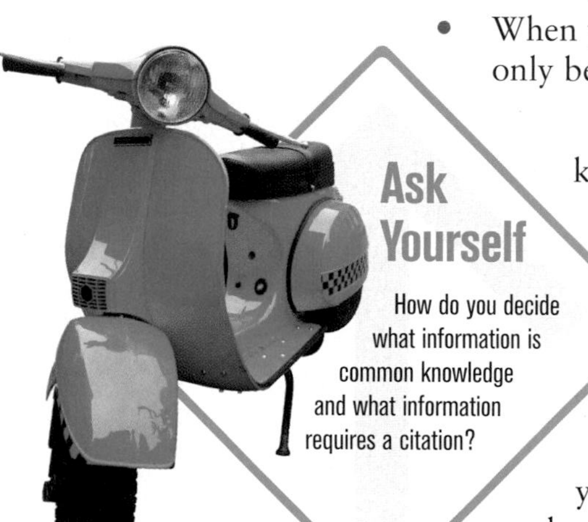

Ask
Yourself
How do you decide what information is common knowledge and what information requires a citation?

For information that is widely known—thought of as common knowledge—there is no need for an in-text citation. For example, it is widely known that plastic water bottles have replaced glass for many beverages and that bottled water consumption has increased dramatically in the past ten years. There is no need to use an in-text citation to acknowledge a source that mentions these facts. In contrast, the fact that Californians lose $26 million a year on unredeemed plastic bottles is information you might find in only one source; consequently, you need an in-text citation to tell your reader where you found that information. If you have any doubt about whether information is common knowledge, it is best to use an in-text citation to indicate where you found it.

You should provide an in-text citation immediately after any quotation, fact, or statistic that appears in your paper. The citation should be placed in parentheses at the end of the sentence where the information appears. Place the period *after* the in-text citation. The information you include in your in-text citation depends on the type of publication you cite and on how you identify the source in your writing.

Author name(s). For both traditional and electronic sources for which you have the author's name, include the last name in the in-text citation *unless* you refer to the author by name prior to the information you are citing (in which case only include the page number/s).

> *Waste News* suggests that Californians lose $26 million a year on unredeemed plastic bottles. That is, the consumer pays the deposit and the bottle is never returned (Johnson 1).

The student integrates an important statistic into her essay.

She cites the author's last name and the relevant page number in her in-text citation.

Titles. If there is no author listed for a source, include the entire title (if it is short) or a shortened version before the page number in your in-text citation, *unless* you have already mentioned it in the sentence (in which case only include the page number/s).

> In Mexico, polyethylene terephthalate (PET) plastic bottles are fast replacing glass and metal. Producers hope the technology is soon available for packaging beer in plastic ("Resins" 40).

This in-text citation indicates a source, but no author or title is given. There is no page number shown, which means this is an Internet source.

Page numbers. For traditional print sources, such as books and magazines, that have page numbers, include the specific page number(s) where the information (fact, statistic, quotation) you are citing can be found. If the author and title of the work being cited are both included in the sentence, only the page number(s) should be included in the citation.

> In his article in *Environment* magazine, Robert Nicholson reports, "Plastic bottles have to be sorted by color and type of resin, and all extraneous materials have to be removed; in many cases, these processes have to be done by hand" (6).

The student integrates a complete quotation into her essay.

On first reference to this source, the student uses the author's full name; therefore, she only includes the page number in parentheses.

Many Web sites do not use page numbers; however, if they do, include the page number in your citation. If the site uses paragraph numbers, include them, preceded by *para.* or *paras.* (Brown paras. 5-14).

Introducing Quotations

Practice using a variety of verbs to introduce your sources: *says, reports, states, explains, argues, observes*. The more variation you use when you set up your quotations, the smoother the integration process.

> Darryl Young, from the California Department of Conservation, <u>notes</u> that plastic beverage bottles have become "as common as a cell phone" (qtd in Johnson 1).

The student integrates a partial quotation into her essay. She uses the authority's full name; "qtd in Johnson" in the in-text citation indicates Johnson used this quotation in his article.

Here are a couple of other ways she could integrate the quotation:

> Darryl Young, from the California Department of Conservation, <u>points out</u> that plastic beverage bottles have become "as common as a cell phone" (qtd in Johnson 1).

Darryl Young, from the California Department of Conservation, indicates that plastic beverage bottles have become "as common as a cell phone" (qtd in Johnson 1).

Be sure to distinguish between partial and complete quotations, observing the rules for capitalization and punctuation. (See Chapter 15 for additional information on quotations.)

Complete Quotation

The student uses only the author's last name because she has already referred to him earlier in her paper.

Nicholson points out, "Plastic bottles have to be sorted by color and type of resin, and all extraneous materials have to be removed; in many cases, these processes have to be done by hand" (6).

Partial Quotation

The student refers to the name of the magazine to set up this quotation. In parentheses, she cites the last name of the author.

Moreover, according to *Look Japan,* we are now at a point where PET bottles can be made from recycled plastic, which "will decrease waste volume and reduce consumption of the petroleum resources used to make PET plastic" (Yoshihiro 24).

In your citations, provide only enough information to help your reader clearly identify your source. Do not include the names of publishing companies or Internet addresses. Save this information for your list of works cited.

DOCUMENT SOURCES

Once known as the bibliography, the works cited section of your paper provides the reader with publication information. Listing your sources is a matter of academic honesty. When you process information, you must take care not to plagiarize. When you integrate sources into your essay, you should tell your reader your sources of information. Include only those sources you used for facts and statistics, details on people and places related to your topic, and quotations. How you document your sources depends on the academic discipline of the course for which you write the paper.

In social science courses you are likely to use guidelines published by the American Psychological Association (APA). In humanities courses, including English, you will use guidelines published by the Modern Language Association (MLA). The Modern Language Association's *MLA Handbook for Writers of Research Papers,* sixth edition, is a comprehensive treatment of documentation issues (the seventh edition will be available in the spring of 2009). You can also find information on MLA guidelines online at many university writing center websites, such as Purdue's Online Writing Lab (OWL): http://owl.english.purdue.edu/owl.

The following guidelines for MLA style are based on the *MLA Style Manual and Guide to Scholarly Publishing,* third edition (2008).

GENERAL GUIDELINES FOR CITING SOURCES

According to MLA guidelines, your works cited list should be organized in the following way:

- List sources in alphabetical order by author's last name; or, if there is no author given, list alphabetically by the first word of the title.
- Double-space within and between all entries.
- Indent the second line and all subsequent lines for each entry.
- Include specific publication information according to the type of source you have used.

Cite Different Types of Sources

How you cite a source depends on the kind of source it is. There are traditional sources, such as newspaper articles, magazine articles, professional journal articles, and books. There are electronic sources like Web sites and listservs, and there are articles retrieved from a service, such as InfoTrac. Here are examples of the most common sources you will use. After each description of the form is an example of an actual source.

Newspaper

Author(s). "Title of Article." *Name of Newspaper* Date: Section Page. Medium of Publication.

Glater, Jonathon D., and Karen W. Arenson. "Lenders Sought Edge Against U.S. in Student Loan." *New York Times* 15 Apr. 2007: A1+. Print.

For sources with more than one author, the source is alphabetized by the last name of the first author; all other authors are first name first.

Magazine

Author(s). "Title of Article." *Title of Source* Date: Pages. Medium of Publication.

Fowles, Jib. "The Whipping Boy." *Reason* Mar. 2001: 27. Print.

Titles of articles are surrounded by quotation marks; names of magazines are in italics or underlined.

Book by One Author

Author. *Title of Book*. City: Publisher, Date of Publication. Medium of Publication.

Friedman, Thomas. *The World Is Flat: A Brief History of the Twenty-First Century*. New York: Farrar, Straus and Giroux, 2006. Print.

Books by Two or Three Authors

Levitt, Stephen D., and Steven J. Dubner. *Freakonomics: A Rogue Economist Explores the Hidden Side of Everything.* New York: HarperCollins Publishers. 2005. Print.

Book by More than Three Authors

Belenky, Mary Field, et al. *Women's Ways of Knowing.* New York: Basic Books, 1986. Print.

Two or More Books by the Same Author

Three typed hyphens are used to replace the same author's name in the second citation.

Friedman, Thomas. *The World Is Flat: A Brief History of the Twenty-first Century.* New York: Farrar, Straus and Giroux. 2006. Print.

---. *Hot, Flat, and Crowded: Why We Need a Green Revolution—And How It Can Renew America.* New York: Farrar, Straus and Giroux. 2008. Print.

Article from Anthology

Author. "Title of Article." *Title of Anthology.* Ed. Name of Editor. Edition Number. City: Publisher, Date of Publication. Page(s). Medium of Publication.

White, E. B. "Once More to the Lake." *The Bedford Reader.* Ed. X. J. Kennedy, et al. 6th ed. New York: St. Martin's Press, 1994: 120-26. Print.

Web Site Article that Only Appears Online

An article for which no author is given is alphabetized by the first word of the title.

Use *N.p.* if no information on publisher and *n.d.* if there is no date of publication.

Author(s). "Title of Article." *Title of Web Site.* Name of Publisher. Date of Publication. Medium of Publication. Date of Access.

"'It's Just Harmless Entertainment.' Oh Really?" *Parents Television Council.* Parents Television Council. n.d. Web. 21 Oct. 2008.

Print Article Accessed Via Internet

Author(s). "Title of the Article." *Magazine Title* Year of Publication: page number(s). *Title of Web Site/Database.* Medium of Publication. Date of Access.

"Resin: Opportunities Downstream." *Chemical Week* 29 Mar. 2006: 40(1). *Academic OneFile.* Web. 19 Oct. 2008.

EXERCISE 16-4 Integrating and Documenting Sources

Directions: *Read the following essay and identify the student's use of source material in the essay. Then respond to the questions that follow.*

ASSIGNMENT Does TV pose a real threat to young people? Drawing upon research, defend your viewpoint on this issue.

Pothin 1

Randy Pothin
Prof Toma
Soc 188
November 16, 2008

Trouble with the Tube

They watch in the morning. Then they come home and watch after school. Don't forget every single night. Some children even watch TV in bed. All this television cannot be good for children. They could be reading or playing outside, exercising their imaginations, doing anything besides sitting there like zombies or couch potatoes watching a show they have already seen twenty-five times. Nevertheless, that's the way it is nowadays. TV is a negative fact of life, impacting education, health, and behavior.

One problem with TV is how much time it takes away from schoolwork. According to the Parents Television Council, a group of over 800,000 parents who would like to improve the quality of television, the average American kid watches twenty-five hours of television a week and plays video games for seven hours. It is hard to see how young people can find time to do any schoolwork. Consider the average eleventh grader who is having a hard time in her classes. She does all of her homework sitting in front of the TV. Some nights she may not do any homework at all because she is watching *Friends* reruns. There is only one solution: turn off the TV.

Another problem with TV is its impact on children's health. The physical ramifications of a sedentary lifestyle are enormous and not always obvious until a health crisis occurs. Type II Diabetes in children, caused by poor eating habits, too much fast food, and too little physical activity, is at an all time high. High-blood pressure is also on the rise in children, teenagers, and young adults. According to *Pediatric News,* "Adolescents who had television sets in their bedrooms had less physical activity, poorer dietary habits, and worse school performance than did adolescents without bedroom TVs" (Walsh). As little as an hour each day of moderate physical activity reduces the risk of these health issues substantially. However, many young people do not find time for even this small amount of exercise.

Yet another problem with TV is sex and violence. Sex sells. Evidently so does violence. That's what people want to see. The Parents Television Council reports that by eighteen years of age, the average American child has seen over 10,000 murders and 200,000 acts of violence on TV. Not all acts of violence kids see on TV are imaginary. Some are real, too real, and must have an impact. Surely if kids see violence, they become violent. Jib Fowles, writing for *Reason* magazine, points out that television's "sinister reputation lives on," even though there is no evidence that it actually causes kids to be aggressive (27). He may be right, but what about copy-cat crime? The

The student begins with specific details.

THESIS STATEMENT
The writer puts the thesis statement at the end of the introduction.

TOPIC SENTENCE
The student begins with a focused topic sentence.
He cites statistical information from a website.

He ends his paragraph with an emphatic plea.

TOPIC SENTENCE
Use of the transition term "another" moves the reader smoothly to the next major point of the essay.

He presents more statistical information.

PARTIAL QUOTATION
Before presenting this opposing viewpoint, the student refers to the source by full name. The page number in the in-text citation indicates this is a multipage article in a traditional print source.

The student repeats "turn it off," echoing the solution posed at the end of the preceding paragraph.

"One thing is true" signals the paper is coming to a close. The conclusion paragraph summarizes content from the essay.

most horrific example is the massacre at Columbine. After it, there were more school shootings. Where do kids get these ideas from if not from television? Then there are young people dealing drugs and shooting each other up in the streets. That probably wouldn't be happening if it weren't for TV. TV glamorizes violence. Turn it off.

One thing is true: American children are fatter now than they have ever been before, and it is partially the fault of TV. The U.S. may be dumber than it used to be, again, the fault of TV. And it is more violent, probably at least partially the fault of TV. There is a bumper sticker going around on some cars. "Kill your TV," it says. It's a violent solution, but maybe that is exactly what we should do. We would be better off without TV, or at least with less of it. Turn it off.

Works Cited

Fowles, Jib. "The Whipping Boy." *Reason* Mar. 2001: 27-28. Print.

Grossman, Dave, and Gloria DeGaetano. *Stop Teaching Our Kids to Kill: A Call to Action Against TV, Movie, and Video Game Violence.* New York: Crown, 1999. Print.

"'It's Just Harmless Entertainment.' Oh Really?" *Parents Television Council.* Parents Television Council. n.d. Web. 21 Oct. 2008.

Walsh, Nancy. "Teens' Bedroom TVs May Hurt Activity Level, Diet, Grades." *Pediatric News.* 42.5 (2008): 24. *Academic OneFile.* Web. 31 Oct. 2008.

DISCUSSION QUESTIONS Answers will vary.

1. What purpose does the student's source material serve in this paper?

____

____

2. Why is there no in-text citation for the Parents Television Council?

____

____

3. Does the list of works cited accurately reflect the works cited in the essay?

____

____

EXERCISE 16-5 Drafting and Revising Your Documented Essay

Directions: *Using your tentative outline as a guide (Exercise 16-3), write a draft of your documented essay. Integrate information from your research into the essay, including in-text citations as needed to document your sources. Provide a list of works cited. When you finish your draft, use the checklist below to focus your work revising and editing your essay.*

DOCUMENTED ESSAY CHECKLIST

_____ My essay has an introduction, body, and conclusion.

_____ My thesis is focused.

_____ My body paragraphs have focused topic sentences and specific supporting details.

_____ I repeat key words and use transition words and sentences.

_____ My conclusion brings the essay to a close.

_____ I use facts and statistics, cases and examples, and quotations from my reading.

_____ Where appropriate, I provide in-text citations for the sources I use.

_____ I include a list of works cited in line with MLA guidelines.

_____ I have proofread my paper for spelling, capitalization, common errors, and sentence variety.

Gateway

TOPIC 13: Compiling a Works Cited Page (MLA) and a Reference Page (APA)
www.mhhe.com/goingplaces

GOING PLACES

GETTING THE MOST MILEAGE FROM TIMED WRITING

The Heat Is On

Pressure. We have all felt it. There is intensity in the air, a sense of urgency, and a lump in your throat. In an academic setting, the greatest pressure arrives at exam time, though regular quizzes and in-class writing may constantly keep you on your toes. And, fortunately or unfortunately, this stress does not end with graduation. Throughout life, you will face high-stakes, time-sensitive situations, and the sooner you learn to cope with such scenarios, the better. If you can write a well-crafted essay in the pressure cooker of a classroom, you will find it that much easier to deal with "pressurized" situations in your nonacademic life. It is 11:00 p.m. on April 15, and you suddenly realize you forgot to file your taxes—no problem, right?

DISCUSSION

Turn and talk to a classmate about writing under pressure—a specific time when you performed (or did not perform) well under pressure. When and where? What subject? How did you prepare for the writing?

Showing What You Know

Instructors cannot grade you on what you know; it is what you can *show* you know that counts. No matter how well prepared you are, if you write an incoherent, threadbare essay exam, your instructor will likely assume that your knowledge and ideas are just as incoherent and threadbare. Bridging the gap between what you have learned and what you can write is an essential academic skill. Learning to write an effective exam essay is an important move toward closing this gap. The techniques you use to master the essay exam will help you surmount other academic tasks as well.

BRAINSTORM

Brainstorm a list of steps to prepare for writing under pressure. What can you do at home to prepare in advance? What can you do in the classroom, as you write, that will help you be successful?

Working Against the Deadline

The working world is filled with deadlines. Clients need answers, projects must be submitted, bosses demand reports . . . and all this work has to be completed by a specific time on a particular day. Even the best-prepared professionals sometimes find themselves in the deadline crunch, with work that needs to be done yesterday. Unfortunately, time pressure is never an excuse for lack of quality. Mastering the ability to work well in a limited amount of time will benefit you greatly in any work setting. If you can approach a time-sensitive situation calmly and work rationally toward its conclusion, you will be a valuable contributor to whatever field you work in.

DISCUSSION

Turn and talk to a classmate about working under pressure on the job. How do you maintain your composure and guarantee you do your best work?

Writing in Class: Short Answer and Essay Tests

CHAPTER 17

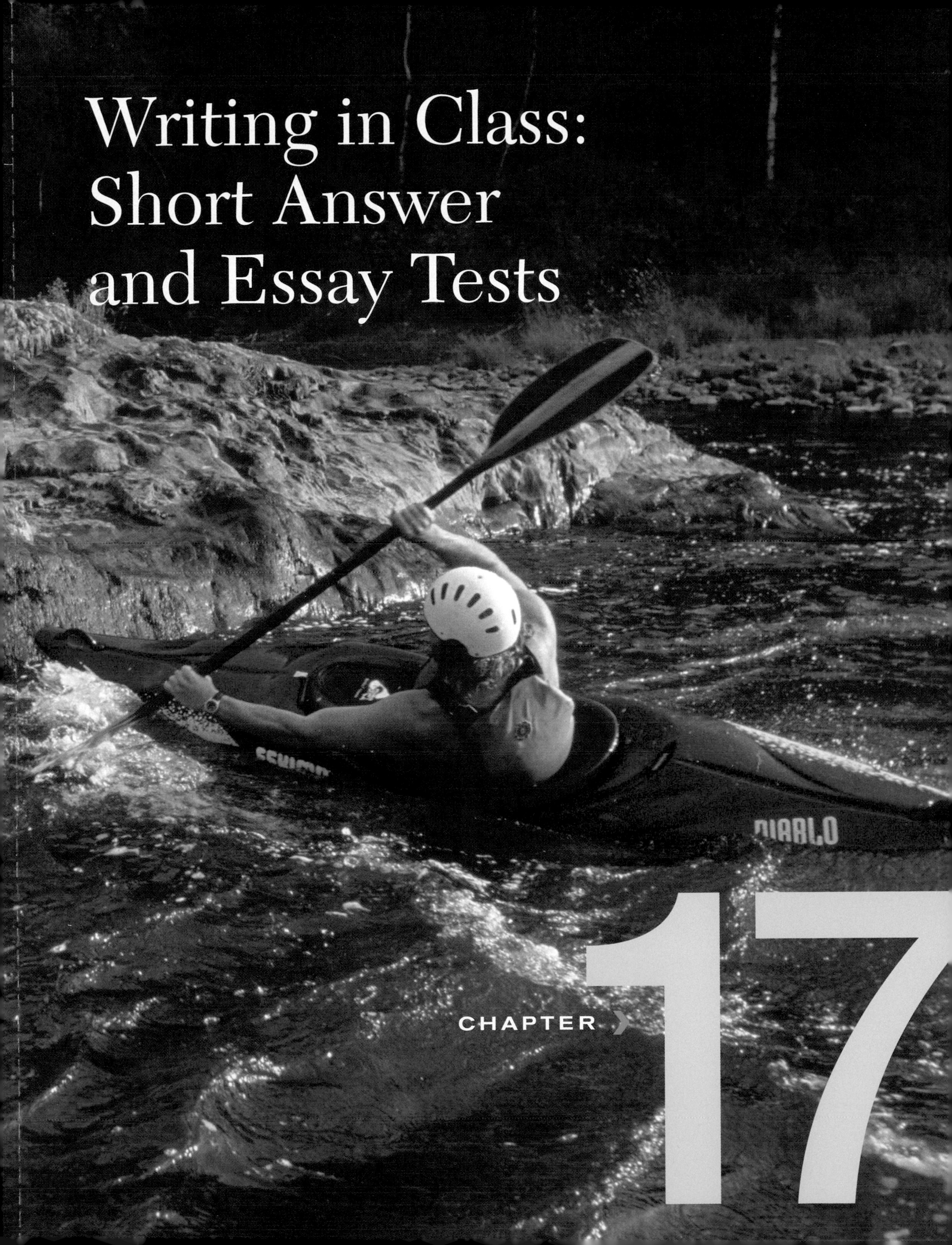

CHAPTER OVERVIEW

- THE IN-CLASS ESSAY AT A GLANCE
- ELEMENTS OF IN-CLASS WRITING
- TYPES OF IN-CLASS WRITING
  - Sentence-Length Short Answers
  - Paragraph-Length, Short Essay Answers
  - Essay-Length Answers
  - How to Prepare for In-Class Writing

THINK FIRST

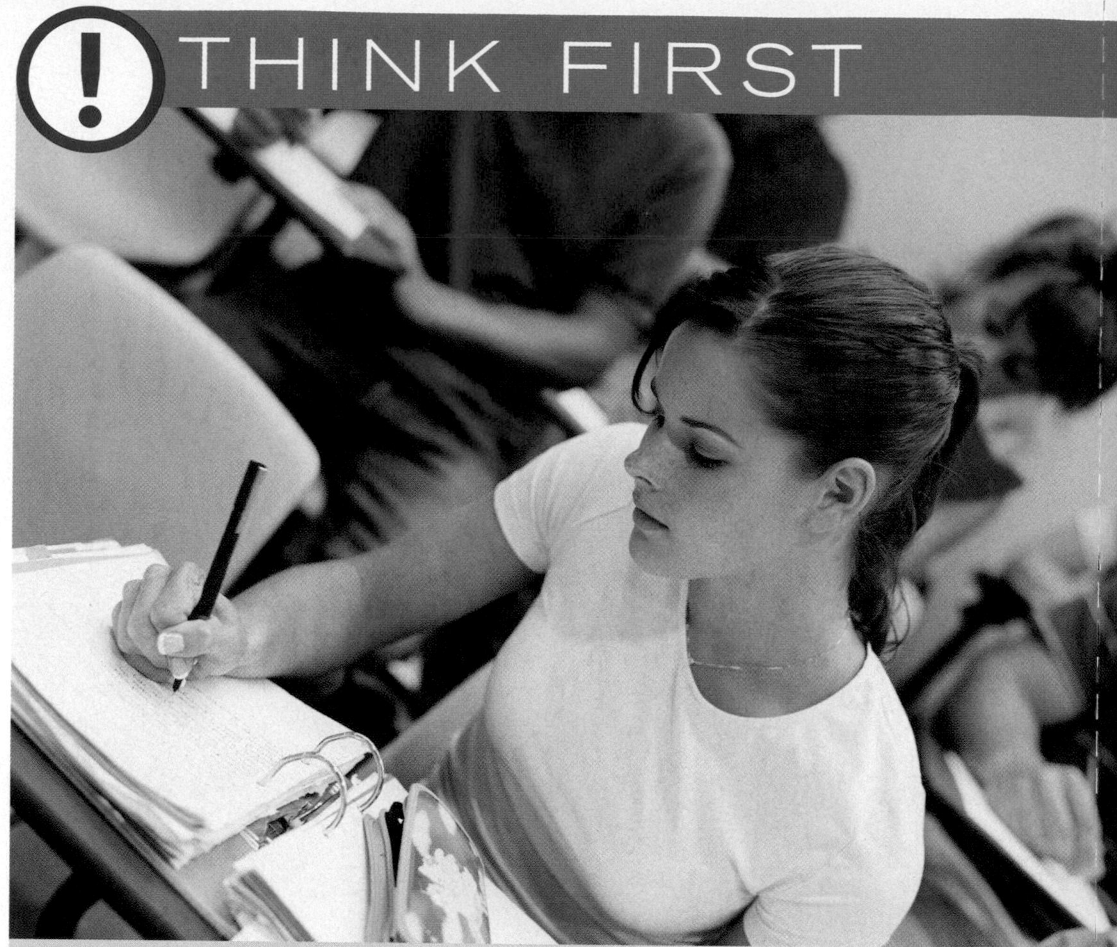

Write a paragraph discussing what you know about studying for and writing in-class exams. Cite and discuss specific classes and the instructors who provided you with this instruction. Organize your paragraph by looking first at those ideas and strategies that are not as useful and then move to more useful ones.

At a Glance

THE IN-CLASS ESSAY AT A GLANCE

Like the paragraphs and essays you have practiced writing in this course, effective in-class writing includes topic sentences, supporting details, and transitions to make connections within and across paragraphs. You do not have a lot of time, so in-class writing gets to the point. Introductions and conclusions are held to a minimum. If you want to persuade your instructor that you know the content, you have to make detailed references to the material covered in your answer. Details matter. Finally, in-class writing is usually not personal in focus. Unless you are specifically asked to talk about yourself, it is a good idea to maintain a steady focus on the question and how it relates to course content.

The In-Class Essay at a Glance

ASSIGNMENT Discuss the research we have reviewed on homework in this unit of study. What is its connection to learning and academic achievement? How important is age and grade level? Please relate your answer to your own preparation for college. You may use notes during the exam period.

The research on the role of homework in academic achievement has been contradictory; some studies say homework improves learning and achievement; others caution against assigning too much homework, especially drills.

Studies support two conflicting views of homework's role in learning and academic achievement. **Some of the most interesting research** comes from two Penn State researchers. In the article "Too Much Homework" the researchers state that many instructors use homework as a drill for memorization. Homework should be used for helping students understand and comprehend course content. If homework is all drill and repetition, that is not good. **On the other hand,** in the *Atlantic Monthly* study, Jonathon Rauch argues that homework is the best way of increasing "time on task." According to his research, American students spend far less time doing homework than students in other countries. Rauch cites the National Assessment of Educational Progress, which indicates that American seventeen-year-olds do less than one hour of homework each night. Those

THESIS STATEMENT
The writer provides a general overview of her response to the assignment.

TOPIC SENTENCE
The writer echoes key terms from the essay question.

SUPPORTING DETAILS
The student refers to specific articles by title. The articles describe research on her subject. She reports what they say.

ORDER AND TRANSITIONS
She uses a transition phrase to show she is shifting to a contrasting view of homework.

In addition to summarizing major points, the student uses a short quotation to demonstrate her knowledge of the material.

students who do have homework learn more and achieve more. Harris Cooper, an educational psychologist says, "The effect of homework can be impressive." Homework, according to these experts, is valuable, but there are limits.

TOPIC SENTENCE
The student goes immediately to the next major point in the assignment.

SUPPORTING DETAILS
The student draws on other research the class has covered, demonstrating she has mastered the content.

TRANSITION
This sentence allows the student to switch to a contrasting view.

In addition to summarizing major points, the student uses a short quotation to demonstrate her knowledge of the material.

Studies also show that age or grade level should be taken into consideration when homework is assigned. In the article "Yes, Johnny, Homework Is Important" researchers from the American Psychological Association mention that doing homework in lower grades is important, helping students develop study skills, even though the benefits of study at home might not show immediately. **However,** homework can also have a negative effect on younger students. Too much homework can result in unfavorable attitudes toward school in lower grades. Rauch also points out this negative effect. He writes, "For young children homework appears not to be particularly helpful." It can turn young kids off to learning. The problem is worse in homes in which parents cannot or do not help young children with homework. If parents do not make homework come first, students may think that it is not that important and not complete their assignments. Worse, in those homes where parents cannot help, children may associate homework with frustration and anger. For homework to be effective, teachers have to assign the right amount. Further, if they communicate well with parents, homework is more likely to improve academic achievement.

TOPIC SENTENCE
In this part of her answer, the student shifts to first person, talking about herself. This paragraph addresses the third part of the essay question.

Evidently the National Assessment of Educational Progress did not talk to my school; at my high school, homework was a given, and there was a lot of it. The school offered advanced placement courses, which always had college levels of homework. On a regular basis, I would come home with about four to five hours a night needed for studying and doing homework. It was a stressful time then, but I learned about time management. Now I am in college, and I see that I was well prepared by my high school for the demands of college.

PEER CONVERSATION

DISCUSSION QUESTIONS

1. How would you describe the introduction of this essay?
2. This essay is a mixture of fact and opinion. Where do you see the student expressing her opinion?
3. Reread the assignment. How is the organization of the essay based on the assignment?

ELEMENTS OF IN-CLASS WRITING

Because in-class writing is timed, it is important to quickly determine the focus of the assignment and how much detail to provide in your answer.

- ***The assignment:*** An assignment may be a question, a series of questions, or a series of statements directing your attention to the focus of your writing. In the at-a-glance example in this chapter, the student responds to a series of statements.
- ***Topic sentences:*** Topic sentences echo key terms from the assignment. Assignments written as a series of questions or statements usually take multiple paragraphs to answer. In the at-a-glance example, the student writes a paragraph focusing on each specific part of the assignment.
- ***Specific details:*** An essay exam demonstrates how much you know about the subject matter in question. The answer you formulate to an essay question refers to facts, examples, proper names and dates, and important concepts covered by in-class learning and the textbook.

TYPES OF IN-CLASS WRITING

In-class writing is widely used to evaluate learning in college classes. While the content may vary from class to class, most instructors have similar expectations. They look for answers written in complete sentences. They also look for detailed answers that show you have paid attention in class and retained important course content. You will encounter in-class writing that falls into three categories:

- Sentence-length short answers
- Paragraph-length short answers
- Essay-length answers

Sentence-Length Short Answers

You will often use sentence-length short answers for definitions. Answers should be formulated in complete sentences. An effective sentence-length definition begins with the term to be defined, contains a present-tense linking verb (for example, *is* and *are*), and ends with an elaborated idea. Here are two responses in which a student is asked to define the term *precipitation*.

Inadequate Definition

> Precipitation—rain.

Satisfactory Definition

> Precipitation *is* any form of water or moisture that condenses in the upper atmosphere and falls to earth, including snow, sleet, rain, mist, and dew.

The first definition is incomplete—both in what it says about precipitation and how it is formulated. In contrast, the second definition is detailed and specific. It is also a complete sentence.

The form of an effective short-answer definition varies. For the sake of practice, use this template, which shows you how to elaborate on a this-is-that statement:

This-Is-That Statement

Alliteration is a literary device.

Education is a process.

This-Is-That Statement + Elaboration

Alliteration is a literary device in which two or more consecutive words begin with the same consonant.

Education is a process that imparts a body of knowledge and trains the minds of students.

EXERCISE 17-1 Sentence-Length Short Answers

Directions: *Write definitions for the following terms using the examples above as templates. Consult a dictionary if necessary, but do not copy the definitions. Be sure to write in complete sentences.* Answers will vary.

1. ethics ______________________________

____

2. mitochondria ______________________________

____

3. collaboration ______________________________

____

4. activist ______________________________

____

5. latitude ______________________________

____

EXERCISE 17-2 Defining Key Terms in Your Courses

Directions: *Select important terms from another course (or courses) you are taking and define them on a piece of paper. If necessary, use study guides as well* *as textbooks from your courses to find relevant ideas and details to help you formulate your definitions. Use the same sentence structure you practiced in Exercise 17-1.*

Paragraph-Length, Short Essay Answers

Paragraph-length, short essay answers will be evaluated on three qualities: focus, number and relevance of supporting details, and grammatical and mechanical correctness. To focus your paragraph-length answer, identify the key terms in the question. Make those terms part of the topic sentence of your paragraph. Try to repeat the terms at least once in the paragraph-length answer.

Short Essay Question: State one drawback or problem with using the philosophy of utilitarianism.

Key Terms: one drawback, problem, philosophy of utilitarianism

Topic Sentence: One drawback to using the philosophy of utilitarianism is that actions or ways of life that have no observable use or effect cannot be evaluated as good.

In Part II, you learned about the different patterns of organization and how to write effective paragraphs using them. Read questions carefully to see if they ask for answers related to a specific pattern—for instance, examples, causes or effects, or a comparison of two ideas. (See Table 17-1 for

TABLE 17.1

PATTERNS OF ORGANIZATION AND TEST QUESTIONS

Pattern of Organization	Test Question Language to Notice
Description	*Describe . . .*
Example	*Discuss the two (three, four . . .) main . . .*
Narration	*Tell what happened when . . .*
Process	*Explain how . . .*
Classification	*What types of . . .*
Cause and effect	*Explain why . . .* *What were the consequences of . . .*
Comparison and contrast	*How is . . . similar to . . .* *How does . . . differ from . . .* *How has . . . changed . . .*
Definition	*Define . . .*
Argument	*Make a case for . . .* *State your opinion . . .*

language that indicates which pattern of organization you should use when answering a specific question.) If the question asks you to discuss the three main consequences of the New Deal, you should provide an answer with three main points. Moreover, your discussion of the three points should have roughly equal emphasis. For a 15-point question, you can assume that each of the main points in your answer is worth 5 points.

Short Essay Question: Explain three ways in which mass media acts as an agent of gender socialization during childhood.

Key Terms: three ways, mass media, gender socialization, childhood

Topic Sentence: The mass media acts as an agent of gender socialization during childhood in three important ways.

Pattern of Organization: illustration and example

Finally, always use proper grammar and mechanics in any writing you do in college. You may think, "Well, this is not an English class, so how I write is not as important as what I write." Nothing could be further from the truth. All your college instructors care about the way you write. You will never be criticized for writing clear sentences and using correct grammar. On the contrary, using proper grammar and mechanics will add points to your score, while poorly edited writing will lead to points being deducted.

EXERCISE 17-3 Short Essay Answers

Directions: *Underline the key terms in the following short essay questions and indicate what pattern of organization you would use in your answers to them.*

1. What were some of John Quincy Adams's concerns in his deliberations on the *Amistad*?

Pattern of Organization: example

2. In what way is the gene "selfish" in Dawkins's view? What is the primary consequence of the gene being selfish?

Pattern of Organization: example, cause and effect

3. Explain how Steinbeck did both primary and secondary research as he prepared to write *The Grapes of Wrath.*

Pattern of Organization: process

4. Describe two general differences between Puritan and Native American societies.

Pattern of Organization: comparison and contrast

5. Explain three challenges in studying past Native American culture and family life.

Pattern of Organization: example

Essay-Length Answers

On an essay test, you will be evaluated on your essay's focus, inclusion of supporting details, and mechanical and grammatical correctness. You may use more than one pattern of organization as you formulate your answer. If you do not know what the essay question will be in advance, prepare for the test by anticipating possible questions. (See the list of tips for test preparation on page 395.)

Here are some suggestions for what to do at the beginning and during an essay exam to provide the best possible answers.

At the Beginning of an Essay Test

1. Underline key terms in the essay question.
2. Drawing on your memory of the material you have studied, or a pretest outline you made, list key terms, concepts, and details from the course content that you must mention in your essay.
3. Identify patterns of organization that will help you organize and focus your answers.

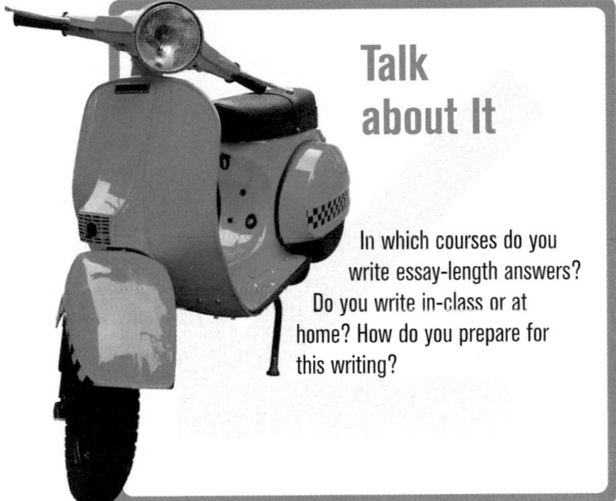

Talk about It

In which courses do you write essay-length answers? Do you write in-class or at home? How do you prepare for this writing?

While Writing Your Essay Answer

1. Include key terms from the test question in your first sentence.
2. Get to the point. Avoid introduction paragraphs and wordy preludes.
3. When ideas occur to you as you write, make quick changes and additions to your outline.
4. Place check marks in the margin of your paper to signal those areas that require attention during the editing phase of your writing.
5. Use the pattern of organization called for in the question. If you are asked to cite examples, be sure to explain each example using relevant details. If you are asked to discuss causes and effects, be sure to use those key terms and provide sufficient elaboration.
6. Keep an eye on your outline. Check off key details you have integrated into the essay; make a point of mentioning additional key terms, concepts, and details from the course in your answer.
7. Leave enough time at the end of the exam period for proofreading. Look for check marks you have made in the margin. Erase or lightly cross out misspelled words or grammatical errors and make corrections. Unless you are told otherwise, do not copy your paper over.

EXERCISE 17-4 **Essay-Length Answers**

Directions: *Read the following essay questions and underline the key terms in each. Indicate what pattern of organization you would use in answering each question and how many paragraphs you would need for a detailed answer. (***Suggestion:*** Plan to write one or two paragraphs for each key term in the test question.)*

EXAMPLE

American History Test Question: Explain the concept of "impressments" and its consequences in U.S. and British relations.

Pattern(s) of Organization: definition, cause and effect

Number of Paragraphs: one on impressment, two on consequences for U.S.-British relations

1. What were your perceptions of geography before signing up for this class? Has your initial view of geography changed? If so, how and why? What do you see as the value of utilizing geography's approach to address contemporary problems and issues?

Pattern(s) of Organization: comparison and contrast, cause and effect, example

Number of Paragraphs: three to four paragraphs minimum

2. Define the "shadow" side of the personality. Use Goffman's ideas on the "presentation of self" to explain how the shadow side develops. Discuss one of your shadow traits and use Goffman's ideas to explain how it developed.

Pattern(s) of Organization: definition, process, example

Number of Paragraphs: three to four paragraphs minimum

3. Relate the three characteristics of tragedy we discussed in class to Arthur Miller's *Death of a Salesman*. What, in your opinion, makes this a peculiarly American tragedy? In your answer, refer to at least three characters in detail.

Pattern(s) of Organization: argument, example

Number of Paragraphs: three to four paragraphs minimum

EXERCISE 17-5 In-Class Writing in Your College Courses

PEER CONVERSATION

Directions: *Survey members of your class for the types of writing they have done on tests. If possible, collect specific questions for four or five tests. Analyze the language of each test question and circle the type of answer required (sentence, paragraph, or essay), list the key terms, recommend the best thinking and writing strategies for answering the question, and estimate the number of paragraphs (if an essay) required to answer it.*

How to Prepare for In-Class Writing

Students who perform well writing in class have a reliable preparation process. Preparation consists of both general and specific actions. On the day of the test, you should be physically and mentally ready to do your best work. Here are some tips for general preparation. Use these for any test situation.

GENERAL TIPS FOR TEST PREPARATION

- Get a good night's rest.
- Eat a good breakfast.
- Find out when and where the exam is, how long it will be, what its value is in your overall grade in the class.
- Arrive early, with the necessary materials (pencil, pen, paper, dictionary).
- Read all the directions carefully.
- Budget your time properly based on the number of questions and the point values of questions.

Along with being physically and mentally ready, it is important to study the material you will be tested on to the best of your ability. Most instructors indicate what will be emphasized in their exams. As they lecture, they may explicitly state, "this material will be on the exam," or they may underscore important themes through repetition, notes and outlines on the board, and the use of PowerPoint presentations. Take full advantage of all these clues to what will be on the exam. There are also a number of specific actions you can take to get ready for a test.

SPECIFIC TIPS FOR TEST PREPARATION

- Review all notes you took during lectures and class discussions.
- Review the course syllabus and outline, circling unit titles and themes.
- Review reading material, particularly any study guides provided by the textbook.
- Review previous quizzes and tests.
- Review any annotations you made when you read the textbook.
- Generate possible questions based on the themes and topics your instructor places most emphasis on in class and lectures.
- Formulate answers to possible questions. Think of a thesis statement, identify the main points that support it, write an outline, and practice drafting an answer. Doing so will help you remember information and make it easier for you to write under pressure.

The Simple Sentence

CHAPTER OVERVIEW

- An Introduction to the Simple Sentence
- Find Subjects and Predicates
- The Subject
  - *Nouns*
  - *Pronouns*
  - *Gerunds*
  - *Tips to Find the Simple Subject*
  - *Prepositional Phrases*
  - *Questions and Commands*
- The Predicate
  - *Action Verbs*
  - *Linking Verbs*
  - *Helping Verbs and Verb Phrases*

The simple sentence is a building block for more sophisticated thinking and writing. Learning the grammar and mechanics of the simple sentence will enable you to write more complicated and effective sentences. Good writing begins with the simple sentence.

An Introduction to the Simple Sentence

A simple sentence expresses a complete thought. It makes a meaningful statement that another person can process and respond to.

MULTILINGUAL TIP
Typical word order in English is subject, verb, object. Do not omit the subject.

Awakened by the sound of gunfire in the distance.

Two blocks from our house is a park with a playground.

The first example does not express a complete idea. There is reference to gunfire, but nothing definitive is said about the gunfire. *Who was awakened? What happened?* The second example, in contrast, expresses a complete idea. The reader can process and respond to the statement. *That's interesting. Do you ever go to this park?*

EXERCISE 18-1 **The Sentence as Complete Idea**

Directions: *Write* CI *next to each of the following items that expresses a complete idea.*

_____ 1. Sparkling blue eyes with a dash of gold in the middle.

__CI__ 2. A look of pure distrust enveloped their cola-stained faces.

_____ 3. Girls and boys holding hands, most of them dancing, swaying back and forth to the music as if they were hypnotized.

__CI__ 4. We met back in November of 2000.

__CI__ 5. I was living life day by day, wondering what tomorrow would bring.

_____ 6. A normal day with many phases and challenges that await.

_____ 7. Every Friday on the eve of C-day as we called it.

__CI__ 8. We would go to Autozone to get materials for our job.

_____ 9. As I sit thinking back a couple years to my childhood days.

__CI__ 10. It seems like yesterday that we met.

Find Subjects and Predicates

A sentence contains two parts: a subject and a predicate. The **subject** is who or what a sentence is about. The **predicate** contains the verb and related words and phrases to express the action or state of being of the subject. In the example below, the subject of the sentence is underlined; the predicate is double-underlined.

MULTILINGUAL TIP
In a simple sentence, the subject usually comes before the predicate.

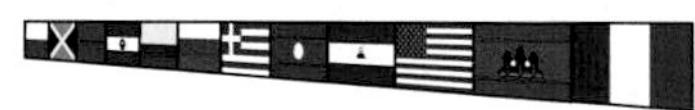

The entire **Wilson family** *drove* to the seashore on Sunday.

Usually the subject and predicate of a sentence can be reduced to one word each: the simple subject and the simple verb. The simple subject of the sentence is *family*, and the simple verb, or action, of the sentence is *drove*.

In the next example, the subject is underlined, the predicate double-underlined. The simple subject of this sentence is *hair*, and the simple verb, or action, of the sentence is *blew*.

Alice's long dark **hair** *blew* in the salty ocean breeze.

Hint: To find the verb in a sentence, look for the word that expresses action and has tense (places the sentence in the past, present, or future). For instance, in the preceding example, the verb *blew* can be written in different tenses: *blow, will blow, had blown*.

EXERCISE 18-2 Identifying the Complete Subject and Predicate

Directions: *Identify the subject and predicate in each of the following sentences. To find the verb, look for the word that expresses action or can be written in different tenses. Underline the complete subject; double-underline the complete predicate.*

1. The elderly woman with the funny hat walked her dog around the subdivision every morning.
2. Robert caught five salmon after getting skunked on his first day of fishing.
3. The ladies in the neighborhood swap ideas about gardening every year in April.
4. The county health department declared the food supply to be safe.
5. Scientists who study outer space no longer consider Pluto to be a planet.
6. Each student sketches the parts of the cell before writing a description of the lab activity.
7. Computer technology, more than any other consumer product, gets better and cheaper with every passing year.
8. Years ago auto manufacturers worried very little about alternative fuels and their possible use in the near future.
9. Dutch elm disease totally wiped out most of the trees in our community.
10. Mrs. Howard will join the bridal party later this evening.

The Subject

The subject of a sentence is usually found near the beginning of the sentence. The subject performs the action in the sentence or is the main focus of the sentence. The most common simple subjects to look for in a simple sentence are nouns, pronouns, and gerunds.

TYPES OF SUBJECTS		
Noun	person, place, thing, or idea	Unemployment is on everyone's mind these days.
Pronoun	a word taking the place of a noun	It has increased in the past sixteen months.
Gerund	a word for an activity, ending in *-ing*	Finding a good job is easier for those with a college degree.

Nouns

A **noun** names a person, place, thing, or idea, and it can be the subject of a sentence.

> The little **girl** on the plane *cried* through much of the flight.

This sentence has three nouns: *girl, plane,* and *flight.* The noun acting as subject comes near the beginning of the sentence. This sentence is primarily about the girl. She performed the action in the sentence. She cried. *Girl* is the simple subject of the sentence.

MULTILINGUAL TIP

Do not use subject and pronoun for the same grammatical function: "The little girl ~~she~~ cried through much of the flight."

Pronouns

Pronouns take the place of nouns or other pronouns.

TYPES OF PRONOUNS		
Personal Pronouns	**Indefinite Pronouns**	
I you she he we they	it all each few none any either neither something everything several	somebody someone anybody anyone everyone one

They eliminate endless repetition in our speaking and writing. Just as nouns can be the subject of a sentence, a pronoun replacing a noun can also be the subject of a sentence.

> The little girl on the plane cried through much of the flight.
>
> Near the end of the flight, she finally went to sleep.

In this example, the pronoun *she* substitutes for "the little girl" and acts as the subject of the second sentence. The little girl did something: She went to sleep. *She* is the subject of the second sentence.

Gerunds

A **gerund,** the *-ing* form of a verb, is the name of an activity. Activities such as running, reading, thinking, or stopping can also be the subject of a sentence.

> The little girl on the plane cried through much of the flight.
>
> Near the end of the flight, she finally went to sleep.
>
> Flying can be very difficult for small children.
>
> It can also be hard on people around them.

Here we see the gerund *flying* act as the subject of the third sentence. In that sentence, flying is what is being talked about.

How to Find the Simple Subject

The simple subject is the most important part of the complete subject. To identify the simple subject of a sentence, ask the following questions:

1. Who or what did the action?
2. What is being described?

The simple subject is usually a noun or pronoun. It is the doer of the action or the thing being described. The answers to these questions will be the simple subject of the sentence.

> The supervisor's **statements** about female employees *got him in a lot of trouble.*

Who or what did the action? Who or what is being described? The supervisor's *statements* did the action. They got the supervisor in trouble.

> The underground parking **structure** was *crammed* with construction equipment.

Who or what did the action? Who or what is being described? The underground parking structure is described as crammed. Therefore, the *structure* is the simple subject of the sentence.

EXERCISE 18-3 Identifying the Simple Subject

Directions: *Find the simple subjects in the following sentences. Write the one-word simple subject in the space provided. Then indicate whether it is a noun, pronoun, or gerund by circling the correct answer in the list.*

1. Offenders of whatever age and social class are promptly arrested and put in jail.

Offenders ________ are promptly arrested and put in jail.

(noun) pronoun gerund

2. They then pay a significant fine and are asked to attend classes designed to improve their behavior.

They ________ pay a significant fine and are asked to attend classes designed to improve their behavior.

noun (pronoun) gerund

3. Finding just the right electronic toys on the market today is a big headache for parents of small children at Christmastime.

Finding ________ is a big headache for parents of small children at Christmastime.

noun pronoun (gerund)

4. It takes hours of time and commitment.

It ________ takes hours of time and commitment.

noun (pronoun) gerund

5. Swimming across the English Channel was Alison Streeter's goal from a very early age.

Swimming ________ was Alison Streeter's goal from a very early age.

noun pronoun (gerund)

6. Hovering over the city, the storm clouds dumped five inches of rain on a community already suffering the effects of inclement weather.

Clouds ________ dumped five inches of rain on a community already suffering the effects of inclement weather.

(noun) pronoun gerund

7. Nobody at the meeting expected things to end with a resolution to change school policy in such a drastic way.

Nobody ________ expected things to end with a resolution to change school policy in such a drastic way.

noun (pronoun) gerund

8. The eccentric old gentleman living above the barber shop, a decorated World War II veteran and a gifted photographer, will exhibit his photos and talk about his life in the next college cultural activities event.

Gentleman ________ will exhibit his photos and talk about his life in the next college cultural activities event.

(noun) pronoun gerund

9. The living will, a document that expresses an individual's end-of-life wishes, can make a family's and a physician's decisions easier at difficult times.

Will ________ can make a family's and a physician's decisions easier at difficult times.

(noun) pronoun gerund

10. Sitting around swapping stories and generally taking it easy is my idea of well-spent holiday time.

Sitting ________ is my idea of well-spent holiday time.

noun pronoun (gerund)

Subjects and Prepositional Phrases

A prepositional phrase consists of a preposition and an object. The phrase provides information about time and place, stating the relationships between one noun and another. A list of common prepositions used at the beginning of prepositional phrases can be found in the box on page 403.

Do not confuse the object of the preposition with the simple subject of the sentence.

The **singer** *in the band* is still unavailable.

Here the prepositional phrase is "in the band": *in* is the preposition, "band" is the object. Ask, *Who or what did the action? Who or what is being described?* "Singer" is the thing being described; "in the band" describes the simple subject "singer."

The sentence states that the singer is unavailable. Note that the sentence does not say the band is unavailable. "Band" is part of the complete subject, but it is not the simple subject of the sentence. Here is another example:

> The **owner** *of the professional football team* will sell his interest to the highest bidder.

"Owner" is the subject. The owner will sell his interest. The prepositional phrase "of the professional football team" describes "owner." "Team" is not the subject. The team is not selling; the owner is selling.

COMMON PREPOSITIONS

about	above	across	after	against
along	among	around	at	before
behind	below	beneath	beside	between
beyond	but	by	despite	during
except	for	from	in	inside
into	like	near	of	off
on	onto	out	outside	over
past	since	through	throughout	till
to	toward	under	underneath	until
up	upon	with	within	without

EXERCISE 18-4 Simple Subjects and Prepositional Phrases

Directions: *Cross out the prepositional phrases and circle the simple subject in each of the following sentences.*

1. ~~For the next three weeks~~, science classes will meet ~~in temporary classrooms~~.
2. The piping plover population, ~~along with other beach-nesting birds~~, has been threatened ~~by cats and dogs~~.
3. The largest organ ~~in the body~~ is the skin.
4. Most salespeople ~~in the organization~~ go ~~on calls with their computers under their arms~~.
5. All rescue operations ~~except those involving the military~~ are halted ~~until further notice~~.
6. The study ~~of nutrition and its impact on health~~ deserves greater emphasis ~~in medical education~~.
7. Alcohol consumption ~~among high school students~~ is ~~on the rise~~.

Talk about It
Check your last paper. How many prepositional phrases did you use? What do you notice about prepositional phrases and punctuation?

8. ~~In the opinion of most health care professionals~~, a sedentary lifestyle is more dangerous ~~for your health~~ than smoking.

9. Investors, ~~in a state of shock over recent revelations~~, scrambled ~~for cell phones~~.

10. Readers ~~of detective fiction, along with assorted film buffs~~, showed up ~~for the book signing~~ early Saturday evening.

Subjects in Questions and Commands

To find the simple subject in a question, turn the question into a statement that answers the question.

Question: Why can't Bill stop smoking?

Statement: Bill can't stop smoking because he is nervous.

Simple Subject: Bill

Question: When will classes begin?

Statement: Classes will begin on August 23.

Simple Subject: Classes

In commands, the simple subject is always "you." It is understood that "you" is the subject, so it is not necessary to write "you" as the subject.

Look for the lost keys.

This is a command, also known as an imperative. *Who should look for the keys? **You** should look for them.*

EXERCISE 18-5 Simple Subjects, Questions, and Commands

Directions: *Find the simple subjects in the following sentences. Rewrite questions as statements that answer the question, and circle the simple subject of the statement. For commands, rewrite the sentence using "you" for the subject.*

1. When did your mother get out of the hospital?

My mother got out of the hospital on Monday.

2. At the beginning of class, open your books and take out your homework.

At the beginning of class, you open your books and take out your homework.

3. What is the most important idea about being an American?

The most important idea about being an American is freedom.

4. Before the plane pushes back from the jetway, be sure to fasten your seatbelt.

Before the plane pushes back from the jetway, you be sure to fasten your seatbelt.

5. Never underestimate the power of a good idea whose time has come.

You never underestimate the power of a good idea whose time has come.

6. When did the black mold first appear to affect the atmosphere in your home?

The black mold first appeared to affect the atmosphere in my home last month.

7. In the interest of maintaining a quality work environment, please refrain from smoking on the premises.

In the interest of maintaining a quality work environment, you refrain from smoking on the premises.

8. How does a college athlete attend hours of practices every week and also maintain a good grade point average?

A college athlete attends hours of practices every week and also maintains a good grade point average by setting up a schedule.

9. Where is the best pizza in town?

The best pizza in town is at Stromboli's, on Warren Avenue.

10. Divide and conquer.

You divide and conquer.

EXERCISE 18-6 Additional Practice Finding Simple Subjects

Directions: *Apply what you have learned in Exercises 18-2, 18-3, and 18-4 to find the simple subjects of the following sentences. Write the simple subjects in the space provided. For sentences written as commands, write "you" in the space provided.*

1. Before buying a dog, the Corwins visited an animal shelter located in the city.

Corwins

2. For information on home economics and saving money, listen to the "Money Man" on WKNX.

You

3. He will never steer you wrong.

He

4. Don't leave home without your American Express card.

You

5. Arriving late is never a good idea.

Arriving

6. What is the worst thing that can happen in a national election?

The worst thing

7. Flying over the devastation left by Hurricane Katrina, rescue workers and journalists alike watched intently for survivors.

Flying

8. We never have quite enough time.

We

9. Open your test booklets and begin work.

You

10. The best math teacher I ever had was Mr. Nustad.

Teacher

The Predicate

All sentences have a predicate. The **predicate** consists of the verb, which expresses an action or a state of being in the past, present, or future, as well as words and/or phrases that modify the verb.

Action Verbs

Your writing often focuses on a series of events or actions. In these instances, you rely heavily on action verbs. An **action verb** expresses the action of the subject. When you analyze a sentence, use the subject to help identify the action verb. Ask these questions:

What did the subject do?

What action took place?

Also, you will know you have found the action verb if you can write it in different tenses.

The oldest **sister** always *worked* harder than the rest of the family.

The subject of this sentence is "sister." What did the sister do? What action took place? The action verb is *worked*. It states what action the subject ("sister") did. The complete predicate, *always worked harder than the rest of the family*, describes how the sister worked. Note that the verb can be written in different tenses: *my sister worked, my sister works, my sister will work*.

EXERCISE 18-7 Identifying Action Verbs

Directions: *Underline the simple subjects and double-underline the action verbs in the following sentences. To be sure you have found the action verbs, write each one in the past, present, and future tense in the space provided.*

1. For the next three weeks, sciences classes will meet in temporary classrooms.

Action Verb: met, meet, will meet

2. Dogs threatened the piping plover population and other beach-nesting birds.

Action Verb: threatened, threaten, will threaten

3. The number of cosmetic surgeries increased dramatically.

Action Verb: increased, increase, will increase

4. Most salespeople in the organization go on calls with their computers under their arms.

Action Verb: went, go, will go

5. All rescue operations except those involving the military halted until further notice.

Action Verb: halted, halt, will halt

6. The study of nutrition and its impact on health deserves greater emphasis in medical education.

Action Verb: deserved, deserves, will deserve

7. Alcohol consumption among high school students reached alarming new levels.

Action Verb: reached, reaches, will reach

8. In the opinion of most health care professionals, a sedentary lifestyle poses almost as much danger to your health as smoking.

Action Verb: posed, poses, will pose

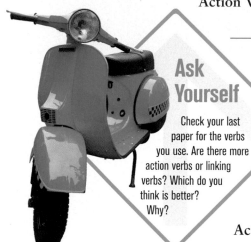

Ask Yourself

Check your last paper for the verbs you use. Are there more action verbs or linking verbs? Which do you think is better? Why?

9. Investors, in a state of shock over recent revelations, scrambled for cell phones.

Action Verb: scrambled, scramble, will scramble

10. Readers of detective fiction, along with assorted film buffs, showed up for the book signing early Saturday evening.

Action Verb: showed, show, will show

Linking Verbs

A linking verb connects a subject to the words that explain or describe it. (See the box below for a list of linking verbs.) These explanatory, descriptive words follow the verb and are called the **subject complement.**

All the **girls** *looked* beautiful.

The linking verb *looked* connects the subject "girls" to the word that describes them. The subject complement "beautiful" describes the girls.

The oldest **sister** *is* the hardest worker of the family.

The linking verb *is* connects the subject "sister" to the word that describes her. The subject complement "worker" describes the sister.

COMMON LINKING VERBS	
am	shall be
are	could have been
is	will be
can be	would be
was being	have been
has been	may have been
may be	must have been
were	

Other Linking Verbs

appear	become
feel	grow
look	seem
smell	sound
taste	

EXERCISE 18-8 **Identifying Linking Verbs**

Directions: *Underline the simple subjects, circle the linking verbs, and double-underline the subject complements in the following sentences. To be sure you have found the linking verbs, write each one in the past, present, and future tense in the spaces provided.*

1. Taking a few days off work seemed like a good idea.

Linking Verb: seemed, seems, will seem

2. The color of the gourds grew faint in the weeks after harvest.

Linking Verb: grew, grows, will grow

3. Being a smoker in the state of California is not easy.

Linking Verb: was, is, will be

4. I felt like a teenager again.

Linking Verb: felt, feel, will feel

5. My mother's disciplining style is aggressive.

Linking Verb: was, is, will be

6. Some distractions may be for the better.

Linking Verb: were, are, will be

7. The main problem many adult students face is financial.

Linking Verb: was, is, will be

8. Vanessa's battle would be very difficult one minute, hardly noticeable the next.

Linking Verb: was, is, will be

9. The children feel betrayed, unloved, and angry.

Linking Verb: felt, feel, will feel

10. My grandfather was an interesting man.

Linking Verb: was, is, will be

MULTILINGUAL TIP

Helping verbs are used to form tenses except for present and simple past.

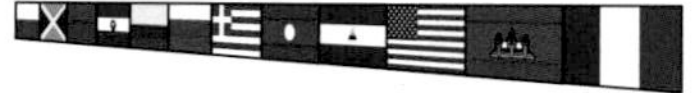

Helping Verbs and Verb Phrases

A **verb phrase** contains a helping verb and a main verb. **Helping verbs** may be used with either action verbs or state of being verbs to convey when something happened and to form questions. (A list of common helping verbs can be found in the box on page 411.) Verb phrases are used to express the tense of actions and states of being with greater precision.

The **girls** *are sitting* on the left side of the classroom.

The helping verb *are* locates this action in the present tense. Joined with *sitting*, the verb phrase describes a continuous action, possibly an action that is not generally the case. (Compare this with "The girls *sit* on the left side of the room," suggesting that the girls *usually* or *always* sit on the left side of the room.) The complete verb phrase "are sitting" is the action of the subject "girls."

England *has been* a good friend to the United States.

The verb phrase *has been* links the subject "England" to the subject complement "friend." The sentence suggests England was and continues to be a friend. (Compare "England was a good friend to the United States," which suggests the friendship no longer exists.)

COMMON HELPING VERBS			
am	are	is	was
were	do	did	can
may	must	has	have
had	be	been	shall
will	could	would	should

EXERCISE 18-9 Identifying Helping Verbs and Verb Phrases

Directions: *Underline the simple subjects and double-underline the helping verbs in the verb phrases in the sentences that follow.*

EXAMPLE

Young drivers have been known to drive with their radio on and their cell phone pressed to their ear, while eating a fast-food lunch.

1. Under other circumstances, Darrell would have gone to the University of California on a football scholarship.
2. Friday night we will eat with the Shepherds at the Adobe Grill downtown.
3. That summer all the team members were working on basic skills.
4. To get your student ID, you should go to the Registrar's Office in the Hallisey Building.
5. The student's amazing skill with high-level math may have been noticed in her high school years.
6. The drama coach is often seen sitting in his office, wearing a white scarf and smoking a pipe.
7. Rogers had been pulled aside from surgical procedures a number of times because of his poor attendance and tardiness.
8. Telling a child no, without any real explanation, will sometimes cause a rebellious attitude to develop.
9. Some people can't imagine doing anything without modern technological devices.
10. The other students would make fun of the kid's clothes and accent.

EXERCISE 18-10 Putting It All Together

Directions: *Underline the simple subject and double-underline the verb and any helping verbs in the sentences that follow.*

EXAMPLE:

My girlfriend took me to a fast-food restaurant for dinner a few weeks ago.

1. The experience was terrible.
2. The lines extended to the door.
3. I did not want to stay.
4. We actually stood in line for forty-five minutes.
5. She entertained me the whole time.
6. Even in a bad experience like this, we always have fun.
7. We were having so much fun, some of the other customers gave us dirty looks.
8. In the end the manager offered everyone coupons as an apology for the wait.
9. I will never go back to that place again.
10. My girlfriend knows plenty of other good places to eat.

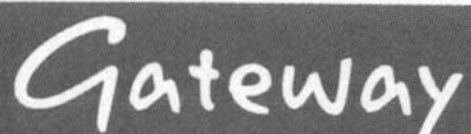

TOPIC 14: Sentence Building Blocks
www.mhhe.com/goingplaces

EXERCISE 18-11 **Observing Your Verbs**

PEER CONVERSATION

Directions: *Go to a public place on campus and observe events taking place around you. Write a paragraph-length description of the scene and the action. When you finish, double-underline all verbs and helping verbs in your sentences. Count the number of linking verbs and action verbs in your writing. Compare your writing and your use of verbs to the work of two or three classmates.*

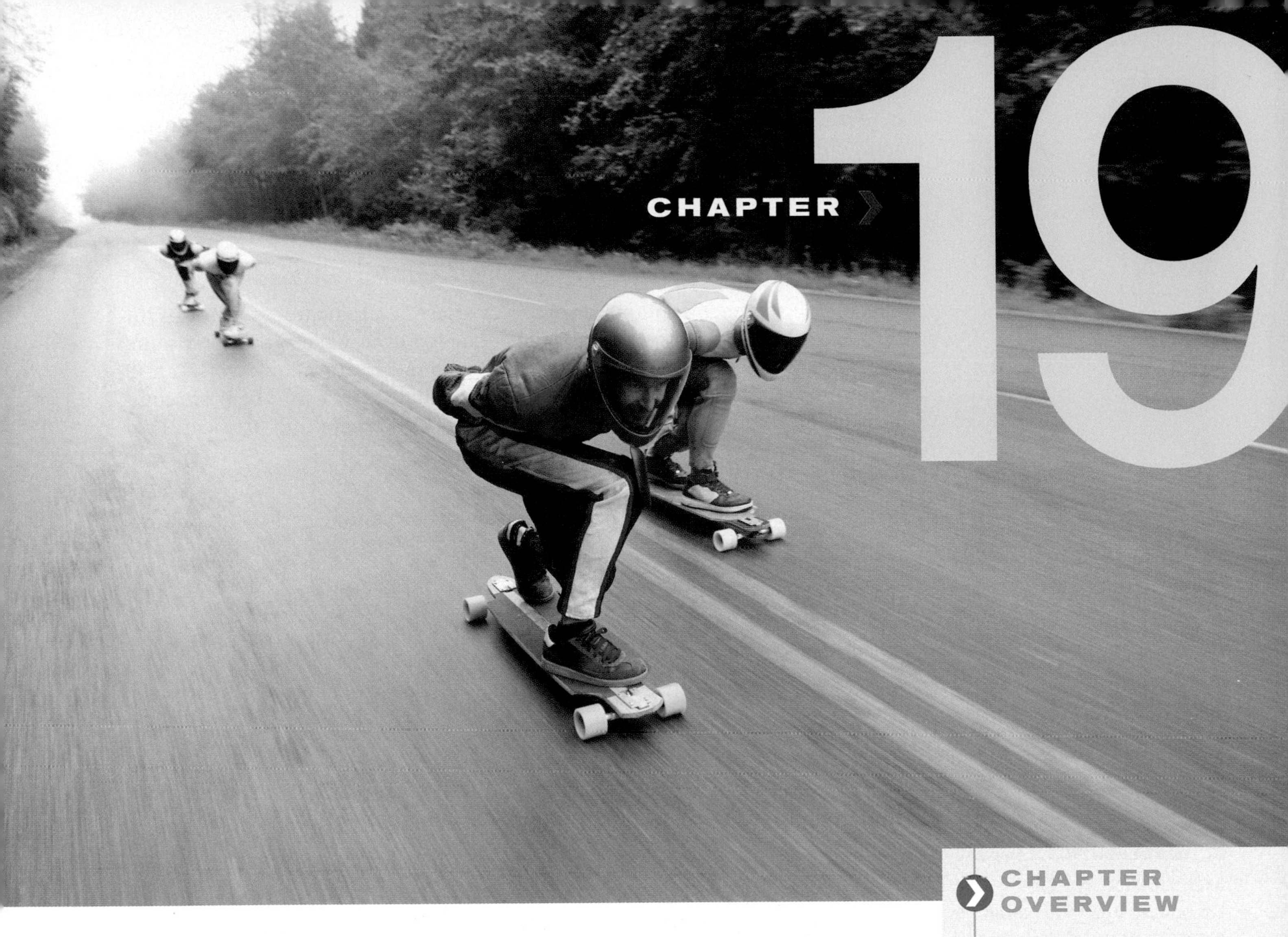

CHAPTER 19

Beyond the Simple Sentence: Compounds, Coordination, and Subordination

CHAPTER OVERVIEW

- Build on the Simple Sentence
  - *Compound Subjects*
  - *Compound Predicates*
- The Compound Sentence and Coordination
  - *Use a Comma and a Conjunction*
  - *Use a Semicolon and a Conjunctive Adverb*
  - *Use a Semicolon*
- The Complex Sentence and Subordination
  - *Subordination and the Relative Clause*

The simple sentence is the building block for richer, more complex sentence structures. There are a variety of ways to expand the simple sentence using compound forms and complex forms.

Build on the Simple Sentence: Compound Subjects and Compound Predicates

The simple sentence contains one subject and one predicate. It is useful for making simple, straightforward statements. However, what if the details and ideas you write about are not simple? Compound forms enable you to talk about more than one subject and action in a single sentence. The most common compound forms are compound subjects and compound predicates.

Compound Subjects

In a **compound subject,** two or more subjects are connected by a conjunction—usually *and* or *or.*

Simple Sentence: On Friday, **Bob** *drove* to the seashore alone. *Who else drove to the shore?*

Simple Sentence: **Alice** drove to the seashore.

Compound Subject: On Friday, **Bob and Alice** *drove* to the seashore together.

Note: No punctuation is used before or after the conjunction when the compound consists of two subjects. In the case of three or more subjects in a compound subject, use a comma before the conjunction.

MULTILINGUAL TIP

Do not use a pronoun after a compound subject: "Irish setters, Brittany spaniels, and beagles they make good hunting dogs."

Simple Sentence: Irish setters *make* good hunting dogs. *What other breeds make good hunting dogs?*

Simple Sentence: Brittany spaniels *make* good hunting dogs.

Simple Sentence: Beagles *make* good hunting dogs.

Compound Subject: Irish setters, Brittany spaniels, and beagles *make* good hunting dogs.

EXERCISE 19-1 Identifying Compound Subjects

Directions: *Underline the compound subjects in the following sentences. Circle the coordinating conjunctions.*

EXAMPLE

Snow, ice, and rain made it impossible for people to travel far at Thanksgiving this year.

1. A bouquet of flowers and a box of candy are popular gifts on Valentine's Day.
2. Mustard and onions on a hot dog cannot be beat.
3. Angelica or I will be at the concert early enough to get a front-row seat.
4. The windows in the house, the roof on the barn, and the car's windshield were all damaged in Saturday's storm.

5. Bicycle racing and women's volleyball are two exciting but frequently overlooked sports.

EXERCISE 19-2 Adding Compound Subjects

Directions: *Rewrite each of the following sentences so that it has a compound subject. For help creating the compound subject, respond to the question provided and write a sentence. Use commas for three or more compound subjects. Be sure to change verbs so they agree with your compound subject.* Answers will vary. Example answers shown.

EXAMPLE

A bowl of vegetable soup makes a great lunch.

What else makes a great lunch?

A bowl of vegetable soup, sandwich on rye bread, and a slice of cheese make a great lunch.

1. Less exposure to light in the winter months causes a form of depression called "seasonal affective disorder."

What else causes a form of depression called "seasonal affective disorder"?

Less exposure to light in the winter months and cold weather in winter cause a form of depression called "seasonal affective disorder."

2. Not washing their hands is a common reason why children catch the common cold.

What are other reasons that children catch the common cold?

Not washing their hands and using each other's drinking glass are common reasons children catch the common cold.

3. A trip to the seashore can be a very restful vacation.

What else can be a very restful vacation?

A trip to the seashore or just staying home and relaxing can be a very restful vacation.

4. Being on time for work enhances an employee's possibilities for getting a raise.

What else enhances an employee's possibilities for getting a raise?

Being on time for work, putting in extra effort, and trying to learn something new every day enhances an employee's possibilities for getting a raise.

5. The Great Stock Market Crash of 1929 was an important event in American history.

What were some other great events in American history?

The Great Stock Market Crash of 1929, the Great Depression, and World War II were important events in American history.

Compound Predicates

A sentence with a **compound predicate** has two or more predicates that share the same subject. Like the compound subject, the compound predicate enables you to express more complex details and ideas.

> **Simple Sentence:** The **telephone** *rang* in the middle of the night.
>
> *What else did the telephone do?*
>
> **Simple Sentence:** The **telephone** *woke* up the baby.
>
> **Compound Predicate:** The **telephone** *rang* in the middle of the night and *woke* up the baby.

Note: No punctuation is used before or after the conjunction when the compound consists of two predicates (see example above). However, when three predicates form the compound predicate, as in the following example, use a comma before the conjunction.

> **Simple Sentence: Computers** *distract* employees from their work.
>
> *What else do computers do?*
>
> **Simple Sentence: Computers** *diminish* production.
>
> **Simple Sentence: Computers** *increase* costs.
>
> **Compound Predicate: Computers** *distract* employees from their work, *diminish* production, and *increase* costs.

EXERCISE 19-3 Identifying Compound Predicates

Directions: *Underline the compound predicates in the following sentences. Circle the coordinating conjunctions.*

1. My accountant invested my money but made very poor choices.
2. We sat on the dock, watched the blue water glisten in the sun, and talked about old times.

3. The doctor sent a bill and charged me for two visits instead of one.

4. Conway wants a raise and has complained about his job assignment.

5. My friend complains about her boyfriend constantly but still dates him.

EXERCISE 19-4 Adding Compound Predicates

Directions: *Rewrite each of the following sentences so that it has a compound predicate. For help creating the compound predicate, respond to the question provided by writing one or two new sentences. Then combine the sentences by putting the predicates together. Use commas for compound predicates of three or more. Circle the verbs in each predicate.* Answers will vary. Example answers shown.

EXAMPLE

Squirrels built a nest in the apple tree.
What else did the squirrels do?

Squirrels built a nest in the apple tree, jumped onto the bird feeders, and ate every scrap of food they could find.

1. Thomas moved out of his parents' house.

What else did Thomas do?

Thomas moved out of his parents' house, rented his own apartment, and set up housekeeping on his own.

2. After the storm, the National Guard came to town.

What else did the National Guard do?

After the storm, the National Guard came to town, set up rescue activities, and helped restore electrical service.

Write a sentence about a daily routine, using a compound predicate to list actions you do to accomplish this routine.

3. On the evening of July 4, the kids lit firecrackers.

What else did the kids do?

On the evening of July 4, the kids lit firecrackers and toasted marshmallows over the campfire.

4. For a healthy diet, consumers should avoid transfats.

What else should consumers do?

For a healthy diet, consumers should avoid transfats and increase their consumption of complex carbohydrates.

5. The artist took out his sketch book.

What else did the artist do?

The artist took out his sketch book, sharpened his pencils, and began drawing.

The Compound Sentence and Coordination

Simple sentences that are connected form a **compound sentence.** Making use of **coordination,** the compound sentence comes in three forms. Three different approaches to coordination enable you to express the logical relationships between details and ideas:

1. Coordination using a comma and a conjunction
2. Coordination using a semicolon and a conjunctive adverb, followed by a comma
3. Coordination using a semicolon

Use a Comma and a Conjunction

You can combine two simple sentences by replacing the period after the first sentence with a comma and a coordinating conjunction.

Simple Sentence: Gordon's sister got married young.

Simple Sentence: She has been happy ever since.

Compound Sentence: Gordon's sister got married young, and she has been happy ever since.

The conjunction you use establishes a logical connection between the two sentences. Here is a list of common coordinating conjunctions and the logical connections they imply.

COORDINATING CONJUNCTIONS AND THEIR LOGICAL CONNECTION

and	*means*	in addition
but, yet	*means*	exception or contrast
or, nor	*means*	options or alternative
so, for	*means*	logical conclusion

Here are some examples of compound sentences that illustrate the logical connections that can be made by using coordinating conjunctions:

Simple Sentence: She says good things about marriage.

Simple Sentence: Not every young married person does.

Compound Sentence: She says good things about marriage, but not every young married person does.

The coordinating conjunction suggests contrast or an exception.

Simple Sentence: Some young people took full-time work right away.

Simple Sentence: They became parents too soon.

Compound Sentence: Some young people took full-time work right away, or they became parents too soon.

The coordinating conjunction suggests options or alternatives.

Simple Sentence: Getting married is a big responsibility.

Simple Sentence: You want to be sure you have chosen the right partner.

Compound Sentence: Getting married is a big responsibility, so you want to be sure you have chosen the right partner.

The coordinating conjunction expresses a logical conclusion.

Note: In a compound sentence, a comma is placed before the conjunction. In the case of very short sentences—such as "I sat and I waited"—a comma does not have to be used.

EXERCISE 19-5 Choosing Coordinating Conjunctions

Directions: *Choose a coordinating conjunction to connect each of the following sentences to make it into a compound sentence. Write the conjunction you choose in the space provided. Remember that when you insert a conjunction in place of a period, you need to put a comma before the conjunction.* Answers will vary. Example answers shown.

EXAMPLE

My car stalled out this morning. It was inexpensive to repair.

, but ______________________________

1. I will bring the desserts. You can bring the drinks.

, and ______________________________

2. Britta and Clem wanted to know how to salsa at their wedding. They took ballroom dancing lessons.

, so ______________________________

3. Erica did not apply to the nursing program this semester. She did not even sign up for classes.

, nor did she ______________________________

4. Latasha was unwilling to go to the football game. She was willing to go the movie.

, yet ______________________________

5. My worst subject in school was geometry. I also was also terrible in choir.

, but ______________________________

EXERCISE 19-6 Commas and Compound Forms

Directions: *Some of the sentences below are simple sentences with compound subjects or predicates. Others are compound sentences.*

- *Circle the conjunctions in all the sentences.*
- *Add commas to the compound sentences. Do not add commas to compound subjects or compound predicates. Some of the sentences are correct as written.*

EXAMPLE

E-mail is now used by nearly everyone, (and) many businesses have websites to advertise their products and services. (Insert comma after "everyone.")

1. I saw a car standing by the side of the road this morning, (and) the tire was flat.
2. I hate doing the dishes and detest taking out the garbage, (but) those are the jobs I have to do.
3. My sister's boyfriend went to France last summer, (and) this summer she wants to go.
4. My mom works afternoons and doesn't really have time to cook dinner. correct as written
5. My boyfriend (and) I go to the grocery store (and) buy the ingredients for the meal we decide to make. correct as written
6. We like to make salads a lot, (so) we always buy some kind of vegetables to go with the meal.
7. We usually make something that is simple (and) doesn't require a whole lot of cooking time. correct as written
8. We often make spaghetti (or) taco salad. correct as written
9. My mom likes refried beans (and) guacamole. correct as written
10. I mostly cut up the vegetables (and) cook the meat, (and) my boyfriend sets the table and does the dishes afterward.

EXERCISE 19-7 Compound Sentences in Your Writing

Directions: *For each of the following subjects, write a compound sentence in the space provided. Use a variety of conjunctions.* Answers will vary.

EXAMPLE

horses

In the nineteenth century city horses generated huge amounts of manure, so a large segment of the population found work transporting manure out of the city every day.

1. sleep

2. summer fun

3. health care

Use a Semicolon and a Conjunctive Adverb

You can combine two simple sentences by replacing the period with a semicolon and a conjunctive adverb followed by a comma. A **conjunctive adverb** is a connecting word, like a conjunction, that makes a logical connection between two ideas.

> **Simple Sentence:** One of my coworkers came late today.
>
> **Simple Sentence:** He was completely distracted and unable to do his job properly.
>
> **Compound Sentence:** One of my coworkers came late today; furthermore, he was completely distracted and unable to do his job properly.

Furthermore expresses the logical connection between these two simple sentences. Like coordinating conjunctions, conjunctive adverbs express the logical connection between two sentences. They also function as transition words. The following box shows a list of conjunctive adverbs.

CONJUNCTIVE ADVERBS

accordingly	indeed
again	moreover
as a result	nevertheless
also	otherwise
besides	then
consequently	therefore
finally	thus
furthermore	on the other hand
however	in contrast
in addition	in fact

MULTILINGUAL TIP

Write conjunctive adverbs carefully. Avoid errors like these: as ~~the~~ a result, ~~in~~ on the other hand.

Remember that the semicolon is a strong mark of punctuation, almost as strong as a period. For this reason, it replaces the period after *today* in the preceding example; the comma after *furthermore,* in contrast, marks the pause of an introductory modifier.

Simple Sentence: Digital photography is becoming more popular all the time.

Simple Sentence: Most of my friends now have digital cameras.

Compound Sentence: Digital photography is becoming more popular all the time; indeed, most of my friends now have digital cameras.

Here, *indeed* expresses the logical connection between these two simple sentences.

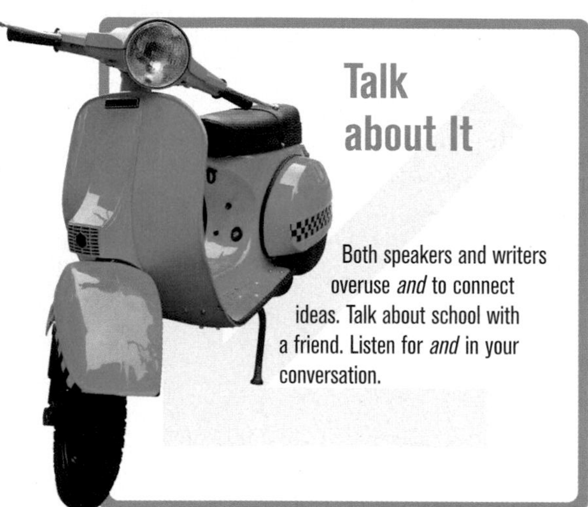

Talk about It

Both speakers and writers overuse *and* to connect ideas. Talk about school with a friend. Listen for *and* in your conversation.

Use a Semicolon

In cases where you are expressing clearly related or contrasting ideas, consider using a semicolon alone.

Simple Sentence: Life in the country tended to be dull.

Simple Sentence: Life in the city provided too much stimulation.

Compound Sentence: Life in the country tended to be dull; life in the city provided too much stimulation.

Simple Sentence: My father is pretty quiet in social gatherings.

Simple Sentence: My mother will talk your ear off.

Compound Sentence: My father is pretty quiet in social gatherings; my mother will talk your ear off.

EXERCISE 19-8 **Compound Sentences, Conjunctive Adverbs, and the Semicolon**

Directions: *Using the list of conjunctive adverbs on page 421, combine the following sentences using a semicolon and a conjunctive adverb that expresses the logical relationship between the two sentences. In the case of contrasting sentences, just use a semicolon. Write the changes in the space provided.* Answers will vary. Example answers shown.

1. The team lost five consecutive games. The coach continued to practice basic skills and work toward their first victory.

games; nevertheless, the coach

2. Mutual funds offer better growth over time than savings accounts. Most young investors choose the mutual fund option.

accounts; consequently, most

3. Fast foods typically have high calorie counts. They have high salt and fat contents.

counts; moreover, they

4. My younger brother went to medical school. My older brother went to law school.

school; my older

5. Having drunk so much coffee, Parker was in an agitated state when he arrived at the doctor's office. His blood pressure was much higher than usual.

office; as a result, his

6. The store-bought pumpkin pies did not sell well at the bake sale. The home-baked pies practically flew out the door.

sale; the

7. Trish scored very high on her entrance exams and interviewed very well. She was offered a generous scholarship.

well; accordingly, she

8. We attended the same college, took the same classes, and were guided by a stern, yet loving advisor. She was my glimpse into the real world of the operating room.

advisor; in addition, she

9. According to the Centers for Disease Control and Prevention, around 63 percent of all adults consume alcohol. Around 32 percent of those consume five or more drinks a day.

alcohol; moreover, around

10. We initially purchase technological gadgets to make our lives easier. Those good intentions erode over time and become something else.

easier; however, those

COORDINATION SUMMARY

Comma and Coordinating Conjunction

- Traffic stopped in the tunnel for forty-five minutes, but no one in our car seemed to mind.

Semicolon, Conjunctive Adverb, and Comma

- The neighbors on our right are enthusiastic about gardening and yard work; in contrast, those on the left work on the inside of their house.

Semicolon

- A small car is for economy; a large car is for space and convenience.

EXERCISE 19-9 **Putting It All Together**

Directions: *The following paragraphs consist of simple sentences. On a separate sheet of paper, use all three approaches to coordination—(a) comma and conjunction; (b) semicolon, conjunctive adverb, and comma; or (c) semicolon—to create three compound sentences within each paragraph.* **Answers will vary.**

1. We met in high school. We were both first-year students. He was very focused and spontaneous. He would make anyone laugh. He was a very good friend. He always helped me out. I really needed the help then. We played football together all four years of high school. During football he would push others to do their best. Chris was an amazing individual. After school he volunteered to do landscaping for our church on the weekends and during the summer. This saved the church a lot of money. He even won an achievement award for this. He was always helping out others.

2. Soon Vanessa felt a little better. She returned to work. She found herself still in pain at times. This didn't bother her though. She was determined to get on with her life. She wanted to accomplish all the goals she had set for herself. First she returned to work. Then she went back to school. She started off taking one class a semester. She made sure she could handle the sickness, work, and the workload of college again. Soon she was taking two, then three classes. She was comfortable with this workload. It was difficult trying to manage working, going to school, and still cooking and cleaning her home. She was determined. She found the time and strength to get it done. She graduated with a bachelor's degree in business.

3. There are times when the parent and child are at an impasse. Both are speechless and storm away. There is nothing left to do but yell and scream at each other. One or the other decides to stop. Maybe the child takes something the parent says completely the wrong way. The child attacks with unkind words or insults. Maybe the parent fights back. The two will fight for hours on end. It is sad. These conflicts start with a miscommunication. Both individuals are too stubborn to give up the fight. Both truly want it all to end. There is a perfect balance of power in this communication between the parent and the child. Neither gives in. Neither actually achieves ultimate victory.

The Complex Sentence and Subordination

Subordination occurs when an independent clause (containing a subject and verb) is made into a dependent clause by joining it to another independent clause using a **subordinating conjunction.** Sentences making use of subordination are called **complex sentences.** If they are separated, the subordinate elements do not express a complete thought.

Notice the effect the subordinating conjunction has on an independent clause:

Riley mowed the lawn.

After Riley mowed the lawn.

The first statement is an **independent clause.** It states a complete idea. However, when the subordinating conjunction *after* is placed in front of the independent clause, it no longer expresses a complete idea: "After Riley mowed the lawn." What happened? By itself, the dependent clause does not make a statement.

After Riley mowed the lawn, she went swimming next door.

The added language completes the statement. Notice that "she went swimming next door" is an independent clause. It stands alone, whereas the first part has to be part of the whole sentence to make sense. The following box is a list of subordinating conjunctions.

SUBORDINATING CONJUNCTIONS

after	so that
although	though
as	unless
as long as	until
because	when
before	whenever
even though	whereas
if	wherever
in order that	whether
provided that	while
since	

MULTILINGUAL TIP

Do not use "because" or "although" with conjunctions that mean the same thing: "Although a good-looking guy asked me to dance, ~~yet~~ I turned him down.

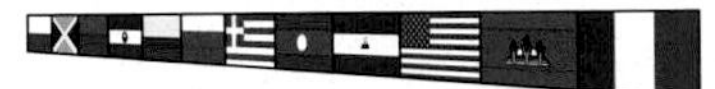

In the following example, notice the effect a subordinating conjunction has on two simple sentences that are combined to form a complex sentence:

Simple Sentence: A great-looking guy asked me to dance.

Simple Sentence: I turned him down.

Complex Sentence: Although a great-looking guy asked me to dance, I turned him down.

Although expresses the logical relationship between these two simple sentences. The underlined section of the sentence, beginning with the subordinating conjunction *although,* has become a dependent clause. It can no longer stand alone as a complete sentence. It "depends" on the rest of the sentence, "I turned him down."

When the dependent clause of a complex sentence comes first, use a comma to attach it to the rest of the sentence. Use a comma to set off a dependent clause at the end of a sentence only if the dependent clause reads like an afterthought, adding nonessential information. Afterthoughts often begin with the subordinating conjunctions *although, though,* and *whereas.*

Salespeople need a comfortable car because they spend a lot of time on the road.

I turned down a great-looking guy who asked me to dance, although I regretted it later.

In the first sentence, the subordinate section, beginning with *because,* adds essential information. The sentence expresses a cause and effect relationship. In contrast, the subordinate section in the second sentence, beginning with *although,* adds nonessential information. It reads like an afterthought.

EXERCISE 19-10 Selecting the Right Subordinating Conjunction

Directions: *Review the list of subordinating conjunctions on page 425. Then read the following simple sentences and select a subordinating conjunction that expresses the logical relationship between the ideas in each one. Add commas as needed.*

EXAMPLE

Andrew studied hard for the exam and did well, while______ Matthew barely opened a book and did poorly. (insert comma before "while")

1. Although______ I am not winning, I like playing the game.
2. After______ I played in the game, I went to the dance at the youth center.
3. I study every night from seven until midnight so that______ I can get a scholarship for college. no comma needed
4. Whether______ you go or not, I plan to see the Degas art exhibit on dance.
5. My boss requires all his employees to submit vacation requests six months in advance because______ he wants to accommodate as many as possible. no comma needed
6. Stephen King is a very popular novelist, though______ most literary critics do not think of him as a "serious" writer.
7. I do not want to go to the movies, although______ you might persuade me to change my mind.
8. Although______ I always wanted a dog, my brother's allergies kept us from having one.
9. Mark broke his hand while______ he was moving scenery around the stage. no comma needed
10. If______ you decide to quit your job, let me know so that I can apply for it.

EXERCISE 19-11 Dependent Clauses and the Comma

Directions: *For each of the following pairs of sentences, select a subordinating conjunction from the list on page 425 and use it to combine them. Write the subordinating conjunction you choose with punctuation as needed in the space provided.* Answers will vary. Example answers shown.

EXAMPLE

Sarah cooked on a gas range at work. At home she used an electric range.

Although Sarah . . . , at home. . . .

1. Early tools used in logging were the ax and the chain saw. Now tractors and helicopters make heavy work lighter.

While early . . . , now tractors. . . .

2. CEOs want the public to see them as "all American." They want their shareholders to know they will do anything to make a buck.

. . . American," whereas they. . . .

3. Most of the family was very supportive during this time. No one suffered too much.

. . . time so that no one. . . .

4. Another big draw, "the summer blockbuster," comes along. Movie executives bank their futures on it.

When another . . . , movie, ...

5. "Be cool, stay in school" was always the motto of schools when I was growing up. Not everyone stayed in school.

. . . growing up, although not everyone. . . .

6. I started working at Wilson's Leather in Southland Mall. I stumbled in there looking for a Christmas present for my boyfriend.

. . . Mall after I stumbled. . . .

Ask Yourself

Do you insert too many commas or too few commas? What do you see in this exercise that applies to your writing?

7. Throngs of windows shoppers descend upon the local malls and shopping centers. There has been a media blitz announcing big sales and huge savings on consumer goods.

. . . centers because there has been. . . .

8. Students and teachers work together and show mutual respect. The classroom is a welcoming place.

Provided that students . . . , the classroom. . . .

9. The government has increased the tax on tobacco. Being a smoker is not easy.

Since the government . . . , being a smoker. . . .

10. This is a day everyone is excited about. We're going back to Tennessee for our family reunion.

. . . about since we're. . . .

MULTILINGUAL TIP
Who and *that* replace a person; *that* and *which* replace a thing.

Subordination and the Relative Clause

A **relative clause** begins with one of the relative pronouns: *that, which,* or *who.* A relative clause can appear at the beginning, in the middle, or at the end of a sentence. In the following examples the relative pronouns are in bold and the relative clauses are underlined.

> **Which** guitar player they would choose was not immediately clear.
>
> The band members **who** heard Phil first immediately asked him to join the band.
>
> Then Phil completely took over a band **that** had been struggling for quite some time.

When you combine sentences using a relative clause, you add information about a person or a thing. Usually the relative pronoun comes immediately after the person or thing being modified. Which band members? The band members who Phil heard first. Which band? A band that had been struggling for quite some time. A relative clause adds the detail needed to specify a person or thing. *That one,* the clause says. *We're talking about that one.* In the following examples, the relative clauses are in bold.

> A news journalist covered the story. *Which news journalist?*
>
> A news journalist **who happened to be on the scene** covered the story.

> A car can be expensive to operate. *Which car?*
>
> A car **that requires a lot of repairs** can be expensive to operate.

Punctuation can be required for some relative clauses. When the information is an afterthought, when it is not essential information, add commas. When this nonessential information comes at the end of the sentence, use a comma before the relative pronoun. In the following examples, the relative clauses are in bold.

> Staubach signed autographs for the kids **who were working at the stadium.**

In this sentence, the relative clause "who were working at the stadium" provides essential information: It tells which kids got autographs, so a comma is not used.

> Both the man and my father come from Parma, **which is a small town in Iowa.**

Here the relative clause provides nonessential information because the town is named and specified. Therefore, the relative clause is set off with a comma.

If the nonessential clause is in the middle of a sentence, you need a pair of commas. Look at the following examples.

> Roger Staubach, **who played quarterback for the Dallas Cowboys,** stopped by the store the other day and bought an ice cream cone.

In this sentence, because the subject of the sentence is named, the relative clause is considered nonessential information and is therefore placed between a pair of commas.

A man **who was a childhood friend of my father's** invented superglue.

In this example, "a man" is neither named nor specified, so the relative clause provides essential information for determining who the man is, and no commas are necessary.

EXERCISE 19-12 Adding Relative Clauses

Directions: *Add a relative clause to each of the following sentences and rewrite them in the space provided. Use commas as needed.* Answers will vary. Example answers shown.

EXAMPLE

Gerald Ford who ______________________________ did not want to be president.

Gerald Ford, who became president when Richard Nixon resigned, did not want to be president.

1. My psychology class which ______________________________ has completely changed my mind about human nature.

My psychology class, which meets on Tuesday and Thursday at 9:40 a.m , has completely changed my mind about human nature.

2. The clothes that ______________________________ will be ready by four o'clock tomorrow.

The clothes that you dropped off at the cleaners last week will be ready by four o'clock tomorrow.

3. Our family ended up going for a short vacation in August which ______________________________ .

Our family ended up going for a short vacation in August, which was very unusual for a family that loves the snow.

4. The flowers that ______________________________ are now on sale at the local market for half what you paid.

The flowers that you bought at the flower shop on the corner are now on sale at the local market for half what you paid.

5. When we were kids, we always waited for the crash and flash of thunderstorms which ______________________ .

When we were kids, we always waited for the crash and flash of thunderstorms, which scared the daylights out of me but delighted my little sister.

6. The nation's dependence upon oil which ______________________ leads to continuing vulnerability.

The nation's dependence upon oil, which has increased with each passing year, leads to continuing vulnerability.

7. School lunch programs that ______________________ actually contribute to problems with obesity in this country.

School lunch programs that are intended to help kids actually contribute to problems with obesity in this country.

8. Be sure to buy a computer that ______________________ .

Be sure to buy a computer that has a large hard drive and lots of RAM.

9. Train travel which ______________________ hardly exists in many American cities.

Train travel, which can be a perfectly stress-free way of commuting to and from work, hardly exists in many American cities.

10. Most zoo animals that ______________________ are probably quite happy in their confinement.

Most zoo animals that we think are suffering in captivity are probably quite happy in their confinement.

EXERCISE 19-13 Combining Sentences Using Relative Clauses

Directions: *Use relative clauses to combine the following sentences. Add commas as needed.* Answers will vary. Example answers shown.

EXAMPLE

The Volt was an electric car. We saw it at the most recent auto show.

The Volt was an electric car that we saw at the most recent auto show.

1. The construction trades once provided thousands of secure jobs everywhere in the United States. The construction trades are now booming only in certain parts of the country.

The construction trades, which once provided thousands of secure jobs everywhere in the United States, are now booming only in certain parts of the country.

2. There is an antique market at the edge of town every second Saturday. That is not often enough for some enthusiasts.

There is an antique market at the edge of town every second Saturday, which is not often enough for some enthusiasts.

3. Scuba diving is a popular sport in the Caribbean. It appeals to the brave-at-heart.

Scuba diving, which appeals to the brave-at-heart, is a popular sport in the Caribbean.

Talk about It

Short sentences are easy to write and punctuate. How do you usually combine sentences to make your writing more sophisticated?

4. The ferry boats used to run between the city and the island every twenty minutes. They were replaced by a four-lane bridge five years ago.

Ferry boats that used to run between the city and the island every twenty minutes were replaced by a four-lane bridge five years ago.

5. Elective surgeries are not covered by most health insurance policies. These surgeries are primarily cosmetic in nature.

Elective surgeries that are primarily cosmetic in nature are not covered by most health insurance policies.

6. Methane gas is used by some municipalities. The gas is generated at landfills.

Methane gas, which is generated at landfills, is used by some municipalities.

7. Charles Dickens's *David Copperfield* is still one of my favorite novels. I first read it when I was in high school.

Charles Dickens's *David Copperfield,* which I first read when I was in high school, is still one of my favorite novels.

8. Burning leaves has been banned in many parts of the country. The smell of burning leaves is intoxicating.

Burning leaves, the smell of which is intoxicating, has been banned in many parts of the country.

9. During my time as a camp counselor, I gave speeches on a regular basis. Giving speeches never bothered me in the least.

During my time as a camp counselor, I gave speeches on a regular basis, which never bothered me in the least.

10. Most people sleep better at night if the temperature in the house is lowered. Lowering the temperature is made easy by a programmable thermostat.

Most people sleep better at night if the temperature in the house is lowered, which is made easy by a programmable thermostat.

EXERCISE 19-14 Editing and Subordination

Directions: *The following paragraphs consist entirely of simple sentences. On a separate sheet of paper, combine the sentences using subordinating conjunctions and relative pronouns. Use commas as needed.* Answers will vary.

1. I quit smoking for a variety of reasons. The first reason was inconvenience. I did not enjoy carrying my pack of cigarettes everywhere. It took up space in my pocket. It was just one more thing to worry about. There was another reason I quit smoking. The worst part about smoking was the smell. Smoke got on my clothes. That was bad enough. The smell got in my hair and on my breath. It was hard to get rid of the smell. I smoked for seven years. At first, the price was not that bad. Then the state started taxing tobacco. Next thing I knew, it was two, three, then four dollars a pack. That was another reason to quit. I woke up and looked at my bank account. It was pretty pathetic. I realized how much money I could save if I quit smoking. So I quit. I quit cold

turkey. The nicotine craving never got that bad. My hands needed to be doing something. I ended up chewing on coffee straws every time I had a craving for a cigarette. I needed to do that for a couple of weeks. Now I never think of having a cigarette. I am much better off.

2. Consider the young male student and his computer use. His parents buy him a computer to help with his homework. He uses it only for school. One day in his room he logs into a chat room to talk about the local football team. He begins to lose track of time. He chats with friends from various messaging services. The Internet becomes a secondary social environment. He tries to do his homework. His friends distract him. This causes him to fall behind in his responsibilities. In his free time he explores other uses for his computer. Soon he downloads illegal music, chats with friends at all hours, and looks for ways to access to age-restricted sites. The line blurs between responsible use of technology and letting technology have far too much of a place in his life.

3. Some people can be cruel. The classroom can be a very unwelcoming place. I was in elementary school. There was a foreign student named Katya. She had not been in the United States very long. She had a thick Polish accent. The other students made fun of her clothes and the way she spoke. She became socially withdrawn, had few friends, and ended up changing schools. This is a perfect example of cruelty in the classroom. This cruelty is often directed at new students. That is so unfortunate. If kids were more accepting of different types of people and cultures, it would help newcomers feel welcome.

Ask Yourself

What punctuation will you try to use in your writing? In what kinds of sentences?

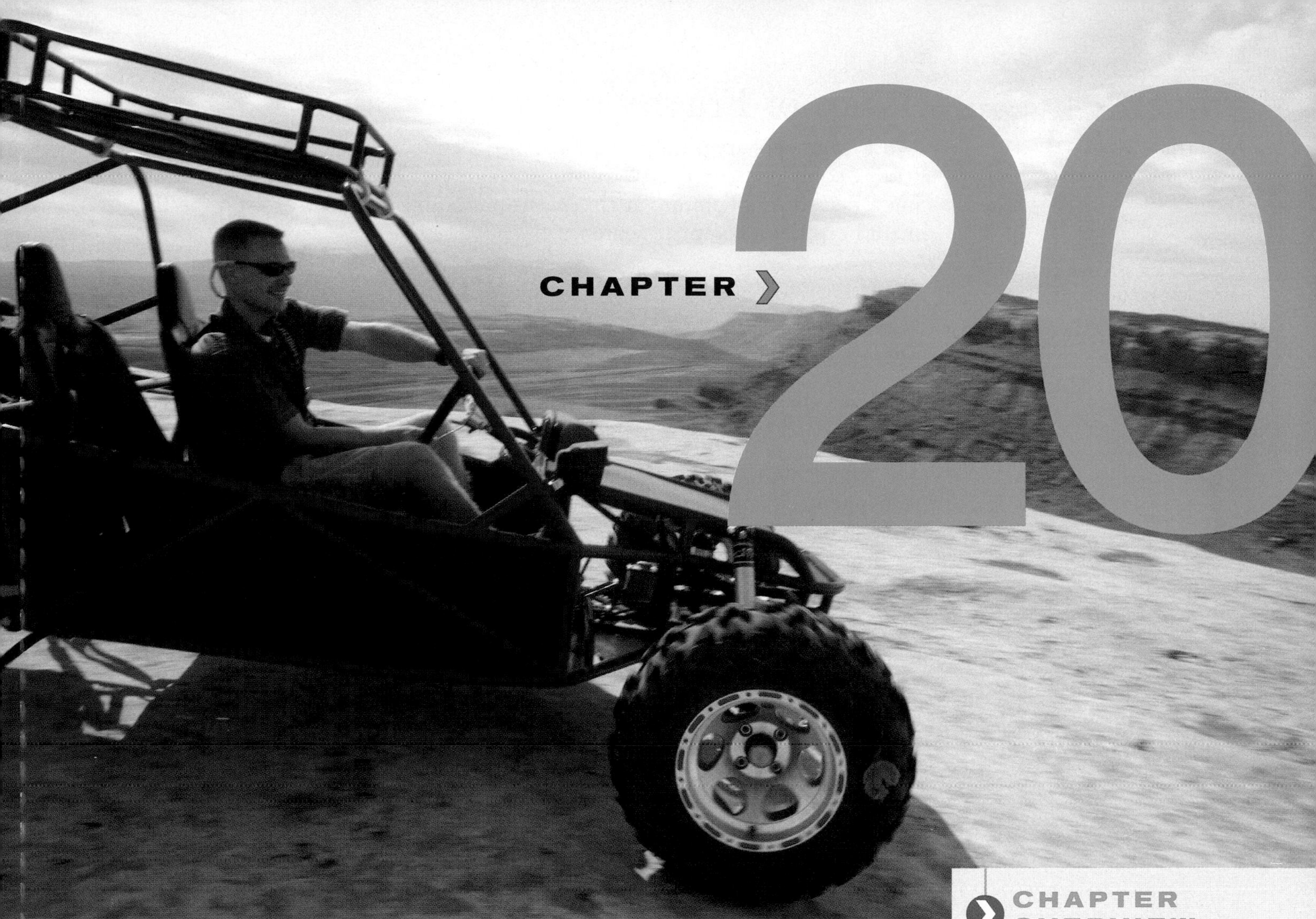

CHAPTER 20

The Sentence Fragment

CHAPTER OVERVIEW

- Types of Fragments
  - *Noun Phrase*
  - *Adjective Phrase*
  - *Prepositional Phrase*
  - *Verbal Phrase*
  - *Dependent Clause*

Readers of college writing expect you to write in complete sentences. A **complete sentence** contains a subject and a verb and states a complete idea that a reader can take in, understand, and respond to. A complete sentence can also be identified by the use of a capital letter at the beginning and a period, question mark, or exclamation point at the end. A **sentence fragment** does not contain either a subject or a verb, and it does not express a complete thought.

MULTILINGUAL TIP

Common errors: using commas to link complete thoughts, omitting subjects and/or verbs, using subordinate clauses as a complete sentence.

Types of Fragments

Most fragments are phrases, verbals, or dependent clauses that are detached from a complete sentence. While most fragments can be corrected by changing a period to a comma, at times it is preferable to add words so the fragment becomes a complete sentence.

Noun Phrase Fragments

Noun phrases are modifiers at the beginning or end of a sentence. Watch for phrases that sound like an afterthought.

> The construction project downtown was a regular danger zone. A disaster waiting to happen.

The first sentence is a complete sentence. The fragment, "a disaster waiting to happen," is a noun phrase that describes "danger zone." It sounds like an afterthought, an additional descriptive detail the writer has added. By itself, "a disaster waiting to happen" does not express a complete idea. Correct the fragment by attaching it to the complete sentence or by adding words to make the fragment a complete sentence.

> The construction project downtown was a regular danger zone, a disaster waiting to happen.

> The construction project downtown was a regular danger zone. It was a disaster waiting to happen.

Adjective Phrase Fragments

Adjective phrase fragments also become detached at the beginning or end of complete sentences. Watch for a phase that sounds introductory.

> Way too smart and generous for his own good. The technician invented programs that were sold by his company with little compensation in return.

The second sentence is a complete sentence. The fragment, "way too smart and generous for his own good," is an adjective phrase that describes "the technician." By itself, "way too smart and generous for his own good" does not express a complete idea. It sounds like introductory information, which should be connected to the main sentence with a comma, not a period. Correct the fragment by attaching it to the complete sentence or by adding words to make the fragment a complete sentence.

> Way too smart and generous for his own good, the technician invented programs that were sold by his company with little compensation in return.

> The technician was way too smart and generous for his own good. He invented programs that were sold by his company with little compensation in return.

Prepositional Phrase Fragments

Prepositional phrases occasionally become loose threads the writer needs to tie up in editing. Watch for afterthoughts.

> The nursing students' real stress is felt once they begin their clinical rotations. Usually in the third semester of the program.

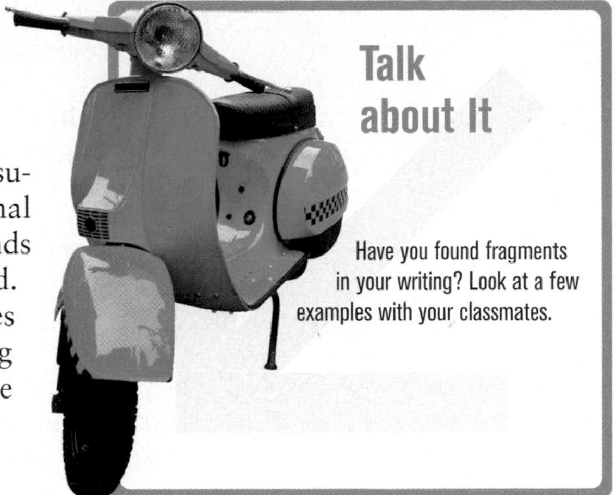

Talk about It
Have you found fragments in your writing? Look at a few examples with your classmates.

The first sentence is a complete sentence. The fragment, "usually in the third semester of the program," is a prepositional phrase that modifies *begin* in the complete sentence. It sounds like an afterthought, a descriptive detail the writer has added. By itself, "usually in the third semester of the program" does not state a complete idea. Correct the fragment by attaching it to the complete sentence or by adding words to make the fragment a complete sentence.

> The nursing students' real stress is felt once they begin their clinical rotations, usually in the third semester of the program.

> The nursing students' real stress is felt once they begin their clinical rotations. This usually happens in the third semester of the program.

Verbal Phrase Fragments

Verbals are either -ing forms (participles) or "to" forms (infinitives). They become sentence fragments when they are detached from the beginning or end of a complete sentence. Watch for -ing forms and "to" forms coming at the beginning of a sentence.

> Robert put off his homework all weekend. Waiting until late Sunday night to start it.

> To the surprise of his physics teacher. Robert, a natural born genius, scored 100 percent on the test, even without studying.

These fragments can be corrected by attaching them to the complete sentence (the first sentence in the first example, the second sentence in the second example) or by adding words to make the fragments complete sentences.

> Robert put off his homework all weekend, waiting until late Sunday night to start it.

> Robert put off his homework all weekend. He waited until late Sunday night to start it.

> To the surprise of his physics teacher, Robert, a natural born genius, scored 100 percent on the test, even without studying.

> He surprised his physics teacher. Robert, a natural born genius, scored 100 percent on the test, even without studying.

Learn to listen for sentence completeness. Always read your work out loud, giving periods a good long pause, as you listen for complete ideas. In addition, look for noun, adjective, prepositional, and verbal phrases.

EXERCISE 20-1 Noun, Adjective, Prepositional, and Verbal Phrase Fragments

Directions: *Underline the phrases in the following items. Correct the fragments by connecting them to a complete sentence or by adding words to make them complete sentences and write your answers in the space provided.* **Answers will vary.**

1. How do I use math in my life now? I'll cite just one important example. Cutting coupons for shopping and knowing how much I'm actually saving. It's the best way to save money.

   I cut coupons when I shop so I know how much I'm actually saving.

2. There's no better feeling than driving a shiny red car, with the top down and the hum of the large motor under the hood. The feeling of power and control, sheer excitement. You can't help thinking, "Don't I look cool?"

   It gives you the feeling of power and control, sheer excitement.

3. As a kid, there were many things I did to pass the time. Everything from playing video games, to riding bikes, to playing sports. What made it even better was the fact that I was surrounded by really good friends.

   . . . time, everything from playing video games, to riding bikes . . . ,

4. With a stern voice, my mother told me to get in the car. And to get ready to go home. I knew then I was in big trouble.

   . . . car and to get ready to go home.

5. From helping my little brothers with homework to taking the garbage out every Monday. I really had a lot of responsibilities. A kid's work was never done.

   . . . Monday, I really had a lot of responsibilities.

6. Working under extremely hot conditions. Chasing golf balls, cleaning golf balls, and cleaning golf clubs after every use. This was an ideal job for me. I got lots of sun, and every once in a while I played some free golf.

   I worked under extremely hot conditions, chasing golf balls, . . .

7. I taught the campers how to blow bubbles with their fingers when we washed our hands. It gave me a feeling I will never forget. Just to see their smiling faces every time I taught them something new or just played with them.

. . . a feeling I will never forget, just to see their smiling faces . . .

8. The job I now have has some good and bad qualities. I'm a food server, which gives me excellent experience with people. All types of people. Which also helps me develop patience.

. . . experience with all types of people, which also helps me develop patience.

9. I started working when I was fifteen years old. I worked at Meijers. I was too young to be a cashier. I was a bagger, which was more than just bagging groceries. My job was cleaning the entranceways. Getting change for the cashiers. Finding items that customers forgot and putting back items that customers did not want. It wasn't the world's greatest job, but it got me started earning money.

. . . entranceways, getting change for the cashiers, finding items . . . did not want.

10. Then came high school. It started out just like elementary school. The teachers calling me Debra and my friends calling me Debbie. Some things never change.

. . . school, the teachers calling me Debra and my friends calling me Debbie.

Dependent Clause Fragments

A dependent clause fragment can occur either before or after the independent clause to which it belongs. Watch for subordinating conjunctions at the beginning of a sentence. (See page 425 in Chapter 19 for a list of subordinating conjunctions.)

> I was asked to submit transcripts for the committee to review. As soon as I possibly could.

The first sentence is a complete sentence. The fragment, "as soon as I possibly could," can be joined to the complete sentence or made into a complete sentence.

> I was asked to submit transcripts for the committee to review as soon as I possibly could.

> I was asked to submit transcripts for the committee to review. They wanted them as soon as possible.

Watch also for sentences beginning with one of the relative pronouns, such as *that, which, who,* and *whoever.* Fragments with relative clauses often sound like afterthoughts.

The argument then turned violent. Which didn't change anyone's mind.

The first sentence is a complete sentence. The fragment, "which didn't change anyone's mind," can be corrected by joining it to the independent clause or by making it into a complete sentence.

The argument then turned violent, which didn't change anyone's mind.

The argument then turned violent. The fighting didn't change anyone's mind.

When you read your work out loud, give periods a good long pause as you listen for complete ideas; watch for subordinating conjunctions. Read and listen carefully to all sentences that begin with a subordinating conjunction.

EXERCISE 20-2 Fragments and Dependent Clauses

Directions: *Circle subordinating conjunctions and relative pronouns in the following sentences. Underline any sentence fragments you find. Correct the fragments by connecting them to a complete sentence or by adding words to make them complete sentences and write your answer in the space provided. Some are correct as written.* Answers will vary. Example answers shown.

1. When will I ever have to know how many degrees are in an octagon? The answer is never, unless I become an engineer. Which I choose not to be. So all those engineers can just enjoy their math. I'm doing fine without it.

The answer is never, unless I become an engineer, which I choose not to be.

2. When we first moved to this country, I would help my dad balance his checkbook. Usually after he had mailed out all of his bills. Some math knowledge came in handy then.

. . . I would help my dad balance his checkbook, usually after he had . . .

3. I currently work as a waiter. More than likely, technology will not take my job. Unless they build robots to serve people, I'm going to be all right. Although not too many people are in my shoes. At least I can say for the time being that I'm not worried about new technology.

Although not too many people are in my shoes, at least I can say . . .

4. Smoking should be banned in restaurants. Because some people have asthma, and secondhand smoke in public places makes them sick. That's just the simple fact of the matter.

. . . restaurants. Some people have asthma, . . .

5. Once, without permission, I gave a lot of my mother's things to charity. Which made her pretty mad. When we sat down and talked about it, my mother didn't look mad anymore. For the next few years, until I grew out of it, my mom designated a charity box for everyone in the family to contribute to.

. . . to charity, which made her pretty mad.

6. When people ask questions about my name, it gives me a story to tell. About my father, how I was named after him, and how he got his name. No one believes it, but it's true.

. . . a story to tell, about my father, how I was named after him, and how he got his name.

7. There are some famous people who have the same name I do, for instance, Gary Shandling. Another is Gary Peters. Who was a senator.

. . . Peters, who was a senator.

8. When I was nine years old, my brother, my friend, and his brother. We used to collect chestnuts. We had buckets full of chestnuts. We polished them and put them in our rooms on display. Eventually I heard someone refer to them as "buckeyes."

. . . his brother used to collect chestnuts.

9. I played a lot of sports when I was a kid. On some teams I became a leader, which I valued a lot because it made me the person that I am today.

correct as written

10. I worked in customer service. That meant all the upset people came to me. I handled all the Better Business Bureau complaints. Which meant

Ask Yourself

Subordinating conjunctions and relative pronouns can help you find fragments. Do those words occur in fragments you have written this semester?

talking to some irate people and getting them results. Sometimes I really wanted to quit.

. . . complaints, which meant talking . . .

EXERCISE 20-3 **Putting It All Together**

Directions: *Underline each fragment in the following sentences. Correct the error by joining the fragment to the appropriate sentence or by making it a complete sentence and writing your answer in the space provided. Some of the sentences may be correct.* Answers may vary. Example answers shown.

1. Every day I used to kick the fence and throw rocks and sticks at the neighbors' dogs, hoping they would get dirty or hurt. I was only four years old. I didn't care about those dogs.

correct as written

2. One day on our way to the store. My dad and I had an incident with this angry dog. It was a warm Friday afternoon.

. . . store, my dad . . .

3. The thought of safety didn't enter my mind. I stared in awe at this beast charging in my direction, ready to devour me. Just as it closed in, my guardian angel scooped me up from behind and placed me on top of the car.

correct as written

4. As I look back on it now, I really don't think the dog was going to hurt me. Because it didn't bite my dad or even really bark. But ever since then, I have been scared of my neighbors' dogs.

. . . to hurt me, because it didn't . . .

5. I really learned my lesson in this summer job. Which was to keep an eye on infants and what they have in their mouths. I also learned to help an infant when its life is in danger.

. . . job, which was to keep . . .

6. Once my friends found the perfect spot for the prank, they unloaded their gear. The most important of which were the Polaroid camera, a recorder, and a flashlight. My duty was lookout. I had to let the other boys know if the security guard was around.

. . . their gear, the most important of which were . . .

7. I never saw a real gun until I was ten years old. When a guy drove up to me and pulled a gun on me. I was never so scared in my life.

. . . ten years old, when a guy drove . . .

8. We played "jailbreak" when we were kids. The bad guy would be thrown into our makeshift jail, and moments later, he or she would break out. Repeating the same cycle of running, hopping fences, and eventually getting caught. We had fun like this the entire summer.

. . . break out, repeating the same cycle of . . .

9. I wasn't afraid of crossing the bridge itself. I was just afraid of falling into the water below. The bridge seemed like it was a million miles long, and time seemed to slow down. I thought we would never get to the other side.

correct as written

10. The sun had gone down. It was a cool night. Sitting by the riverbank, smoking our first cigarettes. We felt like the coolest guys alive.

Sitting by the riverbank, smoking our first cigarettes, we felt . . .

EXERCISE 20-4 Editing Fragments in Paragraphs

Directions: *Read the following paragraphs and underline the fragments. On a separate sheet of paper, correct the fragments by altering the punctuation or revising the wording.* Answers will vary.

1.

I had been driving for only a couple months. My father had just purchased a brand-new Ford F-150 pickup truck. I was taking a music class at night. While en route to my instructor's home. I was headed westbound on West Road, crossing Allen Road. Out of nowhere, I got broadsided by another car. He took out the whole side of the truck. From the front bumper to the tailgate. Try to explain this to your dad right after he told you to be extra careful with the car. Something that he had worked so hard for. It was the worst feeling of my life. I had destroyed his car in a matter of minutes. There was no escaping his wrath. I had no control of the situation.

home, I was

truck, from

car, something

2.

Math can be very difficult. Maybe it is all the numbers, the formulas, and the boring work. Nowadays there are hundred-dollar calculators that pretty much do the work for you. Some people are opposed to using

	calculators in class. I can see not using them in grade school, when you
basics, for	are just learning the basics. For example, addition and subtraction and
	then your multiplication and division tables. Kids should know that stuff
	right away and not need help from calculators to do things like that. They
calculator, until	should not be allowed to use a calculator. Until around the sixth grade. At
play because	that point calculators should be brought into play. Because most kids will
	have a good understanding of basic math. In addition, they will have to be-
years, for	come familiar with calculators for the coming years. For example, the high
	school classes that require a calculator. In high school, calculators become
	essential for math and other subjects.

3.

	Looking at myself and my two best friends just proves how much the
	times have changed. Each of us lives a very different life. Yet one thing
I go to school full-time and work only	separates us from our mothers. We had options. I am a typical college
	student. At school full-time and working only part-time as a waitress. My
	friend Lynn chose to get a job straight out of high school. She is a full-
Marisa, who	blown workaholic. Finally, there is Marisa. Who had a child right out of
	high school. She manages a full-time job and a child all on her own. Now
	which one of us works the hardest? The answer is that we all work equally
path while	hard. We have chosen our own paths. While remaining the best of friends
	and thriving off one another.

TOPIC 15: Sentence Structure
www.mhhe.com/goingplaces

Comma Splices and Run-Ons

CHAPTER OVERVIEW

- Comma Splices
  - *Identify Comma Splices*
  - *Correct Comma Splices*
- Run-Ons
  - *Identify Run-Ons*
  - *Correct Run-Ons*

Sometimes college writers, aiming for long sentences, overlook the most basic rule in writing: Put a period at the end of a sentence. This chapter looks at long sentences gone wrong, sentences that can be easily fixed with end punctuation or by using what you have learned about coordination and subordination.

Comma Splices

A **comma splice** occurs when two complete sentences are connected with a comma. Correct a comma splice with a period or by forming a compound or complex sentence.

Identify Comma Splices

If you can substitute a period for a comma in a sentence and make two separate, complete sentences, then you have a comma splice. Consider this example:

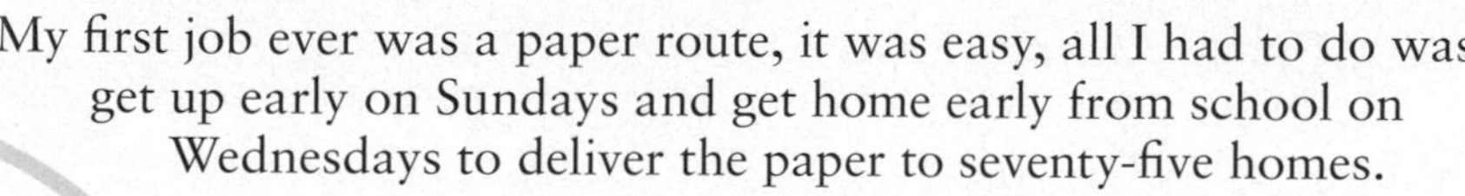

My first job ever was a paper route, it was easy, all I had to do was get up early on Sundays and get home early from school on Wednesdays to deliver the paper to seventy-five homes.

Writer's Response

Search your papers for a comma splice. Then describe what a comma splice is using the example from your writing.

There are three complete sentences in this example. Each sentence expresses a complete idea and can be written as a separate sentence:

1. My first job ever was a paper route.
2. It was easy.
3. All I had to do was get up early on Sundays and get home early from school on Wednesdays to deliver the paper to seventy-five homes.

Putting a period at the end of each complete sentence corrects these comma splices.

My first job ever was a paper route. It was easy. All I had to do was get up early on Sundays and get home early from school on Wednesdays to deliver the paper to seventy-five homes.

EXERCISE 21-1 **Comma Splices and Simple Sentences**

Directions: *Read the following sentences and circle the commas. Identify the simple sentences. Where you see a comma splice, change the comma to a period and write the correction in the space provided.*

1. I believe everyone is intelligent in at least one field, take my brother John, for instance. He's a businessman.

   . . . field. Take . . .

2. Year after year he would save up his money for his big break, finally it happened. He opened up a restaurant with his friend. A couple of years passed, he was constantly fighting with his friend because they both wanted to do different things.

   . . . break. Finally. . . . passed. He . . .

3. I never lie to my parents about anything major. I'd rather have them know what I'm doing, they were kids once too.

   . . . I'm doing. They . . .

4. My mother does a good job keeping the house together. Even though she's a single parent, she takes care of her responsibilities and makes sure everyone is taken care of, I have to give her a lot of credit.

   . . . care of. I . . .

5. The customer came in for his car. The boss said, "You don't owe us anything, it's on us." The customer just stood there. I will never forget the look on his face. He was extremely happy.

. . . owe us anything. It's on us."

Correct Comma Splices

When you find a comma splice, you can make a decision about sentence variety. If you put a period at the end of a sentence, you will never be wrong. You will have concise, emphatic sentence structure.

However, there are more options available to you when you edit comma splices. For example, you can replace a comma with a conjunction; replace a comma with a semicolon, conjunctive adverb, and a comma; or replace a comma with a subordinating conjunction. (See Chapter 19 for additional information and practice on coordination and subordination.)

Add an Appropriate Conjunction after the Comma

Here's a comma splice:

> I've been going to school for thirteen years, I'm beginning to realize how important it is.

This comma splice can be corrected by adding an appropriate conjunction after the comma:

> I've been going to school for thirteen years, and I'm beginning to realize how important it is.

See Chapter 19, page 418, for a list of coordinating conjunctions.

Substitute a Semicolon for the Comma and Add a Conjunctive Adverb Followed by a Comma

Here is another comma splice:

> College is simply a lot harder than high school was, I have a lot more homework to do every day.

This comma splice can be corrected by replacing the comma with a semicolon and adding a conjunctive adverb followed by a comma:

> College is simply a lot harder than high school was; moreover, I have a lot more homework to do every day.

See Chapter 19, page 421, for a list of conjunctive adverbs.

Use the comma-conjunction and semicolon-conjunctive adverb options when they make sense and sound right.

EXERCISE 21-2 Correcting Comma Splices Using Conjunctions and Conjunctive Adverbs

Directions: *Underline the comma splices in each of the following items. Then correct them, using one of these three options: (a) replace the comma with a period, (b) add a conjunction after the comma, or (c) replace the comma with a semicolon and a conjunctive adverb followed by a comma.* **Answers will vary. Example answers shown.**

1. The first time I ever saw a real celebrity I was ten years old. A TV personality named Arnold Stang walked out of a restaurant, he looked just like he did on TV, only smaller.

. . . out of a restaurant. He looked . . .

2. When I was a kid, I was very curious about guns. I never touched a real handgun, I saw and heard one once.

. . . handgun; however, I . . .

3. The doctor said everything he tested for was positive. I couldn't believe it, I was allergic to eighty-two things.

. . . believe it. I was . . .

4. I'm glad I got the tests over with. Now my doctor and mom won't bug me about it, that will be a great relief.

. . . it, and that . . .

Ask Yourself

Which five conjunctive adverbs are you most likely to use? Can you write a sentence for each?

5. Ah, the last days of summer. It was a cool night, the sun had just gone down.

. . . night, and the sun . . .

6. When I was a kid, I thought I would always love dogs. I had one of my own, her name was Lady. She was a big brown retriever.

. . . own. Her name . . .

7. It was a hot June morning, I was coming back from McDonald's when I saw one of my neighbors, Mark, playing with a neighbor's dog.

. . . morning. I was . . .

8. This dog was horrible, it would not stop barking, it kept slobbering on my new shoes, and it would not listen to anything I said.

. . . horrible; for example, it would not stop barking. It . . .

9. This thing was crazy, it tried attacking me every time I cut the grass or cleaned my swimming pool.

. . . crazy; indeed, it . . .

10. One afternoon I got mad at our cat when she was hissing at me, I started yelling back at her, from that time on she has been a lot nicer to me.

. . . me; consequently, I started yelling back at her. From . . .

Add an Appropriate Subordinating Conjunction

Like coordinating conjunctions and conjunctive adverbs, subordinating conjunctions establish a logical relationship between consecutive ideas. Look at the following example:

> Some of the problems you have are brought on by yourself, others are caused by your friends. The important thing is recognizing what needs to be fixed and taking care of business.

The comma splice can be corrected, and the relationship between the two statements indicated through the addition of a subordinating conjunction after the comma.

> Some of the problems you have are brought on by yourself, **while** others are caused by your friends.

Here is another example:

> I worked hard to change things in my life, everything seemed to remain the same. It was easy to get discouraged, but I didn't lose hope. In the end, everything came out okay.

Once again, the comma splice occurs at the beginning of the short paragraph. The logical relationship between the two statements here can be indicated through the addition of a subordinating conjunction at the beginning of the sentence.

> **Even though** I worked hard to change things in my life, everything seemed to remain the same.

See Chapter 19, page 425, for a list of subordinating conjunctions.

EXERCISE 21-3 Correcting Comma Splices Using Subordinating Conjunctions

Directions: *Underline the comma splices in each of the following items. Then correct them either by using a subordinating conjunction with a comma or by using a period at the end of the sentence. Some items may have more than one comma splice.* Answers will vary. Example answers shown.

1. When we have company over, I don't have to worry about putting the cat in a different room, she won't come out from her hiding spot.

. . . different room. She . . .

2. Our cat is also an indoor cat, she rarely wants to go outside, I am happy about that.

Because our cat is also an indoor cat, she . . . outside. I . . .

3. The math teacher started solving a problem on the board I studied every step, she asked me to do the same problem on the board. I did the problem, and I got it right. I was so happy. From that day I started liking math, that was six years ago.

As the math teacher . . . board, I studied . . . step. When she . . . board,

I did . . . it right. From . . . math. That . . .

4. When I was in the seventh grade, I was at a school dance, a boy approached me and asked me to dance, but I turned him down.

. . . dance. A boy . . .

5. Then came freshman year, it was time to enter high school. It was a brand-new experience.

. . . year, when it was . . .

6. I see people smoking, I have the urge to ask them if I can have one, I just turn away my head instead.

Whenever I see people smoking, I have . . . one. I just . . .

7. Most teenagers want to smoke because they think it makes them look cool. Some smoke because their mom and dad tell them not to, others are rebellious and do it just to disobey.

. . . not to, while others . . .

8. There is too much homework, kids are losing out on fun after school, parents can help, they can monitor their kids' homework, they can meet with principals and discuss the amount of homework that kids receive.

Because there is too much homework, kids . . . school. Parents can help.

They . . . homework, and they . . .

9. My mother is a calm person, she just loves to chat and laugh with her children, occasionally she gets a little excited. You want to watch out then.

. . . person. While . . . children, occasionally . . .

10. Joe and I went to the same school, we went everywhere together, we often spent the night at each other's houses on the weekend.

Because Joe and I . . . school, we . . . together. We . . .

EXERCISE 21-4 Putting It All Together

Directions: *Find the comma splices in the following paragraphs. Rewrite the paragraphs and underline your corrections. Try to use all of the methods listed for correcting comma splices: (a) replace the comma with a period; (b) add a conjunction and a comma; (c) replace the comma with a semicolon, a conjunctive adverb, and a comma; or (d) add a subordinating conjunction.* Answers will vary.

death; indeed, media

trouble. They

1. Violence has become the answer to many teenagers' frustrations in life. The introduction to violence starts when they are very small. Television dramas show everything from guns to blood and death, media glamorizes the violent behavior. Teens relate to these dramas and feel violence is the way to end their depression. Another important cause of violence is a lack of family structure. Those teens lacking love and family structure often are in trouble, they all too often take out their

troubles through violent actions. Finally, violence may be seen as a cry for help or a way to get attention for some adolescents. Teens see that the only time they are noticed is when they become violent, hurt others, or cause trouble, sometimes they are scared or confused and do not know how to properly express or release those emotions, then violence becomes the vent through which they release steam.

trouble. Sometimes
emotions. Then

2. Some men think the women's movement as it stands today makes it difficult for men and women to enjoy an old-fashioned relationship. This is true to the point that I have to watch practically everything I say and do. It bothers me that I can't compliment a woman on how she looks, it's not sexist, it is just appreciation. I still like to open the door for a woman and pay for dinner, I do so with the hope that she won't consider it sexual harassment. At one time these kinds of things were just simple manners. Take a look at our parents, they treated each other with respect. I don't know about you, but I sometimes wish I lived in the olden days. Today it is important for women to be treated as equals, in the workplace. Nevertheless, we need to understand that being courteous is sometimes just that, being courteous. Being equal is important, that does not mean we cannot just be nice.

looks. It's
dinner, and I
parents. They
important; however, that

3. Attitudes about credit cards can vary a great deal, depending on when a person is born. My grandfather is old school, he purchased his last truck with $15,000 in $20 bills he had been socking away for years. Then there are people like my parents, who prefer to make their purchases without the long savings period. They got their first taste of plastic in the mid 80's and never looked back, they enjoy the ability to spend what they want, when they want it, and simply make their planned monthly payments to eliminate debt. If for some reason their cards are lost or stolen, the bank replaces them in 7–10 days, forgiving any unauthorized purchases. These days my parents are educated on the dangers and benefits of a credit lifestyle. They believe that plastic makes their lives easier. Being a generation X'er, I have learned to walk a fine line between cash and credit. On one hand, I am terrified of identity theft, I prefer to carry cash. On the other hand, the reality is that I cannot make a hotel reservation, rent a car, or take advantage of shopping online without a credit card. Our society is a credit culture, there are purchases you cannot make without a credit card. I have learned to walk a fine line between cash and credit, I am both old school and new school. (237 words)

school. He
back because they enjoy
hand, since I . . .
culture; consequently, there
credit. I

Run-Ons

Like a comma splice, a **run-on** is an error involving two complete sentences. Whereas a comma splice occurs when two complete sentences are joined by a comma, a run-on sentence has no connecting punctuation. The sentences simply run together.

Identify Run-Ons

Consider this example:

> I remember the day we met I was swimming to the raft in the lake. This guy went speeding by on a wave runner he was so close I could almost reach out and touch him later that day I ran into him in town.

There are five complete sentences in this example. Each sentence expresses a complete idea and can be written as a separate sentence:

1. I remember the day we met.
2. I was swimming to the raft in the lake.
3. This guy went speeding by on a wave runner.
4. He was so close I could almost reach out and touch him.
5. Later that day I ran into him in town.

This series of consecutive actions can be expressed in concise simple sentences:

> I remember the day we met. I was swimming to the raft in the lake. This guy went speeding by on a wave runner. He was so close I could almost reach out and touch him. Later that day I ran into him in town.

End punctuation brings your writing into focus. It helps you see your ideas clearly, giving you an opportunity to edit, combine sentences, and vary sentence length and structure.

EXERCISE 21-5 Run-Ons and the Simple Sentence

Directions: *Underline the run-ons in the following sentences. Insert a period at the end of each complete sentence. Write your corrections in the space provided.*

1. Don't get me wrong I enjoyed where I worked and what I was doing, but it was not enough I wanted more.

   . . . wrong. I enjoyed . . . enough. I wanted more.

2. After thinking about my employment prospects, I came to a decision I decided I do not want to be a secretary for the rest of my life I want to be a registered nurse.

   . . . decision. I decided . . . life. I want . . .

3. I tried skipping class while in the eighth grade my friends didn't that is when my trouble with school began I spent some time in detention after school I met a couple of bad characters there.

   . . . grade. My friends didn't. That . . . began. I . . . after school. I met . . .

4. I think I watched too much TV when I was a kid it must have had some effect on me I didn't spend enough time on schoolwork even now I watch too much TV, and it affects my grades.

   . . . a kid. It must . . . me. I didn't . . . schoolwork. Even now . . .

5. I guess it wasn't the type of work that was important to me it was the place I work that led me to a change of attitude that was my value system then that's my value system now.

   . . . to me. It was . . . attitude. That . . . then. That's . . .

Correct Run-Ons

You can correct a run-on in much the same way you would a comma splice. Because you are joining two simple sentences, you can use the options for coordination and subordination that you learned in Chapter 19. These include adding an appropriate conjunction and a comma; adding a semicolon, conjunctive adverb, and a comma; or adding an appropriate subordinating conjunction.

Note: The most important thing to remember is that you do not correct a run-on by placing a comma between the two simple sentences. Doing so makes a run-on into a comma splice.

Add an Appropriate Conjunction and a Comma

Here is a run-on sentence:

> My son tries hard in school it takes him a little longer to get good grades.

The error can be corrected by the addition of a comma and an appropriate conjunction.

> My son tries hard in school, **but** it takes him a little longer to get good grades.

Talk about It
Are your sentences long or short? Are you more inclined to write comma splices or run-ons?

Add a Semicolon, a Conjunctive Adverb, and a Comma

Here is a run-on sentence:

> I had five hard classes last semester my hardest class was economics.

The error can be corrected by adding a semicolon and a conjunctive adverb followed by a comma.

> I had five hard classes last semester**; however,** my hardest class was economics.

Use the comma-conjunction and semicolon options when they make sense and sound right.

EXERCISE 21-6 **Correcting Run-Ons with Conjunctions and Conjunctive Adverbs**

Directions: *Underline the run-ons in the following sentences. Then correct the errors using one of these three options: (a) add a period at the end of the sentence; (b) add a comma followed by a conjunction; or (c) add a semicolon and a conjunctive adverb followed by a comma. Some items may not need correction.* Answers will vary. Example answers shown.

1. Usually the drive down to Florida would take about nine hours if my mom was driving, it would take twelve.

... nine hours; however, if my ...

2. He purposely mixed his languages together to make me confused it took years for me to catch on to this.

. . . confused, and it . . .

3. My aunt is a very important person in my life she is my great-aunt, my grandmother's baby sister. She's my mother's favorite aunt, that is why we are so close.

. . . life. She is. . . . aunt, so that is why we are so close.

4. Uncle Pete enjoys playing golf two or three times a week during golf season in the off-season he bowls.

. . . season; however, in . . .

5. My favorite knickknack is a jade elephant it was given to me as a gift.

. . . elephant. It . . .

6. One of my ceramic eggs has green and gold designs all over it and around the rim of the egg itself. This egg opens up, and it has a working clock inside.

correct as written

7. My sister is a friend to everyone she is more than a friend to me she is my best friend she is the person I confide in the most.

. . . everyone, but . . . me. She . . . friend. In fact, she . . .

8. It's hard enough just being in high school my friend turned high school into a roller coaster of love-hate situations our freshman year was great we would spend the weekend at each other's houses and study together we sang a duet in our choir's spring festival. Then things changed.

. . . school. My . . . situations. For example, . . . great. We . . . together; in addition, . . .

9. I thought about the decision for quite a while I decided that I did not care. She had her turn now I would get mine.

. . . while. Then, I decided. . . . turn. Now . . .

10. I'm using basketball as a tool to reach my goal of becoming an engineer it is not just a game to me it is my life.

. . . engineer. Consequently, it . . . me. It is . . .

Add an Appropriate Subordinating Conjunction

The two simple sentences in a run-on can also be joined using a subordinating conjunction. (See the list of subordinating conjunctions in Chapter 19 on page 425.) The connecting words establish a logical relationship between the two sentences in the run-on.

The trash collectors come every morning at 7:30 I usually take out the garbage the night before.

The logical relationship in the first sentence is cause and effect. This relationship can be indicated by using a subordinating conjunction and a comma to join the simple sentences.

Because the trash collectors come every morning at 7:30, I usually take out the garbage the night before.

To develop a feel for sentence variety, use both coordination and subordination when you proofread for and correct run-on sentences.

EXERCISE 21-7 Correcting Run-Ons Using Subordinating Conjunctions

Directions: *Underline the run-ons in the following sentences. Then correct them either by inserting a subordinating conjunction with a comma or by using a period at the end of the sentence.* Answers will vary. Example answers shown.

1. Many people still do not use seatbelts when they drive seatbelts save lives.

. . . drive, even though . . .

2. The time and place were set all I had to do was complete the task.

After . . . set, all I had . . .

3. I turned to say goodbye to my cousin and his friends they were gone seconds later I realized why their bus had actually arrived five minutes early.

When . . . friends, they . . . gone. Seconds . . . why. Their . . .

4. I had to use a lot of heavy machinery it was hard work somehow I managed and actually began to like what I was doing.

. . . machinery; it was hard work, although somehow . . .

5. When I was little, I was not much of a collector all I collected was dolls my friends would ask me if they could hold one of my dolls I just said no.

. . . collector. All . . . dolls. When . . . dolls, I . . .

6. My uncles are twins they are the bosses of their catering company they prepare food for any kind of occasion they say they like wedding receptions the best it looks like a cool job.

. . . twins. They . . . company. Although . . . occasion, they . . . the best. It . . .

7. I realize everyone has problems some people just have more than others that is the way it is.

. . . problems, although . . . others. That is . . .

8. My brother Jim and his friend Joe stopped at the fireworks store they spent a couple hundred dollars each I went inside and decided to buy some I only had about twenty dollars to spend.

When my . . . store, they . . . each. I . . . some, even though . . .

9. All of a sudden Emily wanted to leave we started walking out the alarm went off. The manager came out and asked us if we had stolen anything. Never in my life had I stolen anything Emily was another story.

. . . leave. We . . . out when the alarm. . . . anything, whereas Emily . . .

10. I misbehaved the teacher told me to get out and go home I was excluded from the play I figured I went back the next day and apologized maybe she would let me back in the play that didn't work she told me she already had someone else to play my part.

After I misbehaved . . . home. I . . . play. I figured if . . . the play. That . . . work. She . . .

EXERCISE 21-8 Proofreading for Comma Splices and Run-Ons

Directions: *Read the following sentences. Mark those that are comma splices CS and those that are run-ons RO. Some sentences may have more than one error. Correct the errors using one of these four options: (a) add a period at the end of the sentence; (b) add a comma and a conjunction; (c) add a semicolon and a conjunctive adverb; or (d) add a subordinating conjunction.* Answers will vary. Example answers shown.

Ask Yourself

Which errors are easier to identify and correct, comma splices or run-ons? Why?

CS 1. My first job was Franklin Wright Settlements. I started that job the summer of 2004, I was fourteen years old. I was really excited the whole summer about that job. So I did my best.

. . . 2004, when I was . . .

RO 2. Even strangers teach me things. Sometimes it doesn't matter who it is if it means something to me or relates to me, somehow I never forget it.

. . . it is. If it . . .

RO 3. It's not his fault he was born with AIDS what can he do about that?

. . . AIDS. What . . .

CS,CS 4. I operate a forklift, it is hard to drive, but at the end of the day I feel like I did something. The thing I hate about my job is my boss, she always tries to do things too fast and always wants to be right.

. . . forklift. It is. . . . boss, because she . . .

RO,CS 5. I try to drink orange juice it prevents me from catching colds, I really like the taste of it.

. . . juice. It . . . colds; moreover, . . .

RO 6. I think that when you're sixteen or seventeen, you don't think about the value of your job you just want to work so you can earn money to go shopping with friends and blow your money on whatever grabs your attention.

. . . your job. Indeed, you . . .

RO,CS 7. When I was trying to quit smoking, I never wore the patch it is not that I didn't want to put one on it is just that I always forgot.

. . . patch. It is . . .; it is . . .

CS 8. It was very interesting to meet the travelers who had no knowledge of Pennsylvania, to them it was just another place to have a business meeting.

. . . Pennsylvania; indeed, to . . .

CS,RO 9. Then one day I started doing time cards, making beds, and working overtime while still getting paid only eight dollars an hour, I tried to talk to my boss but it wasn't any help, so I finally said goodbye to that job. I really did enjoy that job it was fun and diverse every day.

. . . hour. I tried . . . job. It was . . .

CS 10. How I got my name is very simple, I was born, my parents looked in the phone book and selected the first name they liked.

. . . simple. When I was . . .

Gateway

TOPIC 15: Sentence Structure
www.mhhe.com/goingplaces

CHAPTER OVERVIEW

- Verbs and Verb Agreement
  - *Verbs*
  - *Subject and Verb Agreement*
  - *Additional Verb Agreement Problems*
- Irregular Verbs
- Consistent Verb Tense

Verb Errors: Agreement, Irregular Verbs, and Consistency

The English you are accustomed to hearing and speaking may differ from the English used in the college classroom. If it is, you need to make a "code shift." For example, in an informal setting, you might say that you "seen" a good movie. In the college classroom or workplace, you say that you "saw" a good movie. What sounds fine in an informal setting may not be acceptable in formal written English. Code shifting requires paying attention to verbs.

Verbs and Verb Agreement

TOPIC 17: Agreement
www.mhhe.com/goingplaces

Verbs

Verbs either express actions or link subjects to modifiers. They also state when something happens—in the past, the present, or the future.

Most college teachers assign homework every day.

This sentence is about college teachers and homework, but the heart of the sentence is the verb, *assign*. The verb expresses the action, what college teachers *do*.

Most college teachers assigned homework every day.

Most college teachers will assign homework every day.

Verbs also place the action in the past, present, or future. In the first sentence, *assigned* indicates an action that took place in the past. In the second sentence, *will assign* indicates an action that will take place in the future.

A SIMPLE TEST FOR ACTION VERBS

To find the action verb in a sentence, ask these questions:

- What is happening?
- When is it happening?

When you identify the word or words that answer these questions, you have found the verb in the sentence.

Verbs can also link subjects to modifiers. A modifier can be another noun or an adjective. A noun gives the subject another name, whereas an adjective ascribes a quality to the subject.

The committee chairperson is a tyrant.

The committee chairperson is serious.

In the first sentence the verb links the subject, "chairperson," to a noun, *tyrant*; in the second sentence, it is linked to an adjective, *serious*. Like action verbs, linking verbs also express time: past, present, and future.

The hurricane disaster was widespread. (*past tense*)

The hurricane disaster will be a wake-up call. (*future tense*)

In these examples the verb links the subject first to an adjective, *widespread,* then to a noun, *a wake-up call,* first in past tense, then in future tense.

COMMON LINKING VERBS		
is	feel	remain
are	get	seem
was	grow	smell
were	sit	sound
appear	look	taste
become	prove	turn

EXERCISE 22-1 Identifying Verbs

Directions: *Underline subjects once and verbs twice in the sentences below. Indicate in the space provided whether the verb is an action verb (A) or a linking verb (L).*

A 1. All the new employees wanted overtime.

L 2. The situation between the neighbors and the new resident turned out fine.

L 3. At first all the reading in psychology class seems excessive.

A 4. Work stoppages in the transportation sector will complicate people's travel plans this summer.

L 5. Efforts to beautify the state were vigorous and well funded.

L 6. The arguments against young people giving a year or two of national service are much less persuasive than those in favor of service.

A 7. New technologies emerge every day and transform the workplace practically over night.

A 8. Opinions vary on the best summer activities for college graduates.

A 9. The cook will taste the sauce and pronounce it ready to serve.

L 10. Both the coach and the players remain confident in the team's prospects for the coming year.

Subject and Verb Agreement

Subject and **verb agreement** occurs when the subject and verb of a sentence go together properly. Subjects of sentences can be singular or plural. For subject and verb to agree, present tense verbs must also be singular or plural. Singular subjects take singular verbs; plural subjects take plural verbs. Here are some guidelines for editing subject and verb agreement.

MULTILINGUAL TIP

In present tense, third-person singular verbs end in "s" or "es." Do not confuse this ending with the plural of nouns, "s" or "es." He likes to read novels.

Regular Verbs in Present Tense

Most verbs in English are regular. That means you apply the same rule to all of them. With regular verbs in present tense, third-person singular has an -s ending. The table shows the present tense forms of the verb *to like.*

to like	Singular	Plural
First person	I *like*	we *like*
Second person	you *like*	you *like*
Third person	he/she/it *likes*	they *like*

Notice that verbs following he/she/it have the "s" sound.

I start school in September.

Football practice starts early in August.

My cousin plans to go out for football this year.

The first game of the season falls on a Saturday this year.

EXERCISE 22-2 Verb Agreement and Regular Verbs

Directions: *Underline subjects and double underline the correct verbs for each of the sentences below.*

1. The crazy bus driver on Illinois Avenue (sing/sings) out each bus stop when he (feel/feels) happy.
2. Passengers (like/likes) to ride his bus for that reason.
3. We usually (sit/sits) halfway back on the bus and (wait/waits) for him to start singing.
4. Sometimes he (drive/drives) one-handed and (play/plays) the harmonica.
5. Company regulations (require/requires) drivers to minimize interaction with passengers.
6. I (know/knows) this because my uncle (drive/drives) the bus on Fuller Avenue.
7. You just never (know/knows) what surprises (await/awaits) you on a city bus.
8. Afternoon traffic (get/gets) heavy.
9. Passengers (appreciate/appreciates) his singing.
10. It (make/makes) time pass a little faster.

EXERCISE 22-3 Verb Agreement and Regular Verbs

Directions: *Read the following paragraph. Correct the verb agreement errors you find.*

My mother is a great role model for me and my brother. She works, goes to school, clean the house, cooks, and still finds time to help us out when she can. She reads to my little brother, explains things, and breaks words down to their simplest meanings. She is a role model because she cares about whether my brother understand things and how he behaves in school. She is also a very good cook. We don't go out to eat as much as I would like to. I tell her that food in restaurants smell good. Not only that, but the food always taste good too. She agrees with me, but then she help me understand that food cost less when we cook it at home. Finally, my mother is an outgoing woman. She will help anyone who need help. If someone ask her for some spare change, she will dig down deep in her purse and find a little something. Then she say to us: Help others. Work hard so you don't find yourself in a bad situation, but always remember the poor. My mother work hard and tries her best to raise us well.

cleans the house
breaks words down
understands things
smells good
tastes good
helps me
costs less
needs help
asks her
says to us
works hard

Irregular Verbs in Present Tense: *Be, Have, Do*

Irregular verbs are those that do not follow the pattern shown above. Notice, however, that the third-person singular retains the "s" sound on the end of the verb.

to be	Singular	Plural
First person	I *am*	we *are*
Second person	you *are*	you *are*
Third person	he/she/it *is*	they *are*
to have	**Singular**	**Plural**
First person	I *have*	we *have*
Second person	you *have*	you *have*
Third person	he/she/it *has*	they *have*
to do	**Singular**	**Plural**
First person	I *do*	we *do*
Second person	you *do*	you *do*
Third person	he/she/it *does*	they *do*

EXERCISE 22-4 Agreement and Irregular Verbs

Directions: *Underline subjects and choose the correct verbs for each of the sentences below. Be sure to choose present tense forms of* to be, to have, *and* to do.

1. After my two best friends, I am__________ the best basketball player on the block.

2. They do__________ not practice very much, but somehow they have__________ better skills.

3. Some people say basketball is ________ a waste of time.

4. It does ________ take up a lot of time, if you let it.

5. My friends and I are ________ careful not to get carried away.

6. Homework is ________ important.

7. Jobs are ________ important, too.

8. I have ________ a job, and one of my friends has ________ a job.

9. We are ________ very busy people.

10. Still, if we do ________ not play some ball at least once a week, we have ________ a tendency to get a little nervous.

Agreement and Irregular Verbs in Past Tense

In the simple past tense, agreement problems occur only with the irregular verb *to be.*

to be	Singular	Plural
First person	I *was*	we *were*
Second person	you *were*	you *were*
Third person	he/she/it *was*	they *were*

The neighborhood school grounds are always open for public use.
The neighborhood school grounds were always open for public use.
The neighborhood school is fully Internet-ready.
The neighborhood school was fully Internet-ready.

EXERCISE 22-5 Agreement and Irregular Verbs in Past Tense

Directions: *Underline subjects and choose the correct past tense form of* to be *for each of the sentences below.*

1. There was ________ never any doubt about who would move out of the house first.

2. People were ________ talking a lot about organizing a ski trip, but no one was ________ actually doing anything yet.

3. You were ________ not really cool if you were ________ still living at home.

4. At the time, I was ________ working thirty hours a week, and my parents were ________ eager for me to live at home and go to school.

5. My friend, Tanya, on the other hand, was ________ working forty hours a week, and her mother was ________ always giving her a hard time.

6. My other good friends, Deena and Pam, were______ not working at all.

7. One night there was______ an incident.

8. I don't know what happened, but at midnight, Tanya was______ on my front doorstep.

9. Were______ there any good reasons for her to continue living at home?

10. We talked all night and saw that there were______ no good reasons, and the next day she was______ ready to pack up and go.

Talk about It

Who do you know who is good at grammar and finding verbs? Why is knowing about verbs important?

EXERCISE 22-6 Agreement and Irregular Verbs in Present and Past Tense

Directions: *Read the following sentences and underline the subjects. Then double underline the verb that agrees with the subject of the sentence. Read the simple subject and verb together to listen for the single "s" sound.*

1. Before the Kyoto Summit, many fingers (was/were) pointed at assumed guilty parties.
2. Gifford Pinchot's belief was that "all natural resources (was/were) for the benefit of humans."
3. When we came outside, a police officer (was/were) sitting right in front of our house.
4. My uncles (go/goes) to every sporting event they can think of.
5. Then one afternoon I (was/were) watching TV, and I heard the motorcycle start up.
6. We had lunch at the Olive Garden. The food (was/were) excellent.
7. Over time, graphing calculators (has/ have) become standard equipment in the classroom.
8. Now women (is/are) visible everywhere in the workplace.
9. My second reason for favoring the war on drugs (has/have) to be the effects drugs have on newborn babies.
10. Almost all businesses (do/does) at least some of their work on the Internet these days.

EXERCISE 22-7 Missing Verb Endings

Directions: *Read the following sentences and edit for missing verb endings. Add -d and -ed, -s, and -es endings as needed. Some items may have more than one verb error.*

1. For a number of reasons it is easy to understand why he feel the way that he do.

. . . he feels the way that he does.______

2. My grandfather always made us do various chores around the house. He also watch everyone that came to the door from his favorite chair.

He also watched . . .

3. My aunt's complexion was dark brown. She had no wrinkles. She use Oil of Olay on her skin.

She used Oil of Olay . . .

4. This aunt still calls me Baby Bobby. How old do I have to be before she stop calling me that?

. . . before she stops . . .

5. I have grown to respect the person who live down the street from me. He has encourage me to work hard at everything I do and not to let anybody stop me.

. . . who lives. . . . has encouraged me . . .

6. The first time I got into trouble, my own people did not come to visit, but our pastor did, and I change because of him.

. . . I changed . . .

7. The job he do make a difference to many young teens.

. . . he does makes . . .

8. I took one look at our new math teacher and judge his character wrong.

. . . judged his character . . .

9. My grandmother remembers a lottery number based on my birthday. She still remember the first time she play it, but she can't remember my name.

. . . still remembers the first time she played it . . .

10. In her spare time, she like to read and do crafts such as floral arrangements.

. . . she likes to . . .

Additional Verb Agreement Problems

In addition to knowing regular and irregular verbs, it helps to recognize sentence constructions in which verb agreement can be confusing.

Compound Subjects

A compound subject may be two subjects joined by *and* or three or more subjects in a series ending with *and*.

Simple Subject: The bicycle gets people around town in many European cities.

Compound Subject: Bicycles and motorcycles get people around town in many European cities.

Compound Subject: Bicycles, motorcycles, and cars get people around town in many European cities.

Hint: To check for the correct verb, substitute a singular pronoun for simple subjects and a plural pronoun for compound subjects.

Simple Subject: The bicycle gets kids around town in many European cities.

Substitute Singular Pronoun: It gets people around town in many European cities.

Compound Subject: Motorcycles and cars get people around town in many European cities.

Substitute Plural Pronoun: They get people around town in many European cities.

Compound Subject: Bicycles, motorcycles, and cars get people around town in many European cities.

Substitute Plural Pronoun: They get people around town in many European cities.

EXERCISE 22-8 Verb Agreement and Compound Subjects

Directions: *Underline the simple or compound subject in each sentence below and choose the verb that agrees with it. Substitute a pronoun for the subject to test your answer and write the sentence, using the pronoun, in the space provided.*

1. Technology (is/are) essential in most lines of work.

It is essential in most lines of work.

2. Clever use of language and creative graphics (keep/keeps) the child interested in reading.

They keep the child interested in reading.

3. Music and painting (express/expresses) the way people feel.

They express the way people feel.

4. A good diet (is/are) essential to maintaining health.

It is essential to maintaining health.

5. People's jobs (define/defines) who they are.

They define who they are.

6. If a longer school day and a program to get more parents involved in education (doesn't/don't) work, then what is the answer?

If they don't work, then what is the answer?

7. Working in a pharmacy, taking care of a family, and going to school full time (was/were) all I could handle.

They were all I could handle.

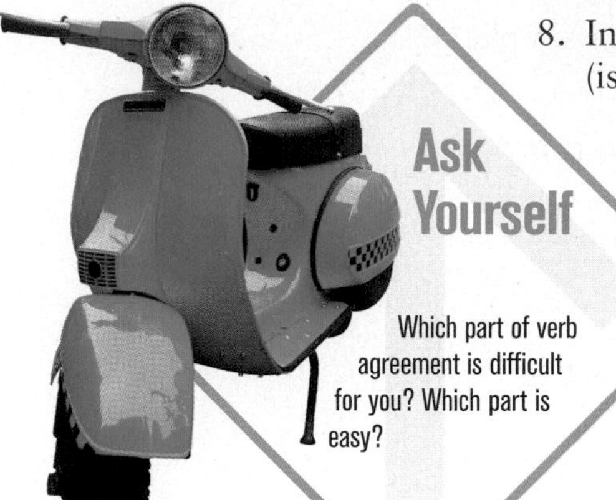

Ask Yourself
Which part of verb agreement is difficult for you? Which part is easy?

8. In large group settings, my interests and the interests of others (is/are) completely different.

They are completely different.

9. I usually got As and Bs. Class participation and attendance (was/were) not all that was needed to do well in the class.

They were not all that was needed to do well in the class.

10. The number of healthy people (has/have) been increasing over the past few years.

It has been increasing over the past few years.

Verb-First Sentences

In sentences beginning with the words *here* and *there* the subject comes after the verb. To choose the verb that agrees with the subject, put the subject in front of the verb.

Here at last was the one perfect job for me to do.
The perfect job for me was here.

There /have been many fingers pointed at assumed guilty parties.
Many fingers have been pointed at assumed guilty parties.

In these sentences, "here" and "there" are not the subjects. The subjects come after the verbs—"the job *was*" and "many fingers *have*."

Sentences with Relative Pronouns

In complex sentences, relative pronouns "repeat" the subject and are either singular or plural:

The peaches that (fall/falls) to the ground (rot/rots) quickly.
Peaches fall.
Peaches rot.
The peaches that fall to the ground rot quickly.

The main part of this sentence is "peaches rot quickly." The relative clause tells which peaches. The relative pronoun *that* echoes the plural subject "peaches" and consequently takes a plural verb.

The neighborhood kid who (stop/stops) by our house (is/are) always welcome.
Kid stops.
Kid is welcome.
The neighborhood kid who stops by our house is always welcome.

The main part of this sentence is "kid is welcome." The relative clause "who stops by our house" specifies which kid. *Who* echoes the singular subject "kid" and therefore takes the singular verb.

EXERCISE 22-9 Editing for Subject and Verb Agreement

Directions: *Underline simple subjects and double underline verbs in the following sentences. Correct verb agreement errors by writing in the correct verb in the space provided. Some of the sentences may be correct as written.*

1. There are things a person can do to get better grades and improve himself as a student.

correct as written

2. There has been many situations in which people recognized me from the competitions I entered.

There have been . . .

3. The areas that I need to work on is attending classes, keeping up with material, and paying attention in class.

The areas . . . are

4. These are a few strategies that has worked for me and is bound to make you a successful student.

. . . strategies that have worked . . . are bound . . .

5. Some people have to work at their talents; then again there is some who just has them naturally.

. . . there are some . . . have them . . .

6. The strong family values that influence his work habits makes this person stand out above the rest.

. . . values . . . make . . .

7. I know there is many distractions while you are driving.

. . . there are many distractions . . .

8. So that is my suggestions on how to become a more alert and safe driver.

. . . those are my suggestions . . .

9. Common team injuries include pulled muscles, which is usually a result of not stretching before exercising.

. . . which are . . .

10. You can imagine the looks that was on their faces when they saw me.

. . . that were on their faces . . .

EXERCISE 22-10 Additional Practice Editing for Subject and Verb Agreement

Directions: *Underline simple subjects and double underline verbs in the following sentences. Correct verb agreement errors in the space provided. Some of the sentences may be correct as written.*

1. I didn't know anyone who worked in the store, but when I started, there was a couple of good-looking women.

. . . there were a couple of good-looking women.

2. This experience taught me that there is many great people out in the world.

. . . there are many great people . . .

3. I rode my bike around town, trying to find someone who would be generous enough to keep a few little kittens. I didn't get home until late. There was no kittens left in my backpack.

There were no kittens . . .

4. My favorite game show is "Jeopardy," which airs every night during the week at 7:30 and is hosted by Alex Trebek.

correct as written

5. My skills working with animals gets better all the time.

. . . skills . . . get better . . .

6. I did not like working at the optical company. The people who worked there was older than I was and not very friendly.

The people . . . were older . . .

7. Secular holidays are any holidays established by a society or government that has no religious bearing.

Secular holidays . . . that have . . .

8. There has been times growing up when I would have enjoyed having a different name.

There have been times . . .

9. Upkeep and maintenance of bicycles is relatively inexpensive.

Upkeep and maintenance . . . are . . .

10. There is all kinds of different exercises a person can do to improve muscle mass.

There are all kinds . . .

Irregular Verbs

You make most past tense verbs in English by adding -ed. Further, that past tense form also serves as the past participle, the form preceded by a helping verb.

To look is a regular verb. Here is its present, past, and participle forms:

Present: I look for my keys every time I leave the house.

Past: I looked for my keys this morning.

Past Participle: Often I have looked for my keys without finding them.

Writer's Response
Sometimes verb agreement errors are hard to "hear." Why is that? What can you do if you don't hear them?

Now consider the irregular verb *to find*.

Present: I find my keys in the most unlikely places.

Past: This morning I found them under the couch.

Past Participle: Often I have found them in the bathtub.

If you know your irregular verbs, you know not to write "I finded them under the couch." There are plenty of irregular forms that are less obvious. For this reason, you may be inclined to make mistakes like these:

I seen a good movie last night (should be *saw*)

My prized possession got broke last night. (should be *broken*)

The major most often chose by freshmen is psychology. (should be *chosen*)

At the end of this chapter are some tables of irregular verbs to help you stay aware of possible mistakes.

Irregular Past Tense Verbs

There are four types of irregular past tense forms, shown in the following tables.

1.

PAST AND PAST PARTICIPLE ARE THE SAME		
Present	Past	Past Participle
bring	brought	brought
build	built	built
buy	bought	bought

Students bring pen and paper to class with them.

Students brought paper and pen to class with them.

Students should have brought paper and pen to class with them.

2.

PRESENT, PAST, AND PAST PARTICIPLE ARE ALL DIFFERENT		
Present	**Past**	**Past Participle**
forget	forgot	forgotten
forgive	forgave	forgiven
freeze	froze	frozen

The fruit crop freezes in December.
The fruit crop froze in December.
The fruit crop has frozen in December.

3.

PRESENT, PAST, AND PAST PARTICIPLE ARE ALL THE SAME		
Present	**Past**	**Past Participle**
cut	cut	cut
hurt	hurt	hurt

He hurts his wrist.
He hurt his wrist.
He has hurt his wrist.

4.

PRESENT AND PAST PARTICIPLE ARE THE SAME		
Present	**Past**	**Past Participle**
run	ran	run
become	became	become

The crowd becomes unruly.
The crowd became unruly.
The crowd has become unruly.

Refer to the tables of irregular verbs at the end of the chapter when you do exercises in this book. You can also use them as a reference as you learn to listen for these irregular verbs.

EXERCISE 22-11 Proofreading for Irregular Verbs

Directions: *Read the following sentences and underline the verbs. Using the tables at the end of the chapter as your guide, substitute corrected verb forms as needed in the space provided. Some sentences may be correct as written.*

1. The recent slowdown in economic activity has hurt the housing industry. Lawmakers have rose to the challenge in the past and provided tax incentives to stimulate demand; the president, however, has forbade his aides to consider such a stimulus at this time.

Lawmakers have risen. . . . however, has forbidden . . .

2. Athletes at Central University has always rose to the challenge when they needed to. Now that the football team has lost three consecutive games, the coach has spoke forcefully to the players about the importance of spirit, dedication, and perseverance.

. . . have always risen. . . . coach has spoken . . .

3. The candidate has ran a good campaign. She stands an excellent chance of being sent to Washington, D.C.

. . . has run . . .

4. The children had hid for so long in the woods that they no longer remembered the way back to their campsite.

. . . had hidden . . .

5. After Cleary had drunk so much, he ventured out on the road, which had froze to glare ice and was perilous for even the best of drivers.

. . . had frozen . . .

6. She has taught me how great a Crock-Pot is, and I use mine all the time. She has also gave me many tips on cleaning and cooking.

. . . has also given . . .

7. In the morning it was a clear day, and the sun shone on everything.

correct as written

8. The problem with late night pizza parties is that after you have ate all that food and went to bed, you have no desire to get up and exercise the next morning.

. . . have eaten all that food and gone to bed, . . .

9. After Suzanne was thrown from her horse, she was taken to the hospital, treated for broken ribs, then sent home. She rode again as soon as her ribs started to feel better.

correct as written

10. For as long as I can remember, we have flew Northwest Airlines to go to Minneapolis to visit my grandparents, and we have come to trust them to get us to our destination on time.

. . . have flown Northwest Airlines . . .

Consistent Verb Tense

In college writing, readers look for a consistent use of the present or past tense. The agreement of one verb tense with another is called *consistency.*

MULTILINGUAL TIP
This is a common ESL error.

Inconsistent: It was a beautiful summer day. My brother and I had found ourselves sitting on our rusty swing set with nothing to do.

In the example above, the student uses two different forms of the past tense: *was* and *had found.* To be consistent, the student should use one form: *was* and *found.* When possible, use simple verb tenses. Usually one-word verbs are preferable to more complex forms.

Consistent: It was a beautiful summer day. My brother and I found ourselves sitting on our rusty swing set with nothing to do.

Watch out for auxiliary verbs—such as *can/could, will/would,* and *may/might*—and keep them consistent with the tense you establish.

Inconsistent: This time we agreed that we will study together.

Consistent: This time we agreed that we would study together.

More often than not, consistency errors occur because of inattention. Be alert when you check your writing for these (and other) common errors.

EXERCISE 22-12 Proofreading for Inconsistent Verb Tense

Directions: *Read the following sentences and underline the verbs. Then correct errors in verb tense consistency in the space provided. Some may be correct as written.*

1. I believe that if people are dependable, it helps a great deal. They could make a positive contribution to the world.

They can make . . .

2. I would always be the cop, which means catching and arresting my friend. When I catch him, he would always cry, stomp his feet, and say I was cheating.

. . . which meant . . . . I caught him, . . .

3. My stepfather came to me first and asks who drove his truck without permission.

. . . asked who . . .

4. My parents always used to brag about how I am the perfect child.

. . . I was the perfect child.

5. The few times my father tried to make dinner, he could not make it taste as good as my mother's cooking.

correct as written

6. As soon as the fire cracker exploded, we all take off running.

. . . took off running.

7. One morning my sister and I were walking to school, and we meet up with some of our friends.

. . . we met up . . .

8. A lot of people play their music loudly just to get attention. For example, my friend Moe had a system in his car, and he always turns up the sound.

. . . has a system . . .

9. One time when I was eight or nine years old, I asked my mother if I can go outside and play with friends.

. . . if I could go . . .

10. When I was a kid, most of the kids pass their time collecting football cards, basketball cards, and baseball cards.

. . . passed their time . . .

IRREGULAR VERBS: PAST AND PAST PARTICIPLE ARE THE SAME					
Present	**Past**	**Past Participle**	**Present**	**Past**	**Past Participle**
bring	brought	brought	meet	met	met
build	built	built	pay	paid	paid
buy	bought	bought	say	said	said
catch	caught	caught	seek	sought	sought
deal	dealt	dealt	sell	sold	sold
feed	fed	fed	send	sent	sent
feel	felt	felt	shine	shone	shone
fight	fought	fought	sit	sat	sat
find	found	found	sleep	slept	slept
have	had	had	spend	spent	spent
hear	heard	heard	stand	stood	stood
hold	held	held	swing	swung	swung
keep	kept	kept	teach	taught	taught
lay	laid	laid	tell	told	told
lead	led	led	think	thought	thought
leave	left	left	understand	understood	understood
lose	lost	lost	win	won	won
make	made	made			

IRREGULAR VERBS: PRESENT, PAST, AND PAST PARTICIPLE ARE ALL DIFFERENT					
Present	**Past**	**Past Participle**	**Present**	**Past**	**Past Participle**
be	was/were	been	hide	hid	hidden
begin	began	begun	know	knew	know
blow	blew	blown	lie	lay	lain
break	broke	broken	ride	rode	ridden
choose	chose	chosen	ring	rang	rung
do	did	done	rise	rose	risen
drink	drank	drunk	see	saw	seen
drive	drove	driven	shake	shook	shaken
eat	ate	eaten	sing	sang	sung
fall	fell	fallen	speak	spoke	spoken
fly	flew	flown	spring	sprang	sprung
forbid	forbade	forbidden	steal	stole	stolen
forget	forgot	forgotten	swim	swam	swum
forgive	forgave	forgiven	take	took	taken
freeze	froze	frozen	tear	tore	torn
get	got	gotten	throw	threw	thrown
give	gave	given	wake	woke/waked	woken/waken
go	went	gone	wear	wore	worn
grow	grew	grown	written	wrote	written

IRREGULAR VERBS: PRESENT, PAST, AND PAST PARTICIPLE ARE ALL THE SAME					
Present	**Past**	**Past Participle**	**Present**	**Past**	**Past Participle**
burst	burst	burst	let	let	let
cut	cut	cut	quit	quit	quit
hurt	hurt	hurt	read	read	read

TOPIC 18: Verb Tenses, Moods, and Voices
www.mhhe.com/goingplaces

IRREGULAR VERBS: PRESENT AND PAST PARTICIPLE ARE THE SAME		
Present	**Past**	**Past Participle**
become	became	become
come	came	come
run	ran	run

CHAPTER OVERVIEW

- Pronoun Agreement
  - *Detect Errors in Pronoun Agreement*
  - *Indefinite Pronouns and Agreement*
- Pronoun Case
  - *Compound Subjects and Objects, Sentences with* Than *and* As
- Pronoun Consistency

Pronoun Agreement, Case, and Consistency

We constantly slip up when speaking, and no one corrects us. The error goes unnoticed, or because it is considered slightly bad manners to correct another person's speech. Even more than verbs, we get pronouns wrong when we speak. Pronoun errors to look for in your writing involve agreement, case, and consistency.

Pronoun Agreement

MULTILINGUAL TIP

In English, the pronoun does not agree with the noun it modifies: "Marie showed me her rings."

Pronouns are words that take the place of nouns. They eliminate repetition and enable you to manage more information when you speak and write.

> Last night after soccer practice I ate pizza with all my buddies. The pizza was delicious. My friend Phil paid for the pizza. Phil likes pizza too, but Phil prefers that someone else pay for the pizza.

Notice the repetition of the words *pizza* and *Phil.* In the following sentences, this repetition is eliminated by the use of pronouns.

> Last night after soccer practice I ate pizza with all my buddies. It was delicious. My friend Phil paid for it. He likes pizza too, but he prefers that someone else pay for it.

Table 23-1 shows a list of commonly used pronouns.

Agreement occurs when a pronoun agrees in number with the noun to which it refers, called the **antecedent.** Singular antecedents take singular pronouns. Plural antecedents take plural pronouns.

> Smoking stinks. It also poses terrible health risks. I just don't understand why people would want to pollute the air and risk their health at the same time.

In these sentences, *it* is a singular pronoun that refers to "smoking," a singular antecedent. *Their* is a plural pronoun that refers to "people," a plural antecedent. In both cases, the pronouns and antecedents agree in number.

> My sister was very athletic when she was a kid. She could do just about anything. Her favorite sport was gymnastics. It appealed to her because it was a performance, almost like dance.

The antecedent "sister" is followed by a number of singular pronouns: *she, she, her,* and *her.* The singular pronoun *it* refers to the singular antecedent "gymnastics." **Note:** Some nouns in English are singular in meaning even though they end in "s." *Economics, ethics,* and *mathematics* are other examples.

TABLE 23-1

COMMON PRONOUNS			
Subjective	**Objective**	**Possessive**	**Reflexive**
I	me	my	myself
you	you	your	yourself
it	it	its	itself
she	her	her	herself
he	him	his	himself
we	us	our	ourselves
they	them	their	themselves

EXERCISE 23-1 Identifying Pronouns and Their Antecedents

Directions: *Underline the pronouns and circle the antecedents in the following sentences. Write them in the space provided and indicate whether they are singular or plural.*

1. Some parents today neglect teaching their children the importance of saving money.

their/parents, plural

2. Drugs can be a huge problem. They can even destroy a person's life.

they/drugs, plural

3. One time, I was watching Oprah, and she asked members of the audience to raise their hands to show if they would have preferred being raised at a day care center rather than at home.

I, singular; she/Oprah, singular; their/audience, plural; they/audience, plural

4. A teacher definitely affects learning. Her voice, attitude, personality, and even her penmanship create this unique feeling of character you cannot get from staring at a computer screen.

her/teacher, singular; her/teacher, singular; you, singular

5. I knew a boy who was so full of life. He was also full of surprises.

I, singular; he/boy, singular

6. So this neighbor called my parents. He told them that he had caught everything my friend and I did on tape. We got in a lot of trouble.

he/neighbor, singular; my, singular; them/parents, plural; we/my friend and I, plural

7. It was a beautiful summer day, yet my brother and I found ourselves sitting on our rusty swing set with nothing to do.

it, singular; my brother and I/ourselves, plural; our/my brother and I, plural

8. I bought a new sound system for my car. It was so loud that people ran for cover every time they heard it.

I, singular; it/sound system, singular; my, singular; they/people, plural; it/sound system, singular

9. It is amazing how many people are working out of their houses these days.

it, singular; their/people, plural

10. A father who cannot manage time properly can lose the most important thing in his life, and that's the love of his family.

his/father, singular; his/father, singular

Detect Errors in Pronoun Agreement

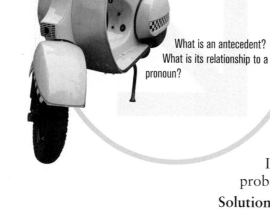

Writer's Response

What is an antecedent? What is its relationship to a pronoun?

One of the most common errors in spoken English involves pronoun agreement. In fact, this grammatical misstep is so common that even radio and television professionals frequently make statements like this:

> If an older person (*singular*) applies for a job, they (*plural*) will probably be overlooked.

They is a plural pronoun that refers to a singular antecedent, "person." The pronoun and antecedent do not agree in number.

In formal English, it would be preferable to say and write one of the following:

> If older people (*plural*) apply for a job, they (*plural*) will probably be overlooked.

Solution: Make the antecedent plural to agree with the plural pronoun.

> If an older person (*singular*) applies for a job, he or she (*singular*) will probably be overlooked.

Solution: Make the pronoun singular to agree with the singular antecedent.

> An older person who applies for a job will probably be overlooked.

Solution: Revise the sentence to eliminate the pronoun in question.

Because of the gap between what you hear in spoken English and what is required in college writing, agreement errors can be difficult to detect and correct. It is good practice to examine plural pronouns every time they occur.

> Every person (*singular*) has talents and special abilities. Their (*plural*) talents and abilities make them (*plural*) who they (*plural*) are and determine the impression they (*plural*) make on other people.

The pronouns here are all plural: *their, them, they*, and *they*. The antecedent is singular: "person." (Think every single person.) The pronouns in this sentence, then, are not in agreement with their antecedent. Because there are four pronouns for one antecedent, it makes sense to make the antecedent plural. However, there are two other options as well:

People (*plural*) have talents and special abilities. Their (*plural*) talents and abilities make them (*plural*) who they are and determine the impression they (*plural*) make on other people.

Solution: Make the antecedent plural to agree with the plural pronouns.

Every person (*singular*) has talents and special abilities. His or her (*singular*) talents and abilities make that person who he or she (*singular*) is and determine the impression he or she (*singular*) makes on other people.

Solution: Make the pronouns singular to agree with the singular antecedent.

Every person has unique talents and abilities that make an impression on other people.

Solution: Revise the sentence to eliminate the pronouns in question.

Your goal when correcting these errors is to produce a sentence that both sounds good and retains the meaning of the original sentence. In the preceding examples, the first revision sounds the best and expresses the same idea as the original sentence.

EXERCISE 23-2 Editing Pronoun Agreement Errors

Directions: *Underline the pronouns and circle the antecedents in the following sentences. Then determine whether the antecedents and the pronouns agree. Use one of these three solutions to correct any errors and write the corrected sentences in the space provided:*

- *Make an antecedent plural to agree with a plural pronoun.*
- *Make a pronoun singular to agree with a singular antecedent.*
- *Revise the sentence and eliminate the pronoun in question.* Answers will vary. Example answers shown.

1. When a person is under the influence of a drug, they are less inhibited and do things that they normally would not do.

First option: When people are under the influence of a drug, they are less inhibited and do things that they normally would not do.

2. There are many ways a person can protect themselves from other drivers on the road. One is defensive driving. The person driving next to you might not realize they are crossing into your lane.

First option: There are many ways people can protect themselves from other drivers on the road. One is defensive driving. The person driving next to you might not realize he or she is crossing into your lane.

3. Not every driver is as good as they should be, but that does not mean we are all doomed.

Third option: Not every driver is careful all the time, but that does not mean we are all doomed.

4. This person has gone through many hardships in their life.

Third option: This person has gone through many hardships in life.

5. The strengths of this course would be that the student can work at their own pace and set their work schedule around the rest of their life.

First option: The strengths of this course would be that students can work at their own pace and set their work schedule around the rest of their lives.

6. A good waitress should make it her duty to satisfy the customer, regardless of their ethnic or financial background.

Second option: A good waitress should make it her duty to satisfy the customer, regardless of his or her ethnic or financial background.

7. A child has a vivid imagination, the ability to create things that do not exist, before the cruel adult world gets hold of them.

First option: Children have vivid imaginations, the ability to create things that do not exist, before the cruel adult world gets hold of them.

8. Whether it is a nine-to-five office job or a stay-at-home mom's job, every woman has something that they are committed to every day.

Third option: Whether it is a nine-to-five office job or a stay-at-home mom's job, every woman has a number of commitments every day.

9. If a teacher pronounces my name right after the first try, I give them a lot of respect.

First option: If teachers pronounce my name right after the first try, I give them a lot of respect.

10. When I meet a guy for the first time, they always ask my name.

Second option: When I meet a guy for the first time, he always asks my name.

Indefinite Pronouns and Agreement

In spoken English, speakers frequently use plural pronouns with indefinite pronouns (see box). Although these indefinite pronouns sound plural, they are clearly singular in meaning.

INDEFINITE PRONOUNS	
one	everyone
nobody	everybody
anyone	someone
anybody	somebody

Someone (*singular*) always parks their (*plural*) car too close to mine.

Everyone (*singular*) brought their (*plural*) own lunch on the trip to the museum.

There are three solutions (the same ones discussed earlier) to correct agreement errors involving these indefinite pronouns: Make the antecedent plural, make the pronoun singular, or revise the sentence to eliminate the pronoun in question.

People (*plural*) always park their (*plural*) cars too close to mine.

Someone (*singular*) always parks his or her (*singular*) car too close to mine.

Someone always parks too close to my car.

All the visitors (*plural*) brought their (*plural*) own lunches on the trip to the museum.

Everyone (*singular*) brought his or her (*singular*) own lunch on the trip to the museum.

Everyone brought a lunch on the trip to the museum.

Ask Yourself
Proofread your papers for indefinite pronouns. Do you use the correct pronouns? Check your work.

As always, your goal is to choose the revision that sounds the best and retains the meaning of the original sentence.

EXERCISE 23-3 Indefinite Pronouns and Pronoun Agreement

Directions: *Underline the pronouns and circle the antecedents in the following sentences. Use the space provided to rewrite the sentences so that the pronouns and antecedents agree. Use one of these three solutions to correct the errors:*

- *Make an antecedent plural to agree with a plural pronoun.*
- *Make a pronoun singular to agree with a singular antecedent.*
- *Revise the sentence and eliminate the pronoun in question.* Answers will vary. Example answers shown.

1. When somebody is addicted, they will want to try stronger and more dangerous drugs.

Third option: An addict will want to try stronger and more dangerous drugs.

2. Happiness is something everyone needs in their life.

Third option: Happiness is something everyone needs in life.

3. When someone has a good attitude, they bring everyone else's spirit up.

Third option: A good attitude brings everyone else's spirit up.

4. No matter what occupation one has or how large their income is, if they are happy with their lives, that is the best fortune they could ask for.

First option: No matter what occupation people have or how large their income is, if they are happy with their lives, that is the best fortune they could ask for.

5. Sometimes one's ignorance can get the best of their principles.

Third option: Sometimes ignorance can get the best of a person's principles.

6. Anybody can succeed. They just have to try hard enough to get what they want.

Second option: Anybody can succeed. He or she just has to try hard enough to get what he or she wants.

7. I need someone who will not turn their back on me.

Second option: I need someone who will not turn his or her back on me.

8. I feel my mother does a good job of keeping the house together. Even though she is a single parent, she makes sure everyone is taken care of and their needs are met.

Third option: I feel my mother does a good job of keeping the house together.

Even though she is a single parent, she makes sure everyone's needs are met.

9. Each person is smart in their own way.

Second option: Each person is smart in his or her own way.

10. I hope everyone has someone in their lives that they can truly respect as much as I do my neighbor.

Third option: We all need someone in our lives that we can truly respect as much as

I do my neighbor.

Types of Pronouns

Pronouns can have a variety of functions in a sentence. Pronouns can act as the subject of a sentence or as the object of a preposition or verb. They can also indicate possession. Table 23-2 presents these three types of pronouns.

MULTILINGUAL TIP
Avoid confusion between your/yours, her/hers, our/ours, their/theirs.

1. **Subjective pronouns** are used as the subject of a sentence:

   We foreign language students are a competitive bunch.

   She called home on her new cell phone and said hello to her sister.

   After waking up late, he skipped breakfast and went directly to work.

TABLE 23-2

THREE TYPES OF PRONOUNS		
Subjective	**Objective**	**Possessive**
I	me	my/mine
you	you	your/yours
it	it	its
he	him	his
she	her	her/hers
we	us	our/ours
they	them	their/theirs
who	who/whom	whose

2. **Objective pronouns** are used as the objects of verbs and prepositions:

The principal called us down to the office.

My father gave me some good advice.

Robert went with me to Florida last spring.

3. **Possessive pronouns** are used to indicate possession:

Young people spend much of their time online these days.

Their shopping online is a particularly interesting development.

If the subject of the sentence is an -ing word preceded by a personal pronoun, the pronoun should be possessive case:

Daniel decided to join the Marines. His *going* into the military was a very big decision.

Incorrect: Him/He *going* into the military was a very big decision.

We all went to ground zero in New York City. Our *being* there was important to everyone.

Incorrect: Us/We *being* there was important to everyone.

EXERCISE 23-4 **Identifying Subjective, Objective, and Possessive Pronouns**

Directions: *Underline the pronouns in the following sentences, write them in the space provided, and indicate whether they are subjective, objective, or possessive pronouns. Some sentences will have both subjective and objective pronouns.*

Talk about It

With a classmate, identify the types of pronouns you used in your last paper. Are there any pronoun choices you question?

1. This kid I met on vacation is the same age as I am.

I-subjective; I-subjective

2. When my parents got home, they found me sitting in the kitchen reading the newspaper.

my-possessive; they-subjective; me-objective

3. After a while, he opened up a business. It was rough in the beginning, but now the business is doing extremely well.

he-subjective; it-subjective

4. Every day after school, I used to play baseball with my friends.

I-subjective; my-possessive

5. My parents thought my going to Daytona on spring break was a mistake.

my-possessive; my-possessive

6. For the past three years I have gone to the finals, but I haven't been able to win.

I-subjective; I-subjective

7. He attended the same school I did.

he-subjective; I-subjective

8. He was younger than she was, but he was also the boss.

he-subjective; she-subjective; he-subjective

9. Her brothers all have their own car, whereas she still takes the bus.

her-objective; their-possessive; she-subjective

10. I followed her to a room, where she did the paperwork and called the cops. She left as I waited for what seemed a half an hour. Then she came back with the security guard, who began to interrogate me.

I-subjective; her-objective; she-subjective; she-subjective; I-objective; she-subjective;

who-subjective; me-objective

Compound Subjects and Objects, Sentences with Than *and* As

Subjective and objective pronoun errors occur frequently in sentences with compound subjects and objects and in sentences with *than* and *as.*

Compound Subjects and Objects

Compound subjects and objects put two pronouns together with the conjunction *and.*

Compound Subject: Me *and* Bill got scholarships

Compound Object: The boss gave Bill *and* I a bonus.

Because pronoun errors commonly occur in spoken English, to some people these sentences might sound correct. The best way to detect incorrect pronoun usage is to make a compound sentence into two separate sentences and then put them back together:

Me got a scholarship. Bill got a scholarship.

I got a scholarship. Bill got a scholarship.

Correct: Bill *and* I got a scholarship.

The boss gave Bill a bonus. The boss gave I a bonus.

The boss gave Bill a bonus. The boss gave me a bonus.

Correct: The boss gave Bill *and* me a bonus.

It is preferable to make "I" the second of two subjects in sentences with two compound subjects. In sentences with three subjects, make "I" last: as in, "Professor Janes, Mr. Hacker, and *I* attended the council meeting last Tuesday."

Do not use reflexive pronouns in place of subjective or objective pronouns:

Bill and myself got a scholarship.
Correct: Bill *and* I got a scholarship.

The boss gave Bill *and* myself a bonus.
Correct: The boss gave Bill *and* me a bonus.

Talk about It

Read the examples under "Sentences with *Than* and *As*." Which sentences sound right to you? What clue helps you choose the right pronoun?

Sentences with *Than* and *As*

Sentences that express comparisons are formed with *than* and *as*. These sentences actually combine two ideas.

I finished the test early.
You finished the test earlier.
You finished the test earlier *than* I did.

Speakers and writers frequently choose the wrong pronoun in these sentences.

Incorrect: She grew so much faster than me.
Incorrect: He played tennis well, but not as well as me.

To detect pronoun errors in comparative forms, make the sentence two separate sentences and then put them back together:

Incorrect: She worked faster *than* me.
She worked fast. I worked fast.
Correct: She worked faster *than* I (worked).

Incorrect: He played tennis too, only not *as* well as me.
He played tennis well. I played tennis well.
Correct: He played tennis well, only not *as* well as I (played).

EXERCISE 23-5 **Proofreading for Errors in Pronoun Case**

Directions: *Read the following sentences and underline the subjective and objective pronouns. In the space provided, write pronouns you would insert as needed. Some sentences may be correct as written.*

1. Most of the people I met on vacation were older than me.

. . . than I (am).

2. When they got home, they found Rachel and I in the kitchen reading the newspaper.

. . . Rachel and me . . .

3. After a while, my sister and him opened up a business. It was rough in the beginning, but now the business is doing extremely well.

. . . my sister and he . . .

4. Every day after school, me, Dan, and Ron used to play baseball with some friends.

. . . school, Dan, Ron, and I . . .

5. Rhonda and myself were selected to chair the orientation meeting at the college.

Rhonda and I . . .

6. For the past three years, Cheryl and me have made it to the dance contest finals, but we have not been able to win.

. . . Cheryl and I . . .

7. He attended the same school as me.

. . . same school as I (did).

8. She was as young as him, but she was also his boss.

. . . young as he (was) . . .

9. Her brothers all have their own cars, whereas her and her sisters still take the bus.

. . . whereas she and her sisters . . .

10. At the end of the unit of study, the instructor asked Janet and me to act as tutors. We agreed to it.

correct as written

Pronoun Consistency

Depending on your subject matter, one pronoun will be more appropriate to use than another. If you write about yourself, you will probably use the first person: *I, me, my*. If you write about a social issue or problem, you may choose the pronoun *it* to refer to the problem—racism, for example—and the pronoun *they* to refer those who are affected by the problem. It is difficult to avoid some shifting from one pronoun to another, but be aware of these shifts and try to be consistent.

Inconsistent

I had a great experience in high school band class. I learned to play an instrument and went to competitions with the band. I had a great time at these competitions. The director was great. He always pushed you to do your best.

The first-person pronoun is appropriate when you write about yourself.

In this example the writer shifts from first person (*I, me, my*) to second person (*you, your*).

I is first person. The shift to second person—*you* and *your*—is conversational but inconsistent. For formal writing, such as you do in college, try to minimize the use of *you*.

Consistent

I had a great experience in high school band class. I learned to play an instrument and went to competitions with the band. I had a great time at these competitions. The director was great. He always pushed me and my fellow band players to do our best.

The use of *me* and *our* is more consistent than *you* and *your*.

Here's another example:

The student begins with first-person plural (*we, us, our*).

Here she shifts to second person (*you*).

Inconsistent

Our class took part in a "city beautiful" program. We were assigned to groups and took responsibility for keeping a section of the city clean. This is a good program. It taught you to take pride in where you live. Once you finished, you sort of wanted to show off your city.

The shift from *we* to *you* is inconsistent pronoun use.

Consistent

Our class took part in a "city beautiful" program. We were assigned to groups and took responsibility for keeping a section of the city clean. This is a good program. It taught us to take pride in where we live. Once we finished, we sort of wanted to show off our city.

Consistent pronoun use, like consistent verb tense, is an important characteristic of academic writing. Consistent pronoun use makes your writing more coherent and connected. Practice consistently avoiding first- and second-person pronouns, when it is possible and appropriate to do so.

EXERCISE 23-6 Proofreading for Consistent Pronoun Use

Directions: *Read the following sentences and underline the pronouns. Cross out incorrect pronouns and write your corrections to make the pronoun use consistent in the space provided.* Answers will vary. Example answers shown.

1. We have a tendency to pick up something quick for dinner on ~~your~~ way home, instead of going home and taking time to cook dinner. It's convenient. However, eating carry-out on a regular basis can get costly.

. . . our way home . . .

2. ~~A person~~ doesn't always have to be happy all the time. There are many different emotions we go through. ~~You~~ simply have to expect that.

We don't. . . . we go through. We simply . . .

3. The most important thing ~~an employer~~ looks for is trust. ~~You~~ don't want an employee to cheat ~~you~~ when the ~~employer~~ turns ~~his or her~~ back.

. . . thing employers look. . . . They don't . . . them when they turn their back.

4. I took the test and waited nervously for the results. The level of ~~your~~ score would give ~~you~~ the opportunity to go further.

. . . The level of my score would give me . . .

5. Collecting rocks was easier than collecting seashells because ~~you~~ could find them everywhere. I made use of the rocks I found. I painted them, decorated them, or decorated with them. But mostly I collected them and kept them in my room.

. . . because I could . . .

TOPIC 19: Pronouns
www.mhhe.com/goingplaces

6. I also learned that by helping people in need ~~you~~ can really make a difference.

. . . in need I can . . .

7. With a cat, ~~you~~ set out her food and she's happy. I don't have to walk her every day or let her outside to use the bathroom.

. . . cat, I set . . .

8. Having a cold is dreadful ~~to me~~ because ~~you~~ feel horrible and just wish it would go away.

. . . is dreadful because a person feels . . . horrible . . . and just wishes . . .

9. The cellular phone has had a big impact on my life. ~~You~~ can reach anyone, anywhere, at any time.

. . . I can . . . reach

10. I tried to drive and use my cell phone a couple of times. I was so distracted it was horrifying. I became unaware of my surroundings to such a great degree. It was like driving in a dream, and nothing around ~~you~~ was real.

. . . nothing around me was real.

CHAPTER OVERVIEW

- Adjectives
- Adverbs and the -ly Ending
- *Good/Well, Bad/Badly, Real/Really*
- Adjectives: Comparatives and Superlatives
- Adverbs: Comparatives and Superlatives
- Hyphenated Adjectives

Adjectives and Adverbs

If you want to sound like a college student, you need to get your adjectives and adverbs working properly. In casual conversation, there is a high tolerance for adjective and adverb error. If you make a mistake, as long as you are understood, it is unlikely that you will be corrected. For that reason, adjective and adverb errors can easily slip into your writing. However, nothing distracts an academic reader from your message as quickly as one of these slips. If you want to do *well* (not *good*), learn the difference between an adjective and an adverb.

Adjectives

MULTILINGUAL TIP
Unlike some other languages, the adjective usually appears before the word it modifies in English. It does not agree in number or gender.

Adjectives modify nouns and pronouns. They provide information about quantity and quality. In most cases, adjectives are found right next to the noun they modify, usually directly *before* the noun.

The team's **last** game was its **best** game. (adjectives modify noun *game*)

The **visiting** artist changed his **preferred working** hours soon after arriving on campus. (adjectives modify nouns *artist* and *hours*)

In some sentences with linking verbs—such as *is/are, was/were, seem/seems*—adjectives come after the verb.

We are **vulnerable.**

Mrs. Kraft seems **happy.**

Also, in the case of indefinite pronouns—such as *someone, something,* or *anything*—the adjective comes after the pronoun.

Someone **special** called me last night.

Anything **good** to read will be on his desk sooner or later.

MULTILINGUAL TIP
Distinguish between past participles and present participles used as adjectives.

EXERCISE 24-1 Identifying Adjectives

Directions: *Underline adjectives in the sentences below. Circle the noun each adjective modifies.*

1. There were three steps leading to the porch of the brick bungalow.
2. When the horse and buggy arrive, you sit on the comfortable bench seat and take a long ride. You feel great.
3. His pants were faded and threadbare.
4. Toward the end of the school year, she threw a tea party and told all of the students they had to bring bone china for it.
5. This classic sandwich, a club pita, contains sliced ham, turkey, lean bacon, and crispy lettuce.
6. Cooking is therapeutic, an enjoyable activity. Mozart had his piano. I have my gleaming cleavers and trusty skillets. I am always happy in the kitchen. Anything complex is what I like to cook.
7. Outdoor work is annoying. In winter, the weather is freezing cold. Shoveling heavy snow can be a health risk.
8. A good reason to not live in the city is endless traffic. It can be bad. Imagine living in the middle of rush hour on Broadway.
9. Organization is an important skill needed for online education. Even if adequate time is allotted, success requires time management and the ability to meet deadlines.
10. I was on my high school swim team, and every day I dreaded the long practice hours and endless drills.

EXERCISE 24-2 **Choosing Adjectives**

Directions: *Fill in the blank and provide an adjective for each of the nouns below.* **Answers will vary.**

1. the ______________________ question
2. a(n) ______________________ opportunity
3. these ______________________ interruptions
4. my ______________________ phobia
5. a(n) ______________________ friend
6. the ______________________ mail delivery
7. her ______________________ objection
8. your ______________________ responsibility
9. a(n) ______________________ need
10. our ______________________ coworkers

Adverbs and the -ly Ending

Adverbs modify verbs, adjectives, and other adverbs. They provide information about how or when an action occurs. Most adverbs can be easily spotted because of their -ly ending. In fact, many adverbs are merely adjectives with -ly endings. (**Note:** In the case of adjectives ending in "y," remember to change the "y" to "i.")

Saturday's game was an **easy** victory over State. (adjective modifies noun *victory*)

Our team **easily** beat State. (adverb modifies verb *beat*)

Along with the -ly ending, you can tell adverbs by the fact that they can sometimes be moved around in a sentence and be placed before or after the verb, or at the beginning or end of the sentence.

Our team **easily** beat State.

Our team beat State **easily.**

James **gradually** came to his senses.

Gradually James came to his senses.

EXERCISE 24-3 **Adverbs and the -ly Ending**

Directions: *Complete the sentences below by selecting adverbs from the following list. In cases where an adjective is needed, remove the -ly ending.* **Answers will vary. Example answers shown.**

consistently	immediately
continuously	initially
diligently	instantly
eventually	quickly
frequently	seriously
greatly	superbly

1. Marisa initially ________ considered going away to school.
2. She eventually ________ considered the alternative option of staying home.
3. Once she started, she immediately ________ saw that she had made the right decision.
4. In high school, Marisa was not a serious ________ student.
5. She preferred instant ________ gratification to the continuous ________ drudgery of homework.
6. As a college student, she decided to take things seriously ________ .
7. She studied frequently ________ and diligently ________ .
8. She quickly ________ saw the results of her superb ________ efforts.
9. Her grades were greatly ________ improved.
10. Her new approach produced consistently ________ better grades than those she earned in high school

EXERCISE 24-4 Proofreading for -ly Endings

Directions: *Proofread the sentences below for adverbs missing -ly endings. Underline the error and add -ly where needed.*

1. The failure rate in new marriages in this country is frightening. People get married, try it for a while, and then when the real work starts, they just give up. The problem is that not everyone takes marriage serious. Like everything in modern life, marriage is temporary. (seriously)
2. The Buick LeSabre is a full-size vehicle, great for transportation. It has four doors, automatic windows, and locks. The color is tan, which is a very neutral color. It runs smooth and floats like a boat. (smoothly)
3. Not punishing a person can have long-term effects. An individual needs to see there are consequences for his actions. If there is no follow through after someone does something wrong, he might think he can commit a crime easy. The next thing you know, he is in real trouble. (easily)

4. There have been lots of studies of how men and women are alike and different. Mostly they are different. The writer Deborah Tannen has written extensively about how men and women think and speak different. Her goal is to help people get along better. (differently)

5. Since starting school, I have been working in the social science department of the college. I work close with a lot of people who are educated. I listen to them speak. I try to imitate their vocabulary. (closely)

Good/Well, Bad/Badly, Real/Really

Common slips in conversation find their way into college writing. *Good, bad,* and *real* are adjectives; they modify nouns and pronouns. *Well, badly,* and *really* are adverbs; they modify verbs, adjectives, and other adverbs.

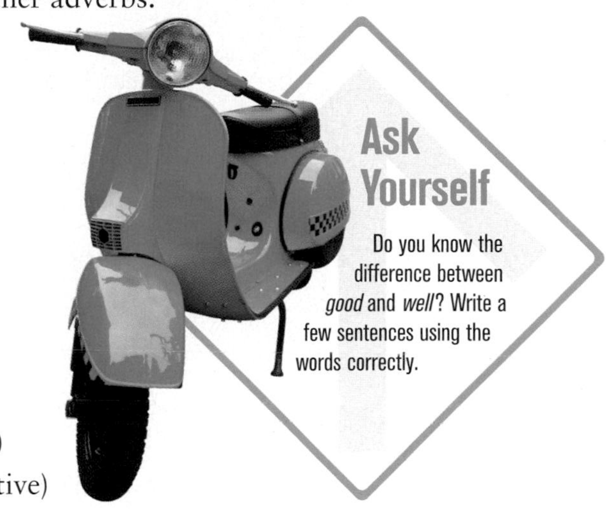

Ask Yourself
Do you know the difference between *good* and *well*? Write a few sentences using the words correctly.

The members of the study group did **good** work. (adjective-noun)

Their work was **good.** (noun-adjective)

They worked **well** together. (verb-adverb)

Their study time was **well** worth the effort. (adverb-adjective)

The ski instructor regretted the **bad** weather. (adjective-noun)

The ski conditions were **bad.** (noun-adjective)

Many of her pupils skied **badly** as a result. (verb-adverb)

The lesson was **badly** received all around. (adverb-adjective)

Marie's mother makes **real** mayonnaise. (adjective-noun)

It **really** makes a difference in some of her sandwiches. (adverb-verb)

Her vegetable roll-up tastes **really** good. (adverb-adjective)

EXERCISE 24-5 *Good/Well, Bad/Badly, Real/Really*

Directions: *Underline the correct modifiers in the sentences below. For each choice, circle the words that are modified.*

1. Our family vehicle is a (real/really) (good/well) car. It is very spacious. It has many miles on it, but the engine still runs pretty (good/well).
2. A (bad/badly) organized store means the flow of traffic on the floor is (bad/badly) and individual workers cooperate (bad/badly).
3. I am (real/really) motivated right now to get my work done and do (good/well) in school. Sometimes older students have to wait a (good/well) long time to come back to school.
4. We all agreed that Cooper's (bad/badly) reputation was (good/well) earned. He ran the meetings (bad/badly), as he tended to be overbearing and not (good/well) suited to getting people to work (good/well) together.
5. The coach was an all-around (good/well) guy. He taught us (real/really) discipline. He always pushed players to study hard, to make (good/well) decisions in their personal lives, and to do (good/well) on the field.

6. As far as future work is concerned, Willis is in a (good/well) position. In fact, he is (good/well) positioned to take a (good/well) entry-level job and run with it (good/well) into the future.
7. I think Henderson writes (good/well) books. Nevertheless, his first couple publications were (bad/badly) received. Some critics object to his confrontational style. He handles their criticisms (good/well). When they criticize him, he attacks them in return.
8. My child was (real/really) ill for a number of years. Now, by the grace of God, he is doing (good/well). We can thank the hospital staff for their (good/well) work.
9. After the argument, everyone felt (bad/badly). It was agreed that a (real/really) long cooling-off period would be helpful.
10. Hallie's job with Disney worked out really (good/well). It was a (bad/badly) needed jumpstart to her career in marketing.

Adjectives: Comparatives and Superlatives

An adjective assigns a quality to the noun it modifies. There are degrees of modification.

A statement

A **sad** statement (adjective)

A **sadder** statement (comparative)

The **saddest** statement (superlative)

In most cases the degree of modification is indicated by suffixes.

1. For one-syllable adjectives and two-syllable adjectives ending in "y," add the -er suffix to comparative adjectives; add the -est suffix for the superlative.

   close closer closest

   jolly jollier jolliest
2. For all other adjectives, use *more* and *most* to indicate degree.

   controversial more controversial most controversial
3. Learn to recognize the irregular comparatives and superlatives shown in Table 24-1.

TABLE 24-1

IRREGULAR ADJECTIVES		
Adjective	**Comparative**	**Superlative**
good	better	best
bad	worse	worst
little	less	least
much many some	more	most
far	further	furthest

Note: Use *little, less,* and *least* for indefinite amounts; use *few, fewer,* and *fewest* for things that can be counted.

4. Do not use *more* and *most* with the -er and -est suffixes:

Incorrect:	hard	more harder	most hardest
Correct:	hard	harder	hardest

Note: Be sure to use *than* (not *then*) in sentences expressing a comparison.

Economics was harder **than** U.S. History Before 1800.

5. Use the comparative when talking about two things; use the superlative when talking about more than two things.

Jordan was the **taller** of the two boys. (*not* "the tallest")

Of all the jobs I worked, the one that paid **best** was the warehouse job. (*not* "that paid better")

EXERCISE 24-6 Adjectives: Comparatives and Superlatives

Directions: *Underline the correct adjectives in the following sentences.*

1. The success of a product will be enhanced if the marketing is (more broad/broader).
2. Everyone has had a teacher who preferred some students over others. This is the (most common/commonest) grievance students have.
3. In my computer class the teacher would always send me on the (craziest/most crazy) errands.
4. After taking both pre-calculus and first semester calculus, Jane decided pre-calculus was (the more difficult/the most difficult) of the two.
5. One time our class was being a little loud. When the teacher first asked us to quiet down, we did not the first time. The second time he asked us, we still did not hear him. The third time he threw the (most awful/awfulest) fit.
6. You can meet the (shyest/most shy) person at a party. Get that person away from the crowd, and he or she will open up and be the (most outgoing/outgoingest) individual you have ever met.
7. This particular breed of dog is the (most calm/calmest), (most friendly/friendliest) animal you could ever hope to find.
8. In our family there was a fair amount of conflict, maybe because my mother was (educater/more educated) than my dad.
9. It is common to find large numbers of seniors walking in malls for exercise. They like malls because weather is not a factor. They like mornings because (less/fewer) teens are there at that time.
10. If we were more accepting of different types of people and cultures, it would help people feel (welcomer/more welcome).

Writer's Response

Write three sentences about movies using *good, better,* and *best.*

Adverbs: Comparatives and Superlatives

Like nouns, verbs can also be modified in degrees. That is, you can express not only how an action takes place—fast—but differences in how it takes place: *fast, faster, fastest.* Degrees can be positive, comparative, and superlative.

Comparatives and superlatives define quality. Discuss the places in your day where defining quality is important.

1. Add -er and -est to one-syllable adverbs, such as *fast, close, near,* and *late.*

   The semester went by **fast**.

   The semester went by **faster** than I expected.

   The semester goes by **fastest** when you are very busy.

2. Use *more* and *most* to form the comparatives and superlatives in longer adverbs.

   One tutor **quickly** answers questions.

   This tutor answers questions **more quickly** than the others.

   The tutor who answers questions **most quickly** is the most popular tutor.

EXERCISE 24-7 **Adverbs: Comparatives and Superlatives**

Directions: *Insert the correct comparative or superlative adverb form of the adjective in parentheses.*

1. (quick) I am meeting and getting to know people more quickly this year than I did last year.
2. (close) Out of all the debate teams in the competition, our team came the closest to getting a perfect score.
3. (serious) The current crop of new employees takes the job more seriously than the previous one and earns as much as possible.
4. (discreet) The professor could not have asked for the class's attention more discreetly.
5. (tactful) The morning bus driver handles disturbances and angry riders more tactfully than the afternoon driver.
6. (smooth) Out of the two landings observed, it was agreed the aircraft touched down more smoothly the first time.
7. (fierce) The battles fought most fiercely were those in which the combatants defended against invaders on their own soil.
8. (clear) Once the smoke cleared, I saw my situation more clearly than I had in a long time.
9. (efficient) The operation that is run most efficiently is most likely to realize the best profit.
10. (rapid) Out of all the sectors of the economy, the one that has recovered most rapidly is information technology.

Hyphenated Adjectives

When you bring two or more words together to modify a noun, you create a **hyphenated adjective.**

If you have a question about refunds, the **go-to** person is the Registrar.

After the patient comes home from the hospital, a visiting nurse comes on an **as-needed** basis.

Hyphenated adjectives precede the nouns they modify. *Go-to* is a hyphenated adjective that modifies the word *person. As-needed* modifies the word *basis*. Avoid hyphenated adjectives that are longer than three or four words.

Your exam will consist of ten **fill-in-the-blank** questions.

Those **eighteen-year-old** volunteers have transformed the department.

Unusually long hyphenated adjectives can usually be written as straightforward sentences:

When we first met, she was definitely a **you-will-not-dance-with-me-tonight-or-probably-ever-for-that-matter** kind of girl.

When we first met, she had a look on her face that said, "You will not dance with me tonight or probably ever, for that matter."

EXERCISE 24-8 Hyphenated Adjectives

Directions: *Find strings of words that function as adjectives in the following sentences. Add hyphens as needed. Write the hyphenated adjectives and nouns they modify in the space provided.*

1. To get an up to date source I went to an ABC News article to research this topic a little further.

up-to-date source

2. Parents should be explaining to their children that the happily ever after movies are just pretend, and nobody's life is actually like that.

happily-ever-after movies

3. My mom, no longer able to be a stay at home mom, went to work cutting hair to support us.

stay-at-home mom

4. It did not take him long to realize that he was in a no win situation and that he could not do this alone.

no-win situation

5. Parents must do their homework when searching for a day care provider. They should ask questions about daily events. One of the most important factors is the staff to student ratio.

staff-to-student ratio

6. The U.S. Congress debated the need for national regulatory standards regarding child care needs. Currently the responsibility is a state by state matter, with each state handling its own standards.

state-by-state matter

7. She wore long dresses every day, that came down to her sock and sandal covered feet.

sock-and-sandal-covered feet

8. As I came upon the reduce your speed sign, I took my foot off the gas.

reduce-your-speed sign

9. I purchased a beautiful white sleeveless dress with a split up the front right leg to wear to the ball.

front-right leg

10. I attended an all girls school, which by definition eliminated the potential for too much interaction with boys.

all-girls school

Gateway

TOPIC 20: Adjectives and Adverbs
www.mhhe.com/goingplaces

EXERCISE 24-9 **Proofreading Practice**

Directions: *Proofread the paragraphs below for adjective and adverb errors. Underline errors and write your corrections in the margin.*

most extreme
is blinded occasionally
easily

Blizzards are one of the extremest weather conditions that can make driving a dangerous task. There are several conditions created by a blizzard that can impair one's ability to drive. The obvious factor is that heavy snow decreases visibility. The driver becomes almost blind. Then heavy amounts of snow pile up on the road, creating slick conditions that cause vehicles to lose traction. After snow accumulates, cars driving over the road warm the pavement enough to melt the snow, which then freezes into ice. This is especially hazardous in the evening and nighttime when the patches of ice cannot be seen as easy. Snow is not the only weather condition that is dangerous. Rain is very unsafe to drive in as well.

really
slick
carelessly

Driving in a thunderstorm can be real dangerous. Like snow, rain can decrease visibility to zero. Along with affecting visibility, a downpour can render windshield wipers ineffective at clearing the windshield. The rain can also cause the road to become slickly and dangerous. Slippery roads like this increase the braking time needed to stop. If a person slams on the brakes, the car can skid out of control. Hydroplaning can occur if water has collected on the road and if a person drives careless. The car literally floats across the road. On side streets water can accumulate near the curb causing the vehicle to pull into the curb.

is worse
fewer

Both types of weather conditions can be treacherous. Most people would agree that snow is the worst. This fact is evident because less drivers venture out in a blizzard.

CHAPTER OVERVIEW

- Commas
  - *Commas and Conjunctions*
  - *Commas and Introductory Modifiers*
  - *Commas and Interrupters*
  - *Commas in a Series*
- Semicolons and Colons
- Quotation Marks
- Apostrophes

Punctuation

If I get all my commas in the right place, my writing will be okay. Right? Not exactly. Punctuation matters, but the content of your writing matters more. Your task is to minimize punctuation errors because they distract the reader from the content of your writing. In earlier chapters you saw that punctuation goes along with good sentence structure. In this chapter you revisit how to use commas, semicolons, and colons. You also practice using quotation marks and apostrophes properly.

Commas

Most student writers use too many commas. They think, "I'm pausing in this sentence, so I must need a comma." While it is true that the comma signals a pause, correct usage relies on understanding the role of the comma: It joins related parts of a sentence to one another.

Gateway

TOPIC 23: End Punctuation and Commas
www.mhhe.com/goingplaces

Commas and Conjunctions

The conjunctions *and, but,* and *or* often link pairs of terms that do not require commas. One of the most common punctuation errors is placing a comma before a conjunction when it is not needed.

Incorrect: My mother, and my sisters explained to me that lying will get me nowhere in life.

Correct: My mother and my sisters explained to me that lying will get me nowhere in life.

Incorrect: My father loves to chat, and laugh with his children.

Correct: My father loves to chat and laugh with his children.

For more explanation of punctuation and independent clauses, see the section on coordination in Chapter 19.

In these examples, the conjunction *and* joins two nouns, *mother* and *sisters,* and two verbs, *chat* and *laugh.* Generally, when you put two things together with *and* or *or,* you do not use a comma. However, a comma is required before a comma that joins two complete sentences (or independent clauses):

Comma Required: I agree that discipline is needed, but I don't think corporal punishment is the answer.

Comma Required: I wasn't making very much money, and my social life was beginning to suffer.

The comma and conjunction in these two examples are equivalent to a period.

I agree that discipline is needed. I don't think corporal punishment is the answer.

I wasn't making very much money. My social life was beginning to suffer.

Whenever you want to use a comma with a conjunction, ask yourself, "Could I put a period here instead? Is what comes before and after the conjunction a complete sentence?" If the answer is yes, the comma is probably needed.

EXERCISE 25-1 Commas and Conjunctions

Directions: *Circle all conjunctions in the following sentences and if any commas are needed, indicate where you would put them in the space provided. Some may be correct as written.*

1. I got into trouble often (and) for the stupidest reasons (and) a lot of the time it was at the dinner table.

. . . reasons, and a lot . . .

2. I tried not to make trouble (or) be a burden to anyone (but) I was human.

. . . anyone, but I . . .

3. It was morning and I was alone with some matches and my curiosity.

. . . morning, and I . . .

4. At first, it was a small fire but it increased quickly because it was summer and very dry.

. . . fire, but it . . .

5. I tried to put out the fire with some water but it was futile and the flames rose higher and higher.

. . . water, but it was futile, and the flames . . .

6. I worked frantically to put out the fire but sometimes foolishness and bad luck conspire against a person.

. . . fire, but sometimes . . .

7. I shouted at my little sister to help and she did her best. We worked together at it but it did not help and soon the fire was out of control.

. . . help, and she did. . . . at it, but it . . . help, and soon . . .

8. The fire trucks came wailing and shrieking and the firefighters put out the fire.

. . . shrieking, and the firefighters . . .

9. The damage was minimal but having the water and smoke in the house meant big trouble.

. . . minimal, but having . . .

10. It was a difficult time when my father got home that night and saw everything that had happened.

no comma necessary

Commas and Introductory Modifiers

Introductory words, phrases, or clauses at the beginning of a sentence are called **introductory modifiers.** Sentences starting with introductory modifiers include a natural pause. The pause occurs where the intonation falls, and this is where the comma should be placed.

> *As I sat alone at the picnic table,* Joanna and her boyfriend began to dance.

The box on page 506 provides a list of two kinds of words that signal an introductory modifier.

Writer's Response
Commas and conjunctions connect items in lists. Write two sentences: 1) list subjects you study; 2) list activities you enjoy.

SIGNAL WORDS FOR INTRODUCTORY MODIFIERS

Subordinating Conjunctions

after	if	until
although	in order that	when
as	provided that	whenever
as long as	since	whereas
because	so that	wherever
before	though	whether
even though	unless	while

Conjunctive Adverbs

accordingly	furthermore	otherwise
again	however	then
as a result	in addition	therefore
also	indeed	thus
besides	moreover	on the other hand
consequently	nevertheless	in fact
finally		

These words all signal an introductory pause, which is marked by a comma. The same pause comes after a prepositional phrase that precedes an independent clause.

Subordinating conjunction

Since *there were a number of short-answer questions on the sociology exam*, students were required to bring bluebooks to class.

Conjunctive adverb

Moreover, a multiple-choice section of the test called for a Scantron sheet for answers.

Prepositional phrase

At *the end of the exam period*, students were also given a chance to have a short conference with the professor.

In all of these examples, the comma marks the dividing line between the main sentence and the modifier that introduces it.

EXERCISE 25-2 Commas and Introductory Words, Phrases, and Clauses

Directions: *Look for introductory words, phrases, and clauses in the following sentences. Read each of the sentences out loud. Listen for the natural pause where the intonation falls. Using the space provided, indicate where the commas should be placed.*

1. When I have worries on my mind my grandmother is always there to let me know that everything will be just fine.

. . . mind, my grandmother . . .

2. Money also causes great debate between both groups. Indeed it is a primary cause of conflict.

. . . Indeed, it . . .

3. Once I got in high school I had chores to do in my house.

. . . high school, I . . .

4. She was the nicest woman in the whole world, and she loved me a lot. But although we were best friends we were very different, and we would fight a lot. She was such a perfectionist.

. . . best friends, we were . . .

5. When I was in the sixth grade a French teacher told me my name was French, and when I was in the seventh grade a Spanish teacher told me my name was Spanish.

. . . grade, a French . . . grade, a Spanish . . .

6. When I was in college some of my friends and I used our "soap opera" names. A soap opera name was your middle name and the name of the street you lived on. My name was Dawn Michigan.

. . . school, some . . .

7. After a short time the officer let us go, and when we went into the house Derrick's dad started to yell at us.

. . . time, the officer . . . house, Derrick's dad . . .

8. After five minutes or so my dad would come out just as mad as my mom, and she would say, "I already spanked him."

. . . or so, my dad . . .

9. If you were not good you knew what would happen to you, and the punishment would not be a time-out.

. . . not good, you knew . . .

10. In most cases an adult tone of voice gave the impression of authority, and you knew they were in charge.

. . . cases, an adult . . .

Commas and Interrupters

Use a pair of commas to insert a parenthetical word, phrase, or clause into the middle of a sentence. **Parenthetical modifiers,** as they are sometimes called, interrupt the natural flow of the sentence. The commas act like parentheses and thus are used in pairs. For example:

The teacher would say our first and last names when he called on one of us. His name was Mr. Cowell.

The teacher, *Mr. Cowell,* would say our first and last names when he called on one of us.

Eric was the first name my parents chose for me. It means a powerful leader or king.

Eric, *which means a powerful leader or king,* was the first name my parents chose for me.

My sister is always picky about where she eats. She is picky for a variety of reasons.

My sister, *for a variety of reasons,* is always picky about where she eats.

When an interrupter comes at the end of a sentence, it sounds like an afterthought. The parentheses are formed by the comma and the period at the end of the sentence:

I was in the eighth grade. That made me fourteen years old.

I was in the eighth grade, *which made me fourteen years old.*

It was starting to get late in the evening. It was maybe around midnight.

It was starting to get late in the evening, *maybe around midnight.*

EXERCISE 25-3 **Commas and Interrupters**

Directions: *Read the following sentences and identify the parenthetical modifiers. Those coming in the middle of a sentence will need two commas; those coming at the end will need one comma. Indicate where commas are needed by using the space provided.*

1. My friend with his chiseled good looks and quick wit couldn't master the task of inserting an IV in a patient while in the back of a speeding ambulance.

My friend, with his chiseled good looks and quick wit, couldn't . . .

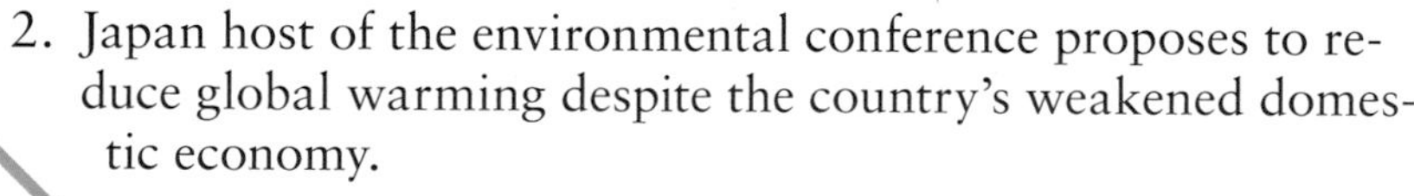

Ask Yourself
Does an interrupter contain essential information or nonessential information?

2. Japan host of the environmental conference proposes to reduce global warming despite the country's weakened domestic economy.

Japan, host of the environmental conference, proposes to reduce global warming, despite . . .

3. Failure to take action to reverse this cycle however would mean a world in peril.

. . . this cycle, however, would mean . . .

4. My friend always went to the mall with her friends. Every time she went, her mother gave her a time to be back which was 10:00 p.m.

. . . back, which was 10:00 p.m.

5. I choose to be honest even if the truth hurts someone.

. . . honest, even if . . .

6. A couple of weeks later after days and nights of terrible arguments he filed for divorce.

. . . later, after days and nights of terrible arguments, he . . .

7. In the summer of 1996 the year my father passed away my brothers and I all began to receive Social Security checks.

. . . 1996, the year my father passed away, my . . .

8. The rule is that you receive the checks until you're nineteen or graduate from high school whichever comes first.

. . . school, whichever comes first.

9. We had a long talk which consisted mostly of her telling me what she'd been up to for the last ten years.

. . . talk, which consisted . . .

10. The only downside to memory enhancement for humans is that they will remember everything such as annoying songs on the radio.

. . . everything, such as annoying . . .

Commas in a Series

Use commas in a list of three or more items. Lists can consist of nouns, verbs, adjectives, phrases, or clauses.

1. **Series of Nouns:** At the shop, I pushed the cart while he picked up the items we needed, such as wet and dry towels, wheel cleaner, car wash detergent, car wax, a buffer, and tire gloss.

2. **Series of Adjectives:** Todd was a cool name. It sounded tough, mean, and just plain cool.

3. **Series of Clauses:** Once you lose control of a child, he will end up doing what he wants, what his friends want, but definitely not what you want him to do.

4. **Series of Verb Phrases:** When I came back outside, the ball wasn't on the porch. It had rolled off the porch, hit the hood of my dad's car, and put a huge dent in it

In college writing, readers expect you to use a comma before the conjunction and the last item in a series:

> I read the newspaper, a few magazines, and an occasional novel.

EXERCISE 25-4 Commas in a Series

Directions: *Identify items in a series in the following sentences. Using the space provided, indicate where you would add commas as needed.*

1. My friends live for clubs. They go to clubs every weekend stay up all night and sleep all day.

. . . go to clubs every weekend, stay up all night, and sleep . . .

2. There's no need to run around with your feathers all up your chest sticking out and a nasty look on your face. Nobody is impressed with that kind of attitude.

. . . your feathers all up, your chest sticking out, and a nasty . . .

3. You don't need to dress like a man cut your hair like a man and act like a jerk to let people know you're equal to a man.

. . . dress like a man, cut your hair like a man, and act . . .

4. People do goofy things when they use drugs. These can include saying inappropriate things acting crazy and committing crimes.

. . . saying inappropriate things, acting crazy, and committing crimes.

5. Every day computers become more outdated complex and confusing. System conflicts and programming errors hinder access to the Internet and cause delays and downtime.

. . . more outdated, complex, and confusing. . . .

6. I was waiting for my nephew to come around the corner with his hair sticking up from his nap. I thought we would get into his secret cupboard and have a snack. He never came. I walked over to the cupboard opened it and had some crackers. That's how I said good-bye.

. . . walked over to the cupboard, opened it, and had . . .

7. One task I despise is cleaning the basement. It takes up too much time. My kids have a different point of view. They enjoy cleaning the basement because they get to run around like maniacs listen to music and drive me crazy at the same time. I sometimes wonder if they enjoy the cobwebs dust and bugs.

. . . run around like maniacs, listen to music, and drive. . . . the cobwebs, dust, and bugs.

8. She's a young intelligent beautiful classy woman. She's also bright and sexy.

a young, intelligent, beautiful, classy . . .

9. We had a black BMW 740ii Series with black-tinted windows large eighteen-inch chrome wheels and a bad-boy aura. We nicknamed it the Baron.

. . . black-tinted windows, large eighteen-inch chrome wheels, and . . .

10. My nephew is eight years old. His poor bicycle is covered with dust. You can hardly tell what color it is. Jim would rather spend hours on the couch watching TV eating chips and playing his video games.

. . . watching TV, eating chips, and playing his video games.

EXERCISE 25-5 **Putting It All Together**

Directions: *Identify and punctuate items in a series in the following sentences. Rewrite the sentences in the space provided, inserting commas as necessary to set off introductory and parenthetical modifiers and before conjunctions introducing independent clauses.*

1. After I finish school I go home do my homework and then go out to have fun.

After I finish school, I go home, do my homework, and then go out to have fun.

2. Learning to take on responsibility is important. If you are a responsible young adult when you want to go away to college get a job or move away from home your mom and dad won't have second thoughts.

If you are a responsible young adult, when you want to go away to college, get a job, or move away from home, your mom and dad won't have second thoughts.

3. The other night my friend came over to my house drunk got sick and then passed out.

The other night my friend came over to my house drunk, got sick, and then passed out.

4. When it comes to art history I can remember the artist's daily routine his or her relatives and in most cases what drugs he or she took but I forget the title of his or her most famous piece of art.

When it comes to art history, I can remember the artist's daily routine, his or her relatives, and in most cases what drugs he or she took, but I forget the title of his or her most famous piece of art.

Talk about It

With a classmate, compose a sentence about music with items in a series.

5. Jake and I love to play watch and just talk about football. Unfortunately not all the other friends we play football with share our enthusiasm. If it were up to me and Jake we would have everyone play every day.

Jake and I love to play, watch, and just talk about football. Unfortunately, not all the other friends. . . . If it were up to me and Jake, we would have everyone play every day.

6. The season seems to sneak up on us and then all of a sudden it is 105 degrees in the shade and the heat is scorching the grass baking the earth and turning everything to dust.

The season seems to sneak up on us, and then all of a sudden it is 105 degrees in the shade, and the heat is scorching the grass, baking the earth, and turning everything to dust.

7. Where I work sometimes a car is parted out which means the parts are sold the proceeds go to charity and someone's life is made a little easier.

Where I work, sometimes a car is parted out, which means the parts are sold, the proceeds go to charity, and someone's life is made a little easier.

8. The principal wanted to send me home because of my tank top short skirt and slingback sandals. Honestly I was very angry and did not agree with his decision. As a matter of fact I had a big argument with him.

The principal wanted to send me home because of my tank top, short skirt, and slingback sandals. Honestly, I was. . . . As a matter of fact, I had a big argument with him.

9. The artist still puts on his best clothes and goes for a stroll around the village every night. If someone recognizes him and asks him about a painting he smiles stops and gives generous explanations of his work.

The artist still puts on his best clothes and goes for a stroll around the village every night. If someone recognizes him and asks him about a painting, he smiles, stops, and gives generous explanations of his work.

10. After an hour of lecturing my kids about the television their future and the importance of education I cool off for a while give them some

breathing room and then look in on them to see if they have started their homework.

After an hour of lecturing my kids about the television, their future, and the importance of education, I cool off for a while, give them some breathing room, and then look in on them to see if they have started their homework.

Semicolons and Colons

Semicolons and colons are strong marks of punctuation, almost as strong as periods. Used correctly, they express the relationship of ideas within sentences.

Semicolons

MULTILINGUAL TIP
Compare the use of semicolons in your native language with English usage.

1. Use a semicolon between two complete sentences that express closely related or contrasting ideas.

    These nicknames did not say anything meaningful about my personality; they just made fun of my name.

    Charity is not doing something you have to do; it is doing something that you want to do.

2. Use a semicolon with a conjunctive adverb to link two related sentences.

    Big cars have a lot of room; consequently, people who carry around a lot of stuff are likely to buy them.

    My grandfather is in a nursing home; however, he is in control of all his faculties.

3. Use a semicolon for items in a series that need internal punctuation.

    When I was a kid, I mowed lawns, a job I kind of liked; weeded the flower beds, which I liked less than mowing; and washed windows, a job I totally hated.

Colons

1. Use a colon to connect a list to a complete sentence. The list can come either before or after the complete sentence.

    So that was our idea of fun: running, hopping fences, and screaming like maniacs.

    Building hot rods, fixing a leaking water pump, or fixing a flat tire: It's all fun to me.

2. Use a colon between two complete sentences when the second sentence explains the first or when one is general and the other is specific. **Note:** The second sentence can begin with either a lowercase letter or a capital letter.

    My mother was sad: she was mourning the loss of her mother.

    To be successful today, young people need to learn a valuable lesson: Get the best education you can.

3. Other situations for using colons are before a quotation or to separate titles and subtitles:

After a long pause, the judge lifted her eyes from her desk and spoke: "The court has decided to rule in favor of the defendant."

The title of her paper was *West Side Story: Romeo and Juliet Made Modern*.

EXERCISE 25-6 **Using Semicolons and Colons**

Directions: *Insert semicolons and colons in the following sentences as needed. In the space provided, briefly explain your reason for using the punctuation mark you chose.* Answers will vary. Example answers shown.

EXAMPLE

The food there was amazing. They had everything, duck, steak, and roast beef.

The food there was amazing. They had everything: duck, steak, and roast beef. (Chose a colon because it is used to connect a list to a complete sentence.)

1. The police academy allowed us to handle two types of guns. Machine guns and hand pistols.

The police academy allowed us to handle two types of guns: machine guns and hand pistols. (Colon used to connect a list to a complete sentence.)

2. Although we had the same name, we were different in every other way. She was the oldest child in her family. I was the middle. She was chubby. I was thin. She had two brothers. I had three.

. . . She was the oldest child in her family; I was the middle. She was chubby; I was thin. She had two brothers; I had three. (Semicolons used between pairs of complete sentences that express contrasting ideas.)

3. First I had doubts about police work. However, I changed my mind when the recruiter started telling me about the benefits. Pay for college tuition, self-discipline, or even better a motorcycle.

. . . ; however, I changed my mind when the recruiter started telling me about the benefits: pay for college tuition, self-discipline, or, even better, a motorcycle. (Semicolon used with a conjunctive adverb to link two related sentences. Colon used to connect a list to a complete sentence.)

4. For kids who play in the street, there are two significant things to be aware of. Motor vehicles and human nature.

For kids who play in the street, there are two significant things to be aware of: motor vehicles and human nature. (Colon used to connect a list to a complete sentence.)

5. A dog owner has to walk his dog every day or let it outside to use the bathroom. In contrast, I simply set out food for my cat and keep her litter box clean.

. . . bathroom; in contrast, I simply set out food for my cat and keep her litter box clean. (Semicolon used between contrasting statements; semicolon used before a conjunctive adverb.)

Talk about It

With a classmate, compose a sentence that uses a semicolon properly.

6. I hoped I would never see this customer again. I didn't get mad because she didn't tip me. I was mad at the fact that she was so rude.

. . . tip me; I was mad at the fact that she was so rude. (Semicolon used between contrasting statements.)

7. I learned a lot from this experience. Don't be greedy and take what you're given.

I learned a lot from this experience: Don't be greedy and take what you're given. (Colon used when the second sentence explains the first.)

8. I learned that spanking a child does not indicate parental failure. It can be a necessary measure that teaches kids right from wrong. Parents should use corporal punishment.

I learned that spanking a child does not indicate parental failure; it can be . . . (Semicolon used between contrasting statements.)

9. I say teach real math first. Allow kids to use a calculator once they have the basics in place.

I say teach real math first: Allow kids to use a calculator once they have the basics in place. (Colon used when the second sentence explains the first.)

10. I will name my son one of three names. It could be Richard because that is the name of my deceased father. It could be Mick for a friend of mine. Then again, it could be Nicolas for Nicolas Cage, my favorite actor.

I will name my son one of three names: It could be Richard because that is the name of my deceased father; it could be Mick for a friend of mine; then again, it could be Nicolas for Nicolas Cage, my favorite actor. (Colon used when the second sentence explains the first, and semicolon used for items in a series that need internal punctuation.)

Quotation Marks

A **quotation** is language you borrow from someone else. Place quotation marks around words that are clearly not your own. These words might be speech you write in the form of dialogue, or they might be a phrase, sentence, or multi-sentence passage you borrow from a newspaper, a magazine, or a book.

You always use a pair of quotation marks, one where the quotation begins and one where it ends. When you write quotations, observe punctuation conventions both before and after the quote.

Complete-Sentence Quotations

A complete-sentence quotation is preceded by a comma or a colon and begins with a quotation mark and a capital letter. It ends with a period, question mark, or exclamation mark, which goes inside the closing quotation mark.

> My father looked up from his work. He said, "Hand me that end wrench."
>
> Every so often, the thoughtful citizen should look up from her personal pursuits and ask, "Where is this country going?"

Partial Quotations

A quotation that is less than a complete sentence, such as a word or phrase, is not preceded by a comma and does not begin with a capital letter (unless the first word is a proper noun). Periods always go inside quotation marks.

> My name means "dark-skinned" in Arabic.
>
> The brochure refers to Sanibel Island as "Florida at its best."
>
> It says right on the side of the cigarette pack that smoking can cause "fetal injury, premature birth, and low birth weight."

EXERCISE 25-7 **Using Quotation Marks**

Directions: *Using the space provided, correct errors in the use of quotation marks, correcting the punctuation and capitalization as necessary.*

1. I learned very little in the sixth grade. Consequently, I was held back. Teachers said I had a very difficult time "Concentrating and absorbing the information" that was needed in order to pass that grade.

. . . time "concentrating and absorbing the information" . . .

2. I ran home screaming "It's alive"!

I ran home screaming, "It's alive!"

3. One thing I recall from my younger days is when we played "spy".

One thing I recall from my younger days is when we played "spy."

4. I was afraid for my sister that night. I told my mom "Please don't let her go, because the weather is really bad out there".

I told my mom, "Please don't let her go, because the weather is really bad out there."

5. The next day I woke up to the phone ringing, and I heard my aunt talking to somebody. I heard her say Oh my God, what happened? And right there and then I started crying because I knew something had happened to my sister.

I heard her say, "Oh my God, what happened?" . . .

6. When we finally got to the hospital, we had to wait in the emergency room. I was sitting with my head down when my uncle said there's your dad.

. . . I was sitting with my head down when my uncle said, "There's your dad."

7. Come on, man. Try it. It won't hurt. It makes you feel good. These are just some of the temptations teens have to deal with these days. Words such as these can affect a teen's life greatly.

"Come on, man. Try it. It won't hurt. It makes you feel good." These . . .

8. Every time I introduce myself to people, and I tell them my name is Val, they always respond by saying "what, short for Valerie?" Sometimes they say "let me guess. You were born on Valentine's Day!"

. . . saying, "What, short for Valerie?" Sometimes they say, "Let me guess. You were born on Valentine's Day!"

9. The doctor looked up at the mother and said she was going to have "A little princess".

The doctor looked up at the mother and said she was going to have "a little princess."

10. "Here" Steve said. Then he handed me the keys to the car.

"Here," Steve said. Then he handed me the keys to the car.

Indirect Quotations

Indirect quotations paraphrase what someone said. They do not require quotation marks. Indirect and direct quotations differ in their use of pronouns and verb tense:

> **Direct:** My father looked up from his work and said, "Hand me an end wrench."
>
> **Indirect:** My father looked up from his work and told me to hand him an end wrench.
>
> **Direct:** A friend saw me walking back to the locker room, so he pulled up and asked, "Do you want a ride home?"
>
> **Indirect:** A friend saw me walking back to the locker room, so he pulled up and asked me if I wanted a ride home.

EXERCISE 25-8 Indirect Quotations

Directions: *Using the space provided, rewrite the following quotations as indirect quotations.* Answers may vary. Example answers shown.

1. When I asked the teacher if I could make up the assignment, she said, "I don't think so."

When I asked the teacher if I could make up the assignment, she said she didn't think so.

Writer's Response
Tell about an important conversation with a family member. Use both direct and indirect quotes to tell who said what.

2. My son is always telling me, "I hope my comic book collection is worth something someday."

My son is always telling me that he hopes his comic book collection is worth something someday.

3. When I stepped in the house, my mother asked me, "What's wrong?"

When I stepped in the house, my mother asked me what was wrong.

4. I asked my uncle, "Do you know anything about constellations, and if you do, can you help me?"

I asked my uncle if he knew anything about constellations, and if he did, if he could help me.

5. Our neighbor's son grew up saying, "I will never do drugs."

Our neighbor's son grew up saying he would never do drugs.

6. I stopped, got out of my car, and asked him, "What is going on?"

I stopped, got out of my car, and asked him what was going on.

7. Being in a hurry I thought, "I won't forget."

Being in a hurry I thought that I wouldn't forget.

8. I asked her if she gets bored reading all these books. She said, "No, I love reading them."

I asked her if she gets bored reading all these books. She said no and that she loves reading them.

9. With this suspicious look on their faces, they politely asked us, "Where did you get the money?"

With this suspicious look on their faces, they politely asked us where we got the money.

10. When he asked about the spelling of my name, I said, "My parents could not spell."

When he asked about the spelling of my name, I said that my parents could not spell.

Internal Quotations and Titles

A special use of quotation marks is required when you have an internal quotation. In these cases, the quotation within the quotation is surrounded by single quotation marks.

> One official was quoted as saying, "When we are faced with 'the lesser of two evils,' when we make a choice, we are still choosing an evil."

'The lesser of two evils' is the quote within the quote.

Use quotation marks around the titles of newspaper articles, essays, short stories, poems, and songs.

> A newspaper article titled "Cruising Alaska, This Time on Land" describes the amazing sights to be seen from an automobile.
>
> The only Walt Whitman poem I remember from high school is "When Lilacs Last in the Dooryard Bloom'd."

EXERCISE 25-9 **Internal Quotations and Titles**

Directions: *Edit the following sentences, adding quotation marks as needed. Some of the sentences may be correct as written.*

1. Perhaps because it is written in the form of a very long question, many people have difficulty remembering the words to The Star Spangled Banner.

   . . . "The Star Spangled Banner."

2. The song, as musicologist Mark Adler notes, "begins with the question Oh, say can you see, and continues with a number of subordinate clauses."

   . . . with the question 'Oh, say can you see,' . . ."

3. Adler suggests that America the Beautiful might be a better national anthem.

   . . . that "America the Beautiful" might be . . .

4. One of the most important American poems in contemporary poetry is Allen Ginsberg's Howl.

   . . . Allen Ginsberg's "Howl."

5. An exasperated linguist remarked, "One problem with young people's speech today is their overuse of "you know."

   . . . remarked, "One problem with young people's speech today is their overuse of 'you know.'"

Apostrophes

Possessive Forms

MULTILINGUAL TIP
Compare how your native language forms the possessive.

Apostrophes are used to indicate possession or ownership. In the case of singular nouns, including those ending in "s" and plural nouns not ending in "s," add an apostrophe and an "s" (*'s*) to indicate possession: for example, *the store manager's attention, Chris's book, the children's toys*. In the case of plural nouns ending in "s," simply add the apostrophe: for example, so many *mammals' habitats*.

EXERCISE 25-10 Possessive Forms and Apostrophes

Directions: *Complete the table below. Put together the possessors and objects listed. Add apostrophe plus "s" to those possessors that do not end in "s":* my brother's Ford Mustang, most women's career plans. *Add just an apostrophe to possessors that end with an "s": the* delegates' conference.

EXAMPLE

my brother	Ford Mustang	my brother's Ford Mustang
most women	career plans	most women's career plans
the delegates	conference	the delegates' conference

1.	a kid	first role model	a kid's first role model
2.	kids	first role models	kids' first role models
3.	the book	last chapter	the book's last chapter
4.	most books	last chapters	most books' last chapters
5.	the child	good fortune	the child's good fortune
6.	children	good fortune	children's good fortune
7.	the airlines	responsibility	the airlines' responsibility
8.	my job	biggest drawbacks	my job's biggest drawbacks
9.	the boss	pet peeves	the boss's pet peeves
10.	that man	bad attitude	that man's bad attitude
11.	most movies	earnings	most movies' earnings
12.	the idea	power	the idea's power
13.	modern music	audience	modern music's audience
14.	a woman	time to act	a woman's time to act
15.	my neighbors	French poodle	my neighbors' French poodle

Contractions

An apostrophe can be used to replace a missing letter in **contractions**—words that have been created by dropping letters or combining some of the sounds from two or more words:

cannot	can't
have not	haven't
it is	it's

Note: The words *its* is the possessive form of the pronoun *it*. Writers often accidentally interchange "it's" ("it is") and "its" ("belonging to it"). Be on the lookout for this common mistake when proofreading your work. Also, bear in mind that contractions are considered informal, more appropriate to use in conversation than in writing. For that reason, many readers of college writing prefer students to minimize their use of contractions

Plurals

A frequent error made by writers is the addition of apostrophes to simple plurals, as illustrated in the following example:

> I didn't like dog's when I was a kid.

Here, the word *dogs* is a simple plural; it means "more than one dog." The inclusion of the apostrophe indicates the possessive, belonging to the dog, rather than the fact that there is more than one dog. Therefore, the apostrophe is not needed. Be aware of this common pitfall when proofreading your writing.

EXERCISE 25-11 Proofreading for Apostrophes

Directions: *Edit the following sentences. Delete apostrophes from plurals. Proofread for* its/it's *errors. Eliminate unnecessary contractions. In the space provided, write corrections of the errors you find.*

1. Television has made many advances since it's debut.

its

2. The news let's you know what's happening around your city, state, and country right away.

lets; what is

3. There were five of us: one sister, three brother's, and myself.

brothers

4. It's Christmas, always a good time for us to catch up on the latest news in the family.

It is

5. When I first get to work, I don't do anything except check inventory. It doesn't matter what else is happening. That's my first responsibility.

do not, does not, That is

6. It makes sense to society that mother's carry a child for nine months, care for it when it is born, listen and meet it's needs, feed it when it is hungry, and reassure it that it is going to be safe and happy all it's life.

mothers; its needs; its life

7. Let's say things have improved somewhat. We are in the twenty-first century, and women are playing role's that were once dreamt about but have now become reality.

Let us; roles

8. Every morning the cat will sit with me as I'm having my coffee. At night, I know when it's time for bed because that's when she comes out of her hiding spot.

I am; it is; that is

9. I don't want to take the chance of having too many friend's that might hurt me one day. It's hard to trust anyone.

do not; friends; It is

10. The age of electronic education is here, and like everything it has it's advantages and it's disadvantages.

its

EXERCISE 25-12 Editing for Apostrophe Errors

Directions: *Read the following sentences to determine whether the correct possessive form is being used. Correct any errors you find in the space provided. Some sentences are correct as written.*

1. Every kid's idea of fun is different.

correct as written

2. My mother read every novel by Charles Dickens. She says the book's portraits of miserable children interested her.

books' portraits

3. I used to work in the childrens' department.

children's department

4. The airline's pilots refused to cross the picket lines that day.

correct as written

5. My job's benefit package includes dental insurance.

correct as written

6. His cousins' real trouble began when their stepfather lost his job.

correct as written

Ask Yourself
What type of apostrophe error are you most likely to make?

TOPIC 24: Other Marks of Punctuation
www.mhhe.com/goingplaces

7. I read in this mornings' paper about a mans' journey around the globe in a hot air balloon.

this morning's paper; man's journey

8. This movies' content is too violent for little kids to see.

movie's

9. He was obsessed with time travel. The ideas appeal was both complete freedom and the chance to meet historical people.

idea's

10. My sisters workplace closed suddenly. Now they are unemployed.

sisters' workplace

Mechanics

CHAPTER OVERVIEW

- Spelling
  - *Basic Spelling Rules*
  - *Commonly Misspelled Words*
  - *Commonly Misused Words*
- Capitalization
- Numbers
- Abbreviations

Everyone misspells words occasionally, omits a capital letter, forgets to write out numbers from one to nine, or uses an incorrect abbreviation. This chapter provides a few strategies to identify and correct errors in spelling, capitalization, numbers, abbreviations, and confusing words that sound alike.

Spelling

To ensure you spell correctly, use a dictionary (including a misspeller's dictionary) and a thesaurus when you write. Learn to use spell-check on your computer. Finding a reliable proofreading partner can also help you eliminate recurring mechanical errors.

Gateway

TOPIC 26: Spelling and Hyphenation
www.mhhe.com/goingplaces

Spelling Tips

1. **Keep a vocabulary or word log.** Make a list of words you frequently misspell. Then study these words and write them multiple times.
2. **Be vigilant while writing and proofreading.** As you draft a paper, underline words that look misspelled. Check these words as you proofread your paper.
3. **Use a dictionary.** Don't wait until you proofread. Use your dictionary as you draft. In addition to definitions, a dictionary will help you with prefixes, suffixes, word combination, and word splits.
4. **Use a misspeller's dictionary.** Organized in alphabetical order, a misspeller's dictionary is a quick reference to find the correct spelling of a word. You can also identify the common errors you make. Here is a sample from *The McGraw-Hill Dictionary of Misspelled and Easily Confused Words.*

Wrong	Correct
buleten	bul•le•tin
evassion	eva•sion
particepant	par•tic•i•pant

5. **Use spell-check.** Computer spell-checks underline and correct words you misspell. Unfortunately, spell-check has limitations and is no substitute for a good proofreading partner.

Basic Spelling Rules

Memorizing a few basic rules will help you spell correctly. These rules pertain to vowel combinations, suffixes, and plural spellings.

Rule 1: *ie* and *ei*

Words with the letters *ie* and *ei* are frequently misspelled. To avoid these spelling errors, remember this saying: *i* before *e* except after *c* or when sounding like *a* as in neighbor or weigh.

Examples

_i_ before _e_: chief, field, believe, or niece
except after _c_: deceive, receive, or ceiling
sounding like _a_: freight or vein

There are always exceptions to a rule. When in doubt, consult a dictionary.

Exceptions

eight	seize
science	counterfeit

EXERCISE 26-1 **Using *ie* or *ei***

Directions: *Insert ie or ei in the blanks to correctly spell the following words.*

1. for_ei_gn
2. br_ie_f
3. y_ie_ld
4. pr_ie_st
5. suffic_ie_nt
6. gr_ie_f
7. rel_ie_ve
8. w_ei_ght
9. fr_ie_nd
10. handkerch_ie_f

Rule 2: Suffixes

Suffixes are endings that are added to words. Remember the following rules to avoid misspelling words when you add suffixes to them.

1. Words ending in *e*.
   - **Drop the final *e* in a word if the suffix begins with a vowel, such as *-ed* or *-ing*.**

     rake + ed = raked

     care + ing = caring
   - **Drop the final *e* in a word when it is preceded by a vowel.**

     true + ly = truly

     argue + ment = argument
   - **Drop the final *e* in a word when you add the suffixes *-able* or *-ous*.**

     advise + able = advisable

     ridicule + ous = ridiculous

     Exception: If eliminating a silent *e* creates confusion, keep it.

     mile + age = mileage
   - **Keep the final *e* in a word if the suffix begins with a consonant.**

     home + less = homeless

     care + ful = careful
   - **Keep the final *e* in a word if it follows a soft *c* or *g*.**

     trace + able = traceable

     outrage + ous = outrageous

2. Words ending in *y*.
   - **Change the *y* to an *i* at the end of a word when it follows a consonant.**

     happy + ness = happiness

     ready + ly = readily
   - **Keep the *y* at the end of a word if it follows a vowel.**

     portray + ed = portrayed

     habitual + ly = habitually

- **Keep the *y* at the end of a word if you are adding the suffix -ing.**

  play + ing = playing

  copy + ing = copying

3. Words ending in a consonant.
   - **Double the final consonant in a single syllable word when it follows a single vowel.**

     wet + er = wetter

     trap + ing = trapping
   - **Do *not* double the final consonant in a single syllable word when it does not follow a single vowel.**

     mark + er = marker

     crow + ing = crowing
   - **Double the final consonant when the word has more than one syllable, the consonant follows a single vowel, and the last syllable of the word will be stressed once the ending is added.**

     forget + ing = forgetting

EXERCISE 26-2 Adding Suffixes

Directions: *Combine each word and suffix. Spell the new word correctly.*

1. stubborn + ness stubbornness
2. appoint + ment appointment
3. control + er controller
4. run + ing running
5. propel + ed propelled
6. benefit + ed benefited
7. move + er mover
8. remove + able removable
9. write + ing writing
10. fame + ous famous

Rule 3: Plurals

To improve your spelling, remember these rules for making nouns plural.

1. **Add *s* to most singular nouns to make them plural.**

   frog + s = frogs

   lemon + s = lemons
2. **Add *-es* to singular nouns ending in *s, ss, z, zz, x, sh, ch,* or *tch.***

   bus + es = buses

buzz + es = buzzes

sex + es = sexes

wish + es = wishes

church + es = churches

watch + es = watches

3. **Add *-ies* to singular nouns ending in a consonant plus *y*. Change the *y* to *i* and add *-es*.**

   baby + es = babies

   party + es = parties

   Exception: Add *s* to proper nouns that end in *y*.

   Mondays   Kennedys   Wendys

   Will all the Wendys in the senior class report to the office?

4. **Words ending in *o*.**
   - **Add *s* when the word ends in a vowel plus *o* combination.**

     studio + s = studios

     rodeo + s = rodeos
   - **Add *-es* when the word ends in a consonant plus *o* combination.**

     mosquito + es = mosquitoes

     potato + es = potatoes
   - **Some words that end in *o* can be made plural by adding *s* or *es*.**

     avocado + s = avocados   avocado + es = avocadoes

5. **Irregular nouns are made plural in different ways. Memorize the nouns that are irregular.**

   child = children

   mouse = mice

   woman = women

   goose = geese

   ox = oxen

   person = people

   tooth = teeth

EXERCISE 26-3 Creating Plural Nouns

Directions: *Make the nouns plural and spell them correctly.*

1. rodeo ___rodeos___
2. lady ___ladies___
3. donkey ___donkeys___
4. hero ___heroes___
5. comedy ___comedies___

6. goose geese

7. fox foxes

8. class classes

9. chief chiefs

10. bench benches

11. ghetto ghettoes

12. zoo zoos

13. radio radios

14. kiss kisses

15. foot feet

Commonly Misspelled Words

Learn to edit for commonly misspelled words, such as *always* (allways), *parallel* (paralel), *special* (specal), and *surprise* (suprize). Table 26-1 shows a list of the words most commonly misspelled by writers of all ages.

Keep a list of words you misspell. Use memory aids to help you remember correct spelling. For example, underline or circle the misspelled part of the word:

Misspelled	Correctly Spelled
usualy	usually
definate	definite
sophmore	sophomore

You can use common memory aids like "remember that skiing uses two poles so you spell *skiing* with two *i*s in the middle," or make up your own. Here are memory strategies for *a lot* and *argument,* which are frequently misspelled.

Misspelling	Correct Spelling	Memory Strategy
alot	a lot	*A lot* is two words because it is not just one thing. It is a lot of things.
arguement	argument	To win an argument you must have an idea that sticks in someone's head. The correct spelling of argument has the word *gum* in it.

EXERCISE 26-4 Your Frequently Misspelled Words

Directions: *On a sheet of paper, make a list of ten words you frequently misspell. Select these words from your papers or review the table of commonly misspelled words (Table 26-1). Create a chart like the one for* a lot *and* argument *to study the words. Write the misspelled words, then the correct spellings. Underline the letters where the errors occur. Write a strategy or memory aid you can use to remember the correct spelling of each word.*

TABLE 26-1

COMMONLY MISSPELLED WORDS			
a lot	dining	license	psychology
absence	disappoint	lightning	receiving
ache	dying	loneliness	recognize
across	eighth	maneuver	relevant
address	embarrassing	marriage	restaurant
aisle	environment	mathematics	rhythm
always	equivalent	meant	roommate
among	especially	minimum	schedule
analyze	familiar	missile	seize
appearance	fascinate	mortgage	secretary
argument	flexible	mysterious	separate
attendance	foreign	necessary	sincerely
believe	formerly	noticeable	skiing
business	friend	ninety	sophomore
beautiful	fulfill	occurrence	special
beginning	generally	opinion	subtle
calendar	gesture	parallel	succeed
campaign	grammar	paralysis	surprise
career	government	paralyze	technique
category	grief	particular	therefore
cemetery	height	peculiar	transferred
campaign	humorous	perceive	truly
changeable	illegal	perform	until
compelled	immediately	physically	usually
conscientious	independent	preference	valuable
convenient	intelligence	prejudice	weight
defendant	interrupt	probably	weird
definite	irrelevant	procedure	woman
description	knowledge	proceed	women
dilemma	leisure	profession	written

Commonly Misused Words

Spelling is often complicated by the fact that some words sound alike, look alike, or both. For example, the words *knew* and *new* look and sound alike but have different spellings and different meanings. They are also different parts of speech.

PARTS OF SPEECH
All words serve a specific purpose or function in a sentence. The part of speech is the name of that purpose or function.

There are eight parts of speech: noun, pronoun, adjective, verb, adverb, preposition, conjunction, and interjection.

Knew and New

knew: (verb) to know or to understand

Ricardo **knew** how to operate the fork-lift.

new: (adjective) just created or unfamiliar

A **new** president is sworn into office.

Develop a system to help you master these words. Some commonly confused words have a unique feature that helps you remember how to spell them and how to use them.

principle principal (the principal is the head of a school and your *pal*)
incite insight (insight provides the sight to understand something)

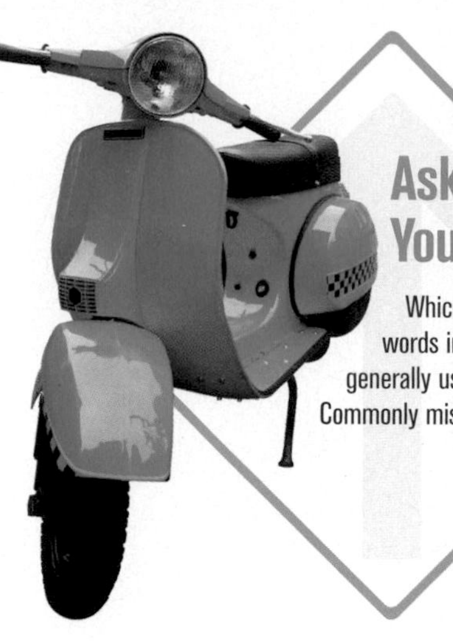

Ask Yourself
Which of the words in Set 1 do you generally use correctly? Commonly misuse?

However, not all words with different meanings have unique spellings that allow you to distinguish between them, so having a reference book handy or using the reference tools on your computer will help.

Commonly Misused Words—Set 1

accept—except

- **accept:** (verb) to receive, to understand, to allow in
  I was pleased to **accept** the nomination for class secretary.
- **except:** (preposition) otherwise, than, to the exclusion of; (conjunction) unless; or (verb) to take out
  Everyone **except** five new students attended the rally.

advice—advise

- **advice:** (noun) opinion given as to what to do
  The physicist provided **advice** on how to understand the problem.
- **advise:** (verb) to give advice
  Wilson would **advise** the president to veto the tax bill, but the president would not listen.

all ready—already

- **all ready:** (adjective or adverb/verb or noun) everyone or everything is ready to go or prepared
  The judges were **all ready** to begin the barbecue taste test.
- **already:** (adverb) previously
  The engineers had **already** triple-checked the missile prior to blast-off.

all right—alright

- **all right:** (adverb or adjective) satisfactory; adequate, safe
  The outfielders were **all right** after lightning hit left field.
- **alright:** (adjective or adverb) disputed spelling of *all right*

all together—altogether

- **all together:** (adjective) gathered; united
  When the children were finally found, they were **all together.**
- **altogether:** (adverb) completely; thoroughly
  It was a completely different situation altogether.

choose—chose

- **choose:** (present tense verb) to select or decide
  The committee must **choose** the theme for the festival.
- **chose:** (past tense verb) to select or decide
  After the meeting, the committee **chose** the theme for the festival.

conscious—conscience

- **conscious:** (adjective) having awareness; being mentally awake
  Conscious of the traffic problems, the bus driver chose another route.
- **conscience:** (noun) having a sense of morality and choosing to do good
  My **conscience** guides me to make good choices in my life.

hear—here

- **hear:** (verb) to perceive sound; to listen
  The audience could **hear** the violins echo the main melody.
- **here:** (adverb) a place or location
  We decided to camp **here** because the trees would shade our tent.

its—it's

- **its:** (pronoun) possessive form of *it*
  The starving dog ate **its** food quickly.
- **it's:** (pronoun/verb) the contraction for *it is*
  It's easy to find a phone number using yellowpages.com.

knew—new

- **knew:** (verb) past tense of know; understood
  Denise **knew** how to drive a motorcycle.
- **new:** (adjective) just created or unfamiliar
  A **new** president was sworn into office.

leave—let

- **leave:** (verb) to depart a place or to allow a person or thing to remain
  Please **leave** the papers on the kitchen table so I can mail them.
- **let:** (verb) to give an opportunity; assign; allow
  Let me mail the letters when I go to the store.

lay—lie

- **lay:** (verb) to place a thing onto something
  Lay the books on the book cart, and the librarian will put them on the shelf.
- **lie:** (verb) to rest in a horizontal position
  Lie on the couch and relax before dinner.

loose—lose—loss

- **loose:** (adjective) not fastened; detached
  Tightening the **loose** wires repaired the faulty light.
- **lose:** (verb) not able to keep or find something
  More people will **lose** jobs with a weak economy.
- **loss:** (noun) the result of losing a person or thing; failing to gain or win
  The financial **loss** was too large to ignore, and the company closed its doors.

raise—rise

- **raise:** (verb) to lift a person or thing; to increase the amount; to grow
  The farmer will **raise** a variety of crops: corn, wheat, and alfalfa.
- **rise:** (verb) to move upward; ascend; respond
  The team will **rise** to the challenge to beat their opponents.

set—sit

- **set:** (verb) to place a thing down or onto something
  He **set** the basket on top of the picnic table.
- **sit:** (verb) to rest in a sitting position
  Please **sit** in the lobby and wait for the next available agent.

than—then

- **than:** (conjunction) used to make a comparison between two things
  I am taller **than** the doorway, so I always duck when I enter the house.
- **then:** (adverb) indicating a time period or a future time period
  First, I picked up my laundry, and **then** I went to the post office.

their—there—they're

- **their:** (pronoun) possessive pronoun of *they*; to show possession of a person, place, or thing
  The family checked into **their** suite at the resort.
- **there:** indicating a place or position or point
  There are three reasons that I cannot go to the party.
- **they're:** (pronoun and verb) the contraction for *they are*
  The bridesmaids are late for the wedding. **They're** caught in traffic.

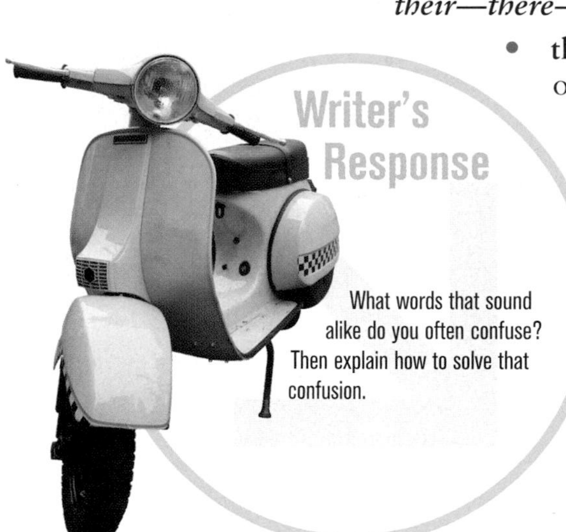

Writer's Response

What words that sound alike do you often confuse? Then explain how to solve that confusion.

to—too—two

- **to:** (preposition) indicating action toward a person, place, or thing
  Robert mailed the package **to** his sister in California.
- **too:** (adverb) also; very; excessive amount
  I wanted to go **too.**
  I ate **too** many calories at lunch, so dinner has to be mostly vegetables.
- **two:** (adjective) the number 2
  I read **two** chapters before class this morning.

whose—who's

- **whose:** (pronoun) inquiring about ownership of a person, place, or thing
  Whose tennis shoes are sitting in the hallway?
- **who's:** (pronoun and verb) the contraction for *who is*
  Who's going to buy the tickets for the football game next month?

your—you're

- **your:** (pronoun) indicating ownership by a specific person
  Your son causes frequent disruptions and may be suspended.
- **you're:** (pronoun and verb) the contraction for *you are*
  You're causing frequent disruptions in class and may be suspended.

EXERCISE 26-5 Self-Assessment of Commonly Misused Words—Set 1

Directions: *Read the following sentences and underline the correct word in the parentheses for each one. Use the definitions above to help you select the correct word.*

1. I have (all ready/already) packed the children's books in those boxes, so they are (all ready/already) to go.
2. I (hear/here) there is a (knew/new) restaurant downtown, but anyplace you choose is (all right/alright) with me.
3. (Their/There/They're) is more to eat at the party (than/then) you imagine.
4. If you have to (leave/let) early, please (leave/let) me know at the beginning of the class.
5. I never give (advice/advise) to friends, but (your/you're) an exception (to/too/two) my rule.
6. If we go (all together/altogether), (whose/who's) driving to the game?
7. I will (choose/chose) a new course for my schedule, so I can (raise/rise) my grades.
8. I am (conscious/conscience) of the confusion between the (to/too/two) political groups, but I (accept/except) your facts and will reconsider.
9. If you let the rope (loose/lose/loss), I can (lay/lie) it flat on the ground.
10. Before (its/it's) too late, (sit/set) down and talk about your decision.

EXERCISE 26-6 Spelling Challenges from Set 1

Directions: *Score Exercise 26-5 to identify words you need to add to your spelling log. Create a memory aid like the one in the box for each word or pair of words that gave you difficulty. Then write a sentence for each word and study the words before you test yourself again using the additional self-assessment tests online.*

EXAMPLE: *WHOSE* AND *WHO'S*

Whose is a pronoun used to ask who owns a person, place, or thing.

Who's is the contraction of *who is*.

- **Whose** doll was left on the front porch?
- **Who's** going to wash the dishes after dinner?

Commonly Misused Words—Set 2

allowed—aloud

- **allowed:** (verb) past tense of *allow*; to permit

  The professor **allowed** his class to turn in their papers late.
- **aloud:** (adverb) loudly

  The whole congregation heard the little boy talking **aloud** during the sermon.

behalf—behave

- **behalf:** (noun) interest, support, or benefit a person or group

  The daughter spoke on **behalf** of her extremely ill father.
- **behave:** (verb) to act in a certain way

  Please **behave** properly while we wait for our food to come.

breath—breathe

- **breath:** (noun) air inhaled or exhaled

  Take a **breath** before you talk to calm yourself.
- **breathe:** (verb) to inhale and exhale

  Back up and give him room to **breathe.**

capital—capitol

- **capital:** (adjective and noun) primary or main; a punishment requiring the death penalty; an accumulation of money

  The owner had enough **capital** that he was able to expand his store.
- **capitol:** (noun) a building in which governments of states or nations meet; a city where a state locates its government

  The legislature will meet in the **capitol** to discuss immigration laws.

clothes—cloths

- **clothes:** (noun) clothing

  I bought new **clothes** with my birthday money.
- **cloths** (noun) fabric or material

  The mechanic used some old cloths to clean the windows and instrument panels of the car.

complement—compliment

- **complement:** (noun) something that improves or enhances a person, place, or thing

  Creamy coleslaw is a **complement** to the sharp taste of barbeque ribs.
- **compliment:** (verb) to express respect or praise

  The senators **complimented** the committee on a thoughtful review of educational policies.

hole—whole

- **hole:** (noun) an opening; a flaw

  A gaping **hole** was left after the car crashed into the building.
- **whole:** (adjective) an entire thing; a system or group working together

  The **whole** office attended the retirement party.

know—no

- **know:** (verb) to understand or have knowledge of

  First-year students **know** they must learn to study and manage their time effectively.
- **no:** (adjective or adverb) not any; used to express a negative choice

  There are **no** carrots left in the refrigerator.

lead—led

- **lead:** (verb) present tense; to guide or show

  The conductor is going to **lead** the orchestra to success.
- **led:** (verb) the past tense of *lead*; to guide or show

  The team captain cheered his teammates as he **led** them to a victory.

passed—past

- **passed:** (verb) past tense of *pass*; to give or transfer an object or person from one place to another; to act in order to gain credit, certification, or permission

  The legislature **passed** a law to restrict dumping chemicals into rivers.
- **past:** (adjective, adverb, or noun) a time period that has already occurred

  In the **past** months, an infestation of butterflies ate my crops.

  In the **past,** women were unable to vote.

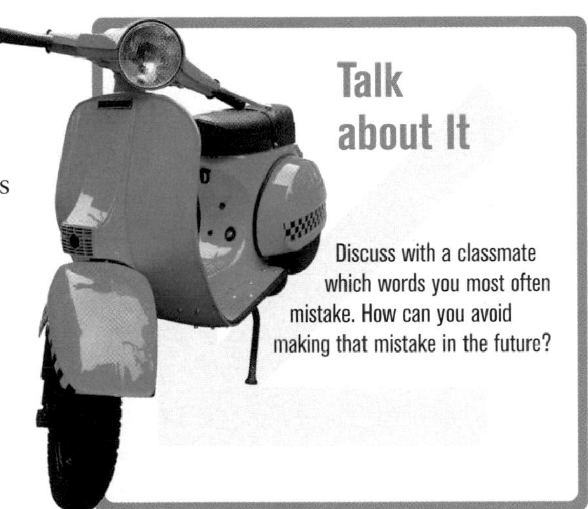

Talk about It

Discuss with a classmate which words you most often mistake. How can you avoid making that mistake in the future?

propose—purpose

- **propose:** (verb) to suggest an idea or action

  I **propose** we do not consider cutting costs by reducing medical care.
- **purpose:** (noun) a reason to do or have a person, place, or thing.

  Aesthetic beauty is the primary **purpose** for planting flowers and shrubs.

safe—save

- **safe:** (noun) a place to keep valuable things; (adjective) protected from harm or worry

  I put my diamond necklace in the **safe** in the hotel lobby.

  The basement is a **safe** place during a tornado.
- **save:** (verb) to keep; to rescue from danger

  You can **save** lives by telling people about the dangers of smoking.

scared—scarred

- **scared:** (verb) past tense of *scare*; to be frightened
  The small boy was **scared** by the trick-or-treaters.
- **scarred:** (noun) having a scar or a feeling of being damaged
  The small boy's face was **scarred** after the dog bit him.

scene—seen

- **scene:** (noun) a place; a view or stage setting; a sequence of action
  The third **scene** in the play portrays the fears of new parents.
- **seen:** (verb) past participle of *see*; to have the experience of seeing; to come to know
  Bystanders were frightened by the accident they had just **seen.**

threw—through

- **threw:** (verb) past tense of *throw*; to toss
  The pitcher **threw** three straight fastballs to strike out the batter.
- **through:** (preposition) to go from one place to another; to complete a direct passage
  The needle went **through** the thick carpet with ease.

were—where

- **were:** (verb) past tense of *to be*; to be in a place; to be doing an action
  You **were** at the market all afternoon.
- **where:** (conjunction, adverb, and noun) at or in a place or position
  Where are you going after class?

EXERCISE 26-7 Self-Assessment of Commonly Misused Words—Set 2

Directions: *Read the following sentences and underline the correct word in the parentheses for each one. Use the definitions above to help you select the correct word.*

1. My brother's face was (scared/scarred) when a kid (threw/through) a rock at him.
2. My cousin often created a huge (seen/scene) at home; he would (behalf/behave) better at school.
3. My yoga instructor reminds us to (breath/breathe) deeply as we stretch.
4. Since I gained weight, I am always hunting through my (clothes/cloths) trying to find an outfit that is (loose/lose) enough to wear.
5. There is no talking (allowed/aloud) in my sign language class.
6. (Threw/Through) the (passed/past) few months, gas prices have doubled.
7. My (hole/whole) family loves bargain shopping, and my sister will drive fifteen miles to (safe/save) even a single dollar.

8. (Know/No) matter how unpleasant a summer job might be, you have to remember that the primary (propose/purpose) is to make money.
9. I always wanted to (lead/led) a tour of the (capitol/capital).
10. She (complemented/complimented) her employee for a job well done.

EXERCISE 26-8 Spelling Challenges from Set 2

Directions: *Score Exercise 26-7 to identify the words you need to add to your spelling log. Create a memory aid like the one in the box for each word or pair of words that gave you difficulty. Then write a sentence for each word and study the words before you test yourself again using the additional self-assessment tests online.*

EXAMPLE: *PASSED* AND *PAST*

Passed is a verb used to state an action that has already occurred.

Past is a noun used to indicate a past time or experience.

- Greg **passed** the store and had to turn around and go back.
- The argument was in the **past** and not worth talking about.

Commonly Misused Words—Set 3

altar—alter

- **altar:** (noun) a table or platform used for worship
  The priest stepped up to the **altar** to offer communion.
- **alter:** (verb) to change
  Your comments did not **alter** my opinion of the movie.

Writer's Response
Write a short paragraph about the environment. Use *affect* or *effect* in your paragraph.

affect—effect

- **affect:** (verb) to influence or to make an impression on
  Carbon monoxide **affects** the quality of the air.
- **effect:** (noun) the result of an action or event
  The **effects** of carbon monoxide are a concern for environmentalists.

brake—break

- **brake:** (noun) a device used to stop a vehicle; (verb) to stop a vehicle;
  I stepped on the **brake** to miss the dog running in front of my car.
  To avoid swerving, truck drivers **brake** hundreds of feet before a stop.
- **break:** (noun) an intermission in a show, game, or event; (verb) to damage something; to separate into parts
  There will be a fifteen-minute **break** in the middle of the show.
  My sons **break** their toys because they throw them around.

council—counsel

- **council:** (noun) a group of people who meet to provide advice

  The teacher's **council** recommends reading nightly to your children.
- **counsel:** (noun) advice, a person hired to provide advice

  The company hired legal **counsel.**

  My best **counsel** for new parents is to worry less and laugh more.

cite—site—sight

- **cite:** (verb) to state facts or information

  Three coaches **cite** injuries as the biggest challenge for high school football teams.
- **site:** (noun) location of a building, park, or monument

  I walked the **site** with the architect to understand the future building.
- **sight:** (noun) a thing that is seen; the ability to see something

  Margaret's furniture in her new house is a **sight** to behold.

  The blind man miraculously regained his sight.

coarse—course

- **coarse:** (adjective) rough or harsh; poor quality

  The ground salt has a **coarse** texture.
- **course:** (noun) class or lecture series; a way to act

  I signed up for a cooking **course** on pasta and sauces.

desert—dessert

- **desert:** (noun) a geographic location that is hot, dry, and sandy; (verb) to leave or abandon a person or thing

  The **desert** blooms in the spring each year.

  Soldiers who **desert** their posts are severely punished.
- **dessert:** (noun) the last course in a meal, usually sweet

  Dessert is my favorite part of the meal, so I always eat it first.

discreet—discrete

- **discreet:** (adjective) respecting privacy; keeping quiet about personal issues

  A **discreet** nurse avoids discussing a patient's health in front of visitors.
- **discrete:** (adjective) distinct part of something

  Reading requires a child to learn a series of **discrete** skills in order to recognize known and unknown words.

do—due

- **do:** (verb) to act; to accomplish a task

  I **do** five sets of crunches every morning to strengthen my abdominal muscles.
- **due:** (adjective) when a debt is owed; a date required to pay a debt or obligation

  I sent my payment after the bill's **due** date.

fourth—forth

- **fourth:** (noun) one quarter of a whole; related to number 4

  Give me a **fourth** of the pie to take home.
- **forth:** (adverb) moving forward

  The driver rocked his car back and **forth** to get out of the snow bank.

moral—morale

- **moral:** (adjective or noun) the significance of a lesson; the point of a story

  The **moral** of the story is simple: Trying and failing is better than giving up.
- **morale:** (noun) mental or emotional attitude

  The USO works to keep up the army's **morale.**

principal—principle

- **principal:** (noun) a person in charge of a school; the sum of a loan that is being repaid; (adjective) a primary influence or person

  The **principal** called five boys to his office for causing a food fight.

  The **principal** investor vetoed the decision to raise employee salaries.
- **principle:** (noun) a rule, law, or code; the essential nature or concept

  There are five **principles** for a successful work ethic.

quiet—quite

- **quiet:** (adjective or noun) a state of peace and rest; (adjective) being free from noise; gentle

  My vacation in the woods gave me the **quiet** and calm that I needed.
- **quite:** (adverb) wholly, completely

  I am **quite** sure the man on the left stole my purse.

real—really

- **real:** (adjective) not false; actual

  The blonde's hair was **real.**
- **really:** (adverb) truly; unquestionably; very

  The race was loaded with **really** dangerous curves.

stationary—stationery

- **stationary:** (adjective) not moving, not changing place or position

  I ride a **stationary** bike every night as I watch television.
- **stationery:** (noun) paper or materials to write notes or letters

  The company's **stationery** has a letterhead featuring the president's photograph.

Ask Yourself
Which of the words in Set 3 do you generally use correctly? Commonly misuse? Why?

EXERCISE 26-9 Self-Assessment of Commonly Misused Words—Set 3

Directions: *Read the following sentences and underline the correct word in the parentheses for each one. Use the definitions to help you select the correct word.*

1. I was (real/really) hungry, so I ate an appetizer, salad, entrée, and two (deserts/desserts).
2. The (council/counsel) voted on a noise abatement law to create a (quite/quiet) and serene environment for our town.
3. The (coarse/course) requires you to (cite/site/sight) specific examples of (moral/morale) (principles/principals).
4. William has difficulty keeping secrets: he has never been very (discreet/ discrete).
5. I purchased new (stationary/stationery) for the office.
6. The doctor told Bill that although he did not (brake/break) any bones, any further (affects/effects) from the accident would take months to appear.
7. The (principal/principle) brought (fourth/forth) a new set of rules to be approved by the Board of Education.
8. It is illegal to (altar/alter) your driver's license.
9. Students knew work was (do/due) at the beginning of the week.
10. A good speller must learn dozens of (discreet/discrete) rules.

EXERCISE 26-10 Spelling Challenges from Set 3

Directions: *Score Exercise 26-9 to identify the words you need to add to your spelling log. Create a memory aid like the one in the box for each word or pair of words that gave you difficulty. Then write a sentence for each word and study the words before you test yourself again using the additional self-assessment tests online.*

EXAMPLE: *AFFECT* AND *EFFECT*

Use alphabetical order. *Affect* begins with an "a" so it comes first alphabetically. A cause is an action that happens before the effect or result. *Affect* is a verb. *Effect* is the result of the action. It is also a noun.

- The cheery new paint **affected** the student's attitudes toward learning.
- The **effects** of the flood were still visible a month later.

Capitalization

Capitalization is used to distinguish between **proper nouns**—words that are the specific names of people, places, and things—and **common nouns**—words that refer to general categories or types of people, places, and things.

Common Nouns	Proper Nouns
woman	Deanna Wiltzer
day	Tuesday
month	July
city	Hong Kong
country	England

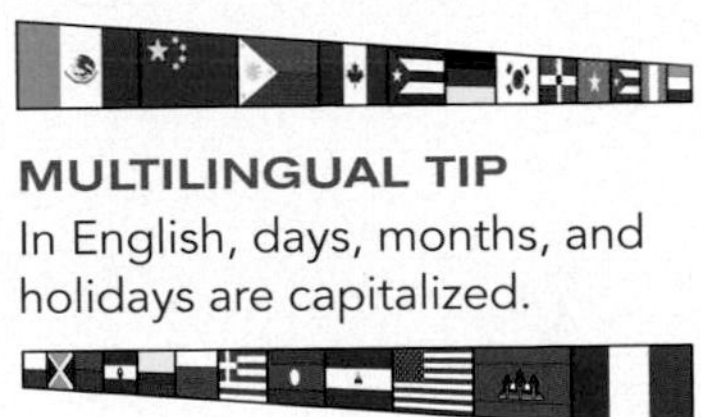

MULTILINGUAL TIP
In English, days, months, and holidays are capitalized.

Capitalization is also used to indicate the first word of a sentence, the titles of books and newspapers, and job titles. Here are some guidelines for capitalization.

1. **Capitalize the first word of a sentence.**

   Don't drop out of high school if you want a job.

   Machines replace people in more and more unskilled jobs each year.

2. **Capitalize proper nouns (specific people, places, and things).**

   - **Specific people (including the pronoun *I*)**

Karen Hicks	Sting
Albert Einstein	I
D. H. Lawrence	

   - **Races, nationalities, cultures, ethnic groups, and languages**

Japanese	Hispanic
African American	Portuguese

   - **Religions, religious followers, and religious/sacred texts**

Baptist	Bible
Semitic	Torah
Jesuit priests	Quran

   - **Governmental organizations, company names, other institutions, or brand names**

World Wildlife Fund	Consumers Energy
Irvine Police Department	Phi Kappa Delta
McDonald's	Tostito

   - **Social, political, sports, and other organizations**

YMCA	Student Activities Safety Association
Loyal Order of the Moose	Clutterers Anonymous
FactCheck.Org	

   - **Specific places (continents, countries, regions, counties, cities, towns, addresses, and so on)**

Africa	Oakland
Brazil	New York City
the Southwest	Gingellville, Michigan
256 W. Saginaw Street	

- **Specific things (buildings, monuments, famous objects, titles of works, and so on)**

Eiffel Tower	Crown Jewels
Lincoln Memorial	*The Hymns of Atharvan*
Wrigley Field	*Zarathushtra*
Cloud Gate	

- **Days of the weeks, months, holidays, and religious holidays (Note: Seasons are not capitalized.)**

Thursday	Yom Kippur
December	Eid al Fitr
Labor Day	Mardi Gras

- **Historical time periods, events, movements, and documents**

Renaissance	Expressionist movement
Industrial Revolution	Constitution
World War II	*Brown v. Board of Education*

3. **Capitalize formal and informal titles.**
   - **Capitalize job titles or positions** when the title appears before the name, but **not** when it comes afterward or separately from a name.

chairperson	Chairperson Benger
senator	Senator Kennedy
doctor	Doctor Franklin

   The aide looked frantically for **Senator Kennedy.**

   He could not find the **senator** anywhere.

4. **Capitalize the titles of relatives when they are used to replace proper names or appear immediately before proper names.**

   After my parent's divorce, **Mother** kept in close contact with **Aunt** Maria.

5. **Capitalize the following words when they serve as proper nouns:**
   - **Directions** such as north, south, east, or west when they refer to a geographic region and do not compass directions: the Southwest, the Northeast.
   - **Course titles** when they name a specific course: Introduction to Anthropology, Apprentice Drafting, Calculus 101.

EXERCISE 26-11 Proper Nouns

Directions: *Select the sentence that uses the correct form of capitalization from each of the pairs below.*

__b__ 1.

a. Yosemite national park is nearly 1,200 square miles of mountains, valleys, and spectacular waterfalls.

b. Yosemite National Park is nearly 1,200 square miles of mountains, valleys, and spectacular waterfalls.

a 2.

a. Thousands of teens head south to Florida for spring break.

b. Thousands of teens head South to Florida for spring break.

b 3.

a. The Senators from Oregon will arrive shortly.

b. The senators from Oregon will arrive shortly.

a 4.

a. Technological weapons used in the Gulf War changed warfare.

b. Technological weapons used in the Gulf war changed warfare.

b 5.

a. I'm taking English 101 and archeology 232 this semester.

b. I'm taking English 101 and Archeology 232 this semester.

b 6.

a. the southwest is facing a dire water shortage (Severe water shortages affect 400 million people).

b. The Southwest is facing a dire water shortage (severe water shortages affect 400 million people).

b 7.

a. Learning spanish on DVD is easier than I thought.

b. Learning Spanish on DVD is easier than I thought.

a 8.

a. I had an interview with the Advisory Council on Historic Preservation.

b. I had an interview with the Advisory Council on historic preservation.

a 9.

a. Tell the cab driver to drop you at 34667 N. Wilshire Boulevard.

b. Tell the cab driver to drop you at 34667 N. Wilshire boulevard.

a 10.

a. After the surgery, the surgeons and Doctor Moss spoke with the family.

b. After the surgery, the Surgeons and Doctor Moss spoke with the family.

Talk about It

What is the difference between common and proper nouns?

PUNCTUATION ALERT
1. Underline titles of books, newspapers, and magazines.
2. Use quotation marks for titles of poems, articles, stories, documents, works of art, TV shows, and songs.

Another rule for capitalization is that the titles of publications should be capitalized. Titles of books, newspapers, magazines, poems, articles, stories, documents, films, TV shows, plays, tapes, and works of art all have a single rule for capitalization: **Capitalize the first word, last word, and all other words except articles, conjunctions, and prepositions.** Prepositions of five letters or longer may be capitalized.

Book: *The No-Nonsense Guide to the Art of Dating*
Newspaper: *New York Times*
Magazine: *Arts & Crafts Homes and the Revival*
Poem: "The Love Song of J. Alfred Prufrock" by T. S. Eliot
Article: "Looking for Love in Baghdad" by Bobby Ghosh
Story: "Eyes of a Blue Dog" by Gabriel García Márquez
Document: "The Fugitive Slave Law of 1793"
Work of Art: "Still Life with Three Puppies" by Gauguin
TV show: "Law & Order: Special Victims Unit"
Song: "Because of You" by Kelly Clarkson

EXERCISE 26-12 **Titles of Publications**

Directions: *Underline the words that should be capitalized in the following titles.*

1. "the road not taken"
2. *the freedom writers diary: how a teacher and 150 teens used writing to change themselves and the world around them*
3. "seventeen hits and a sigh of relief for the yankees"
4. the mona lisa
5. *black and decker: the complete guide to home masonry*
6. *us weekly*
7. "new pacman xbox is swan song for founder"
8. *harry potter and the goblet of fire*
9. "you give love a bad name"
10. "stem cell industry set to break out"

Numbers

Here are the basic rules for writing numbers.

1. **Spell out numbers that start a sentence.**

   Two Russian spacewalkers will attach a micrometeorite shield to the space station.

2. **Spell out numbers consisting of one or two words.** Use figures for numbers that require more than two words.

   - I had **eight** jobs before I found one I really liked.
   - The local food store has **three hundred** employees.
   - I love music and have **325** CDs in my collection.

3. **Hyphenate all compound numbers.**

   Seventy-five top companies were cited for creating a quality work environment.

4. **Use figures for most dates, addresses, percentages, fractions, decimals, scores, statistics, pages, and time.**
   - **Dates:** One of the most famous dates in history is **July 4, 1776.**
   - **Addresses:** My new address is **1455 West 42nd Street.**
   - **Percentages:** I always wait for the ultimate price of **75 percent** off the original price.
   - **Scores:** The Cubs won with a final score of **7 to 5.**
   - **Statistics:** In 2001 over **1 million** immigrants entered the United States.
   - **Surveys:** Recent surveys indicate **9 out of 10** dentists recommend fluoride.
   - **Divisions in Books:** I am currently reading the *Complete Letters and Speeches of Charles Dickens,* and I am on **page 358 in Chapter 5 of Volume 2.**
   - **Time:** I have a meeting at **9:37 a.m.** exactly to discuss the budget.

MULTILINGUAL TIP

In American English, the month is followed by the day and the year: July 4, 1776.

5. **Spell out simple fractions and use hyphens.** Use figures for mixed fractions.
   - **One-fourth** of new employees doubt their ability to be successful.
   - I anticipate my salary will increase by 3½ percent next year.

6. **Spell out larger numbers (five million dollars or $5 million).**
   - The new hospital addition will cost **five million dollars.**
   - The new hospital addition will cost **$5 million.**

7. **Spell out decades (eighties) or use complete (1980s) or incomplete numerals ('80s).** Do not use an apostrophe between the year and the "s" (1980s or '80s). Choose one approach and be consistent.

   I love the early rock and roll music of the **'60s,** even though I was a teenager during the disco era of the **'80s.**

8. **Spell out noon, midnight, and time when using *o'clock*.**

   We work eight-hour shifts at the hospital. We change shifts at **eight o'clock, four o'clock, and midnight.**

EXERCISE 26-13 **Numbers**

Directions: *Determine if the numbers underlined below are written correctly. Write a C at the beginning of an item if the number is written correctly. If it is not, write the corrected version in the space provided below.*

_____ 1. 25 drivers qualified in the first round of the Indianapolis 500.

Twenty-five

__C__ 2. The Dow Jones fell 100 points in the last week.

C 3. Five men were stranded in a snowstorm for two days in Colorado.

____

C 4. The Rolling Stones have sold over 200,000 albums.

____

____ 5. In a single year 16 coral reefs were destroyed by changes in the environment.

sixteen

____ 6. 33 years ago the Endangered Species Act began protecting wildlife.

Thirty-three

C 7. Can a dog that loses 0.25 percent of its body weight in a week be healthy?

____

____ 8. Just over 100 Turkish troops chased Kurdish gorillas into Iraq.

one hundred

C 9. Drought in the 2000s will grow more dramatic in the 2010s because of global warming.

____

____ 10. The new store hours will be one o'clock to 10 o'clock on Saturday.

ten o'clock

Abbreviations

Use an abbreviation, such as FBI or YMCA, only when you are sure a reader will understand it. Here are the basic rules for writing abbreviations.

1. **Write the full title the first time you use it, followed by the abbreviation in parentheses.** Then use the abbreviation throughout the rest of the paper.

   Due to the requirements of **No Child Left Behind (NCLB)**, local school boards are concerned about funding **NCLB.**

2. **Use standard abbreviations for titles used before or after a proper name.** Do not abbreviate a title if it is not used with a proper name.

   Mr. William McDougal
   George P. Wilson Sr.
   Dr. Rachel Russio
   Prof. Michael Bates
   Zavira Cussins DDS
   Ms. Shree Zabawa
   George P. Wilson Jr.
   David White MD
   Michelle Anderson PhD

3. **Capitalize abbreviations of agencies of government, corporations, and call letters of radio and television stations.**

NASA	IBM
FDA	102.1 NICE
DOD	

4. **Use BC, AD, a.m., p.m., No., and $ with specific dates, times, numbers, and amounts only.**

510 BC	7:35 a.m.
AD 476	No. 3
3:15 p.m.	$100

5. **Avoid using overused or inappropriate abbreviations.**

Avoid	**Use**
i.e.	that is
e.g.	for example
etc.	and so forth, and so on
lb.	pound
Mon.	Monday
Xmas	Christmas
Jan.	January
Am Lit.	American Literature
MO	Missouri

EXERCISE 26-14 Abbreviations

Directions: *Determine if the underlined abbreviations are written correctly. Write a C above abbreviations that are correct. Correct errors by writing the corrections on the lines provided.*

1. The prof. in my poli. sci. 327 course required we visit the ACLU Web site.

professor, Political Science, American Civil Liberties Union (ACLU)

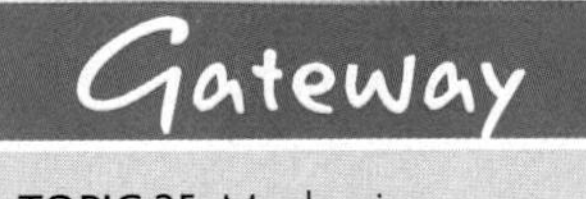

TOPIC 25: Mechanics
www.mhhe.com/goingplaces

2. Ben Farmer Sr. (C) visits the YMCA (C) daily to work out, meet friends, drink coffee, etc.

and so forth

3. On Tuesday and Thurs., it costs only $5.00 (C) for walk-ins at the barbershop.

Thursday

4. AZ, NM, UT, and CO are the four states that meet at Navajo Nation's Four Corners Monument.

Arizona, New Mexico, Utah, and Colorado

5. The Federal Bureau of Investigation (FBI) (C) is looking for new FBI (C) agents who can speak Arabic languages.

Words Matter

All of us watch our language around young children. Films, music, and television rate their content and sometimes restrict access to young viewers. Words matter, which is why you censor topics and the language you use depending on the setting and audience. You may talk to your friends in one way, talk in class and to your college instructors in another, and engage in work conversations in still another. To function effectively, it is necessary to develop a filter for language and adjust vocabulary to fit the situation. Some people call this code switching.

DISCUSSION

Turn and talk to a classmate about what it means to you to code switch. When do you switch your vocabulary? Where? Why?

The College Speaker

In college you develop an academic voice. Especially when talking in class, the way you present your ideas impacts your relationships with classmates and instructors. Your vocabulary can affect your grades and your success in college. Over time you absorb the language in your textbooks and readings; you use it in your thinking, speaking, and writing. For example, it would be difficult to answer a question on earthquakes for a geology exam without words like *plate tectonics, mantle,* or *lithosphere.* It is your responsibility to increase your vocabulary every day. Do you identify essential vocabulary as you read, take notes, or listen to your instructor or classmates? Do you use this academic language in your conversations with classmates?

BRAINSTORM

Think about the language you are consciously trying to stop using or start using in your college courses. What courses present the biggest challenge for you? What strategies are you currently using to increase your vocabulary?

Language on the Job

The language you use on the job translates to money in your pocket. Dealing with customers, coworkers, or bosses, your ability to communicate puts you on the track for more responsibility or a job that you find interesting and challenging. In addition, communication is a two-way street. Being a careful listener is as important as being a thoughtful speaker. Listen carefully. What words do customers use to explain their problems? What is the tone of their request or demand? Do customers understand the problem or are they confused? Many employers train their employees in listening techniques and methods for identifying what a customer needs. This training makes sense at work. Moreover, communication is a 24-7 job. To be truly effective you need to speak precisely and listen carefully both at work and at home.

RESUME BUILDER

Talk to a classmate about communication at work. How do you communicate with your customers, coworkers, or bosses? Is communication generally effective? How might you improve it?

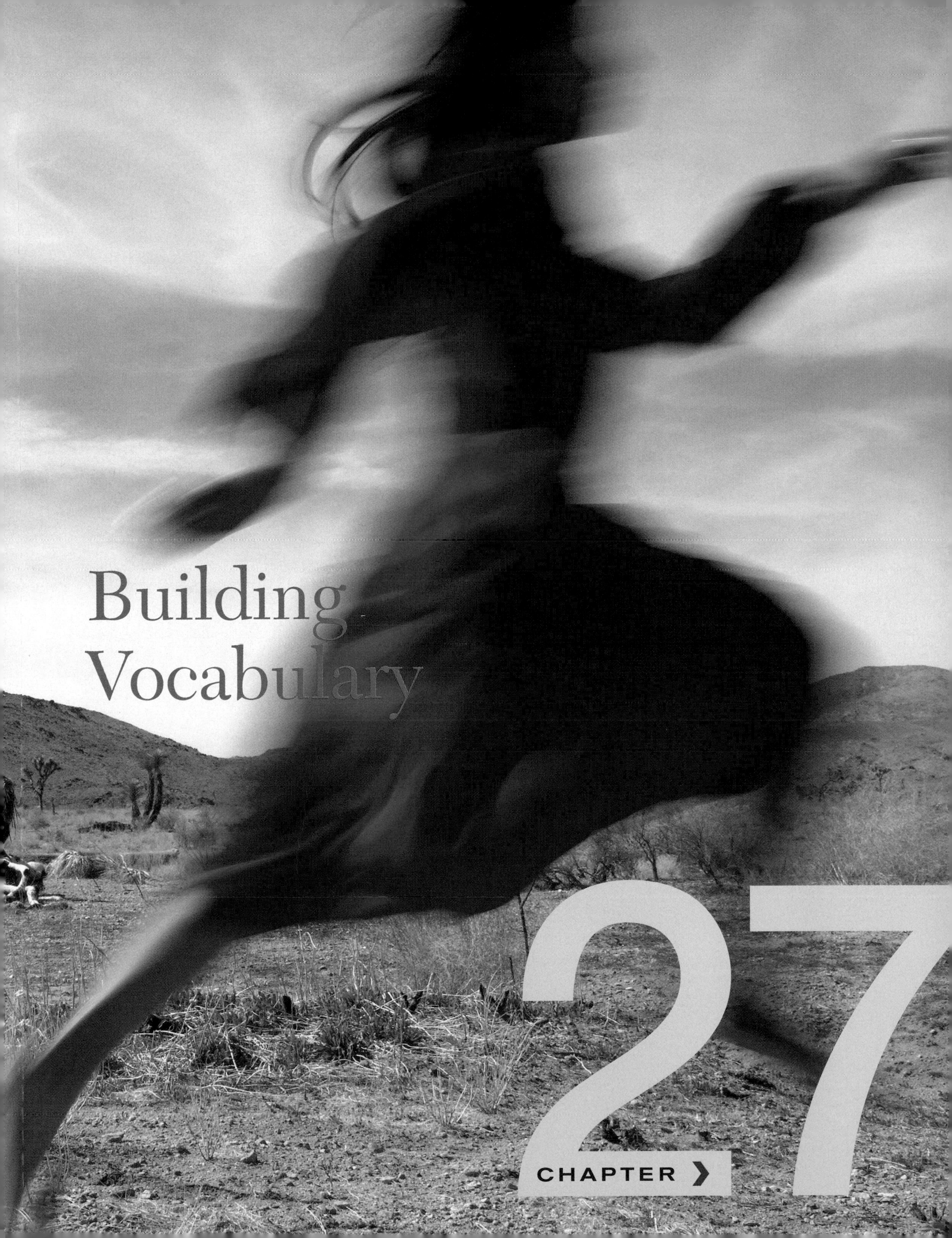

Building Vocabulary

CHAPTER 27

CHAPTER OVERVIEW

- Collect Vocabulary Daily
- Use a Dictionary and Thesaurus
- Improve Word Choice
  - *Precise Nouns and Verbs*
  - *Tone*
  - *Denotation and Connotation*
  - *Appropriate Word Choice*

THINK FIRST

Suppose you are faced with an irate or challenging customer or coworker. What makes a situation like that tense? What do you listen for in a customer's speech? What do you ignore? Write a paragraph in which you describe the process you will use to ensure you are listening critically when faced with challenges at work.

How do I build my vocabulary? This is a good question, because a rich vocabulary is essential to meet the speaking, reading, and writing challenges of college courses. Some words you acquire in conversation with friends; others you learn at school, at home, or on the job. Use the following strategies to build your vocabulary as you speak, read, write, or edit your college papers.

- Collect vocabulary daily.
- Use a dictionary and thesaurus when you read and write.
- Improve word choice.

Collect Vocabulary Daily

Each day add a few words to your vocabulary. All of your subjects in college have basic vocabularies. Simply select a few essential words used in your class discussions, lectures, or textbooks. Five new words a day add up to twenty-five new words a week. If five words are too many, add two words a day. Even two new words a day add up to 10 new words a week, 40 new words a month, 150 new words in a semester. Use the following four-step approach to select, record, study, and use new words.

Step 1: Create a List of New Words

- Carry a small notebook to list new vocabulary words, or reserve ten pages in the back of your notebook for this purpose.
- Use a note card or other piece of paper as a bookmark where you can write new words as you read.

Step 2: Select Words for Your Vocabulary List

- Gather technical vocabulary that is necessary to talk or write effectively about a subject.
- Look for unfamiliar words that appear repeatedly in your textbooks.
- Focus on essential words that name important concepts or appear in questions at the end of a reading or in your assignments.

Step 3: Create a Vocabulary Notebook to Study New Words You Collect

- Copy each word from your vocabulary list into your vocabulary notebook.
- Write the source of the word (where you encountered it).
- Write a brief description of the word's meaning. Consider the context in which you read or heard the word, and consult a dictionary or glossary if necessary.
- Write an original sentence to practice using the word, and leave space to write more practice sentences later.

Step 4: Use Each New Word in Speaking and Writing, and Review New Words Periodically

- Challenge yourself to use new words appropriately during class discussions or informal conversations.
- Incorporate new words into your academic or personal writing.
- Review the words in your vocabulary notebook, and write additional sentences for each word after you become more comfortable using it.

Shown below are several sample entries from a student's vocabulary notebook.

Word: toolbar **Source:** home—e-mail and Internet

Meaning: a bar usually placed above an electronic document or website that contains a menu of tools or shortcuts

Practice Sentence(s): I put links to music, news, and weather on my Internet **toolbar** to help me find information quickly.

WHY COLLECT THESE WORDS?

Toolbar is a basic word for any computer user. Your college courses will require you to have computer knowledge and understand basic computer-related vocabulary.

Resolve might be part of on-the-job etiquette, but you can use it in speaking and writing in your college courses.

Word: resolve **Source:** work—employee handbook
Meaning: to clear up; to find an answer to
Practice Sentence(s): Whenever possible, **resolve** customer complaints immediately. For complicated problems, ask a manager to help you **resolve** the complaint.

The word *thermal* could be used in a technology course, but it is used in other subjects as well. For example, geology, geography, textiles, and meteorology are just a few fields in which it is used.

Word: thermal **Source:** course—Applied Technology
Meaning: the study of the impact of temperatures on materials
Practice Sentence(s): Thermal analysis studies the dramatic changes that occur when plastic is exposed to heat or cold: Cold makes it like glass while heat makes plastic like rubber.

PEER CONVERSATION

EXERCISE 27-1 **Collect Five Words**

Directions: *On a sheet of paper, list five words you want to add to your vocabulary. Select words that you have read or heard in the last day or two at school, work, or home. On a second sheet of paper, use the word study approach described above to organize and examine the five words you have selected. List each word and note its source. Write a brief description of the word's meaning. Then write a practice sentence using the word. When you have finished, talk to a classmate and explain why these five words are important to add to your vocabulary.* Answers will vary.

Use a Dictionary and Thesaurus

ONLINE DICTIONARIES
- Merriam-Webster Online at www.m-w.com
- Cambridge Dictionaries Online at dictionary.cambridge.org

ONLINE THESAURUS
- Roget's Thesaurus at education.yahoo.com/education/thesaurus

Expanding your reading and writing vocabulary is a lifelong process. However, you can speed up your vocabulary growth by investing in a dictionary and a thesaurus. Also add an online dictionary and thesaurus to your "Favorites" menu.

Every time you read, you have an opportunity to acquire new vocabulary. If you do not know a word, you can use the context in which it appears to help you figure out its meaning. For example, you might not know the meaning of the word *furtive,* but you can use information in surrounding words or sentences to figure out what it means.

The dog made a *furtive* retreat under the table after he stole a hotdog.

The phrase "under the table" provides details you can use to guess that the meaning of the word *furtive* is "sneaky or secretive."

Sometimes, however, you need to use a dictionary to determine a word's meaning as you read. A dictionary can also be useful when you write, helping you select the proper words to express your ideas. A thesaurus, which provides lists of synonyms, is another useful resource for expanding your writing vocabulary.

Get Acquainted with a Dictionary

Dictionaries provide definitions and other detailed information about words. By using a dictionary, you will learn the history of a word, how to pronounce it, all of its meanings, and its part of speech or function in a sentence. *The American Heritage Dictionary* provides the following information on the word *soul.*

PRONUNCIATION GUIDE
This is a one syllable word that is pronounced with a long "o" sound.

PART OF SPEECH
n. – Indicates "soul" is a noun.

DEFINITIONS
Soul has a range of definitions, from the religious sense to expressing the meaning associated with African-American culture.

soul (sōl) *n.* **1.** The animating and vital principle in humans, credited with the faculties of thought, action, and emotion and often conceived as an immaterial entity. **2.** The spiritual nature of humans, regarded as immortal, separable from the body at death, and susceptible to happiness or misery in a future state. **3.** The disembodied spirit of a dead human **4.** A human: *"the homes of some nine hundred souls"* (Garrison Keillor). **5.** The central or integral part; the vital core: *"It saddens me that this network . . . may lose its soul, which is after all the quest for news"* (Marvin Kalb). **6.** A person considered as the perfect embodiment of an intangible quality; a personification: *I am the very soul of discretion.* **7.** A person's emotional or moral nature: *"An actor is . . . often a soul which wishes to reveal itself to the world but dare not"* (Alec Guiness). **8.** A sense of ethnic pride among Black people and especially African Americans, expressed in areas such as language, social customs, religion, and music. **9.** A strong, deeply-felt emotion conveyed by a speaker, a performer, or an artist. **10.** Soul music. [Middle English, from Old English *sāwol.*]

ILLUSTRATIONS of the word are used in a sentence or phrase.

ORIGIN OR ETYMOLOGY OF THE WORD
The word comes to modern English from Middle English, and before that, from Old English.

EXERCISE 27-2 A Dictionary Definition

PEER CONVERSATION

Directions: *Turn to a classmate, and answer the following questions.*

- *Does this dictionary entry for the word* soul *contain any information or definitions that you found new or unexpected? Explain your answer.*
- *Do you think that reading and discussing this dictionary entry will help you remember various meanings of the word* soul*? Explain your answer.*

Use a Dictionary Effectively

The following tips will help you use dictionaries most effectively and save you time.

- ***Look for the root or main part of a word.*** Some words may have a suffix, such as *conciseness* or *indifferently.* You will find the meaning for *conciseness* by searching for the word *concise* and the meaning for the word *indifferently* by looking for *indifferent.*

- *Pay attention to a word's part of speech.* If you know what part of speech a word is, look for the definitions that are the same part of speech. For example, if you are looking up a verb, or action word, look for definitions that follow the abbreviation *v.* which stands for "verb."
- *Read all the definitions before choosing the one that best fits your word.* A word can have multiple meanings, so you need to identify the one that makes the most sense based on the way the word is used in the sentence.
- *Reread the passage in which the word appears.* Use the context of the sentence to help you select the accurate meaning for a word.

EXERCISE 27-3 Using a Dictionary I

Directions: *Use a dictionary to find the primary or most common meaning of each of the words below. List its part of speech and pronunciation. Then read the sentence that follows and use context to determine if the common meaning is correct. If not, write the correct definition and part of speech for the word.*

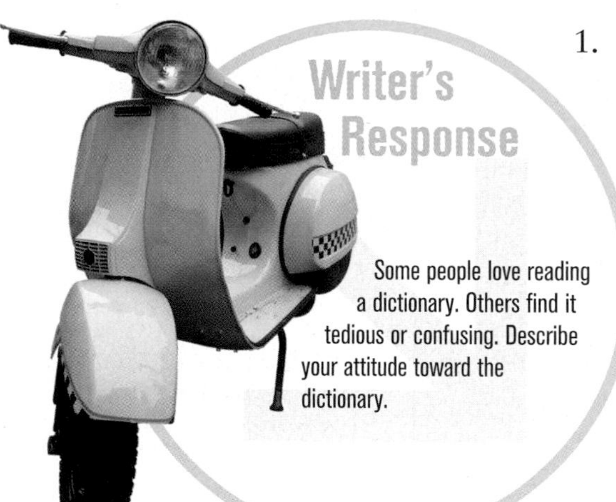

Writer's Response
Some people love reading a dictionary. Others find it tedious or confusing. Describe your attitude toward the dictionary.

1. **club**

Primary Definition: a heavy stick used as a weapon

Part of Speech: noun **Pronunciation:** club (kləb)

My friends started a **club** to raise funds for clean water.

(noun) a group of persons organized for a common cause

2. **flutter**

Primary Definition: to move in a quick, flapping motion

Part of Speech: verb **Pronunciation:** flut•ter (flə-t´ər)

A heart **flutter** can be a symptom of a serious problem.

(noun) an abnormal spasm or rapid beating

3. **justify**

Primary Definition: to demonstrate or be just or right

Part of Speech: verb **Pronunciation:** jus•ti•fy (jəs´tə´fī´)

Please **justify** your choice to sit silent instead of describing your actions.

Primary definition is correct.

4. **root**

Primary Definition: the underground portion of plant that serves as support and draws and stores food

Part of Speech: noun **Pronunciation:** root (rüt)

Cheerleaders **root** for the team.

(verb) to give encouragement or cheer

5. **separate**

Primary Definition: to set, keep, or come apart; divide or become divided

Part of Speech: verb **Pronunciation:** sep•a•rate (sep′ə′rət′)

Spring is the best time to **separate** mature plants.

Primary definition is correct.

EXERCISE 27-4 Using a Dictionary II

Directions: *Read the passage below. As you read, use context to determine the meaning of the boldfaced words. Underline the words that help you determine the meaning of a boldfaced word and select the correct meaning from the multiple-choice options below. Use a dictionary to help you select the correct meaning, if necessary.*

from *Care of the Soul*
by THOMAS MOORE

Care of the soul is a fundamentally different way of regarding daily life and the (1) **quest** for happiness. The emphasis may not be on problems at all. One person might care for the soul by buying or renting a good piece of land, another by selecting an appropriate school or program of study, another by painting his house or his bedroom. Care of the soul is a continuous process that concerns itself not so much with "fixing" a central (2) **flaw** as with attending to the many details of everyday life, as well as to major decisions and changes.

Care of the soul may not focus on the personality or on relationships at all, and therefore it is not psychological in the usual sense. Tending to things around us and becoming (3) **sensitive** to the importance of home, daily schedule, and maybe even the clothes we wear, are ways of caring for the soul. When Marsilio Ficino wrote his self-help book, *The Book of Life*, five hundred years ago, he placed emphasis on choosing colors, spices, oils, places to walk, countries to visit—all very concrete decisions of everyday life that day by day either support or disturb the soul. We think of the (4) **psyche,** if we think of it at all, as a cousin to the brain and therefore something essentially internal. But ancient psychologists taught that our own souls are inseparable from the world's soul, and that both are found in all the many things that make up nature and (5) **culture.**

c 1. quest

a. wonder

b. investigation

c. pursuit

b 2. flaw

a. a crack or tear

b. a defect

c. steady actions

a 3. sensitive

a. highly perceptive

b. logical

c. easily hurt

b 4. psyche

a. fortune teller

b. soul or mind

c. psychiatry

c 5. culture

a. morals

b. courage

c. behavior of a civilization

Get Acquainted with a Thesaurus

Ask Yourself

Do you find a thesaurus easier or more difficult to use than a dictionary? Why?

A thesaurus helps you select the word that will most precisely express what you want to say. Like a dictionary, a thesaurus lists words in alphabetical order. Unlike a dictionary, a thesaurus does not provide definitions. Instead, it provides **synonyms** or words that have essentially the same meaning as the word you are looking up. A thesaurus also provides **antonyms**—words that have opposite meanings to the ones you are researching. On the facing page is a thesaurus entry for the word *explain*.

Use a Thesaurus Effectively

- Read all the synonyms before choosing one to replace your word.
- Use the context of your sentence to help you make your choice. Choose strong, precise words to make your point.
- Consider the tone of a word. Writers often choose words to create an emotional impact on the reader.
- Use a dictionary to find the meaning of unfamiliar synonyms: although synonyms have essentially the same meanings, they are not always exactly the same, and you want to find the word that most precisely expresses your point.
- Do not use a word just because it sounds sophisticated. Well-chosen simple words can be just as effective as more complex words if they accurately state what you want to say.

PART OF SPEECH
v.—indicates that *explain* is a verb.

SYNONYMS
Syn.—indicates that the words listed have similar meanings.

explain, *v.*—*Syn.* interpret, explicate, account for, elucidate, illustrate, clarify, illuminate, make clear, describe, expound, teach, manifest, reveal, point up *or* out, demonstrate, tell, refine, read, translate, paraphrase, render, put in other words, decipher, assign a meaning to, construe, define, disentangle, justify, untangle unravel, make plain, unfold, come to the point, put across, throw light upon, show by example, restate, rephrase, get to, annotate, comment *or* remark upon *or* on, make *or* prepare *or* offer an explanation *or* an exposition (of), resolve, clear up, get right, set right, put (someone) on the right track, unscramble, spell out, go into detail, get over, get to the bottom of, figure out, speak out, emphasize, cast light upon, get across *or* through, bring out, work out, solve, make oneself understood; both (D): hammer into one's head, put in plain English.—*Ant.* puzzle, confuse*, confound.
explorer, *n.*—*Syn.* adventurer, traveler, pioneer, wayfarer, pilgrim, voyager, space traveler, investigator, inventor, seafarer, mountaineer, mountain climber, scientist, globe-trotter, navigator, circumnavigator, spelunker, creator, founder, colonist, Conquistador.

ALPHABETICAL ENTRIES

USAGE
(D)—indicates that these synonyms may be considered informal for some audiences.

ANTONYM
Ant.—indicates that the words listed have opposite meanings.

PART OF SPEECH
n.—indicates that *explorer* is a noun.

EXERCISE 27-5 Using a Thesaurus

Directions: *The following sentences all contain the word* explain. *For each sentence*

- *Underline the words that clarify the meaning of the word* explain *(the words that provide context clues).*
- *Use the thesaurus entry for the word* explain *above to select two effective synonyms and one weak one and write them in the space provided.* Answers will vary. Example answers shown.

1. To understand a poem, a reader must be able to **explain** how the metaphors and symbols create the poet's meaning.

Good Choices: interpret, explicate

Weak Choice: get over

2. **Explain** what you mean when you use the term *audience* in a college paper on how to write well.

Good Choices: define, clarify

Weak Choice: justify

3. **Explain** your outrageous behavior at the birthday party last night.

Good Choices: justify, account for

Weak Choice: emphasize

EXERCISE 27-6 **Thesaurus Work**

Directions: *Read the following passage paying attention to the tone of the boldfaced words. Then look up each word in a thesaurus. In the list under the passage, write five to ten synonyms for each word and underline the words that could serve as good replacements for the boldfaced words. Finally, determine the tone John Simpson creates with his word choice.* Answers will vary. Example answers shown.

from "Tiananmen Square"
by JOHN SIMPSON

It was humid and airless, and the streets around our hotel were empty. We had set out for Tiananmen Square: a big, conspicuous European television team—reporter, producer, cameraman, sound-recordist, translator, lighting man, complete with gear. A cyclist rode past, shouting and pointing. What it meant we couldn't tell. Then we came upon a line of soldiers. Some of them had bleeding faces; one cradled a broken arm. They were walking slowly, **limping.** There had been a battle somewhere, but we couldn't tell where.

When we reached Changan Avenue, the main east–west thoroughfare, it was full of people as in the days of the great demonstrations—a human river. We followed the **flow** of it to the Gate of Heavenly Peace, under the **bland,** moonlike portrait of Chairman Mao. There were hundreds of small groups, each concentrated around someone who was **haranguing** or lecturing the others, using the familiar, heavy public gestures of the Chinese. Other groups had formed around radios tuned to foreign stations. People were moving from group to group, pushing in, **crushing** round a speaker, arguing, moving on, passing along any new information.

1. limping: walk lamely, proceed slowly, shuffle, lag, stagger, totter, dodder, hobble, falter

2. flow: current, movement, progress, stream, tide, river, flood, ebb, surge, influx, outpouring, effusion, gush, spurt, spout, dribble, oozing

3. bland: flat, dull, insipid, affable, urbane, agreeable, pleasant

4. haranguing: lecture, discourse, sermon

5. crushing: to break into small pieces, smash, pulverize, powder; to bruise severely, press, mash, bruise; to defeat utterly, overwhelm, force down

6. What tone is created by these words? The words emphasize the terror, anger, fear, and bewilderment of the reporters who were trying to understand what had just occurred as they walked toward Tiananmen Square.

Write with a Dictionary and Thesaurus

Using a dictionary and thesaurus when you write can improve your diction as they provide you with options to express your ideas clearly and precisely. To meet the challenge of writing sophisticated paragraphs and essays on any subject, use the following three steps. Look at the example below. Here, the word *quarreled* does not capture the writer's intended meaning.

> At a public hearing, the senators **quarreled** over new legislation, expressing serious concern about the impact the legislation could have on their constituents.

Step 1. Rephrase the Main Idea of the Sentence to Better Understand Its Meaning

> The senators do not agree with each other about the proposed law because they are worried about its possible effect on citizens.

Step 2. Use a Thesaurus to Find Synonyms

With a thesaurus, you can look up synonyms for the word you want to replace, and select a word that best fits the meaning of the sentence. Well-chosen, simple words are more effective than sophisticated words that sound smart but are confusing. Remove the suffix and look up *quarrel.* Choose a word that is the same part of speech.

> dispute, disagree, argue, fight, differ, clash, lock horns, bicker, squabble, debate, battle, wrangle, feud, contend

If you like a synonym but are not sure of its meaning, look it up in the dictionary. *Argue* or *debate* both suggest the senators are putting forth reasons for or against a particular point of view; however, *bicker, squabble,* or *wrangle* suggest the senators lack logic and are emotional or childish.

Step 3. Replace the Word and Revise the Sentence

If you decide that *debate* is the best synonym for *quarrel* in the context of your sentence, you would revise the sentence as follows:

At a public hearing, senators **debated** the legislation, expressing serious concern about the impact the legislation could have on their constituents.

Replacing the word *quarreled* with the synonym *debated* successfully suggests the senators were logical and reasonable as they discussed the bill.

EXERCISE 27-7 Three Steps to Improved Word Choice

Directions: *Use the three-step approach to improve word choice in the following sentences. Replace the boldfaced word in each sentence with a more precise synonym from the list provided. Feel free to use a dictionary to clarify the exact meaning of the words you select.* Answers will vary. Example answers shown.

1. Newspapers **stress** stories about murders and tragedy to sell papers.

Rephrase the main idea of the sentence.

Newspapers stress bad news by putting it in the headlines and on the front page to draw people's attention to the emotion and drama.

Underline two synonyms for *stress* that fit the sentence.

stress (verb) 1. EMPHASIZE, accent, underscore, underline, accentuate, highlight, spotlight, play up.

Replace the word and revise the sentence.

Newspapers **highlight** stories about murders and tragedy to sell papers.

2. The professor recommended Alfonse to serve as a resident advisor in the dormitory because he was responsible, organized, and **nice** to his classmates.

Rephrase the main idea of the sentence.

The professor thinks Alfonse would make a good resident advisor in the dorm because he's reliable and treats other students well.

Underline two synonyms for *nice* that fit the sentence.

nice (adjective) 1. APPEALING, pleasing, attractive, agreeable, pleasant, satisfactory, desirable, enjoyable; 2. LIKABLE, charming, kind, considerate, gracious, amiable, sweet, well-mannered, genial, cordial, thoughtful, good-hearted; 3. UPRIGHT, virtuous, moral, chaste, genteel, seemly; 4. REFINED, delicate, proper, correct, seemly, appropriate.

Replace the word and revise the sentence.

The professor recommended Alfonse to serve as resident advisor in the dormitory because he was responsible, organized, and **considerate** of his classmates.

3. Exercising to maintain a healthy and fit body **remains** important throughout life.

Rephrase the main idea of the sentence.

People should always exercise throughout their lives to have healthy and fit bodies.

Underline two synonyms for *remains* that fit the sentence.

remain (verb) 1. STAY, wait, sit tight, stay put, hold; 2. ENDURE, continue, abide, keep on, persist.

Replace the word and revise the sentence.

Exercising to maintain a healthy and fit body **continues** to be important throughout life.

Improve Word Choice

Increasing your vocabulary and using a thesaurus and a dictionary will improve your writing. However, you can also improve your writing by paying close attention to **diction,** or word choice. Careful word choice helps a writer create a specific mental picture for a reader. To improve word choice, use precise nouns and verbs, select words to create a tone, and monitor your choices. As you become more conscious of how and why you are using specific words, your vocabulary will also improve.

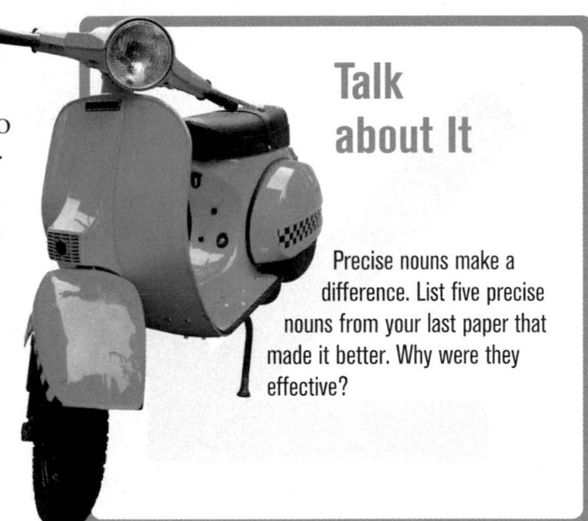

Talk about It

Precise nouns make a difference. List five precise nouns from your last paper that made it better. Why were they effective?

Precise Nouns and Verbs

Powerful writing begins with use of precise nouns and verbs. Shift general diction into precise diction by replacing vague or overused nouns and verbs with more specific words that fit the context of your writing.

Read the following sentence:

> The high winds caused the hiker to pull his **jacket** closed as he **walked** up the mountain.

In this sentence, the boldfaced words are too general to create a specific image in the mind of the reader. To improve the diction, the general noun

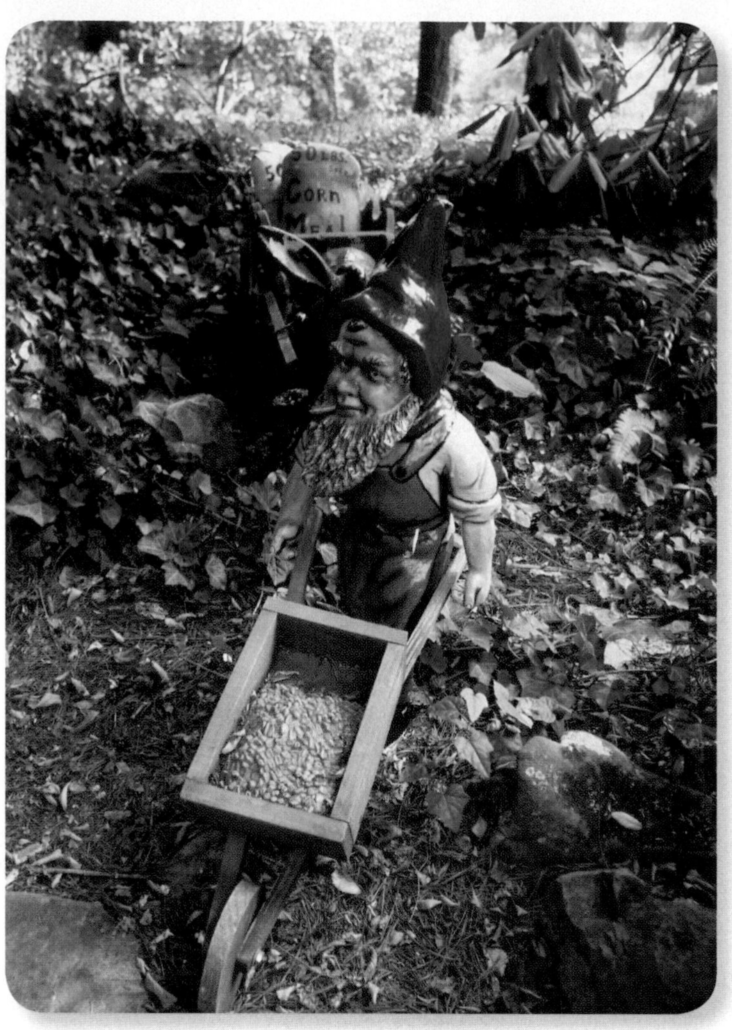

jacket could be replaced with a more precise noun such as *anorak, cardigan, bomber jacket, pea coat,* or *parka.* Similarly, the vague word *walked* could be replaced with a more precise verb such as *traipsed, trekked, marched, wandered, trudged,* or *strolled.*

Here is one way the writer could effectively revise the sentence:

> The high winds caused the hiker to pull his **parka** closed as he **trudged** up the mountain.

In the revised sentence, the writer emphasizes the difficulty of the hike by helping readers visualize the hiker struggling in high winds. The word *jacket* is replaced by *parka,* a specific type of coat designed to withstand difficult weather. The verb *trudged* replaces the general word *walked* and is more effective in conveying the difficulty of the climb.

Tone

Writers choose specific words to express an attitude or tone in their writing. Writing can be formal or informal, positive or negative. Writers consider an audience as they plan and write.

College essays are written for a single reader, your professor. In college writing, the style is generally formal, and your words are chosen to express a view or attitude toward an academic subject. You might explain the destructive consequences of a historical event or examine the positive influences of an effective exit strategy for businesses.

Look at the photograph here and read the sentences related to it that define basic tones in writing. Words chosen to create the tone are underlined in each sentence.

- **Formal Tone:** A formal tone may be objective, clinical, instructive, factual, or informative. The following sentence illustrates a factual tone.

  Landscape <u>designers</u> use <u>garden statues</u> as <u>focal points</u> to express the personality of the homeowner.
- **Informal Tone:** An informal tone may be sentimental, emotional, nostalgic, or sarcastic. The following sentence illustrates a sarcastic tone.

  <u>Pot-bellied</u> ceramic gnomes <u>scattered</u> around a lawn are an <u>eyesore</u>, not landscaping.
- **Positive Tone:** A positive tone may be hopeful, enthusiastic, appreciative, confident, or optimistic. The following sentence illustrates an appreciative tone.

  Garden gnomes create a <u>playful</u> <u>element</u> in any garden and suggest the homeowner <u>loves</u> <u>fun</u>.

- **Negative Tone:** A negative tone may be angry, accusing, scornful, or critical. The following sentence illustrates an angry tone.

  There should be a neighborhood watch initiated to remove all unsightly and ridiculous lawn art, and the garden gnome should be the first item thrown in the trash.

Denotation and Connotation

Effective word choice not only improves and clarifies your writing, but also helps you create a tone that matches your purpose. Words have two types of meaning: denotative and connotative.

Denotation is the exact dictionary definition of a word. Words can have a variety of dictionary meanings or denotations.

> **lift** (verb) 1. the act of raising something; 2. the act of stealing; 3. the beginning of flight as in *lift off*; (noun) 1. a ride; 2. an elevator; 3. a machine designed to raise something.

Connotation is the implied meaning of a word that conveys an emotion and creates an emotional response in a reader. The word *lift* denotes the act of raising something up or moving something from one place to another. It can also suggest or connote power, change, or growth. In the sentence that follows, *lift* means *to raise the level* of morale. However, it also has a positive connotation and suggests power and improvement.

> The management team planned to restructure expectations and **lift** morale.

As you select words, consider both the denotation (dictionary meaning) and connotation (implied or suggested meaning). Use a dictionary or thesaurus to aid you.

EXERCISE 27-8 Precise Word Choice

Directions: *Read the following paragraph. To achieve a more formal tone, change the writer's word choice by replacing the boldfaced words. Consider denotation and connotation as you select more precise words as replacements.* Answers will vary. Example answers shown.

PEER CONVERSATION

Don Meeker, an environmental graphic designer, believes sign design is a form of social activism. One of his first projects saved lives. He (1) **contrived** a sign system for the country's rivers and waterways after the Army Corps of Engineers discovered over 200 people were drowning each year, and most of them around (2) **just before morning or just as it was getting to be night** when visibility was reduced. Meeker designed a sign using yellow (3) **glow-in-the-dark** sign material that kept its shine during the dark morning and evening hours. Next, his team began a (4) **really hard** study of highway roads signs across the 46,871 miles of Interstate highways. (5) **Old** drivers had difficulty finding the important information on roads cluttered with signs. While researching road signs, his team examined signs almost 80 years old that were unreadable at night. Highway engineers suggested making these letters bigger, but Meeker rejected this (6) **high dollar** solution. After years of research, his team designed Clearview, a font easier to read from a distance that reduced the glare and blur at night and increased visibility. Watch for it on a road sign near you.

1. contrived: designed, engineered

2. just before morning or just as it was getting to be night: dawn or dusk

3. glow-in-the-dark: luminescent

4. really hard: intricate or complex

5. Old: Elderly

6. high dollar: expensive

Appropriate Word Choice

When you are thinking about which word to use in a given writing situation, ask yourself, Who is my audience? For the majority of your college papers you will be writing for your instructor or professor. He or she will expect you to use formal English. This means you should avoid using informal language such as jargon, idioms, slang, and clichés. You should also avoid sexist language.

1. **Jargon** is specialized or technical language used by professionals and other groups. It is not always familiar to a general audience. Here is an example from the business world:

   Money market accounts offer competitive yields and easy access to cash.

   Here, the phrase "competitive yields" means the account offers competitive interest rates. If you are writing a paper for a business course, you could expect to use this term and have it understood by your reader. However, if you were writing for a general audience, it would be more effective to avoid jargon and use simpler words that any reader could understand.

   Money market accounts offer the opportunity to earn interest and to access cash easily.

2. **Idioms** are commonly used phrases that mean something different from the literal meanings of the words they contain. For example, a person might say his aunt "kicked the bucket" or your friend might say she needs to "burn the midnight oil" in order to finish a project. What these statements mean is that the person's aunt died and that your friend needs to stay up late to finish a task. Although idioms are commonly used in speech, it is best to avoid using them in formal academic writing.
3. **Slang** is informal, casual language used in everyday speech. It is acceptable to use within your circle of friends or daily life but is too informal for college courses.

   My friend looks like an airhead because she parties constantly, then pulls all-nighters to cram for tests.

   Above, slang is used to create a colorful description of a friend. Here is the sentence written in formal English.

   My friend looks like she is not intelligent because she goes to parties constantly and stays up all night to study just before a test.

4. **Clichés** are expressions that are overused and no longer surprising or interesting. Everyone can complete these phrases: Busy as a (bee); selling like (hotcakes); light as a (feather). If you want to make your writing fresh and interesting, avoid clichés.

COMMON CLICHÉS

better late than never	playing with fire
beyond a shadow of a doubt	sink or swim
blind as a bat	starting at the bottom of the ladder
cool as a cucumber	the bottom line
crystal clear	tried and true
hard as a rock	water under the bridge
last but not least	what comes around goes around
like a bull in a china shop	white as a ghost

5. **Sexist language** can directly or indirectly stereotype men or women. Sometimes it is easy to recognize, for example, calling a woman "a babe" is sexist. However, it might not be so clear that referring to a nurse or doctor as a "male nurse" or a "lady doc" is also sexist. In these examples, the suggestion is that nurses are usually female, and doctors are typically male. Avoid sexist language by using gender neutral language. See the box for examples.

GENDER NEUTRAL LANGUAGE

Sexist Terms	Gender Neutral Terms
actor, actress	actor
anchorman, anchorwoman	anchor
chairman	chairperson
clergyman	member of the clergy, pastor
fireman, policeman	firefighter, police officer
foreman	supervisor
mailman	mail carrier
salesman	sales associate
stewardess, steward	flight attendant
woman engineer	engineer

EXERCISE 27-9 Appropriate Word Choice

Directions: *Read each sentence below and identify any informal language (jargon, idioms, slang, or clichés) or sexist language. Underline the informal or sexist language usage (word or phrase). In the space provided, identify the kind of informal language being used, and then rewrite the sentence using a more precise word or phrase.* Answers will vary. Example answers shown.

EXAMPLE

The sales associate happily offered assistance to the hunk trying to coordinate a shirt and tie.

(sexist language) The sales associate happily offered assistance to the customer trying to coordinate a shirt and tie.

1. I knew I was nervous when I felt butterflies in my stomach.

(cliché) I knew I was nervous when I felt my stomach begin to churn.

2. The firewoman quickly climbed the extension ladder to rescue the children trapped in a third-floor bedroom.

(sexist language) The firefighter quickly climbed the extension ladder to rescue the children trapped in a third-floor bedroom.

3. Scientists are engaged in gender research to solve the battle of the sexes.

(idiom) Scientists are engaged in gender research to understand the differences between men and women and their impact on social encounters.

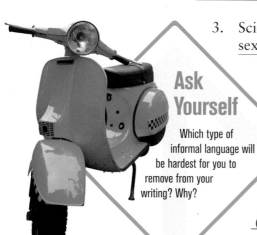

4. Electronic surveillance of the Internet practices of employees borders on invasion of privacy.

(jargon) Tracking the Internet practices of employees borders on invasion of privacy.

Ask Yourself

Which type of informal language will be hardest for you to remove from your writing? Why?

5. It was awesome to be voted president of my dorm, which was a big deal for me.

(slang) I was pleased to be voted president of my dorm because it was a significant personal accomplishment.

GOING PLACES

A VOYAGE INTO CRITICAL READING

The Critical Citizen

All of us are bombarded with information—online, on television, in print, in the classroom, and on the street. To function effectively, it is necessary to hone your critical thinking skills. In other words, you need to learn to reject what is false or inaccurate and to accept what is trustworthy and reliable. You undoubtedly do this already, to some extent. After all, do you really trust a tabloid newspaper as much as the *New York Times* or CNN? But practice is necessary for finer distinctions: Which op-ed piece makes more sense on the issues of the upcoming election? Which candidate should you vote for and why? Consider the ways in which this sort of thinking occurs in other aspects of your life, and ask yourself how you can become a more "critical citizen."

DISCUSSION

Turn and talk to a classmate about what it means to you to be a citizen. What are your responsibilities as a citizen? What does the term "critical citizen" mean to you?

The College Reader

One of the differences between high school and college is the amount of reading required. You have to process a great deal of information. Furthermore, the reading demands vary, from multiple chapter assignments in textbooks to short essays and articles. When you read for college, you need to be aware of what you are reading and what the goal of the reading assignment is. Does the reading provide background? Does it prepare you for a lecture? Does it reflect and reinforce content your instructor presents in class? Does the reading ask you to use classroom knowledge to think critically about a specific case or problem? You do not want to read everything the same way.

BRAINSTORM

Think about the kind of reading you have done so far in college. In what courses was the reading heavy? In what courses was it light? What was the purpose of the reading?

The Critical Worker

All the critical thinking skills covered in this book can be applied directly to the working world. You will be asked to write reports, document patient progress in a hospital or outpatient setting, analyze business records and draw conclusions, problem solve technological problems, and research information on the Internet. The more skills you acquire in school at approaching situations critically, the more valuable you will be as a decision-maker on the job.

RESUME BUILDER

Turn and talk to a classmate about decisions you make (or have made) on the job that require critical thinking. What kind of information do you use to make your decisions? What are the consequences of the decisions you make?

Critical Reading, Thinking, and Writing

CHAPTER 28

CHAPTER OVERVIEW

- Critical Reading
- Five Strategies for Effective Reading
  - *Preview*
  - *Ask Questions*
  - *Connect to Prior Knowledge*
  - *Identify Important Information*
  - *Reread*
- Read with a Pen
- Additional Readings

THINK FIRST

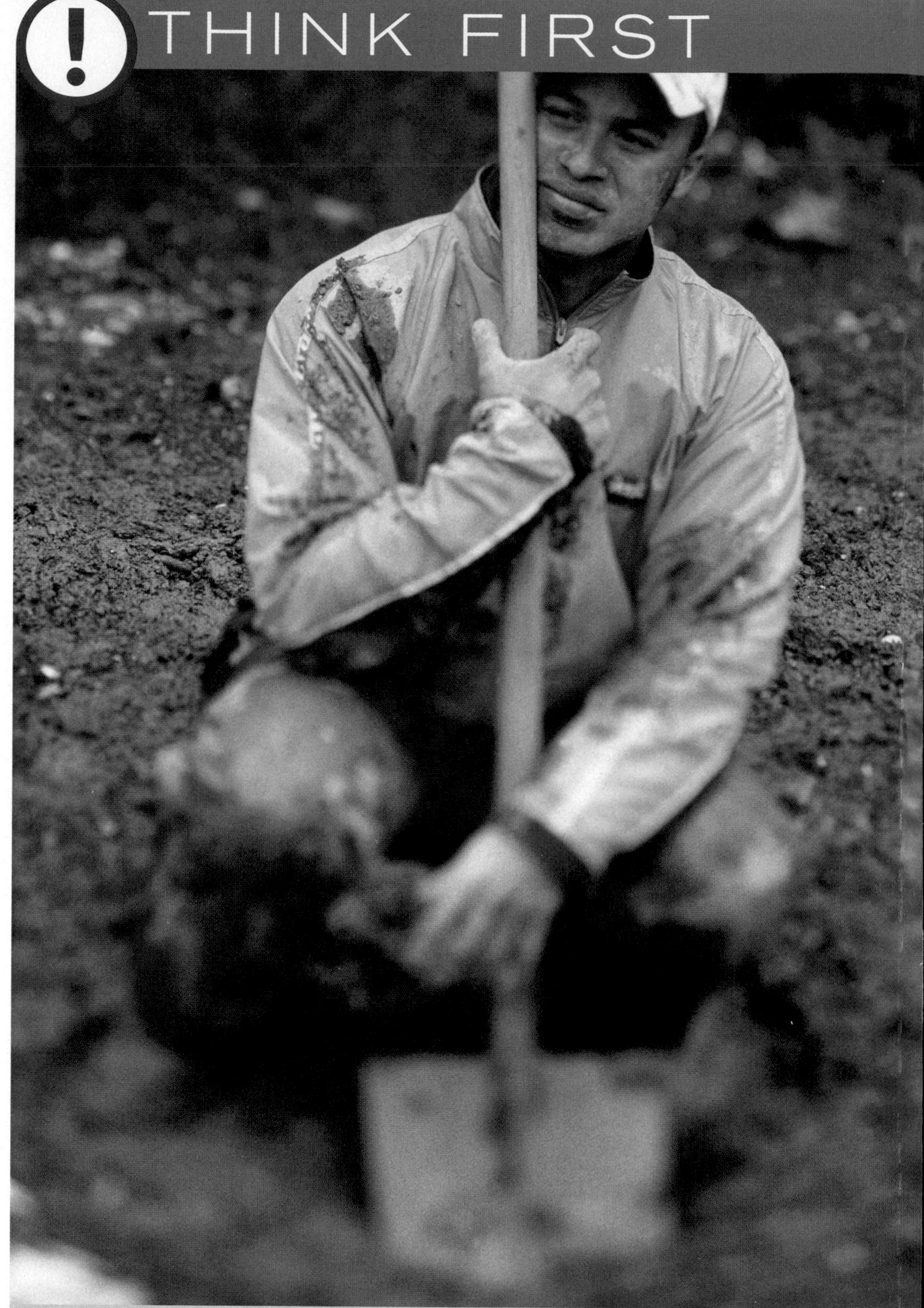

Suppose you could change jobs right now. What would you do? Write a paragraph in which you describe the new job and what it would involve. To what extent would critical reading, thinking, and writing be important in this job?

Critical Reading

What is my approach to reading? If you do not have an answer to this question, then you need to develop an approach. Critical reading is one of the most important skills you develop as a college student. It is a skill that is not limited to written texts: It extends to visual images, graphs, maps, and tables. Whether you are reading, thinking, or writing critically, your understanding will be improved if you have a strategic approach to reading.

Five Strategies for Effective Reading

Effective readers are active and critical readers. They set a purpose for reading before they begin and monitor their understanding as they read. During and after reading, they ask questions to understand the author's purpose. Here are five strategies for active reading that will help you understand what you read, think critically about the material, and draw conclusions about the author's ideas or arguments.

Preview

Previewing a reading allows you to get a general idea of the topic being discussed, how the material is organized, what the author's main points are, and what you already know about the subject. First, ask yourself these questions:

1. What kind of text am I about to read (narrative, essay, nonfiction article, or textbook)?
2. What do I know about the subject that I can use to help me understand it?
3. How is the text organized? Are there subtitles, sections, illustrations, and so on that will help me understand the content?
4. How difficult is the selection? Does it contain technical vocabulary? Will I need a dictionary?

If the reading looks challenging, you may prefer to read it in a quiet room so you can concentrate and have a dictionary nearby for difficult words. The following steps will help you to get an overview of the text.

How to Preview

- ***Read the title.*** This will give you an idea of the general topic of the selection.
- ***Read the introduction or first few paragraphs.*** Authors usually provide a brief overview of their subject and the main points they plan to make at the beginning of a reading or chapter.
- ***Read any headings.*** In textbooks particularly, subheadings provide an outline of the main points of the chapter.
- ***Read the first sentence of each paragraph (or the first sentence under each heading).*** These are often topic sentences and will provide information about what is going to be discussed in a paragraph or section of text.
- ***Look for boxes, visuals, and boldfaced or italicized print.*** All these features are used to highlight information the author considers

important. For example, in textbooks key words and terms are often in boldface font and followed by definitions.

- ***Read the final paragraph.*** Usually authors will summarize their main points at the end of an article or essay. In textbooks you will often find a heading like "Chapter Summary" under which the main points are clearly stated.

EXERCISE 28-1 **Previewing**

Directions: *Preview the following excerpt from a textbook, highlighting the title, headings, introduction, and the first sentence of each paragraph. Then use the highlighted material to answer the questions that follow.*

Edison and the Kinetoscope

from *American Cinema, American Culture* by JOHN BELTON

QUESTION
What does this writer mean by "mass communication"?

CAPTURING TIME

The origins of the cinema lie in the development of mass communication technology. The cinema serves as the culmination of an age that saw the invention of the telegraph (1837), photography (1826–1839), the typewriter (1873), the telephone (1876), the phonograph (1878), roll film (1880), the Kodak camera (1888), George Eastman's motion picture film (1889), Thomas Edison's motion picture camera (1891–1893), Marconi's wireless telegraph (1895), and the motion picture projector (1895–1896).

Edison, who had played a role in the development of the telegraph, the phonograph, and electricity, used the phonograph as a model for his "invention" of the motion picture. Actually, Edison did not so much invent as produce the first motion picture camera, the Kinetoscope. The actual execution of Edison's goal of creating an "instrument which [did] for the eye what the phonograph [did] for the ear" was accomplished through the effort of Edison's assistant, W. K. L. Dickson, which was itself based on earlier work by Étienne-Jules Marey.

PEEPSHOWS VERSUS PROJECTORS

The cinema did not emerge as a form of mass consumption, however, until its technology evolved from its initial format of peepshow into its final form as images projected on a screen in a darkened theater. Edison's Kinetoscope was designed for use in Kinetoscope parlors, which contained only a few individual machines and permitted only one customer to view a short, 50-foot film at any one time. The first Kinetoscope parlors contained five machines. For the price of 25 cents (or 5 cents per machine), custom-

Interior view of Kinetoscope with peephole viewer at top of cabinet.

ers moved from machine to machine to watch five different films (or, in the case of famous prizefights, successive rounds of a single fight).

These Kinetoscope arcades were modeled on phonograph parlors that had proved successful for Edison several years earlier. In the phonograph parlors, customers listened to recordings through individual ear tubes, moving from one machine to the next to hear different recorded speeches or pieces of music. The Kinetoscope parlors functioned in a similar way. More interested in the sale of Kinetoscopes (for roughly $250 apiece) to these parlors than in the films (which cost approximately $10 to $15 each) that would be run in them, Edison refused to develop projection technology, reasoning (quite correctly) that if he made and sold projectors, then exhibitors would purchase only one machine—a projector—from him instead of several Kinetoscopes.

1. What are the origins of the cinema?

the development of mass communication technology

2. Who "invented" the motion picture?

Thomas Edison

3. What was the initial format of the cinema?

the peepshow

4. What were the Kinetoscope parlors modeled on?

phonograph parlors

Ask Questions

Effective readers ask questions before, during, and after reading. For example, the title of the essay "Too Much Homework, Too Little Play" generates a question: How can anyone argue that play is more important than homework? The minute you ask that question, you start to focus your reading to find, understand, and evaluate the evidence the author uses to support his or her point. You might ask yourself other questions that focus your reading: How effective is homework in my experience? What evidence will the author provide? Can I trust his or her point of view?

Questions create active engagement with the text and call to mind your prior knowledge about a topic, helping you understand new ideas and arguments. Every question you ask begs for an answer. Every answer requires you to think and read more carefully.

EXERCISE 28-2 **Asking Questions**

Directions: *Read the first paragraph of "Edison and the Kinetoscope" on page 574, and answer the question in the margin. Then, as you read, ask at least two additional questions and write them in the margin. Underline words or phrases that answer your questions and comment on them.* Answers will vary.

Connect to Prior Knowledge

Connect information you have previously learned or read to the topic of a new reading. Even challenging texts can be mastered if you already know something about the subject. For instance, the essay "How Space Junk Works," on page 601, might remind you of an article you have read or a documentary you have watched about the impact of trash on our environment. As you read, you can use your prior knowledge of a subject to help you understand an author's points and to remember new information by connecting it to what you already know.

EXERCISE 28-3 **Connecting Prior Knowledge**

Directions: *Read "Edison and the Kinetoscope" on page 574. As you read, keep track of what you already know about the subject by writing notes in the margin. Underline the words or phrases that prompt your note taking.*

Identify Important Information

Different types of texts use different techniques to highlight important information. Textbooks use headings, bold and italic fonts, bulleted or numbered lists, color, and icons to announce that important ideas are being discussed. Essays contain a thesis statement that states the purpose of the essay, topic sentences that outline the main ideas of paragraphs, and concluding sentences that emphasize or comment on the essay's purpose. Transition words are used to emphasize important connections between details.

EXERCISE 28-4 **Identifying Important Information**

Directions: *In "Edison and the Kinetoscope" on page 574, the thesis is stated in the first sentence. Identify and underline important facts, details, or examples that support the thesis. Place numbers and brief labels in the margin beside each major point.*

Reread

Plan to reread. Every reader's mind wanders. If you are just reading words and not thinking or you lose your concentration, stop and reread. Reading something once is rarely enough. Here are three reasons to reread:

- ***Improved comprehension:*** As you read, monitor your understanding. At the first sign of confusion stop. You may need to reread a sentence or two or even an entire paragraph or essay in order to figure out what is being said. Be vigilant and continually ask yourself: *Does this make sense? Do I know what is happening?* If the answer is no to either question, stop and reread until you are sure you understand what the author is saying. Do the following things to clarify your comprehension of the material:

1. Summarize the section of the reading that seems confusing.
2. Connect what you are reading to what you know or to what you read earlier in the text.
3. Highlight key words or phrases and write notes in the margin.
4. Ask questions in the margins to set a purpose for further reading.

- ***Improved recall:*** To make sure you have understood what you have read and to help you remember new information, pause occasionally to check your comprehension. Then review sections of the text, words and phrases you highlighted, your margin notes, or the questions you wrote in the margins. Take a moment and answer your questions. If you cannot answer a question, go back and reread the relevant section of text. Doing this will improve your recall of the material.
- ***Expanded vocabulary:*** College readings often contain discipline-specific vocabulary. These words slow down your reading and make it harder to understand what an author is saying. To deal with challenging vocabulary, you can use resources in the text or context clues.

Writer's Response

Describe how you read. Are you easily distracted? How do you stay connected to a reading?

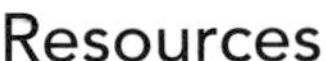

Resources

Some texts define difficult vocabulary in the margin or at the bottom of the page. Many provide a glossary of technical terms at the back of the book. In addition, keep a dictionary by your side as you read. (See Chapter 27, "Get Acquainted with a Dictionary" on page 555 for additional information on using a dictionary.)

Context Clues

Use the context in which a word appears to infer what it means. Context clues—hints in the text—can often help you figure out the meaning of unfamiliar words. There are five types of context clues:

- ***Definition clues:*** The word or phrase is defined immediately after it appears. Definitions can be preceded by terms like "means," "refers to," or "can be defined as." In textbooks, words to be defined are often in **bold** or *italic*. Punctuation—such as commas, dashes, colons, or parentheses—is often used to indicate a definition is about to be provided by setting the explanation off from the word being defined, as in this example:

  Calligraphy, the art of beautiful writing, has gained popularity with brides who want handwritten place cards for their wedding reception.

- ***Synonym clues:*** The word or phrase is restated using a different word or phrase that has the same or a similar meaning. Synonym clues may be preceded by phrases like "in other words," "also known as," "sometimes called," and "that is."

  The lawyer declined filing a lawsuit at this **juncture** in the case. In other words, without more specific information, he had no choice, and at this point in the lawsuit he had to wait.

- ***Antonym clues:*** The word or phrase is explained through the use of words that mean the opposite to it. Antonym clues may be followed by terms like "but," "in contrast," "although," "on the contrary," "instead of," "unlike," "yet," and "however."

  The artist created a series of **melodramatic** conflicts to resolve problems with clients, *unlike* his calm and matter-of-fact business partner who resolved problems with ease.

- ***General meaning clues:*** The clues to the meaning of the word are found in the sentences immediately before or after the unfamiliar word. The reader may need to reread these sentences in order to infer the meaning of the word.

  State governments are playing a major role in identifying the key **sectors** responsible for global warming. By analyzing the role of small businesses and local governments, the state governments are implementing strategies to reduce greenhouse gases, improve air quality, and create jobs that are cost-effective.

EXERCISE 28-5 Rereading

Directions: *Choose one of the readings in this chapter. Read the title and write a note in the margin stating what you imagine the reading will be about. Put a star in the margin at each place you decide to stop, write a question, and reread looking for the answer. As you reread, underline words or phrases that clarify your thinking and answer your question.*

Read with a Pen

A critical reader is an active reader. Your mind is one of the tools you use; a pen or pencil is the other. Always read with a pen or pencil in hand. Apply the strategies of effective readers by interacting with the text. As you read, underline, highlight, circle, or annotate the following information:

- The thesis statement (which states the main idea of the article or selection)
- Topic sentences that state the main ideas of paragraphs
- Key terms and definitions
- Unfamiliar vocabulary (look up new words in your dictionary and write definitions in the margin of the selection)
- Examples and important supporting details or ideas

Then write notes in the margin to explain your underlining or highlighting, ask questions, indicate important information, make connections with prior learning, and note difficult vocabulary or concepts you find challenging to understand.

Here is an essay annotated by a student named George. George's text markings and notes show that he is practicing all five strategies for active reading. Prior to reading, George previewed the text. As he read, he also underlined important information and wrote notes in the margin to make connections between his prior knowledge and what he read. Finally, he asked questions, sought answers to those questions, and noted what he did not understand.

A Simple Glass of Water

by TED FISHMAN

ASK QUESTIONS
Is this essay going to be about the dangers of heat?

CONNECT TO PRIOR KNOWLEDGE
I have read about cities in Texas that have 120° heat waves. People can die, and everyone worries about older people without air conditioning. Plus, the cities ration water and stop people from watering their lawns.

Recently, on a day so blistering in Chicago that authorities issued a heat warning, telling people to stay inside when possible, I was out early with my wife and 10-year-old son, hoping to run errands before the temperature topped 90. Alas, at 9:45 a.m., we were too late, and the heat hit. We wanted water. We went into a coffee shop and ordered a latte for my wife, an iced coffee for my son, and please, a glass of water for me. "I can only give you a small cup," the clerk told me. That would be fine, I told him. He came back with a thimble-sized cup with roughly one ounce of liquid in it. Was it possible to get more? I asked. "No," said the clerk. "That's all we can give out. We do sell water, though."

REREAD
Why is the restaurant trying to make money by selling water on these hot days?

PREVIEW
Topic sentence and maybe the thesis of article.

These days it seems that providing a simple drink of water is not so much an exercise in quenching the thirsty as in soaking them. Worldwide, bottled water is a $35 billion business. Over the next four years, the bottled water market is expected to grow 15 percent annually. That dwarfs the growth rates for fruit beverages, beer and soft drinks, all under 2 percent. Of course, sometimes bottled water does taste better or is more convenient or safer than tap water—and is worth paying for. That's nothing new. More novel is the pervasive push by businesses to sell bottled water by depriving customers of tap water.

CONNECT TO PRIOR KNOWLEDGE
I agree that selling water is a problem. I've noticed that bottled water is everywhere these days. At first I was surprised that people bought it, and I refused to buy it. It should be free. But now I buy it all the time.

For the past few years, the movie theaters I frequent have been declining requests for water, pushing—at $2.50 each—the bottled product instead. Seen a water fountain at a gasoline station lately? Not likely. Bottled water is one of the highest selling items—after cigarettes—in the stations' convenience stores. In restaurants, waiters now frequently ask for your drink order before they bring you tap water, in the hope that you can be talked into buying bottled water. A waitress I asked called this the "beverage greeting" that her manager required her to say before bringing a glass of water.

REREAD
Why is the author changing the subject and talking about Indonesia now?

IDENTIFY IMPORTANT INFORMATION
Underlined key details that illustrate how primitive this region was.

During my travels nearly 20 years ago through Indonesia's coffee-growing regions, I would often stop by a bamboo-thatched lean-to for a drink. Water in the land of the coffee bean rarely comes from a tap; it has to be hauled from wells, strained and boiled.

PREVIEW
The final paragraph reaches a conclusion that consists of a statement and question that emphasizes that not giving people water is inhumane.

Often I was served by rail-thin old men or women in fraying sarongs who subsisted on a few dollars a week. Yet, ask for water and they brought it. At first I asked to pay, not for the water, but for the work behind it. They'd refuse even the smallest coin. The custom of sharing water was too elemental to gum up with finagling.

In India, the Sarai Act mandates that an innkeeper give a free glass of drinking water to any passerby. Indeed, in most places around the world, giving strangers water is the bare minimum of humane behavior. Why is that not so here?

REREAD
Why does the author end the essay with a question? How is this connected to his point about water?

Notice that George uses his prior knowledge of the topic to connect to the reading and to understand the author's point. George underlines the thesis sentence, topic sentences that state main ideas, and important examples, details, and ideas in the selection. As he reads he also asks questions and underlines details that help him answer those questions. As a result, his questions focus his reading and help him understand the author's purpose. In addition, George uses questions to monitor his comprehension. He asks a question when he is confused about what the author is doing. He asks, "Why is the author changing the subject and talking about Indonesia now?" and then he reads on to understand the purpose for that shift.

ADDITIONAL READINGS

This section contains readings on a variety of subjects. Each reading is followed by a few comprehension questions, discussion questions, and writing assignments.

The readings are a valuable way for you to build your vocabulary. *Before you read,* skim the reading and underline any words that are unfamiliar to you. *As you read,* use context (clues in the reading) to help you figure out the meanings of these words. *After reading,* use a dictionary to find definitions of the words for which you could not determine the meaning by using context. Write the definitions in the margin beside the words.

Too Much Homework, Too Little Play

by KATHY SEAL

lunatic: utterly foolish

satirical: using sarcasm to attack vices and follies

1 When I was in junior high school, my parents gave me a typewriter. My friends Amy Neff and Carol Stein often walked with me to my house after school, and we closed my bedroom door and spent the afternoon giggling—or rolling on the carpet, howling with **lunatic** laughter—as we tapped out silly limericks and **satirical** stories on my sage-green Hermes. Once we even wrote a play.

2 Our after-school typing was not homework. We rambled wherever our teenage imaginations took us; we explored words wildly for the pure fun of it, with no exams, report cards or SAT's in mind. We practiced literary risk-taking and problem solving, honed our language skills and learned perseverance, all with no fear of failure—because we were playing. Few children today have time for this kind of after-school play. There's too much homework. Parents' concerns about overload have become a familiar story as schools all over the country pile on homework in a mis-aimed response to criticism that they were teaching too little. Some elementary teachers routinely assign time-consuming work in each of three or four academic subjects every night.

3 Amy Neff, one of the friends who helped me enjoy my typewriter in junior high, learned at a school meeting in May that in fifth grade her 10-year-old daughter would have an hour and a half to two hours of homework seven days a week, plus special projects. "The idea is that, under an **avalanche** of work, children should learn to organize their time efficiently," she wrote to me in an e-mail message. "Nobody has mentioned creativity: ideas, content of what is learned. Just doing LOTS, FAST!" The parents and grandparents of today's children had time for "playing around" with stamp collections or model airplanes, writing a fairy tale, selling lemonade or indulging a fascination with space travel. What many people do not realize is that these kinds of interests and hobbies are just as important as academic learning.

avalanche: an overwhelming amount coming suddenly

4 Many successful adults have a childhood history of freewheeling play. Louis Ignarro, a Nobel Prize winning **pharmacologist,** had six successively complex chemistry sets and played with model rockets. When Letty Cottin Pogrebin, president of the Authors Guild, an association of published writers, was 9, she spent afternoons writing and drawing for a monthly magazine she printed on a primitive press called a hectograph. She charged friends and family 3 cents a copy and then mailed each copy with a 3-cent stamp. She recalls now, "I never understood why the magazine didn't make a profit." But that's just the point: when kids play, they are free to experiment and learn from their experiences, without worrying about how well they're performing.

pharmacologist: a person who studies the effects of drugs on living things

5 Though homework has a clear benefit in high school, there is no research showing that any amount of it advances the education of elementary school kids. They may be stuffing a great deal of information into their heads, but after an hour or two, children lose any eagerness or joy they had in learning. That's important, because research has shown decisively that when children enjoy it, their learning is deeper, richer, and longer-lasting.

6 Parents do have some recourse. They can meet with principals and teachers, organize other parents, and protest. Parents in several communities, including Piscataway, N.J., have prevailed upon school districts to enact homework limits. For their children, at least, there may still be time to indulge in the ancient and powerful **medium** for learning known as play.

medium: a means of communication

COMPREHENSION QUESTIONS

1. According to Seal, how does play differ from homework? Cite two to three examples.

Seal states, "We practiced literary risk-taking and problem solving, honed our language skills and learned perseverance, all with no fear of failure—because we were playing." Examples of her point will vary.

2. List the five kinds of play parents and grandparents engaged in as children.

stamp collecting, building model airplanes, writing fairy tales, selling lemonade, indulging a fascination with space travel

3. Why does play increase learning?

Answers will vary.

DISCUSSION QUESTIONS

1. Seal learned by playing. Which paragraph defines the relationship between learning and play most effectively?
2. Which examples of play best illustrate Seal's point?
3. Why does Seal use the example of parents protesting about homework in her last paragraph?

WRITING ASSIGNMENTS

1. Use process thinking to write a paragraph in which you describe your approach to homework. What process do you use? What is the key detail in the process?
2. Write an essay in which you agree or disagree with Seal's argument. State your position, and support it with facts, examples, and reasons from research or your school experience.
3. Most people would say that they expect to do homework, and it is essential to learning. However, the author questions its usefulness and suggests it reduces learning. What expectations have you faced at school or work that you question? Consider dress codes, attendance policies, grades, or other expectations. Define the purpose and impact of this expectation from your view. Support your view with examples from your school experience or research.

In Defense of Zoos

from *The Life of Pi*
by YANN MARTEL

1 Well-meaning but misinformed people think animals in the wild are "happy" because they are "free." These people usually have a large, handsome predator in mind, a lion or a cheetah (the life of a gnu or of an aardvark is rarely exalted). They imagine this wild animal roaming about the savannah on digestive walks after eating a prey that accepted its lot piously, or going for callisthenic runs to stay slim after overindulging. They imagine this animal overseeing its offspring proudly and tenderly, the whole family watching the setting of the sun from the limbs of trees with sighs of pleasure. The life of the wild animal is simple, noble and meaningful, they imagine. Then it is captured by wicked men and thrown into tiny jails. Its "happiness" is dashed. It yearns mightily for "freedom" and does all it can to escape. Being denied its "freedom" for too long, the animal becomes a shadow of itself, its spirit broken. So some people imagine.

2 This is not the way it is.

3 If you went to a home, kicked down the front door, chased the people who lived there out into the street and said, "Go! You are free! Free as a bird! Go! Go!"—do you think they would shout and dance for joy? They wouldn't. The people you've just **evicted** would sputter, "With what right do you throw us out? This is our home. We own it. We have lived here for years. We're calling the police, you **scoundrel**."

4 Don't we say, "There's no place like home"? That's certainly what animals feel. Animals are territorial. That is the key to their minds. Only a familiar territory will allow them to fulfill the two relentless **imperatives** of the wild: the avoidance of enemies and the getting of food and water. In a zoo, we do for animals what we have done for ourselves with houses: we bring together in a small space what in the wild is spread out. Finding within it all the places it needs—a lookout, a place for resting, for eating and drinking, for bathing, for grooming, etc.—and finding that there is no need to go hunting, food appearing six days a week, an animal will take possession of its zoo space in the same way it would lay claim to a new space in the wild, exploring it and marking it out in the normal ways of its species, with sprays of urine perhaps. Once this moving-in ritual is done and the animal has settled, it will not feel like a nervous tenant, and even less like a prisoner, but rather like a landholder, and it will behave in the same way within its enclosure as it would in its territory in the wild, including defending it tooth and nail should it be invaded. Such an enclosure is subjectively neither better nor worse for an animal than its condition in the wild; so long as it fulfills the animal's needs, a territory, natural or constructed, simply is, without judgment, a given, like the spots on a leopard. One might even argue that if an animal could choose with intelligence, it would opt for living in a zoo, since the major difference between a zoo and the wild is the absence of **parasites** and enemies and the abundance of food in the first, and their respective abundance and **scarcity** in the second. Think about it yourself. Would you rather be put up at the Ritz with free room service and unlimited access to a doctor or be homeless without a soul to care for you?

evicted: forced out; ejected

scoundrel: mean, immoral, or wicked person

imperatives: commands

parasites: plants and animals that live on or in another organism, usually with harmful effects

scarcity: inadequate supply

5 In the literature can be found legions of examples of animals that could escape but did not, or did and returned. There is the case of the chimpanzee whose cage door was left unlocked and had swung open. Increasingly anxious, the chimp began to shriek and to slam the door shut repeatedly—with a deafening clang each time—until the keeper, notified by a visitor, hurried over to remedy the situation. A herd of roe-deer in a European zoo stepped out of their corral when the gate was left open. Frightened by visitors, the deer bolted for the nearby forest, which had its own herd of wild roe-deer and could support more. Nonetheless, the zoo roe-deer quickly returned to their corral. In another zoo a worker was walking to his work site at an early hour, carrying planks of wood, when, to his horror, a bear emerged from the morning mist, heading straight for him at a confident pace. The man dropped the planks and ran for his life. The zoo staff immediately started searching for the escaped bear. They found it back in its enclosure, having climbed down into its pit the way it had climbed out, by way of a tree that had fallen over. It was thought that the noise of the planks of wood falling to the ground had frightened it.

6 But I don't insist. I don't mean to defend zoos. Close them all down if you want (and let us hope that what wildlife remains can survive in what is left of the natural world).

COMPREHENSION QUESTIONS

1. What are the three reasons that Martell gives in support of zoos?

A zoo provides a familiar territory, protection from enemies, and food.

2. Why did the chimpanzee, roe-deer, and bear return to their cages or enclosures?

They were frightened and returned to places that were familiar to them.

3. What is the "moving-in ritual"? How does it affect a wild animal?

finding all the places it needs in the zoo enclosure, such as a lookout, a place for resting, for eating and drinking, for bathing, for grooming, etc. The animal realizes hunting is unnecessary and takes possession of the space by marking the territory with urine.

DISCUSSION QUESTIONS

PEER CONVERSATION

1. Identify Martell's counterargument. What specific facts and examples refute this counterargument and support his position?

2. Does Martell hurt or help his argument when he compares freeing wild animals to freeing people from their homes?
3. In the conclusion, Martell says, "I don't mean to defend zoos. Close them all down if you want." Do you believe him? If not, why does he say this? Explain your answer.

WRITING ASSIGNMENTS

1. Does a zoo educate children, preserve wildlife, or just entertain? Determine your position on the purpose of a zoo. Write a paragraph stating your view. Provide examples to support your view.
2. Write an essay stating the effects of amusement parks, hands-on museums, video game parlors, or organized sports on young children.
3. Write a narrative describing an educational experience you had as a child outside of school. What did you see? What did you learn? Why was it important to you?

Night Walker

by Brent Staples

1 My first victim was a woman—white, well dressed, probably in her early 20s. I came upon her late one evening on a deserted street in Hyde Park, a relatively **affluent** neighborhood in an otherwise mean, **impoverished** section of Chicago. As I swung onto the avenue behind her, there seemed to be a discreet, uninflammatory distance between us. Not so. She cast back a worried glance. To her, the youngish black man—a broad six feet two inches with a beard and billowing hair, both hands shoved into the pockets of a bulky military jacket—seemed menacingly close. She picked up her pace and was soon running in earnest. Within seconds she disappeared into a cross street.

affluent: wealthy; rich

impoverished: poor

2 That was more than a decade ago. I was 22 years old, a graduate student newly arrived at the University of Chicago. It was in the echo of that terrible woman's footfalls that I first began to know the unwieldy inheritance I'd come into—the ability to alter public space in ugly ways. It was clear that she thought herself the quarry of a mugger, a rapist, or worse. Suffering a bout of insomnia, however, I was stalking sleep, not defenseless wayfarers. As a softy who is scarcely able to take a knife to a raw chicken—let alone hold one to a person's throat—I was surprised, embarrassed, and dismayed all at once. Her flight made me feel like an accomplice in tyranny. It also made it clear that I was **indistinguishable** from the muggers who occasionally seeped into the area from the surrounding ghetto. I soon gathered that being perceived as dangerous is a hazard in itself: Where fear and weapons meet—and they often do in urban America—there is always the possibility of death.

indistinguishable: not clearly recognizable

3 In that first year, my first away from my hometown, I was to become thoroughly familiar with the language of fear. At dark, shadowy intersections, I could cross in front of a car stopped at a traffic light and elicit the thunk, thunk, thunk, thunk of the driver—black, white, male, female—hammering down the door locks. On less traveled streets after dark, I grew accustomed to but never comfortable with people crossing to the other side of the street rather than pass me. Then there were the standard unpleasantries with policemen, doormen, bouncers, cabdrivers, and others whose business it is to screen out troublesome individuals before there is any nastiness.

4 I moved to New York nearly two years ago and I have remained an avid night walker. In central Manhattan, the near-constant crowd covers the tense one-on-one street encounters. Elsewhere, things can get very **taut** indeed.

taut: strained; tense

5 After dark, on the warrenlike streets of Brooklyn where I live, I often see women who fear the worst from me. They seem to have set their faces on neutral, and with their purse straps strung across their chests bandolier-style, they forge ahead as though bracing themselves against being tackled. I understand, of course, that the danger they perceive is not a **hallucination.** Women are particularly vulnerable to street violence, and young black males are drastically overrepresented among the **perpetrators** of that violence. Yet these truths are no **solace** against the **alienation** that comes of being ever the suspect, an entity with whom pedestrians avoid making eye contact.

hallucination: the perception of sights and sounds that are not actually present

perpetrators: people who commit crimes

solace: a source of relief

alienation: isolation

6 It is not altogether clear to me how I reached the ripe old age of 22 without being conscious of the **lethality** nighttime **pedestrians** attributed to me. Perhaps it was because in Chester, Pennsylvania, the small, angry industrial town where I came of age in the 1960s, I was scarcely noticeable against a backdrop of gang warfare, street knifings, and murders. I grew up one of the good boys, had perhaps a half-dozen fistfights. In retrospect, my shyness of combat has clear sources. As a boy, I saw countless tough guys locked away; I have since buried several, too. They were babies, really—a teenage cousin, a brother of 22, a childhood friend in his mid-20s—all gone down in episodes of bravado played out in the streets. I chose, perhaps unconsciously, to remain a shadow—timid, but a survivor.

lethality: capable of causing death

pedestrians: walkers

7 The fearsomeness mistakenly attributed to me in public places often has a perilous flavor. The most frightening of these confusions occurred in the late 1970s and early 1980s, when I worked as a journalist in Chicago. One day, rushing into the office of a magazine I was writing for with a deadline story in hand, I was mistaken for a burglar. The office manager called security and, with an ad hoc posse, pursued me through the **labyrinthine** halls, nearly to my editor's door. I had no way of proving who I was. I could only move briskly toward the company of someone who knew me.

labyrinthine: a structure or building with winding passageways that may be difficult to follow without getting lost

8 Relatively speaking, however, I never fared as badly as another black male journalist. He went to nearby Waukegan, Illinois, a couple of summers ago to work on a story about a murderer who was born there. Mistaking the reporter for the killer, police officers hauled him from his car at gunpoint and but for his press **credentials** would probably have tried to book him. Such episodes are not uncommon. Black men trade tales like this all the time.

credentials: evidence showing a person's position and authority

9 Over the years, I learned to smother the rage I felt at so often being mistaken for a criminal. Not to do so would surely have led to madness. I now take precau-

tions to make myself less threatening. I move about with care, particularly late in the evening. I give a wide berth to nervous people on subway platforms during the wee hours. If I happen to be entering a building behind some people who appear skittish, I may walk by, letting them clear the lobby before I return, so as not to seem to be following them. I have been calm and extremely **congenial** on those rare occasions when I've been pulled over by the police.

congenial: friendly; compatible

10 And on late-evening **constitutionals** I employ what has proved to be an excellent tension-reducing measure: I whistle melodies from Beethoven and Vivaldi and more popular classical composers. Even steely New Yorkers hunching toward nighttime destinations seem to relax, and occasionally they even join in the tune. Virtually everybody seems to sense that a mugger wouldn't be warbling bright, sunny selections from Vivaldi's "Four Seasons." It is my **equivalent** of the cowbell that hikers wear when they are in bear country.

constitutionals: walks

equivalent: equal in worth, quantity, or meaning

COMPREHENSION QUESTIONS

1. Staples notes "being perceived as dangerous is a hazard in itself." What stories does he tell to illustrate this observation?

Answers will vary.

2. What is his purpose in mentioning young relatives and friends dead in their twenties?

He contrasts his timid ways, which have helped him survive, to the bravado of his family and friends who acted as tough guys and died on the streets in their teens.

3. What precautions does Staples take to avoid dangerous situations?

He tries not to threaten people. In the evening he moves carefully and creates distance between himself and nervous people on subway platforms. He may pass by an office letting people exit the lobby before he goes in. He is extremely friendly when he is stopped by police, and he whistles Vivaldi.

DISCUSSION QUESTIONS

PEER CONVERSATION

1. Staples connects a series of narratives to illustrate his position. Identify a sentence or two that state his position. Then select the two most effective narratives that illustrate it.
2. Define prejudice. How is Staples a victim of prejudice?
3. Who is the audience for this essay? Support your answer with details from the essay.

WRITING ASSIGNMENTS

1. Write a paragraph comparing or contrasting the precautions you take in public spaces to the precautions Staples takes in public spaces.
2. Write a cause and effect essay about a change of mind you have had. Consider a person, place, thing, or idea. What was your initial viewpoint? What were its origins? What caused you to change your mind? How did this change affect you?
3. Discuss a prejudice that bothers you. Suggest strategies to counteract it. Consider these questions: When and where do you see it? What are its origins?

You've Got Hate Mail

by LYDIE RASCHKA

1 Hate mail confirms a vague, nagging feeling that you've done something wrong. It's a firm tap on the shoulder that says, "The jig is up." So when the first letter came, it was expected. The second, however, was a shock. By the third I was a wreck. How did he know it would take exactly and only three?

2 I started writing a few years ago, after I had a baby. I haven't completely figured out what led me to writing, but it was probably tied up with my son's birth and the attendant emotions that needed sorting.

solitary: living or being alone

void: an empty space

introvert: shy, reserved, inward looking

perilous: dangerous

3 I like the **solitary** work life. I write at a table in the bedroom. I send my ideas out into the **void.** The bedroom seems a safe enough place. I have been told that I am an **introvert.** What on earth makes me want to communicate with strangers in this **perilous** way—standing naked in a field?

4 "You have to expect these things when you are a writer," my father says about the hate mail. "When you're in the public eye, anyone can read what you write."

5 The letters are effective and unsettling, to say the least. I have an unusual name, so he thinks I'm foreign. He calls me "Eurotrash." It's a relief because it means he doesn't really know me—although he makes some pretty accurate guesses. He doesn't know that my parents simply like unusual names.

6 He spells my name correctly. I can only hope he's mispronouncing it. He uses it in ways I've never seen it used before—paired with obscenities and crooked thoughts.

psyche: soul

7 It bothers me that he has written my name and my address three different times on three different envelopes. My name is next to the buzzer outside my building so that people will have easier access to me. I am two doors and one buzzer away from danger. But the mail slips through, into the letter box, into my **psyche.**

8 I call the postal inspector but she never calls me back. One day I leave a message on her machine and I am in tears. Finally she calls. She tells me that let-

ters like these don't usually lead to violence. She says there's nothing we can do; we have to wait until he makes a mistake.

9 My fingers shake when I open the mailbox. I pick through the stack. When a letter arrives I open it quickly. You read your mail. You do.

10 I spend most of a morning sitting in an old school chair at the police station, the kind with a desk attached. The police are standing around. They joke with one another. They drink coffee and ask me what I need in a **skeptical** way, as though there is nothing I can offer that will surprise them.

skeptical: doubting or questioning

11 "I am getting anonymous hate mail," I say.

12 "Is it threatening?" they ask.

13 "Not specifically," I answer. "But the first one had **feces** in it." Sending feces is threatening, in my mind. At the very least it's a health hazard. The policewoman writes down what I say and photocopies the letters. She makes a file.

feces: excrement; waste from the bowels

14 I am vulnerable to people's opinions of me. I partly believe what he says. When I tell my friends and family, I imagine that they partly believe what he says, too. They ask me what I wrote, what he wrote. "What does it matter what I wrote!?" I say. "Do you think I did something to deserve this?!" I can't yell at him, so I yell at them. I want unconditional support from everyone I know. I want protection. I have revealed too much about who I am.

15 I cling to his most obvious mistakes—Eurotrash—in the hope that he has gotten other things wrong, too. He is sarcastic and angry and a good speller. A person can be a good speller and be crazy, right? But still, it's hard that he's a good speller.

16 I try to have **rational** conversations with him in my mind, but it's hopeless. We get nowhere.

rational: logical; sane

17 He owns a dog. It's his dog's feces he has sent. I always thought animal lovers were especially sensitive human beings. In my vulnerable state—in spite of this **blatant** example of insensitivity—dog ownership gives him stature.

blatant: obvious, bold, or intrusive

18 He has decided I'm rich because I live in a certain neighborhood. He has decided I've stolen someone's job because I'm foreign. He attacks my writing and everything he can **eke out** about me from what I have written. But he reveals who he is in his writing, too. He has an aunt and a disabled sister. He doesn't know how much we have in common. He doesn't know that I have a sister and a disabled aunt.

eke out: make or acquire with difficulty

19 I think about changing my byline. I will remove my address from the phone book. I will use only a first initial. I will give up writing. But then he wins, says my editor.

20 I am unable to write for a month, two months. My editor calls. I say I'm not ready. He hires someone else to write on a topic I wanted to write about. I don't trust my motivations. Perhaps there's truth in what he says. I have been flippant. I have been **patronizing.** I have been biased.

patronizing: to be kind or helpful in an arrogant way

21 At home I put the letters in a brown envelope and write "**Anonymous** Mail" in the top right-hand corner, avoiding the word "hate." I make a mental note to throw them away before my son can reach the shelf where I have put them. I don't want him to read these letters that have my name written all over them, with their inaccuracies and **assumptions** and possible wayward truths.

anonymous: no name given

assumptions: thoughts that are not proven; suppositions

22 The feces were wrapped in a piece of foil; they came in a small padded envelope. I threw the feces away, then fished them out again and put them in a

contamination: being infected or made unclean

baggie. I washed my hands with soap, and rubbed them red. I am afraid of **contamination** or disease. I am afraid I will pass on germs to my son.

23 "Here's a little present from my best friend," he writes. The way he uses language is absurd: little present, best friend. He writes in sentences, with periods and commas and capital letters. He ignores the typical friendly greeting—he does not say "Dear."

24 I imagine him in a room, at a desk or a table. I imagine the light in the room, and the clothes tossed on the bed. He has paper and a pen. He pulls up a chair. Something compels him to write. He doesn't know how much we have in common.

COMPREHENSION QUESTIONS

1. What does the letter writer say about Raschka? What faults does he find? Cite examples.

The letter writer calls her Eurotrash and criticizes her writing. He also believes she is foreign because of her name. He criticizes her for taking someone's job.

2. Why does it bother Raschka that the letter writer is a good speller?

His letters are sarcastic and angry. She worries that he is crazy, and somehow because he is a good speller, he is more capable of doing her harm.

3. What do Raschka and the letter writer have in common?

He has an aunt and a disabled sister. She has a disabled aunt and a sister. They are both writers.

DISCUSSION QUESTIONS

PEER CONVERSATION

1. Where does Raschka's narrative convey to the reader her thoughts and feelings about the hate mail she receives?
2. Raschka uses the language and details in the hate mail to understand the person who sent the mail. Reread paragraphs 15, 17, and 23. Do her assumptions seem accurate and support her point in the concluding paragraph?
3. How would you react to the situation described in the reading? Are there other things you might have done to protect yourself?

WRITING ASSIGNMENTS

1. Write a paragraph about a person with whom you do not get along. Describe the person and the source of the conflict between you.
2. Write an essay discussing the positive and negative implications of taking risks. Compare and contrast examples of risk-taking behavior you

see around you. As you cite and discuss these examples, analyze what makes them positive or negative.

3. Fear is a powerful motivator. Discuss some common effects of fear on people, how it drives them to act irrationally. Cite and discuss a number of examples.

The Body of the Beholder

by MICHELE INGRASSIA

1 When you're a teenage girl, there's no place to hide. Certainly not in gym class, where the shorts are short, the T-shirts revealing and the adolescent critics eager to dissect every flaw. Yet out on the hardwood gym floors at Moran Park High, a largely African-American school on Chicago's Southwest Side, the girls aren't talking about how bad their bodies are, but how good. Sure, all of them compete to see how many sit-ups they can do—Janet Jackson's washboard stomach is their model. But ask Diane Howard about weight, and the African-American senior, who carries 133 pounds on her 5-foot 7½ inch frame, says she'd happily add 15 pounds—if she could ensure they'd land on her hips. Or La'Taria Stokes, a stoutly built junior who takes it as high praise when boys remark, "Your hips are screaming for twins!" "I know I'm fat," La'Taria says. "I don't care."

2 In a society that worships at the altar of supermodels like Claudia, Christy and Kate, white teenagers are obsessed with staying thin. But there's growing evidence that black and white girls view their bodies in dramatically different ways. The latest findings come in a study to be published in the journal Human Organization this spring by a team of black and white researchers at the University of Arizona. While 90 percent of the white junior-high and high-school girls studied voiced dissatisfaction with their weight, 70 percent of African-American teens were satisfied with their bodies.

3 In fact, even significantly overweight black teens described themselves as happy. That confidence may not carry over to other areas of black teens' lives, but the study suggests that, at least here, it's a lifelong source of pride. Asked to describe women as they age, two thirds of the black teens said they get more beautiful, and many cited their mothers as examples. White girls responded that their mothers may have been beautiful—back in their youth. Says **anthropologist** Mimi Nichter, one of the study's coauthors, "In white culture, the window of beauty is so small."

anthropologist: a person who studies customs and cultures

4 What is beauty? White teens defined perfection as 5 feet 7 and 100 to 110 pounds—superwaif Kate Moss's vital stats. African-American girls described the perfect size in more attainable terms—full hips, thin thighs, the sort of proportions about which Hammer ("Pumps and a Bump") and Sir Mix-A lot ("Baby Got Back") rap poetic. But they said that true beauty—"looking good"—is about more than size. Almost two thirds of the black teens defined beauty as "the right attitude."

disparity: different or distinct; unequal

5 The **disparity** in body images isn't just in kids' heads. It's reflected in fashion magazines, in ads, and it's out there, on TV, every Thursday night. On NBC, the sitcom "Friends" stars Courteney Cox, Jennifer Aniston and Lisa Kudrow—all of them white and twentysomething, classically beautiful and reed thin. Meanwhile, Fox Television's "Living Single," aimed at an African-American audience, projects a less Hollywood ideal—its stars are four twentysomething black women whose bodies are, well, real. Especially the big-boned, bronze-haired rapper Queen Latifah, whose size only adds to her magnetism. During a break at the Lite Nites program at the Harlem YMCA, over the squeal of sneakers on the basketball court, Brandy Wood, 14, describes Queen Latifah's appeal: "What I like about her is the way she wears her hair and the color in it and the clothes she wears."

6 Underlying the beauty gap are 200 years of cultural difference. "In white, middle-class America, part of the great American Dream of making it is to be able to make yourself over," says Nichter. "In the black community, there is the reality that you might not move up the ladder as easily. As one girl put it, you have to be realistic—if you think negatively about yourself, you won't get anywhere." It's no accident that Barbie has long **embodied** a white-adolescent ideal—in the early days, she came with her own scale (set at 110) and her own diet guide ("How to Lose Weight: Don't Eat"). Even in this **postfeminist** era, Barbie's tight-is-right message is stronger than ever. Before kindergarten, researchers say, white girls know that Daddy eats and Mommy diets. By high school, many have split the world into physical haves and have-nots, rivals across the beauty line. "It's not that you hate them [perfect girls]," says Sarah Immel, a junior at Evanston Township High School north of Chicago. "It's that you're kind of jealous that they have it so easy, that they're so perfect-looking."

embodied: in a definite bodily form

postfeminist: viewpoints emerging in the 1980s responding to the views of feminism (the movements, theories, and philosophies of the inequities between men and women)

7 In the black community, size isn't debated, it's taken for granted—a sign, some say, that after decades of preaching black-is-beautiful, black parents and educators have gotten across the message of self-respect. Indeed, black teens grow up equating a full figure with health and fertility. Black women's magazines tend to tout NOT TRYING TO BE SIZE 8, not TEN TIPS FOR THIN THIGHS. And even girls who fit the white ideal aren't necessarily comfortable there. Super model Tyra Banks recalls how, in high school in Los Angeles, she was the envy of her white girlfriends. "They would tell me, 'Oh, Tyra, you look so good,'" says Banks. "But I was like, 'I want a booty and thighs like my black girlfriends.'"

8 Men send some of the strongest signals. What's fat? "You got to be real fat for me to notice," says Muhammad Latif, a Harlem 15-year-old. White girls follow what they think guys want, whether guys want it or not. Sprawled across the well-worn sofas and hard-back chairs of the student lounge, boys at Evanston High scoff at the girls' **idealization** of Kate Moss. "Sickly," they say, "gross." Sixteen-year-old Trevis Milton, a blond swimmer, has no interest in dating Kate wanna-bes. "I don't want to feel like I'm going to break them." Here, perfection is a hardbody, like Linda Hamilton in "Terminator II." "It's not so much about eating broccoli and water as running," says senior Kevin Mack.

idealization: viewing as perfect; a model to strive for

9 And if hardbodies are hot, girls often need to diet to achieve them, too. According to the Arizona study, which was funded by the National Institute of Child Health and Human Development, 62 percent of the white girls reported dieting at least once in the past year. Even those who say they'd rather be fit than thin

get caught up. Sarah Martin, 16, a junior at Evanston, confesses she's tried forcing herself to throw up but couldn't. She's still frustrated: ". . . I have a big appetite, and I feel so guilty when I eat."

10 Black teens don't usually go to such extremes. **Anorexia** and **bulimia** are relatively minor problems among African-American girls. And though 51 percent of the black teens in the study said that they'd dieted in the last year, follow-up interviews showed that far fewer were on sustained weight-and-exercise programs. Indeed, 64 percent of the black girls thought it was better to be "a little" overweight than underweight. And while they agreed that "very overweight" girls should diet, they defined that as someone who "takes up two seats on the bus."

anorexia: an eating disorder characterized by obsession with weight loss

bulimia: an eating disorder characterized by eating large quantities of food followed by self-induced vomiting

11 The black image of beauty may seem saner, but it's not necessarily healthy. Black women don't **obsess** on size, but they do worry about other white cultural ideals that black men value. "We look at Heather Locklear and see the long hair and the fair, pure skin," says Essence magazine senior editor Pamela Johnson. More troubling, the acceptance of fat means many girls ignore the real dangers of **obesity.** Dieting costs money—even if it's not a fancy commercial program; fruits, vegetables and lean meats are pricier than high-fat foods. Exercise? Only one state—Illinois—requires daily physical education for every kid. Anyway, as black teenagers complain, exercise can ruin your hair—and, if you're plunking down $35 a week at the hairdresser, you don't want to sweat out your 'do in the gym. "I don't think we should obsess about weight and fitness, but there is a middle ground," says the well-toned black actress Jada Pinkett. Maybe that's where Queen Latifah meets Kate Moss.

obsess: think excessively

obesity: being very fat

COMPREHENSION QUESTIONS

1. What is the main point of the reading?

Black and white girls view their bodies in dramatically different ways.

2. How do the two cultures define beauty? Cite examples for each.

Answers will vary.

3. Which view of beauty is saner? Which is healthier?

Black girls' view of beauty is saner; however, both can lead to health problems.

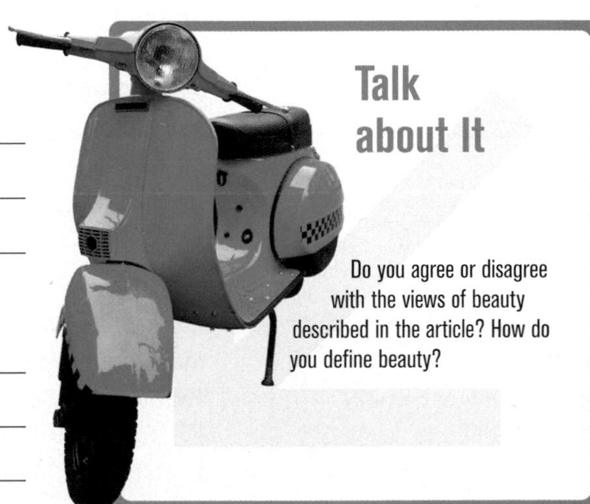

Talk about It

Do you agree or disagree with the views of beauty described in the article? How do you define beauty?

PEER CONVERSATION

DISCUSSION QUESTIONS

1. The essay is organized using comparison and contrast; however, Ingrassia uses more details about one view of beauty to make a point about both views. Why does she do this? Is it effective?
2. How do you think advertising has contributed to the growth in eating disorders among teenage girls?
3. Ingrassia supports her thesis with fact, examples, and details. Which paragraph do you think is most effective? Why?

WRITING ASSIGNMENTS

1. Write a paragraph that categorizes beauty in another way. Provide specific examples to illustrate your categories.
2. Write an essay in which you examine your view of beauty. Cite examples to explore your views in detail.
3. Compare and contrast your view of fashion with a view presented in an advertisement or the view of someone you know.

Dogs Need a Best Friend, Too

by MICHELLE SLATALLA

1 Otto has always slept with Bone.

2 We considered that perfectly normal.

3 But recently our 5-year-old Labrador retriever began to lug Bone everywhere, laying the smelly old piece of rawhide beside him on the floor of whatever room he had chosen for his next nap. He took Bone with him on walks. At mealtime, he arranged Bone **reverently** beside his bowl.

reverently: with deep love or respect

4 At first we didn't worry. Otto has fallen in love before. There was a period when Old Sock was his faithful buddy. He still keeps Slobbery Tennis Ball under the bed for emergencies.

5 What made the Bone situation so worrisome was the escalation. Here was a dog who used to eat the same brand of bone he now considered his best friend. By last week, Otto had gotten to the point where he was propping Bone against a closed bathroom door before settling down to wait for whoever was inside to come out. When the door opened and Bone fell, Otto leapt to cradle his **inanimate** companion with a devotion **reminiscent** of Tom Hanks's love for Wilson the volleyball in "Cast Away."

inanimate: not having life or spirit

reminiscent: a memory; remembering

6 Otto was lonely.

7 This was a variation on the underlying principle that prompted previous family expansions. My husband and I had our first child, Zoe, to keep us company. Later we had Ella for Zoe. Then we had Clementine for Ella. Otto we got for Clem.

8 It seemed only fair for our pet to have a pet. The goldfish, Davis, had not turned out to be the comfort we had hoped when we purchased him for Otto. A year later, their relationship remains distant. And having recently abandoned the idea of a pet rabbit (I concluded that a prey animal might not be comfortable living with an 85-pound dog), that left one logical choice.

9 Who doesn't love a puppy?

10 When I went online to investigate possibilities, I had two goals: to determine which breed would be most suitable and to find a reputable local breeder.

11 I started my search at the American Kennel Club's Internet site, akc.org, where I found detailed descriptions of 153 club-recognized breeds, from affenpinschers (a "wiry-haired terrierlike toy dog") to Yorkshire terriers ("bundles of energy as puppies").

12 I had a sense of the kind of dog I wanted - a breed that was small, lazy and not **prone** to excessive barking - and so was able to weed out many breeds, including beagles ("known to bark as part of their hunting heritage") and cocker spaniels ("may require the help of a professional" for grooming).

prone: to be inclined or having a tendency toward something

13 French bulldogs intrigued me. With adorable bat ears, a small **stature** and a reputation for being "house dogs whose **niche** in life is to be an adored pet," they sounded perfect.

stature: standing height

niche: an especially suitable place or position

14 The next step was to find reputable breeders and talk to them about French bulldogs' **temperaments** and health issues. At the American Kennel Club site, I could click on Breeder Referral to link to A.K.C.-approved national parent clubs for each breed; many list affiliated breeders.

temperaments: natural dispositions

15 "That's a great first step, but the best thing to do after you find the contacts is to go see dogs at shows and events in your area, which our site lists by state," said Gail Miller, an A.K.C. spokeswoman. "There are so many **nuances** with each breed that the only way to find out if a breed is right for you is to actually ask breeders."

nuances: subtle or slight variations

16 The most important things to avoid when searching for breeders online are so-called puppy mills that churn out as many puppies as possible, with more regard for profit than for the health and quality of the dogs.

17 "Responsible breeders breed to improve a breed," said Arlie Amarie Arford, editor of The French Bullytin, "the magazine of record for French bulldogs." The magazine has a Web site at frenchbullytin.com. "But if you pick a breeder just because they have a Web site with a lot of cute puppy pictures on it, you don't know what you are getting."

18 After generations of relatively limited gene pools, purebred dogs tend to have specific health problems. Labrador retrievers like Otto, for instance, are prone to hip problems. Short-muzzled and stocky, most French bulldogs must be delivered by Caesarean section. They tend to have breathing and spinal problems.

19 "French bulldogs are a very manmade breed, they're hothouse orchids," Ms. Arford said. "As a breeder, I don't want people coming back in a year and half saying a dog had a heart attack. I don't want to breed a dog that might snap at a child."

20 "But if you get a puppy shipped to you sight unseen from out of state from one of these breeders whose primary goal is profit," she said, "they may use shortcuts."

ascertaining: finding out with certainty

auxiliary: helping or supplementary

21 Tip-offs include breeders' sites that offer puppies for sale without first **ascertaining** the suitability of prospective homes. Breeders who set prices based on dogs' color rather than their physical structure, those who breed more than seven litters a year or those who advertise **auxiliary** products on their sites also are questionable, Ms. Arford said.

fanatical: unreasonably enthusiastic

arduous: difficult to do

22 When we got Otto, we avoided those problems by going to a highly recommended local breeder who displayed such **fanatical** devotion to her pups that she subjected prospective buyers to an **arduous** interview process, at the end of which she decreed which specific puppy was appropriate for each buyer. How we managed to get Otto I still don't know. After we had signed all the paperwork, assured the breeder we would adhere to her recommended puppy diet and managed to drive away with him, we kept checking the rearview mirror to make sure she wasn't pursuing us to reclaim him.

23 In my current search, the A.K.C. site referred me to the French Bulldog Club of America, at frenchbulldogclub.org, which in turn listed breeders by state. In California, where I live, 14 breeders were listed. Among them were Ron and Edie Parker of Grass Valley, about whom Ms. Arford had spoken highly.

24 Mr. Parker turned out to be a very responsible breeder. During a two-hour phone conversation, he told me he would not sell me one of his dogs because of Otto.

25 "He's more than twice the size of a French bulldog, and that right away puts you on my B-list," Mr. Parker said. "He can potentially injure the small dog, not because he wants to, but by accident. It doesn't take more than one accidental pounce and it's over with. I would say, why don't you call me when you lose your lab?"

26 I also phoned Jane Norris, who also turned out to be a very responsible breeder. During a similarly lengthy conversation, Ms. Norris asked me why I wanted a French bulldog, what my family situation was, whether I had a fenced yard and if I knew that bulldogs overheat easily and should never be left outside alone.

27 I told her about Otto.

alpha: dominate member of a group

28 Ms. Norris, who is expecting two litters in October, said she would not necessarily consider Otto a deal breaker. "If you had a Lhasa Apso and a Shih Tzu, for instance, I would not give you the **alpha** puppy who wants to be king of the mountain," she said. "I would keep your Lab in mind when picking a puppy."

29 She said that if I was still interested, I should call again after her puppies are born.

30 Am I still interested? I'll have to do a lot more research before being persuaded that a hothouse breed like a French bulldog is healthy enough to make a good family pet.

31 In the meantime, luckily we have a sturdy stand-in named Bone.

COMPREHENSION QUESTIONS

1. Why does the writer believe her dog Otto needs a best friend?

Otto lugs a bone around with him. He takes it on walks and sets it next to him when he naps or eats.

2. How can you tell whether a dog breeder is responsible?

Responsible dog breeders improve the breed. They also interview potential buyers to determine if they will provide a suitable home.

3. What makes the writer doubt that a French bulldog would make a good family pet?

French bulldogs are a hothouse breed that require a great deal of attention, and they may not be healthy enough to be a good family pet.

DISCUSSION QUESTIONS

PEER CONVERSATION

1. The essay begins with Slatalla's decision to buy a dog. However, no dogs are ever purchased in the essay. So what is the purpose of the essay?
2. Slatalla's essay contains multiple paragraphs on the same point. Reread the essay and divide it into three or four major sections. Then outline each section to identify the key examples, details, and facts. Explain your divisions and determine how each part helps the writer make her point.
3. Slatalla organizes her essay as a narrative. Would it be easier for a reader to understand her purpose if she used a different pattern of organization? Which pattern would you recommend? Explain your choice.

WRITING ASSIGNMENTS

1. Slatalla's essay explores the concept of company. Write a paragraph in which you illustrate an important concept in your home, such as responsibility, authority, or stress.
2. Write an essay in which you discuss the process of making a responsible decision, such as choosing a college, job, or mate or purchasing a car or home. What issues are important in the decision? What steps would you take to ensure you make a wise decision?
3. It is sometimes said the world can be divided into cat people and dog people, that people can be categorized by the type of animal they love. How would you categorize people? Create two categories you might use to describe people.

Hitting Bottom: Why America Should Outlaw Spanking

by EMILY BAZELON

1 Sally Lieber, the California assemblywoman who proposed a ban on spanking last week, must be sorry she ever opened her mouth. Before Lieber could introduce her bill, a poll showed that only 23 percent of respondents supported it. Some pediatricians **disparaged** the idea of outlawing spanking, and her fellow politicians called her crazy. Anyone with the slightest **libertarian** streak seems to believe that outlawing corporal punishment is silly. More government intrusion, and for what—to spare kids a few swats? Or, if you're pro-spanking, a spanking ban represents a **sinister** effort to take a crucial disciplinary tool out of the hands of good mothers and fathers—and to encourage the sort of permissive parenting that turns kids ratty and rotten.

disparaged: belittled or discredited

libertarian: an advocate of maximizing the rights of individuals

sinister: threatening harm; evil

2 Why, though, are we so eager to retain the right to hit our kids? Lieber's ban would apply only to children under the age of 4. Little kids may be the most infuriating; they are also the most vulnerable. And if you think that most spanking takes place in a fit of temper—and that banning it would gradually lead more parents to restrain themselves—then the idea of a hard-and-fast rule against it starts to seem not so ridiculous.

3 The purpose of Lieber's proposal isn't to send parents to jail, or children to foster care, because of a firm smack. Rather, it would make it easier for prosecutors to bring charges for instances of corporal punishment that they think are **tantamount** to child abuse. Currently, California law (and the law of other states) allows for spanking that is reasonable, age-appropriate, and does not carry a risk of serious injury. That forces judges to referee what's reasonable and what's not. How do they tell? Often, they may resort to looking for signs of injury. If a smack leaves a bruise or causes a fracture, it's illegal. If not, bombs away. In other words, allowing for "reasonable" spanking gives parents a lot of **leeway** to cause pain.

tantamount: equal to

leeway: room for freedom of action

4 Who should we worry about more: The well-intentioned parent who smacks a child's bottom and gets hauled off to court, or the kid who keeps getting pounded because the cops can't find a bruise? This U.N. report on violence against children argues that "The de minimis principle—that the law does not concern itself with **trivial** matters" will keep minor assaults on children out of court, just as it does almost all minor assaults between adults. The U.N. Committee on the Rights of the Child has been urging countries to ban corporal punishment since 1996. The idea is that by making it illegal to hit your kids, countries will make hurting them socially unacceptable.

trivial: unimportant; insignificant

5 The United Nations has a lot of converting to do in this part of the world. Its report cites a survey showing that 84 percent of Americans believe that it's "sometimes necessary to discipline a child with a good hard spanking." On this front, we are in the company of the Koreans, 90 percent of whom reported thinking that corporal punishment is "necessary." On the other side of the spanking map are 19 countries that have banned spanking and three others that have partially banned it.

6 The grandmother of the bunch is Sweden, which passed a law against corporal punishment in 1979. The effects of that ban are cited by advocates on both sides of the spanking debate. Parents almost universally used corporal punishment on Swedish children born in the 1950s; the numbers dropped to 14 percent for kids born in the late 1980s, and only 8 percent of parents reported physically punishing their kids in 2000. Plus, only one child in Sweden died as the result of physical abuse by a parent between 1980 and 1996. Those statistics suggest that making spanking illegal contributes to making it less **prevalent** and also to making kids safer. On the other hand, reports to police of child abuse soared in the decades after the spanking ban, as did the incidence of juvenile violence. Did reports rise because frustrated, spanking-barred parents lashed out against their kids in other ways, or because the law made people more aware of child abuse? The latter is what occurred in the United States when reports of abuse spiked following the **enactment** of child-protective laws in the 1970s. Is the rise in kids beating on each other evidence of undisciplined, unruly child mobs, or the result of other unrelated forces? The data don't tell us, so take your pick.

prevalent: widely used or accepted

enactment: passing into law

7 A similar split exists in the American social-science literature. In a 2000 article in the *Clinical Child and Family Psychology Review,* Dr. Robert Lazelere (who approves of spanking if it's "conditional" and not abusive) reviewed 38 studies and found that spanking posed no harm to kids under the age of 7, and reduced misbehavior when deployed alongside milder punishments like scolding and timeouts. By contrast, a 2002 article in *Psychology Bulletin* by Dr. Elizabeth Gershoff (not a spanking fan) reviewed 88 studies and found an association between corporal punishment and a higher level of childhood aggression and a greater risk of physical abuse.

8 This is the sort of research **impasse** that leaves advocates free to argue what they will—and parents without much guidance. But one study stands out: An effort by University of California at Berkeley psychologist Diana Baumrind to tease out the effects of occasional spanking compared to frequent spanking and no spanking at all. Baumrind tracked about 100 white, middle-class families in the East Bay area of northern California from 1968 to 1980. The children who were hit frequently were more likely to be **maladjusted.** The ones who were occasionally spanked had slightly higher misbehavior scores than those who were not spanked at all. But this difference largely disappeared when Baumrind accounted for the children's poor behavior at a younger age. In other words, the kids who acted out as toddlers and preschoolers were more likely to act out later, whether they were spanked occasionally or never. Lots of spanking was bad for kids. A little didn't seem to matter.

impasse: deadlock

maladjusted: unable to meet demands of interpersonal relationships in daily life

9 Baumrind concluded that it is "*reliance* on physical punishment, not whether it is used at all, that is associated with harm to the child." The italics are mine. While Baumrind's evidence undercuts the **abolitionist** position, it doesn't justify spanking as a regular punishment. In addition, Baumrind draws a telling distinction between "impulsive and reactive" spanking and punishments that require "some restraint and forethought." In my experience as a very occasional (once or twice) spanker, impulsivity was what hitting my kid was all about. I know that I'm supposed to spank my sons more in sorrow than in anger. But does that really describe most parents, especially occasional spankers, when they raise their hand to their children? More often, I think, we strike kids when we're mad—enraged,

abolitionist: a person who works to abolish or destroy something

in fact. Baumrind's findings suggest that occasional spankers don't need to worry about this much. I hope she's right. But her numbers are small: Only three children in her study weren't spanked at all. That's a tiny control group.

10 Baumrind argues that if the social-science research doesn't support an outright ban on spanking, then we shouldn't fight over the occasional spank, because it diverts attention from the larger problems of serious abuse and neglect. "Professional advice that categorically rejects any and all use of a disciplinary practice favored and considered functional by parents is more likely to **alienate** than educate them," she argues. The extremely negative reaction to Lieber's proposed ban is her best proof.

alienate: to drive away or make hostile

11 It's always difficult and awkward—and arguably misguided—to use the law as a tool for changing attitudes. In the case of corporal punishment, though, I'm not sure we'd be crazy to try. A hard-and-fast rule like Sweden's would infuriate and frustrate some perfectly loving parents. It would also make it easier for police and prosecutors to go after the really bad ones. The state would have more power over parents. But then parents have near infinite amounts of power over their kids.

COMPREHENSION QUESTIONS

1. What is the purpose of the proposed law against spanking?

The law would define what is corporal punishment and what is child abuse. It makes it easier for prosecutors to bring child abuse charges against parents.

2. What effect did the spanking ban have in Sweden?

Fewer and fewer parents used spanking as a punishment; only one child died of child abuse injuries caused by a parent between 1980 and 1996. The law made children safer. However, reports of child abuse and juvenile violence increased.

3. What is a "research impasse"? Cite two examples Bazelon uses in her explanation.

In a research impasse, experts cannot make a definitive statement about what research says about a question. A disagreement continues. In the case of spanking, Bazelton reports that studies in both Sweden and the U.S. indicated that making spanking illegal protected kids from harm. In both countries, however, it appeared that child abuse actually increased after the law was passed. Studies in the U.S. also suggest that spanking both reduces aggression and causes aggression. The studies are inconclusive. There is an impasse.

Ask Yourself

Self-monitoring is the key to comprehension. How do you ensure that you understand what you read?

DISCUSSION QUESTIONS

PEER CONVERSATION

1. List the ways Bazelon uses research to support her thesis. Which one is most effective?
2. Bazelon uses Baumrind's research to make a point in paragraph 8. Then she explains this research in paragraphs 9 and 10. Which paragraph most effectively explains the research? Explain how it is effective and why.
3. Can government interfere with parenting by passing too many laws? What is your view on laws that monitor or control parenting decisions?

WRITING ASSIGNMENTS

1. Write a paragraph in which you recall a time you were punished justly or unjustly. What was the effect of the punishment?
2. Punishment is one way to encourage participation or obedience. Write an essay that defines a different practice commonly used by parents, teachers, or bosses to encourage participation or obedience. Consider the following questions: Why is the practice frequently used? Is it appropriate or effective?
3. Would you support a dress code in public schools? Why or why not? Explore pros and cons.

How Space Junk Works

by JOHN FULLER

1 During a visit to the International Space Station, an astronaut is required to make some repairs to the outside of the structure. After gathering the correct tools, donning his spacesuit and proceeding through the airlock, the astronaut begins his spacewalk. His mission—tighten some loose screws on the space station's hull, a potential danger to the crew's safety. After a tense but ultimately successful repair, the astronaut relaxes and removes the wrench from the last bolt. Unfortunately, his relaxation costs him, because a looser grip on the wrench causes it to slip from his hand and fly off into space. The wrench has now become space junk, high-speed pieces of **debris** orbiting the Earth at 17,000 kilometers per hour.

debris: trash, rubbish

2 Humans produce an incredible amount of trash on Earth. In the United States alone, the average person throws away more than 4 pounds of trash every day. The country as a whole produces 251 million tons of garbage in one year [source: EPA]. Because we have our own issues on the ground with littering and overflowing landfills, we might not think too much about space junk aside from a few space stations and a handful of satellites in orbit. But NASA claims there are potentially millions of objects, both small and large, orbiting Earth in a giant cloud of junk.

3 Space junk got its start in the middle of the twentieth century, at the very beginning of the space race. When the Soviet Union launched Sputnik I, the first satellite in history to go into orbit around the Earth, on October 4, 1957, the world paid attention. Although the satellite was small by today's standards—it was about the size of a beach ball—Sputnik still caused a great amount of fear among nations, especially the United States. Along with sparking the space race, the launch worried many Americans because of its association with the nuclear arms race. If the Soviets were capable of putting a satellite into space, they could also strap a nuclear bomb on top and reach a target in a matter of hours.

4 Since this caught everyone off guard, several countries threw resources into space programs—the event directly led Congress to create the National Aeronautics and Space Administration, or NASA. Governments, and now cell phone, television and GPS receiver companies, have launched hundreds of satellites a year since the beginning of the space race. These satellites, along with rockets and other objects sent up into space, make up the majority of space junk.

5 The U.S. Space Surveillance Network, a department that tracks debris floating through space and reports to NASA, observes over 13,000 man-made objects orbiting Earth larger than 4 inches in diameter [source: National Geographic News]. That number has only been increasing, up from 9,000 objects in 2000. The organization estimates there are also millions of much smaller objects floating around, and all of it combined weighs about 5,500 tons. Does all this space junk create any problems for space stations—or even people on the ground?

velocity: speed

6 Although it's hard to believe, many of these objects travel around the Earth at speeds more than 22,000 miles an hour. Anything traveling at a **velocity** this high would cause a considerable amount of damage to a spacecraft if a direct hit occurred. Even a tiny fleck of paint traveling at such a speed is capable of boring a quarter-inch hole into the window of a space station.

7 Because there are so many objects flying around up there, there's concern that collisions between debris will only produce more fragments. Even if we stopped launching spacecraft right now and didn't send a single object into orbit, the amount of debris in space would remain constant until 2055 [source: National Geographic News]. After that, things would actually get worse, because the amount of material already up there would inevitably collide and create even more space junk. Experts are worried this is already happening. The most recent case of such a collision, for instance, happened on January 17, 2005, when a piece of debris from an exploded Chinese rocket smashed into a 31-year-old American rocket that had been left alone. The collision only produced four pieces of debris, but observers fear it's only a matter of time before such pieces create an unstoppable chain reaction.

8 The good news for astronauts is that most space junk is located between 550 and 625 miles above the Earth—the International Space Station flies in orbit at 250 miles high, while space shuttles usually only reach 375 miles above Earth. Space programs are also working on rocket designs that limit the amount of debris created during a launch.

9 For those of us on Earth, is there a possibility space junk could fall back to the ground? Everything in orbit will eventually be pulled back down by Earth's gravity—when that happens depends on how high the object is and how fast it's

going. The higher the altitude, the longer the object will take to fall, and it'll take even longer the faster it's speeding around the Earth. These objects could stay in orbit for thousands of years.

10 And the risks of getting hit on the head? Fortunately, most debris burns up during reentry, and no one has ever been killed by space junk. UK bookmakers note the chances of space junk landing on a person are at least 20 billion to one.

COMPREHENSION QUESTIONS

1. How much space junk is orbiting Earth?

Over 13,000 human-made objects larger than 4 inches in diameter are orbiting Earth. It is estimated that over a million smaller pieces are floating in space as well.

2. Why are experts worried about space junk?

Space junk might hit something important.

3. What might be the long-term impact of cell phones, GPS, and television on space junk?

More satellites will be launched to support this new technology. These satellites will eventually become space junk.

DISCUSSION QUESTIONS

PEER CONVERSATION

1. Space junk is monitored by the U.S. Space Surveillance Network, but should it be reduced?
2. Why does Fuller use a process analysis paragraph to begin the essay?
3. How does Fuller suggest that space junk is a serious problem? List evidence to support your answer.

WRITING ASSIGNMENTS

1. Write a process paragraph explaining how you contribute to the mountains of trash created each day in the world.
2. Technology leaves a large footprint on the earth. Write an essay to contrast the positive and negative ways technology impacts our lives.
3. If you could turn back time, what inventions or customs would you revoke? Consider things people find acceptable that actually create social or environmental problems. Write an essay explaining why these inventions or customs should be eliminated.

The Ice Bear Cometh, Wearing Nothing but a Speedo

by LEWIS GORDON PUGH

1 I was standing at the edge of history two weeks ago, ready to plunge into the frozen waters of a lake beneath Nigards Glacier in Norway in a bid to set a new world record for the longest swim in ice water. A long white tongue of ice stretched down a narrow valley and stopped abruptly in front of the half-frozen lake. It was without a doubt one of the most beautiful places on earth.

2 My team had spent two days cutting a 700-meter-long channel across the lake, just wide enough to get a support boat to a small, turquoise piece of water at the foot of the glacier. I was wearing only a Speedo, a swimming cap and goggles in accordance with English Channel Swimming Association rules. And this time, there were no polar bears, leopard seals, crocodiles or great white sharks to worry about. Nevertheless, I was afraid.

hypothermia: a subnormal body temperature

3 **Hypothermia** could just as easily have destroyed my chances of success. A cardiac surgeon and English Channel swimmer once warned me that it was impossible to swim for any length of time in water that is 32 degrees Fahrenheit. "A normal person will be disabled within seconds," he said, "and dead within two or three minutes."

confounded: confused or bewildered

4 But my view is that nothing is impossible. On my side was the fact that whenever I see cold water, my body instinctively raises its core temperature from 98 degrees to 101 degrees. That may sound insignificant, but in thermo-regulation terms, it is critical. Before I get into icy water, my body is a furnace. It has **confounded** scientists and earned me the nickname the Ice Bear.

5 The man with overall command of the swim was Maj. Gen. Tim Toyne Sewell, the former commandant of the Royal Military Academy Sandhurst. He completed the final safety checks.

6 My safety would be in the hands of Jonathan Dugas, an American sports scientist. Over the past two years, along with Tim Noakes of the University of Cape Town, Dugas conducted the most comprehensive scientific tests ever on humans' ability to withstand extreme cold.

7 Dugas tied a monitor around my chest and attached an antenna to my back so he could record my core body temperature and heart rate, essential data to complete the swim safely.

8 When it was time to jump in, I could not afford the luxury of testing the water. It would only open the door of doubt. My mind coach, Martin Jenkins, stepped forward and said: "Lewis, you are the best cold-water swimmer in the world. You have pioneered more swims than anyone else in history. You are the only person to have swum in all five oceans of the world. And you are the only person to have swum in both the Arctic and the Antarctic. Remember that! Ready, go!"

hyperventilation: deep, extremely rapid breathing

9 I rushed forward and dived straight in. First I gasped, and then gulps of icy water rushed down my throat, mouthful after mouthful, the result of unavoidable massive **hyperventilation.** I forced myself to breathe slowly and calmly, trying not to lose concentration for one second. My skin felt like it was on fire, and my head was pounding.

10 I had to swim six widths of the lake to break the world record. There was ice to the left of me and ice to the right of me. After the first width, I was already thinking that this was a very bad idea. Each stroke was an effort. After a few minutes, the real pain set in, deep inside my core. It was almost unbearable.

11 Driving me forward were scores of children waving Norwegian flags and screaming, "Heia Lewis! Heia!" (Go Lewis! Go!) It was very different from my recent swim in Antarctica, where the only spectators were curious penguins.

12 I struggled through two, then three, then four widths. Jenkins was beside me in the support boat with a white board. He wrote down my core temperature. It had dropped to 99 degrees. I was exhausted, but he would not let me fail. Just two more laps. I struggled to put one arm in front of the other. I forced myself to work harder and harder, but I became slower and slower as the cold tightened around me.

13 Then the final lap. My arms felt like lead, and there was no strength in them. They turned slowly—one, two, three. Finally, I reached the shore, exhausted and frozen. I stood up. My legs were weak, but I made it—I set a world record for the longest swim in ice water—1,200 meters in 23 minutes 50 seconds.

14 Once out of the water, I was at the most dangerous stage. My core body temperature had dropped to 97 degrees, and then it started to plummet as the cold blood in my limbs returned to my core.

15 My team bundled me into a boat and rushed me to the nearest hot shower. Dugas was reading out my temperature—"96, 95, 94, 93 . . ." Finally, it bottomed out at 92.5 degrees, hovered for a few minutes, and slowly started rising. He sighed, and his confident smile reassured me that I was now safe.

16 "You have done it again, Ice Bear—with a little margin," he said. Forty-five minutes later, I had made a full recovery.

17 At the end of every swim, I vow it will be my last, but I break that promise every time. So I have stopped making promises. There are just too many reasons to keep going. So all I can say is that I want to return to that icy continent at the bottom of the world and push the boundaries just a little farther.

18 How far can I swim? Well, anything is possible with courage, determination and the support of an incredible team.

COMPREHENSION QUESTIONS

1. Where did the author go swimming? What was he trying to achieve?

Pugh was at a lake beneath Nigards Glacier in Norway. He was breaking a world's record by swimming six widths of the lake.

2. What advantage does he have over other swimmers when swimming in very cold water?

Pugh's body temperature automatically moves from 98 degrees to 101 degrees when he looks at cold water.

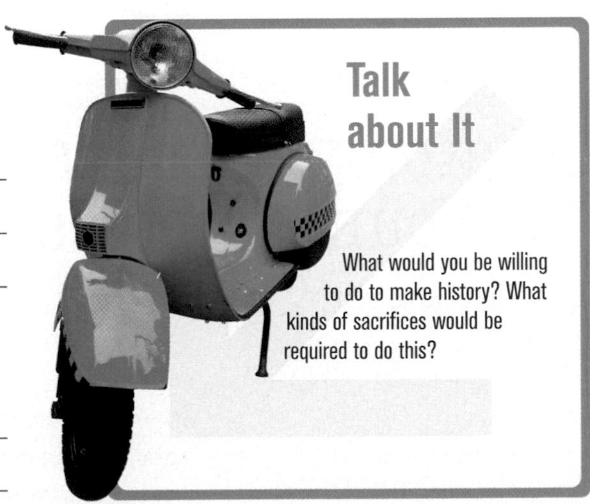

Talk about It

What would you be willing to do to make history? What kinds of sacrifices would be required to do this?

3. Why was getting out of the icy water the most dangerous stage for Pugh?

Pugh's core body temperature dropped to 97 degrees when he was swimming. When he stepped out of the water it plummeted because the cold blood in his arms and legs returned to the core. His temperature dropped to 92.5 degrees, which is dangerously low and could kill him.

PEER CONVERSATION

DISCUSSION QUESTIONS

1. What is hypothermia? How many paragraphs provide information to help a reader understand it? Why is it so important to understand?
2. Pugh describes key points in his courageous swim in the lake beneath Nigards Glacier in Norway. Paragraph 10 is an example of the way he controls his description and compresses time to focus his narrative. Identify another paragraph in which he controls description or compresses time to make a point.
3. Pugh believes he is making history by swimming in the lake and breaking the world record. How important is this event? Support your answer with details from the reading.

WRITING ASSIGNMENTS

1. Do you do anything thrilling but possibly dangerous? Write a cause or effect paragraph to describe how you ensure your safety.
2. Write a mixed-pattern essay that explains the importance of a history-making event that you have witnessed or in which you have participated. What did the event mean to you? What did it mean to the world?
3. Write about a time you pushed yourself to the limits of your endurance. Consider more ordinary physical experiences, such as running or biking.

Anatomy Lessons: A Vanishing Rite for Young Doctors

by ABIGAIL ZUGER

evolved: gradually changed

initiation rite: ceremony to gain membership to a club

1 Over the centuries, dissecting the human body has **evolved** from a criminal offense to a vehicle of mass entertainment to an **initiation rite.** In the Middle Ages, human dissections were forbidden. In 17th century Europe, medical school dissections were open to the public and often attracted unruly crowds cracking obscene jokes. By the 20th century, dissection had become the exclusive pur-

view of scientists and a **mandatory** rite of passage for all doctors. In 18th and early 19th century America, the public repeatedly rioted against doctors and medical institutions accused of dishonoring the dead.

mandatory: required

2 Now, though, the place of dissection in medical education is changing in ways that have not been seen before. The hours devoted to formal anatomy training are sharply down in medical schools. Anatomy instructors are in short supply. Computerized scans and three-dimensional recreations of the human body provide cleaner, more colorful teaching tools than the time-consuming dissections of the past.

3 Some educators say that dissection, as taught to medical students since the **Renaissance,** is on its way out. Others maintain it is becoming more important than ever, not only for teaching the structure of the human body but also for the more subtle lessons it can impart on the meaning of being a doctor. "It is always difficult to decide how much anatomy should be learned by a doctor," said Dr. Frank Gonzalez-Crussi, a retired **pathologist** in Chicago who has written extensively on the history and philosophy of human dissection. Much of the traditional anatomy curriculum is irrelevant to medical practice and might easily be eliminated, Dr. Gonzalez-Crussi said, but there is still no substitute for dissection, which forces the student, willy-nilly, to confront human mortality.

Renaissance: a period of time between the fourteenth and seventeenth centuries that was the beginning of modern science, art, and literature

pathologist: a person who studies the nature of disease

4 Through the mid-20th century, medical students typically spent hundreds of hours dissecting. Working in small groups with scalpels and scissors, they would tease out every major structure in the body, including tendons, arteries and nerves, memorizing dozens of tortuous pathways and hundreds of Latin names in the process. But as the focus of medical science has shifted from whole organs to cells and molecules, more and more teaching hours are consumed by molecular biology and genetics. "Something has to give somewhere," said Dr. Arthur F. Dalley II, director of medical gross anatomy at the Vanderbilt School of Medicine.

5 That something has been anatomy. Surveys show that today's medical students may spend more than 80 percent less time in dissections than did students in the 1950's. The personnel to teach anatomy courses have declined in parallel: anatomy faculty members are aging, Dr. Dalley said, and fewer classically trained graduate students are available to replace them. In many universities, anatomy departments have been engulfed by other departments in the biological sciences. A shortage of donated **cadavers** is not the big problem. Most medical schools receive enough to meet their teaching needs. Anatomical research continues to have practical applications, for example, in the design of new implants or **prosthetic devices.** Still, startling new discoveries in anatomy are uncommon, and money for research is sparse. "It seems that anatomy has fewer and fewer advocates," Dr. Dalley said.

cadavers: corpses used for dissection

prosthetic devices: replacements for missing parts of the body

6 To supplement dissections, medical schools now routinely use computer-based tools, most often C.T. and M.R.I. scans of living patients. Some programs take advantage of the National Library of Medicine's Visible Human Project, which provides radiologic scans and actual digitalized photographs of cross sections of a male and female cadaver. Computer-generated models—like one program that gives the viewer the illusion of flying through the nooks and crannies of a human skull—can clarify tiny, **convoluted** anatomical structures in a way that actual preserved specimens cannot. A handful of schools now pare down

convoluted: characterized by having overlapping coils or folds

anatomy courses by sparing students all hands-on contact with a cadaver. At the University of California at San Francisco, for instance, students learn anatomy by inspecting important structures in cadavers that have already been dissected by an instructor.

7 Even when the details of anatomy and the Latin names fade from a doctor's memory, memories of the experience remain vivid, Dr. Scott-Conner said. Further, drawings and models ignore the huge variability in human anatomy, in which duplicated, misshapen or **aberrant** structures are common. Students who spend time searching for an important nerve or a blood vessel that surfaces nowhere near where it is supposed to be learn a hands-on lesson about the huge range of normal in medicine. Anatomists also emphasize that working with a cadaver elicits a sense of reverence that pictures and models do not.

aberrant: abnormal; deviations from what is normal

8 Now, schools uniformly encourage students to work through their emotions, he said, and also make sure they understand the gravity of the proceedings. "Students are informed at the beginning of the course that gross anatomy is a solemn endeavor and disrespect will not be tolerated," said Dr. Charles Maier, who directs the anatomy course at Case Western Reserve University Medical School. Dr. Maier, like many other course directors, tells students the cadavers are their "first patients," to be treated with all the respect that living patients would command.

9 Funeral services held at the end of anatomy courses emphasize this point. "Many if not most schools have memorial services of one sort or another" Dr. Maier said. The nondenominational service at Case is held at a local cemetery and is similar to a standard graveside ceremony. Family members of the deceased are invited, and afterward, they mingle with the dozens of students who attend. Dr. Maier said he routinely received letters of thanks from families after the events.

COMPREHENSION QUESTIONS

1. Computerized images are replacing dissection in anatomy classes, but they do not teach some important lessons. List three lessons Zuger says dissection teaches that she considers important.

Answers will vary. Some examples might be: (1) provides "subtle lessons on the meaning of being a doctor"; (2) forces "the student to confront human mortality"; (3) creates a "sense of reverence" since a cadaver is the "student's first patient"; (4) dissection is used "in the design of new implants or prosthetic devices."

2. What lessons do computerized images offer that dissection cannot provide?

"Computer-generated models—like one program that gives the viewer the illusion of flying through the nooks and crannies of a human skull—can clarify tiny, convoluted anatomical structures in a way that actual preserved specimens cannot."

3. Why do medical schools hold funerals and memorials for their cadavers after the anatomy class has ended?

They believe cadavers should be "treated with all the respect that living patients would command."

DISCUSSION QUESTIONS

PEER CONVERSATION

1. What is the purpose of this essay? Does Zuger believe dissection should be continued or replaced? Support your answer by citing evidence from the essay.
2. Zuger uses comparison and contrast to analyze the history of and the current trends in anatomy lessons. What transitional words and phrases help a reader see the organization of her discussion and understand the two views of anatomy lessons?
3. What is your opinion on anatomy lessons? Would you prefer a doctor who learned about the human body by watching computer images or by dissecting cadavers?

WRITING ASSIGNMENTS

1. Write a narrative paragraph about a positive or negative experience with a doctor. What made the experience positive or negative? Use a specific office visit or hospital experience to illustrate your point.
2. Write an essay in which you classify doctors to make a point about what makes a good doctor. List the characteristics of each type of doctor. State your position, and support it with facts, examples, and reasons.
3. Colleges and universities decide what classes will prepare individuals for specific careers. What is your opinion of required courses for your degree program? Should colleges rethink required courses or even the methods they use to teach these courses?

Privacy Lost: These Phones Can Find You

by LAURA M. HOLSON

1 Two new questions arise, courtesy of the latest advancement in cell phone technology: Do you want your friends, family, or colleagues to know where you are at any given time? And do you want to know where they are? Obvious benefits come to mind. Parents can take advantage of the Global Positioning System (G.P.S.) chips embedded in many cell phones to track the whereabouts of their phone-toting children.

2 For teenagers and 20-somethings, who are fond of sharing their comings and goings on the Internet, youth-oriented services like Loopt and Buddy Beacon are a natural next step. Sam Altman, the 22-year-old co-founder of Loopt, said he came up with the idea in early 2005 when he walked out of a lecture hall at Stanford. "Two hundred students all pulled out their cell phones, called someone and said, 'Where are you?'" he said. "People want to connect." But such services point to a new truth of modern life. If G.P.S. made it harder to get lost, new cell phone services are now making it harder to hide. "There are massive changes going on in society, particularly among young people who feel comfortable sharing information in a digital society," said Kevin Bankston, a staff lawyer at the Electronic Frontier Foundation based in San Francisco. "We seem to be getting into a period where people are closely watching each other," he said. "There are privacy risks we haven't begun to grapple with."

converts: people who have changed from one way of thinking to another

3 But the practical applications outweigh the worries for some **converts.** Kyna Fong, a 24-year-old Stanford graduate student, uses Loopt, offered by Sprint Nextel. For $2.99 a month, she can see the location of friends who also have the service, represented by dots on a map on her phone, with labels identifying their names. They can also see where she is.

4 One night last summer she noticed on Loopt that friends she was meeting for dinner were 40 miles away, and would be late. Instead of waiting, Ms. Fong arranged her schedule to arrive when they did. "People don't have to ask 'Where are you?'" she said. Ms. Fong can control whom she shares the service with, and if at any point she wants privacy, Ms. Fong can block access. Some people are not invited to join—like her mother. "I don't know if I'd want my mom knowing where I was all the time," she said.

nascent: beginning to form or develop

5 Some situations are not so clear-cut. What if a spouse wants some time alone and turns off the service? Why on earth, their better half may ask, are they doing that? What if a boss asks an employee to use the service? So far, the market for social-mapping is **nascent**—users number in the hundreds of thousands, industry experts estimate. But almost 55 percent of all mobile phones sold today in the United States have the technology that makes such friend-and-family-tracking services possible, according to Current Analysis, which follows trends in technology. So far, it is most popular, industry executives say, among the college set. But others have found different uses. Mr. Altman said one customer bought it to keep track of a parent with Alzheimer's. Helio, a mobile phone service provider that offers Buddy Beacon, said some small-business owners use it to track employees.

6 Consumers can turn off their service, making them invisible to people in their social-mapping network. Still, the G.P.S. service embedded in the phone means that your whereabouts are not a complete mystery. "There is a Big Brother component," said Charles S. Golvin, a wireless analyst at Forrester Research. "The thinking goes that if my friends can find me, the telephone company knows my location all the time, too."

7 Phone companies say they are aware of the potential problems such services could cause. If a friend-finding service is viewed as too intrusive, said Mark Collins, vice president for consumer data at AT&T's wireless unit, "that is a negative for us." Loopt and similar services say they do not keep electronic records of

people's whereabouts. Mr. Altman of Loopt said that to protect better against unwelcome prying by, say, a former friend, Loopt users are sent text messages at random times, asking if they recognize a certain friend. If not, that person's viewing ability is disabled.

8 Clay Harris, a 25-year-old freelance marketing executive in Memphis, says he uses Helio's Buddy Beacon mostly to keep in touch with his friend Gregory Lotz. One night when Mr. Lotz was returning from a trip, Mr. Harris was happy to see his friend show up unannounced at a bar where he and some other friends had gathered. "He had tried to reach me, but I didn't hear my phone ring," Mr. Harris said. "He just showed up and I thought, 'Wow, this is great.'" He would never think to block Mr. Lotz. But he would think twice before inviting a girlfriend into his social-mapping network. "Most definitely a girl would ask and wonder why I was blocking her," he said.

COMPREHENSION QUESTIONS

1. The vice president of AT&T stated: "If a friend-finding service is viewed as too intrusive that is a negative for us." What details in the article would support their claim?

GPS tracking enables family and friends to find users. However, it also allows the company to track users. Users might have concerns about privacy and worry about how companies might use this information.

2. Being connected to friends and family is a huge incentive for having GPS on cell phones. Which examples most effectively support using cell phone GPS? Which examples most effectively argue against using GPS on cell phones?

Cell phone GPS makes it easier for parents to track their children, for friends to find each other. However, GPS reduces privacy; and it can cause conflicts if users do not want parents, spouses, or friends to know their whereabouts. Blocking people from access or not allowing people into the social network can create problems as well.

3. Who might be the biggest consumers of cell phone GPS?

parents and college students

DISCUSSION QUESTIONS

PEER CONVERSATION

1. Evaluate the effectiveness of the introductory paragraph. What is the point of this essay? How do you know?

2. What is your opinion of cell phone GPS? Who would you put on your list of friends who could access your whereabouts?
3. Why does Holson use an example paragraph for her last paragraph? Does this paragraph provide an effective conclusion to the essay?

WRITING ASSIGNMENTS

1. Inventors are observant people who watch and realize that people need something to make life more convenient. Loopt discovered the need for GPS phones as he walked out of a college lecture. Be an inventor. Write a paragraph illustrating and explaining an upgrade to a product you use every day that might make it more efficient or convenient.
2. How have cell phones affected your life? Write a cause and effect essay to identify the impact of cell phones on your daily life.
3. Technology first used for entertainment has also changed learning. For example, bowling alleys introduced overhead scoring. Eventually overheads moved into the classroom. Then televisions moved to projector screens. Now classrooms are switching to computer projectors instead of overhead projectors. How has technology changed the way you learn? Is this a positive or negative change?

The Replacement

by SANFORD J. UNGAR

1 In June 1945, a 43-year-old woman gave birth to a son in Wilkes-Barre, Pa.—a miracle of sorts, but not just because of her age. Tillie and her husband, Max, then 50, had been utterly bereft since their only son, Calvin, died in a military plane crash over Italy 11 months earlier. A 20-year-old navigator in the Army Air Forces, he was like a hero from the movies: a patriot, a charmer and an all-American guy with a great life ahead of him.

2 Cal got up early and worked long hours to help his parents in their grocery store. From an early age, he had a knack for keeping order among his three sisters. He graduated at the top of his high-school class, was a standout debater and had an unusually large circle of friends. When he and his girlfriend, Charlotte, were out on the dance floor, everyone stopped to watch. He had swept her off her feet, and she was waiting for him to come home and marry her.

3 Tillie and Max aged overnight, and everyone knew why. The whole town mourned with them. How unusual, then, that this middle-aged couple **contrived** to create a replacement for Calvin and start over again. Plus, how **fortuitous** that the healthy baby, born so soon after Cal's death, was a boy.

contrived: ingeniously planned

fortuitous: lucky; happening by chance

4 I am that replacement child. I grew up in the shadow of a brother I could never meet or know—his large portrait, in uniform, a permanent fixture on the

living-room wall; his name a part of conversation every day; his reputation and **legacy unassailable.** My sisters managed to persuade our parents not to name me for Calvin, but that made little difference. By all accounts, I looked just like him. I talked like him. I walked like him. My gestures were said to be similar to his. I had many of the same interests. Some of my teachers, having taught him two decades earlier, confused me with him. It was a miracle, all right, and I hated it.

legacy: something handed down from one generation to another

unassailable: not affected by change or doubt

5 The ongoing celebration of my existence was inevitably diluted by, or at least mixed with, my parents' persistent sadness over Calvin's death. My mother wept about him at the slightest **provocation.** Yet just as often she exalted me as her "gift from God." A replacement, yes, but was I really solace for her, or an inescapable reminder of her numbing loss?

provocation: cause, action to incite

6 Growing up, I privately rejected the concept that Calvin and I were brothers in the conventional sense. We had the same parents, but since we had not lived at the same time, how could we have any relationship to each other? I found it unimportant, not to say impossible, to recall the details of his life or his death. During **obligatory** visits to the cemetery as a young child, I would try to avoid looking at his grave. How could I possibly be sad that he died? If he had not, I never would have lived.

obligatory: required responsibility

7 Of course I felt obliged to compete with Calvin, in school and everywhere else. I wanted to be smarter, more accomplished, more interesting and worldly than I imagined him to have been, and yet I dared not reveal this ambition to anyone. I aimed to be the most loyal, loving of children, hoping this might buy me a **reprieve** from hearing about him. When people praised me, I wanted it to be because they admired me in my own right. But Calvin's legacy was everywhere. Twenty years and four and a half months of life: instant martyrdom, and nothing else seemed to matter.

reprieve: temporary relief

8 Over time, however, once I lived beyond him in years, I began to feel a more sympathetic appreciation of my parents' loss. In middle age, when dealing with my own loss—my mother—I began to think of Calvin as an actual person rather than as an annoying legend. Then, eight years ago, during an event in Wilkes-Barre, a **dignitary** leaned over and said to me, "You know, I knew your brother," and he slipped me his business card. Instead of asking him to leave me alone, as I might once have been inclined to do, I found myself saying, "I'd like to talk."

dignitary: a person holding an important or high position

9 Since then, Calvin has become an object of **obsessive** curiosity for me. And sources, though aging rapidly, have appeared everywhere; I've been meeting his high-school friends in the most improbable circumstances. It turns out that Calvin may have been popular to a fault, doing what was necessary to try to please everyone. What a relief, after so many years of living with his perfection, to finally find a flaw or two.

obsessive: excessive

10 At one point I dug up Charlotte's phone number and called her in California. After a long silence, she said, "Sandy, I've been meaning to contact you for about 30 years." She used to hear me on the radio, she said, and I sounded just like Cal. Still do. But how can that be? He lived to be 20, and I'm now 62.

11 Indeed, there are times when I wonder if Calvin and I are really the same person—if, in some mystical way, we share a single soul. These days, to my amazement, I don't mind that idea so much.

COMPREHENSION QUESTIONS

1. In paragraph 4, Ungar lists why he hated being the replacement child. What might be the most difficult part of being so much like Cal? Explain your thinking.

The fact that he was like Cal in so many ways seemed like a miracle to people. Being called a miracle might make Ungar feel like he was not important as a person. He only had value because he replaced Cal.

2. What happened that made Ungar more sympathetic to his parents' loss of Cal?

He became more sympathetic after his mother died, and he began to think of Calvin as a person and not a legend.

3. What flaw did Calvin have that gave Ungar a sense of relief? Why?

"Calvin may have been popular to a fault, doing what was necessary to try to please everyone." This helped Ungar realize that Cal was not perfect.

DISCUSSION QUESTIONS

PEER CONVERSATION

1. Ungar provides three paragraphs of history before he tells the reader that he is the replacement child. Why does he delay giving this piece of information? Is it an effective strategy?
2. Ungar states: "How could I possibly be sad that he died? If he had not, I never would have lived." If the essay's purpose is to define life as a replacement child, why does Ungar ask this question? What is the purpose of this essay?
3. Most of Ungar's essay lists the problems and difficulties of being a replacement child. Were you prepared for the concluding paragraph? What examples, details, and reasons does Ungar provide that help you make sense of this final comment?

WRITING ASSIGNMENTS

1. Which sibling or relative are you most like? Select one person and write a comparison or contrast paragraph to describe how you are alike and different.
2. Write an essay to define sibling rivalry or bonding. Provide examples to illustrate the advantages or disadvantages of sibling rivalry or bonding.
3. What is the right size for a family? How many children are too few? How many children are too many? How did you, your parents, or a close friend or relative decide on the size of their family?

Desperate to Learn English

by ALICE CALLAGHAN

1 Juana and Florencio left the poverty of their rural Mexican village in 1985 and came to Los Angeles to work in the garment district's sweatshops. In 1996, they pulled their three children—all born in Los Angeles—out of school for nearly two weeks until the school agreed to let them take classes in English rather than Spanish.

2 Seventy other poor immigrant families joined this school **boycott** in February 1996, insisting that their children be allowed out of the city's bilingual program, which would not teach English to children from Spanish-speaking homes until they learned how to read and write in Spanish. In the end, the parents prevailed.

boycott: join together in protest; refuse to use, buy, or deal with a product or company

3 Throughout California and elsewhere in the country, many Hispanic parents are worried that bilingual education programs are keeping their children from learning English. These children live in Spanish-speaking homes, play in Spanish-speaking neighborhoods and study in Spanish-speaking classrooms. With little exposure to English in the primary grades, few successfully learn it later. This is why Latino parents are backing a California ballot **initiative** that would end bilingual education for most children in the state. The measure will be put to a vote in June if enough signatures are gathered to put it on the ballot.

initiative: legislation proposed by voters

4 School administrators, Latino politicians, and other **advocates** of bilingual education have **denounced** the measure. They acknowledge the failings of the system, but they insist they can fix it with time. Yet after 25 years, bilingual education has few defenders among Latino parents. In a *Los Angeles Times* poll this year, 83 percent of Latino parents in Orange County said they wanted their children to be taught in English as soon as they started school. Only 17 percent of those surveyed said they favored having their children taught in their native language.

advocates: people who speak in favor of a person or cause

denounced: condemned

5 One reason bilingual education is so **entrenched** is money. Bilingual teachers in Los Angeles are paid extra, up to $5000 a year; schools and school districts receive hundreds of dollars for each child who is designated as having limited **proficiency** in English. About $500 million in state and Federal money supports bilingual educational programs in California. Because such money is not readily relinquished, students languish in Spanish-language classes. Moreover, there are not enough bilingual teachers. In Los Angeles, the shortfall has been so severe that the city has granted emergency credentials to people whose only claim to a classroom lectern is their ability to speak Spanish.

entrenched: deeply established

proficiency: skill or ability

6 Latino parents know that placing their children in English-language classes will not cure the many problems plaguing California schools, where the Latino dropout rate is 40 percent and Latino students have consistently low achievement test scores. Unless these students can learn English, future school **reform** efforts will not help them. Most parents who participated in the school boycott last year labor in garment district sweatshops. Others wait on tables, clean downtown offices or sell fruit or tamales on street corners. All struggle on average monthly incomes of $800. Education is their only hope for a better future for their children. The first step is learning English.

reform: improving measures

COMPREHENSION QUESTIONS

1. What does Callaghan suggest is the motive behind continuing bilingual education in Californian schools?

Bilingual teachers are paid up to $5,000 a year more. Schools receive hundreds of dollars for each child with limited proficiency in English. State and federal money supports bilingual programs—about $500 million a year for California.

2. What points in Alice's argument would you question?

Answers will vary. Some questionable points are: (1) bilingual education is entrenched due to the money involved; (2) districts hire unqualified teachers just to maintain the system.

3. What information would the writer need to add to better support these points?

Answers will vary.

DISCUSSION QUESTIONS

PEER CONVERSATION

1. Callaghan begins with two narrative paragraphs describing families who fought to place their children in English-language classrooms. What is the thesis of this argument essay? Where is it located in the essay? Is this placement effective?
2. What examples and reasons does Callaghan use as counterarguments to her thesis? Are they effective? How you would you vote—for or against bilingual education?
3. What is the purpose of the final examples in the concluding paragraph? Does Callaghan save the most convincing information for last? Would you rearrange the essay?

WRITING ASSIGNMENTS

1. What would you change about your public or private school education? Write a paragraph describing the problem using specific details and reasons. State a solution to the problem and the effects of that solution.
2. Write a mixed-pattern essay explaining how you learned to read, speak well, or write effectively. Include a brief narrative paragraph as well as description of people or places that played a part in your success.
3. Tell about a time you disagreed with the traditional way of behaving. Consider issues of civil, gender, or marital rights. What did you believe? How were your views different from those of others? What did you do? What was accomplished?

TEXT CREDITS

p. 15, From *The Corrosion of Character: The Personal Consequences of Work in the New Capitalism* by Richard Sennett. Copyright © 1998 by Richard Sennett. Reprinted by permission of W.W. Norton & Company, Inc.; p. 16 From Amy Tan, "Mother Tongue." Copyright © 1990 by Amy Tan. First appeared in *The Threepenny Review.* Reprinted by permission of the author and the Sandra Dijkstra Literary Agency.

p. 35, Brenda Peterson, "Growing Up Game" excerpted from *Living by Water: True Stories of Nature and Spirit* by Brenda Peterson. Copyright © Brenda Peterson. Used with permission.

p. 78, From *Nickel and Dimed: On (Not) Getting By in America,* by Barbara Ehrenreich. Copyright © 2001 by Barbara Ehrenreich. Reprinted by permission of Henry Holt and Company, LLC.

p. 102, Excerpt from Yann Martel, *Life of Pi,* p. 19. Copyright © 2001 by Yann Martel, reprinted by permission of Houghton Mifflin Harcourt Publishing Company.

p. 125, G. Pascal Zachary, "Ping: The Risk of Innovation: Will Anyone Embrace It?" *New York Times,* January 20, 2008. Copyright © 2008 by the New York Times. All rights reserved. Used by permission and protected by the Copyright Laws of the United States. The printing, copying, redistribution, or retransmission of the material with express written permission is prohibited.

p. 147, Mark Caldwell, "Polly Want a PhD?" *Discover,* January 2000.

p. 169, Karen Kline, "Younger Siblings, Better Entrepreneurs?" *BusinessWeek,* June 1, 2006. Reprinted by permission.

p. 191, Laurence Steinberg, "Bound to Bicker," *Psychology Today,* December 1987. Reprinted with permission from Psychology Today Magazine. Copyright © 1987 Sussex Publishers, LLC.

p. 214, Arlie Hochschild, *The Time Bind: When Work Becomes Home and Home Becomes Work,* Metropolitan Books, Henry Holt and Co.

p. 235, Thomas Moore, *Care of the Soul,* pp. 3–4. Copyright © 1992 by Thomas Moore. Reprinted by permission of HarperCollins Publishers.

p. 256, From "Last Rights," *The Economist,* June 21, 1997, p. 21. Copyright © The Economist Newspaper Limited, London. Reprinted by permission.

p. 340, From *The Corrosion of Character: The Personal Consequences of Work in the New Capitalism* by Richard Sennett. Copyright © 1998 by Richard Sennett. Reprinted by permission of W.W. Norton & Company, Inc.

p. 345, Abraham Thiombiano, "Dr. Love: Communication flaws between men, women prevalent," *Dixie Sun Online Edition,* Nov. 29, 2006. Reprinted by permission.

p. 347, Charles Wheelan, "Lives Changed in a Split Second," *New York Times,* 1/10/01. Copyright © 2001 New York Times. All rights reserved. Used by permission and protected by the Copyright Laws of the United States. The printing, copying, redistribution, or retransmission of the material with express written permission is prohibited.

p. 349, Ira Berkow, "A Deadly Toll Is Haunting Football," *New York Times,* 7/28/01. Copyright © 2001 New York Times. All rights reserved. Used by permission and protected by the Copyright Laws of the United States. The printing, copying, redistribution, or retransmission of the material with express written permission is prohibited.

p. 351, Jonathon Rauch, "Now, for Tonight's Assignment," *Atlantic Monthly,* November 2004. Reprinted by permission.

p. 352, Hazel Muir, "The violent games people play: as computer games get to look more lifelike is their violence also spilling over into real life?" *New Scientist Magazine,* October 23 2004, p. 26. Reprinted by permission.

p. 355, Rick Weiss, "For First Time, Chimps Seen Making Weapons for Hunting," *Washington Post,* February 23, 2007, p. A1. Copyright © 2007 by The Washington Post. All rights reserved. Used by permission and protected by the Copyright Laws of the United States. The printing, copying, redistribution, or retransmission of the material with express written permission is prohibited.

p. 359, From Deborah Baldwin, "Helping an Old French Art Rise," *New York Times,* Nov. 27, 2003, p. A15. Copyright © 2003 by the New York Times. All rights reserved. Used by permission and protected by the Copyright Laws of the United States. The printing, copying, redistribution, or retransmission of the material with express written permission is prohibited.

p. 555, Definition of "soul" copyright © 2006 by Houghton Mifflin Harcourt Publishing Company. Reproduced by permission from *The American Heritage Dictionary of the English Language, Fourth Edition.*

p. 557, Thomas Moore, *Care of the Soul,* pp. 3–4. Copyright © 1992 by Thomas Moore. Reprinted by permission of HarperCollins Publishers.

p. 559, Definition of "explain" from *Webster's New World Dictionary and Thesaurus,* 2nd ed. Copyright © 2001. Reprinted with permission of John Wiley & Sons, Inc.

p. 559, Definition of "explorer" from *Webster's New World Dictionary and Thesaurus,* 2nd ed. Copyright © 2001. Reprinted with permission of John Wiley & Sons, Inc.

p. 574, John Belton, "Edison and the Kinetoscope," in *American Cinema, American Culture,* pp. 6–8. Reprinted by permission of the McGraw-Hill Companies.

p. 579, Ted Fishman, "A Simple Glass of Water," *New York Times,* 8/23/01. Copyright © 2001 New York Times. All rights reserved. Used by permission and protected by the Copyright Laws of the United States. The printing, copying, redistribution, or retransmission of the material with express written permission is prohibited.

p. 580, Kathy Seale, "Too Much Homework, Too Little Play," *New York Times,* Sept. 3, 2001. Reprinted with permission of the author.

p. 583, Excerpt from Yann Martel, *Life of Pi,* p. 19. Copyright © 2001 by Yann Martel, reprinted by permission of Houghton Mifflin Harcourt Publishing Company.

p. 585, From Brent Staples, "Night Walker" from *Parallel Time: Growing Up in Black and White.* Copyright © 1994 by Brent Staples. Used by permission of Pantheon Books, a division of Random House, Inc. and International Creative Management.

p. 588, Lydie Raschka, "You've Got Hate Mail," Salon, 2/16/01. This article first appeared in *Salon.com,* at http://www.salon.com. An online version remains in the Salon archives. Reprinted by permission.

p. 591, Michele Ingrassia, "The Body of the Beholder," *Newsweek,* April 24, 1995. Copyright © 1995 Newsweek, Inc. All rights reserved. Used by permission and protected by the Copyright Laws of the United States. The printing, copying, redistribution, or retransmission of the material with express written permission is prohibited.

p. 594, Michelle Slatalla, "Online Shopper: Dogs Need a Best Friend, Too," *New York Times,* 9/16/04. Copyright © 2004 New York Times. All rights reserved. Used by permission and protected by the Copyright Laws of the United States. The printing, copying, redistribution, or retransmission of the material with express written permission is prohibited.

p. 598, Emily Bazelon, "Hitting Bottom: Why America Should Outlaw Spanking," www.slate.com, Jan. 25, 2007. Reprinted by permission of Slate.com and Washington Post, Newsweek Interactive. All rights reserved.

p. 601, "How Space Junk Works" by John Fuller, located at howstuffworks.com. Reprinted by permission.

p. 604, Lewis Gordon Hugh, "The Ice Bear Cometh, Wearing Nothing but a Speedo," *New York Times,* May 27, 2006. Copyright © 2006 New York Times. All rights reserved. Used by permission and protected by the Copyright Laws of the United States. The printing, copying, redistribution, or retransmission of the material with express written permission is prohibited.

p. 606, Abigail Zuger, "Anatomy Lessons: A Vanishing Rite for Young Doctors," *New York Times,* March 23, 2004. Copyright © 2004 New York Times. All rights reserved. Used by permission and protected by the Copyright Laws of the United States. The printing, copying, redistribution, or retransmission of the material with express written permission is prohibited.

p. 609, Laura M. Holson, "Privacy Lost: These Phones Can Find You," *New York Times,* Oct. 23, 2007. Copyright © 2007 New York Times. All rights reserved. Used by permission and protected by the Copyright Laws of the United States. The printing, copying, redistribution, or retransmission of the material with express written permission is prohibited.

p. 612, Sanford J. Ungar, "The Replacement," *New York Times,* Sept. 2, 2007. Copyright © 2007 New York Times. All rights reserved. Used by permission and protected by the Copyright Laws of the United States. The printing, copying, redistribution, or retransmission of the material with express written permission is prohibited.

p. 617, Alice Callaghan, "Desperate to Learn English," *New York Times,* August 15, 2007. Reprinted by permission of the author.

PHOTO CREDITS

p. 3, © Henrik Sorensen/Stone/Getty Images; **pp. 4, 5,** © Digital Vision/Getty Images; **p. 15,** © IML Image Group Ltd/Alamy; **p. 21,** © Plush Studios/Blend Images/Getty Images; **p. 22,** © Christoph Wilhelm/Digital Vision/Getty Images; **p. 25,** © PhotoDisc/Getty Images; **p. 43,** © Angelo Cavalli/The Image Bank/Getty Images; **p. 44,** © Pete Ryan/National Geographic/Getty Images; **p. 52,** © Alistair Berg/Digital Vision/Getty Images; **p. 60,** Getty Images; **p. 67,** © Tyler Stableford/The Image Bank/Getty Images; **p. 68,** © Digital Vision; **p. 73,** © AP/Wide World Photos; **p. 78,** © Simon Weller/Reportage/Getty Images; **p. 85,** © Panoramic Images/Getty Images; **p. 86,** © AP/Wide World Photos; **p. 93,** © Royalty-Free/Corbis; **p. 102,** © William West/AFP/Getty Images; **p. 111,** © Thomas Barwick/Digital Vision/Getty Images; **p. 112,** © PhotoLink/Photodisc/Getty Images; **p. 118,** © Ian Shaw/Alamy; **p. 125,** Adam Gault/Getty Images; **p. 133,** © Henrik Sorensen/Photonica/Getty Images; **p. 134,** Getty Images; **p. 138L,** © Daniel Allan/Digital Vision/Getty Images; **p. 138R,** © Marc Romanelli/The Image Bank/Getty Images; **p. 147,** © Ryan David/Boston Globe/Landov; **p. 155,** © Chase Jarvis/UpperCut Images/Getty Images; **p. 156,** Ryan McVay/Getty Images; **p. 164,** Stockbyte/Punchstock Images; **p. 169,** © Claudia Hehr/zefa/Corbis; **p. 177,** © Jonathan Ferrey/Allsport Concepts/Getty Images; **p. 178,** PhotoLink/Getty Images; **p. 183,** © Brownstock Inc./Alamy; **p. 191,** © AP/Wide World Photos; **p. 199,** © Anton Robert/Gallo Images ROOTS RF Collection/Getty Images; **p. 200T,** Dynamic Graphics/JupiterImages; **p. 200B,** Steve Mason/Getty Images; **p. 206,** © PCL/Alamy; **p. 214,** © Radius Images/Alamy; **p. 223,** © Barry Rosenthal/The Image Bank/Getty Images; **p. 224,** Blend Images; **p. 228,** © Brand X Pictures/PunchStock; **p. 235,** © Royalty-Free/Corbis; **p. 243,** © Masakazu Watanabe/Score by Aflo/Getty Images; **p. 244,** © Ryan McVay/Getty Images; **p. 250,** SW Productions/Getty Images; **p. 256,** © Ron Wurzer/Getty Images; **p. 265,** © John Lund/The Image Bank/Getty Images; **p. 266,** S. Alden/PhotoLink/Getty Images; **p. 274,** © Bill Varie/Corbis; **p. 278,** © Alan Marsh/First Light/Getty Images; **p. 299,** © Angelo Cavalli/Photodisc/Getty Images; **p. 300,** Getty Images; **p. 302,** © Gabriela Medina/Blend Images/Getty Images; **p. 313,** © 2007 Getty Images, Inc; **p. 337,** © Kei Uesugi/Taxi Japan/Getty Images; **p. 338,** © Digital Vision; **p. 343,** Digital Vision/Getty Images; **p. 345,** © Royalty-Free/Corbis; **p. 363,** © Rayman/Digital Vision/Getty Images; **p. 364,** © Najlah Feanny/Corbis; **p. 365,** © Ashley Cooper/Corbis; **p. 385,** © Ira Block/National Geographic/Getty Images; **p. 386,** BananaStock/JupiterImages; **p. 397,** © Darryl Leniuk/Digital Vision/Getty Images; **p. 413,** © Darryl Leniuk/Stone/Getty; **p. 435,** © Erik Isakson/Tetra Images/Getty Images; **p. 44,** © Sami Sarkis/Photographer's Choice/Getty Images; **p. 459,** © Photo and Co/Riser/Getty Images; **p. 477,** © Tyler Stableford/Stone/Getty Images; **p. 493,** © IIC/Axiom/Getty Images; **p. 503,** © Joel Kiesel/Iconica/Getty Images; **p. 525,** © James Hager/Robert Harding World Imagery/Getty Images; **p. 551,** © Thomas Northcut/Stone+/Getty Images; **p. 552,** © Bob Daemmrich/PhotoEdit; **p. 564,** © David G. Houser/Corbis; **p. 571,** © Caroline Woodham/Photographer's Choice RF/Getty Images; **p. 572,** © Uli Wiesmeier/zefa/Corbis; **p. 574,** ©NMPFT/SSPL/The Image Works

abbreviations, 548–549
adjective(s), 494
- choosing, 495
- comparative, 498–499
- hyphenated, 501–502
- identifying, 494
- irregular, 498
- phrase fragment, 436, 438–439
- superlative, 498–499

adverb, conjunctive, 421
- comma splices and, 447–448

adverbs
- comparative, 500
- "-ly" ending and, 495–497
- superlative, 500

afterthoughts, 425, 428
American Cinema, American Culture (Belton), 574–575
"Anatomy Lessons: A Vanishing Rite for Young Doctors" (Zuger), 606–609
apostrophes
- editing errors in, 523–524
- plural, 522
- possessive forms of, 520–522
- proofreading for, 522–523

argument essay, 328–331
- focused assignments and, 330
- general assignments and, 330
- imitation assignments and, 330
- refresher, 331

argument paragraph
- audience, 254
- audience, academic, 260
- claims in, 246
- concluding sentence, 255
- correcting, 262
- critical reading of, 258–259
- details in, 246
- editing, 259–262
- editing checklist, 259–260
- elements of, 246
- evidence in, 246
- evidence in, reviewing, 248–249
- first draft checklist, 255
- freewriting, 253
- glancing at, 245–246
- goals, 263
- initial tendency in, 250
- other viewpoints in, 246, 249–252
- prewriting, 253–254
- process of, 252–255
- reflecting on, 263
- revising, 257–259
- revision checklist, 259
- searching, 262
- self-editing, 262
- strengths in, identifying, 263
- taking stand in, 247–248
- topic sentence, 254

authoritative opinion, 372–373

bad/badly, 497–498
Baldwin, Deborah, 359
Bazelon, Emily, 598–601
Belton, John, 574–575
Berkow, Ira, 349–350
bibliography, 378
body, 269, 280–290, 303
"The Body of the Beholder" (Ingrassia), 591–594
brainstorming, 24, 25–26
- for classification paragraphs, 166
- comparison and contrast paragraphs and, 212
- description paragraphs, 75
- example, 26
- for example paragraphs, 99
- process paragraphs and, 140, 144
- side-by-side approach to, 212

Caldwell, Mark, 147
Callaghan, Alice, 617–618
capitalization, 542–546
- publication titles and, 546

Care of the Soul (Moore), 235, 557
cause and effect essay, 319–321
- focused assignments and, 320
- general assignments and, 321
- imitation assignments and, 320
- refresher, 321

cause and effect paragraph
- academic audience and, 194
- audience and, 188–190
- clustering and, 188
- coherence of, 189
- concluding sentence, 190
- correcting, 197
- details, 183–184
- editing, 194–197
- editing checklist, 194
- elements of, 181–182
- first draft, 188–190, 190
- first draft checklist, 190
- focus on, 184, 188–190
- goals in, 197
- multiple causes/one effect in, 180–181
- one cause/multiple effects in, 180
- organization of, 184–186, 188–190
- prewriting, 188
- problem in, 181
- process, 187–190
- progress and, 183
- reading critically, 193
- reflecting on, 197
- revising, 191–194, 195–196
- revision checklist, 193
- satisfaction and, 183
- searching, 197
- selecting assignment for, 187
- self-editing, 197
- situation in, 181
- strengths in, identifying, 197
- success and, 183
- talking and, 188
- time and, 184
- topic sentence, 189
- transitions related to, 189
- unity of, 189

challenges, identifying, 40–41
classification essay, 316–318
- focused assignments and, 318
- general assignments and, 318
- imitation assignments and, 318
- refresher, 318

classification paragraph
- academic audience and, 172
- assignment for, focused, 165
- assignment for, unfocused, 165
- audience for, 166–167
- basis for, 158, 159
- brainstorming for, 166
- categories and, 158
- clustering for, 166
- coherence of, 167
- concluding sentence, 168
- correcting, 175
- editing, 172, 174–175
- editing checklist, 172
- elements of, 158
- examples in, 158
- first draft checklist, 168
- first draft of, 168
- focus of, 166–168
- glancing at, 157–158
- interest and, 159
- organization of, 166–168
- prewriting, 166
- process of, 165–168
- purpose and, 158, 159–160
- reflecting on, 175
- revising, 170–172, 173–174
- searching, 175
- selecting assignment for, 165
- self-editing, 175
- strengths in, identifying, 175
- topic sentence, 167
- unity and, 167

clichés, 567
clustering, 23, 24–25
- cause and effect paragraphs and, 188
- classification paragraphs and, 166
- definition paragraphs and, 227, 232
- examples, 25
- narration paragraphs and, 115, 121–122

colons, 513–516
comma(s), 418–421, 503
- compound forms and, 420
- conjunctions and, 504–505
- dependent clauses and, 426–428
- interrupters and, 507–510
- introductory modifier and, 505–507
- series and, 510–511

comma splice, 445
- conjunctions and, 447–448
- conjunctive adverbs and, 447–448
- correcting, 447–451
- identifying, 446
- proofreading for, 456–457
- simple sentences and, 446–447
- subordinating conjunction and, 449–450

comparison and contrast essay, 321–325
- focused assignments and, 323
- general assignments and, 324
- imitation assignments and, 323
- point-by-point comparison, 325
- refresher, 324
- subject-by-subject comparison, 324

comparison and contrast paragraph
academic audience and, 218
audience and, 212
brainstorming and, 212
coherence in, 212–213
concluding sentence, 213
correcting, 220
critical reading and, 215–217
details in, 206–209
editing, 217–221
editing checklist, 218
elements of, 204
first draft checklist, 214
first draft of, 213–214
focusing on, 212–214
getting started with, 204–205
glancing at, 201–203
goals, 221
organization of, 212–214
point-by-point organization of, 201, 202–203
points of, 205–208
prewriting, 211–212
process of, 210–214
reflecting on, 221
revising, 215–217
revision checklist, 217
rewriting, 215–217
searching, 220
selecting assignment for, 210–211
self-editing, 221
strengths in, identifying, 221
subject-by-subject organization of, 201–202
talking and, 211
topic sentence, 212
unity in, 212–213
conclusion, 269, 291–294, 303
introductions and, 292–293
missteps, 292
conjunction(s), 418–421
choosing, 419
comma splices and, 447–448
commas and, 504–505
subordinating, 424, 425, 449–450, 454–456
content, 9–13
coordination, 418–424
summary, 423
The Corrosion of Character (Sennett), 339–340

Days of Atonement (Rodriguez), 357–358
"A Deadly Toll Is Haunting Football" (Berkow), 349–350
definition essay, 325–328
focused assignments and, 327
general assignments and, 328
imitation assignments and, 327
refresher, 328
definition paragraph
audience and, 233
category in, 226
clustering and, 227, 232
coherence, 233
concluding sentence, 234
correcting, 241
critical reading of, 237
editing, 238–241
editing checklist, 238
elements of, 226–227
establishing territory in, 231
examples and, 226
first draft checklist, 234
first draft of, 234
freewriting, 232
general statements in, 227
getting started in, 227–228
glancing at, 225–226
goals, 241
group in, 226
negatives and, 226–227, 230–231
parts of, 225
prewriting, 232
process of, 231–234
reflecting on, 241
rethinking, 235–236
revising, 235–238
revision checklist, 238
searching, 241
selecting assignment for, 231–232
self-editing, 241
strengths in, identifying, 241
topic sentence, 233
unity, 233
dependent clause, 425
comma and, 426–428
fragment, 439–442
describing people, 72
description essay, 304–307
focused assignments and, 306
general assignments and, 306
imitation assignments and, 306
refresher, 306–307
description paragraph
assignment selection, 74–75
audience, 76
brainstorming, 75
coherence in, 76
comparisons in, 70, 73–74
concluding sentence in, 77
correcting, 83
details in, 71
dominant impression in, 70
editing, 81–83
editing checklist, 81
first draft, 77
first draft checklist, 78
freewriting, 75
getting started with, 70–71
glance at, 69
goals, 83
organization of, 76–77
parts of, 69, 70
prewriting, 75
process, 74–78
reflecting on, 83
revision checklist, 80
searching, 83
self-editing, 83
sensory description in, 70
strengths in, identifying, 83
topic sentence, 76
unity in, 76
"Desperate to Learn English" (Callaghan), 617–618
details
adding, 34
in argument paragraph, 246
cause and effect, 183–184
in comparison and contrast paragraphs, 206–209
cutting, 34
in description paragraphs, 71
in example paragraphs, 88
examples and, 228–230
general to specific, 89–90
irrelevant, 127
minor, 54–55
in narration paragraph, 117–119
ordering, 63–64
ordering, chronological, 64
ordering, importance, 64
ordering, simple to complex, 64
ordering, spatial, 64
organizing, 140–141, 141, 185–186
process paragraphs and, 137, 138
retrieving specific, 291
selecting/elaborating on, 209
specific, 56–57
vague, 56
details, key, 141–142
identifying, 142
details, supporting, 45, 52–57, 284–286
elaborating on, 54–55
in example paragraph, 87
major, 52–54
in narration paragraph, 113
outlines and, 53–54
diction, 563–569
connotation and, 565
denotation and, 565
tone and, 564–565
dictionary, 554–558
effective use of, 555–556
getting acquainted with, 555
documented essay
checklist, 383
elements of, 367
integrating information and, 367
locating information and, 367, 368–371
processing information and, 367, 374–376
revising, 382
"Dogs Need a Best Friend, Too" (Slatalla), 594–597
double-checking, 38

editing, 23. *See also* self-editing
activities, 304
apostrophes and, 523––524
argument paragraph, 259–262
cause and effect paragraph, 194–197
classification paragraph, 172
comparison and contrast paragraph, 217–221
definition paragraph, 238–241
description paragraph, 81–83
essay, 294–296
example paragraph, 105–109

narration paragraph, 128–131
process paragraph, 150–153
pronoun agreement, 481–483
subordination, 432–433
Ehrenreich, Barbara, 78
elaboration, 93–96
narration paragraph, 118
Electric Library, 370
essay. *See also specific types of essays*
assignments, 271–273
checklist, 297, 335
drafting, 294
editing, 294–296
elements of, 269, 302–303
final review, 296, 335
goal of, 284
guidelines for, 295
key terms in, repeating, 288
logical order and, 287–288
with multiple patterns of organization, 331–335
with one pattern of organization, 304–331
organizational pattern in, 286
outline, 269–271, 286
paragraph and, relationship between, 269
plan, 286–288
prewriting, 273
relationship pattern in, 285
topics, 271–273
example essay, 308–310
focused assignments and, 309–310
general assignments and, 310
imitation assignments and, 309
refresher, 310
example paragraph
academic audience and, 106
brainstorming for, 99
coherence in, 100
concluding sentence in, 87, 101
correcting, 108
critical reading and, 103–105
details in, 88
editing, 105–109
editing checklist, 105
elements of, 88
examples in, 88
facts in, 88
first draft checklist, 102
first draft of, 101
focus and, 100
freewriting and, 99
getting started, 88–90
glance at, 87
goals, 109
organizing, 100
parts of, 87
peer papers and, 104
point in, 88
prewriting, 99
process of, 98–101
reflecting on, 109
revising, 103–105
revision checklist, 105
rewriting, 103–105
searching, 108
selecting assignment for, 98–99
self-editing, 108
strengths in, identifying, 109
topic sentence in, 87, 100
unity in, 100
examples, 373
best for last, 96
brainstorming, 26
of categories, 160–161
categories working with, 162–164
categories/topic and, 161–162
chronological, 96
classification paragraphs and, 158
clustering, 25
contrasting, 91–92
cumulative effects of, 100
definition paragraphs and, 226
details and, 228–230
elaborating on, 93–96
in example paragraphs, 88
extended, 92–93
freewriting, 27
piggybacking, 26
as proof, 93
related, 91
similar, 91
simple, 94
transition, 64
transitions based on, 101, 233
transitions for, 168
types of, 91–93

facts, 372
FirstSearch, 371
Fishman, Ted, 579–580
Ford, Henry, 180
form, 5–8
freewriting, 24
argument paragraph, 253
definition paragraphs, 232
description paragraphs, 75
example, 27
example paragraphs, 99
focusing on, 75
Fuller, John, 601–603

Galileo's Daughter (Sobel), 358
General Reference Center Gold, 370
gerunds, 400
goals, 17–19, 40
cause and effect paragraphs and, 197
in comparison and contrast paragraphs, 221
definition paragraph, 241
description paragraph, 83
example paragraph, 109
exercise, 18
narration paragraphs and, 131
process paragraphs and, 139, 153
good/well, 497–498
grammar-check, 38
graphic organizer, 71–72
"Growing Up Game" (Peterson), 35
Gupta, Sanjay, 256

"Helping an Old French Art Rise" (Baldwin), 359
"Hitting Bottom: Why America Should Outlaw Spanking" (Bazelon), 598–601
Hochschild, Arlie, 214–215
Holson, Laura M., 609–612
"Homework, a School Reform that Works" (Rauch), 351–352
"How Space Junk Works" (Fuller), 601–603

"The Ice Bear Cometh, Wearing Nothing but a Speedo" (Pugh), 604–606
idioms, 566
"In Praise of the F Word" (Sherry), 340–341
in-class essay
college course, 394
elements of, 389
essay-length essay, 393–394
paragraph-length short essay answer, 391–392
preparing for, 395
sentence-length short answer, 389–391
tips, 395
types of, 389–394
independent clause, 424
inference, 14–15
InfoTrac, 370
Ingrassia, Michele, 591–594
in-text citations, 376–377
introductions, 269, 303
conclusions and, 292–293
focused, 274
unfocused, 274
writing effective, 274–277
introductory modifiers
commas and, 505–507
signal words for, 506

James, William, 154
jargon, 566
journal, 17

Kline, Karen, 169

library catalog, 371
The Life of Pi (Martel), 102, 583–585
"Lives Changed in a Split Second" (Wheelan), 347–349

Martel, Yann, 102, 583–585
misspelled words, commonly, 530–531
misused words, commonly, 532–542
self-assessment of, 535, 538, 542
mixed pattern essay, 331–335
approach to, determining, 334–335
focused assignments and, 333–334
general assignments and, 334
imitation assignments and, 333
Moore, Thomas, 235, 557
"Mother Tongue" (Tan), 16–17
Muir, Hazel, 352–353

narration essay, 310–313
focused assignments and, 312–313
general assignments and, 313

narration essay *(continued)*
imitation assignments and, 312
refresher, 313
narration paragraph
academic audience and, 129
actions in, 114
actors in, 114
clustering and, 115, 121–122
coherence, 123
concluding sentences in, 113, 124
connections and, 119–120
correcting, 131
details in, specific, 117–119
editing, 128–131
editing checklist, 128
elaboration, 118
elements of, 114, 118
first draft checklist, 125
first draft of, 124–125
focus and, 122
focused, 127
getting started with, 115–117
glance at, 113–114
organization of, 122, 123
outcome in, 114
parts of, 113
peer papers, 128
prewriting, 121–122
problems with, common, 126
process, 120–125
reflecting, 131
revising, 126
revision checklist, 128
scene in, 114
searching, 131
selecting assignment for, 121
self-editing, 131
skeleton, 115
strengths, identifying, 131
supporting details in, 113
talking and, 122
topic sentence in, 113, 123
transitions and, 119–120
unity, 118, 123
Nickel and Dimed (Ehrenreich), 78
"Night Walker" (Staples), 585–588
notes, 373–376
on computer, 373–374
with note cards, 374
noun(s), 400
common, 542–546
phrase fragment, 436, 438–439
plural, 528–530
proper, 542–546
numbers, 546–548

"On Baking" (Sennett), 15–16
"once upon a time," 110
outlines
details and, major supporting, 53–54
essay, 286

paragraph. *See also specific types of paragraphs*
adding to, 34
analyzing, 57–58
coherence, 31, 62, 64–65
cutting from, 34
essay and, relationship between, 269
hook, 60
reorganizing, 34
sentence fragments in, 443–444
structure of, 45–46
transition sentences between, 289–290
unity, 31, 62, 64–65
paragraph organization, 31–32, 59–65
chronological, 31–32
deductive, 59–62
inductive, 60–62
order of importance, 31–32
simple to complex, 31–32
spatial, 31–32
parallelism, 167
paraphrasing, 339–343
guidelines for, 339
practice, 342–343
recognizing effective, 340–341
parenthetical modifiers, 507–510
periodical literature, 370–371
personal connections, making, 14
personality traits, 72
Peterson, Brenda, 35
physical characteristics, 72
piggybacking, 25
example, 26
"Ping: The Risk of Innovation: Will Anyone Embrace It?" (Zachary), 125
plagiarism, 336, 343–346, 373
"Polly Want a PhD?" (Caldwell), 147
predicates, 398–399, 406–408
predicates, compound, 416–418
adding, 417–418
identifying, 416–417
prepositional phrases, 402–404
fragment, 437–439
prewriting, 23–29
as act of discovery, 51
argument paragraph, 253–254
cause and effect paragraphs, 188
classification paragraphs, 166
comparison and contrast paragraphs, 211–212
definition paragraphs, 232
description paragraphs, 75
essays, 273
example paragraphs, 99
narration paragraphs, 121–122
process paragraphs and, 143–144
reviewing, 28–29
strategy, 29
topic sentence and, 50–52
"Privacy Lost: These Phones Can Find You" (Holson), 609–612
problem solving, 246
process essay, 313–316
focused assignments and, 315
general assignments and, 315
imitation assignments and, 315
refresher, 315–316
process paragraph
academic audience and, 150
audience and, 144–145
brainstorming and, 140, 144
coherence of, 145
concluding sentence, 146
correcting, 153
critically reading, 147–150
details and, 137, 138
editing, 150–153
editing checklist, 150
elements of, 136–137, 139
first draft checklist, 146
first draft of, 144–146
focus and, 144–146
goals and, 139, 153
materials and, 136, 137
order and, 137, 138
organization of, 136, 144–146
participants and, 136, 137
prewriting and, 143–144
process of, 143–146
purpose and, 136, 137
reflecting on, 153
revising, 147–150
revision checklist, 150
rewriting, 147–150
searching, 153
selecting assignment for, 143
self-editing, 153
steps and, 137, 138
strengths in, identifying, 153
talking and, 144
topic sentence, 145
unity of, 145
pronoun agreement, 478–485
editing errors in, 481–483
indefinite pronouns and, 483–485
pronouns, 400
antecedents, 479–481
case, 485–489
common, 478
identifying, 479–481
indefinite, 400, 483–485
objective, 486–487
personal, 400
possessive, 486–487
relative, 468–469
subjective, 485–487
pronouns, consistency, 489–490
proofreading for, 490–491
proofreading
for apostrophes, 522–523
for comma splice, 456–457
for irregular verbs, 472–473
peers, 38
for pronoun consistency, 490–491
for run-ons, 456–457
Pugh, Lewis Gordon, 604–606
punctuation, types of, 172
purpose of writing, 4–8

questions, asking, 14
quotations, 292, 354–361, 516–520
choosing, 354
complete, 355, 357, 378, 516
indirect, 518–519
internal, 519–520

introducing, 354–361
partial, 355, 357, 378, 516
in reading, 359

Raschka, Lydie, 588–591
Rauch, Jonathon, 351–352
reading
aloud, 38
between lines, 14
peer papers, 80, 104, 128, 149, 172, 193, 217, 237
with pen, 14, 578–579
quotations in, 359
reading, critical, 13–17, 34–35
argument paragraphs, 258–259
cause and effect paragraphs, 193
classification paragraphs and, 171–172
comparison and contrast paragraphs and, 215–217
definition paragraphs, 237
description paragraphs and, 80
example paragraphs and, 103–105
exercise, 16–17
identifying important information and, 576
narration paragraphs and, 127
previewing and, 573–575
prior knowledge and, 576
process paragraphs, 147–150
questions and, asking, 575–576
rereading and, 576–578
strategies for, 13–15, 573–578
real/really, 497–498
reference books, 371
reflective student, 17–19
reflective writing, 17–18
relative clause, 428–432
adding, 429–430
combining sentences using, 430–432
subordination and, 428–432
"The Replacement" (Ungar), 612–614
response groups, 35–37
forming, 36
guidelines for, 35–36
revision, 23, 33–37
argument paragraph, 257–259
cause and effect paragraph, 191–194, 195–196
classification paragraph, 170–172, 173–174
comparison and contrast paragraph, 215–217
definition paragraph, 235–238
description paragraph, 79–80
documented essay, 382
example paragraph, 103–105
narration paragraph, 126
plan, 36
process paragraph, 147–150
strategies, 34, 304
Rodriguez, Richard, 357–358
run-ons, 451–457
correcting, 453–456
identifying, 451–452
proofreading for, 456–457
simple sentence and, 452

Seal, Kathy, 580–582
self-editing
argument paragraph, 262
cause and effect paragraph, 197
classification paragraph, 175
comparison and contrast paragraph, 221
definition paragraph, 241
description paragraph, 83
example paragraph, 108
narration paragraph, 131
process paragraph, 153
semicolon, 421–422, 513–516
Sennett, Richard, 15–16, 339–340
sentence fragment, 435
adjective phrase, 436, 438–439
dependent clause, 439–442
noun phrase, 436, 438–439
in paragraphs, 443–444
prepositional phrase, 437–439
types of, 436–444
verbal phrase, 437–439
sentence, topic, 30–31, 45, 47–48, 280–284
argument paragraph, 254
cause and effect paragraph, 189
classification paragraph, 167
comparison and contrast paragraph, 212
definition paragraph, 233
in description paragraphs, 76
in example paragraph, 87, 100
focus, 48–50, 282–284
in narration paragraph, 113, 123
prewriting and, 50–52
process paragraph, 145
vague versus specific, 48
sentences
complete, 435
complex, 424–433
relative clauses combining, 430–432
with relative pronouns, 468–469
verb-first, 468
sentences, compound, 420–421
objects and, 487–488
sentences, concluding, 57–59
argument paragraph, 255
cause and effect paragraph, 190
classification paragraph, 168
in comparison and contrast paragraphs, 213
definition paragraphs, 234
in description paragraphs, 77
in narration paragraph, 113, 124
process paragraph, 146
sentences, simple
comma splices and, 446–447
as complete idea, 398
run-ons and, 452
sexist language, 567
Sherry, Mary, 340–341
shortcomings, 54
signal words, 38
"A Simple Glass of Water" (Fishman), 579–580
slang, 566
Slatalla, Michelle, 594–597

Sobel, Dava, 358
sources, 339
acknowledging, 341–342, 356
from anthology article, 380
from book by one author, 379
from book by two authors, 380
from book by more than two authors, 380
document, 378–379
electronic, 380
integrating, 376–378
Internet, 368–370, 380
from magazines, 379
from newspapers, 379
from two or more books by same author, 380
spell-check, 38, 525
spelling. *See also* misspelled words, commonly
basic rules for, 526–530
numbers and, 546–548
tips, 526
Staples, Brent, 585–588
statistics, 371
Steinberg, Laurence, 191
stereotyping, 164
subject(s), 398–406
in commands, 404–405
complement, 408
finding, 401–402
in questions, 404–405
types of, 399
verb agreement and, 461–466, 469–471
subject, compound, 414–416, 466–467
adding, 415–416
identifying, 414–415
verb agreement and, 467–468
subordination, 424–433
editing and, 432–433
relative clause and, 428–432
suffixes, 527–528
adding, 528
summary, 346–353
of journal, 350–353
of magazine, 350–353
of news story, 347–350
practice suggestions, 361

talking, 23
cause and effect paragraphs and, 188
comparison and contrast paragraphs and, 211
narration paragraphs and, 122
process paragraphs and, 144
Tan, Amy, 16–17
t-chart, 72
thesaurus, 559–561
effective use of, 558–559
getting acquainted with, 558
synonyms with, finding, 561
thesis, 280–284, 303
developing, 277–280
focused, 282–284
heavy-handed, 279
reinforcing, 291
writing effective, 277–280

"think in three's," 88–89
thinking, critical, 13–17
  strategies for, 13–15
Time Bind (Hochschild), 214–215
titles, 295–296
  predictability of, 296
"Too Much Homework, Too Little Play" (Seal), 580–582
topic(s), 46–52
  categories/examples and, 161–162
  defining, 28–29
  dividing, 278–279
  essay, 271–273
transitions, 32–33, 100, 303
  based on chronological order, 123–124, 145, 190
  based on comparisons, 213
  based on contrast, 213
  based on example, 101, 233
  based on priority, 101, 123, 145, 234
  cause and effect, 189
  commonly used, 32
  for examples, 168
  examples of, 64
  to express content, 167
  narration paragraphs and, 119–120
  between paragraphs, 289–290
  priority based, 77
  spatial order, 76

Ungar, Sanford J., 612–614

verb agreement
  compound subject and, 467–468
  problems, 466–471
  subject and, 461–466, 469–471
  verbs and, irregular, 463–465
  verbs and, regular, 462–463
verb endings, missing, 465–466
verb phrases, 410–412
  fragment, 437–439
  identifying, 411
verb tense
  consistent, 474
  inconsistent, 474–475
verb-first sentences, 468
verbs
  identifying, 461
  observing, 412
  regular, 462–463
verbs, action, 406–408
  identifying, 407–408
  test for, 460
verbs, helping, 410–412
  common, 411
  identifying, 411
verbs, irregular, 463, 471–473, 475–476
proofreading for, 472–473
verb agreement and, 463–465
verbs, linking, 408–410
  common, 408, 461
  identifying, 409–410
"The Violent Games People Play" (Muir), 352–353
vocabulary, dictionary and, 554–558

Wheelan, Charles, 347–349
works cited, 378
writing process, 23, 303
  checklist, 303

"You've Got Hate Mail" (Raschka), 588–591

Zachary, G. Pascal, 125
Zuger, Abigail, 606–609

THOSE WHO HELPED US GET HERE!

Symposia Participants

Every year McGraw-Hill conducts Developmental Writing Symposia, which are attended by instructors from across the country. These events are an opportunity for McGraw-Hill editors to gather information about the needs and challenges of instructors teaching the Developmental Writing course. They also offer a forum for the attendees to exchange ideas and experiences with colleagues they might not have otherwise met. The feedback we have received has been invaluable and has contributed—directly or indirectly—to the development of *Going Places* and *On the Go*.

Zoe Albright, *Longview Community College*
Jared Aragona, *Scottsdale Community College*
Liz Barnes, *Daytona State College*
Nellie Boyd, *Texas Southern University*
Carol Ann Britt, *San Antonio College*
Carrie Brooks, *Erie Community College, City Campus*
Joann Brown, *Miami Dade College, North*
Lucia Cherciu, *Dutchess Community College*
Julia Cote, *Houston Community College, Southwest*
Ella Davis, *Wayne Community College*
Crystal Echols, *Sinclair Community College*
Karen L. Feldman, *Seminole Community College*
Rita Fernandez-Sterling, *Miami Dade College, Kendall*
Murray Fortner, *Tarrant County College, Northeast*
Holly French, *Bossier Parish Community College*
Lilian Gamble, *Delgado Community College*
Richard Gaspar, *Hillsborough Community College*
Tina Getz, *Pikes Peak Community College*
Rochelle Harden, *Parkland College*
Judy Harris, *Lone Star College, Tomball*
Alan J. Hutchinson, *Des Moines Area Community College*
Bill Jordan, *Joliet Junior College*
Kerry J. Lane, *Joliet Junior College*
Dennis Lee, *American River College*
Donna Matsumoto, *Leeward Community College*
Michelle Nettle, *Fayetteville Technical Community College*
Sheila Otto, *Middle Tennessee State University*
Tracy A. Peyton, *Pensacola Junior College*
Miki Richardson, *Southwest Tennessee Community College, Macon*
Doug Rigby, *Lehigh Carbon Community College*
Valerie Russell, *Valencia Community College, East*
Karin Russell, *Keiser University*
Deneen Shepherd, *St. Louis Community College, Forest Park*
Nancy Trautmann, *Northampton Community College*
Linda Van Vickle, *St. Louis Community College, Meramac*
Maria Villar-Smith, *Miami Dade College, Wolfson*
Mary Warner, *Nashville State Technical Community College*
Arlene Weaver, *Wilbur Wright College*
Paul Wolford, *Walters State Community College*
John Wright, *Central New Mexico Community College*

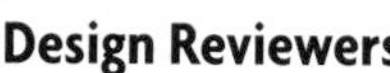

Design Reviewers

Dawn Elmore-McCrary, *San Antonio College*
Zohra Fazal, *Florida Institute of Technology*
Deborah Sanders Felton, *Cleveland State Community College*
Richard Gaspar, *Hillsborough Community College*
L. M. Grow, *Broward College, Central*
Mark Hall, *Central Carolina Community College*
Monique Harris, *University of Wisconsin—Parkside*
Vicki Houser, *Northeast State Community College*
Elizabeth Huergo, *Montgomery College*
Patrick McGuire, *University of Wisconsin—Parkside*
Donna Slone, *Marysville Community & Technical College*
Kelli Wood, *El Paso Community College*

Student Reviewers

Joliet Junior College
Brandon Barrara
William Bills
Mary Borron
Nicole Carmichael
Jonathan Cent
Alexander Dennis
Whitney Draper
Stephanie Elliott
Lauren Filate
Alex Hamilton
Marquis Harmon
Nicole James
Cassandra Link
Latoya Lowe
Katherine Marren
Maggie Nelson
Heidi O'Brien
Payal Patel
Latecia Risden
Nancy Rodriguez
Terry Russell
Aisha Smith
Jacqual Smith
Alex Snieski
Chris Swartz
Anthony Vizek
Feng Wang
Iliana Yankova

Amarillo College
Lanassa Beard
Maria Gonzalez
Cynthia Jones
Lindey Judkins
Kristie Lucero
Hunberto Martinez
Neil Nevarez
Ihudiya Ohuonu
Amber Reed
Kissey Reed
Sayra Valenzulla
Kelly Vitteli
Danella West

Seminole Community College
Jennifer Erskin
Jhon Inalien
Jessica Rodriquez
Karen Sheldon

Pasadena Junior College
Wesley Bailey
Chelsea Bowling
Ian Chace
Dana Eddy
Kristina Fuciarelli
Joseph Martinez
Josh Schocttuner
Jean Stafford
Cassie Williams
Jamie Voorhes

Bossier Parish Community College
Erica Ashby
Zach Brodst
Harvey Cooksen
Amber Hager
Sean Hayes
April Osby
Terry Plant
Frances Small
Ashley Speights
Billy William

South Plains College
Daryus Campbell
Kelci Carter
Cynthia Ewers
Chelsea Joiner
Cruz Lopez
Jamie Nunnelle
Araceli Perez
Courtney Reeves
Matt Roach